Studying Virtual Math Teams

COMPUTER-SUPPORTED COLLABORATIVE LEARNING

VOLUME 11

The *Computer-Supported Collaborative Learning Book Series* is for people working in the CSCL field. The scope of the series extends to 'collaborative learning' in its broadest sense; the term is used for situations ranging from two individuals performing a task together, during a short period of time, to groups of 200 students following the same course and interacting via electronic mail. This variety also concerns the computational tools used in learning: elaborated graphical whiteboards support peer interaction, while more rudimentary text-based discussion forums are used for large group interaction. The series will integrate issues related to CSCL such as collaborative problem solving, collaborative learning without computers, negotiation patterns outside collaborative tasks, and many other relevant topics. It will also cover computational issues such as models, algorithms or architectures which support innovative functions relevant to CSCL systems.

The edited volumes and monographs to be published in this series offer authors who have carried out interesting research work the opportunity to integrate various pieces of their recent work into a larger framework.

Contents

List of Figures

List of Tables

Logs

Authors and Collaborators

VMT Principal Investigators

Gerry Stahl, Information Science, Drexel University, gerry@gerrystahl.net

Wesley Shumar, Anthropology, Drexel University, shumarw@drexel.edu

Stephen Weimar, The Math Forum, Drexel University, steve@mathforum.org

VMT Post-doctoral Researcher

Alan Zemel, Communication & Culture, Drexel University, arz27@drexel.edu

VMT PhD Research Assistants

Murat Perit Çakir, Information Science, Drexel University (from Turkey), mpc48@drexel.edu

Johann W. Sarmiento, Information Science, Drexel University (from Columbia), jsarmi@drexel.edu

Ramon Prudencio S. Toledo, Information Science, Drexel University (from Philippines), ramon.toledo@drexel.edu

Nan Zhou, Information Science, Drexel University (from China), nan.zhou@drexel.edu

VMT Visiting Researchers

Elizabeth S. Charles, School of Education, Dawson College, Canada, echarles@place.dawsoncollege.qc.ca

Fei-Ching Chen, Graduate Institute of Learning & Instruction, National Central University, Taiwan, fcc@cc.ncu.edu.tw

Weiqin Chen, Computer Science, University of Bergen, Norway,
weiqin.chen@infomedia.uib.no

Ilene Litz Goldman, School of Education, Nova University, USA,
irl22@drexel.edu

Martin Mühlpfordt, Computer Science, IPSI Fraunhofer Institute, Germany,
martin.muehlpfordt@gmx.de

Henrry Rodriguez, Computer Science, Royal Institute of Technology, Sweden,
henrry.rodriguez@drexel.edu

Jan-Willem Strijbos, Educational Sciences, Leiden University, the Netherlands,
jwstrijbos@fsw.leidenuniv.nl

Stefan Trausan-Matu, Computer Science, Politehnica University of Bucharest,
Romania, stefan.trausan@cs.pub.ro

Martin Wessner, Computer Science, IPSI & IESE Fraunhofer Institute, Germany,
martin.wessner@iese.fraunhofer.de

Fatos Xhafa, Computer Science, The Open University of Catalonia, Barcelona,
Spain, fxhafa@uoc.edu

Collaborating Researchers

Marcelo Bairral, Math Education, Federal Rural University of Rio de Janeiro,
Brazil, mbairral@ufrrj.br

Sourish Chaudhuri, School of Computer Science, Carnegie Mellon University,
USA, sourish@cmu.edu

Yue Cui, School of Computer Science, Carnegie Mellon University, USA,
ycui@cs.cmu.edu

Terrence W. Epperson, Social Sciences Librarian, The College of New Jersey,
USA, epperson@tcnj.edu

Hugo Fuks, Informatics, Pontifical Catholic University of Rio de Janeiro, Brazil,
hugo@inf.puc-rio.br

Gahgene Gweon, School of Computer Science, Carnegie Mellon University,
USA, gkg@cmu.edu

Timothy Koschmann, Medical Education, Southern Illinois University, USA,
tkoschmann@siumed.edu

Rohit Kumar, School of Computer Science, Carnegie Mellon University, USA,
rohitk@andrew.cmu.edu

F. Frank Lai, Urban Education, Rutgers University at Newark, USA,
ffLai@eden.rutgers.edu

Chee-Kit Looi, Learning Sciences, Nanyang Technological University, Singapore, cheekit.looi@nie.edu.sg

Richard Medina, Information & Computer Sciences, University of Hawai'i, USA, rmedina@hawaii.edu

Mariano Pimentel, Applied Informatics, Federal University of State of Rio de Janeiro (UNIRIO), Brazil, pimentel@unirio.br

Arthur B. Powell, Urban Education, Rutgers University at Newark, USA, powellab@andromeda.rutgers.edu

Traian Rebedea, Computer Science, Politehnica University of Bucharest, Romania, traian.rebedea@cs.pub.ro

Carolyn Penstein Rosé, School of Computer Science, Carnegie Mellon University, USA, cprose@cs.cmu.edu

Daniel D. Suthers, Information & Computer Sciences, University of Hawai'i, USA, suthers@hawaii.edu

Ravi Vatrapu, Information & Computer Sciences, University of Hawai'i, USA, vatrapu@hawaii.edu

Juan Dee Wee, Learning Sciences, Nanyang Technological University, Singapore, johnwee@pmail.ntu.edu.sg

VMT Staff and Consultants

Joel Eden, Information Science, Drexel University, joel.eden@gmail.com

Annie Fetter, The Math Forum, Drexel University, annie@mathforum.org

Rev Guron, The Math Forum, Drexel University, rguron@mathforum.org

Michael Plommer, Software Consultant, Germany, m_plomer@gmx.net

Ian Underwood, The Math Forum, Drexel University, ian@mathforum.org

Part I
Introducing Group Cognition in Virtual Math Teams

Introduction to Part I

Virtual math teams are small groups of learners of mathematics who meet online to discuss math. They encounter stimulating math problems and engage in intense discussions of math issues among peers. It is now technologically possible for students from around the world to gather together in these teams and to share mathematical experiences involving deep conceptual relationships that invoke wonder—the kinds of experiences that can lead to a lifetime fascination with mathematics, science and other intellectual pursuits. The online meeting of students from different backgrounds can spark interchanges and collaborative inquiry that lead to creative insight. The accomplishments of such groups can have productive consequences for the students involved. The meeting can also produce records of the interactions, which researchers can study to understand the group processes involved in collaborative math exploration.

Beginning in 2002, a group of researchers and online-math-education-service providers began the Virtual Math Teams (VMT) Project, which is still active in 2009 as this book goes to press. The mission of the VMT Project is to provide a new opportunity for students to engage in mathematical discourse. We have three primary goals in this project:

- As service providers, we want to provide a stimulating online service for use by student teams from around the world.
- As educational-technology designers, we want to develop an online environment that will effectively foster student mathematical discourse and collaborative knowledge building.
- As researchers, we want to understand the nature of team interaction during mathematical discourse within this new environment.

The VMT Project was launched to pursue these goals through an iterative, cyclical process of design-based research at the Math Forum at Drexel University in Philadelphia, USA. This book reports on some of our progress to date in this effort.

Studying Virtual Math Teams is a diverse collection of chapters about various aspects of the VMT Project and about the group interactions that take place in the VMT environment. Researchers who have been involved with the project in different

3

ways contributed chapters on their findings. Because of the deeply collaborative nature of the project, all the chapters are, at heart, group products. Most of them are written by core members of the VMT research team, which has met together weekly over the years of the project to analyze logs of student interaction in detailed group data sessions. Others are written by researchers who visited the project for several months or who used the VMT environment or data for investigations in their own collaborative research groups.

The collecting of the chapters was initiated at an all-day workshop at the CSCL 2007 international conference, where drafts of many of the chapters were presented and discussed. Early versions of these presentations had been previously critiqued through online sessions conducted within the VMT environment. The researchers involved have profoundly influenced each other's thinking/writing. Furthermore, all chapters have been heavily edited to form a coherent volume with manifold connections and tensions.

The motivation behind the VMT Project and the historical background for this book is provided at length in *Group Cognition: Computer Support for Building Collaborative Knowledge* (Stahl, 2006b). That book covered the author's work for the decade preceding the VMT Project, in which he and his colleagues developed a number of computer systems to support knowledge building, analyzed the interactions that took place by users of those systems and explored theoretical aspects of such group interaction. The book argued for a need to investigate what it termed *group cognition*: the interactive processes by means of which small groups of people can solve problems, build knowledge and achieve other cognitive accomplishments through joint effort. In particular, it proposed studying this in online environments, in which a complete record of the shared interaction could be captured for replay and detailed study. The chapters of *Group Cognition*—mostly written before the VMT Project began—envisioned a research agenda that could elaborate and support its theory of group cognition. The chapters of *Studying Virtual Math Teams* report on the results of implementing that research agenda with the VMT Project and confirm the conjectures or fulfill the promises of the earlier work. They also extend the theory of group cognition substantially with the detail of their empirical findings and the corresponding analyses by the VMT team and its collaborators.

This volume is meant to display the methodology that we have developed through our group interaction with the project data. The Editor and his colleagues have in the past made claims about what microanalysis of chat logs could provide, and it is now time to document this. We do not claim to have invented a completely new approach, having learned enormously from the many social-science researchers referenced in our chapters. However, we have adapted existing approaches to fit the context of our situated work through the inter-animation of our own diverse perspectives on the scientific enterprise. Many of these perspectives will shine through in the individual chapters authored by different people or small groups. As the history of the project emerges from the consecutive pages that follow, the influence of project personnel and visitors will become evident.

In terms of analysis method, our first visiting researchers—Strijbos and Xhafa—introduced us to both the rigors and the limitations of coding. Zemel then provided expertise in the alternative approach of conversation analysis. However, conversation analysis did not quite fit our undertaking, because it is oriented toward physical (rather than virtual) co-presence of participants and because it aims to reveal the interactional methods of participants (rather than assess educational designs). So we gradually adapted conversation analysis, which is traditionally based on a particular style of video transcriptions of informal talk, to replayable chat logs of students doing goal-directed problem solving. Weimar's sensitivity to educational interactions, Shumar's perspective from social theory and ethnographic practice as well as Stahl's focus on design-based research processes all helped to sculpt this into an effective practice. Our gradually emerging findings also modified our approach, such as Sarmiento's research into how students sustain longer episodes than are usually studied in CA, Çakir's analyses of the dialectic between visual/graphical reasoning and symbolic/textual group cognition, and Zhou and Toledo's studies of questioning and resolving differences as drivers of collaborative problem solving.

Despite the sequential development of themes as this book unfolds, the chapters retain the self-contained character of individual essays. The reader is welcome to skip around at will. However, we have also tried to provide some coherence and flow to the volume as a whole, and the ambitious reader may want to follow the over-arching narrative step by step:

- *Part I* provides a gentle introduction to the perspective, vision, technology, theory, methodology and analysis of the VMT Project.
- *Part II* digs deeply into the data, analyzing specific aspects of group interactions that take place in the VMT environment.
- *Part III* investigates higher-level issues of the team discourse, such as small-group agency, problem solving, creativity and reasoning.
- *Part IV* turns to design issues of the online technology that supports the student communication: how to integrate different media and how to structure important functionality.
- *Part V* explores various ways of analyzing and representing the foundational response structure of small-group interaction in chat.
- *Part VI* concludes with the implications of the preceding chapters for a science of group cognition.

Introducing Group Cognition in Virtual Math Teams

Part I offers an introduction to the study of group cognition in virtual math teams. It consists of four chapters written by the Editor on independent occasions (see Notes at end of book) and in varying literary genres (interview, user manual, book review, methodological reflection and case study). They should provide entry for the reader into the orientation and intricacies of the book's material:

- *Chapter 1* is an informal discourse on the Editor's views about how to think about computer support for collaborative learning. It was written at the request of an Italian journal about knowledge building, and is structured as an interview by the journal.
- *Chapter 2* was written for teachers who are interested in using the VMT service with their students. It describes technological and pedagogical aspects. Although the details of the environment have evolved from year to year, the general description in this chapter provides good background for most of the later analyses of student interactions. It is written for potential users—or their teachers—to give a sense of the practical instructional uses of the service.
- *Chapter 3* reproduces a review of a recent book that conceptualizes mathematical learning in terms of discourse. The position elaborated there motivates the VMT orientation to math learning through discursive problem solving. The review then extends the book's approach to apply it to small-group interactions, such as those in the VMT Project. Extended this way, the book's theory of mathematics provides a way of understanding group cognition in collaborative math work.
- *Chapter 4* presents the methodology of the VMT Project analyses: to describe the group practices that the student teams use in doing their collaborative intellectual work. Specifically, this chapter introduces several analyses that appear in later parts of the volume to illustrate the analytic approach. In giving a glimpse of concrete analyses that will follow, it situates them in one way of understanding their significance.
- *Chapter 5* goes into detail on one of the analyses in Chapter 4, providing two competing analyses of the same interaction: one in terms of an individual solving a tricky math problem and the other understanding the solution as a group achievement. The subtle interplay between individual and group phenomena/analyses provides a pivotal theme for the VMT Project, for the theory of group cognition and for the present volume. Without trying to be conclusive, this chapter at least makes explicit the issue that is perhaps the most subtle and controversial in the theory of group cognition.

These essays and the subsequent studies of the VMT Project in Parts II through VI are intended to help you, the reader, to initiate your own studying of virtual math teams (or similar phenomena) and to further your reflections on the associated theoretical and scientific themes.

Chapter 1
A Chat About Chat

Gerry Stahl

Abstract This is an informal discussion from my personal perspective on computer-supported collaborative learning (CSCL). I envision an epical opportunity for promising new media to enable interpersonal interaction with today's network technologies. While asynchronous media have often been tried in classroom settings, I have found that synchronous text *chat* in small workgroups can be particularly engaging in certain circumstances—although perhaps chat can often be integrated with asynchronous hypermedia to support interaction within larger communities over longer periods. More generally, building collaborative knowledge, making shared meaning, clarifying a group's terminology, inscribing specialized symbols and creating significant artifacts are foundational activities in group processes, which underlie internalized learning and individual understanding no matter what the medium. Therefore, I look at the online discourse of small groups to see how groups as such accomplish these activities. This has consequences for research and design about learning environments that foster knowledge building through group cognition, and consequently contribute to individual learning.

Keywords CSCL · group cognition · text chat · math education

Interviewer: Prof. Stahl, can you chat with us a little about your view of research in computer-supported collaborative learning today?

For me, CSCL stands at an exciting turning point today. The field of computer-supported collaborative learning (or, "CSCL") started in the early 1990s as an interdisciplinary effort to think about how to take advantage of the availability of computers for education. In particular, social constructivist ideas were in the air

G. Stahl (✉)
College of Information Science & Technology, Drexel University, Philadelphia, PA, USA
e-mail: gerry@gerrystahl.net

G. Stahl (ed.), *Studying Virtual Math Teams*, Computer-Supported Collaborative
Learning Series 11, DOI 10.1007/978-1-4419-0228-3_1,
© Springer Science+Business Media, LLC 2009

and people thought that personal computers in classrooms could help to transform schooling. Researchers arrived at CSCL from different disciplines and brought with them their accustomed tools and theories. Education researchers and psychologists administered surveys and designed controlled experiments, which they then analyzed statistically to infer changes in mental representations. Computer scientists and AI researchers built systems and agents. Everyone who put in the required effort soon discovered that the problem was a lot harder than anyone had imagined. Progress was made and a research community grew, but existing conceptualizations, technologies and interventions ultimately proved inadequate. Today, I think, people are working at developing innovative theories, media, pedagogies and methods of analysis specifically designed to deal with the issues of CSCL. I feel that we are now poised just at the brink of workable solutions. Perhaps as editor of the *ijCSCL* journal, I have a special view of this, as well as a peculiar sensitivity to the fragility of these efforts.

Of course, I do not want to give the impression that previous work in CSCL was not significant. Certainly, the pioneering work of Scardamalia and Bereiter, for instance, broke crucial new ground—both practical and theoretical—with their CSILE system for collaborative knowledge building. I want to come back to talk about that later. Nevertheless, I think that even the successes like those also demonstrated that the barriers were high and the tools at hand were weak.

Interviewer: **What do you think is the #1 barrier to widespread success of CSCL?**

As someone interested in philosophy, I see a problem with how people conceive of learning—both researchers and the public. The philosophical problem is that people focus on the *individual learner* and conceive of learning as the accumulation of *fixed facts*. But I think that the evidence is overwhelming that social interaction provides the foundation upon which the individual self is built, and that knowledge is an evolving product of interpersonal meaning making. We often cite Vygotsky as the source of these ideas, but there is a rich philosophical literature that he drew on, going back to Vico, Hegel, Marx, Gramsci, Mead, Dewey and many others.

There is an "ideology of individualism" prevalent in our society, with negative consequences for politics, morality, education and thought generally. We need to recognize that the individual is a product of social factors, such as language, culture, family and friends. Even our ability to think to ourselves is an internalized form of our ability to talk with others and of our identity as an inverted image of the other; the mental is a transformed version of the social. When I learn as an individual, I am exercising skills that are based on social skills of learning with others: collaborative learning is the foundation for individual learning, not the other way around.

Standard assumptions about learning are, thus, misleading. Researchers strive to get at the mental representations of individual subjects—through pre/post tests, surveys, interviews, think-aloud protocols and utterance codings—that they assume are driving learning behaviors. But, in fact, learning behaviors are constructed in real time through concrete social interaction; to the extent that the learning is reflected mentally, that is a trace in memory or a retrospective account of what happened in the world. To foster learning, we need to pay more attention to collaborative arrangements, social actors and observable interactions.

Interviewer: **Then do you feel there is a problem with the very concept of learning?**

Yes, the traditional concepts of learning, teaching and schooling carry too much baggage from obsolete theories. If we try to situate thought and learning in groups or communities, then people complain this entails some kind of mystical group spirit that thinks and learns, in analogy with how they conceive of individual thinking and learning as taking place by a little homunculus in the head. That is why I prefer Bereiter's approach of talking about knowledge building. Unfortunately, he was caught up using Popper's terminology of "third world" objects that belong neither to the physical nor mental worlds. What he was really talking about—as he now realizes—was knowledge-embodying *artifacts*: spoken words, texts, symbols or theories. Artifacts are physical (sounds, inscriptions, visible symbols, carved monuments), but they are also meaningful. By definition, an artifact is a man-made thing, so it is a physical body that incorporates a human intention or significance in its design. Knowledge artifacts belong simultaneously in the physical and meaning worlds. Through their progressive reification in physical forms, symbols come to have generalized meanings that seem to transcend the experiential world.

If we now situate knowledge building in groups or communities, we can observe the construction and evolution of the knowledge in the artifacts that are produced—in the sentences spoken, sketches drawn and texts inscribed. There is no mystery here; these are common things whose meanings we can all recognize. They are so familiar, in fact, that we take them for granted and never wonder how meanings are shared and knowledge is created in group interactions or how it spreads through communities. When you consider it this way, the strange thing is to think about learning taking place inside of brains somehow, rather than in the interplay between linguistic, behavioral and physical artifacts. If one carefully observes several students discussing a mathematical issue using terminology they have developed together, drawings they have shared and arguments they have explained, then the learning may be quite visible in these inscriptions. One can assume that each member of the group may go away from the group process with new resources for engaging in math discourses (either alone or in new groups) in the future.

Interviewer: **But can't students learn by themselves?**

Of course, I can also build knowledge by myself, as I am now in typing this text on my laptop. However, that is because I have discussed these and similar issues in groups before. I have had years of practice building ideas, descriptions and arguments in interaction with others. Even now, in the relative isolation of my study, I am responding to arguments that others have made to my previous presentations and am designing the artifact of this text in anticipation of the possible reactions of its potential audiences. The details and significance of this artifact are ineluctably situated in the present context of discourse in the CSCL research community and the scientific world generally. That is why I have chosen a classic dialog genre for its form, in which my utterances partake in a community discourse.

The idea that thoughts exist primarily inside of individual heads is deeply misguided. The ideology of individualism is accompanied by an objectivistic worldview. There is an assumption that stored in the minds of individuals are clear and distinct thoughts ("ideas" or propositions), and that it is the goal of scientific research to discover these thoughts and to measure how they change through learning episodes. However, when knowledge is truly constructed in social interactions, then the thoughts do not exist in advance. What individuals bring to the group is not so much fixed ideas, already worked out and stored for retrieval as though in a computer memory, but skills and resources for understandingly contributing to the joint construction of knowledge artifacts.

Interviewer: **What would be the consequences of rejecting this ideology of individualism?**

Given a view of learning as the increased ability to engage in collaborative knowledge building rather than as an individual possession, CSCL researchers may want to develop new methods to study learning. The old methods assumed that thoughts, ideas and knowledge lived in the heads of individuals and that researchers should find ways to access this fixed content. But if knowledge is constructed within situations of interaction, then (a) there is no ideal (God's-eye-view, objective) version of the knowledge that one can seek and (b) the knowledge will take essentially different forms in different situations. A student's skills of computation will construct very different forms of knowledge in an interactive group discourse, a written test, a visit to buy items in a store, a job adding up customer charges, a laboratory experiment or an interview with a researcher.

If we conceive of learning as situated in its specific social settings and as a collaborative knowledge-building process in which knowledge artifacts are constructed through interaction among people, then we need to give up the idea that learning can be adequately studied in settings that are divorced from the kinds of situations in which we want the learning to be useful. Studying knowledge in laboratories, questionnaires and interview situations will not necessarily reveal how learning takes place in social settings like school and work.

To make matters worse, the traditional methods that are brought to CSCL from other disciplines are often based on theories of causation that arose with the laws of mechanics in physics, dating back to Galileo and Newton. In order to deal with the complexity of nature, early physicists simplified matter into ideal, inelastic billiard balls whose actions and reactions followed simple equations. We cannot simplify the complexity and subtlety of human interaction, of interpersonal gesture, of linguistic semantics and of social strategies into equations with a couple of linear variables without losing what is most important there. Each utterance in a knowledge-building discourse is so intertwined with the history, dynamics and future possibilities of its situation as to render it unique—irreducible to some general model. In phenomena of a human science like CSCL, researchers must treat events as unique, situated, over-determined, ambiguous case studies—rather than as instances of simplistic, deterministic, linear causative general laws—and interpret their meanings with the same sorts of social understanding that the "subjects" or participants brought to bear in constructing the meanings. Too many research hypotheses presume a model of knowledge as pre-existing individual opinions causing group interactions, rather than viewing knowledge as an emergent interactional achievement of the group interactions—subsequently assimilated and retroactively accounted for by individuals.

Interviewer: **How can you have a rigorous science without laws, laboratories, equations, models and quantified variables?**

Let me give you a recent example that I take as a guide for my own research agenda. During the past 50 years, a new discipline was created called conversation analysis (CA). It set out to study informal, everyday conversation and to discover how speakers constructed social order through common, subtle discourse practices that everyone is familiar with and takes for granted. The pioneers of the field took advantage of the latest tape-recording technology and developed forms of detailed transcription that could capture the details of spoken language, like vocal emphasis, timing and overlap. Although meaning making takes unique twists in each conversation, it turned out that there are interesting regularities, typical practices and preferred choices that researchers can identify as being consequential for face-to-face interactions. For instance, they outlined a set of conventional rules that people follow for taking turns in conversations.

In CSCL, we are particularly interested in computer-mediated communication, often among students discussing some subject matter. This is very different in form and content from informal conversation. First, in a medium like text chat people cannot take advantage of vocal emphasis, intonation, facial expression, accent, gesture, pauses or laughter. One does not observe a chat utterance being constructed in time; it appears as a sudden posting. Consequently, postings can never overlap each other, cut each other off or fluidly complete each other's thoughts. Several people can be typing simultaneously—and they cannot predict the order of appearance of their postings. So the whole system of turn taking discovered by CA no longer applies in the same form.

However, chat text has some advantages over speech in that utterances are persistently visible and can be designed with special visual features, such as punctuation, capitalization, emoticons and other symbols. People in chat rooms take advantage of the new affordances for interaction to create their social order. CSCL could study the methods that small groups use to communicate in the new media that we design. The understanding of how people interact at this level in various CSCL environments could inform the design of the technologies as well as influencing the kinds of educational tasks that we ask students to undertake online in small groups.

CSCL researchers can take advantage of the detailed computer logs that are possible from chat rooms just as the CA researchers used meticulous transcripts of tape recordings or videos to study interaction at a micro-analytic level never before possible. Depending upon one's research questions, these logs may allow one to finesse all the issues of videotaping classroom interactions and transcribing their discourse. Of course, one should not get carried away with hoping that the computer can automate analysis. The analysis of human interaction will always need human interpretation, and the production of significant insights will require hard analytic work. The pioneers of CA were masters of both those skills.

Interviewer: **Can you give some examples of text chat analysis that you have conducted?**

First, I have to explain that I do not conduct analysis of text chat on my own—as an individual. I am part of the Virtual Math Teams (VMT) research team that is trying to build the analog of CA for CSCL. When we analyze some chat log, we hold a "data session" with about eight people, so that our interpretations of meanings constructed in the chat have some intersubjective validity. We have been working on a number of different themes, including how small groups in online text chat:

- Propel their discourse with math proposal bid/uptake pairs,
- Coordinate drawing on a shared whiteboard with chat postings to make deictic references,
- Design texts and other inscriptions to be read in specific ways,
- Collaboratively construct math artifacts,
- Bridge back to previous discussions with group memory practices,
- Engage in information questioning and
- Resolve differences between multiple perspectives or alternative proposals.

With each of these themes, we have been discovering that it is possible to uncover regular social practices that recur from group to group, even though most groups have never used our CSCL system before. In each case, the achievements of the groups are constructed interactively in the discourse situation, not premeditated or even conscious. To determine which of these activities the group is engaging in at any given time requires interpretation of the activity's meaning. It cannot be determined by a simple algorithm. For instance, a question mark does not always correspond with an information question; there are many ways of posing a question and many uses of the question mark in chat.

Interviewer: **Why are you focused so much on text chat?**

Actually, I have not always favored chat. My dissertation system was a shared database of design rationale. Next, I developed a CSCL system to support multiple perspectives in threaded discussion. When I later worked on a European Union project, I helped design a system that again featured threaded discussion. It was not until a few years ago that my students convinced me that synchronous chat was a much more engaging online medium than asynchronous forums. I still think that asynchronous media like Knowledge Forum or wikis may be appropriate for longer-term knowledge building in classrooms or communities. But we have found that text chat can be extremely powerful for problem solving in small groups.

The CSCL research community now has a lot of experience with discussion forums. Studies have clearly documented the importance of the teacher's role in creating a knowledge-building classroom. To just tell students in a traditional class to post their ideas in a regular threaded discussion system like Blackboard is doomed to failure: there will be little activity and what gets posted is just individual opinions and superficial agreements rather than knowledge-building interactions.

Chat is different. Although teenagers are used to superficial socializing using instant messaging and texting, they can readily be encouraged to participate in substantive and thoughtful exchanges in text chat. Our studies show that students in our chat rooms are generally quite engaged in knowledge-building activities.

Group size has an enormous impact on the effectiveness of different media. Unfortunately, there is not much research on, for instance, math collaboration by different size groups. Most math education research is still focused on individual learning. Studies of collaboration in math problem solving tend to use dyads. Dyad communication is easy to study because it is always clear what (who) a given utterance is responding to. In addition, the two participants often fall into relatively fixed roles, often with one person solving the problem and the other checking it or asking for clarifications.

Perhaps one of our most interesting findings is that math problem solving can, indeed, be accomplished collaboratively. When we started the VMT Project, we had no idea if the core work of mathematical thinking could be done by a group. The tradition has always pictured an isolated individual deep in silent reflection. Even the studies of dyads generally found that one student would solve the problem and then explain the solution to the other. We found that participants in virtual math teams spontaneously began to explore their problems together, discussing problem formulations, issues, approaches, proposals and solutions as a group. Moreover, students generally found this interaction highly engaging, stimulating and rewarding.

Small groups of three or four active students chatting become much more complex and interesting than an individual thinking aloud or a dyad answering each other. The response structure of postings is still critical to interpreting meaning, but in groups it can become tricky, often leading to interesting confusions on the part of the participants. Roles still surface, but they are often fluid, disputed and emergent, as participants try to position themselves and others strategically in the collaborative-learning dynamic. Here, the construction of knowledge becomes much more of a group achievement, resulting from the intricate semantic intertwining of postings and references rather than being attributable to individuals.

Interviewer: Is that what you mean by your concept of group cognition?

Exactly! Cognition (thinking) is a semantic process, not necessarily a mental—silent, in the head—affair. An idea is a knowledge artifact, like a sentence, that gathers together in a complicated way a network of meanings of words, references, past events, future possibilities and other elements of the context in which the idea is situated. In our chat logs, we can see cognition taking place as knowledge artifacts build up, as words follow upon each other in subtly choreographed sequences to construct new ideas. The meaning can be seen there regardless of whether the words appear silently in the inner voice of one person, heard in the authoritative tones of a speaker, distributed among several interacting voices, in the pages of a book or even in the inanimate form of a computer log. Plato's ideas are as meaningful in a twentieth century edition of his writings as they were in his discourses thousands of years ago among small groups in the Athens marketplace or in seminars at his Academy, although the meaning has certainly shifted in the meantime.

The ideology of individualism gives priority to the thoughts of the individual. However, I believe that the foundational form of knowledge building actually occurs in small groups. Innovative knowledge building requires the inter-animation of ideas that were not previously together. A fertile ground for this exists when a couple of people come together to discuss a common topic. Recent CSCL studies have shown that it is precisely the friction between disparate perspectives that sparks productive knowledge building in the collaborative effort to clarify and/or resolve difference. The kinds of rhetorical and logical argumentation that arise in small-group discourse dealing with misunderstandings, alternative proposals or disagreements are then internalized in the reflection skills of individuals and in the controversies of communities. Thereby, small-group cognition provides the origin for and middle ground between individual cognition and community knowledge building.

Within the CSCL field and related disciplines, the ideology of individualism has been countered by a proposed shift in focus to communities-of-practice and learning communities. In my book, *Group Cognition*, I try to overcome this opposition of unreconciled extremes by pointing to the small group as the social unit that often mediates between individuals and their communities. Consider how groups of friends in a classroom or teams of colleagues in a workplace mediate the knowledge building that takes place there.

In the VMT Project, we have found that small-group collaboration is powerful. It enhances the desired characteristics of intentional learning and knowledge building. Effective collaborative groups not only produce knowledge artifacts that can be shared with a broader community, they also check to make sure that each individual group member understands (and potentially internalizes) the meanings of the group product. In responding to classroom assignments, small groups answer questions from their members and make decisions on how to proceed, thereby assuming agency for their own intentional learning. The group checks its progress and reflects on its conclusions, eventually deciding when they have completed a task and are ready to offer their knowledge to the larger community.

Sociologists of small groups have generally emphasized the negative possibilities of group cognition, such as "group think." Writing in the wake of the era of fascism, sociologists and social psychologists have worried about mob mentality and biases from peer pressure. This emphasis has obscured the potential of group cognition. It is like saying that thinking is dangerous because people might have evil thoughts. The point is to study and understand group cognition so that we can determine what might lead to negative versus positive consequences. Like any form of learning, it is important to provide supportive guidance and appropriate resources.

Interviewer: So what does all this mean for the analysis of online knowledge building?

Today's technology of networked computers offers exciting opportunities for students and for researchers. For students, it opens the possibility to meet with small groups of peers from around the world who share their interests; the recent phenomena of social networking on the Internet are just small indications of the potential for Web-based small-group cognition as a major form of knowledge building in the near future. For researchers, it suggests settings where group cognition can be studied in naturalistic settings. Unfortunately, adequate software environments and educational services are still not provided for students, and appropriate tools and methods are not available for researchers.

In the VMT research group, we are trying to develop a research approach in tandem with designing an online collaborative math service. We have developed a software environment centered on text chat for groups of three to five students. The chat is supplemented with a whiteboard for sketching, a portal for social networking and a wiki for community sharing of group knowledge artifacts. The different components are integrated with referencing tools and social awareness signs. Researchers can replay the logs of sessions like a digital video, providing the control necessary to conduct fine-grained analysis of interactions. The replayer shows everything that the students all saw on their screens during their sessions. Because the students typically did not know anything about each other except what appeared on their screens and had no other contact with each other, the replayed log provides a complete record for analyzing the shared meaning making and joint knowledge building that took place. Because all interaction took place through inscriptions (text and drawings, appearing sequentially), a detailed and accurate rigorous transcript can be automatically provided from the computer log.

The researcher does not have to engage in any preliminary work (such as transcribing video), but can begin by trying to understand the display of the inscriptions in the online environment using normal human interpretive skills, much as the students originally did (although from a research perspective rather than an engaged position). The researcher can then explore the methods used by the students for creating the meanings and social order of their session. We can actually observe the processes of knowledge building and group cognition as they unfolded.

In this interview I have only been able to indicate some of our ideas about group cognition in text chat, as they are developing through the analyses of the VMT research group. In order to convince you of the power of group cognition in chat and of the utility of our analyses to inform CSCL design, it will be necessary to share and reflect upon some of our concrete case studies. We have compiled the chapters of *Studying Virtual Math Teams* specifically to accomplish this.

Interviewer: **Thanks for sharing your views on these important topics.**

Chapter 2
The VMT Vision

Gerry Stahl

Abstract The aim of the Virtual Math Teams (VMT) Project is to catalyze and nurture networks of people discussing mathematics online. It does this by providing chat rooms for small groups of K-12 students and others to meet on the Web to communicate about math. The vision is that people from all over the world will be able to converse with others at their convenience about mathematical topics of common interest and that they will gradually form a virtual community of math discourse. For individuals who would enjoy doing math with other people but who do not have physical access to others who share this interest, the VMT service provides online, distant partners. For societies concerned about the low level of math understanding in the general population, the VMT service offers a way to increase engagement in math discourse. The VMT Project was funded in Fall 2003 by the US National Science Foundation. A collaboration of researchers at Drexel University and The Math Forum, the project is designing, deploying and studying a new online service at the Math Forum.

Keywords Knowledge building · social practices · group cognition · math education

A Report from the Present

The following report on the VMT Project was published in the Fall 2008 issue of *Bridge*, a magazine of the iSchool (the College of Information Science and Technology) at Drexel University. It was written by *Bridge* editor Susan Haine. It provides a view for the public of the project and its vision:

> Society is global. With just the push of a button, the dance of fingers across a keyboard we
> can connect with people and information from all corners of the globe. We network, bank,

G. Stahl (✉)
College of Information Science & Technology, Drexel University, Philadelphia, PA, USA
e-mail: gerry@gerrystahl.net

G. Stahl (ed.), *Studying Virtual Math Teams*, Computer-Supported Collaborative
Learning Series 11, DOI 10.1007/978-1-4419-0228-3_2,
© Springer Science+Business Media, LLC 2009

research and shop worldwide, but we do it all online from the comfort of our homes and offices. *iSchool* Associate Professor Gerry Stahl's research looks beyond the basics of international electronic communication, exploring how groups of people can more effectively learn through computer-supported collaborative learning (CSCL).

Stahl is lead researcher for the Virtual Math Teams Project (VMT) at the iSchool and the Math Forum at Drexel. The project utilizes chat interaction analysis to explore how students solve problems through online discussion and collaboration, with the goal to discover and better understand how groups of people think, come to decisions, solve problems and learn.

"When we started, we didn't even know if collaborative learning could be effective in math because people are so used to thinking about math on their own," Stahl said. "It's not typically considered an area where group interaction is beneficial to the learning process. The first thing we learned through this project is how effective collaborative learning can be, even with math, and how it could be a very effective classroom approach in general. It is a new form of not only math education, but education as a whole. I try to use it in my own iSchool courses."

The VMT service utilizes the Internet to connect students with global sources of knowledge, including other students around the world, information on the Web, and digital resources. Through these links, participants can engage in mathematical discussions which are, according to Stahl, rarely found in schools. Through this collaborative process, participants can challenge one another to understand formulas and problem solving in different ways, better understand one another's perspectives, and explain and defend their own ideas. VMT research shows that through this technique, students not only solve math problems, they better comprehend theories, expand their critical thinking and learn to work as a team. Knowledge is created through group interaction processes—what Stahl calls "group cognition."

"Anyone can benefit from it," Stahl said. "Other research has shown that collaborative small group work can be effective at any level, from Kindergarten through graduate school, and in professional math, even. In particular, though, VMT provides a venue for interacting with peers, and we've found in studying our logs of student interaction, there's a lot of social activity that is highly engaging for students."

This interaction encourages learning, increasing interest. According to Stahl, he plans to expand on the concept of how collaborative group learning can change a student's perception of learning in his next two books. One will be a collection of analyses of data from the VMT Project (this volume); the other will be a book-long reading of a four-hour series of chats by one group of students, discussing in fine detail the many facets of their interaction and joint knowledge building.

Though it may sound simple enough—observing the collaboration and communications among groups of students—the VMT Project has faced a number of challenges, and research plans have continually evolved in order to respond to what was learned about the needed chat environment, problem design, data collection and analysis methodology. Collaborating closely with four PhD students, colleagues at the Math Forum, at the School of Education, at the College of Arts & Sciences, and a series of international visiting researchers, Stahl and his team (see Fig. 2.1) have committed a good deal of time to fine tuning and coordinating a unique combination of pedagogical research, software development, analysis of interaction data and theory about collaborative learning.

"This is a complex research project," Stahl noted. "Nobody comes in with all the background they need in terms of educational theory, software design, etc. For the past four years we experimented with the best ways to collect data and analyze robust, naturalistic data."

According to Stahl's website, the project evolved from a very basic chat service environment to elaborate programming developed specifically for VMT through a relationship with researchers and developers in Germany. This system includes a number of chat tools and thread features with an integrated shared whiteboard for students to construct drawings related to a problem, a wiki for sharing findings with other teams, and a VMT Lobby that allows students to return to chat rooms or locate sequences of rooms arranged by VMT staff

Fig. 2.1 Some of the VMT team

and teachers. The goal in development was to make the software as effective as possible to assist learning, offering students effective tools without overloading them with options. The system supports students in exploring provided math problems, discussing open-ended mathematical situations and creating chat rooms to discuss topics of their own choosing.

The VMT service is available through the Math Forum at Drexel. To date, it has mainly been used by researchers—including labs at CMU, Rutgers, Hawaii, Brazil, Romania and Singapore—working with classroom teachers. The next step is to explore its use at online high schools and by home-schooled students. The end result is a new form of math education, melding technology and worldwide interaction with engrossing discussions and problem solving, offering students a different understanding of what math, learning and knowledge are all about. (Haine, 2008, pp. 2–3)

Historical Background: The Math Forum

The Math Forum manages a website (http://mathforum.org) with over a million pages of resources related to mathematics for middle-school and high-school students, primarily algebra and geometry. This site is well established; a leading online resource for improving math learning, teaching and communication since 1992, the Math Forum is now visited by several million different visitors a month. A community has grown up around this site, including teachers, mathematicians, researchers, students and parents—using the power of the Web to learn math and improve math education. The site offers a wealth of problems and puzzles, online mentoring, research, team problem solving, collaborations and professional development. Studies of site usage show that students have fun and learn a lot; that educators share ideas and acquire new skills; and that participants become increasingly engaged over time.

The Math Forum offers a number of online services, including the following. Most of these services were developed with research funding and volunteer support; some of the established services now charge a nominal fee to defray part of their operating costs:

(a) *The Problem of the Week.* This popular service posts a different problem every other week during the school year in a number of categories, such as math fundamentals, pre-algebra, algebra or geometry. Challenging non-standard math problems can be answered online or offline. Students can submit their solution strategies and receive feedback from mentors on how to improve their presentations. The best solution descriptions are posted on the Math Forum site.
(b) *Ask Dr. Math.* Students and others receive mathematics advice from professionals and expert volunteers.
(c) *Math Tools.* Visitors to the site explore the world of interactive tools for understanding math concepts and communicate with teachers using them in their classrooms, discussing and rating the tools.
(d) *Teacher2Teacher.* Classroom teachers and educators from around the world work together to address the challenges of teaching and learning math.
(e) *Other.* Math Forum staff also provide online mentoring and teacher professional development, lead face-to-face workshops and work with teachers in their math classrooms, under contracts with school districts.
(f) *Virtual Math Teams.* The VMT service builds on the highly successful Problem-of-the-Week (PoW) service. Students who once worked by themselves on PoW problems can now work on more open-ended problems with a group of peers. This can be organized in a variety of ways and can bring many advantages, as discussed in the following sections.

The VMT Service Design

The free VMT service currently consists of an introductory web portal within the Math Forum site and an interactive software environment. The VMT environment includes the VMT Lobby—where people can select chat rooms to enter (see Fig. 2.2)—and a variety of math discussion chat rooms—that each include a text chat window, a shared drawing area and a number of related tools (see Fig. 2.3).

Three types of rooms can be created in the lobby:

a. *Open rooms.* Anyone can enter these rooms and participate in the discussion— see Fig. 2.2, where rooms are listed under math subjects and problem topics.
b. *Restricted rooms.* Only people invited by the person who created the room can enter.
c. *Limited rooms.* People who were not originally invited can ask the person who created the room for permission to join.

This variety allows rooms to be created to meet different situations. For instance, (a) someone can open a room available to the public; (b) a teacher can open a room

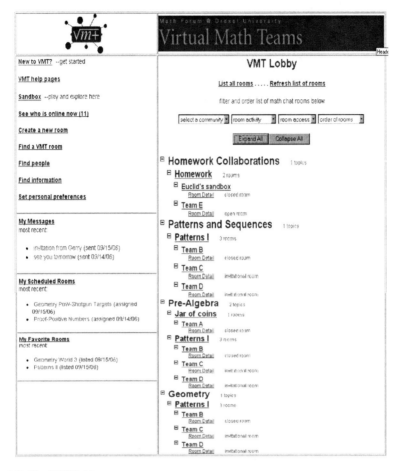

Fig. 2.2 The VMT lobby

for a group of her own students and choose whom else to let in; (c) a person can just invite a group of friends.

Three general types of room topics are presented in VMT rooms:

a. *A math problem*. This could be a problem from the PoW service, or a similar challenging problem that may have a specific answer, although there may be multiple paths to that answer and a variety of explanations of how to think about it. Sometimes, the VMT Project organizes PoW-wows: meetings of small groups of students to chat about a Problem-of-the-Week (PoW-wow logs are analyzed in Chapters 9, 23 and elsewhere).

b. *A math world*. An open-ended math world describes a situation whose mathematical properties are to be explored creatively. The goal may be as much for students to develop interesting questions to pose as for them to work out answers or structural properties of the world. In some years, the VMT Project sponsors a

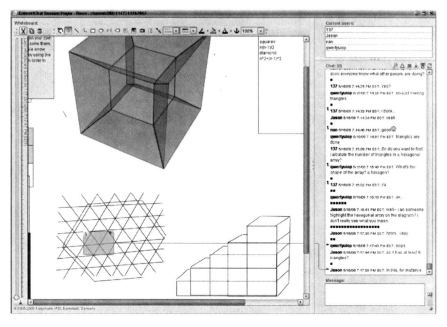

Fig. 2.3 A VMT chat room

VMT Spring Fest: teams from around the world explore the mathematics of an open-ended situation (Spring Fest logs are analyzed in Chapters 6, 7, 8, 10, 26 and others).

c. *Open topic.* These rooms are open for discussion of anything related to math, such as perplexing questions or homework confusions. These rooms have been used for university courses and even for discussions among researchers in the VMT Project (see examples in Chapter 21).

Such flexibility allows the VMT service to be used in a wide range of ways and in limitless combinations and sequences:

1. For instance, teams of students from the same classroom might first use the VMT environment to work together on a series of PoW problems during class time, allowing them to become familiar with the system and build collaboration skills in a familiar social setting.
2. Later they could split up and join groups with students from other schools to explore more open-ended mathematical situations.
3. As they become more advanced users, they can create their own rooms and invite friends or the public to discuss topics that they themselves propose.

Through such sequences, people become more active members of a math-discourse virtual community and help to grow that community.

A New Form of Math Education

The VMT Project explores the potential of the Internet to link learners with sources of knowledge around the world, including other learners, information on the Web and stimulating digital or computational resources. It offers opportunities for engrossing mathematical discussions that are rarely found in most schools. The traditional classroom that relies on one teacher, one textbook and one set of exercises to engage and train a room full of individual students over a long period of time can now be supplemented through small-group experiences of VMT chats, incorporating a variety of adaptable and personalizable interactions.

While a service like PoW or VMT may initially be used as a minor diversion within a classical school experience, it has the potential to become more. It can open new vistas for some students, providing a different view of what mathematics is about. By bringing learners together, it can challenge participants to understand other people's perspectives and to explain and defend their own ideas, stimulating important comprehension, collaboration and reflection skills.

As the VMT library grows in the future, it can guide groups of students into exciting realms of math that are outside traditional high school curriculum, but are accessible to people with basic skills. Such areas include: symbolic logic, probability, statistics, digital math, number theory, infinity, group theory, matrices, non-Euclidean geometries. Many math puzzles and games also build mathematical thinking and stimulate interest in exploring mathematical worlds.

Ultimately, whole curricula within mathematics could be structured in terms of sequences of VMT topics with associated learning resources. Students could form teams to explore these sequences, just as they now explore levels of game environments. A Problem-Based Learning (PBL) approach could cover both the breadth and depth of mathematical fields, just as PBL curricula currently provide students at numerous medical schools with their academic training in face-to-face collaborative teams. In varying degrees, students could pursue their own interests, learning styles, social modes and timing. Assessments of student progress could be built in to the computational environment, supplementing and supporting teacher or mentor judgments. The collaborative, small-group VMT approach would be very different from previous automated tutoring systems that isolated individual learners, because VMT is built around the bringing together of groups of students to interact with one another. (Part II of this volume analyzes the nature of group interactions in VMT.)

Promoting Knowledge Building Through Math Discourse

For most non-mathematicians, arithmetic provides their paradigm of math. Learning math, they assume, involves memorizing facts like multiplication tables and procedures like long division. But for mathematicians, math is a matter of defining new concepts and arguing about relations among them. Math is a centuries-long discourse, with a shared vocabulary, ways of symbolically representing ideas and procedures for defending claims. It is a discourse and a set of shared practices. Learning to talk about math objects, to appreciate arguments about them and to adopt the practices of mathematical reasoning constitute an education in math.

Classical training in school math—through drill in facts and procedures—is like learning Latin by memorizing vocabulary lists and conjugation tables: one can pass a test in the subject, but would have a hard time actually conversing with anyone in the language. To understand and appreciate the culture of mathematics, one has to live it and converse with others in it. Math learners have to understand and respond appropriately to mathematical statements by others and be able to critically review and constructively contribute to their proposals. The VMT Project creates worlds and communities in which math can be lived and spoken.

Students learn math best if they are actively involved in discussing math. Explaining their thinking to each other, making their ideas visible, expressing math concepts, teaching peers and contributing proposals are important ways for students to develop deep understanding and real expertise. There are few opportunities for such student-initiated activities in most teacher-led classrooms. The VMT chat room provides a place for students to build knowledge about math issues together through intensive, engaging discussions. Their entire discourse and graphical representations are persistent and visible for them to reflect on and share. (Part III of this volume describes features of group discourse in VMT.)

Evolving the VMT Service Design

The VMT service was not built from a fixed plan. It evolves. The VMT Project started by building on the success of the PoW service. In 2004, initial VMT sessions were held. Chat rooms were opened using a popular commercial chat system. Small groups of middle-school or high-school students were invited to work together in hour-long sessions on a PoW problem. An adult facilitator opened the room and announced the problem. If the students wanted to share a drawing or if they had technical problems, the facilitator assisted, but otherwise let the students work on their own. These early trials demonstrated that students were skilled at adapting to the chat environment and carrying on interesting mathematical discussions. However, it was clear that the software environment was too impoverished. It was hard to share drawings and to keep track of important ideas.

Later sessions experimented with introducing a shared whiteboard into the chat room (see Chapter 15). This allowed the participants to construct drawings related to the problem, to label the drawings and to post messages that remained visible on the board. This helped to overcome some of the technical difficulties. Unfortunately, it made the interactions more complicated. While some students invented effective group practices for taking advantage of the whiteboard (see Chapter 17 for analysis of innovative ways of pointing at the whiteboard from chat), these were not universally used. It became clear that people needed time to get used to the environment and to learn useful procedures.

More recently, the software environment of chat with whiteboard has been supplemented with a number of additional tools or features designed to support math discourse and online interaction (see Chapter 16). Furthermore, attempts have been made to involve groups of students in sequences of consecutive sessions, in addition to one-shot events. The VMT Lobby was added to allow students to return to chat rooms or to locate sequences of rooms that teachers or VMT staff prepared for them.

Perhaps most importantly, the nature of the problems offered has changed from the PoW format. As discussed above, different rooms have different kinds of topics. Some have individual problems, similar to the problems of the PoW service, but more oriented toward collaborative problem solving. However, other rooms have math worlds. These are open-ended situations, which suggest worlds, objects or patterns and relationships with interesting mathematical properties. In addition, students can open rooms for their own purposes. The nature of the topics and the ways they are presented strongly influence the nature of the interactions that take place in the rooms.

Supporting Math Discourse with Software Tools

Early theories of computer support for group work stressed the need to provide communication media, generally striving to duplicate as much as possible the features of face-to-face communication in situations where people were physically and/or temporally distant. Just as there are advantages (as well as disadvantages) of written communication over verbal, so there are advantages of particular computer-based media over face-to-face. The persistence of the written word in email, chat or threaded discussion is one important factor. In addition to supporting generic communication, it is possible for software environments to support group coordination and math problem solving more specifically.

For instance, the addition of the shared whiteboard to the VMT environment not only facilitated the communication of graphical representations of mathematical situations (like geometry problems), but also allowed for the posting of text messages, equations and summary statements in small text boxes that remained on-screen while chat postings scrolled away. Students could decide to draw in different colors to coordinate simultaneous sketching. It would also be possible to add math symbols, labels for drawings or a simple calculator to help express and compute mathematical relationships.

An important tool in the VMT environment provides the ability to reference from one text posting to a previous one or to a drawing area. This is an example of support for coordination. It helps in chats with several participants because when everyone is typing at once it is hard to tell which previous posting a new one is responding to. Furthermore, the referencing of an area of the whiteboard can support the mathematical work of defining specific areas in a drawing as corresponding to certain math objects.

For the development of the software environment, we began an intensive collaboration with researchers and developers at Fraunhofer Institute-IPSI in Darmstadt, Germany. They had developed a chat system with a shared drawing area and a referencing tool that provided both a form of threading in the chat and an integration of the drawing area with the chat. Their ConcertChat system formed the basis for VMT Chat. Working closely together, we not only improved the functionality of the chat rooms, but also designed a Lobby for finding chat rooms.

It is possible to add many more software tools to VMT Chat. The question is how to control the complexity of learning and using the system as it becomes more complicated. Separating the VMT Lobby, the VMT Chat, Web-based help documents and wiki-based archives of problems, resources and sample solutions is one way to keep each part relatively simple. (Part IV of this volume considers design issues in the VMT collaboration environment.)

Social Practices that Emerge in VMT

Perhaps more important than the design of the technological environment is the establishment of social practices to structure the behavior of participants in the chat rooms. Although this has been largely left up to the students in order to let them make VMT their own world, the VMT Project staff has tried to define expectations about how the space will be used. For instance, the ways in which students are invited to participate in VMT, the decor of the environment and the wordings of the room topics encourage an emphasis on math discourse.

Students enter the VMT environment with their previous experiences and bring along practices they have adopted in their school classrooms and social experiences. They are accustomed to tacitly agreeing upon ways of interacting. They are used to greeting people, starting a conversation topic, proposing new ideas, posing questions, taking turns, asserting themselves, saving face, correcting mistakes by themselves and others, coming to agreements and ending discussions. In VMT, this is all done through posting text in the chat stream and drawing on the whiteboard. It is normally done with strangers who are not visible. The VMT chat environment imposes a set of constraints and opportunities. It has aspects of a math classroom, a video game and an instant messaging exchange, as well as having unique characteristics. Groups of students adapt their familiar social practices to the peculiarities of the VMT chat environment. They spontaneously adopt and share methods of interaction—without necessarily being aware of them or able to explicitly describe them.

As researchers, the VMT staff tries hard to analyze the methods that groups use in VMT sessions (see Chapter 4). While these are in many ways unique to specific groups and sessions, one can also see patterns to the methods and structures to the sessions. Sessions typically start with mutual greetings and socializing. New users of the software spend some time experimenting with the tools or being trained in them. Eventually, someone suggests starting on the math topic and the question of how to begin arises. Math discussion often proceeds through sequences of math proposals, which themselves tend to have a typical structure of group interaction. (Part V of this volume analyzes structures of group interaction in VMT.)

Analysis of group methods used in the VMT Chat environment provides ideas for how to improve the software and the service design. It highlights where students have trouble making progress and where significant learning seems to be taking place.

Mentoring Through Guiding Feedback

A major issue in the design of the VMT service is how to guide the student discourse so that it will build mathematical knowledge related to the given topic. In a traditional classroom, a teacher is present to impose structure, provide informational resources, direct the flow of ideas, evaluate proposals and assess learning. In a Problem-Based-Learning collaborative group, there is a professional mentor present to actively model methods of interaction and argumentation. In the long run for the VMT service, however, it is generally not possible to have an adult facilitator present. The design of the service must itself make up for this lack.

The Math Forum context sets the general tone that mathematics is the central concern. The way that a given chat room topic or math problem is written is designed to establish a certain attitude, expectation and perspective for the discourse to follow. In addition, the VMT experience is designed to encourage democratic discussion, where people know they will be listened to and supported; therefore they feel free to express themselves. Students may develop positive identities as people who enjoy math in situations where math is not a competitive performance that makes some feel stupid and others odd.

As the VMT service has evolved, it has become increasingly important to provide feedback to the students and to encourage them to come back repeatedly. While mentoring cannot be done during most VMT sessions, groups are encouraged to post summaries of their work and to request asynchronous feedback. Sometimes we provide a wiki for students to share their discoveries with other groups working on the same topics. VMT staff can go to a chat room the next day, review what took place, enter some feedback, guidance or suggestions and send the students an email encouraging them to come back to the room to read the feedback and perhaps hold a follow-up group session.

Building a Community of Math Discourse

Ultimately, if students and teachers start to frequent the VMT service, share their group results, engage in multiple sessions and perhaps participate in other activities, they will start to form a user community. Teachers can interact at the site about the design of their favorite VMT math problems and share ways they have integrated VMT into their classrooms. Students can start to know each other from collaborating in groups together. They can participate in sequences of topics that build on each

---

28 G. Stahl

other. They can improve their collaboration and problem-solving skills and then start to mentor newcomers to VMT. As they become experienced with VMT, students and teachers can recommend improvements to the service and suggest variations to the topics.

We live in a society that is very dependent upon knowledge of mathematics, but that does not value mathematical discourse outside of narrow academic or professional contexts. The Math Forum has gradually built an online realm in which a community of math discourse can be found. By virtue of its collaborative focus, the VMT service may be able to help that community prosper.

We are considering related services to help build a collaborative user community. An archive of student discoveries is one possibility that we are exploring using wiki technology, so that students can grow their own repository of discoveries. A teachers' curriculum assistant site is another idea for supporting collaboration among teachers, who may want to know what topics worked for other teachers and share ways of involving students in math discourse. We would like to make the resources of the Math Forum digital library available to VMT participants in a relevant and useful way. And, of course, we are developing training materials (like this chapter, originally written for teachers) for students, teachers and researchers to introduce and explain VMT.

Studying Group Cognition

The VMT Project has the practical goal of establishing a new service at the Math Forum. It approaches this goal through a design-based-research effort that starts simply and develops the design of the service through an iterative process of evaluating the results of trying new features. From a basic research perspective, this is a valid way to explore the nature of collaborative learning and small-group interaction in math chats.

More particularly, the VMT Project generates data illustrating *group cognition.* As virtual teams produce sequences of problem-solving moves, the actions of different participants merge into an integrated discourse. Cognitive results then emerge as achievements of the group as a whole.

The VMT Project was designed as an experimental test-bed that captures lasting traces of collaborative interactions. The chat logs or persistent chat rooms preserve a rather complete record of the collaborative interactions that take place. The interactions involve challenging, creative problem solving of mathematics, including critical reflection on the problem-solving discourse. Thereby, the interactions produce numerous examples of group cognition in which teams produce cognitive results that cannot be attributed to any one individual but that arose out of the interactions among multiple participants situated in the group context. Since the students did not know each other from before the chat and could not observe each other except through the behavior that took place in the chat room, they could only understand each other's messages and actions based on what took place inside the chat room. The same information is available to researchers for understanding the messages and actions, providing an adequate record for analysis of how the group cognition took place. In contrast to classroom studies of face-to-face interaction, there is no need for videotaping and transcription, which introduce potential analytic difficulties.

The VMT Project allows researchers to see how small-group interaction and group cognition take place within a specific set of circumstances—e.g., small groups of K-12 students discussing math—with a particular form of technological mediation—i.e., chat with shared whiteboard and the features of VMT chat rooms. Synchronous math chats are different from forms of communication that have been studied more extensively, like asynchronous threaded discussions of science or face-to-face social conversation. The VMT Project is able to study and document the distinctive nature of math chats and their specific potentials for fostering group cognition. In this way, it illustrates with one small example a much broader vision of engaged learning in online communities of the future. (Part VI of this volume conceptualizes group cognition in VMT.)

Chapter 3
Mathematical Discourse as Group Cognition

Gerry Stahl

Abstract This chapter reviews Anna Sfard's book, *Thinking as communicating: Human development, the growth of discourses and mathematizing* (Sfard, 2008). It highlights insights of the book that are relevant to studying virtual math teams as well as calling for further analysis to situate Sfard's theory within the discourses of CSCL and socio-cultural theory.

Keywords Discourse · participation · math objects · math education

Anna Sfard raised the methodological discourse in the CSCL community to a higher niveau of self-understanding a decade ago with her analysis of our two prevalent metaphors for learning: the acquisition metaphor (AM) and the participation metaphor (PM). Despite her persuasive argument in favor of PM and a claim that AM and PM are as incommensurable as day and night, she asked us to retain the use of both metaphors and to take them as complementary in the sense of the quantum particle/wave theory, concluding that

> Our work is bound to produce a patchwork of metaphors rather than a unified, homogenous theory of learning. (Sfard, 1998, p. 12)

A first impression of her new book is that she has herself now come closer than one could have then imagined to a unified, homogenous theory of learning. It is a truly impressive accomplishment, all the more surprising in its systematic unity and comprehensive claims given her earlier discussion. Of course, Sfard does not claim to give the last word on learning, since she explicitly describes how both learning and theorizing are in principle open-ended. One could never acquire exhaustive knowledge of a domain like math education or participate in a community culture in an ultimate way, since knowledge and culture are autopoietic processes that keep building on themselves endlessly.

G. Stahl (✉)
College of Information Science & Technology, Drexel University, Philadelphia, PA, USA
e-mail: gerry@gerrystahl.net

G. Stahl (ed.), *Studying Virtual Math Teams*, Computer-Supported Collaborative Learning Series 11, DOI 10.1007/978-1-4419-0228-3_3,
© Springer Science+Business Media, LLC 2009

Sfard does not explicitly address the tension between her earlier essay and her new book. To reconcile her two discourses and to assess their implications for the field of CSCL, one has to first review her innovative and complex analysis of mathematical thinking.

Understanding Math Objects

Sfard introduces her presentation by describing five quandaries of mathematical thinking. I will focus on just one of these, which seems particularly foundational for a theory of math cognition, though all are important for math education: What does it mean to *understand* something in mathematics? Sometimes we ask, what is *deep understanding* in math (as opposed to just being able to go through the procedures)?

I am particularly interested in this question because in the VMT research group we are observing the chat of an algebra student who repeatedly says things like, the formula makes sense to him... but he does not see why it should. (In the chat shown in Fig. 3.1, Aznx expresses uncertainty about his understanding of Bwang's proposal about a formula and his ability to explain the formula in response to Quicksilver.) For us as analysts, it is hard to know how Aznx cannot see why the equation is right if it makes sense to him; the nature of his understanding seems to be problematic

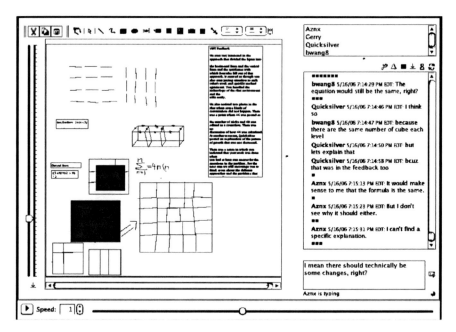

Fig. 3.1 Three students chat about the mathematics of stacked blocks

for him as well as for us (see Chapter 26 in this volume). One assumes that either he "possesses" knowledge about the applicability of the formula or he does not.

According to Sfard's theory, a math object—like the equation that Bwang is proposing in the chat for the number of blocks in stage N of a specific kind of pyramid—is an *objectification* or reification of a discursive process, such as counting the blocks at each stage (see also Wittgenstein, 1944/1956, p. 3f, §3). In fact, we observe the team of students in the chat environment visibly constructing the pyramid pattern in their shared whiteboard. Looking through Sfard's eyes, we can watch the students counting in a variety of ways. Sometimes they are numbering the graphical representations of blocks, other times referencing shared drawings of the blocks from the chat postings, or coordinating the sequential drawing of arranged blocks with the chat discussion in ways that make visible to the other students the enumeration of the pattern (see Chapter 7).

Sfard's central chapters spell out the ways in which math objects are subsequently co-constructed from these counting communication processes, using general procedures she names *saming, reification and encapsulation*. Note, for instance, that Bwang is explicitly engaged in a process of saming: claiming that a set of already reified math objects (previous and current equations the students are discussing) are "the same." He states, "The equation would still be the same, right? ... Because there are the same number of cube[s on] each level." He has reified the counting of the blocks into the form of a symbolic algebraic expression, which looks like an object with investigable attributes, rather than a discursive counting process. If he were a more expert speaker of math discourse, Bwang might even encapsulate the whole set of same equations as a new object, perhaps calling them *pyramid equations*. And so it goes.

In our case study, Aznx, Bwang and Quicksilver engage in four hours of online collaborative math discourse. They consider patterns of several configurations of blocks that grow step by step according to a rule (see also Moss & Beatty, 2006). They develop recursive and quadratic expressions for the count of blocks and number of unduplicated sides in the patterns. They decide what to explore and how to go about it, and they check and question each other's math proposals, collaboratively building shared knowledge. Their group knowledge[1] is fragile, and the team repeatedly struggles to articulate what they have found out and how they arrived at it, encouraged to explain their work by the facilitator, who places the textbox of feedback in their whiteboard. During their prolonged interaction, the group creates

---

[1] The use of the term *group cognition* for referring to the discursive methods that small groups collaboratively use to accomplish cognitive tasks like solving problems often raises misunderstandings because readers apply AM when they see the noun *cognition*. They wonder where the acquired cognitive objects are possessed and stored, since there is no individual physical persisting agent involved. If one applies PM instead, in line with Sfard's theory, then it makes much more sense that discursive objects are being built up within a publicly available group discourse. Conversely, Sfard's view of "thinking as communicating" or what she calls "commognition" ultimately requires a theory of group cognition as its philosophical foundation.

a substantial set of shared drawings and chat postings, intricately woven together in a complex web of meaning.

Sfard describes the discursive construction of math objects, which—as Husserl (1936/1989) said—is *sedimented* in the semiotic objects themselves. To paraphrase and reify Sfard's favorite Wittgenstein quote,[2] the use (the construction process) is embodied in the sign as it's meaning. She lays out the generative process by which a tree of *realizations* is built up through history and then reified by a new symbolic realization that names the tree. The algebraic equation that Bwang proposes is one such symbolic expression. The students have built it to encapsulate and embody various counting processes and graphical constructions that they have produced together. The equation also incorporates earlier math objects that the group has either co-constructed or brought into their discourse from previous experience (e.g., Gauss' formula for the sum of N consecutive integers, previously discussed in their math classrooms).

A centerpiece of Sfard's theory is the definition of a *math object as the recursive tree of its manifold visual realizations.* I will not attempt to summarize her argument because I want to encourage you to read it first hand. It is presented with all the grace, simplicity, insight and rigor of an elegant mathematical proof. It is itself built up from quasi-axiomatic principles, through intermediate theorems, illustrated with persuasive minimalist examples.

It is this definition of math object that, I believe, provides the germ of an answer to the conundrum of deep math understanding. That is, to understand a math object is to understand the realizations of that object. One must be able to unpack or de-construct the processes that are reified as the object. To be able to write an equation—e.g., during a test in school, where the particular equation is indicated—is not enough. To some extent, one must be able to re-create or derive the equation from a concrete situation and to display alternative visual realizations, such as graphs, formulas, special cases and tables of the equation. There is not a single—Platonic ideal or Cartesian necessary and sufficient—definition of the equation's meaning, but a network of inter-related realizations. To deeply understand the object, one must be conversant with multiple such realizations, be competent at working with them, be cognizant of their interrelationships and be able to recognize when they are applicable.

Routines of Math Discourse

Sfard then moves from ontology to pedagogy—from theory of math objects to theory of discourses about such objects, including how children come to participate in these discourses and individualize the social language into their personal math thinking. Based on her intensive work with data of young children learning math,

---

[2]"For a large class of cases—though not for all—in which we employ the word 'meaning' it can be defined thus: the meaning of a word is its use in the language." (1953, p. 20, §43)

she describes with sensitivity and insight how children come to understand words like *number, same, larger* and other foundational concepts of mathematical cognition. It is not primarily through a rationalist process of individual, logical, mental steps. It is a discursive social process—not acquisition of knowledge, but participation in co-construction of realizations. Sfard describes this as participation in social *routines*—much like Wittgensteinian language games. She describes in some detail three types of routines: *deeds, explorations and rituals. Routines* are meta-level rules that describe recurrent patterns of math discourse. Like Sfard's discussion itself, they describe math discourses rather than math objects. *Deeds* are methods for making changes to objects, such as drawing and enumerating squares on the whiteboard. *Explorations* are routines that contribute to a theory, like Bwang's proposal.

Rituals, by contrast are socially oriented. The more we try to understand Aznx's chat postings, the more we see how engaged he is in social activity rituals. He provides group leadership in keeping the group interaction and discourse moving; reflecting, explaining, responding to the facilitator, positioning his teammates, assigning tasks to others. His mathematical utterances are always subtly phrased to maintain desirable social relations within the group and with the facilitator—saving face, supporting before criticizing, leaving ignorances ambiguous, checking in with others on their opinions and understandings, positioning his teammates in the group interaction and assigning tasks to others. Each utterance is simultaneously mathematical and social, so that one could not code it (except for very specific purposes) as simply *content, social* or *off-topic* once one begins to understand the overdetermined mix of work it is doing in the discourse. Similarly, Bwang's explicitly mathematical proposals (explorations) are always intricately situated in the social interactions. Quicksilver often reflects on the group process, articulating the group routines to guide the process. Sfard's analysis helps us see the various emergent roles the students' participations play in their discourse—without requiring us to reduce the complexity of the social and semantic interrelationships.

Just as Vygotsky (1930/1978, 1934/1986) noticed that children start to use new adult words before they fully understand the meaning of the words (in fact, they learn the meaning by using the word), so Sfard argues that children advance from passive use of math concepts to routine-driven, phrase-driven and finally object-driven use. They often begin to individualize group knowledge and terminology through *imitation*. Again, the part of the book on routines requires and deserves careful study and cannot be adequately presented in a brief review. I would encourage the reader to try to apply Sfard's analysis to actual data of children learning math.

In the case of the VMT data, we see Aznx *imitating* his partners' routines and thereby gradually individualizing them as his own abilities. He often makes a knowledgeable-sounding proposal and then questions his own understanding. He does not *possess* the knowledge, but he is learning to *participate* in the discourse. In a collaborative setting, his partners can correct or accept his trials, steering and reinforcing his mimetic learning. During our four-hour recording, we can watch the group move through different stages of interaction with the symbols and realizations of math objects. The students we observe are not fully competent speakers of the language of math; as they struggle to make visible to each other (and eventually through that to themselves) their growing understanding, we as analysts can see both individual understanding and group cognition flowering. We can make sense of the discourse routines and interactional methods with the help of Sfard's concepts.

Participation in the discourse forms of math routines—such as exploration, ritual and imitation—can expose students to first-hand experiences of mathematical meaning making and problem solving. As they individualize these social experiences into their personal discourse repertoire, they thereby construct the kind of deep understanding that is often missing from acquisitionist/transmission math pedagogies (see Lockhart, 2008, for a critique of the consequences of AM schooling).

Situating Math Discourse

Sfard's theory resolves many quandaries that have bothered people about participationist and group cognitive theories, such as: How can ideas exist in discourses and social groupings rather than in individual minds? It provides detailed analyses of how people participate in the discourses of communities—at least within the domain of math discourses, both local and historical. It provides an account of some basic ways in which individual learning arises from collaborative activities. It indicates how meaning (as situated linguistic use) can be encapsulated in symbols. It explains how children learn, and that creativity is possible, while suggesting ways to foster and to study learning. It describes some of the mediations by which public discourses—as the foundational form of knowledge and group cognition—evolve and are individuated into private thinking.

Sfard has done us the great service of bringing the "linguistic turn" of twentieth century philosophy (notably Wittgenstein) into twenty-first century learning science, elaborating its perspective on the challenging example of math education. She shows how to see math concepts and student learning as discourse phenomena rather than mental objects.

The kind of theoretical undertaking reported in this book must restrict its scope in order to tell its story. However, if we want to incorporate its important accomplishments into CSCL research, then we must also recognize its limitations and evaluate its contributions *vis a vis* competing theories. In addition to noting its incomplete treatment of socio-cognitive theory, knowledge building, activity theory, ethnomethodology or distributed cognition, for instance, we should relate it more explicitly to the characteristics of CSCL.

First CSCL. By definition of its name, CSCL differs from broader fields of learning in two ways: its focus on *collaborative learning* (e.g., small-group peer learning) and its concern with *computer support* (e.g., asynchronous online discussion, synchronous text chat, wikis, blogs, scripted environments, simulations, mobile computing, video games). Sfard does not present examples of small-group interaction; her brief excerpts are from dyadic face-to-face discussions or adult-child interviews. Her empirical analyses zero in on individual math skills and development, rather than on the group mechanisms by which contributions from different personal perspectives are woven together in shared discourse. Nor do they take into account the mediation of online interaction by technological environments, so central to CSCL concerns. We now need to extend her general approach to computer-mediated interaction within small groups of students working together on the construction and deconstruction of math objects.

Fine-grained analysis of collaboration requires high-fidelity recordings, which—as Sfard notes—must be available for detailed and repeated study. She makes the tantalizing hypothesis that Piaget's famous distinction between successive developmental stages in children's thinking during his conservation experiments may be a misunderstanding caused by his inability to re-view children's interactions in adequate detail. Tape recordings and video now provide the technological infrastructure that made, for instance, conversation analysis possible and today allows multi-modal observation of micro-genetic mechanisms of interaction and learning. Computer logs offer the further possibility of automatically recording unlimited amounts of high-quality data for the analysis of group cognition.

For instance, in our study (in Chapter 26) of the case shown in Fig. 3.1, we used a Replayer application that lets us step through exactly what was shared by everyone in the chat room. Our Replayer shows the window as the participants saw it and adds across the bottom controls to slow, halt and browse the sequential unfolding of the interaction. This not only allows us to review interesting segments in arbitrarily fine detail in our group data sessions, but also allows us to make our raw data available to other researchers to evaluate our analyses (see Chapter 10 and Chapter 21, where other research groups analyze VMT data). Everyone has access to the complete data that was shared in the students' original experience. There are no selective interpretations and transformations introduced by camera angles, lighting, mike locations, transcription or log format.

Of course, the analysis of group interaction necessarily involves interpretation to understand the meaning-making processes that take place. The analyst must have not only general human understanding, but also competence in the specific discourse that is taking place. To understand Aznx's utterances, an analyst must be familiar with both the "form of life" of students and the math objects they are discussing. As Wittgenstein (1953, p. 223, §IIxi) suggests, even if a lion could speak, people would not understand it. Sfard's talk about analyzing discourse from the perspective of an analyst from Mars is potentially misleading; one needs *thick descriptions* (Geertz, 1973; Ryle, 1949) that are meaning-laden, not "objective" ones (in what discourse would these be expressed?). To understand and describe meanings, one must be to some extent a member of the discourse community—in contrast to the alien life forms from the jungle or outer space.

Sfard's discussion of the researcher's perspective (p. 278f) is correct that analysis requires understanding the data from perspectives other than those of the engaged participants—for instance, to analyze the structures of interactional dynamics and individual trajectories. However, it is important to differentiate this removed, analytic perspective (that still understands and relies upon its understanding of the meaning making) from a behaviorist or cognitivist assumption of objectivity (that claims to recognize only physical observables or hypothetical mental representations). The analyst must first understand the discourse in order to "explore" it from an outsider's meta-discourse, and neither a lion nor an analyst from Mars is competent to do so.

Sfard defines the unit of analysis as the discourse (p. 276). The use of CSCL media for math discourses problematizes this, because the discourse is now explicitly complex and mediated. Although Sfard has engaged in classroom analyses elsewhere, in this book her examples are confined to brief dyadic interchanges or even utterances by one student. In fact, some examples are made-up sentences like linguists offer, rather than carefully transcribed empirical occurrences. Moreover, the empirical examples are generally translated from Hebrew, causing a variety of interpretive problems and lessening the ability of most readers to judge independently the meaning of what transpired. Computer logs allow us to record and review complex interactions involving multiple people over extended interactions. The unit of analysis can be scaled up to include: groups larger than dyads (Chapter 21), the technological infrastructure (Jones, Dirckinck-Holmfeld, & Lindström, 2006), the classroom culture (Krange & Ludvigsen, 2008), or time stretches longer than a single session (Chapter 6). One can observe complex group cognitive processes, such as problem-solving activities—from group formation and problem framing to negotiation of approach and sketching of graphical realizations, to objectification and exploration of visual signifiers, to reflection and individualization. The encompassing discourse can bring in resources from the physical environment, history, culture, social institutions, power relationships, motivational influences, collective rememberings—in short, what activity theory calls the activity structure or actor-network theory identifies as the web of agency.

While Sfard uses the language of sweeping discourses—like the discourse of mathematics from the ancient Greeks to contemporary professional mathematicians—her specific analyses tend to minimize the larger social dimension in favor of the immediate moment. This is particularly striking when she uses terms like *alienation* and *reification* to describe details of concept formation. These terms are borrowed from social theory—as constructed in the discourses of Hegel, Marx and their followers, the social thought of Lukacs, Adorno, Vygotsky, Leontiev, Engeström, Lave, Giddens and Bourdieu. Sfard describes the reification of discursive counting processes into sentences about math objects named by nouns as eliminating the human subject and presenting the resultant products as if they were pre-existing and threatening. She does this in terms that all but recite Marx's (1867/1976, pp. 163–177) description of the fetishism of commodities. However, Marx grounded this process historically in the epochal development of the relations of social practice, the forces of material production and the processes of institutional reproduction. In contrast, Sfard often treats mathematics as a hermetic discourse, analyzable independently of the other discourses and practices that define our world. To her credit, in her concluding chapter she emphasizes the need to go beyond this in future work.

Mathematics develops—both globally and for a child—not only through the inter-animation of mini-discourses from different personal perspectives, but also through the interpenetration of macro-discourses. Math is inseparable from the world-historical rise of literacy, logic, rationalism, individualism, monotheism, capitalism, globalization, science and technology. CSCL theory must account for phenomena across the broad spectrum, from interactional details contained in subtle word choices to the clashes of epochal discourses. While Sfard has indicated a powerful way of talking about much of this spectrum, she has not yet adequately located her theory within the larger undertaking. One way to approach this would be to set her theory in dialog with competing participationist theories in CSCL and the learning sciences.

Continuing the Discourse

Issues of situating math discourse in social practice return us to the quandary of the metaphors of acquisition and participation. Sfard's book works out an impressive edifice of participation theory. Math can be conceptualized as a discourse in which people participate in the social construction of math objects; because of such participation, they can understand and individualize elements of the discourse. In doing so, Sfard follows a path of dialogical and discursive theory starting at least with Bakhtin, Vygotsky and Wittgenstein, and propounded by numerous contemporaries. Within the domain of math discourse, Sfard has pushed the analysis significantly further.

Her argument 10 years ago was that there is something to the metaphor of *objects* of math but that the ontological status of such objects was unclear and was perhaps best described by AM. In addition, she felt that multiple conflicting metaphors breed healthy dialog. Now she has shown that math objects are products of math discourse (so they now exist and make sense within PM). As for healthy dialog, there is plenty of opportunity for controversies among multiple discourses within PM itself. Thus, we can conclude that Sfard is justified in moving to a fully PM metaphor because this stream of thought is capable of resolving former quandaries and it contains within itself an adequate set of potentially complementary, possibly incommensurable discourses to ensure the kind of lively and productive on-going debate that drives science. Sfard has provided us with one of the most impressive unified, homogenous theories of learning; it remains for us to situate that theory within the specific field of CSCL and within the broader scope of competing theoretical perspectives. This includes extending and applying her analysis to group cognition and to computer-mediated interaction. It also involves integration with a deeper theoretical understanding of social and cultural dimensions.

At the other end of the spectrum, one must also resolve the relationship of "thinking as communicating" with the psychological approach to individual cognition as the manipulation of private mental representations. Is it possible to formulate a cognitivist view without engaging in problematic acquisitionist metaphors of a "ghost in the machine" (Ryle, 1949)? Assuming that one already recognizes the mechanisms of math discourse as Sfard has laid them out, how should hypothetical-deductive

experimental approaches then be used to refine models of individual conceptualization and to determine statistical distributions of learning across populations? Questions like these raised by the challenge of Sfard's book are likely to provoke continuing discourse and meta-discourse in CSCL for some time to come, resolving
intransigent quandaries and building more comprehensive (deeper) scientific understandings.

Chapter 4
Interactional Methods and Social Practices in VMT

Gerry Stahl

Abstract Virtual math teams develop innovative methods of interacting within the synchronous text chat VMT environment. New competencies for communication, collaboration and mathematical reasoning emerge as the groups make sense of the complex features of their shared virtual worlds.

Keywords Data session · expository discourse · explanatory discourse · adjacency pair

An Online Math Discourse Community Outside School

At the VMT Project, we are trying to build the foundations for an online community of people around the world who are interested in mathematics. Our focus is on students, rather than professionals or graduate students, so we feature math problems that can be solved with basic knowledge of algebra and geometry. The math education research community stresses the importance of math students discussing their reasoning (NCTM, 1989; Sfard, 2002), but school classrooms continue to be dominated by problem solving by individuals. Therefore, we are creating a place where students can explore and discuss math with other students, either independent of or in parallel with classroom routines.

We are involved in a multi-year effort to design an online math discourse community. Starting very simply from a successful online math problem-of-the-week service and taking advantage of popular off-the-shelf chat software to make it collaborative, we have gradually been evolving a more sophisticated environment involving carefully scripted pedagogical interventions, open-ended math issues and custom software—guided by extensive analysis of student behaviors through cycles of design-based research.

G. Stahl (✉)
College of Information Science & Technology, Drexel University, Philadelphia, PA, USA
e-mail: gerry@gerrystahl.net

G. Stahl (ed.), *Studying Virtual Math Teams*, Computer-Supported Collaborative Learning Series 11, DOI 10.1007/978-1-4419-0228-3_4,

While the ubiquity of networked computers connected through the Internet from homes and schools creates an exciting opportunity for students around the world to explore math together, the practical difficulties are enormous. We are interested in facilitating the development of high-level thinking skills and the deep understanding that comes from engaging in effective dialog (Wegerif, 2006, 2007) and merging personal perspectives (Stahl, 1993b, 2006b), but we find that students are accustomed to using chat and the Internet for superficial socializing. Furthermore, their habits of learning are overwhelmingly skewed toward passive acquisition of knowledge from authority sources like teachers and books, rather than from self-regulated or collaborative inquiry. Finally, attempts to invent technological solutions have failed for lack of regard for issues of social practice. Our experience to date suggests three stubborn challenges that need to be addressed:

- How to deepen the learning that takes place, given that most current examples of learning in online communities remain shallow.
- How to introduce inquiry learning in student-centered informal online communities into social contexts dominated by formal schooling.
- How to integrate pedagogical scaffolding, technological affordances and motivational sociability into a coherent service that fosters a growing community.

In order to address these needs, we have been using our emergent online community as a laboratory for studying the social practices of group cognition "in the wild." In our current phase, virtual math teams are small groups of students who meet in a chat room to discuss mathematical topics. These are typically three or four teenage students who interact for about an hour at a time. The chat rooms are set up by staff of the Math Forum. New students are invited by Math Forum initiatives, although students can subsequently set up their own rooms and invite friends or the online public. These meetings may be encouraged by teachers, but they occur online while the students are at home, in a library or elsewhere. No teacher is present in the room, although a facilitator from the Math Forum may be present to provide guidance in learning how to use the online environment. In the long run, these small, short-lived teams may evolve to become part of a global community of math discourse.

As the researchers who developed the VMT service, we are studying how students do mathematics collaboratively in online chat environments. We are particularly interested in the *social practices* that they develop to conduct their interactions in such an environment. Taken together, these practices define a culture, a shared set of ways to make sense together. The practices are subtly responsive to the chat medium, the pedagogical setting, the social atmosphere and the intellectual resources that are available to the participants. These practices define the ways in which chat groups interactively manage resources and conduct activities.

The VMT service and its technological infrastructure have been systematically designed as an experimental testbed for studying group cognition. The chat room is itself persistent and the drawings and text messaging can be replayed for researchers with their original sequentiality. While many things are not captured that may take place for individual participants at their distributed physical locations, most of what enters into the group interactions and is necessary for its analysis is readily available to researchers. Subtle communication cues that are hard to specify in the description of face-to-face communication have been largely excluded from the text-based interaction.

We have adapted the scientific methodology of conversation analysis (Livingston, 1987; Pomerantz & Fehr, 1991; Psathas, 1995; Sacks, 1962/1995; Sacks, Schegloff, & Jefferson, 1974; ten Have, 1999) to the micro-analysis of online, text-based, mathematical discourse. We adopt an ethnomethodological (Garfinkel, 1967; Heritage, 1984) focus on the methods that participants use to make shared sense of what they are jointly doing. In this chapter, we summarize some of our preliminary findings about how small groups make sense collaboratively in settings like VMT. For instance, we distinguish between expository and exploratory modes of narrative, showing alternative ways individual and group knowledge can be intertwined. The negotiation of communication genres like these involve the constitution of the group as such.

At a finer granularity, the sequentiality of chat messages can become confused without the turn-taking conventions of face-to-face communication. Both participants and analysts must learn how to reconstitute and represent the response structure that drives interaction. At this level, we analyze a proposal-response pair that is typical in math chats and look at the referencing patterns that determine chat threading when this pair is successfully completed and when it fails. Often, math proposals involve deictic references to math objects. Accomplishing such references without physical gestures can be challenging; they require support from special software functionality.

More generally, we investigate how these groups construct their shared experience of collaborating online. While answers to many questions in computer-mediated interaction have been formulated largely in terms of *individual* psychology, questions of collaborative experience require consideration of the *group* as the unit of analysis. Naturally, groups include individuals as contributors and interpreters of content, but the group interactions have structures and elements of their own that call for special analytic approaches. When groups work well, they can succeed in accomplishing high-order cognitive tasks—like inquiry, problem-solving, generalization and insight—as a group. We call this *group cognition* (Stahl, 2006b).

Using the kinds of practices analyzed in this chapter, small groups construct their collaborative experience. The chat takes on a flow of interrelated ideas for the group, analogous to an individual's stream of consciousness. The referential structure of this flow provides a basis for the group's experience of intersubjectivity, common ground and a shared world.

As designers of educational chat environments, we are particularly interested in how small groups of students construct their interactions in chat media with different technical features (Lonchamp, 2006). How do they learn about the meanings that designers embed in the environment and how do they negotiate the practices that they will adopt to turn technological possibilities into practical means for mediating their interactions? How can we design with students the technologies, pedagogies and communities that will result in desirable collaborative experiences for them?

The analysis of social practices summarized in this chapter points to the potential of text-based chat to provide an effective medium for computer-supported collaborative learning outside of school settings. In many contexts, chat is more engaging than the asynchronous media often used in education. However, text messaging and chat as normally practiced by teenagers is customarily a medium of informal socializing, not of group knowledge building. Creating a virtual place, a technological infrastructure and a set of social practices to foster more serious group cognition requires coordinated design based on detailed analysis of usage in settings like virtual math teams. Much of our effort goes into analyzing the social practices of our pioneer users.

Research Methodology for Recording Social Practices and Group Cognition

In chat settings, participants exchange textual postings. This is the sole visible basis for interaction, communication, mutual understanding and collaborative knowledge building within a generic chat environment. For the moment, let us consider such a generic chat room. In addition to the content of the typed postings, their order, sequentiality and timing typically play a significant role in how the postings are understood (O'Neill & Martin, 2003). The participants log in with a chat "handle" that is associated with their postings; the wording of this handle may imply something about the person so named. The postings by a given participant are linked together as his (or hers?) via the handle. Furthermore, we assume that the participants come to the chat room with specific expectations and motivations—in our case, because it is part of the Math Forum site and may be recommended by a teacher, parent or friend. Thus, there is an open-ended set of factors that may enter the chat from its socio-cultural context. There is also more-or-less shared language (e.g., English and basic math terminology) and culture (e.g., contemporary teen subculture and classroom math practices) that can play a role in the chats.

The current VMT environment is quite complex compared with generic chat. In addition to the chat window, there is a shared whiteboard for drawing diagrams, geometric figures, tables of numbers and text boxes (see Fig. 2-2 in Chapter 2). The chat and text boxes support mathML mathematical notation. Both the chat and the whiteboard are persistent, and their history can be scrolled by the users. There are social awareness messages indicating who is currently typing and drawing or entering and leaving the chat room. Many students participate in multiple sessions, and Math Forum staff often provide feedback in the chat room between sessions, which the students can read later. Recently, we have added a wiki, where students from different teams can post results and respond to what others have discovered. To support our research, we now have a replay facility in which we can view the whole interaction process in real time or fast-forward and step through the interaction with the chat, drawing and awareness notices all coordinated. This gives us a tool for analysis that is analogous to digital video for face-to-face interaction, but without all the complications of lighting, camera angles, transcription and synchronization.

Moreover, there is nothing going on "off camera" that affects the interaction because everything that was visually shared by the participants is replayed for us.

To study what takes place among students in chat rooms, we hold interaction analysis *data sessions* (Jordan & Henderson, 1995). A number of researchers collaboratively take a careful look at chat logs and discuss what is taking place in these meetings. Focus is directed toward brief extracts that present interactions of analytic interest to the research group. The chat log reveals to the researchers what was visible to the student participants. The researchers can take into account the institutional context in which the chat took place when it is made relevant within the chat discourse. As members of the broader society to which the students also belong, the researchers largely share a competent understanding of the culture and language of the chat. Thus, they are capable of making sense of the chat because they see the same things that the participants saw and can understand them in similar ways. Moreover, by repeatedly studying the persistent log of the chat and by bringing their analytic skills to it, researchers who have made themselves familiar with this genre can make explicit many aspects of the interaction that were taken for granted by participants in the flow of the moment. By working as a group, the researchers can minimize the likelihood of idiosyncratic analyses. We also work individually, studying transcripts and writing about them, but we periodically bring our analyses to the group for feedback and confirmation.

Ethnomethodology provides a further theoretical justification for the ability of researchers to produce rigorous analyses of recorded interactions. This has to do with the notion of *accountability* (Garfinkel, 1967; Livingston, 1987). When people interact, they typically construct social order (such as conducting a fun chat or developing a math solution) and may produce social objects (like textual postings). These objects are accountable in the sense that they were tacitly designed to reveal their own significance. A brief text posting, for instance, is written to be read in a certain way (Livingston, 1995); its choice of wording, syntax, references and placement in the larger chat are selected to show the reader how to read it (see Chapter 14). The account that a chat posting gives of itself for the other students in the chat can also be taken advantage of by the researchers. The researchers in a data session discuss the log in order to agree on the accounts of the postings, individually and in their interactive unity.

The social structure and the accountability of human interactions make it possible for researchers to draw generalized understandings from the analysis of unique case studies. Interactions in the VMT setting and elsewhere are extremely dependent upon the specific momentary circumstances of the interactional context that they sequentially build and the physical or socio-cultural context that they repeatedly index. Therefore, the data of student interactions is not reproducible and cannot in general be compared under conditions of experimental control. However, the social structures that people construct during their interactions necessarily have a generality. Otherwise, if every event had a unique significance, people would not be able to understand each other. Shared understanding is the basis for human interaction and it relies upon the generality of the structures that are interactionally created. These structures may vary within limits from culture to culture and in reaction to different mediational circumstances. Students in an English-language chat in Singapore might interact differently from adults in an asynchronous discussion forum in Scotland. However, experienced researchers can make sense of events in both contexts by taking into account the contextual differences. As the analyses that will be summarized in this chapter have shown us, there are basic patterns of interaction that students repeatedly call upon to discuss math. At the same time, even minor changes in technology support may cause participants to invent new forms of meaning making in reaction to the affordances and barriers that they enact in their online environments.

The VMT service has been developed through a design-based research approach to co-evolve the software, pedagogy, mathematics and service through an iterative process of trial, analysis and design modification. The software started with generic, commercial and educational chat systems and now involves development of a research prototype. The pedagogy started with principles of mathematics education and computer-supported collaborative learning and is now incorporating efforts to build a user community engaged in discussing math and facilitating collaborative practices. The math problems started out using the same Problems-of-the-Week offered to individuals and are now providing opportunities for groups to explore open-ended mathematical worlds as well as to work on issues that the participants generate themselves. The service started as occasional offerings and is now gearing up for continuous availability supported by as-needed monitoring and feedback.

As the trials progress, we analyze the resultant logs in the ways indicated in this chapter and use our results to inform our redesign of the software, pedagogy, mathematics and service. Thereby, ethnomethodologically-informed interaction analysis provides the analytic component of design research, a component that is not often specified in discussions of design-based research (Koschmann, Stahl, & Zemel, 2007). In this sense, the usage of our insights into how students interact in chat is at odds with the usual practices of ethnomethodology and conversation analysis, which claim not to impose researcher or designer interests on their data. While we try to understand what the student participants are up to in their own terms and how they are making sense of the activity structure that we provide for them, we are doing this in order to motivate our subsequent design decisions. Our goal is not just to understand the student meaning-making processes, but also to use that understanding to modify the VMT service to allow groups to engage more effectively in math discourse.

Participant Methods for Discussing Math Online

In order to understand the experience of people and groups collaborating online in our Virtual Math Teams service at the Math Forum, we look in detail at the captured interactions. We conceptualize the patterns of interaction that we observe as *methods*. This is a concept that we take from ethnomethodology (Garfinkel, 1967). Ethnomethodology is a phenomenological approach to sociology that tries to describe the methods that members of a culture use to accomplish what they do, such as how they carry on conversations (Sacks et al., 1974) or how they "do" mathematics (Livingston, 1986). In particular, the branch of ethnomethodology known as conversation analysis (Sacks, 1962/1995) has developed an extensive and detailed scientific literature about the methods that people deploy in everyday informal conversation and how to analyze what is going on in examples of verbal interaction.

Methods are seen as the ways that people produce social order and make sense of their shared world. For instance, conversation analysis has shown that there are well-defined procedures that people use to take turns at talk. There are ways that people use to determine when they can speak and how they can signal that others may take a turn at conversation (Sacks et al., 1974).

We adopt the general approach of conversation analysis, but we must make many adaptations to it given the significant differences between our chat logs and informal conversation. Our data consists of chat logs of student messages about mathematics. The messages are typed, not spoken, so they lack intonation, verbal stress, accent, rhythm, personality. The participants are not face-to-face, so their bodily posture, gaze, facial expression and physical engagement are missing. Only completed messages are posted; the halting process of producing the messages is not observable by message recipients (Garcia & Jacobs, 1998, 1999). The messages are displayed in a particular software environment and the messages are designed by their posters to be read and responded to in that environment (Livingston, 1995). The textual messages are persistent and may be read or ignored at will, and may be re-read later—although they scroll off-screen after several other postings appear. Several participants may be typing messages at the same time, and the order of posting these messages may be unpredictable by the participants (see Chapter 21). Consequently, messages do not necessarily appear immediately following the messages to which they are responding. In addition to these features of chat, our logs are concerned with mathematics and are created within educational institutional contexts—such as the Math Forum website and sometimes school-related activities or motivations. Thus, the chats may involve building mathematical knowledge, not just socializing and conversing about opinions or everyday affairs.

These differences between our chats and normal conversation mean that the rules of turn taking, etc. have all been transformed. What remains, however, is that people still develop methods for creating and sustaining social order and shared meaning making. Chat participants are skilled at creating and adapting sophisticated methods that accomplish their tasks in these unique environments. It is the analyst's job to recognize and describe these methods, which are generally taken for granted by the participants.

Among the student chat methods of interest to us are the interactional means that the students use:

- To introduce each other
- To adapt to institutional settings
- To socialize; to have fun; to flirt
- To get to know each other better
- To establish interpersonal relations or roles

- To form themselves into groups
- To define a problem to work on
- To start working on a problem
- To agree on how to proceed
- To bring in math resources
- To clarify a point
- To make a proposal
- To ask a question
- To resolve a difference of opinion
- To remember a past event
- To tell a story
- To justify a claim
- To negotiate a decision
- To reference an object
- To count items together
- To step through an analysis
- To agree on solutions
- To stop problem solving.

Our style of discourse analysis follows from our interest in identifying methods or social practices shared by group members. These are structural elements, interaction rules or social orderings, which are broadly accepted and generally taken for granted. When we analyze a log, we are not primarily interested in describing the surface content, because the organization of the interaction has less to do with the contents than with relations among them. We are also not primarily interested in assumptions about individual motivations and conceptions, except to the extent that these are visibly expressed so as to play an interactional role. We take the stated meaning to be a property of the discourse, as a carefully structured complex of symbols and meaningful artifacts. Nor do we assume that the social order has a pre-determined character, but insist on identifying the order as an emergent property—along with the meaning—of the discourse. It is the task of analysis to identify these properties from the data, as shared by the group and subsequently visible to the researchers.

Expository and Exploratory Discourse

Although our ethnomethodological chat analysis methodology modeled on conversation analysis has so far yielded the most insight into our data, we are pursuing a variety of approaches including coding (see Chapters 20 and 22), statistical (Chapter 23) and ethnographic (Chapters 11 and 27) investigations. These independent approaches can shed important light on the data and inform each other. Ethnographic analyses of the socio-cultural context, such as the classroom experiences of individual chat participants or their other activities in the Math Forum community help to clarify the personal motivations and the math resources that students bring into the chat (Renninger & Shumar, 1998).

In our project, a statistical analysis led to an interesting conversation analytic result. A statistical comparison of codes between chats in which students had time to work on math problems individually prior to the chats (condition A) and those where they first saw the problem in the collaborative chat context (condition B) led to a puzzling anomaly (see Chapter 23). While most of the chats in both conditions were clustered together, one chat from each condition clustered more with the chats from the other condition. A conversation analysis of the two anomalous chats led to a distinction between *expository narrative* and *exploratory inquiry*; this distinction was already discussed in the CSCL literature (Mercer & Wegerif, 1999), but we discovered it independently and only later learned of the existing analysis.

In conversation analytic terms, this is largely a difference in turn-taking methods. In *exposition*, one person makes a bid to "tell a story" about how they solved a problem. The other group members offer the expositor an extended turn at talking (or posting). The expositor dominates the discourse, providing a sequential account across several unusually long turns. The other group members listen (read) attentively, provide brief encouraging exclamations, pose questions and provide an audience. In a math problem-solving session, there may be multiple expositions concerning subsequent parts of the problem solution, possibly by different people.

In *exploratory inquiry*, the turns are more equally shared as the group collectively investigates the problem and co-constructs a solution path. The steps in exploration may each involve several participants, with one person proposing a move and others agreeing, making the move or challenging it. The distinction of exposition versus exploration roughly parallels that between cooperation (people dividing up tasks to reach a common goal) and collaboration (people working together on each task) (Dillenbourg, 1999).

The statistical quandary was resolved by noticing that the anomalous chat from condition A consisted largely of collaborative exploration despite the fact that the students may have had a chance to produce their own solutions in advance. In the anomalous chat from condition B, the students took time in the chat to first work out at least partial solutions on their own before contributing to the chat; they then provided expositions on what they found. These examples demonstrate that external conditions do not mechanically determine the methods that people use to interact. In fact, it is common for students in a chat to alternate between cooperative expository and collaborative exploratory sequences of interaction. Thus, the identification of methods must be determined through careful analysis of the social order that structures the discourse and that is spontaneously created by the participants in their on-going interaction—rather than by hypothesizing causal mechanisms based on objective designed conditions.

The Group of Individuals

The difference between cooperative exposition and collaborative exploration in math problem-solving chats is related to the difference between individual solution and group solution. A given math chat log can be ambiguous as to whether it should be analyzed as a set of contributions from individual thinkers or whether it should be analyzed as a group accomplishment. Often, it is helpful to view it both ways and to see an intertwining of these two perspectives at work (see Chapter 5).

We tried an experiment where we had students solve standard math problems individually and then solve the same problems in chat groups. In the group that we tracked, the group not only correctly solved all the problems that were solved by any one member of their group individually, but also solved some that no one did by themselves. Here is one that was solved by the group:

> Three years ago, men made up two out of every three Internet users in America. Today the ratio of male to female users is about 1 to 1. In that time the number of American females using the Internet has grown by 30,000,000, while the number of males who use the Internet has grown by 100%. By how much has the total Internet-user population increased in America in the past three years?
>
> (A) 50,000,000 (B) 60,000,000 (C) 80,000,000 (D) 100,000,000 (E) 200,000,000

When we first looked at the chat log, it appeared that one student (Mic) who seemed particularly weak in math was clowning around a lot and that another (Cosi) managed to solve the problem herself despite this distraction in the chat room.

In thinking about why Cosi could solve this problem in the group context but not alone, we noticed that she was not simply solving the problem as one would in isolation (e.g., setting up algebraic equations), but was interacting with the group effort. In particular, Dan, Mic and Hal had set up a certain way of approaching the problem and of exploring possible solutions. Cosi was reflecting on the group approach and repairing problems in its logic. The numbers, words and considerations that she used were supplied by the context of on-going interactive activities and shared meanings.

If we combine the proposals from Mic, Dan, Hal and Cosi, they read like the cognitive process of an individual problem solver:

> How can I figure out the increase in users without knowing the total number of internet users? <Mic> It seems to all come from the 30,000,000 figure. <Dan> 30,000,000 is the number of increase in American females. Since the ratio of male to female is 1 to 1, <Mic> the total of male and female combined would be 60,000,000. <Hal> No, I think it must be more than 60,000,000 because the male and female user populations can't get higher at equal rates and still even out to a 1 to 1 ratio after starting uneven. No, I made a mistake; the total must be less than 60,000,000. It could be 50,000,000, which is the only multiple-choice option less than 60,000,000. <Cosi> Very smart. <Dan>

Clearly, Cosi made some contributions to the group that were key to the group solution. They were acknowledged as such. Cosi was termed "very smart"— although this could equally well be said of the group as a whole. While no individual in the group could see how to solve the problem, everyone contributed to exploring it in a way that rather efficiently led to a solution. In particular, Mic—who was weak in math—used clowning around as an extremely effective way to facilitate the group process. By joking and laughing a lot, the group relieved some of the pressure to solve a problem that was beyond any individual's reach and to open a social space in which ideas could be put forward without fear of being judged harshly. Through non-threatening forms of critique and repair, the group solved the problem.

Attributing the solution to the group rather than to the sum of the individuals in the group can be motivated by seeing that the construction of mathematical meaning in the solution process was done *across* individuals. That is, meaning was created by means of interactions among individual contributions (postings) to the chat—such as through what are called *adjacency pairs* in conversation analysis—more than by individual postings construed as expressing a series of personal mental representations.

Math Proposal Adjacency Pairs

In an early chat of the VMT Project using AOL's Instant Messenger, a popular chat environment, we observed a repeated pattern of interaction that we have since found to be common in math chats. Log 4-1 is an excerpt from that chat (line numbers added; handles anonymized):

Log 4-1.

17.	Avr	(8:23:27 PM):	i think we have to figure out the height by ourselves
18.	Avr	(8:23:29 PM):	if possible
19.	pin	(8:24:05 PM):	i know how
20.	pin	(8:24:09 PM):	draw the altitude'
21.	Avr	(8:24:09 PM):	how?
22.	Avr	(8:24:15 PM):	right
23.	Sup	(8:24:19 PM):	proportions?
24.	Avr	(8:24:19 PM):	this is frustrating
25.	Avr	(8:24:22 PM):	I don't have enough paper

In this log we see several examples of a three-step pattern:

- A proposal bid is made by Avr in lines 17 and 18 for the group to work on: **"I think we have to . . ."**.
- The bid is taken up by someone else (Pin in line 19) on behalf of the group: **"I know how"**
- There is an elaboration of the proposal by members of the group. The proposed work is begun, often with a secondary proposal for the first sub-step, such as Pin's new proposal bid in line 20.

The third step initiates a repeat of the three-step process:

- A proposal bid is made by Pin in line 20 for the group to work on: **"Draw the altitude"**
- An acceptance is made by someone else (Avr in line 22) on behalf of the group: **"Right!"**
- There is an elaboration of the proposal by members of the group. The proposed work is begun, often with a secondary proposal for the first sub-step, such as Sup's new proposal bid in line 23.

But here the pattern breaks down. It is unclear to us as analysts what Sup's proposal bid, **"Proportions?"** is proposing. Nor is it responded to or taken up by the other group members as a proposal. Avr's lines 24 and 25 ignore it and seem to be reporting on Avr's efforts to work on the previous proposal to draw the altitude. Breakdown situations are often worth analyzing carefully, for they can expose in the breach practices that otherwise go unnoticed, taken for granted in their smooth execution.

Our analysis of Sup's "failed proposal" (see Stahl, 2006b, chap. 21) helps to specify—by way of counter-example—the conditions that promote successful proposals in math chats: (a) a clear semantic and syntactic structure, (b) careful timing within the sequence of postings, (c) a firm interruption of any other flow of discussion, (d) the elicitation of a response, (e) the specification of work to be done and (f) a history of helpful contributions. In addition, there are other interaction characteristics and mathematical requirements. For instance, the level of mathematical background knowledge assumed in a proposal must be compatible with the expertise of the participants and the computational methods must correspond with their training.

We call the three-step pattern described above a *math proposal adjacency pair*. It seems to be a common interaction pattern in collaborative problem solving of mathematics in our chats. We call this a form of "adjacency pair" in keeping with conversation analysis terminology (Duranti, 1998; Schegloff, 1991), even though in chat logs the parts of the pair may not appear adjacent due to the complexities of chat postings: e.g., line 22 responds to line 20, with line 21 intervening as a delayed response to line 19. As we see in other chats, however, not all student groups adopt this method.

Deictic Referencing and Threading

The more we study chat logs, the more we see how interwoven the postings are with each other and with the holistic Gestalt of the interactional context that they form (see esp. Parts II, V and VI of this volume). The importance of such indexicality to creating shared meaning was stressed by Garfinkel (1967). There are many ways in which a posting can reference (index or point to) elements of its context. Deictic referencing (verbal pointing) is one important form of this. Vygotsky noted the central role of physical pointing for mediating intersubjectivity in his analysis of the genesis of the infant-and-mother's co-constructed pointing gesture (1930/1978, p. 56). Our past analysis of face-to-face collaboration emphasized that spoken utterances in collaborative settings tend to be elliptical, indexical and projective ways of referencing previous utterances, the conversational context and anticipated responses (Stahl, 2006b, chap. 12).

So, we provide support for pointing in chat. The VMT environment not only includes a shared whiteboard, but it also has functionality for referencing areas of the whiteboard from chat postings and for referencing previous postings (see Fig. 4-1). The shared whiteboard is necessary for supporting most geometry

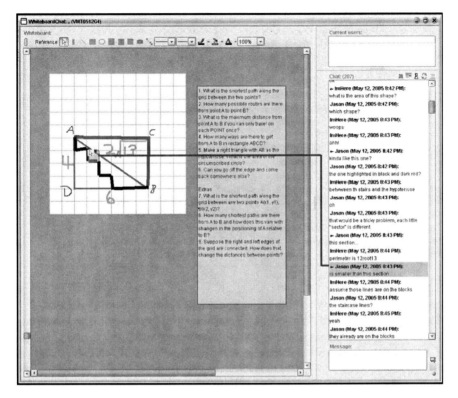

Fig. 4-1 Screen view of the VMT environment with referencing

problems. Sharing drawings is not enough; students must be able to reference specific objects or areas in the drawing. The whiteboard also provides opportunities to post text where it will not scroll away. The graphical references (see the blue line from a selected posting to an area of the drawing) can also be used to reference one or more previous postings from a new posting, in order to make the threads of responses clearer in the midst of "chat confusion" (see Chapter 21).

In one of our first chats using the VMT environment with a shared whiteboard, the students engaged in a particularly complex interaction of referencing a figure in the whiteboard whose mathematics they wanted to explore (see Chapter 17). Log 4-2 is the chat log from Fig. 4-1 (line 12 of the log is selected in the figure; graphical references to the whiteboard are indicated in the log by **"[REF TO WB]"**).

Line 1 of the chat textually references an abstract characteristic of a complex form in the whiteboard: **"the area of this shape"**. The software function to support this reference failed, presumably because the student, ImH, was not experienced in using it and did not cause the graphical reference line to point to anything in the drawing. With line 5, Jas provides a demo of how to use the referencing tool. Using the tool's line, a definite textual reference (**"the one"**) and the use of line color and thickness in the drawing, lines 5 and 6 propose an area to act as the topic of the chat.

Log 4-2.

1	ImH:	what is the area of this shape? [REF TO WB]
2	Jas:	which shape?
3	ImH:	nwoops
4	ImH:	ahh!
5	Jas:	kinda like this one? [REF TO WB]
6	Jas:	the one highlighted in black and dark red?
7	ImH:	between th stairs and the hypotenuse
8	Jas:	oh
9	Jas:	that would be a tricky problem, each little "sector" is different
10	Jas:	this section [REF TO WB]
11	ImH:	perimeter is 12root3
12	Jas:	is smaller than this section [REF TO WB]
13	ImH:	assume those lines are on the blocks
14	Jas:	the staircase lines?
15	ImH:	yea
16	Jas:	they already are on the blocks

Line 7 makes explicit in text the definition of a sub-area of the proposed area. Line 8 accepts the new definition and line 9 starts to work on the problem concerning this area. Line 9 references the problem as "that" and notes that it is tricky because the area defined does not consist of standard forms whose area would be easy to compute and add up. It refers to the non-uniform sub-areas as little **"sectors"**. Line 10 then uses the referencing tool to highlight (roughly) one of these little sectors or **"sections"**. Line 12 continues line 10, but is interrupted in the chat log by line 11, a failed proposal bid by ImH. The chat excerpt continues to reference particular line segments using deictic pronouns and articles as well as a growing vocabulary of mathematical objects of concern: sectors, sections, lines, blocks.

Progress is made slowly in the collaborative exploration of mathematical relationships, but having a shared drawing helps considerably. The students use multiple textual and graphical means to reach a shared understanding of mathematical objects that they find interesting but hard to define. In this excerpt, we start to get a sense of the complex ways in which brief textual postings weave dense webs of relationships among each other and with other elements of the collaborative context (see Chapter 26).

Group Cognition in Math Chats

Our goal in the VMT Project is to provide a service to students that will allow them to have a rewarding experience collaborating with their peers in online discussions of mathematics. We can never know exactly what kind of subjective experience they had, let alone predict how they will experience life under conditions that we design for them. Our primary access to information related to their group experiences comes from our chat logs. The logs capture what student members see of their group on their computer screens. We can even replay the logs so that we see how they unfolded sequentially in time. Of course, we are not engaged in the interaction the way the participants were, and recorded experiences never quite live up to the live version because the engagement is missing. We do test out the environments ourselves and enjoy the experience, but we experience math and collaboration differently than do middle-school students.

We also interview students and their teachers, but teenagers rarely reveal much of their life to adults. So we try to understand how collaborative experiences are structured as interpersonal interactions. The focus is not on the individuals as subjective minds, but on the human, social group as constituted by the interactions that take place within the group.

During VMT chats, students work on math problems and themes. In solving problems and exploring math worlds or phenomena, the groups construct sequences of mathematical reasoning that are analogous to proofs. Proofs in mathematics have an interesting and subtle structure. One must distinguish: the problem situation; the exploratory search for the solution; the effort to reduce a haphazard solution path to an elegant, formalized proof; the statement of the proof; and the lived experience of following the proof (Livingston, 1986, 1987). Each of these has its own structures and social practices. Each necessarily references the others. To engage in mathematics is to become ensnarled in the intricate connections among them. To the extent that these aspects of doing math have been distinguished and theorized, it has been done as though there is simply an individual mathematician at work. There has been virtually no research into how these could be accomplished and experienced collaboratively—despite the fact that talking with others about math has for some time been seen as a priority in math education.

In the most successful VMT chats, meaning is created at the group unit of analysis rather than by particular individuals. If the group experience is a positive one for the participants, they may want to return. Many chats end with people making plans to get together again. In some experiments, the same groups attended multiple sessions. Eventually, we would like to see a community of users form, with teams re-forming repeatedly and with old-timers helping new groups to form and to learn how to collaborate effectively.

The recognition that collaborative groups constitute themselves interactionally and that their sense making takes place at the group unit of analysis has fundamental methodological implications for the study of collaboration. The field of computer-supported collaborative learning (CSCL) was founded a decade ago to pursue the analysis of group meaning making (Stahl, Koschmann, & Suthers, 2006). We view the research described in this volume as a contribution to that CSCL tradition.

In this chapter, we have summarized several analyses of methods that virtual math teams have used to create shared meaning and to pursue their problem-solving discourse. Most of these analyses are worked out in detail in later chapters of this volume. The discussion of math adjacency pairs already appeared in the final chapter of (Stahl, 2006b) (which anticipated the studies of this volume) and in (Stahl, 2006d), so it is not included in this volume.

Chapter 5
From Individual Representations
to Group Cognition

Gerry Stahl

Abstract More than we realize it, knowledge is often constructed through interactions among people in small groups. The Internet, by allowing people to communicate globally in limitless combinations, has opened enormous opportunities for the creation of knowledge and understanding. However, a major barrier to taking advantage of this opportunity remains the lack of adequate groupware. To design more powerful software that can facilitate the building of collaborative knowledge, we need to better understand the nature of group cognition—the processes whereby small groups develop their understanding. We need to analyze interaction at both the individual and the group unit of analysis in order to understand the variety of processes that groupware should be supporting. This chapter will look closely at an empirical example of knowledge being constructed by a small group and suggest implications for groupware design. It will first analyze the chat interaction as the expression of individual thinking and then re-analyze it as the sequential unfolding of group exploration of a math problem that no individual in the group was able to solve on their own.

Keywords Individual   learning   ·   group   problem   solving   ·   group cognition · referencing · groupware

Individual Learning in Groups

Groupware is software that is specifically designed to support the work of groups. Most software in the past, in contrast, has been designed to support the work of individuals. The most popular applications—such as word processors, Internet browsers and spreadsheets—are structured for use by one individual at a time. Software for communication among people—like an email program—assumes a model of communication as transmission of messages from one person to other individuals.

G. Stahl (✉)
College of Information Science & Technology, Drexel University, Philadelphia, PA, USA
e-mail: gerry@gerrystahl.net

G. Stahl (ed.), *Studying Virtual Math Teams*, Computer-Supported Collaborative Learning Series 11, DOI 10.1007/978-1-4419-0228-3_5,
© Springer Science+Business Media, LLC 2009

Building on these examples, one could design groupware to support groups conceived of as sets of individuals. Such software would allow individuals to express their mental ideas, transmit these expressions to other people, receive expressions transmitted from other people and make sense of received messages as expressions of the ideas in the heads of the other people (as in Shannon & Weaver, 1949). Possibilities for improving these designs might be conceived in terms of "increasing the bandwidth" of the transmissions, probably taking face-to-face communication as the "gold standard" of communication with a wide bandwidth of many channels (words, intonation, gaze, facial expression, gesture, body language).

Until recently, most research about groups has focused on the individual people in the group as the cognitive agents. For instance, research on cooperative learning in the 1970s (still in Johnson & Johnson, 1989), assumed that knowledge resided in the individuals, and that group interaction was most useful as a way of transferring knowledge from one individual to another or as a way of motivating individuals to perform better. Educational research on groups typically measured learning in terms of individual test outcomes and tried to study what is going on in the minds of the individuals through surveys, interviews and think-aloud protocols. Similarly, research in social psychology about small groups conceptualized the groups as sets of rationally calculating individuals seeking to maximize their own advantages. This broad tradition looks to the individual as the unit of analysis, both to understand what takes place in the behavior of individuals working within groups and to measure quantitative learning or knowledge-building outcomes of the individuals in group contexts.

In the 1990s, the individualistic approach was thoroughly critiqued by theories of situated cognition (Suchman, 1987), distributed cognition (Hutchins, 1996), cultural–historical activity theory (Engeström, 1999) and ethnomethodology (Garfinkel, 1967), building on philosophies of phenomenology (Heidegger, 1927/1996), mediation (Vygotsky, 1930/1978) and dialog (Bakhtin, 1986a). These new approaches rejected the view that cognition or the construction of knowledge takes place exclusively in the isolated minds of individuals, and showed how it emerges from concrete situations and interpersonal interactions. One consequence that could be drawn from this would be to analyze cognition at the small-group unit of analysis, as in many cases a product of social interaction within the context of culturally-defined rules or habits of behavior.

An alternative approach for designing groupware, based on such a group conception of cognition would provide functionality to support the working of a group as an organic whole, rather that just supporting the group members as individuals and treating the group as the sum of its parts. In the past, a number of researchers have tried to develop groupware that supports the functioning of the group itself, such as the formation of groups (Wessner & Pfister, 2001), intertwining of perspectives (Stahl & Herrmann, 1999) and negotiation of group decisions (Stahl, 2002a; Vogel, Nunamaker, Applegate, & Konsynski, 1987).

This chapter reports on our analysis of a group of students working on a set of math problems in an online chat room. We are interested in seeing how they work together using a minimal system of computer support in order to see what forms of interaction might be supported by groupware with special functionality designed to increase the effectiveness of the collaboration.

In order to capture both the individual and the group contributions to discourse and to compare their results, we arranged an experiment with a combination of individual and group work. It consists of an individual phase where the knowledge of the individuals can be objectively assessed, followed by a group phase in which the references and proposals can be analyzed at both the individual and the group units of analysis. By seeing what the individuals knew before they participated in the group phase, it should be possible to see what the group interaction added.

In the VMT Project (see Chapters 4 and 23), we have characterized two different general patterns of chat discourse: *expository narrative* and *exploratory inquiry* (compare Mercer & Wegerif, 1999). These are two common methods of conducting online discourse that embody different relationships of the group to its individual members.

As briefly discussed in the previous chapter, expository narrative involves one person dominating the interchange by contributing more and longer texts (Sacks, 1962/1995). Basically, the normal turn-taking procedure in which members take roughly equal and alternating turns is transformed in order to let one person narrate an extended story or explanation. For instance, if a student has already solved a math problem that the group is working on, that student might propose their solution or indicate that they have a solution and the others might request an explanation of the proposed solution. There would still be some forms of interaction, with members of an audience asking questions, encouraging continuation, indicating understanding, raising questions, etc. But in general, the proposer would be allowed to provide most of the discourse. In conversation, this kind of pattern is typical where one member narrates a story or talks in detail about some events or opinions (Bruner, 1990). Exposition in math has its own characteristics, such as providing mathematical warrants for claims, calculating values, addressing issues of formal logic, etc. But it follows a turn-taking profile similar to that of conversational narrative.

Exploratory inquiry has a different structure. Here, the group members work together to explore a topic. Their texts contribute from different perspectives to construct some insight, knowledge, position or solution that cannot be attributed to any one source but that emerges from the "inter-animation of perspectives" (Bakhtin, 1986b; Wegerif, 2006). Exploratory inquiries tend to take on the appearance of group cognition. They contrast with expository narratives in a way that is analogous to the broad distinction between *collaboration* and *cooperation* (Dillenbourg, 1999). Collaboration involves a group of people working on something together, whereas cooperation involves people dividing the work up, each working by themselves on their own part and then joining their partial solutions together for the group solution. Expository narratives tend to take on the appearance of cooperation, where individuals contribute their own solutions and narrate an account of how they arrived at them. In a rough way, then, exploratory and expository forms of discourse seem to reflect group versus individual approaches to constructing shared knowledge.

We will now analyze our experiment involving a group of college students in an online chat discussing a series of math problems. We will try to tease apart the individual and the group contributions to meaning making, knowledge building and problem solving. We conducted the experiment using a set of well-defined math problems, for which it is clear when an individual or a group arrives at the correct answer. We gave the students an opportunity to solve the problems on their own—as individuals—with pencil and paper. We then had them enter an online chat room and decide as small groups on the correct answers. By collecting the individual papers and logging the chat, we obtained data about the individual and the group knowledge, which we can objectively evaluate and compare.

The students were given 11 problems on two sheets of paper with room to show their work and to give their answers. The problems were a variety of algebra and geometry problems, some stated as word problems. Most required some insight. They came from the Scholastic Aptitude Tests (SAT), which are taken by high school students in order to apply to colleges in the United States. They are primarily multiple-choice questions with five possible answers, only one of which is correct.[1]

For the individual phase of the experiment, the students had 15 minutes to complete the problems working silently with paper and pencil. Most students stopped work before the time was up. Their papers were collected and new sheets of paper with the same questions were distributed. The students were then instructed to work in randomly assigned groups and to solve the same problems online. They worked together in chat rooms for 39 minutes.

In this chapter, we analyze the results of one group of five students who worked together in one chat room group. None of the college students in this group did impressively well on the test as an individual. They each got two or three questions right out of the eleven (see Table 5.1) for a score of 18% or 27%.

Table 5.1 Problems answered correctly by individuals and the group

	1	2	3	4	5	6	7	8	9	10	11	Score (%)
Hal		X	X					X				27
Dan			X	X								18
Cosi			X				X		X			27
Mic					X		X					18
Ben			X					X				18
Group	X	X	X	X			X	X	X	X	X	82

For the experiment's group phase, the students worked in a chat room using Blackboard's group chat facility without a shared whiteboard. The software is simple and familiar to the students. The students did not know each other and did not have any information about each other except for the login names. They had not worked together before and had not participated in a chat like this before. The result

---

[1]The eleven questions and the complete chat log are available at: http://GerryStahl.net/publications/conferences/2005/criwg

of the group work was that the group decided upon the correct answers to 9 of the 11 problems, for a group score of 82%. Thus, the group did considerably better than any of the individual students.

However, it seems that each of the correct group answers can be attributed to one of the students. Although each student got only two or three answers right, together at least one of them correctly answered questions 2, 3, 4, 5, 7, 8, 9. No one understood question 1, and the group did not get this answer either. Question 2 was correctly answered by Hal, who persuaded the group. Question 3 was correctly answered by everyone except Mic. Question 4 was correctly answered by Dan. Question 5 gave the group a lot of frustration because no one could figure it out (although Mic had gotten it right on his paper); they eventually accepted the correct answer from someone outside the group. No one understood question 6, and the group got it wrong. They got question 7 right (following Cosi and Mic). Only Hal got question 8, but he persuaded the others. (Ben also got it on his paper, but did not participate in the group discussion.) Cosi got the answer to question 9. No one got questions 10 or 11, so the group had to work on these together. The discussion of question 10 was particularly interesting. As we will see, Cosi got the answer to question 10 during the group-work phase (although she had not gotten it on her individual-work paper), and explained it to the others. Hal got question 11 right and the others accepted it (although he had not gotten it on his paper).

So it appears as though the math problems were actually *solved by individuals*. The group responded to proposed answers. In instances where there were competing answers or other issues, the group required the proposer to give an account, defense or explanation. This resulted in an expository form of discourse where one member proposed an answer and explained why it was right. Although the group was not experienced in working together, they succeeded in selecting the best answers that their members could come up with. The result of the group cooperation was to achieve a sum of their best individual results.

It is particularly interesting to observe how the group negotiated their group answers given proposals from various members. In some cases, everyone proposed the same answer and it was easy to establish a consensus. In certain other cases, only one person proposed an answer and the others simply went along with it. In more interesting cases, when someone proposed an answer that contradicted other people's opinions or was questionable for some other reason, the proposer was required to give an explanation of their proposal. We do not have space here to analyze each of the negotiations: how they were begun, how people contributed, how the discussion was continued, how decisions were made and how the group decided to move on to a new problem (see Chapter 9 for an analysis of how a group resolves differences among its members). In particular, we cannot go into the integration of social chatter and math reasoning or fun making and decision making. Rather, we will take a look at the discussion of question 10, which was particularly interesting because no one had already solved this problem and because we can see the solution emerging in the discourse.

Question 10 is a difficult algebra word problem. It would take considerable effort and expertise to set up and solve equations for it. The group manages to finesse the complete algebraic solution and to identify the correct multiple-choice answer through some insightful reasoning. Question 10 is:

> Three years ago, men made up two out of every three Internet users in America. Today the ratio of male to female users is about 1 to 1. In that time the number of American females using the Internet has grown by 30,000,000, while the number of males who use the Internet has grown by 100%. By how much has the total Internet-user population increased in America in the past three years?
>
> (A) 50,000,000 (B) 60,000,000 (C) 80,000,000 (D) 100,000,000 (E) 200,000,000

The core discussion of this question takes place in the chat excerpt shown in Log 5-1.

Log 5-1.

Line	Time	Name	Message	Interval
350	4:31:55	Mic	how do we do this..	
351	4:31:59	Mic	without knowing the total number	0:00:04
352	4:32:01	Mic	of internet users?	0:00:02
			. . ..	
357	4:32:23	Dan	it all comes from the 30000000	
358	4:32:23	Mic	did u get something for 10?	0:00:00
359	4:32:26	Dan	we already know	0:00:03
360	4:32:44	Mic	30000000 is the number of increase in american females	0:00:18
361	4:33:00	Mic	and since the ratio of male to female	0:00:16
362	4:33:02	Mic	is 1 to 1	0:00:02
363	4:33:09	Mic	thats all i got to give. someone finish it	0:00:07
364	4:33:10	Mic	haha	0:00:01
365	4:33:18	Cosi	haha you jackass	0:00:08
366	4:33:20	Mic	haha	0:00:02
367	4:33:21	Dan	hahaha	0:00:01
368	4:33:26	Mic	u all thought i was gonna figure it out didnt	0:00:05
369	4:33:27	Mic	u	0:00:01
370	4:33:28	Mic	huh?	0:00:01
371	4:33:28	Hal	it would be 60,000,000	0:00:00
372	4:33:30	Mic	hal	0:00:02
373	4:33:31	Mic	its all u	0:00:01
374	4:33:33	Mic	see	0:00:02
375	4:33:34	Mic	i helped	0:00:01
376	4:33:54	Cosi	ok, so what's 11 – just guess on 10	0:00:20
			. . ..	
386	4:34:45	Mic	lets get back to 5	
387	4:34:47	Cosi	i think it's more than 60,00000	0:00:02
388	4:34:57	Mic	way to complicate things	0:00:10
389	4:35:03	Cosi	haha sorry	0:00:06
390	4:35:05	Mic	life was good until you said that	0:00:02
391	4:35:07	Mic	:(	0:00:02
392	4:35:18	Cosi	they cant get higher equally and even out to a 1 to 1 ratio	0:00:11

Log 5-1. (continued)

Line	Time	Name	Message	Interval
393	4:35:27	Cosi	oh, no wait, less than that	0:00:09
394	4:35:32	Cosi	50000000	0:00:05
395	4:35:34	Cosi	yeah, it's that	0:00:02
396	4:35:36	Cosi	im pretty sure	0:00:02
397	4:35:37	Mic	haha	0:00:01
398	4:35:38	Mic	how?	0:00:01
399	4:35:57	Cosi	because the women pop had to grow more than the men in order to even out	0:00:19
400	4:36:07	Cosi	so the men cant be equal (30)	0:00:10
401	4:36:11	Mic	oh wow...	0:00:04
402	4:36:16	Mic	i totally skipped the first sentencwe	0:00:05
403	4:36:16	Cosi	therefore, the 50,000,000 is the only workable answer	0:00:00
404	4:36:19	Dan	very smart	0:00:03
405	4:36:21	Cosi	Damn im good	0:00:02

We can see here that the group is meandering somewhat in trying to solve problem 10. Mic raises the question of how to solve it (lines 350–352). Dan suggests that the 30,000,000 figure is key, and Mic tries to build on this suggestion. But Mic ends his attempt with a laugh, clowning around that he was only pretending to figure out the problem. Hal proposes that the answer is 60,000,000 (line 371), but then Cosi complicates matters by questioning this answer (line 387).

Having rejected Hal's proposal, Cosi proceeds to solve the problem on her own. She reasons that the male and female population cannot grow by the same amount from uneven numbers to arrive at equal numbers (line 392). From this, she concludes that the answer is 50,000,000. She announces that she is "pretty sure" of this answer (line 396). At this point, it seems that Cosi has solved the problem on her own.

Mic responds to the statement that Cosi is only "**pretty sure**" and not positive by requesting an explanation of how Cosi arrived at her opinion that the answer is 50,000,000—and not the 60,000,000 that Hal proposed (line 398).

In the following lines (399, 400, 403), Cosi provides an account of her reasoning. If the females grew by 30,000,000 then the males must have grown by less than that. Therefore, the total growth must have been less than 60,000,000. The only answer listed that meets this condition is 50,000,000—so that must be the correct answer.

Cosi's extended turn providing an exposition of her thinking is interrupted only by Mic (lines 401, 402), who simultaneously affirms Cosi's approach, provides an excuse for not having solved the problem himself, and admits to not having read the problem carefully in the first place. In this way, Mic continues to move the group toward making good decisions about which proposed answers to accept while himself playing the fool. Dan speaks on behalf of the group (line 404), accepting Cosi's answer and proof by praising her as "**very smart**," to which she responds (line 405), "**Damn, I'm good**." In the subsequent discussion, both Hal and Mic agree with Cosi's solution. Cosi is anxious to move on to another problem and finally says (line 419), "**ok great, im smart, lets move on**."

From our analysis, we can see the advantages that have long been claimed by other researchers for collaborative learning (summarized in Strijbos, Kirschner & Martens, 2004). A number of students each contributed their best ideas. Some students knew some answers, some others, and together they arrived at a position where they effectively shared the whole set of best answers that any of them had to start with. In addition, the group work sustained their time-on-task beyond what any one student was willing to do, arriving at correct answers for the final two problems.

According to the foregoing analysis, the actual mathematical reasoning was done by individual minds. The group was able to take the results of these individual achievements and gather them together in a particularly effective way. In the end, all members of the group had the opportunity to know more correct answers than they could arrive at on their own. It may not be obvious that every student could then solve all the problems on their own, but there were a number of indications in the chat that students gained insights into aspects of the problem solving that we can assume would stay with them as individual learning outcomes.

In this experiment, we were able to see how the group took good advantage of the distributed knowledge of its members, even though the group had not had any previous experience working together and had no external scaffolding from the teacher or the software in how to collaborate. As researchers, we know which students were able to solve which problems on their own and we could then observe how they interacted to solve the problems in the group context. Furthermore, we had a simple, objective measure of mathematical skill based on correct answers to standardized SAT problems. We observe that a group of students who individually scored 18–27% was able to score 87% when working together. Furthermore, this impressive result can be understood in terms of simply making good decisions about which proposals to listen to on each problem and then spending more engaged time-on-task on the two final problems. The experiment—analyzed at the individual unit of analysis—confirms the advantages of online collaborative (or, rather cooperative) problem solving.

Group Cognition in Online Math

In the previous section, the work of the student group was interpreted primarily at the individual unit of analysis. The problem solving was discussed as the accomplishment of individuals. The group decisions were discussed as a form of voting or consensus building among people who largely made up their minds individually. In many cases, individuals did not hold strong opinions about the answers to the problems and therefore left the group decision up to other individuals—who might have a higher likelihood of knowing the correct answer—by remaining silent. However, it is also possible to analyze the chat differently, taking the group as the unit of analysis.

The central point of the alternative approach is that the meaning constructed in a group discourse is often the result of the subtle ways in which utterances of different speakers or writers interact, rather than through a simple addition of ideas expressed or represented in the individual utterances. In this view, the solutions, decisions or ideas are seen as emerging from the semantics of the chat as it unfolds, rather than taking them as expressions of thoughts that exist in the minds of the individual students independently of their interactions.

Perhaps the greatest problem in understanding how groups work is to clarify the relation of individual to trans-individual contributions to the group meaning making. Clearly, individual group members may have ideas of their own that they introduce into the discourse. Their utterances may have to wait for the right moment in the conversational flow and they might have to design their *contributions* to fit into the discourse context in order to be accepted as useful proposals with a chance of being taken up, but they also may bring with them some premeditated meaning constructed by their proposer. Individuals also play a necessary role as the *interpreters* of the group meaning in an on-going way as they respond to the discourse (Stahl, 2006b, chap. 16). On the other hand, the formative roles of adjacency pairs and other references among utterances underline the importance of analyzing meaning making at the *group unit of analysis*, not just interpreting the utterances of individuals.

A more detailed analysis of the negotiations of the answers for questions 1 through 9 in the experiment shows that the group had methods for interacting that were quite effective in making good decisions. They had subtle ways of coalescing the individual group members into a collective that could work through the set of math problems, discover solutions and decide which solutions to adopt as the group's answers. This suggests that the problem-solving methods used by the group of students is qualitatively different from the methods they use individually to solve problems. Another way of putting it is that *the group collaboration brings additional methods at the group unit of analysis that supplement the individual cognitive methods of problem solving*. It may be important to distinguish these different classes of methods at the different levels of analysis, as well as to see subsequently how they work together.

In defining his concept of the *zone of proximal development*, Vygotsky sharply distinguished between what a student could accomplish individually and what that same student could accomplish when working with others (Vygotsky, 1930/1978, p. 86): "It is the distance between the actual developmental level as determined by independent problem solving and the level of potential development as determined through problem solving under adult guidance or in collaboration with more capable peers." Based on psychological experiments, Vygotsky argued that what children "could do only under guidance, in collaboration and in groups at the age of three-to-five years they could do independently when they reached the age of five-to-seven years" (p. 87). In the chat, we have seen that older students can also achieve significantly more in collaborative groups than independently—and we have seen the methods of group interaction that one particular group adopted in this one case study to accomplish that.

We can also revisit the solving of problem 10 as a group achievement. Of course, the sequence of recorded events—the lines in the chat log—are the same. But now we no longer attribute the source of the messages to the individuals as the "expression" of internal mental ideas that they have worked out in advance. Rather, we look for evidence in the details of the log of how messages are responses to each other.

Mic's opening question (lines 350–352) is based on the problem statement. The problem asks how much the population has increased. A straightforward calculation of this increase might involve subtracting from the total number of Internet users now the corresponding figure for three years ago. But the two numbers needed for such a calculation are missing from the problem statement. The problem only gives indirect clues. The problem statement thereby calls for a less direct strategy. Mic's messages respond to this implicit requirement by making it explicit.

Dan responds to Mic's question by proposing an approach for coming up with a strategy. He says (lines 357 and 359), "**It all comes from the 30,000,000 we already know.**" In other words, the strategic key is to start with the clue about the number of females having grown by 30,000,000.

Note that to analyze the log we must disentangle line 358 from the middle of the two fragments of Dan's text and re-join Dan's text (see Chapter 20 on chat threading). Mic's question (line 358) is posted at the same time as Dan's proposal, and as a consequence it is ignored and left as a failed proposal (Stahl, 2006b, chap. 21).

Mic's next turn (lines 360–364) picks up on the 30,000,000 figure from Dan and tries to take it further by adding the fact that came before that figure in the problem statement, namely that "**Today the ratio of male to female users is about 1 to 1.**" Mic puts this forward and asks for the group to continue to develop the strategy.

Mic's contribution is not the expression of some rational problem solving that we might speculate took place in Mic's mind. In fact, his contribution—if considered as an individual proposal with math content—only vaguely suggests a mathematical logic. It was primarily an interactive move to keep the group effort going. Following Dan's posting to the chat, there was an unusually long pause of 18 seconds. In face-to-face conversation, a pause of a few seconds is embarrassingly long and exerts considerable pressure on the participants to make another contribution; in chat, 18 seconds can have a similar effect. So Mic repeats Dan's reference to 30,000,000. Following another pause of 16 seconds, Mic adds the reference to the 1-to-1 ratio. He then explicitly calls on the other group members to join in. He admits that he cannot take it further himself, and he laughs.

Cosi, Dan and Mic have a good laugh at Mic's expense, taking his contribution as a practical joke, as an attempt to look like he was making a significant mathematical contribution and then stopping short of delivering. This fills in an otherwise discouraging silence during which no one knows how to advance mathematically with the problem. The laughter lightens up the interaction, allowing people to throw ideas into the mix without worrying that they will necessarily be taken too seriously if they are only partial, or even wrong. After Mic's jackass-like behavior, any other contribution would seem an improvement. In fact, Mic's proposal and request are taken up.

Hal then proposes that the answer "**would be 60,000,000**" (line 371). This is a direct consequence of finishing Mic's partial proposal. If there are 30,000,000 females (line 360) and the ratio of males to females is 1 to 1 (lines 361–362) and you want to know the total number (line 351), then the conclusion that "**it would be 60,000,000**" is at hand. Mic takes this to be the answer to problem 10 and tries to take partial credit for it by pointing out, "**u see I helped**" (lines 373–375).

At that point, Cosi suggests the group should go on to problem 11 and "*just guess*" on 10 (line 376). This declines to affirm Mic's acceptance of 60,000,000 as the answer to question 10, but does so without raising this as a topic for further group discussion. Without making a decision about 10, the group goes on to all decide that the answer to problem 11 is C (lines 378–385, spanning just half a minute), as already stated by Hal in line 353.

Mic then summarizes the group's status as: "**So we got B for 10 and c for 11; lets get back to 5**" (lines 384–386). At this point, Cosi objects to Mic's continued assumption that Hal's 60,000,000 is the answer to problem 10. Mic and Cosi joke about their disagreement. Again, the group's light-hearted attitude avoids the potential of disagreements within the group becoming disruptive of the group functioning.

Cosi then formulates an argument (line 392) why the answer cannot be 60,000,000. The male and female populations cannot get higher equally (i.e., by 30,000,000 each) because they have to even out from unequal numbers according to the problem statement. After formulating this text, Cosi checks and then corrects her previous claim that "**I think it's more than 60,000,000**" (line 387): "**Oh, no wait, less than that: 50,000,000**" (lines 393–394).

Cosi is somewhat hesitant about her revised claim. First she checks it and says, "**Yeah, it's that**" (line 395), followed by the hedge, "**Im pretty sure**" (line 396). Mic continues the laughter and then requests an account of how Cosi is pretty sure that the answer should be 50,000,000.

After a 19 second pause, Cosi takes the extended expository turn that Mic had offered her and the others had left open. She lays out a concise account or proof of her claim. Her argument concerns the increase in the number of females and the ratios of male to female users—the issues raised at the beginning of the group discussion by Dan and Mic. It is plausible that Cosi used the 19-second pause to reflect upon the solution that the group had come to and that her contributions had completed. Thus, her well-worked-out retrospective account seems like the expression of her mental work in constructing the narrative explanation, although her earlier contributions to solving the math of the problem seemed more like spontaneous reactions to the flow of the group discourse.

A solution to problem 10 carried out from scratch using algebraic methods that translated the word problem into a set of equations to be solved for unknown values would have looked very different from Cosi's argument. Her contributions to the chat did not express an independent, individual approach to the problem. Rather, they were responses to preceding contributions. Cosi's texts performed checks on the previous texts and extended their arguments in directions opened up and called for by those previous contributions. Although Dan, Mic and Hal did not carry out the further steps that their own contributions required, they succeeded in starting a discourse that Cosi was able to repair and complete.

This analysis of the log excerpt gives a more group-centered view of the *collaborative solving* of the math problem by the group. Of course, at the level of individual postings, each contribution was that of an individual. But it is not necessary to see those contributions as expressions of prior private mental activities. Rather, they can be seen as responses to the previous texts, the context of the problem-solving task (e.g., the elements of the problem 10 text) and elicitations of contributions to come. These ties of the individual postings to the sequentially unfolding group discourse can be seen in the form of the postings themselves. Single utterances do not stand on their own, but make *elliptical references* to previous mentionings, *indexical references* to matters in the physical and discourse situation and *projective references* to anticipated future responses or actions of other people (see Stahl, 2006b, chap. 12). The references weave a temporal fabric of discourse that defines the meaning of each text within its narrative context. Thus, the individual contributions are incorporated into a problem-solving dialog at the group unit of analysis, which is where the meaning of the log is constructed.

In weaving the discourse fabric, groups use different methods. We have discussed two methods of group discourse used in math problem solving in this chat: exploratory inquiry and expository narrative. In the excerpt concerning problem 10, we have seen that the group first explores a solution path by different students making small contributions that build on each other sequentially. When a candidate answer is reached that someone is "pretty sure" about, that person is asked to provide an extended account or proof of the answer. Thus, Cosi participates first in the joint exploratory inquiry and then provides an expository narrative. Both these methods are interactive discourse methods that involve responding to requests, structuring texts to be read by other group members and eliciting comments, questions and uptake.

Conversation analysts have identified *adjacency pairs* as a powerful way in which meaning is interactively constructed. An adjacency pair is a set of utterances by different people that forms a smallest meaningful unit of interaction (Duranti, 1998). For instance, a greeting or a question cannot meaningfully stand alone. You cannot meaningfully express a greeting or a question without someone else being there in the discourse to respond with a return greeting or an answer. The other speaker may ignore, decline or respond to your greeting or question, but your utterance cannot be a greeting or a question without it addressing itself to a potential respondent. The respondent may just be an imaginary dialog partner if you are carrying out the dialog in your mind (see Bakhtin, 1986a). Adjacency pairs are fundamental mechanisms of social interaction; even very young speakers and quite disabled speakers (e.g., advanced Alzheimer sufferers) often respond appropriately to greetings and questions. Adjacency pairs are important elements for weaving together contributions from different participants into a group discourse.

When I analyzed a different online chat of mathematics problem solving, I defined an adjacency pair that seemed to play a prominent role. I called it the *math proposal adjacency pair* (Stahl, 2006b, chap. 21). In that chat, a math proposal adjacency pair consisted of a problem-solving proposal by one person followed by a response. The proposal addressed the other students as a group and required one or more of them to respond to the proposal on behalf of the group. The proposal might be a tactical suggestion, like "**I think we should start with the 30,000,000 figure.**" Alternatively, it might be a next step in the mathematical solution, like "**They can't get higher equally and even out to a 1 to 1 ratio.**" The response might simply be "*k*": okay, that's interesting, what's next? The pattern was that progress in problem solving would not continue after someone made a proposal until the group responded to that proposal. If they responded affirmatively, a next step could then be proposed. If they responded with a question or an objection, then that ("dispreferred") response would have to be resolved before a next proposal could be put forward. It was important to the group that there be some kind of explicit uptake by the group to each proposal. A counter-example proved the rule. One participant made a failed proposal. This was an attempt to suggest a strategy involving proportions. But the proposer failed to formulate his contribution as an effective first part of a math proposal adjacency pair, and the rest of the group failed to take it up with the necessary second pair-part response.

In the chat we are analyzing now, the math proposal adjacency pairs have a somewhat different appearance. We can identify proposals in, for instance, lines 352, 357, 360, 362, 371, 387, 392 and 394. None of these is followed by a simple, explicit response, like "ok." Rather, each is eventually followed by the next proposal that builds on the first, thereby implicitly affirming it. This is an interesting variation on the math-proposal-adjacency-pair method of problem solving. It illustrates how different groups develop and follow different group methods of doing what they are doing, such as deciding upon answers to math problems. However, each of these methods is readily understandable by us as a way for groups to pursue math problem solving with sequences of proposals.

If we combine the proposals from Mic, Dan, Hal and Cosi, they read like the cognitive process of an individual problem solver:

> How can I figure out the increase in users without knowing the total number of Internet users? It seems to all come from the 30,000,000 figure. 30,000,000 is the number of increase in American females. Since the ratio of male to female is 1 to 1, the total of male and female combined would be 60,000,000. No, I think it must be more than 60,000,000 because the male and female user populations can't get higher at equal rates and still even out to a 1 to 1 ratio after starting uneven. No, I made a mistake; the total must be less than 60,000,000. It could be 50,000,000, which is the only multiple-choice option less than 60,000,000.

Mathematical problem solving is a paradigm case of human cognition. It is common to say of someone who can solve math problems that he or she is smart. In fact, we see that taking place in line 404. Here, the group has solved the problem by constructing an argument much like what an individual might construct. So we can attribute group cognition or intelligence to the group (see Stahl, 2006b, esp. chap. 19).

Unfortunately, the group of students in the chat log does not seem to attribute the problem solving intelligence to itself, but only to one of its members, Cosi. Because she takes the final step and arrives at the answer and because she provides the narrative account or proof, Dan says of her, "**very smart**" (line 404). Later (line 419), Cosi agrees, downgrading the self-praise by using it to close the discussion of problem 10 and of her role in solving it by proposing that the group move on to a remaining problem: "**Ok great, im smart, lets move on**." Casting Cosi as the smart one who solves problems leaves Mic cast as the jackass or class clown when in fact Mic is very skilled at facilitating the chat so that the whole group solves problems that neither Mic nor the others solved independently.

There is an ideology of individualism at work here that encourages both educational researchers and student participants to view problem solving as an accomplishment of individuals rather than groups. This has serious consequences for the design and adoption of groupware to support problem solving, as well as for research methodology and student learning. If groupware designers tried to support collaborative interactions, then they might design more than just generic communication platforms for the transmission of expressions of personal ideas. Researchers studying the use of groupware could focus on processes of collaboration and the methods that groups used to solve problems—as opposed to treating only individuals as cognitive agents. Then research methods might focus more on conversation analysis (Sacks, 1962/1995), video analysis (Koschmann et al., 2007) and their application to discourse logs, rather than predominantly on surveys and interviews of individual opinions. If students using groupware conceived of their work as interactively achieving a group solution, they might take more advantage of groupware collaboration features and might structure their textual contributions more explicitly as parts of an interwoven fabric of collaborative knowledge-building group discourse. Everyone might begin to see collaboration as more than just a way of pooling individual knowledge, and as a source of knowledge building in its own right—with group cognitive methods that overcome some of the limitations of individual cognition.

Groupware to Support Group Cognition

The first step in thinking about the design of groupware today is to understand the methods that groups use to accomplish problem solving, scientific inquiry, decision making, argumentation and the other tasks that they want to do. Generic communication platforms developed to meet the needs of hierarchical corporations and bureaucracies will continue to make new technologies available in response to market pressures. Within education, course management systems to support the administration of distance education will proliferate under their own economic drives. But those developments are almost exclusively guided by a philosophy of individual cognition and the transfer of representations of mental contents.

The preceding analysis of a case study of group cognition suggests a variety of new design principles. Clearly, one or two case studies are not enough to inform a new approach to groupware design. This chapter has only suggested the kind of analysis that is needed to investigate and characterize the methods that groups of students might use to do their work collaboratively. Different age groups, tasks, cultures and environments will introduce considerable variety in how groups constitute themselves, define their work, socialize, problem solve, persuade, guide, decide, conclude, etc. Nevertheless, a number of principles can already be suggested. It is important to start thinking about groupware design because ideas for innovative functionality and prototypes of new components will have to be tried out with online groups and the resultant logs analyzed. One cannot know how new technologies will lead to new member methods without such investigation.

Here are some very preliminary suggestions for groupware design principles.

Persistency and Visibility

Make the group work visible and persistent so that everyone in the group can easily see what all members have accomplished. Ideally, important contributions should stand out so that people do not have to search for them, but are made aware of them with little or no effort. This is a non-trivial requirement, since the work of a group quickly becomes too extensive for everyone to read and keep track of it. The software must somehow help with this.

Deictic Referencing

As discussed above, the references from one message to another or to objects in the problem context are essential to the meaning making. Software could make these references visible under certain conditions. Patterns of references among proposals, adjacency pairs and responses between different group members could also be displayed in order to give participants indicators about how their group interaction is going.

Virtual Workspaces

Ideally, the groupware would encourage noticing, recognizing and reflecting on related contributions. There should certainly be group workspaces for different kinds of work to be done together, creating shared artifacts. For instance, there could be group workspaces for taking notes and annotating them, for jointly navigating the Internet, for constructing shared drawings, for building formal arguments together, for collecting shared annotated bibliographies and other lists or collections. Issues of turn taking, ownership, privacy, credit assignment and control become important here.

Shared and Personal Places

It may be useful to distinguish and sometimes to separate individual and group work (Stahl, 2002a). Individual whiteboards for students to sketch out ideas before sharing them or to maintain personal summaries of the joint work may be useful. However, it may be important to make even the individual work visible to everyone. Group accomplishments build on the individual contributions. Even contributions that the proposer does not consider significant may, as we have seen above, provide a key to progress of the group. In addition, group members often want to know what people are doing when they are not active in the group. Content should move fluidly from place to place. The individual work should be intimately intertwined with the shared work to avoid distracting attention away from the joint effort.

Computational Support

Of course, a major advantage of having groupware systems running on computers is that they can provide computational support to the work of their users. Computers can filter or tailor different views or computational perspectives (Stahl, 2006b, chap. 6) of materials in the chat or workspaces, as well as providing search, browsing and annotating facilities. They can play various moderator roles.

Access to Tools and Resources

Another advantage of the networked computer infrastructure is that groupware can provide structured access to information, tools and other resources available on the Internet, for instance in relevant digital libraries and software repositories.

Opening New Worlds and (Sub-) Communities

Finally, Internet connectivity allows for groups and their members to participate in larger online communities and to interact with other groups—either similar or complementary. Groupware could facilitate the building of open-ended networks of individual, group and community connections, or the definition of new sub-communities.

Allowing Natural Language Subtleties

While computer support brings many potential advantages, it also brings the danger of destroying the extreme flexibility and adaptability of the natural language used in conversation and group interactions. Groupware designs should be careful not to impose rigid ontologies and sets of allowable speech acts for the sake of enabling automated analyses. It should permit the use of overloaded, multiple functioning, subtle linguistic expression that is not reified, stereotyped, coded or packaged, but that opens space for interpretation, engagement, creativity, problem solving. As we saw in the chat, even a simple laugh can perform multiple complex roles simultaneously. Chat is a vibrant form of human interaction in which people exercise their creativity to invent linguistic novelties such as abbreviations, contractions, emoticons and new ways of interacting textually. Groupware should support this, not cramp it.

The VMT Project was designed to explore possibilities for supporting group cognition and to provide a testbed for analyzing online small-group problem solving in the paradigmatic domain of mathematics. The following Parts of this volume report on different aspects of the VMT Project.

Part II
Studying Group Cognition in Virtual Math Teams

Introduction to Part II

This Part of the book is intended to demonstrate how the VMT research team studies group cognition in virtual math teams. It provides four case studies of specific excerpts from the VMT data corpus, which each explore some aspect of the ways in which small groups may structure their work: through the creation and maintenance of a joint problem space, the coordination of work done in different media, the elaboration of questioning and the resolution of alternative proposals.

The chapters of Part II arose through a particularly clear synthesis of group and individual effort. Each presents core ideas of a doctoral dissertation, and in that sense is the result of a mighty individual effort by its author. On the other hand, each arose out of the collaborative work of the VMT Project team and reflects perspectives and insights that cannot be attributed to any individual, but owe their emergence to the complex of experiments, analyses, discussions and theories of the ever-changing research group. For several years, the four authors represented in Part II spent their Wednesdays engaged in VMT research meetings and data sessions, in which the VMT trials, technology, pedagogy, analysis and presentations were all collaboratively planned and conducted. As graduate research assistants in the VMT Project, the authors served as chat room mentors, software developers, data coders, conference presenters and in other hands-on roles.

To anyone who participated in the weekly project meetings, the influence of the core team leadership is unmistakable: Zemel consistently oriented us toward ethnomethodological issues and sustained the rigor of the chat analysis; Weimar kept the discourse tied to issues of collaborative learning; Shumar repeatedly introduced larger sociological considerations and Stahl maintained the focused research agenda. Many other researchers from diverse backgrounds and perspectives joined the research group for various periods, lending invaluable influences. The dissertation themes reflected in the chapters of this part were, of course, frequently discussed in the project meetings and data sessions. In addition, these chapters—like most in this volume—were heavily edited to contribute to a unified presentation.

One could well apply the concepts of these chapters to the process of collaborative knowledge building that has taken place in the VMT Project as itself a group process. The *problem space* of the research project was originally specified only in terms of a general vision of future possibilities for math education and a vague conception of group cognition. As the problem space became clearer to one individual or another, it had to be explained to colleagues and maintained in the face of the innumerable barriers and differences of perspective that constantly arose. *"Bridging" discontinuities* of changing times, constraints, personnel and technology was a recurrent task. What occurred in one aspect of the project had to be related to other aspects to maintain an integrated project. Central *research questions* were co-constructed and continuously tweaked or re-conceptualized by the group. *Differences of perspective* in the evolving interdisciplinary team had to be respected and exploited as well as resolved to take advantage of productive tensions.

As interesting as an analysis of the Project collaborative processes would be, we lack a full documentation of it; our data on student sessions in VMT chat rooms is far more adequate for the kind of microanalysis that is needed. The following chapters therefore turn to a close inspection of the student data, attempting to elucidate how small groups in the VMT environment manage the social organization of their collective work. Four important features of online group interaction are explored and reflected upon in the context of case studies that each focus on a couple minutes of chat.

It is often assumed that case studies do not lead to generalizable findings of theoretical import. Although the following four chapters each focus on specific cases of interaction, they should be understood within the contexts of the larger dissertations, which each consider multiple similar cases in comparable detail. Furthermore, the four dissertations—of which the chapters of Part II can be considered first drafts—each distill in different ways what has been learned more generally and less explicitly from the VMT Project as a multi-year team research effort. Our sense of group work informally synthesizes rather diverse data from numerous virtual math teams and from a number of detailed analyses of brief excerpts. The VMT data corpus includes well over a thousand student-hours of chat in 370 session logs, covering a broad array of different experimental contexts. Most of these chats involved K-12 students working on math topics in groups of 3–6. Some involved college students or researchers—with as many as a dozen typing in the same chat room. Students came from around the US, as well as a few from Brazil, Singapore and Scotland. Some seemed to be mathematically gifted, but others were probably average and some were considered at-risk. The technology for early VMT sessions consisted of familiar commercial chat systems; by 2005 a system with chat and a shared whiteboard integrated by graphical referencing was used; and in 2006, this was expanded to include a lobby, a tabbed interface and a wiki repository. The math topics evolved from algebra and geometry challenge problems from the Math Forum's Problem-of-the-Week (PoW) service to more open-ended topics like the grid world and patterns of sticks and squares.

For a variety of reasons, some of the chat logs were considered better data than others for analyzing the mechanisms of group cognition. In the spring and summer of 2004, an intensive effort was put into coding ten simple chat sessions (PoW-wows)—as discussed in Part IV. The VMT Spring Fest 2005 and 2006 sessions brought student groups back for sequences of four hour-long sessions, providing a glimpse into longer-term development of group dynamics and group learning. VMT data sessions in Spring 2008 systematically reviewed from beginning to end

Team B's series of sessions in Spring Fest 2006, and VMT data sessions in Fall 2008 reviewed Team C's. Chapter 6 in this volume looks at an excerpt from the VMT Spring Fest 2005 data. Chapter 7 follows a sequence of activities in Team C's second session during Spring Fest 2006. Chapter 8 analyzes a different aspect of interaction from Team C's first session. Chapter 9 goes back to Powwow 10 to look at purely textual interaction. In each chapter, the specific, highly situated analysis presents a concrete instance of phenomena that are visible—in their rich variety and individuality—throughout the VMT data corpus.

Of course, all the cases considered in this volume are confined to the specifics of the VMT Project, with its unique technology, pedagogy, etc. That is why this volume is called *Studying Virtual Math Teams*—to signal that its conclusions are restricted to this special context. Nevertheless, the chapters in Part II are perhaps notable for the ways in which their analyses of case-study data shed light on some of the most theoretically fundamental and elusive themes of CSCL, semiotics, information science and learning science. In particular, each of the four chapters addresses a major issue that has been influential in the CSCL research literature. Taken as a whole, they significantly advance our understanding of the nature and mechanisms of group cognition, as should gradually become clear by the end of this volume.

Chapter 6: The Joint Problem Space

In order to engage in shared work as a group, there must be a task to work on together—what activity theory refers to as the "object" of the group activity. This must be more than simply a statement of a problem that was given to the group, but needs to be worked out as a "problem space" to which the group can orient itself in an on-going and practical way. Chapter 6 looks at how a group establishes and maintains its "joint problem space." The chapter considers the origins of this construct in early theories of cognitive science and in later revisions—versions more influenced by situated cognition—within CSCL. It then develops a richer description based on analysis of the joint problem space's role in VMT chats. The new analysis grew out of an attempt to understand how groups maintain their continuity of interaction across discontinuities. It is therefore able to extend our understanding of how a joint problem space is maintained by stressing the sequential and temporal aspects of "bridging" methods that are typically employed by virtual math teams to overcome discontinuities that threaten to disrupt their effort. The joint problem space is now seen to integrate: (a) social aspects (which transform participants into "members" of the interactional group), (b) domain content concerns (such as the group's characterization of their problem to be solved) and (c) temporal relations (the past, present and future as they are constituted in the unfolding sequentiality of the group interaction). This joint problem space structures the work and discourse of the group, providing a shared understanding of the references and concerns that are expressed in utterances and behaviors of the individual group members. This analysis replaces the easily misunderstood metaphor of common ground with a richer construct.

Chapter 7: Coordination of Visual, Narrative and Symbolic Interaction

Chapter 7 considers how work in the joint problem space is conducted when the online environment combines textual postings and graphical drawing media, as in a VMT chat room with shared whiteboard. The chapter carefully considers the approaches of seminal CSCL studies of multimodal interaction before formulating its own analysis of how students coordinate their group work within the VMT dual-interaction space. By looking closely at the methods a student group uses to coordinate chat postings with carefully choreographed inscriptions on the shared whiteboard, it shows how deep understanding of math can be effectively promoted through the organization of visual, narrative and symbolic reasoning. Although drawings, text and mathematical symbols build knowledge and convey meaning through very different semiotic systems, in VMT sessions they are tightly coordinated and mutually informing. Students new to the environment spontaneously develop and share methods of connecting and coordinating work in these media. Mathematical insight is often best grounded in visual reasoning with concrete instances, where relationships can be seen and understood at a visceral level. These insights can be pointed out to others through narratives, which instruct them to see in the proper way. In mathematics, symbolic expressions are effectively employed to articulate, formalize and generalize understandings of relationships, providing means for symbolic manipulations that lead to further conclusions and to different forms of comprehension. The math artifacts that emerge from group work that coordinates visual, narrative and symbolic reasoning are not simple objects, but concepts that can only be understood through the coordination of their multiple realizations in these different types of media. The coordination of group work in the three realms supports deep mathematical understanding (as opposed to rote learning) of individuals by fostering understanding of the multiple realizations of math artifacts. It also enriches the joint problem space of the group's effort by interconnecting the semantic relationships of the three realms within a shared network of meaning.

Chapter 8: The Co-Construction of Questioning

In *Group Cognition* (Stahl, 2006b, ch. 21, esp. p. 454f; 2006e), it was suggested that VMT chats were largely driven by "math proposal adjacency pairs." These are interactions in which one participant makes a proposal bid to the group for the group's work and this is accepted or rejected by another group member on behalf of the group. While this suggestion could be supported by subsequent analysis of VMT data, Chapters 8 and 9 pursue additional driving forces: questioning and the resolution of differences. Chapter 8 undertakes an analysis of questioning as an interactive achievement. Rather than seeing a question posed in a chat as an outward expression of an individual's mental idea or of an individual's request for information, it looks at the methods of formulating and taking up a bid at questioning to see how the meaning and function of the questioning are negotiated interactively. In analogy to the analysis of math proposal adjacency pairs, it contrasts a "failed" question with a successful questioning in order to clarify the conditions for the possibility of success. Questioning is seen to be a potentially complex group process, incorporating a wide variety of interactional methods. A question can be part of a math proposal adjacency pair, putting forward a tentative proposal or reacting to a proposal bid. Questioning within a group can extend across a much longer sequence of adjacency pairs, advancing (or not) the problem-solving trajectory of the group. This analysis of questioning as an interactional achievement of a group—as opposed to a query in an individual mind—signals an innovative interactional approach to information science, with its conceptualizations of knowledge and information seeking, which often underlie CSCL theories.

Chapter 9: Resolving Differences

Neo-Piagetian varieties of CSCL, at least, locate the power of collaboration in the attempt to overcome conflicting perspectives, with their attendant psychological tensions. Chapter 9 deals with the inter-animation of perspectives—the notion that multiple views or approaches can be productive for creative knowledge building in collaborative groups—by looking to see how the alternative perspectives actually interact with each other in group problem-solving efforts. The analysis in this chapter illustrates how the eventual resolution of a difference in approach to a problem can drive the group to solve the problem in a way that none of the participants would have individually. Here, two or more math proposal adjacency pairs—initiated by different individuals, operating from within contrasting perspectives on the group topic—enter into conflict with each other. The group may take up this conflict and work through it across a longer sequence of postings, rather than just quickly accepting or rejecting each proposal on its own. As with questioning, such a group activity can drive the work of the group for a significant period. The group response to "cognitive conflict" and the subsequent inter-animation of different perspectives can impel learning at both the individual and group level, as it sustains the chat interaction. The result of the resolution of differences—like that of longer sequences of questioning—can be an expansion of the joint problem space; group participants subsequently have a richer shared understanding of the object of their collaborative undertaking.

Through the four studies of Part II, the characteristic structure of a VMT problem-solving session is explored. The four case studies delve deeply into the details of specific interactions in order to uncover typical methods of group interaction in this kind of setting and to reveal underlying structures of group meaning that are co-constructed in the process. Each of these chapters presents excerpts from recordings of actual VMT sessions and analyzes the interactional work that is taking place. Thereby, they provide case studies that illustrate the kind of analysis that takes place in VMT data sessions. The studies of Part II offer some of the best examples of the kind of chat interaction analysis that is recommended by this volume. The reader is encouraged to make the effort to follow these analyses line by line. The devil is in the details, and some of these interactions are divinely devilish.

Chapter 6
The Sequential Co-Construction of the Joint Problem Space

Johann W. Sarmiento-Klapper

Abstract Theories of collaborative learning have identified the central role of the joint problem space in coordinating work and establishing intersubjective understanding. The concept of problem space had its inception within the information-processing perspective as a characterization of individual problem-solving activity. It was then reformulated and extended within the learning sciences. Based on a detailed analysis of sustained online collaborative problem-solving activity by a small group of students over multiple sessions, we propose that the theory of the joint problem space should now be further expanded. In addition to the dimensions of social relations and domain content, which are increasingly recognized in the learning sciences, we argue for the salience of the temporal dimension. Our analysis shows that the joint problem space is co-constructed at the group unit of analysis through the temporal and sequential orientation to inter-subjective meaning making.

Keywords Joint problem space · knowledge artifacts · deictic field · temporality · sequentiality

The challenge of appropriately identifying and describing the activities that form the contexts in which learning and knowledge building take place lies at the core of inquiry in the learning sciences. As Sfard (1998) has argued, the metaphors that we use to characterize learning work as lenses that focus our attention on particular aspects of learning interactions, while obscuring or ignoring others. Names and descriptions of features, resources and activities within an educational setting serve as the building blocks for structuring inquiry about learning and its dynamics. In this chapter we investigate the construct of the "joint problem space" (JPS) as a metaphor for the social order that is established in small-group problem-solving interactions. We trace the development of this concept within the learning sciences and consider what it might mean in an analysis of actual student interactions.

J.W. Sarmiento-Klapper (✉)
College of Information Science & Technology, Drexel University, Philadelphia, PA, USA
e-mail: jsarmi@drexel.edu

G. Stahl (ed.), *Studying Virtual Math Teams*, Computer-Supported Collaborative
Learning Series 11, DOI 10.1007/978-1-4419-0228-3_6,
© Springer Science+Business Media, LLC 2009

Theory within the learning sciences is largely fueled by the tension between socio-cognitive and socio-cultural traditions. This tension appears in Sfard's contrast of the acquisitionist and participationist metaphors, in allegiances to Piaget versus Vygotsky, in quantitative as opposed to descriptive methodologies and in individualistic or social foci. The concept of JPS has straddled this divide since its inception. Through our fine-grained analysis of the way that the JPS is co-constructed in an informative case study, we have come to the conclusion that the JPS should be understood as fundamentally a result of group interaction rather than individual cognition. To demonstrate this, we will return to the origin of the earlier concept of *problem space* in the heyday of cognitive science. We will then trace the application of this characterization of individual cognition to the group phenomenon of *joint problem space*. More recent studies of small group collaboration highlight *content and relational dimensions* of the JPS. Our empirical analysis suggests a third structural dimension: *temporal sequentiality*.

The JPS can now be seen as a *socio-temporal-semantic field*, co-constructed through interactions such as collective remembering and providing the basis for shared understanding of meaning. Processes of *group cognition* both sustain and are sustained by the JPS. The JPS is seen as an *interactional* phenomenon at the small-group unit of analysis, rather than as a convergence of mental representations of individuals as is often understood within theories of cognitive change and common ground. That is, the JPS is established and maintained through the sequential relationship of interactions among group participants as they build upon past actions, current situations and future opportunities of their group activity. Individual mental representations are possible spin-offs of the JPS, rather than causes of it.

Problem Spaces

Joint activity—the kind of activity that can take place when multiple participants engage with each other collaboratively—offers a uniquely advantageous context for the investigation of human reasoning. Not only are the reasoning processes that characterize joint activity visibly distributed across multiple participants (e.g., Hutchins, 1996), but they are also essentially shaped by the way that material and conceptual artifacts are integrated into activity (Vygotsky, 1930/1978) and the way that activity evolves over time (Reimann, 2007). For instance, Teasley and Roschelle (1993) analyze the recordable discourse of dyads using a physics software simulation to explore concepts such as velocity and acceleration, and propose the notion of a joint problem space (JPS) to explain how collaborative activity gets structured in this context. The JPS "knowledge structure" was presented as integrating: goals, descriptions of the current problem state and awareness of available problem-solving actions. The space was characterized as being "shared" in the sense that both members of the dyad oriented to its construction and maintenance.

At first glance, the concept of a "joint problem space" may appear closely related to the original concept of "problem space" advanced within the information-processing perspective on human problem solving, which originated in the collaborative work of Newell and Simon (1972). Newell and Simon concentrated on building a "process theory" describing the performance of individual "intelligent adults in our own culture," working on short and "moderately difficult problems of a symbolic nature" (p. 3), where "motivation is not a question and emotion is not aroused" (p. 53). To achieve this, they explicitly excluded group activity as well as "long-term integrated activities" involving multiple episodes of action over longer periods of time (p. 4). Central to their theory is the idea that to solve a task or problem, one must "adapt" to the environment presented by the problem (the "task environment") by constructing an *internal representation* of the problem's relevant elements (a "problem space"). The concept of problem space was then introduced as a "neutral and objective way of talking about the responses of the subject, including his internal thinking responses, as he goes about dealing with the stimulus situation" (p. 59).

This space, mostly viewed as internal or mental but sometimes related to external resources as well (e.g., Kotovsky & Simon, 1990), is commonly presented as a graph with nodes and links. A person is assumed to understand a task correctly when she has successfully constructed a problem space representation containing or "encoding": a set of states of knowledge including the initial state of the problem, the goal state and the necessary intermediate states, as well as operators for changing from one state into another, constraints determining allowable states and moves, and any other encodings of knowledge such as problem-solving heuristics and the like (pp. 59, 810). Problem solving proceeds as the subject works from the initial state in her mental space, purposefully creating and exploring possible solution paths, testing and evaluating the results obtained. This process is commonly characterized as "search" on the problem space—and search, as an activity, becomes the central phenomenon theorized. The level of detail offered about candidate search processes is, undoubtedly, one aspect in which this theory rivals other less specified proposals. For instance, search methods such as breadth first, depth first, branch and bound, bidirectional, heuristic best first, hill climbing, etc. have been offered as descriptions of the processes followed by human problem solvers in different contexts (Newell, 1980).

The Joint Problem Space

The characterization of the joint problem space advanced by Teasley and Roschelle (1993), despite superficial similarities to the information-processing concept of problem space, goes beyond simply being a collective reformulation of it. From their perspective, social interaction in the context of problem-solving activity occurs in relation to a shared conception of the problem which is in itself constituted through the collaborative process of coordinating communication, action and representation in a particular context of activity; not restricted to or primarily driven by individual mental states.

This perspective—as well as the authors' method of analysis—is closely related to the ethnomethodological position regarding the nature of shared agreements as "various social methods for accomplishing the member's recognition that something was said-according-to-a-rule, and not the demonstrable matching of substantive matters." From this perspective, a common understanding becomes a feature of an interaction (an operation, in Garfinkel's terms)—"rather than a common intersection of overlapping sets" (Garfinkel, 1967, p. 30), as discussions of "shared mental models" (Salas & Fiore, 2004) or "common ground" (Clark & Brennan, 1991) sometimes seem to portray. A "shared agreement" or a "mutual conception of the problem" is then the emergent and situated result of the participants' interactions tied to their context of activity. In the words of Roschelle and Teasley, it is "the coordinated production of talk and action by two participants (that) enabled this construction and maintenance (of the joint problem space) to succeed" (1993, p. 254).

Beyond the identification of relevant resources, an effective account of the problem-solving process requires a description of the fundamental activities involved. Roschelle (1992) presents a summary description of such activities associated with the JPS when he states that the process of the students' incremental achievement of convergent meaning through interaction can be characterized by four primary features of activity, synthesized in Fig. 6.1.

(a)	The production of a deep-featured situation, in relation to
(b)	The interplay of physical metaphors, through the constructive use of
(c)	Interactive cycles of conversational turn-taking, constrained by
(d)	The application of progressively higher standards of evidence for convergence.

Fig. 6.1 Primary features of achieving convergent conceptual change

A Joint Problem Space in VMT

Testing and expanding the proposed construct of the JPS requires, then, the ability to recognize these features in interaction. In order to do this and to support the next steps in our exploration of the construct of problem space, we would like to introduce here one particular problem situation used as part of the Virtual Math Teams (VMT) project (Fig. 6.2).

One could argue that the task presented here does not properly specify a problem yet. The "problem" at hand is, rather, to create a problem. Within the information-processing perspective, the foundational activities that contribute to the creation of a problem are, in fact, poorly understood. As a recent review of psychological research on problem solving stated, "problem-solving research has not revealed a great deal about the processes involved in problem recognition, problem definition and problem representation" (Pretz, Naples, & Sternberg, 2003, p. 9). It is only after a problem space has presumably been constructed internally in the mind of a subject, at least partially, that one can start to trace the solution process as a search process.

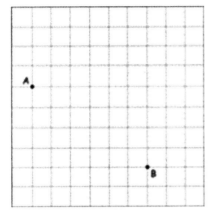

Pretend you live in a world where you can only travel on the lines of the grid. You can't cut across a block on the diagonal, for instance Your group has gotten together to figure out the math of this place. For example, what is a math question you might ask that involves these two points?

Fig. 6.2 Grid-world task

However, observing the early phases of problem solving can, indeed, inform us about how problem spaces are constituted in interaction and how some of the features of collaborative activity described by Roschelle contribute to this important phase. For instance, in our study of the ways that small online groups in VMT engaged with the task in Fig. 6.2, we observed a number of activities that could help characterize certain aspects of the early phases of the creation of a problem space. The groups often identified and appropriated specific elements of the task, and purposefully and iteratively structured them into a problem situation. Resources such as graphical manipulations (e.g., grid annotations), related mathematical concepts (e.g., straight distance), constraints (e.g., you can only travel on the lines of the grid) or analogous problems were used to construct and evolve a set of possible inquiries about this world.

We can characterize these constructions as creating a "deep-featured situation" in the sense that they embody the sustained exploratory activities of the participants. As an example, many groups promptly oriented to finding the shortest distance between points A and B in the grid world, a familiar problem to school-aged students. Some purposefully attended to the constraints of the grid world while others simply ignored them and proceeded to explore diagonal distances. Building on this initial problem, many groups embarked on the problem of finding the number of shortest paths between any two points on the grid. Fig. 6.3 contains some snapshots of the graphical artifacts the different groups created in the shared whiteboard of the VMT environment to help constitute a problem from the original situation.

In this particular situation, potential problems were repeatedly defined as sets of artifacts with specific properties (e.g., constraints), sometimes constituted as "discoverables." Multiple trajectories of reasoning were explored, sometimes in concerted fashion, others in parallel. A central aspect of the group's activity seemed to be concerned with "adding structure" to the resources used for thinking. From an

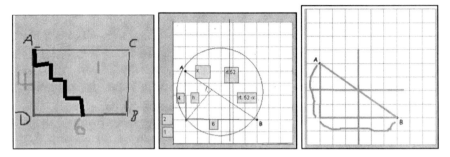

Fig. 6.3 Snapshots of grid-world problem resources created by VMT groups

interactional perspective it certainly does not seem appropriate to characterize such activities as search, although, on the other hand, one could agree that a "space" or network of problem objects and relations was being constructed and that specific features of the resources available were being attended to.

Metaphors played a role in some instances but perspectives, or points of view, seemed more interactionally relevant. In this context, the groups did not necessarily orient to the application of "progressively higher standards of evidence for convergence" but, within those teams that seemed more intensively engaged with the grid world as an expansive situation to think with, they seemed to orient strongly to the continuity and sustainability of their inquiry. In other words, when a confusion arose that interfered with their interaction, the group would engage in repair activities until the problems were rectified to the point at which unproblematic continuation of their task-oriented interaction could continue. Overall, these collective problem-solving activities appear to be much more interactive than what the original concept of search in a mental problem space may have suggested—as Kirsch (2009) has eloquently argued for in relation to individual problem solving as well.

Next, we continue to trace the evolution of the concept of problem space within the learning sciences and explore its role in defining the relevant elements that characterize engagement with problem-solving and knowledge-building activity in different contexts.

Content and Relational Spaces

Barron (2000, 2003) investigated triads of 6th grade students engaged in collaborative mathematical problem solving. Her analysis proposed that it was necessary to differentiate between the social and cognitive aspects of the interactions observed and investigate the ways in which both are interwoven in the establishment of a joint problem-solving space, especially when attempting to characterize successful and unsuccessful collaboration. Both cognitive and social aspects are, in a sense, integrated in the features of collaborative activity described by Roschelle (1992) and reproduced in Fig. 6.1. However, Barron's analysis illuminates a new set of specific activities that the participants engaged in when explicitly orienting to this duality, attending to social and cognitive factors in the development and maintenance of a "between-person state of engagement" (p. 349), which resembles the joint conception of the problem proposed by Teasely and Roschelle. Interestingly, patterns of interaction related to a group's inability to attend to common aspects of the problem or to coordinate their reciprocal participation while solving the problem were particularly salient in groups that failed to achieve and maintain "mutual engagement" and, as a result, were unable to capitalize on the ideas and proposals of the group members (p. 311). As a result, Barron proposed a dual-space model of collaboration integrating a *content space* pertaining to the problem being solved and a *relational space* pertaining to the ways that participants relate to each other. Naturally, these two spaces are not separate entities but essentially mutually constitutive of each other. Participants simultaneously "attend to and develop" such spaces.

Similar proposals have been made, for instance, in the field of Small-Group Research since Bales (1953) first proposed his principle of "equilibrium," which states that a group continuously divides its attention between instrumental (task-related) needs and expressive (socio-emotional) concerns. More recently, McGrath (1991) suggested in his "Time, Interaction and Performance" theory that work groups orient towards three "inseparably intertwined" functions: working on the common task together (production function), maintaining the communication and interaction among group members (group-well-being function) and helping the individual member when necessary (member-support function) (p. 151). Poole and van de Ven (2004) also suggested that group decision-making discussions can be characterized by three intertwining "tracks" of activity and interaction: task progress, relational track and topical focus. The task track concerns the process by which the group accomplishes its goals, such as doing problem analysis, designing solutions, etc. The relation track deals with the interpersonal relationships among group members (e.g., sharing personal information or engaging in social joking). The topic track includes a series of issues or concerns the group has over time. Interspersed within these tracks are breakpoints, marking changes in the development of strands of work.

The power that these proposals have to advance our understanding of group activity lies, however, not in their ability to name dimensions of interaction or group functions, but in their ability to appropriately characterize and describe the activities in which groups engage. Consequently, the value of Barron's proposal, in our opinion, lies in her careful way of calling our attention to the interactional methods employed by the students to orient to and constitute the "responsivity" and "connectedness" (p. 353) of their content and relational spaces. In her descriptions, we see participants' degrees of competence in attending and relating to their own "epistemic process" while "tracking and evaluating others' epistemic processes" (p. 310). Similar descriptions have been provided by Engle and Conant in their discussion of "positioning" (Engle, 2006; Engle and Conant, 2002). In order to expand these concepts, next we extend the type of group phenomena studied from brief collaborative interactions to longitudinal sequences of joint activity, and attempt to inquire about ways in which the concepts of "joint problem space" and "dual problem space" are adequate for understanding them.

Continuity of Joint Problem Spaces in VMT

The joint problem space is an intersubjective space of collective meaning emerging from the active engagement of collectivities in problem solving, combining both "cognitive" and "social" aspects. Arguably, *the difficulty of constructing and maintaining a joint problem space represents the central interactive challenge of effective collaborative knowledge building and learning.* In fact, several studies have shown that what determines the success of the collaborative learning experience is the interactional manner in which this intersubjective problem space is created and used (Barron, 2003; Dillenbourg, Baker, Blaye, & O'Malley, 1996; Hausmann, Chi, & Roy, 2004; Koschmann et al., 2005; Wegerif, 2006). Furthermore, the complexity of the challenge of maintaining a JPS arises when—as in many naturalistic settings—joint activity is dispersed over time (e.g., in multiple episodes of joint activity, long-term projects, etc.) and distributed across multiple collectivities (e.g., multiple teams, task forces, communities, etc.). As a result of these discontinuities or gaps in group interaction, sustained collaborative learning in small virtual groups and online communities of learners might require that co-participants "bridge" multiple segments of their interactions as they interact over time. Motivated by the need to understand such bridging activities, we set out to investigate the challenges associated with discontinuities of interaction over time.

Within the VMT online community, participating teams might engage in multiple, collaborative sessions over time, they might work on several related tasks over time and learn about the work of other teams. To explore whether VMT teams employ specific methods oriented towards overcoming the discontinuities of time, tasks and participation, we conducted a study with five virtual math teams during Spring 2005. These teams were each formed with about four non-collocated upper middle-school and high-school students selected by volunteer teachers at different schools across the United States. The teams engaged in synchronous online math interactions for four hour-long sessions over a two-week period. They used the VMT online environment with chat and shared whiteboard. A new virtual room was provided for each of the sessions, so that participants did not have direct access to the records of their prior interactions. In the first session, the teams were given a brief description of the grid-world presented in Fig. 6.2, where one could only move along the lines of a grid. The students were asked to generate and pursue their own questions about this mathematical world. In subsequent sessions, the teams were given feedback on their work as well as on the work of other teams, and were encouraged to continue their collaboration. Because of the sequential framing of the tasks provided and the continuous relevance of the properties of the grid world, we considered this a potentially advantageous setting for the investigation of members' methods related to continuity of knowledge building. We examined recordings of each of the 18 sessions, paying special attention to the sequential unfolding of the four problem-solving episodes in which each team participated, to the ways that prior activities were used as resources for later teamwork, and also to the ways that changes in team membership triggered issues of continuity.

As a result of our analysis, we identified a number of instances where the teams were engaged in several types of "bridging activity" aimed at overcoming discontinuities emerging over the multiple episodes of interaction. All teams, although in varying levels of intensity, engaged in bridging activities over time. In summary, the instances of bridging identified involved methods related to (a) narrating or *reporting* past doings as resources for constructing a new task, (b) *remembering* collectively and (c) *managing* the history of the team, among others. Constant comparison through different instances of bridging activity in the entire dataset led to our initial characterization of the structural elements that define these activities and their interactional relevance. Our analysis of the dynamics of bridging activity echoes the construction and maintenance of a "joint problem space" (Roschelle & Teasley, 1995) and also agrees with the proposal that such a space integrates "content" and "relational" dimensions (Barron, 2003). However, throughout our analysis of all instances of bridging activity, we noticed that a third element of interaction reoccurred as a resource and a relevant concern of the participants: the temporal and sequential unfolding of activity (see Fig. 6.4).

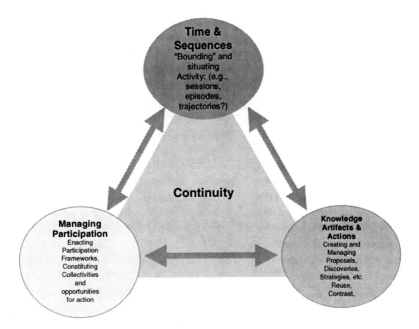

Fig. 6.4 Three dimensions of interaction in bridging work

Time and Sequences

To illustrate each of the three dimensions of interaction identified, let's turn to an actual instance of bridging activity. The conversation reproduced in Log 6-1 illustrates how a team constituted past team activity as a resource for framing a current problem-solving task.

Log 6-1.

144	mathis:	letz start working on number 8
145	bob1:	we already did that yesterday
146	qw:	we did?
147	mathis:	but we did it so that there was only right and down
148	bob1:	i mean tuesday
149	mathis:	i guess we will do it with left and up?
150	qw:	It would be almost the same.
151	bob1:	it's (|x2-x1|+|y2-y1|-2) choose (|x2-x1|-1)
152	bob1:	try it if you like
153	mathis:	nah
154	mathis:	if you are so sure
155	bob1:	i'm not
156	bob1:	actually
157	bob1:	take out the -2 and the -1
158	mathis:	then letz check it

The first of the three basic interactional dimensions that seem to be at play in bridging activity corresponds to the creation, referencing, manipulation, assessment and re-use of a set of knowledge artifacts. This involves constituting the problem-at-hand, identifying which resources are relevant to it, creating tasks, constituting aspects of the problem situation and its resources as known or unknown, among other activities Despite the brevity of the interaction excerpt captured in Log 6-1, we can recognize some of these knowledge artifacts (e.g., problem number 8, **"only right and down"**, " **left and up"**, **"(\|x2-x1\|+\|y2-y1\|-2) choose (\|x2-x1\|-1)"**, etc.). We can get a glimpse of ways in which they are attended to and manipulated (e.g., **"only right and down"** is debated as being almost the same as **"left and up"**, the formula provided is offered for assessment, etc.). Interwoven with the development and use of knowledge artifacts, we also identified the active management of participation as a second relevant dimension at play in this case of bridging activity. From this perspective, teams were actively oriented towards, for instance, who was and was not involved in an activity, who could or should speak about a particular matter and how, which activities (e.g., assessing and responding to assessments) were allocated to participants, etc.

In essence, the participants orient to the development in interaction of specific participation frameworks (Goffman, 1981) which "position" team members in relation to each other, to the resources at hand and to the activities they are engaged in. This positioning activity, for example, situated participants as problem-solving peers, experts, explainers, etc. In addition, the activities they engage in over time position them with different types of access, rights and duties with respect to relevant knowledge artifacts. Log 6-1 illustrates this, especially toward the end of this passage, when Bob1 attempts to position Mathis as someone who could do the checking of his solution formula. After Mathis declines and Bob1 states his lack of confidence in the correctness of the formula, a new participation framework gets enacted, in which the group together can engage in the work necessary to check and possibly correct the solution provided for this problem.

The first two dimensions of interaction observed—the use of knowledge artifacts and the orientation to participation frameworks—match very closely the "content" and "relational" spaces theorized by Barron. However, a recurring third element present in episodes of bridging activity captured our attention additionally, both because of its centrality in the interactions analyzed as well as because of its novelty within the theoretical frameworks considered. The third dimension involves the temporal or sequential organization of experience. Temporality and sequentiality are constructs that are often taken for granted and are only recently recovering their centrality in analyses of joint activity (e.g., Arrow, Poole, Henry, Wheelan, & Moreland, 2004; Lemke, 2001; Reimann, 2007; Sawyer, 2003). Our analysis suggests, however, that in the types of interactions that we observed, participants orient to time and sequence as central resources for the organization of their collaborative activity. As can be seen in Log 6-1, VMT participants visibly oriented to what was done in a different episode of activity or at a different time (lines 145–148), to the relationship between what was done before and what is being done now (lines 149–150), or to what possible actions might be available at a particular moment as related to what had been achieved so far (lines 152–158). Current problem-solving work is situated with respect to its temporal position and to sequences of (past and future) related activities. Participants mark their statements with past, present and future tenses (**"letz start"**, **"we already did"**, **"we will do it"**, **"try it"**, **"then letz check it"**) to co-construct a time line and to structure sequences of referenced or proposed activities.

The Organization of a Deictic Field Through Collective Remembering

Log 6-2 illustrates a case in which another team is collectively engaged in trying to reconstruct parts of their previous session while initiating their current problem-solving activity. Remembering of past activity unfolds as a collective engagement in which different team members participate dynamically. Some of the current team members were not present in the previous session, and yet they are instrumental in the reconstruction of that past and in shaping its current relevance. This was the fourth session of team E. Toward the beginning of the session (8:22:09 PM) the facilitator (MFMod) suggested in the chat that during the summer the team members could work with their friends on a new problem he posted: the **"circle problem"**. Later, he added that they could pursue the circle question in **"this chat"** if they wanted or **"any other questions and worlds"** that they thought of. Following about a minute of silence, the facilitator posted a message in which he reported how in the previous session the team had **"worked on finding a formula for the number of shortest paths between any two points A and B on the grid (. . .) explored multiple possibilities and figured out that x+y and x^2+y^2 work (where x and y correspond to the # of units you need to travel along the x and y axis to get from A to B), but only for some points, not all"**. Then he suggested that they could continue **"exploring more cases"** and see if they could find **"a general formula"**, work on the circle problem he had posted earlier, or on any other problem from the **"original questions"** presented at the beginning of their VMT experience. The team then oriented toward finding a task for themselves, and the following interaction (Log 6-2) took place:

Log 6-2.

119	8:27:42	drago:	ok
120	8:30:11	gdo:	where did u guys last leave off
			(graphical reference from 120 to 119)
121	8:31:20	MFmod:	I think that the above section I wrote is where the group last was
			(graphical reference from 121 to 114)
122	8:31:36	MFmod:	yes?
123	8:31:42	drago:	well
124	8:31:48	gdo:	i dont remember that
125	8:31:51	drago:	actually, my internet connection broke on Tuesday
126	8:31:56	drago:	so I wasn't here
127	8:32:12	MFmod:	so maybe that is not the best place to pick up
128	8:32:14	estric:	i wasnt able to be here on tuesday either
129	8:32:50	gdo:	how bout u meets
130	8:33:01	meets:	uh...
131	8:33:11	meets:	where'd we meet off....
132	8:33:16	meets:	i remember
133	8:33:22	gdo:	i was in ur group
134	8:33:24	meets:	that we were trying to look for a pattern
135	8:33:27	gdo:	but i didn't quite understand it
136	8:33:34	gdo:	can u explain it to us again meets
137	8:33:38	meets:	with the square, the 2by 2 square, and the 3by2 rectangle
138	8:33:42	meets:	sure...
139	8:33:45	meets:	so basically...
140	8:33:45	gdo:	o yea
141	8:33:49	gdo:	i sort of remember
142	8:33:55	meets:	we want a formula for the distance between poitns A and B
143	8:34:02	drago:	yes...
144	8:34:05	meets:	ill amke the points
			(Meets draws two points on the existing grid on the shared whiteboard)
145	8:34:09	MFmod:	since some folks don't remember and weren't here why don't you pick up with this idea and work on it a bit

Log 6-2 (continued).

			(Meets labels the two points on the grid A and B)
146	8:34:55	meets:	okay
147	8:34:59	meets:	so there are those poitns A and B
148	8:35:08	meets:	(that's a 3by2 rectangle)
149	8:35:28	meets:	we first had a unit square
			(Meets draws the lines of a 3 by 2 rectangle with points A and B in its opposing corners)
150	8:35:44	meets:	and we know that there are only 2 possible paths......

This sequence involves a number of interesting interactional features. In particular, a set of temporal and sequential markers (e.g., **Tuesday, last, again**) and the mixing of different verb tenses are used to index prior events and constitute a present task. In the facilitator's feedback, the declarative assertions constructed with past-tense verbs (e.g., **"you worked on finding a formula"**, **"you explored multiple possibilities"**, **"you figured out that x+y and x^2+y^2 work"**, etc.) were followed by future-oriented suggestions: **"you may want to continue exploring more cases and see if you can find a general formula,"** **"you can work on the problem I posted earlier."** The uptake by the team of the task assessments and proposals made by the facilitator also involved similar resources. Gdo's request in line 120 for a report of where the group **"last"** left off seems to use a communicative marker that allows parties in conversation to segment or index specific portions of experiences and relate them in ways that allow them to form sequences of participation and activity. Gdo is orienting the group back to a specific aspect of **"last Tuesday,"** and after Drago and Estric both positioned themselves as not having participated in last Tuesday's session, Meets is then asked directly in lines 129 and 136 to re-produce a past (**"again"**) explanation for the rest (**"us"**).

One of the things that is remarkable about the way this interaction unfolds is the fact that although it might appear as if it was Meets who individually remembered what they were doing last time, the activity of remembering unfolds as a collective engagement in which different team members participate. This is accomplished by marking and using time as a central resource to organize participation and to advance their current problem solving. To organize their present activity, they reproduce a sequence of previously constructed cases (the unit square, the 2×2 square and the 3×2 rectangle) and link them to knowledge artifacts and the related knowledge of the group (e.g., stating in line 150 that for the unit square **"we know that there are only 2 possible paths"** from one corner to the opposite corner).

In fact, later in this interaction there is a point where Meets remembers the fact that they had discovered that there are six different shortest paths between the opposite corners of a 2×2 grid but he reports that he can only **"see"** four at the moment. Drago, who did not participate in the original work leading to that finding, is able to see the six paths and proceeds to invent a method of labeling each point of the grid with a letter so that he can name each path and help others see it (e.g., **"from**

B to D there is BAD, BCD ..."). After this, Meets was able to see again why it is that there are six paths in that small grid and together with Drago, they proceeded to investigate, in parallel, the cases of a 3×3 and a 4×4 grid using the labeling and enumeration method just created.

All of these resources—the knowledge artifacts used and referenced, the sequential organization of cases and the temporal markers of prior activity—are organized in different ways with relation to the participants in a temporal or sequential space. The concept of "deictic field" developed by Hanks (1992) seems especially useful to define the relationship between this new "space" and Barron's content and relational spaces. Hanks describes the deictic field as composed first by "the positions of communicative agents relative to the participant frameworks they occupy," for example, who occupies the positions of speaker and addressee as well as other relevant positions. Second, the deictic field integrates "the positions occupied by objects of reference," and finally "the multiple dimensions whereby the former have access to the latter" (p. 193). From this perspective, participants constitute, through interaction, the relevant relative dimensions whereby they are to manage the positioning of agents and relevant objects of reference.

The method of labeling the grid intersections and using this to name paths provided a shared organization of the deictic field as visually available in the shared whiteboard. Chat messages and textboxes could then reference paths unambiguously and concisely to facilitate not only the on-going group work, but even the group remembering of past work. The remembering could then use the labeling and naming conventions to visualize, comprehend, check, itemize, understand and apply the remembered achievement within the current situation. In the interaction recorded in Log 6-2, the three dimensions are intimately intertwined or unified. Participation is managed so that people who were or were not present in the previous session could nevertheless be included in remembering the knowledge constructed then. The knowledge artifacts (paths, formulae, procedures for exploring patterns) of the past were situated in the present work and enhanced with the labeling. The temporal discontinuity between sessions was bridged and the sequentiality of the group work was organized within the newly elaborated deictic field that the group incorporated in their joint problem space.

Sustaining Group Cognition

In our analysis of interactions like those recorded in Logs 6-1 and 6-2, we have observed that the content and relational dimensions are, in fact, relevant to collaborative problem-solving teams. Moreover, in expanding the range of phenomena analyzed to include longitudinal interactions across discontinuities, we have also uncovered *time and the sequential unfolding of interaction as a third relevant and important dimension of activity*. In Log 6-2, for instance, the interactional field is being constituted by the participants to include problem-related objects and communicative agents associated with a prior interaction, and in doing so they position themselves and those resources within specific participation frameworks. The content objects (e.g., knowledge artifacts) and the relations among people (e.g., social positioning) are located within a temporal field, which provides a context for situating past, present and future events, for pointing to the events as temporally structured and for ordering utterances in their sequential relationships. Our central claim is that this temporal/sequential dimension is as essential to understanding collaborative interactions as are the content and relational dimensions. The three dimensions are inextricably interwoven and constitute the joint problem space. Such interdependency can be seen as characterizing the longitudinal knowledge building of activity systems like the Virtual Math Teams.

The theory of group cognition takes as one of its central principles the dialectical relationship between social interaction and the construction of meaning. Meaning is not viewed as pre-existing in the minds of individuals, but as something that is constituted in the discourse within the group (Stahl, 2006b, chap. 16). Nor is the group viewed as pre-existing as a set of people, but as a functional unit that constitutes itself in the interaction of its members when they position themselves within their group activity. From this perspective, the social organization of action and the knowledge embedded in such action are emergent properties of moment-by-moment interactions among actors, and between actors and the objects and the activity systems in which they participate collectively. The content space and the relational space, in Barron's terms, are mutually constitutive from this perspective.

Group cognition theory offers a candidate description for how the dynamic process of building knowledge might intertwine the content and relational spaces: "Small groups are the engines of knowledge building. The knowing that groups build up in manifold forms is what becomes internalized by their members as individual learning and externalized in their communities as certifiable knowledge" (Stahl, 2006a, p. 16). Thus, small-group interaction can play a pivotal mediating role in the interplay between individual cognition (and the relations among the individuals) and communities of practice (and the knowledge objects that they share). Time as the sequential organization of activity seems to be a resource and an aspect of interaction that plays a significant role in how communities, groups and individuals achieve knowledge through small-group interaction. We have caught a glimpse or two of how temporality is marked and sequentiality is established within the discourse of small groups in VMT (see also Chapter 26).

In our analysis of how small groups "sustain" their group cognition while engaged in brief episodes of online mathematical problem solving, we alluded to two ways in which time might be an important element of individual episodes of problem-solving activity. On the one hand, the collaborative activity involved in solving a problem can be "spread across" hundreds of micro-level interactions. On the other hand, individuals might internalize or individualize the meaning co-constructed through interactions and "sustain" the group cognition by engaging in later individual or group work. In either case, groups are described as sustaining their social and intellectual work by "building longer sequences of math proposals, other adjacency pairs and a variety of interaction methods" (Stahl, 2006e, p. 85).

The analysis presented here of interactions that bridge gaps across sessions confirms and extends these findings by suggesting that in longitudinal interactions, temporal and sequential resources are central to constituting activity as continuous by constructing and maintaining a joint problem space. Interaction is taken here in the full sense that ethnomethodologists give it, as the "ongoing, contingent co-production of a shared social/material world," which, as Suchman argues "cannot be stipulated in advance, but requires an autobiography, a presence and a projected future" (Suchman, 2007). Our characterization in this chapter only provides a tentative framework to organize our developing understanding of collaborative learning and knowledge building over time. We have just began the work of describing in detail the interactional methods that allow teams to construct and manage this expanded problem "field" by interweaving content, relational and temporal aspects of interaction.

Chapter 7
The Organization of Graphical, Narrative and Symbolic Interactions

Murat Perit Çakir

Abstract In order to collaborate effectively in group discourse on a topic like mathematical patterns, group participants must organize their activities so that they have a shared understanding of the significance of their utterances, inscriptions and behaviors—adequate for sustaining productive interaction. Some methodologies applied in CSCL research—such as the widespread coding-and-counting quantitative analysis genre—systematically ignore the sequentiality of actions and thereby miss the implicit referencing, which is essential to shared understanding. The VMT Project attempts to capture and analyze the sequential organization of references and inter-relationships among whiteboard inscriptions, chat postings, mathematical expressions and other elements of virtual math team activities in order to understand the mechanisms of group cognition.

Here, we report the results of a case study of collaborative math problem-solving activities mediated by the VMT multimodal online environment. We employ ethnomethodological conversation analysis techniques to investigate moment-to-moment details of the interaction practices through which participants organize their chat utterances and whiteboard actions as a coherent whole. In particular, we observe that the sequential construction of shared drawings and the deictic references that link chat messages to features of those drawings and to prior chat content are instrumental in the achievement of shared understanding (intersubjective reciprocity) among the team members. We characterize this foundational precondition of collaboration as the co-construction of an indexical field that functions as a common ground for group cognition. The integration of graphical, narrative and symbolic semiotic modalities in this manner also facilitates joint problem solving by allowing group members to invoke and operate with multiple realizations of their mathematical artifacts, a characteristic of deep learning of math.

Keywords Dual-interaction space · multimodal interaction · unit of analysis · persistence · animation · reference

M.P. Çakir (✉)
College of Information Science & Technology, Drexel University, Philadelphia, PA, USA
e-mail: mpc48@drexel.edu

G. Stahl (ed.), *Studying Virtual Math Teams*, Computer-Supported Collaborative
Learning Series 11, DOI 10.1007/978-1-4419-0228-3_7,
© Springer Science+Business Media, LLC 2009

Computer-supported collaborative learning is centrally concerned with the joint organization of interaction by small groups of students in online environments. The term "collaborative learning" is a gloss for *interaction that is organized for the joint achievement of knowledge-building tasks* such as problem solving in domains like school mathematics. Rather than using the term "collaborative learning," which carries vague and contradictory connotations, we prefer the term "group cognition" to refer to activities where several students organize their joint interaction to achieve such collective cognitive accomplishments as planning, deducing, designing, describing, problem solving, explaining, defining, generalizing, representing, remembering and reflecting as a group.

In this chapter, we present a case study of an 18-minute-long excerpt from the VMT Spring Fest 2006. We look at some ways in which the students organized their joint efforts. Our observations here are consistent with our impressions from more than a hundred student-hours of interaction in the VMT data corpus.

The issue that we address in the following pages is: *How do the students in our case study organize their activity so they can define and accomplish their tasks as a group within their online environment?* This is necessarily a pivotal question for a science of CSCL (see Chapter 28). It involves issues of meaning making, shared understanding and common ground that have long been controversial in CSCL.

The problem of coordination is particularly salient in the VMT software environment, which is an instance of a dual-interaction space (Dillenbourg, 2005) (see also Chapter 15), requiring organization across multiple media, each with their own affordances. We have found that the key to joint coordination of knowledge building is sequential organization of a network of indexical and semantic references within the group discourse (see Chapter 26). We therefore analyze sequential interaction at the group level of description, using ethnomethodologically inspired chat interaction analysis rather than quantitative coding, in order to maintain and study this sequential organization. Thereby, we arrive at a view of mathematical knowledge building as the coordinated production and use of visual, narrative and symbolic inscriptions as multiple realizations of co-constructed mathematical objects.

While we have elsewhere presented theoretical motivations for focusing on *group discourse organization* as fundamental for CSCL, in this chapter we foreground our *analysis of empirical data* from a VMT session. We derive a number of characteristics of the joint organization of interaction from the details of the case study. The characteristics we describe are to some extent specific to the technological affordances of the VMT environment, to the pedagogical framing of the chat session and even to the unique trajectory of this particular group interaction. Nevertheless, the characteristics are indicative of what takes place—with variations—in similar settings. After the analytic centerpiece of the chapter, we discuss *methodological implications* for CSCL analysis, including what it means to take the *group* as the unit of analysis. We then contrast our approach to leading *alternative approaches* in CSCL. This discussion focuses particularly on multi-modal interaction in a *dual-interaction space* and on related conceptions of *common ground*, concluding with summary remarks on *sequential analysis*. The chapter proceeds through the following topics:

- The problem of group organization in CSCL
- A case study of a virtual math team
- Implications for CSCL chat interaction analysis
- The group as the unit of analysis
- Other approaches in CSCL to analyzing multimodal interaction
- Grounding through interactional organization
- Sequential analysis of the joint organization of interaction.

The Problem of Group Organization in CSCL

A central issue in the theory of collaborative learning is how students can solve problems, build knowledge, accomplish educational tasks and achieve other cognitive accomplishments *together*. How do they share ideas and talk about the same things? How do they know that they are talking about, thinking about, understanding and working on things in the same way? Within CSCL, this has been referred to as the problem of the "attempt to construct and maintain a shared conception of a problem" (Roschelle & Teasley, 1995), "building common ground" (Baker, Hansen, Joiner, & Traum, 1999; Clark & Brennan, 1991) or "the practices of meaning making" (Koschmann, 2002). We have been interested in this issue for some time. *Group Cognition* (Stahl, 2006b) documents a decade of background to the VMT research reported here: its Chapter 10 (written in 2001) argued the need for a new approach. It pointed out that some CSCL methods of analysis—which reduce subtle networks of linguistic interaction to counts of codes—reify the flow of discourse and miss the temporal structure that is important for understanding the meaning making.

Knowledge building in CSCL has traditionally been supported primarily with asynchronous technologies (Scardamalia & Bereiter, 1996). Within appropriate educational cultures, this can be effective for long-term refinement of ideas by learning communities. However, in small groups and in many classrooms, asynchronous media encourage mere exchange of individual opinions more than co-construction of progressive trains of joint thought. We have found informally that synchronous interaction can more effectively promote group cognition—the accomplishment of "higher order" cognitive tasks through the coordination of contributions by individuals within the discourse of a small group. We believe that the case study in this chapter demonstrates the power of group interaction in a largely synchronous environment; the coordination of interaction in an asynchronous interaction would be quite different in nature as a result of very different interactional constraints.

In CSCL settings, interaction is mediated by a computer environment. Students working in such a setting must enact, adapt or invent ways of coordinating their understandings by means of the technological affordances that they find at hand (Dohn, 2009). The development and deployment of these methods is not usually an explicit, rational process that is easily articulated by either the participants or analysts. It occurs tacitly, unnoticed, taken-for-granted. In order to make it more visible to us as analysts, we have developed an environment that makes the coordination of interaction more salient and captures a complete record of the group interaction for detailed analysis. In trying to support online math problem solving by small groups, we have found it important to provide media for both linguistic and graphical expression. This resulted in what is known within CSCL as a *dual-interaction space*. In our environment, students must coordinate their text chat postings with their whiteboard drawings. A careful analysis of how they do this reveals as well their more general methods of group organization.

The analysis of our case study focuses on episodes of interaction through which an online group of students co-constructs mathematical artifacts across dual-interaction spaces. It looks closely at how group members put the multiple modalities into use, how they make their chat postings and drawing actions intelligible to each other, and how they achieve a sense of coherence among actions taking place across the modalities to which they have access. We base our discussion, analysis and design of the affordances of the online environment on the methodical ways the features of the software are put into use by the students.

In Chapter 6 above, we saw how the problem-solving work of a virtual math team is accomplished through the co-construction and maintenance of a *joint problem space* (Teasley & Roschelle, 1993). This figurative space—that supports group interaction and the shared understanding of that interaction by the participants—not only grounds the *content* of the team's discourse and work, but also ties together the *social* fabric of the relations among the team members as actors. In addition, we saw that the joint problem space has a third essential dimension: *time* or sequence. The construction of the joint problem space constitutes a shared temporality through bridging moves that span and thereby order discontinuous events as past, present and future (Sarmiento-Klapper, 2009). This can be seen, for instance in the use of tenses in group-remembering discourses. More generally, the joint problem space provides a framework of sequential orderings, within which temporal deictic references, for example, can be resolved.

In this chapter, we further investigate how a virtual math team achieves a group organization of its activities such that the group can proceed with a sense of everyone understanding each other and of working collaboratively as a group. We do this through a fine-grained analysis of the group's interaction in a VMT session in which they formulate, explore and solve a geometry problem. Their work takes place in graphical, narrative and symbolic media—supported technologically by the shared whiteboard, text chat and wiki pages of the VMT environment. We pay particular attention to how graphical inscriptions, textual postings and symbolic expressions in the different media are closely coordinated by the group members, despite the differences of the media.

We pursue an ethnomethodological approach to analyzing the activities of the group members in their own terms. They set themselves a task, propose how to proceed step by step and explain to each other how to understand their actions. We try to follow the explanations, which are available in the inscriptions, postings and expressions—particularly when the sequentiality of these allows the complex references among them to be followed.

The establishment of group order in small-group interaction is always strongly dependent upon the media, which mediate interaction. In the case of VMT chats, there is an intricate set of technological media, including text chat, a shared white-board, a community wiki and graphical references from chat to whiteboard. The central part of this chapter explores the different characteristics of the VMT media by observing how the students use them. Of particular interest are the ways in which a group coordinates activities in the different graphical and textual media. From a math-education perspective, it is also insightful to see how the visual and narrative understandings feed into the development and understanding of symbolic expressions.

By the end of the chapter, we will see how the group organization of graphical, narrative and symbolic resources in interaction continuously produce and reproduce the joint problem space of the group's effort. This coordination is revealed through sequential analysis, in which the consequence of one action in one medium following another in another medium is seen as mutually constitutive of the meaning of those actions. The sequential web of activity across the VMT media—woven by semantic and indexical references among them—forms the joint problem space within which problem content, participant relationships and temporal progress are all defined in a way that is shared by the group. We can see the "indexical field" (Hanks 1992) formed by the group activities as the source of grounding that supports the intersubjectivity of the group effort. In contrast to psychological or psycholinguistic models of common ground, the fact that team members believe they have understandings in common about what each other is saying and doing is not a result of exchanging individual mental opinions, but is a function of the indexical organization of the group interaction.

The joint problem space—as the foundation of group cognition—is not a mental construct of a set of individuals who achieve cognitive convergence or common (identical) ground through comparing mental models anymore than it is a figment of some form of group mind. Rather, it is a system of interconnected meanings formed by a weaving of references in the group discourse itself (Chapter 26). In this chapter, we analyze the methods the students used to co-construct this indexical field.

In our case study, the organization of group meaning making takes place across media—in accordance with the specific affordances of the different media. Furthermore, the grounding of the students' symbolic mathematical understanding can be seen as related to their visual and narrative understandings—or, rather, the various understandings are intricately interwoven and support each other. We trace this interweaving through our approach to the interactional analysis of sequential coordination at the group unit of analysis.

A Case Study of a Virtual Math Team

The excerpts we present in this chapter are obtained from a problem-solving session of a team of three students who participated in the VMT Spring Fest 2006. This event brought together several teams from the US, Scotland and Singapore to collaborate on an open-ended math task on geometric patterns. Students were recruited anonymously through their teachers. Members of the teams generally did not know each other before the first session. Neither they nor we knew anything about each other (e.g., age or gender) except chat handle and information that may have been communicated during the sessions. Each group participated in four sessions during a two-week period, and each session lasted over an hour. An adult from the research project moderated each session; the facilitators' task was to help the teams when they experienced technical difficulties, not to participate in the problem-solving work.

During their first session, all the teams were asked to work online on a particular pattern of squares made up of sticks (see Fig. 7.1). For the remaining three sessions the teams were asked to come up with their own shapes, describe the patterns they observed as mathematical formulas, and share their observations with other teams through a wiki page. This task was chosen because of the possibilities it afforded for many different solution approaches ranging from simple counting procedures to more advanced methods involving the use of recursive functions and exploring the properties of various number sequences. Moreover, the task had

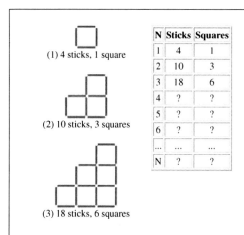

N	Sticks	Squares
1	4	1
2	10	3
3	18	6
4	?	?
5	?	?
6	?	?
...	...	...
N	?	?

(1) 4 sticks, 1 square

(2) 10 sticks, 3 squares

(3) 18 sticks, 6 squares

Session I

1. Draw the pattern for N=4, N=5, and N=6 in the whiteboard. Discuss as a group: How does the graphic pattern grow?
2. Fill in the cells of the table for sticks and squares in rows N=4, N=5, and N=6. Once you agree on these results, post them on the VMT Wiki
3. Can your group see a pattern of growth for the number of sticks and squares? When you are ready, post your ideas about the pattern of growth on the VMT Wiki.

Sessions II and III

1. Discuss the feedback that you received about your previous session.
2. **WHAT IF?** Mathematicians do not just solve other people's problems - they also explore little worlds of patterns that they define and find interesting. Think about other mathematical problems related to the problem with the sticks. For instance, consider other arrangements of squares in addition to the triangle arrangement (diamond, cross, etc.). **What if** instead of squares you use other polygons like triangles, hexagons, etc.? Which polygons work well for building patterns like this? How about 3-D figures, like cubes with edges, sides and cubes? What are the different methods (induction, series, recursion, graphing, tables, etc.) you can use to analyze these different patterns?
3. Go to the VMT Wiki and share the most interesting math problems that your group chose to work on.

Fig. 7.1 Task description

both algebraic and geometric aspects, to allow us to observe how participants put many features of the VMT software system into use. The open-ended nature of the activity stemmed from the need to agree upon a new shape made by sticks. This required groups to engage in an open-ended problem-solving activity, as compared to traditional situations where questions are given in advance and there is a single "correct" answer—presumably already known by a teacher. We used a traditional pattern problem (Moss & Beatty, 2006; Watson & Mason, 2005) to seed the activity and then left it up to each group to decide the kinds of shapes they found interesting and worth exploring further.

All the problem-solving sessions were conducted in the VMT environment. The VMT online system has two main interactive components that conform to the typical layout of systems with dual-interaction spaces: a shared drawing board that provides basic drawing features on the left, and a chat window on the right (Fig. 7.2). The online environment has features specifically designed to help users relate the actions happening across dual-interaction spaces (Chapter 15). One of the unique features of this chat system is the referencing support mechanism that allows users to visually connect their chat postings to previous postings or objects on the whiteboard via arrows (see the last posting in Fig. 7.2 for an example of a message-to-whiteboard reference). The referential links attached to a message are displayed until a new message is posted. Messages with referential links are indicated by an arrow icon in the chat window, and a user can see where such a message is pointing by clicking on it at any time.

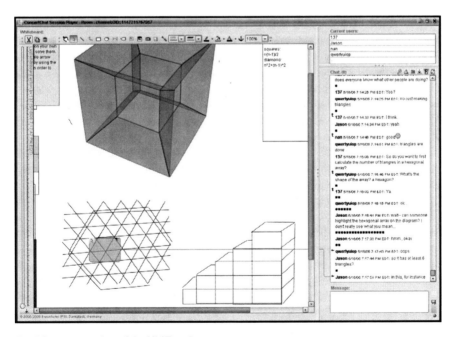

Fig. 7.2 A screen-shot of the VMT environment

In addition to the explicit referencing feature, the system displays small boxes in the chat window to indicate actions performed on the whiteboard. This awareness mechanism allows users to observe how actions performed in both interaction spaces are sequenced with respect to each other. Moreover, users can click on these boxes to move the whiteboard back and forth from its current state to the specific point in its history when that action was performed. Chat messages and activity markers are color coded to help users to keep track of who is doing what in the online environment. In addition to standard awareness markers that display who is present in the room and who is currently typing, the system also displays textual descriptions of whiteboard actions in tool-tip messages that can be observed by holding the mouse either on the object in the whiteboard or on the corresponding square in the chat window.

Studying the meaning-making practices enacted by the users of CSCL systems inevitably requires a close analysis of the process of collaboration itself (Dillenbourg et al., 1996; Stahl et al., 2006). In an effort to investigate the organization of interactions across the dual-interaction spaces of the VMT environment, we consider the small group as the unit of analysis (Stahl, 2006b), and we appropriate methods of ethnomethodology and conversation analysis to conduct sequential analysis of group interactions at a micro-level (Psathas, 1995; Sacks, 1962/1995; ten Have, 1999). Our work is informed by studies of interaction mediated by online text-chat with similar methods (Garcia & Jacobs, 1998, 1999; O'Neill & Martin, 2003), although the availability of a shared drawing area and explicit support for deictic references in our online environment substantially differentiate our study from theirs.

The goal of this line of analytic work is to discover the commonsense understandings and procedures group members use to organize their conduct in particular interactional settings (Coulon, 1995). Commonsense understandings and procedures are subjected to analytical scrutiny because they are what "enable actors to recognize and act on their real world circumstances, grasp the intentions and motivations of others, and achieve mutual understandings" (Goodwin & Heritage, 1990, p. 285). Group members' shared competencies in organizing their conduct not only allow them to produce their own actions, but also to interpret the actions of others (Garfinkel & Sacks, 1970). Since group members enact these understandings visibly in their situated actions, researchers can discover them through detailed analysis of the members' sequentially organized conduct (Schegloff & Sacks, 1973).

We conducted numerous VMT Project data sessions, where we subjected our analysis of the excerpts below to intersubjective agreement (Psathas, 1995). This chapter presents the outcome of this group effort together with the actual transcripts so that the analysis can be subjected to external scrutiny. During the data sessions we used the VMT Replayer tool, which allows us to replay a VMT chat session as it unfolded in real time based on the timestamps of actions recorded in the log file. The order of actions—chat postings, whiteboard actions, awareness messages—we observe with the Replayer as researchers exactly matches the order of actions originally observed by the users. This property of the Replayer allowed us to study the sequential unfolding of events during the entire chat session, which is crucial in making sense of the complex interactions mediated by a CSCL environment (Koschmann et al., 2007).

In this case study, we focus on a sequence of excerpts obtained from a single problem-solving session of a virtual math team. We are concerned with how the actors contribute to the group meaning making as they proceed. This example involves the use and coordination of actions involving both the whiteboard and chat environment. It therefore served as a useful site for seeing how actors, in this local setting, were able to engage in meaningful coordinated interaction.

The team has three members: Jason, 137 and Qwertyuiop, who are upper-middle-school students (roughly 14 years old) in the US. In the following subsections we will present how this team co-constructed a mathematical artifact they referred to as the **"hexagonal array"** through a coordinated sequence of actions distributed between the chat and whiteboard spaces, and how they subsequently explored its properties by referring to and annotating shared drawings on the whiteboard. In particular, we will highlight how whiteboard objects and previous chat postings were used as semiotic resources during the collaborative problem-solving activity. This will show how chat and whiteboard differ in terms of their affordances for supporting group interaction. We will see how these differences are enacted and used in complementary ways by team members to achieve mutual intelligibility of their actions across multiple interaction spaces.

Availability of the Production Processes

Log 7-1 is taken from the beginning of the team's third session. The team has already explored similar patterns of sticks and become familiar with the features of

Log 7-1.

Line	Time	Chat handle	Chat message or *<whiteboard action>*
	7:07:52 - 7:11:00	137	*<137 draws a hexagon shape and then splits it up into regions by adding lines. Figure 7.3 shows some of the key steps in 137's drawing performance>*
1	7:11:16	137	Great. Can anyone make a diagram of a bunch of triangles?
	7:11:16 - 7:11:49	137	*<137 deletes the set of lines he has just drawn>*
2	7:11:51	Qwertyuiop	just a grid?....
	7:11:54 - 7:12:01	137	*<137 moves some of the older drawings away>*
3	7:12:07	137	Yeah...
4	7:12:17	Qwertyuiop	ok...
	7:12:23 - 7:14:07	Qwertyuiop	*<Qwertyuiop draws a grid of triangles in the space opened up by 137. Figure 7.4 shows some of the steps in Qwertyuiop's drawing actions>*

the VMT online environment during their prior sessions. The drawing actions at the beginning of this excerpt were the first moves of the session related to math problem solving.

At the beginning of this excerpt, 137 performs a series of drawing actions. 137's actions on the whiteboard include the drawing of a hexagon first, then three diagonal lines and finally lines parallel to the diagonals and to the sides of the hexagon whose intersections eventually introduce some triangular and diamond-shaped regions. Moreover, 137 also performs some adjustment moves—for instance between the 4th and 5th snapshots in Fig. 7.3—to ensure that three non-parallel lines intersect at a single point, and the edges of the hexagon are parallel to the lines introduced later as much as possible. Hence, this sequence of drawing actions suggests a particular organization of lines for constructing a hexagonal shape. (Fig. 7.3 shows six snapshots corresponding to intermediary stages of 137's drawing actions: 137 initiates his drawing actions with six lines that form the hexagon in stage 1. Then he adds three diagonal lines in step 2. The 3rd snapshot shows the additional two lines drawn parallel to one of the diagonals. The 4th snapshot shows a similar set of two parallel lines added with respect to another diagonal. The 5th snapshot shows slight modifications performed on the new set of parallel lines to ensure intersections at certain places. The 6th snapshot shows the final stage of 137's drawing.)

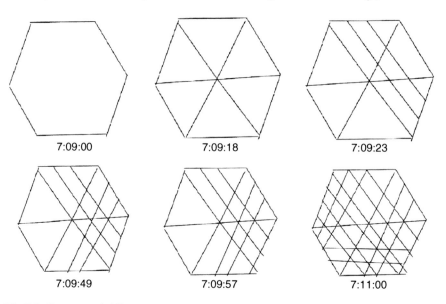

Fig. 7.3 Six stages of 137's drawing actions obtained from the Replayer tool

137's chat posting in line 1 that follows his drawing effort (which can be read as a self-critical, sarcastic **"great"**) suggests that he considers his illustration inadequate in some way. He makes this explicit by soliciting help from other members to produce **"a diagram of a bunch of triangles"** on the whiteboard, and then removing the diagram he has just produced (the boxes following this post-

ing in Fig. 7.5 correspond to deletion actions on the whiteboard). By removing his
diagram, 137 makes that space available to other members for the projected drawing activity. Qwertyuiop responds to 137's query with a request for clarification
regarding the projected organization of the drawing (**"just a grid?"**). After 137's
acknowledgement, Qwertyuiop performs a series of drawing actions that resemble the latter stages of 137's drawing actions, namely starting with the parallel
lines tipped to the right first, then drawing a few parallel lines tipped to the left,
and finally adding horizontal lines at the intersection points of earlier lines that
are parallel to each other (see Figs. 7.4 and 7.5). Having witnessed 137's earlier actions, the similarity in the organizations of both drawing actions suggest
that Qwertyuiop has appropriated some key aspects of 137's drawing strategy, but
modified/re-ordered the steps (e.g., he didn't start with the hexagon at the begin-

Fig. 7.4 The evolution of Qwertyuiop's drawing in response to 137's request

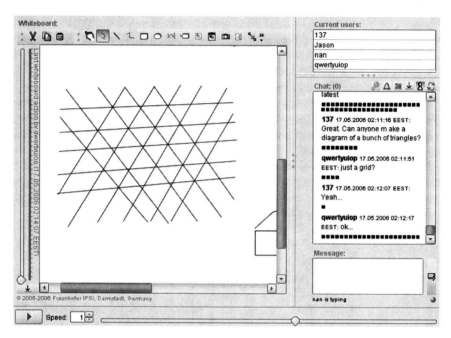

Fig. 7.5 The interface at the 12th stage of Fig. 7.4

ning) in a way that allowed him to produce a grid of triangles as a response to 137's request.

The key point we would like to highlight in this episode is that *the availability of the sequencing of the drawing actions that produces a diagram on the shared whiteboard can serve as a vital resource for collaborative sense-making*. As seen in Log 7-1, 137 did not provide any explanation in chat about his drawing actions or about the shape he was trying to draw. Yet, as we have observed in the similarity of Figs. 7.3 and 7.4, the orderliness of 137's actions has informed Qwertyuiop's subsequent performance. The methodical use of intersecting parallel lines to produce triangular objects is common to both drawing performances. Moreover, Qwertyuiop does not repeat the same set of drawing actions, but selectively uses 137's steps to produce the relevant object (i.e., a grid of triangles) on the whiteboard. Qwertyuiop does not initially constrain his representational development by constructing a hexagon first, but allows a hexagon (or other shapes made with triangles) to emerge from the collection of shapes implied by the intersecting lines. Thus, Qwertyuiop's performance shows us that he is able to *notice a particular organization* in 137's drawing actions, and he has *selectively appropriated and built upon* some key aspects of 137's drawing practice. As we will see in the following logs,[1]

---

[1] For instance, after Qwertyuiop declares the completion of the grid in line 11, 137 anchors Qwertyuiop's drawing to the background at 7:15:47 (see Log 7-3). Since such a move preserves the positions of the selected objects and the objects affected by the move includes only the lines recently

the group's subsequent use of this drawing will provide us additional evidence that Qwertyuiop's diagram serves as an adequate response to 137's request.

This excerpt highlights a fundamental difference between the two interaction spaces: whiteboard and chat contributions differ in terms of the availability of their production process. As far as chat messages are concerned, participants can only see who is currently typing,[2] but not what is being typed until the author decides to send the message. A similar situation applies to *atomic* whiteboard actions such as drawing an individual line or a rectangle. Such actions make a single object appear in the shared drawing area when the user releases the left mouse button; in the case of editable objects such as textboxes, the object appears on the screens of the computers of all chat participants when the editor clicks outside the textbox. However, the construction of most shared diagrams includes the production of multiple atomic shapes (e.g., many lines), and hence the sequencing of actions that produce these diagrams is available to other members. As we have observed in this excerpt, the availability of the drawing process can have interactionally significant consequences for math-problem-solving chats due to its instructionally informative nature. For instance, in Fig. 7.4 transitions from stages 1 to 2 and 7 to 8 show modifications performed to achieve a peculiar geometric organization on the shared workspace. In short, the whiteboard affords an *animated evolution* of the shared space, which makes the *visual reasoning process* manifest in drawing actions *publicly available* for other members' inspection.

Mutability of Chat and Whiteboard Contents

Another interactionally significant difference between the chat and the whiteboard interaction spaces, which is evidenced in the excerpt above, is the difference in terms of the mutability of their contents. Once a chat posting is contributed, it cannot be changed or edited. Moreover, the sequential position of a chat posting cannot be altered later on. If the content or the sequential placement of a chat posting turns out to be interactionally problematic, then a new posting needs to be composed to repair that. On the other hand, the object-oriented design of the whiteboard allows users to re-organize its content by adding new objects and by moving, annotating, deleting, reproducing existing ones. For instance, the way 137 and Qwertyuiop repaired their drawings in the excerpt above by re-positioning some of the lines they drew earlier to make sure that they intersect at certain points and/or that they are parallel to the edges of the hexagon illustrates this difference. Such demonstrable tweaks make the mathematical details of the construction work visible and relevant to observers, and

---

added by Qwertyuiop, 137's anchoring move seems to give a particular significance to Qwertyuiop's recent drawing. Hence, 137's anchoring move can be treated as an (implicit) endorsement of Qwertyuiop's drawing effort in response to his previous request.

[2] While a participant is typing, a social awareness message appears under the chat entry box on everyone else's screen stating that the person "is typing" (see Fig. 7.5). When the typist posts the message, the entire message appears suddenly as an atomic action in everyone's chat window.

hence serve as a vital resource for joint mathematical sense making. By seeing that Qwertyuiop successively and intentionally adjusts lines in his whiteboard drawing to appear more parallel or to intersect more precisely, the other group members take note of the significance of the arrangement of lines as parallel and intersecting in specific patterns.

While both chat and whiteboard in VMT support persistence, visibility and mutability, they do so in different ways. A chat posting scrolls away gradually, whereas a drawing may be rearranged or even erased by anyone at any time. Chat conventions allow one to replace (i.e., follow) a mistyped posting with a new one, much as conversational conventions allow spoken utterances to be retracted, repaired or refined. The mechanisms of the two mediational technologies are different and the characteristics of their persistence, visibility and mutability differ accordingly. Collaborative interaction in the dual-space environment is sensitively attuned to these intricate and subtle differences.

Monitoring Joint Attention

The excerpt in Log 7-2 immediately follows the one in Log 7-1, where the team is oriented to the construction of a triangular grid after a failed attempt to embed a grid of triangles inside a hexagon. As Qwertyuiop is adding more lines to the grid, the facilitator (Nan) posts two questions addressed to the whole team in line 5. The question not only queries about what is happening now and whether everybody knows what others are currently doing, but the placement of the question at this point in interaction also problematizes the relevance of what has been happening so far. 137's response in lines 6 and 8 treat the facilitator's question as a problematic intervention. Qwertyuiop's response indicates he is busy with making triangles and hence may not know what others are doing. Jason acknowledges that he is following what has been going on in line 9. These responses indicate that the team members

Log 7-2.

5	7:14:09	Nan	so what's up now? does everyone know what other people are doing?
	7:14:12	Qwertyuiop	*< Qwertyuiop adds a line to the grid of triangles>*
6	7:14:25	137	Yes?
7	7:14:25	Qwertyuiop	no-just making triangles
	7:14:32	Qwertyuiop	*< Qwertyuiop adds a line to the grid of triangles>*
8	7:14:33	137	I think … [*REF to line 6*]
9	7:14:34	Jason	Yeah
	7:14:36	Qwertyuiop	*< Qwertyuiop adds a line to the grid of triangles>*
10	7:14:46	Nan	good :-)
11	7:14:51	Qwertyuiop	Triangles are done
12	7:15:08	137	So do you want to first calculate the number of triangles in a hexagonal array?

have been following (perhaps better than the facilitator) what has been happening on the whiteboard so far as something relevant to their task at hand.

In this excerpt, the facilitator calls on each participant to report on his/her understanding of the activities of other participants. There was an extended duration in which no chat postings were published while whiteboard actions were being performed by Qwertyuiop. Because it is not possible for any participant to observe other participants directly, it is not possible to monitor a class of actions others may perform that (1) are important for how we understand ongoing action but (2) do not involve explicit manipulation of the VMT environment, actions like watching the screen, reading text, inspecting whiteboard constructs, etc. The only way to determine if those kinds of actions are occurring is to explicitly inquire about them using a chat posting.

Past and Future Relevancies Implied by Shared Drawings

Following Qwertyuiop's announcement in line 11 of Log 7-2 that the drawing work is complete, 137 proposes that the team calculate "**the number of triangles**" in a "**hexagonal array**" as a possible question to be pursued next. Although a hexagon was previously produced as part of the failed drawing, this is the first time someone explicitly mentions the term "**hexagonal array**" in this session. What makes 137's proposal potentially intelligible to others is the availability of referable resources such as whiteboard objects, and the immediate history of the production of those objects such that the proposal can be seen to be embedded in a sequence of displayed actions. 137's use of "**So**" to introduce his proposal presents it as a consequence of, or a making explicit of, what preceded. His suggestion of it as a "**first**" (next) move implies that the drawings opened up multiple mathematical tasks that the group could pursue, and that the proposed suggestion would be a candidate for a next move. In other words, the objects on the whiteboard and their visually shared production index a horizon of past and future activities. The indexical terms in 137's proposal (like "**hexagonal array**") not only rely on the availability of the whiteboard objects to propose a relevant activity to pursue next, but also modify their sense by using linguistic and semantic resources in the production to label or gloss the whiteboard object and its production. This allows actors to orient in particular ways to the whiteboard object and the procedures of its co-construction—providing a basis for coordinated joint activity. The joint activity acquires a temporal structure that is defined by the details of chat wording, the animation of graphical construction and the sequentiality of proposing.

Methods for Referencing Relevant Objects in the Shared Visual Field

Bringing relevant mathematical objects to other members' attention often requires a coordinated sequence of actions performed in both the chat and whiteboard interaction spaces. The episode following 137's proposal (Log 7-3) provides us with an appropriate setting to illustrate how participants achieve this in interaction. Following 137's proposal in line 12, both Qwertyuiop and Jason post queries for clarification in lines 13 and 16, respectively, which indicate that the available referential resources were insufficient for them to locate what 137 is referring to with the term **"hexagonal array."** Jason's query in the chat is particularly important here since it explicitly calls for a response to be performed on the shared diagram, i.e., in a particular field of relevance in the other interaction space. Following Jason's

Log 7-3.

11	7:14:51	Qwertyuiop	Triangles are done
12	7:15:08	137	So do you want to first calculate the number of triangles in a hexagonal array?
13	7:15:45	Qwertyuiop	What's the shape of the array? a hexagon? <REF to 12>
	7:15:47	137	<137 locks the triangular grid that Qwertyuiop has just drawn>
14	7:16:02	137	Ya <REF to line 13>
15	7:16:15	Qwertyuiop	ok....
	7:16:18 - 7:16:35	137	<137 performs a few drawing actions and then erases them>
16	7:16:41	Jason	wait- - can someone highlight the hexagonal array on the diagram? i don't really see what you mean...
	7:16:45 - 7:17:28	137	<137 adds new lines to the grid on the whiteboard which gradually forms a contour on top of the grid. Figure 7.6 shows some of the performed by 137>
17	7:17:30	Jason	Hmm.. okay
18	7:17:43	Qwertyuiop	Oops <REF to Whiteboard>
19	7:17:44	Jason	so it has at least 6 triangles?
20	7:17:58	Jason	in this, for instance <REF to Whiteboard>
	7:18:03 - 7:18:17	137	<137 completes the contour by adding more lines, which forms a hexagon>
21	7:18:53	137	How do you color lines?
22	7:19:06	Jason	There's a little paintbrush icon up at the top
23	7:19:12	Jason	it's the fifth one from the right
	7:19:13 - 7:19:20	137	<137 begins to change the color of the lines that form the contour to blue>
24	7:19:20	137	Thanks.
25	7:19:21	Jason	There ya go :-)
	7:19:25 - 7:19:48	137	<137 finishes the coloring. Now the contour is highlighted in blue>
26	7:19:48	137	Er... That hexagon.
27	7:20:02	Jason	so... should we try to find a formula i guess

query, 137 begins to perform a sequence of drawing actions on the shared diagram. He adds a few lines that gradually begin to enclose a region on the triangular grid[3] (see Fig. 7.6).

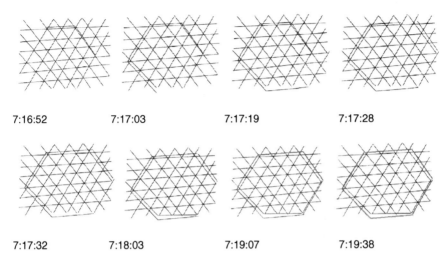

7:16:52   7:17:03   7:17:19   7:17:28

7:17:32   7:18:03   7:19:07   7:19:38

Fig. 7.6 Snapshots from the sequence of drawing actions performed by 137

When the shared diagram reaches the stage illustrated by the 4th frame in Fig. 7.6, Jason posts the message **"hmmm… okay"** in line 17, which can be read as an acknowledgement of 137's performance on the whiteboard as a response to his recent chat query. Since no chat message was posted after Jason's request in line 16, and the only shared actions were 137's work on the whiteboard, Jason's chat posting can be read as a response to the ongoing drawing activity on the whiteboard. As it is made evident in his posting, Jason is treating the evolving drawing on the shared diagram as a response to his earlier query for highlighting the hexagonal array on the whiteboard: the question/answer adjacency pair is spread across the two interaction spaces in an unproblematic way.

Following provisional acknowledgement of 137's drawing actions on the whiteboard, Jason posts a claim in line 19. This posting is built as a declarative: **"so it has at least 6 triangles,"** with a question mark appended to the end. The use of **"so"** in this posting invites readers to treat what follows in the posting as a consequence of the prior actions of 137. In this way, Jason is (a) proposing a defeasible extension of his understanding of the sense of 137's actions and (b) inviting others to endorse or correct this provisional claim about the hexagonal array by presenting this as a query using the question mark.

---

[3] In the meantime, Qwertyuiop also performs a few drawing actions near the shared drawing, but his actions do not introduce anything noticeably different since he quickly erases what he draws each time.

In line 20 Jason provides further specificity to what he is indexing with the term **"it"** in line 19 by highlighting a region on the grid with the referencing tool of the VMT system. The textual part of the posting makes it evident that the highlighted region is an instance of the object mentioned in line 19. Moreover, the 6 triangles highlighted by the explicit reference recognizably make up a hexagon shape altogether. Hence, Jason's explicit reference seems to be pointing to a particular stage (indexed by **"at least"**) of the hexagonal array to which the team is oriented (see Fig. 7.7).

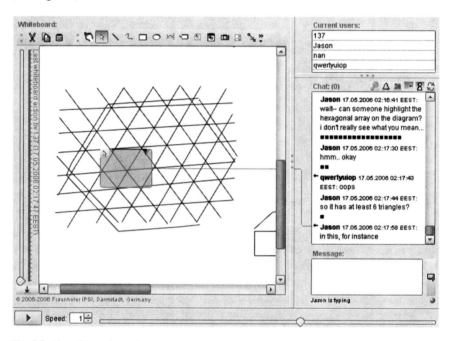

Fig. 7.7 Use of the referencing tool to point to a stage of the hexagonal array

In other words, having witnessed the production of the hexagonal shape on the whiteboard as a response to his earlier query, Jason displays his competence by demonstrating his recognition of the hexagonal pattern implicated in 137's graphical illustration. 137's drawing actions highlight a particular stage of a growing pattern made of triangles—stage N=3, as we will see in Fig. 7.9. However, recognizing the stick-pattern implicated in 137's highlighting actions requires other members to project how the displayed example can be grown and/or shrunk to produce other stages of the hexagonal array. Thus, Jason's description of the shape of the "hexagonal array" at a different stage—N=1—is a public display of his newly achieved comprehension of the significance of the math object in the whiteboard and the achievement of "indexical symmetry" among the parties involved with respect to this math object (see Chapter 14).

Although Jason explicitly endorsed 137's drawing as an adequate illustration, the small boxes in the chat stream that appear after Jason's acknowledgement in line 17 show that 137 is still oriented to and operating on the whiteboard. In line 21, 137 solicits other members' help regarding how he can change the color of an object on the board, which opens a side sequence about a specific feature of the whiteboard system. Based on the description he got, 137 finishes marking the hexagon by coloring all its edges with blue, and he posts **"that hexagon"** in line 25. This can be read as a chat reference to the whiteboard shape enclosed by the blue contour, and as a response to other members' earlier requests for clarification.

In this excerpt, we have observed two referential methods enacted by participants to bring relevant graphical objects on the whiteboard to other group members' attention. In the first case, 137 *marked the drawing* with a different color to identify the contour of a hexagonal shape. As evidenced in other members' responses, this was designed to make the hexagonal array embedded in a grid of triangles visible to others. Jason demonstrated another method by using the explicit referencing tool to support his *textual description* of the first stage of the pattern. Both mechanisms play a key role in directing other members' attention to features of the shared *visual field* in particular ways. This kind of deictic usage isolates components of the shared drawing and constitutes them as relevant objects to be attended to for the purposes at hand. As we shall see, these guided shifts in visual focus of the group have strategic importance for the group's mathematical work. Hence, such referential work establishes a fundamental *relationship between the narrative and mathematical terminology used in text chat and the animated graphical constructions produced on the whiteboard*. The shared sense of the textual terms and the inscriptions co-evolve through the referential linkages established as the interaction sequentially unfolds in both interaction spaces.

In Log 7-3, the group tentatively proposes a major mathematical insight—that a hexagon can be viewed as six symmetric triangular areas. It is a visual achievement. It emerges from a visual inspection by Jason of 137's graphical diagram, based on Qwertyuiop's method of visually representing hexagons as patterns of triangularly intersecting lines. By literally focusing his eyes on a smallest hexagon in the larger array and counting the number of triangles visible within a hexagonal border, Jason discovers that there are at least six triangles at the initial stage of a hexagon with one unit on each side. We will see how the group visualizes the generalization of this picture to other stages. However, it is already interesting to note that Jason not only observes the composition of a small hexagon out of six triangles, but he conveys this to the rest of the group in both media. He posts chat line 19 and then references from chat line 20 to a visually highlighted view in the whiteboard, so that his *visual* understanding can be shared by the group as well as his *narrative* description in his claim. The next step for the group will be to formulate a *symbolic* mathematical expression of this claim.

Whiteboard Visualizations, Chat Narratives and Wiki Symbolisms

The excerpt in Log 7-4 immediately follows Log 7-3. The way 137 uses both interaction spaces in this episode highlights another important aspect of collaborative

Log 7-4.

27	7:20:02	Jason	so… should we try to find a formula i guess
28	7:20:22	Jason	input: side length; output: # triangles
29	7:20:39	Qwertyuiop	It might be easier to see it as the 6 smaller triangles.
30	7:20:48	137	Like this? <REF to line 29>
	7:20:53	137	<137 draws a red line>
	7:20:57	137	<137 draws a red line>
	7:21:00	137	<137 draws a red line>
31	7:21:02	Qwertyuiop	Yes
32	7:21:03	Jason	Yup
	7:21:03	137	<137 moves the second red line>
	7:21:05	137	<137 moves the second red line again. It is positioned on the grid
33	7:21:29	Qwertyuiop	Side length is the same…
34	7:22:06	Jason	Yeah

problem-solving work in an environment like VMT. Since participants can contribute to only one of the interaction spaces at a time, they cannot narrate their whiteboard actions simultaneously with chat postings, as can be done with talking about a whiteboard in a face-to-face setting. However, as we will observe in 137's use of the whiteboard in Log 7-4, participants can achieve a similar interactional organization by coordinating their actions in such a way that whiteboard actions can be seen as part of an exposition performed in chat.

Jason brings the prior activity of locating the hexagonal array on the shared drawing to a close with his so-prefaced posting in line 27, where he invokes the task of finding a formula that was mentioned by 137 earlier. Jason provides further specificity to the formula he is referring to in the next line (i.e., given the side length as input the formula should return the number of triangles as output). In line 29 Qwertyuiop takes up Jason's proposal by suggesting the team consider the hexagonal array as six smaller triangles to potentially simplify the task at hand. In the next line, 137 posts a question phrased as **"like this?"** which is addressed to Qwertyuiop's prior posting, as indicated by the use of the referential arrow. Next, we observe the appearance of three red lines on the shared diagram, which are all added by 137. Here, 137 demonstrates a particular way of splitting the hexagon into six parts: the image on the left of Fig. 7.8 corresponds to the sequence of three whiteboard actions represented as three boxes in the chat excerpt. After 137 adds the third line whose intersection with the previously drawn red lines recognizably produces six triangular regions on the shared representation, Qwertyuiop and Jason both endorse 137's demonstration of a particular way of splitting up the hexagonal shape.

One important aspect of this organization is directing other members' attention to the projected whiteboard activity as a relevant step in the sequentially unfolding exposition in chat. For instance, the deictic term **"this"** in 137's chat line 30 refers to something yet to be produced, and thereby projects that there is more to follow the current posting, possibly in the other interaction space. Moreover, the use of the referential link and the term **"like"** together inform others that what is about

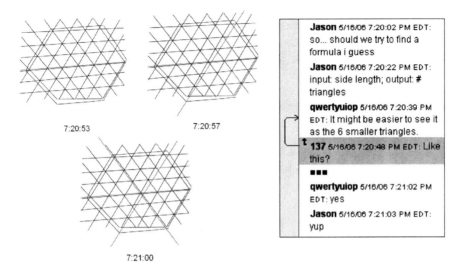

Fig. 7.8 137 splits the hexagon into 6 parts

to be done should be read in relation to the message to which 137 is responding. Finally 137's use of a different color marks the newly added lines as recognizably distinct from what is already there as the background, and hence noticeable as a demonstration of what is implicated in recent chat postings.

Again, the progress in understanding the mathematics of the problem is propelled through visual means. In response to Jason's proposal of finding a formula, Qwertyuiop suggests that **"it might be easier to see it"** in a certain way. Jason's proposed approach might be difficult to pursue because no one has suggested a concrete approach to constructing a formula that would meet the general criteria of producing an output result for any input variable value. By contrast, the group has been working successfully in the visual medium of the whiteboard drawing and has been literally able to "see" important characteristics of the math object that they have co-constructed out of intersecting lines. Jason has pointed out that at least six triangles are involved (in the smallest hexagon). So, Qwertyuiop proposes building on this in-sight. 137 asks if the way to see the general case in terms of the six small triangles as proposed by Qwertyuiop can be visualized by intersecting the hexagon array with 3 intersecting lines to distinguish the six regions of the array. He does this through a visual construction, simply referenced from the chat with his **"Like this?"** post.

By staring at the final version of the array (the 3rd stage in Fig. 7.8), all members of the group can see the hexagon divided into six equal parts at each stage of the hexagonal pattern. Near the intersection of the red lines, they can see a single small triangle nestled in each of the six regions. As will be evidenced in Log 7-5, within the larger hexagon delimited by the blue lines, they can see a set of $1+3+5=9$ small triangles in each of the six larger triangular regions. Similarly, midway between stage $N=1$ and stage $N=3$, one can visually observe $1+3=4$ small triangles in each

Log 7-5.

34	7:22:13	Jason	so it'll just be x6 for # triangles in the hexagon
35	7:22:19	137	Each one has 1+3+5 triangles.
36	7:22:23	Jason	but then we're assuming just regular hexagons
37	7:22:29	Qwertyuiop	the "each polygon corrisponds to 2 sides" thing we did last time doesn't work for triangles
38	7:23:17	137	It equals 1+3+...+(n+n-1) because of the "rows"?
39	7:24:00	Qwertyuiop	yes- 1st row is 1, 2nd row is 3...
40	7:24:49	137	And there are n terms so... n(2n/2)
41	7:25:07	137	or n^2 <REF to line 40>
42	7:25:17	Jason	Yeah
43	7:25:21	Jason	then multiply by 6
44	7:25:31	137	To get 6n^2 <REF to line 43>

region. The new view, scaffolded by 137's red lines, entails *visual reasoning* that leads to mathematical deductions. As soon as Qwertyuiop and Jason see 137's construction, they both concur with it as the easier way to see the mathematical pattern of triangles in the hexagonal array. The visual reasoning supported by whiteboard and narrated textually in the chat will lead in the next episode to symbolic reasoning for posting in the wiki.

A first glance at the chat logs might suggest that the group is narrating their problem-solving process in the chat and illustrating what they mean by "napkin" drawings in the whiteboard, to use Dillenbourg and Traum's (2006) metaphor. However, a second look reveals that the most significant insight and sharing is occurring in the whiteboard, more along the lines of a visual "model" metaphor. Perhaps the best way to describe what is going on is to say that the group is very carefully coordinating their work in the dual space as a whole to achieve a shared progression of understanding of the pattern problem. This is accomplished with an efficiency and effectiveness that could not be achieved in either a purely textual chat system or a purely graphical whiteboard. Although in this view the chat and whiteboard both function as symmetric parts of a coordinated whole—in which chat references drawing, and drawing illustrates chat—it is important to differentiate their roles as well.

Using Representations of Specific Instances as a Resource for Generalization

Immediately following the previous excerpt the team moves on to figuring out a general formula to compute the number of triangles in a hexagonal pattern. In line 34 of Log 7-5, Jason relates the particular partitioning of the hexagon illustrated on the whiteboard to the problem at hand by stating that the number ("#") of triangles in the hexagon will equal 6 times ("x6") the number of triangles enclosed in each partition. In the next posting, 137 seems to be indexing one of the six partitions with the phrase "each one." Hence, this posting can be read as a proposal about the number of triangles included in a partition. The sequence of numbers in the expression "**1+3+5**" calls others to look at a partition in a particular way. While 137 could have simply said here that there are 9 triangles in each partition, he instead organizes the numbers in summation form and offers more than an aggregated result. His expression also demonstrates a systematic method for counting the triangles. In other words, his construction is designed to highlight a particular orderliness in the organization of triangles that form a partition. Moreover, the sequence includes increasing consecutive odd numbers, which implicitly informs a certain progression for the growth of the shape under consideration.

About a minute after his most recent posting, 137 offers an extended version of his sequence as a query in line 38. The relationship between the sequence for the special case and this one is made explicit through the repetition of the first two terms. In the new version the "…" notation is used to substitute a series of numbers following the second term up to a generic value represented by "**n+n-1,**" which can be recognized as a standard expression for the nth odd number. Hence, this representation is designed to stand for something more general than the one derived from the specific instance illustrated on the whiteboard. 137 attributes this generalization to the concept of "**rows,**" and solicits other members' assessment regarding the validity of his version (by ending with a question mark). 137's use of the term "**rows,**" seems to serve as a pedagogic device that attempts to locate the numbers in the sequence on the nth stage of the hexagonal pattern (see Fig. 7.9 for an analyst's illustration of the generalized hexagonal pattern). For stages 1, 2 and 3, the hexagonal shape has $6*(1) = 6$, $6*(1+3) = 24$, $6*(1+3+5) = 54$ triangles, respectively.

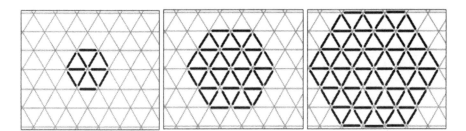

Fig. 7.9 A reconstruction of the first three iterations of the geometric pattern

Qwertyuiop's endorsement of 137's proposal comes in line 39. He also demonstrates a row-by-row iteration on a hexagon, where each number in the sequence corresponds to a row of triangles in a partition. In other words, Qwertyuiop elaborates on 137's statement in line 38 of the chat by displaying his understanding of the relationship between the rows and the sequence of odd numbers. Although he does not explicitly reference it here, Qwertyuiop may be viewing the figure in the whiteboard to see the successive rows. The figure is, of course, also available to 137 and Jason to help them follow Qwertyuiop's chat posting and check it.

Then 137 proposes an expression for the sum of the first **n** odd numbers in line 40.[4] Jason agrees with the proposed expression and suggests that it should be multiplied by **6** next. In the following line, 137 grammatically completes Jason's posting with the resulting expression. In short, by virtue of the agreements and the co-construction work of Jason and 137, the team demonstrates its endorsement of the conclusion that the number of triangles would equal **$6n^2$** for a hexagonal array made of triangles. As the group collaboratively discovered, when **n** equals the stage number (as "input" to the formula), the number of triangles is given by the expression **$6n^2$**.

The way team members orient themselves to the shared drawing in this episode illustrates that the drawings on the whiteboard have a figurative role in addition to their concrete appearance as illustrations of specific cases. The particular cases captured by concrete, tangible marks on the whiteboard are often used as a resource to investigate and talk about general properties of the mathematical objects indexed by them.

Another important aspect of the team's achievement of a general expression in this episode is the way they transformed a particular way of *counting* the triangles in one of the partitions (i.e., a geometric observation) into an algebraic mode of investigation. This shift from a visual method led the team members to recognize that a particular sequence of numbers can be associated with the way the partition grows in subsequent iterations. The shift to this symbolic mode of engagement, which heavily uses the shared drawing as a resource, allowed the team to go further in the task of generalizing the pattern of growth by invoking algebraic resources. In other words, *the team made use of multiple realizations (graphical and linguistic) of the math object (the hexagonal array) distributed across the dual interaction space to co-construct a general formula* for the task at hand.

Chat Versus Whiteboard Contributions as Persistent Referential Resources

In all of the excerpts we have considered so far, the shared drawing has been used as a resource within a sequence of related but recognizably distinct activities. For instance, the group has oriented itself to the following activities: (1) drawing a grid of triangles, (2) formulating a problem that relates a hexagonal array to a grid of triangles, (3) highlighting a particular hexagon on the grid, (4) illustrating a particular way to split the shape into six smaller pieces, and (5) devising a systematic method to count the number of triangles within one of the six pieces. As the group oriented to different aspects of their joint task, the shared diagram was modified on the

---

[4] 137 makes use of Gauss's method for summing this kind of series, adding the first and last term and multiplying by half of the number of terms: $(1 + n + n - 1)*n/2 = 2n*n/2 = n^2$. This method was used by the group and shared in previous sessions involving the stair pattern that is still visible in the whiteboard.

whiteboard and annotated in chat accordingly. Yet, although it had been modified and annotated along the way, the availability of this shared drawing on the screen and the way participants organize their discussion around it highlights its persistent characteristic as an ongoing referential resource. In contrast, none of the chat postings in prior excerpts were attributed a similar referential status by the participants. As we have seen, in each episode the postings responded or referred either to recently posted chat messages or to the visual objects in the shared space.

The textual chat postings and the graphical objects produced on the whiteboard differ in terms of the way they are used as referential resources by the participants. The content of the whiteboard is persistently available for reference and manipulation, whereas the chat content is visually available for reference for a relatively shorter period. This is due to the linear growth of chat content, which replaces previous messages with the most recent contributions inserted at the bottom of the chat window. Although one can make explicit references to older postings by using the scroll-bar feature, the limited size of the chat window affords a referential locality between postings that are visually (and hence temporally) close to each other.

By contrast, objects drawn in the whiteboard tend to remain there for a long time. They are often only erased or moved out of view when space is needed for drawings related to a new topic. While they may be modified, elaborated or moved around, whiteboard objects may remain visible for an entire hour-long session or even across sessions. Like the chat, the whiteboard has a history scrollbar, so that any past state of the drawing can be made visible again—although in practice students rarely use this feature. Although both media technically offer a persistent record of their contents, the visual locality of the whiteboard—the fact that graphical objects tend to stay available for reference from the more fleeting chat—qualifies it as the more persistent medium as an interactional resource. This notion of persistence does not imply that the shared sense of whiteboard objects is fixed once they are registered to the shared visual field. As they continue to serve as referential resources during the course of the problem-solving effort, the sense of whiteboard objects may become increasingly evident and shared, or their role may be modified as participants make use of them for varying purposes.

Implications for CSCL Chat Interaction Analysis

In this case study we investigated how a group of three upper-middle-school students put the features of an online environment with dual-interaction spaces into use as they collaboratively worked on a math problem they themselves came up with. Our analysis has revealed important insights regarding the affordances of systems with dual-interaction spaces. First, we observed that the whiteboard can make visible to everyone the animated evolution of a geometric construction, displaying the *visual reasoning* process manifested in drawing actions. Second, whiteboard and chat contents differ in terms of *mutability* of their contents, due to the object-oriented design of the whiteboard, which allows modification and annotation of past contributions.

Third, the media differ in terms of the *persistence* of their contents: whiteboard objects remain in the shared visual field until they are removed, whereas chat content gradually scrolls off as new postings are produced. Although contents of both spaces are persistently available for reference, due to linear progression of the chat window, chat postings are likely to refer to visually (and hence temporally) close chat messages and to graphical whiteboard objects. Finally, the whiteboard objects *index* a horizon of past and future activities as they serve as an interactional resource through the course of recognizably distinct but related episodes of chat discussion.

Our analysis of this team's joint work has also revealed methods for the organization of collaborative work, through which group members co-construct mathematical meaning sedimented in semiotic objects distributed across the dual interaction spaces of the VMT environment. We observed that bringing relevant math artifacts referenced by indexical terms such as **"hexagonal array"** to other members' attention often requires a coordinated sequence of actions across the two interaction spaces. Participants use explicit and verbal references to guide each other about how a new contribution should be read in relation to prior contents. Indexical terms stated in chat referring to the visible production of shared objects are instrumental in the reification of those terms as meaningful mathematical objects for the participants. Verbal references to co-constructed objects are often used as a resource to index complicated and abstract mathematical concepts in the process of co-constructing new ones. Finally, different representational affordances of the dual interaction spaces allow groups to develop multiple realizations of the math artifacts to which they are oriented. Shared graphical inscriptions and chat postings are used together as semiotic resources in mutually elaborating ways. Methods of coordinating group interaction across the media spaces also interrelate the mathematical significances of the multiple realizations.

Overall, we observed that actions performed in both interaction spaces constitute an evolving historical context for the joint work of the group. What gets done now informs the relevant actions to be performed next, and the significance of what was done previously can be modified depending on the circumstances of the ongoing activity. As the interaction unfolds sequentially, the sense of previously posted whiteboard objects and chat statements may become evident and/or refined. In this way, the group's joint problem space is maintained.

Through the sequential coordination of chat postings and whiteboard inscriptions, the group successfully solved their mathematical challenge, to find a formula for the number of small triangles in a hexagonal array of any given side-length. Their interaction was guided by a sequence of proposals and responses carried out textually in the chat medium. However, the sense of the terms and relationships narrated in the chat were largely instantiated, shared and investigated through observation of visible features of graphical inscriptions in the whiteboard medium. The mathematical object that was visually co-constructed in the whiteboard was named and described in words within the chat. Finally, a symbolic expression was developed by the group, grounded in the graphic that evolved in the whiteboard and discussed in the terminology that emerged in the chat. The symbolic mathematical result was then posted to the wiki, a third medium within the VMT environment. The wiki is intended for sharing group findings with other groups as part of a permanent archive of work by virtual math teams.

Our case study in this chapter demonstrates that it is possible to analyze how math problem solving—and presumably other cognitive achievements—can be carried out by small groups of students. The students can define and refine their own problems to pursue; they can invent their own methods of working; they can use unrestricted vocabulary; they can coordinate work in multiple media, taking advantage of different affordances. Careful attention to the sequentiality of references and responses is necessary to reveal *how* the group coordinated its work and how that work was driven by the reactions of the group members' actions to each other. Only by focusing on the sequentiality of the actions can one see how the visual, narrative and symbolic build on each other as well as how the actions of the individual students respond to each other. Through these actions, the students co-construct math objects, personal understanding, group agreement and mathematical results that cannot be attributed to any one individual, but that emerge from the interaction as complexly sequenced.

This analysis illustrates a promising approach for CSCL research to investigate aspects of group cognition that are beyond the reach of alternative methods that systematically ignore the full sequentiality of their data.

The Group as the Unit of Analysis

For methodological reasons, quantitative approaches—such as those reviewed in the next section—generally (a) constrain (scaffold) subject behaviors, (b) filter (code) the data in terms of operationalized variables and (c) aggregate (count) the coded data. These acts of standardization and reduction of the data eliminate the possibility of observing the details and enacted processes of unique, situated, indexical, sequential, group interaction (Stahl, 2006b, chap. 10). An alternative form of interaction analysis is needed to explore the organization of interaction that can take place in CSCL settings.

In this chapter, we focused on small-group interactions mediated by a multimodal interaction space. Our study differs from similar work in CSCL by our focus on groups larger than dyads whose members are situated outside a controlled lab environment, and by our use of open-ended math tasks where students are encouraged to come up with their own problems. Moreover, we do not impose any deliberate restrictions on the ways students access the features of our online environment or on what they can say. Our main goal is to investigate how small groups of students construe and make use of the "available features" of the VMT online environment to discuss mathematics with peers from different schools outside their classroom setting. In other words, we are interested in studying interactional achievements of small groups in complex computer mediations "in the wild" (Hutchins, 1996).

Our interest in studying the use of an online environment with multiple interaction spaces in a more naturalistic use scenario raises serious methodological challenges. In an early VMT study where we conducted a content analysis of collaborative problem-solving activities mediated by a standard text-chat tool in a similar scenario of use, we observed that groups larger than dyads exhibit complex interactional patterns that are difficult to categorize based on a theory-informed coding scheme with a fixed/predetermined unit of analysis (Chapter 20). In particular, we observed numerous cases where participants post their messages in multiple chat turns, deal with contributions seemingly out of sequence and sustain conversations across multiple threads that made it problematic to segment the data into fixed analytic units for categorization. Moreover, coming to agreement on a code assignment for a unit that is defined *a priori* (e.g., a chat line) turned out to be heavily dependent upon how the unit can be read in relation to resources available to participants (e.g., the problem description) and to prior units (Chapter 22). In other words, the sense of a unit not only depends on the semantic import of its constituent elements, but also on the occasion in which it is situated (Heritage, 1984). This often makes it possible to apply multiple categories to a given unit and threatens the comparability of cases that are labeled with the same category. More importantly, once the data is reduced to codes and the assignments are aggregated, the complex sequential relationships among the units are largely lost. Hence, the coding approach's attempt to enforce a category to each fixed unit without any consideration to how users sequentially organize their actions in the environment proved to be too restrictive to adequately capture the interactional complexity of chat (Chapter 23). Moreover, the inclusion of a shared drawing area in our online environment made the use of a standard coding schema even harder due to increased possibilities for interaction. The open-ended nature of the tasks we use in our study makes it especially challenging to model certain types of actions and to compare them against ideal solutions.

The issue of unit of analysis has theoretical implications. In text chat it is tempting to take a single posting as the unit to be analyzed and coded, because a participant defined this as a unit by posting it as a message and because the chat software displays it as a visual unit. However, this tends to lead the analyst to treat the posting as a message from the posting individual—i.e., as an expression of a thought in the poster's mind, which must then be interpreted in the minds of the post readers. Conversation analysis has argued for the importance of *interactions* among participants as forming more meaningful units for analysis. These consist of sequences of multiple utterances by different speakers; the individual utterances take each other into account. For instance, in a question/answer "adjacency pair," the question elicits an answer and the answer responds to the question. To take a pair of postings such as a question/answer pair as the analytic unit is to treat the interaction within the group as primary. It focuses the analysis at the level of the group rather than the individual. As mentioned, in online text chat, responses are often separated from their referents, so the analysis is more complicated. In general, we find that the important thing is to trace as many references as possible between chat postings or whiteboard actions in order to analyze the interaction of the group as it unfolds (Chapter 26). As seen in our case study, it is through the co-construction of a rich nexus of such references that the group weaves its joint problem space.

Analysis at the group unit of analysis focuses on the co-construction, maintenance and progressive refinement of the joint problem space. This is a distinctive analytic task that takes as its data only what is shared by the group. Whatever may go on in the physical, mental or cultural backgrounds of the individual participants is irrelevant unless it is brought into the group discourse. Because the students know nothing about the gender, age, ethnicity, accent, appearance, location, personality, opinions, grades or skills of the other participants other than what is mentioned or displayed in the chat interaction, these "factors" from the individual and societal levels can be bracketed out of the group analysis. Survey and interview data is unnecessary; individual learning trajectories are not plotted. The VMT Project has been designed to make available to the analyst precisely what was shared by the student group, and nothing else.

Relatedly, the notion of common ground (see section on grounding below) as an abstract placeholder for registered cumulative facts or pre-established meanings has been critiqued in the CSCL literature for treating meaning as a fixed/denotative entity transcendental to the meaning-making activities of inquirers (Koschmann, 2002). The common ground that supports mutual understanding in group cognition or group problem solving is a matter of semantic references that unfold sequentially in the momentary situation of dialog, not a matter of comparing mental contents (Stahl, 2006b, pp. 353–356). Committing to a reference-repair model (Clark & Marshall, 1981) for meaning making falls short of taking into account the dynamic, constitutive nature of meaning-making interactions that foster the process of inquiry (Koschmann, LeBaron, Goodwin, & Feltovich, 2001).

As we saw in the preceding case study, the understanding of the mathematical structure of the hexagon area did not occur as a mental model of one of the students that was subsequently externalized in the chat and whiteboard and communicated to the other students. It emerged in the discourse media in a way that we could witness as analysts. It consisted of the layering of inscriptions (textual and graphical) that referenced one another. The referential network of group meaning can be observed in the way that deictic and indexical expressions are resolved. The three students each contribute to the progressive development of the shared meaning by responding appropriately to the on-going state of the discourse. This is a matter of linguistic skill—including ability in discussing mathematical matters—not of articulating mental representations. It is surprising from a rationalist perspective how poor students are at explaining (Chapter 26), reproducing (Koschmann & LeBaron, 2003) or even recalling (Chapter 6) what they did in the group when they are no longer situated in the moment.

Given these analytical and theoretical issues, we opted for an alternative to the approaches reviewed below that involve modeling of actions and correct solution paths or treating shared understanding as alignment of pre-existing individual representations and opinions. In this chapter we built on our previous work on referencing math objects in a system with chat and a whiteboard (Chapter 17); we presented a "micro-ethnographic" (Streeck & Mehus, 2005) case study using interaction analysis (Jordan & Henderson, 1995). We focused on the *sequence of actions* in which the group co-constructs and makes use of *semiotic resources* (Goodwin, 2000a) distributed across dual interaction spaces to *do* collaborative problem-solving work. In particular, we focused on the joint organization of activities that produce graphical drawings on the shared whiteboard and the ways those drawings are used as resources by actors as they collaboratively work on an open-ended math task. Through detailed analysis at the group unit of analysis, we investigated how actions performed in one workspace inform the actions performed in the other and how the group coordinates its actions across both interaction spaces.

Other Approaches in CSCL to Analyzing Multimodal Interaction

In this section we review previous investigations by other CSCL researchers. Their studies focus on the interactions mediated by systems with multimodal interaction spaces to support collaborative work online. Our review is not meant to be exhaustive, but representative of the more advanced analytical approaches employed. We have selected sophisticated analyses, which go well beyond the standard coding-and-counting genre of CSCL quantitative reports, in which utterances are sorted according to a fixed coding scheme and then statistics are derived from the count of utterances in each category. Unlike the simple coding-and-counting studies, the approaches we review attempt to analyze some of the structure of the semantic and temporal relationships among chat utterances and workspace inscriptions in an effort to get at the fabric of common ground in dual-interaction online environments.

Multimodal interaction spaces—which typically bring together two or more synchronous online communication technologies such as text chat and a shared graphical workspace—have been widely used to support collaborative learning activities of small groups (Dillenbourg & Traum, 2006; Jermann, 2002; Mühlpfordt & Wessner, 2005; Soller & Lesgold, 2003; Suthers et al., 2001). The way such systems are designed as a juxtaposition of several technologically independent online communication tools carries important interactional consequences for the users. Engaging in forms of joint activity in such online environments requires group members to use the technological features available to them in methodical ways to make their actions across multiple spaces intelligible to each other and to sustain their joint problem-solving work.

The communicative processes mediated by multimodal interaction spaces have attracted increasing analytical interest in the CSCL community. A workshop held at CSCL 2005 specifically highlighted the need for more systematic ways to investigate the unique affordances of such online environments (Dillenbourg, 2005). Previous CSCL studies that focus on the interactions mediated by systems with two or more interaction spaces can be broadly categorized under: (1) prescriptive approaches based on models of interaction and (2) descriptive approaches based on content analysis of user actions.

(1) The *prescriptive modeling approach* builds on a content-coding approach by devising models of categorized user actions performed across multimodal interaction spaces, for example:

   (a) Soller and Lesgold's (2003) use of hidden Markov models (HMM) and

(b) Avouris, Dimitracopouiou, and Komis (2003) object-oriented collaboration analysis framework (OCAF).

In these studies, the online environment is tailored to a specific problem-solving situation so that researchers can partially automate the coding process by narrowing the possibilities for user actions to a well-defined set of categories. The specificity of the problem-solving situation also allows researchers to produce models of idealized solution cases. Such ideal cases are then used as a baseline to make automated assessments of group work and learning outcomes.

(2) The *descriptive approach* informed by content analysis also involves categorization of user actions mediated by multimodal interaction spaces, applying a theoretically informed coding scheme. Categorized interaction logs are then subjected to statistical analysis to investigate various aspects of collaborative work such as:

(c) The correlation between planning moves performed in chat and the success of subsequent manipulations performed in a shared workspace (Jermann, 2002),

(d) The relationship between grounding and problem-solving processes across multiple interaction spaces (Dillenbourg & Traum, 2006),

(e) A similar approach based on cultural-historical activity theory (Baker et al., 1999), and

(f) The referential uses of graphical representations in a shared workspace in the absence of explicit gestural deixis (Suthers, Girardeau, & Hundhausen, 2003).

We will now review each of these studies:

(a) Soller and Lesgold's modeling approach involves the use of Hidden Markov Models (HMM) to automatically detect episodes of effective knowledge sharing (Soller & Lesgold, 2003) and knowledge breakdowns (Soller, 2004). The authors consider a programming task where triads are asked to use object-oriented modeling tools to represent relationships among well-defined entities. The task follows a jigsaw design where each group member receives training about a different aspect of the shared task before meeting with other members. The group sessions are hosted in the Epsilon online environment, which includes a text-chat area and a shared workspace. The workspace provides basic shapes that allow users to diagrammatically represent entities and relationships. Participants are required to select a sentence opener to categorize their contributions before posting them in the chat window. The authors manually extract segments from their corpus where each member gets the opportunity to share the unique knowledge element he/she was trained in with other group members. Some of these episodes are qualitatively identified as ideal cases that exemplify either an instance of effective knowledge sharing or a knowledge breakdown, completely based on the results of post-tests. For instance, a segment is considered an effective knowledge-sharing episode provided a chance for demonstrating the unique knowledge element comes during the

session, the presenter correctly answers the corresponding questions in both pre-
and post-tests, and the explanation leads at least one other member to correctly
answer the corresponding question(s) in the post-test. The sequence of categorized
actions (including chat postings and workspace actions) that correspond to these
ideal cases is used to train two separate HMMs for the breakdown and effective
knowledge sharing cases, respectively. An HMM computes the probability of a certain kind of action immediately following another; it thus captures certain aspects
of sequentiality. These models are then used to automatically classify the remaining
episodes and to assess team performance. However, the method is seriously limited
to recognizing connections among actions to those based on immediate sequences
of codes. While this can capture adjacency pairs that are important to conversation,
it misses more distant responses, interrupted adjacency pairs, temporal markings
and semantic indexes. The authors apparently make no specific distinction between
workspace and chat actions as they build their HMMs over a sequence of interface actions. Moreover, the relationship between object diagrams constructed in the
workspace and the explanations given in chat do not seem to be considered as part
of the analysis. Hence, it is not clear from the study how a successful knowledge-
sharing episode is achieved in interaction and whether the way participants put the
affordances of both interaction spaces into use as they explain the materials to each
other have had any specific influence on that outcome. Although they were reported
to be successful in classifying manually segmented episodes, HMMs computed over
a sequence of categorized actions seem to obscure these interactional aspects of the
coordination of chat and workspace.

(b) The modeling approach outlined in Avouris et al. (2003) and Komis, Avouris,
and Fidas (2002) proposes a methodology called the object-oriented collaboration
analysis framework (OCAF) that focuses on capturing the patterns in the sequence
of categorized actions through which dyads co-produced objects in a shared task
space. The collaborative tasks the authors used in their online study included the
construction of database diagrams with well-defined ontological elements such as
entities, relationships and attributes. In this problem-solving context the final representation co-constructed in the shared workspace counted as the group's final
solution. The OCAF model aims to capture the historical evolution of the group's
solution by keeping track of who contributed and/or modified its constituent elements during the course of an entire chat session. The authors not only consider
direct manipulation acts on specific elements but also chat statements through which
actors propose additions/modifications to the shared diagram or agree/disagree with
a prior action. The chat and drawing actions are categorized in terms of their functional roles (e.g., agree, propose, insert, modify, etc.). The mathematical model
includes the sequence of categorized actions and the associations among them. The
model is then used to gather structural properties of interactions (e.g., how contributions are distributed among dyads, what functional role each contribution plays) and
to trace how each action performed in the interface is related to other actions. This
modeling approach differs from similar approaches in terms of its specific focus on
the objects co-constructed in the shared workspace. The model captures the sequential development of the shared object by keeping track of the temporal order of

contributions made by each user. However, it is not clear from the study how the model could deal with the flexibility of referential work. For instance a chat posting may refer to multiple prior postings or to a sub-component of a more complicated entity-relationship diagram by treating several elemental objects as a single object. In other words, a model trying to capture all possible associations between individual actions in a bottom-up fashion may miss the flexibility of referential work and obscure the interactional organization.

(c) Jermann (2002) employs a coding scheme to study the correlation between planning moves in the chat area and the success of subsequent manipulations performed on the shared simulation in the Traffic Simulator environment. The shared task involved students tuning red-green periods of four traffic lights in the simulation to figure out an optimal configuration to minimize the waiting time of cars at intersections. The workspace could be manipulated in specific ways by users. The workspace also includes a dynamic graph that shows the mean waiting time for the cars. The goal of the task is to keep the mean value below a certain level for two minutes. The study included additional experimental cases where dynamically updated bar charts are displayed to provide feedback to users about their level of participation. The logs of recorded sessions are coded in terms of their planning and regulatory content. The nature of the task allowed authors to numerically characterize different types of work organizations in terms of the distribution of manipulations performed on four possible traffic lights. The authors complement this characterization with number of messages posted, number of manipulations done and the types of messages as captured in the coding scheme. The study reported that dyads who coordinated their actions across both interaction spaces by planning what to do next (i.e., task regulation) and discussing who should do what (i.e., interaction regulation) in chat before manipulating the simulation performed better (i.e., achieved the objective more quickly). The interaction meters were not reported to have significant effects on promoting task and interaction regulation. The work of high performance groups are characterized with phrases like "posted more messages," "more frequent postings," "talked relatively more than they executed problem solving actions," "monitor results longer," "produced elaborated plans more frequently" in reference to the tallied codes, frequency of messages and duration of activity. Although the main argument of the chapter highlights the authors' interest in sequential unfolding of regulatory moves, the way the employed quantitative approach isolates and aggregates the actions obscures the temporal connections and sequential mechanisms constituting different forms of regulation moves.

(d) Dillenbourg and Traum (2006) employ a similar methodology to study the relationship between grounding and problem solving in an online environment including a shared whiteboard and a text-chat area. In this study the participants were grouped into dyads and asked to collaboratively work on a murder-mystery task. The authors framed their analysis along the lines of Clark and Brennan's (1991) theory of grounding (at least applied at the micro level of individual utterances) and theories of socio-cognitive conflict. The study reports two kinds of uses of the dual spaces to facilitate grounding during problem solving: a "napkin" model and a "mockup" model. The authors hypothesized that the whiteboard would be mainly used to disambiguate dialogues in the chat window via basic illustrations (i.e., the napkin model). However, the authors report that the dyads used the whiteboard for organizing factual information as a collection of text boxes, and the chat component was mainly used to disambiguate the information developed on the whiteboard (i.e., the mockup model). The authors attributed this outcome to the nature of the task, which required users to keep track of numerous facts and findings about the murder case, and the difference between the two media in terms of the *persistency* of their contents. Since participants organized key factual information relevant to the problem at hand on the shared whiteboard during their experiments, the authors attributed a shared external memory status to this space and claimed that it facilitated grounding at a broader level by offering a more persistent medium for storing agreed upon facts. The study succeeds in highlighting the important role of medium persistence, even if it does not specify the methods by which students exploited such temporal persistence.

(e) Baker et al. (1999) provide a theoretical account of collaborative learning by bringing together the processes of grounding and appropriation from psycholinguistics and cultural-historical activity theory (CHAT), respectively. In their study they focus on the interactions mediated by the C-Chene software system where dyads are tasked to co-construct energy models that account for storage, transfer and transformation of energy (Baker & Lund, 1997). The models for energy-chains are constructed in a shared workspace that allows the addition of annotated nodes and directed edges. Participants also have access to a chat area that can be customized with sentence openers, which are claimed to promote reflective contributions, reduce typing effort and minimize off-task discussion. The interface is designed to allow only one user to produce a contribution in a given interaction interval. The users need to press a button to switch between dual interaction spaces. Hence the possibility of parallel or overlapping work (e.g., one user drawing on the board as the other is typing a message) is ruled out on the grounds that this would hinder collaboration. The dyads also could not overlap in typing since they need to take turns to use the dialog box where they type their messages. However, it is possible for a user to interrupt his/her partner through a special prompt, which asks whether it is okay to take the turn. If the partner agrees, then the turn is passed to the other user. The study reported that dyads who used the structured interface exhibited more reflective and focused discussion. The authors point to limitations involved with constraining user actions to fixed categories, but they argued that some of the sentence openers they used correspond to generic speech acts that were used for multiple purposes in the course of interaction.

(f) Suthers et al. (2003) investigate the *referential* uses of shared representations in dyadic online discourse mediated by the Belvedere system. This environment has a chat area as well as a shared workspace where dyads can co-construct evidence maps to represent their arguments as a set of categorized textboxes linked to each other (Suthers et al., 2001). The study compares face-to-face and online cases to investigate how dyads use the system as a conversational resource in each case as they work on a shared task that involves developing hypotheses about the spreading of a disease at a remote island. Categories for deictic uses such as finger pointing, cursor-based deixis, verbal deixis and direct manipulation of objects are identified and applied to the session logs. Based on the distributions of these categories for each case, the authors report that dyads in the online case made use of verbal deixis and direct manipulation of shared objects to compensate for the limitations of the online environment to achieve referential relationships across dual interaction spaces. Moreover, the study reports that such referential links are more likely to be observed between temporally proximal actions. For instance, a chat posting including a deictic term is likely to be read in relation to a node recently added to the shared representation.

Our review of relevant work in the CSCL literature highlights some common threads in terms of methodological approaches and theoretical orientations.[5] First, these studies all focus on the group processes of collaboration, rather than treating it as a mere experimental condition for comparing the individuals in the groups. Second, they employ a content-coding approach to categorize actions occurring in multiple interaction spaces. In most cases, representational features like sentence openers or nodes corresponding to specific ontological entities are implemented in the interface to guide/constrain the possibilities for interaction. Such features are also used to aid the categorization of user actions. The categorization schemes are applied to recorded logs and subjected to statistical analysis to elicit interaction patterns.

The analytic thrust of these studies is to arrive at quantitative results through statistical comparisons of aggregated data. To accomplish this, they generally have to restrict student actions in order to control variables in their studies and to facilitate the coding of student utterances within a fixed ontology. We fear that this unduly restricts the interaction, which must be flexible enough to allow students to invent unanticipated behaviors. The restrictions of laboratory settings make problematic experimental validity and generalization of results to real-world contexts. Even more seriously, the aggregation of data—grouping utterances by types or codes rather than maintaining their sequentiality—ignores the complexity of the relations among the utterances and actions. According to our analysis, the temporal and semiotic relations are essential to understanding, sharing and coordinating meaning, problem solving and cognition. While quantitative approaches can be effective in testing model-based hypotheses, they seem less appropriate both for exploring the problem of interactional organization and for investigating interactional methods, which we feel are central to CSCL theory.

Despite the accomplishments of these studies, we find that their approaches introduce systematic limitations. Interactional analysis is impossible because coherent

---

[5]We do not intend to minimize the contributions of the particular papers or authors reviewed. On the contrary, we have selected exemplary CSCL studies in order to make a methodological comparison. The quantitative studies may be effective in pursuing their research questions, but their approaches are inadequate for understanding common ground qualitatively. Some of these authors have also adopted case-study approaches more recently; to take only examples from one of the labs, see the studies of deixis, interactional up-take and narrative structure in (Dwyer & Suthers, 2006; Suthers, 2006b; Yukawa, 2006).

excerpts from recorded interactions are excluded from the analysis itself. (Excerpts are only used anecdotally, outside of the analysis, to introduce the features of the system to the reader, to illustrate the categorization schemes employed or to motivate speculative discussion). Moreover, most studies like these involve dyads working on specific problem-solving contexts through highly structured interfaces in controlled lab studies in an effort to manage the complexity of collaboration. The meanings attributed by the researchers to such features of the interface need to be discovered/unpacked by the participants as they put them into use in interaction—and this critical process is necessarily ignored by the methodology. Finally, most of these papers are informed by the psycholinguistic theory of common ground, and are unable to critique it systematically. By contrast—as we shall see in the following section—our analysis of the joint organization of interaction in the case study positions us to understand how the group grounds its shared understanding in interactional terms at the group level.

Grounding Through Interactional Organization

The coordination of visual and linguistic methods (across the whiteboard and chat workspaces) plays an important role in the establishment of common ground through the co-construction of references between items in the different media within the VMT environment. Particularly in mathematics—with its geometric/algebraic dual nature—symbolic terms are often grounded in visual presence and associated visual practices, such as counting or collecting multiple units into a single referent (Goodwin, 1994; Healy & Hoyles, 1999; Livingston, 2006; Sfard, 2008; Wittgenstein, 1944/1956). The visually present can be replaced by linguistic references to objects that are no longer in the visual field, but that can be understood based on prior experience supported by some mediating object such as a name—see the discussion of mediated memory and of the power of names in thought by Vygotsky (1930/1978, 1934/1986). A more extended analysis of the co-construction of mathematical artifacts by virtual math teams, the complementarity of their visual, semantic and symbolic aspects, their reliance on pre-mathematical practices and processes of reification into concepts are beyond the scope of this chapter and require comparison of multiple case studies (see Çakir, 2009). However, for this chapter it is important to understand something of how the interactional organization that we have observed here functions to ground the group's understanding of their math object (the hexagonal array) as a shared group achievement.

As implied in the OCAF study (Avouris et al., 2003) mentioned in the previous section, investigating grounding and problem-solving processes in online dual-interaction environments like VMT requires close attention to the relationships among actions performed in multiple interaction spaces. Our case study illustrates some of the practical challenges involved with producing mathematical models that aim to exhaustively capture such relationships. For instance, the hexagonal array that was co-constructed by the team draws upon a triangular grid that is formed by three sets of parallel lines that intersect with each other in a particular way. In other words, these objects are layered on top of each other by the participants to produce a shape recognizable as a hexagon. Despite this combinatoric challenge, a modeling approach can still attempt to capture all possible geometric relationships among these graphical objects in a bottom-up fashion. However, when all chat messages referring to the whiteboard objects are added to the mix, the resulting model may obscure rather than reveal the details of the interactional organization through which group members discuss more complicated mathematical objects by treating a collection of atomic actions as a single entity. Terminology co-constructed in the chat-and-whiteboard environment—like **"hexagonal array"**—can refer to complexly defined math objects. What is interesting about the student knowledge building is how they aggregate elements and reify them into higher-order, more powerful units (Sfard, 2008). A model should mirror this rather than to simply represent the elements as isolated.

The challenges involved with the modeling approach are not limited to finding efficient ways to capture all relationships among actions and identifying meaningful clusters of objects. The figurative uses of the graphical objects present the most daunting challenge for such an undertaking. For instance, the team members in our case study used the term **"hexagonal array"** to refer to a mathematical object implicated in the witnessed production of prior drawing actions. As we have seen in the way the team used this term during their session, **"hexagonal array"** does not simply refer to a readily available whiteboard illustration. Instead it is used as a *gloss* (Garfinkel & Sacks, 1970) to talk about an imagined pattern that grows infinitely and takes the shape illustrated on the whiteboard only at a particular stage. In the absence of a fixed set of ontological elements and constraints on types of actions a user can perform, modeling approaches that aim to capture emergent relationships among semiotic objects distributed across multiple interaction spaces need to adequately deal with the retrospective and prospective uses of language in interaction. Rather than relying upon a generic approach to modeling imposed by the researchers, our ethnomethodological approach aims to discover the unique "model"—or, better, the specific meaning—that was constructed *by the group* in its particular situation.

In another study discussed earlier, Dillenbourg and Traum (2006) offer the napkin and mockup models in their effort to characterize the relationship between whiteboard and chat spaces. In short, these models seem to describe two use scenarios where one interaction space is subordinated to the other during an entire problem-solving session. The complex relationships between the actions performed across both interaction spaces in our case made it difficult for us to describe the interactions we have observed by committing to only one of these models, as Dillenbourg and Traum did in their study. Instead, we have observed that in the context of an open-ended math task, groups may invoke either type of organization, depending upon the contingencies of their ongoing problem-solving work. For instance, during long episodes of drawing actions where a model of some aspect of the shared task is being co-constructed on the whiteboard (as in our first excerpt), the chat area often serves as an auxiliary medium to coordinate the drawing actions, which seems to conform to the mockup model. In contrast, when a strategy to address the shared task is being discussed in chat (as in the excerpt where the group considered splitting the hexagon into six regions), the whiteboard may be mainly used to quickly illustrate the textual descriptions with annotations or rough sketches, in accordance with the napkin model. Depending on the circumstances of ongoing interaction, participants may switch from one type of organization to another from moment to moment. Therefore, instead of ascribing mockup and napkin models to entire problem-solving sessions, we argue that it would be more fruitful to use these terms as glosses or descriptive categories for types of interactional organizations group members may invoke during specific episodes of their interaction.

Another provocative observation made by Dillenbourg and Traum is that the whiteboard serves as a kind of shared external memory where group members keep a record of agreed-upon facts. In their study the dyads were reported to post text notes on the whiteboard to keep track of the information they had discovered about a murder-mystery task. This seems to have led the authors to characterize the whiteboard as a placeholder and/or a shared working memory for the group, where agreed-upon facts or "contributions" in Clark's sense are persistently stored and spatially organized. As Dillenbourg and Traum observed, the scale of what is shared in the course of collaborative problem solving becomes an important issue when a theory operating at the utterance level like contribution theory (Clark & Marshall, 1981) is used as an analytic resource to study grounding processes that span a longer period of time. Dillenbourg and Traum seem to have used the notion of persistence to extend common ground across time to address this limitation. In particular, they argued that the whiteboard grounds the solution to the problem itself rather than the contributions made by each utterance. In other words, the whiteboard is metaphorically treated as a physical manifestation of the common ground. We certainly agree with this broadening of the conceptualization of common ground, although we do not see the whiteboard as just a metaphor or externalization of a mental phenomenon. Rather, *common ground is established in the discourse spaces* of text chat and graphical whiteboard. Their differential forms of persistence provide a continuing resource for sharing, modifying and remembering the group meaning of joint artifacts and products of group cognition.

In our case study, we have observed that the whiteboard does not simply serve as a kind of shared external memory where the group keeps a record of agreed upon facts, opinions, hypotheses or conclusions. The shared visible communication media are places where the group does its work, where it cognizes. Ideas, concepts, meanings, etc. can *subsequently* be taken up by individuals into their personal memories as resources for future social or mental interactions. There is no need to reduce group meaning to identical individual mental contents or to hypothesize a mysterious "group mind" as the location of common ground—the location is the discourse medium, with all its particular affordances and modes of access.

In our sessions, the whiteboard was primarily used to draw and annotate graphical illustrations of geometric shapes, although users occasionally posted textboxes on the whiteboard to note formulas they had found (see Fig. 7.2 above). While the whiteboard mainly supported visual reasoning—and textual discussion or symbolic manipulation occurred chiefly in the chat stream—actions were carefully, systematically coordinated across the media and integrated within an interactionally organized group-cognitive process. As we have illustrated in our analysis, the fact that there were inscriptions posted on the whiteboard did not necessarily mean that all members immediately shared the same sense of those graphical objects. The group members did considerable interactional work to achieve a shared sense of those objects that was adequate for the purposes at hand. For instance, the crosshatched lines that Qwertyuiop originally drew became increasingly meaningful for the group as it was visually outlined and segmented and as it was discussed in the chat and expressed symbolically.

Hence, the whiteboard objects have a different epistemic status in our case study than in Dillenbourg and Traum's experiment. Moreover, the participants did not deem all the contents of the whiteboard relevant to the ongoing discussion. For instance, Fig. 7.2 above shows a snapshot of the entire whiteboard as the team was discussing the hexagonal pattern problem. The figure shows that there are additional objects in the shared scene like a blue hypercube and a 3-D staircase, which are remnants of the group's prior problem-solving work. Finally, the sense of previously posted whiteboard objects may be modified or become evident as a result of current actions (Suchman, 1990).

In other words, group members can not only reuse or reproduce drawings, but they can also make subsequent sense of those drawings or discard the ones that are not deemed relevant anymore. Therefore, the technologically extended notion of common ground as a placeholder for a worked-out solution suffers from the same issues stated in Koschmann and LeBaron's (2003) critique of Clark's theory. As an abstract construct transcendental to the meaning-making practices of participants, the notion of common ground obscures rather than explains the ways the whiteboard is used as a resource for collaborative problem solving.

Instead of using an extended version of common ground as an analytical resource we frame our analysis using the notion of "indexical ground of deictic reference," which is a notion we appropriated from linguistic anthropology (Hanks, 1992). In face-to-face interaction, human action is built through the sequential organization of not only talk but also coordinated use of the features of the local scene that are made relevant via bodily orientations, gesture, eye gaze, etc. In other words, "human action is built through simultaneous deployment of a range of quite different kinds of semiotic resources" (Goodwin, 2000a, p. 1489). Indexical terms and referential deixis play a fundamental role in the way these semiotic resources are interwoven in interaction into a coherent whole.

Indexical terms are generally defined as expressions whose interpretation requires identification of some element of the context in which it was uttered, such as who made the utterance, to whom it was addressed, when and where the utterance was made (Levinson, 1983). Since the sense of indexical terms depends on the context in which they are uttered, indexicality is necessarily a relational phenomenon. Indexical references facilitate the mutually constitutive relationship between language and context (Hanks, 1996). The basic communicative function of indexical-referentials is "to individuate or single out objects of reference or address in terms of their relation to the current interactive context in which the utterance occurs" (Hanks, 1992, p. 47).

The specific sense of referential terms such as *this, that, now, here* is defined locally by interlocutors against a shared indexical ground. Conversely, the linguistic labels assigned to highlighted features of the local scene shapes the indexical ground. Hence, the indexical ground is not an abstract placeholder for a fixed set of registered contributions. Rather, it signifies an emergently coherent field of action that encodes an interactionally achieved set of background understandings, orientations and perspectives that make references intelligible to interlocutors (Zemel, Koschmann, LeBaron, & Feltovich, 2008).

Despite the limitations of online environments for supporting multimodality of embodied interaction, participants make substantial use of their everyday interactional competencies as they appropriate the features of such environments to engage with other users. For instance, Suthers et al.'s (2003) study reports that deictic uses of representational proxies play an important role in the interactional organization of online problem-solving sessions mediated by the Belvedere system. The authors report that participants in the online case devised mechanisms that compensate for the lack of gestural deixis with alternative means, such as using verbal deixis to refer to the most recently added text nodes and visual manipulation of nodes to direct their partner's attention to a particular node in the shared argument map.

In contrast to the Belvedere system, VMT offers participants additional resources such as an explicit referencing mechanism, a more generic workspace that allows producing and annotating drawings, and an awareness feature that produces a sense of sequentiality by embedding indicators for drawing actions in the sequence of chat postings. Our case study shows that despite the online situation's lack of the familiar resources of embodied interaction, team members can still achieve a sense of shared access to the meaningful objects displayed in the dual interaction spaces of the VMT environment. Our analysis indicates that coherence among multiple modalities of an online environment like VMT is achieved through group members' development and application of shared methods for using the features of the system to coordinate their actions in the interface.

Through coordinated use of indexical-referential terms and highlighting actions, team members help each other to literally "see" the objects implicated in the shared visual field (Goodwin, 1994) and to encode them with locally specified terminology for subsequent use. They demonstrate how to "read" graphical as well as textual objects through the way the objects are built up sequentially and are spatially arranged in relation to each other through sequences of actions. The deictic references that link chat messages to features of graphical inscriptions and to prior chat content are instrumental in the sequential achievement of indexical symmetry, intersubjectivity or common ground.

Sequential Analysis of the Joint Organization of Interaction

To sum up, the focus of our ethnomethodological inquiry is directed towards documenting how a virtual team achieved intersubjectivity and coherence among their actions in an online CSCL environment with multiple interaction spaces. We looked at the moment-to-moment details of the practices through which participants organize their chat utterances and whiteboard actions as a coherent whole in interaction—a process that is central to CSCL. We observed that referential practices enacted by the users are essential, particularly in the coordinated use of multimodalities afforded by environments like VMT. The referential uses of available features are instrumental not only in allocating other members' attention to specific parts of the interface where relevant actions are being performed, but also in the achievement of reciprocity (intersubjectivity, common ground, shared understanding, group cognition) among actions in the multiple interaction spaces, and hence a sense of sequential organization across the spaces.

In our case study, we have seen the establishment of an indexical ground of deictic references co-constructed by the group members as an underlying support for the creation and maintenance of their joint problem space. We have seen that nexus of references created interactionally as group members propose, question, repair, respond, illustrate, make visible, supply symbols, name, etc. In the VMT dual-media environment, the differential persistence, visibility and mutability of the media are consequential for the interaction. Group members develop methods of coordinating chat and drawing activities to combine visual and conceptual reasoning by the group and to co-construct and maintain an evolving shared indexical ground of their discourse.

In this chapter, we have *reconceptualized the problem of common ground from an issue of sharing mental representations to a practical matter of being able to jointly relate semiotic objects to their indexed referents*. The references do not reside in the minds of particular actors, but have been crafted into the presentation of the chat postings and drawing inscriptions through the details of wording and sequential presentation. The references are present in the data as affordances for *understanding* by group participants as well as by analysts (Stahl, 2006b, chap. 17). The *meaning* is there in the visual presentation of the communication objects and in the network of interrelated references (Chapter 26), rather than in mental re-presentations of them. The understanding of the references is a matter of normally tacit social practice, rather than of rationalist explicit deduction. *The references can be explicated by analysis, but only if the structure of sequentiality and indexicality is preserved in the data analysis and only if the skill of situated human understanding is applied.*

In our case study of an 18-minute excerpt taken from a four-hour group chat, three students construct a diagram of lines, triangles and hexagons, propose a math pattern problem, analyze the structure of their diagram and derive an algebraic formula to solve their problem. They propose their own creative problem about mathematical properties; gradually construct a complex mathematical object; explore related patterns with visual, narrative and symbolic means; express wonder; gain mathematical insight and appreciate their achievement. They do this by coordinating their whiteboard and chat activities in a synchronous online environment. Their accomplishment is precisely the kind of educational math experience recommended by mathematicians (Livingston, 2006; Lockhart, 2008; Moss & Beatty, 2006). It was not a mental achievement of an individual, but a group accomplishment carried out in computer-supported discourse. *By analyzing the sequentiality and indexicality of their interactions, we explicated several mechanisms of the group cognition by which the students coordinated the group meaning of their discourse and maintained an effective joint problem space.*

The coordination of visual and textual realizations of the mathematical objects that the students co-construct provides a grounding of the algebraic formulas the students jointly derive using the line drawings that they inspect visually together. As the students individualize this experience of group cognition, they can develop the deep understanding of mathematical phenomena that comes from seeing the connections among multiple realizations (Sfard, 2008) (Chapter 3). Our case study does not by any means predict that all students can accomplish similar results under specific conditions, but merely demonstrates that such group cognition is possible within a synchronous CSCL setting and that a fine-grained sequential analysis of interaction can study how it is collaboratively accomplished.

Chapter 8
Question Co-Construction in VMT Chats

Nan Zhou

Abstract In an online collaborative context like VMT chats, questions are often not simple, well-defined queries for information, but should be understood as situated moves within the group dynamic of the problem-solving effort. The object of the questioning is itself an emergent property of the interaction, through which the meaning is successively interpreted, refined and converged upon by the details of how the question is built, read and responded to. Questioning can play an integral role in the social relations among the participants, either positioning individuals as more or less competent or else maintaining peer standings. Question/response interactions are key to pursuing group problem-solving strategies, building a joint problem space and sustaining the team discourse. In this chapter, we analyze a questioning episode in which the social aspects are particularly clear and interesting, and where the details of the questioning have dramatic consequences for the group process.

Keywords Questioning · information behavior · situated expertise · participation

Chat Questioning and Math Competence

In the VMT Project we invited students to come to chat with their peers in small groups about non-routine math problems designed for them that we thought might be interesting and might encourage mathematical thinking. Different from tutoring sessions, VMT chats stress peer interaction among students and collaboration working on a math problem. Usually a moderator is present in a chat session to explain what the group is expected to do, but not to give the group math help. The moderator remains in the session mainly to address logistical and technical issues. It is up to the student team itself to organize its own interaction and discuss the math problem.

N. Zhou (✉)
College of Information Science & Technology, Drexel University, Philadelphia, PA, USA
e-mail: nan.zhou@drexel.edu

G. Stahl (ed.), *Studying Virtual Math Teams*, Computer-Supported Collaborative
Learning Series 11, DOI 10.1007/978-1-4419-0228-3_8,
© Springer Science+Business Media, LLC 2009

While a general math topic is given, including several issues to explore, the students must to a large extent define the questions they will pursue.

We all know that competence in a particular matter is not always distributed equally among participants in an interaction. The chat setting makes the study of this distribution possible because subtle displays of one's own competence or of attitudes toward the competence of another that are possible through body language in face-to-face settings must be made more explicit online. In VMT, some groups may consist of students from different grade levels; participants may or may not have experience in prior VMT sessions; some may have looked at the problem and tried to solve it before they joined the chat while others have not. In terms of competencies, we notice that some students display higher mathematical fluency, e.g. working with equations; some are better at verbally expressing themselves while others are better at conceptualizing problems visually. Even though many of the differences in expertise, talent, ability, knowledge, understanding, etc. may exist, not all of them are made relevant to the interaction. Differences only become relevant to the organization of participation in the group when they are made so by participants—which can be done in a variety of ways. In other words, it is the local and situated differences that are of interactional relevance. The issue of relative competence often interacts with the student questioning processes.

This chapter explores how it is possible to sustain a productive peer relationship in an online group when there are relevant differences among actors in expertise, talent, ability, knowledge, or understanding. Pursuing this line of inquiry allows us to look into the mechanisms underlying peer-group interaction. How such *group mechanisms* may support or inhibit *individual learning* has become an important topic for current research on learning and instruction (Barron, 2003; Cohen, Lotan, Abram, Scarloss, & Schultz, 2002; Schwartz, 1995). When there are differences in competence, actors need to work out among themselves the social order and the organization of their interaction. In this chapter, we look at how differences are attended to by participants in a collaborative peer group as part of the mechanism by which a group of students collaborate and manage the organization of their participation in ongoing chat interaction around problem solving. In particular, we examine the ways members of a small group (a) introduce differences in situated competencies as interactionally relevant, (b) organize their interaction to attend to these differences and (c) effect repairs where possible or find ways to proceed where repair is ineffective.

There are many ways that differences in competency can be introduced as interactionally relevant. Posing a question is often one way of accomplishing this. For example, an actor can ask a question about what is going on, or indicate there is a problem of understanding, or the actor can show the need for assistance by taking a particular kind of "next step" in a sequentially unfolding set of actions, etc. Acting as less competent than others does not mean the actor is not "membered" (Garfinkel & Sacks, 1970) as a participant in the ongoing interaction. It means the actors have constituted as relevant a particular difference in the distribution of presumed or actual competence among themselves. When a questioner asks certain kinds of questions, she constitutes and makes relevant differences in expertise, knowledge, etc. as a matter for the recipients to attend to. Thus, not only is the questioner asking a recipient about the matter at hand, she is also instantiating their relationship in terms of the organization of their participation in the interaction (e.g., as questioner and answerer). In examining our data of students' interaction in VMT chats, we have noticed that *question-response pairs* are frequently invoked for attending to differences in local expertise and competency. For instance, asking a question may imply that the addressee(s) are likely to be able to provide some information that the questioner does not know.

When actors put forward certain questions that do not address explicitly their standing as participants in the interaction, matters of difference in knowledge, understanding, expertise, etc., can be addressed in ways that preserve a peer relationship between questioner and respondent. When actors make the organization of participation explicit in the question-response construction as a matter to be addressed, then the nature of the relationships among interactants becomes a matter of concern that needs to be addressed. Issues of differences in knowledge, understanding, expertise, etc., are then made relevant in terms of the way those relationships are worked out.

Thus, one way that actors maintain peer relationships is by not addressing potential differences in competence explicitly as an interactional issue in question-response interactions. In this chapter, we show how actors *build a question and build a response* that allows the questioner and the respondent to attend to their relationship by addressing the matter at hand rather than by explicitly mentioning their relationship itself. Through the data analysis we present, we illustrate how we came to understand this.

The Context of the Case Study

The data consists of excerpts taken from chat sessions of Team C in the VMT Spring Fest 2006. This event featured teams who participated in four consecutive sessions over a two-week period. During the four sessions, there were some changes in the membership of some groups. For example, Team C had a newcomer joining at the beginning of the second session but a participant of the first session did not return. Teams were given the same set of problems, which initially required that they find the patterns of growth for a certain shape of stacked squares made up of sticks. In later sessions, the teams made their own shapes using squares and sticks and explored the pattern of growth of the number of squares and sticks in these shapes.

The first part of Team C's work that we analyze is from the first of the four sessions. It includes one episode that is split in six excerpts and two complimentary short excerpts from later in the session. Nish is a latecomer who joined about 10 minutes after other participants began working on the problem. Prior to Nish's arrival, the other three participants had worked out formulas to describe the pattern of growth for the number of sticks. Thus, when Nish arrived, the other participants were busy discussing their formulas. The moderator made two requests asking the group to bring Nish up to speed, the first of which did not receive much attention from the group members, who were engaged in their task at hand. In response to the second request from the moderator, two participants, Jason and David, gave Nish brief instructions on how to reload the previous messages in the chat room. David also provided a summary of their findings, including how they found out the pattern of the number of squares and the number of sticks. They then moved on with the task they were engaged in, which was to write up their findings and post those findings on a wiki to share with other teams. The excerpts we analyze here start about 10 minutes after Nish joins the chat.

Making Differences Relevant: Question Construction

In a peer group engaged in math problem solving, competence—either in doing math, in being a member, or in other matters—is not always equally distributed among participants in an interaction. When differences in competencies become relevant matters among participants, participants use conventional methods to attend to those differences. Indicating a problem of understanding like Nish did at the beginning of the episode (see Log 8-1) or asking a question are among those methods to introduce differences as interactionally relevant. We analyze the excerpt in Log 8-1 to show how a particular method is used by participants to make differences relevant to the ongoing interaction. When a member of a peer group explicitly puts forward the issues regarding actors' participation such as competency, discussion on such issues may be avoided by participants. This allows the peer relationship to be preserved. The excerpt illustrates how Nish's posting at line 126 brings interactional trouble for the participants and how a *question* is constructed through the interaction.

Log 8-1.

126	06.45.11	Nish	just to clarify sumthing, i am not overwhelmingly good at math as u guys seem to be, so it may take me more time than u guys to understand sumthing..
127	06.45.44	Moderator	can you tell us what's puzzling you?
128	06.46.07	Jason	are we allowed to post images on the wiki? I could just download TeX real quick and get the summation notation in a small graphic
129	06.46.12	Nish	the derivation of the number of squares

At line 126, Nish produces a report in which he (a) offers a self-assessment of his own math competency and (b) appends to this a description of his performance and participation in the ongoing activity of the assembled participants as a consequence of this difference. The fact that this report is a self-assessment made by Nish and the organization of participation is explicitly referenced in it (**"so it may take me**

more time than u guys to understand sumthing") may have made Nish's posting a problematic matter for the participants. It reifies knowledge relations among participants in that the self-assessment is produced by making comparison of oneself to other actors among the group as a collectivity. The report calls on members of the collectivity to organize their participation to address the issues—i.e., differences among actors made relevant within it—which involves a discussion about one of the actors rather than about a mathematical matter. This problematic nature of the matter is underscored by the fact that there is a thirty-four second interval during which none of the participants responds (even though Nish's posting is addressed to all the participants as a collectivity, i.e. **"u guys"**), and no other observable activity happens in the system, either in the chat or on the whiteboard, which is rather a noticeable silence for a chat in a small group like this.

Membership in a peer group—i.e., being a peer in the group—involves entitlements and obligations to act, such as asking a question, responding to a request or producing an account. Entitlements of a member are accorded unless otherwise called into question by specific actions. In this excerpt, Nish could have asked a question regarding his problem, but he chooses to make a report instead. If we take a closer look at the setting where the interaction takes place, we come to a better understanding of why Nish chooses not to ask a question. The session is set up for equal participation of all students. The expectation and entitlement of equal participation are also reinforced by the moderator's reiterated request for bringing Nish "up to speed" and the group's effort to summarize what they have done for Nish and to give him directions for viewing their previous discussion in response to the request. As a latecomer, it is natural for Nish to feel the need to participate. However the group is oriented to some current task, and asking a question irrelevant to it becomes a delicate matter since it takes the risk of interrupting the ongoing work. In other words, it is always possible to pose a question during a chat, but it must be appropriately situated. Nish's question about the group's previous work is not appropriate to the current interactional context. So Nish must engage in some interactional work to prepare a new context for his questioning.

In such an imbalanced power situation with its asymmetry of social obligations, structuring a report like Nish does is probably done out of consideration of being minimally intrusive yet still sending out the message, "I'd like to participate." It is also a request, negotiating how one can participate and be part of the group. Later in the chapter, we will analyze an excerpt taken from the second session of the same group, which serves as a contrasting case where a newcomer asks a question regarding a similar problem in understanding, as a way to demonstrate how the method chosen by a group member to make differences relevant to the interaction is very much locally situated.

One function of Nish's report is probably to initiate instructional work by eliciting questions from other participants to probe his problem in understanding. Such instructional work may be dis-preferred, thus avoided in a peer group in order to maintain peer relationships. Problems of participation may therefore arise, where repair becomes a relevant activity. One way to characterize the posting and the subsequent inactivity of the other participants from an interactional perspective is that there was an interruption in the progression of the interaction. One consequence of an interruption in progress is that something needs to be done to restore it if the interaction is to continue. Problems of progressivity call for repair work of some sort: Nish, whose posting led to the lengthy period of inactivity, would have to produce a next posting, or some other participant would need to do so. Given Nish's initial posting, what a next posting could be and who would produce it are a source of interactional trouble for the participants. In this case, a next posting is produced by the Moderator who asks, **"can you tell us what's puzzling you?"** (at 6:45:44).

This posting in a question form is quite clearly addressed to Nish, showing that the moderator has recognized there might be a problem of some sort that Nish has—possibly with understanding—which he is trying to indicate and presumably asking for help from the group. By using **"us"**, the moderator is acting on behalf of the group. The response that it is calling for is thus designed to be directed to the group as a collectivity. It positions the group as recipients and entitles them to respond to whatever Nish may articulate in the subsequent posting. In other words, the posting from the moderator does the work of recognizing the differences (either in math expertise or understanding) as made relevant by Nish's report, and bringing the issue up to the group to deal with. It also puts Nish in the position of providing more specific information about his problem.

By responding to the moderator's inquiry, Nish's response at line 129, confirms with the moderator that there is some trouble in terms of his understanding of what the group has produced and in particular with **"the derivation of the number of squares."** Though line 129 is not in an inquisitive form, combined with the moderator's question that it is responding to, it constitutes a *question* in its own right, articulating Nish's problem and at the same time indicating the need for assistance and calling upon the group to act: How did the group derive the number of squares? Posing a question of this kind instantiates the epistemic stance of Nish—that he does not know how the expression for the number of squares was mathematically derived—in relation to the group, positioning Nish as an actor seeking help from the group, and treating the group as entitled to offer the resource to address the epistemic differences. It is now up to the group to determine what an appropriate response should consist of and to work out among themselves who would actually produce or deliver the response.

How the Differences Are Attended To: Response Construction

In reviewing our data, we found that participants attend to differences in math as indicated in a question regarding math topics promptly without interactional trouble, in contrast to the lack of response to differences regarding an actor's competency. Differences in competence may come from a variety of sources, for example, math skills, understanding or experience in the group, just to name a few. It is consequential for the interaction what kind of differences the participants highlight and how they treat them. Our analysis of the subsequent data excerpt in Log 8-2 shows that

Log 8-2.

130	06.46.21	Jason	oh
131	06.46.31	Jason	so you see in the list a column for "N"
132	06.46.50	Jason	when n=1, we have 1 square; for n=2, 3; and for n=3, 6
133	06.47.00	Jason	we came up with a formula to find the total number of squares for any number N squares and count them
134	06.47.16	Jason	the purpose of the formula is so that you don't have to draw out the squares and count them
135	06.47.39	Nish	um yes
136	06.47.41	Nish	i know
137	06.47.51	Nish	but how did u get that formula

the difference made relevant in the interaction is treated by the group as an experience of being in the group while that part of work was getting done, instead of treating it as knowledge or as a conceptual deficit in math. In the postings from 130 to 134, Jason gives Nish a recap of what the group did by providing an *historical account of the group's work*.

How a difference is treated by the group as such is an interactional and procedural matter for the participants. When the difference is introduced by Nish as interactionally relevant to the group, the announcement at the beginning of the excerpt (line 126) is a report regarding his own math competence in relation to others in the group: **"i am not overwhelmingly good at math as u guys seem to be."** Even though such a report is signaling the need for assistance, it may not be clear to participants (including the moderator) what the particular problem might be, as shown in the lack of response from the participants and the following intervention from the moderator.

How participants treat the differences probably accounts for the discrepancy between what the question may be asking and the response being provided as we take a closer look at the data.

In the five subsequent postings starting with line 130, Jason produces an account of the group's work as a response to address Nish's problem. These postings start with **"oh"** as a separate line, which is a marker of displaying his understanding of the request and also indicates there is more subsequent posting to come. He first directs Nish's attention to **"a column for 'N',"** which is stated in the original problem description, and explained what the group has done: **"we came up with a formula to find the total number of squares for any number N."** The use of the pronoun **"we"** and past tense (as in **"came up"**) suggest that this is produced as an historical account of what the group did earlier in the session, before Nish's joining. However, there seems some disconnect between the group's problem-solving steps provided in the two postings in line 132 and 133. The first one lists the number of squares for N from 1 to 3 whereas the following jumps to stating the result that the group found a formula for **"the total number of squares for any number N."**

This leaves out the mathematical reasoning on how the number of squares is generalized to N. These sequential postings from Jason end with a statement of the purpose of the formula: **"so that you don't have to draw out the squares and count them."** If we pay attention to the timestamp of those postings, we notice that they are being posted in a consecutive manner: there is only a few seconds before the next posting appears.

After the last posting from Jason at 6:47:16, the next posting appears 23 seconds later at line 135 from Nish: **"um yes"**. This noticeable time elapse marks the completion of Jason's production of the response, delivered in five individual postings, and projects subsequent action of relevancy. The fact that there is no uptake by other participants indicates that what Jason has produced may have been treated as being endorsed by the group as appropriate to address Nish's question.

Reformulation of a Question

It is up to the questioner to assess the adequacy of a response to a question (Sacks, 1962/1995). The completion of Jason's production of the response calls on Nish to act upon it. In the following three postings by Nish, **"um yes"**, followed by a separate line, **"i know,"** together with a subsequent question, constitute a *dispreferred* response. In a situation like this when a request for help is made and a subsequent explanation (which is rather elaborate in this case) provided, a preferred response would be acknowledging the usefulness of the explanation so that the interaction could progress without trouble. A dis-preferred response usually involves extra interactional efforts from the respondent such as providing explanation or an account. In face-to-face interaction, one could use a variety of ways to indicate a dis-preferred response, such as frowning, using disapproval or hesitant tone, etc. In chat, there has to be effort made to indicate such, which means a chat message has to be constructed to be read as dis-preferred, such as a posting being preceded by **"um"** in this case. The subsequent **"i know"** indicates that the response provided has not answered the question because what it explains was already clear to the questioner. This also shows that Nish understands much of what went on in the group, but he is specifically asking for help on a particular matter of mathematics—**"the derivation of the number of squares."**

A question from Nish, **"but how did u get that formula"** (line 137), with a preface **"but"** is posed immediately following the two short postings. The dispreferred response consisting of the three consecutive postings constitutes an assessment of what Jason has provided in answering Nish's initial question. The question in line 137 can be seen as a reformulation of the initial one. It is constructed in the interaction among question-response-evaluation using the response and the initial question as resources. If recipients can and do reasonably infer that **"i know"** refers to the math content of the response, then the reformulated question is distinguishing (a) the mathematical derivation of the formula from (b) a recounting of its role in the past group process.

How does the discrepancy arise between the response provided and what the request for help may be asking for? Nish's initially posed "question" constructed through interaction with the moderator—**"the derivation of the number of squares** (is puzzling me)"—does not reveal to the group what he already knew. The question could be interpreted as asking about either (a) the particular mathematical manipulation of deriving the formula from a series of numbers or (b) the problem-solving steps that lead to the posted formula. The differences could be conceptual—as in lack of certain knowledge—or procedural—as caused by Nish's earlier absence from participation. In this episode of peer interaction, the fact that the group treats the differences as the latter seems to suggest there might be certain preferences in a peer group like this for treating differences as differences in group experiences rather than in personal competencies. Actors won't presume incompetence of any sort unless there is strong enough evidence to make it relevant. In our case, the data in later excerpts show that the group finally assumes Nish's incompetence as relevant and makes it explicit after the interactional troubles have accumulated to a certain point. At that point, the organization of participation in the group is consequently changed and the peer relationship is not maintained any more, as we will see.

Doing Situated Expertise: Co-Construction of the Response to a Question

In the analysis of Log 8-3, we show how situated expertise is effected by group members collaboratively—how the group organizes its interaction to attend to the differences and effects repairs when possible or finds ways to proceed when repair turns out to be ineffective.

Log 8-3.

138	06.48.00	Jason	Oh	Ref to WB
139	06.48.11	Moderator	i believe so	Ref to WB
140	06.48.12	Jason	uh, basically you try to find a pattern in the total number of squares first	
141	06.48.47	Jason	We found a formula for that which we'll post on the wiki	
142	06.49.00	David	if you look at the patterns row by row, it's 1 + 2 + 3 + 4 + however many rows there are	

We see that Jason positions himself as the recipient (or one of the recipients) of the question, thereby acting as a local situated expert. He appears to be the first one who picks up Nish's question and provides a response, which is presented in three individual postings. It starts with **"oh"** as a single posting (line 138), a marker signaling more to come in subsequent postings, which also serves as an indicator of expressing his increased understanding of the question, which his upcoming response is going to address.

This line 138 also has an explicit reference to the whiteboard, indicated in the log by **"Ref to WB."** The reference appears as an arrow attached to the message in the chat environment (Fig. 8.1), which is a feature of this environment that allows users to make explicit reference from a current message to previous chat message or to an area on the shared whiteboard. If we follow this reference of **"oh,"** we can see it is pointing to the **"Formula for total # of squares: n(1+n)/2"** in a text box created by the group on the shared whiteboard. The use of the graphical reference here serves to confirm Jason's understanding of the deictic reference made in Nish's question, **that formula**, therefore to establish their shared reference to the object, i.e., the specific formula as the common ground that the question-response interaction is based on. By making the deictic reference publicly visible to the group, it also creates an opportunity for other members' assessment and invites participation from them to help construct a response together.

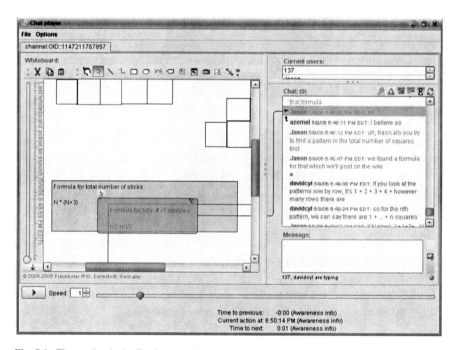

Fig. 8.1 The session in the Replayer tool

The use of **"uh,"** at the beginning of Jason's next posting (line 140) also displays hesitance of some sort, possibly in the appropriateness of the upcoming content as a response to the question being posed. The response being provided here is presumably some kind of repair attempt that seeks to address the trouble that is made relevant by Nish's dis-preferred reply. It is a reformulation of what Jason previously provided, which the reformulated question is projecting. However, Jason's response is not particularly different from the earlier response he provided, which the current one is meant to repair: he is reporting the work the group did (**we found a formula**) and also what the group was oriented to (**for that which we'll post on the wiki**), but not focusing on how the formula, **n(n+1)/2**, is mathematically derived. Such a report may be oriented toward giving the questioner an explanation from a higher-level problem-solving perspective by providing the steps the group has gone through. It is rather interesting that Jason insists on providing a response similar to the previous one just made, which has already been assessed by Nish in his dis-preferred response as not being appropriate since he already **"knew"** it. This suggests that actors are conservative of the trajectories they take in interaction, and it requires a considerable amount of work to get people to shift focus onto things other than what they have been working on in interaction. It is routinely the case that people must, over multiple turns at talk and interaction, work out their troubles. The trouble itself may only become evident in the process of working it out, which in our case is demonstrated by the fact that other members jump in later to offer alternative ways to address the trouble. It also seems to suggest a preference members in a peer group may have in what constitutes an appropriate response to address a newcomer's question in order to **"catch up"**—which is reviewing group experience over providing conceptual math knowledge, as exhibited earlier when the differences are attended to. This may help explain why Nish originally stressed his need for help with math because he wanted an explanation of the derivation of the formula, not the problem-solving steps the group went through that Jason insists on providing.

There is a pause of 35 seconds between Jason's two separate postings at line 140 and 141, which is an interactionally significant duration in a chat like this. A further, closer look at what happens during this period as we step through the unfolding interaction using the VMT Replayer tool reveals that there is a 12 second interval between when the posting at line 140 appears and the next awareness information **"Jason is typing"** shows, immediately followed by another awareness information **"David is typing"** just 2 seconds later. The finished messages anticipated by the awareness information are posted later in line 141 and line 142. Although Jason's posting in line 140 is explaining what the **"first"** step should be, therefore projecting subsequent postings by him on following steps, the 12 second interval during which no observable activity takes place nevertheless indicates the possibility of some interactional trouble and opens up the space for any participants including Nish, the questioner, to address that trouble. It allows the questioner to assess the response or other group members to construct an appropriate response to the question together. David offers a way of addressing the question as an alternative to Jason's response, implying that there may be another relevant kind of response, different from the one Jason has produced.

David starts Log 8-4 by describing how the pattern of the number of squares grows "row by row" in relation to the number of rows. He then continues to present how the pattern is being generalized to the Nth, which is very similar to what Jason posts in the following line (144) that appears only 3 seconds later. Jason's posting

Log 8-4.

143	06.49.24	David	so for the nth pattern, we can say there are 1 + ··· + n squares	
144	06.49.27	Jason	if N rows: 1+2+3+ ··· N	
145	06.49.57	Jason	so then we incorporated the formula for finding the sum of an arithmetic series	
146	06.50.12	David	there's a formula for finding the sum of consecutive integers, which (when starting from 1) is: n(n+1)/2	
147	06.50.17	137	so you use gaussian sum to get n(n+1)/2	Ref to123
148	06.50.25	Jason	that's it	Ref to146
149	06.50.35	David	and as Jason said, it works for arithmetic sequences in general	

"if N rows: 1+2+3+ ··· N" does not stand alone as a meaningful and coherent statement if not read together with David's posting at line 142. It fits seamlessly into the sequential unfolding of the posting just as David's subsequent one does. When we replay the session in real time, the awareness information in the system shows that Jason started composing his message after David's first one was posted and while David's second posting was still being composed. Analysis of the sequential relation of messages suggests that line 144 posted by Jason is built on David's first posting.

This excerpt displays an instance of how a group engages in doing situated expertise collaboratively by taking up and building on each other's postings and endorsing other's contributions. Jason and David respectively present that there is an existing formula (**"for finding the sum of an arithmetic series"** or **"for finding the sum of consecutive integers"**) ready to use, which they **"incorporated"**, as stated by Jason in line 145. David also explicitly provides the formula: **n(n+1)/2**. This contribution is similarly made by the other participant, 137, in the next line that comes just 5 seconds later, where he refers to the formula as the **"gaussian sum"** and also presents the formula explicitly.

David's statement about the formula in line 146 is endorsed by Jason: **"that's it,"** with reference pointed to it using the reference tool (line 148). In his subsequent posting, David also explicitly endorses Jason in line 149 using explicit reference **"as Jason said"** and direct quote with slightly changed wording, i.e. arithmetic sequences in general vs. an arithmetic series. From line 142 to 149 within the period of one and a half minutes or so, the postings from three different participants—namely Jason, David, and 137—align with and build on each other. Together, they construct a rather coherent and complete explanation, at least from the three question recipients' perspective, in response to Nish's question.

How Making the Relationship Explicit Changes Participation

In our case, the group completes the construction of a response to the posed question. The completion is marked by David's endorsement of Jason's explanation regarding the formula and the noticeable 16 seconds elapse that follows where no more posting from the three participants is made. The completion of the question-response pair puts Nish, the questioner, into the position of reacting to the response provided, e.g. making an assessment of it. Nish's response does not come out until 16 seconds later in a very brief form, displaying great hesitation and uncertainty: **"hmm. . ."** Again, Nish presents a dis-preferred response to the proffered explanation. The hesitation marker posted at line 150 of Log 8-5 prepares recipients for the initial indication of uptake at line 151, **"isee,"** and the possible production of a contrastive beginning with **"but . . ."** (as we saw earlier, at line 137). Nish does not produce a contrastive posting. From the Replayer tool, we notice that Jason starts composing his message about the same time as Nish starts composing his reply, which he posts at the same time as Nish's second short acknowledgement **"isee."**

Log 8-5.

150	06.50.51	Nish	hmm. . .
151	06.50.56	Nish	isee
152	06.50.56	Jason	on a side note, you'll be doing stuff of similar sort next year in Algebra II
153	06.51.01	Nish	thanks
154	06.51.11	David	ok so let's finish the problem

It may be the case that Jason's post at line 152, **"on a side note, you'll be doing stuff of similar sort next year in Algebra II,"** was produced and posted in such a way as to circumvent further specification of Nish's query. Another feature of this post at line 152 is that it (a) problematizes Nish's math skill level and competence (as indicated by the remark that Nish will not be exposed to the kind of problem they are working on until the following academic year) and (b) makes the matter of Nish's competence available as a matter of public concern to all parties to the interaction. Nish thanks the group promptly without further comments. David then orients the group to the business that they were working on prior to this whole question-response sequence by proposing the task **"ok so let's finish the problem."** Nish does not challenge this bid to move on and stops asking further questions regarding the same topic.

The most notable feature of this last portion of the sequence is that there is a shift in topicalization from the mathematics to the skill level of the participant. This constitutes a change in the organization of participation among members that, as subsequent interaction displays, changes the nature and distribution of entitlements, obligations, expectations, etc., among participants. One question left for us to wonder is how such noticeable change of the organization of participation happens. Here we offer explanations from a perspective combining conversation-analytic and peer-group-interactional approaches.

In their response to Nish's question, the three participants treat the formula **n(n+1)/2** as something already existing that has been **"incorporated"** (in Jason's words) into the construction of their problem solution. By offering this as established knowledge, they assume this knowledge is available and accessible to all, including the questioner. That there were questions about the formula does not mean necessarily that the questioner is incompetent, at least initially. It is only when others have attempted to respond and these responses (a) are deemed by respondents to be adequate ways of addressing expectable troubles with respect to the formula, but (b) do not resolve the questioner's troubles, that an alternative source of the trouble may be investigated or proposed to account for the apparent failure of the responses to resolve the problem. In this case, Jason presents the fact that Nish has not studied this material and cannot be reasonably expected to competently understand it.

Up till now, the differences made relevant by Nish's first statement and subsequent question have been attended to by the group as differences in situated, local expertise. The participation and interaction have been organized around addressing the differences at hand as topical, i.e., mathematical matters rather than issues of personal competency. Jason's posting in line 152 however made the issue of relationship itself—i.e., a person's competence or incompetence—a matter of concern. By saying that Nish will **"be doing stuff of similar sort next year in Algebra II,"** Jason comments on Nish's studied math preparation, which interactionally serves as a mechanism to shut down this line of discussion. The peer relationship is not maintained anymore, which means certain entitlements of being a peer no longer exist, such as asking a further question regarding the same topic. Such a breakdown does not however necessarily mean that the peer relationship is never to be restored. In fact, there are ways a member like Nish in this situation may try to establish the peer relationship again.

In the rest of the session, Nish remains silent for most of the time except at one point (about 6 minutes after his last posting in line 153), when he poses a very carefully phrased question about what a summation is (Log 8-6, line 175). This probably is an attempt made by Nish to get engaged in the ongoing discussion of

Log 8-6.

175	06.56.58	Nish	hope this doesnt sound too stupid, but wuts a summation *(two lines that are not relevant to this thread of discussion are omitted here)*	
177	06.57.34	137	The sum of all terms from a to b	Ref to 175
178	06.57.36	Jason	http://en.wikipedia.org/wiki/ Sigma_notation	
180	06.58.11	Jason	don't worry Nish, you'll learn all about it next year	

the group as a way of trying to maintain the possibility of participation and to re-establish the peer relationship. We also see that the question is posed in an artful way of "bracketing" the relationship issue by making the competency issue explicit by the questioner himself. By starting the question with a self-conscious statement **"hope this doesnt sound too stupid,"** the questioner is thus minimizing the chance of a similar judgment being made by the recipients of the question, i.e., the peers in the group.

This question is responded to by participant 137 with a direct answer, **"The sum of all terms from a to b"** and also by Jason with a URL pointing to a Wikipedia article, which presumably contains the information to answer Nish's question. Following his response to Nish, Jason also makes a comment similar to the one he made earlier that addresses the personal competency issue (but not the topic of the question itself): **"don't worry Nish, you'll learn all about it next year."** The way the question is taken up by Jason—by providing a pointer to the resource rather than an answer to the question—shows the change of the participation within the group, besides what has been made evident by Nish's lack of participation and his discreetly constructed question. Making the issue of incompetence explicit again shuts down Nish's chance of getting involved in the group discussion and re-establishing the peer relationship. As a matter of fact, Nish remained silent through the rest of the session until near the end. After the three other participants left the chat, which is approximately fourteen and a half minutes after Nish's question on the summation, Nish posts the following: **"sorry bout holdin u guys up"** (at 07:12:24). When the moderator thanks him, Nish seems puzzled and is not sure whether that is a compliment (Log 8-7).

Log 8-7.

273	Moderator	thanks for slowing them down and getting them to explain	07.13.16
274	ssjnish	?	07.13.27
275	ssjnish	was thqat supposed to be a compliment...?	07.13.46

Nish's self disclosure of his feeling again confirms that the way the relationship issue was made explicit as a matter of interactional concern proved consequential for the subsequent organization of participation in the group.

A Contrasting Case

Now we will provide a contrasting case in order to reveal how participants choose methods for making differences in understanding and expertise interactionally relevant. This illustrates how a question can be constructed to indicate the need for assistance while at the same time demonstrating the questioner's competence of being a member. In this episode of interaction, a newcomer to the group poses a question regarding the same formula in the data we have previously seen, and a response is provided that turns out to address the question properly without any observable interactional trouble.

Log 8-8 starts near the beginning of the second session by the same group. Jason and 137 have joined the session, waiting for others including Nish and David to come. A newcomer Qwer who was not in the first session has just joined. In response to the moderator's request to **"bring Qwer up to speed,"** Jason briefly describes what the group did in the last session and orients the newcomer to the resources in the environment including the formula, the discussion and the online wiki.

Log 8-8.

333	Jason	ok, so with this aside– i guess we should discuss our feedback from the last session	07.18.07	
334	Moderator	make sure you bring Qwer up to speed	07.18.34	Ref. to 333
335	Jason	ok	07.18.41	
336	Jason	for the problems last session, we came up with formulas to find the values for the columns	07.19.35	Ref. to 332
337	Qwer	in the view topic thing?	07.20.02	
338	Jason	You can see them to the left of this text; our formula for the total number of sticks or squares for any number N is given	07.20.03	
339	Jason	yes	07.20.09	Ref. to 337
340	Qwer	ok	07.20.12	
341	Jason	that was the problem we were given	07.20.17	
342	Jason	remains of our discussion is on the whiteboard and online wiki	07.20.39	

About three minutes later, Qwer poses a question regarding the formula **"how did you get n(1+n)/2."** That comes after some account of mathematical reasoning steps, which are composed together within the same posting (line 345, Log 8-9). A response is then produced and provided by Jason. It starts with Jason's signature marker **"oh"** just seven seconds later in a separate posting as an opener to his

Log 8-9.

345	Qwer	n=3 is 3+2+1 squares, n=4 is 4+3+2+1 squares ··· how did you get n(1+n)/2	07.23.35
346	Jason	oh	07.23.42
347	Jason	that's the formula for finding a series of consecutive numbers	07.23.53
348	Jason	1+2+3+4+ ··· n = ((n)(n+1))/2	07.24.08

upcoming explanation that consists of two parts: a sentence on what the formula is (i.e., **for finding a series of consecutive numbers**) and a mathematical equation that demonstrates this notion. Participants, including both the questioner and the respondent, then move on to other topics about some newly introduced features of the chat environment, which is not included in the log here. No further problems or issues are raised and the response is treated as appropriate in addressing the posed question. This marks the completion of the question-response interaction, which only takes about half a minute.

By reviewing the data of the two episodes of question-response interaction—involving Nish and involving Qwer—we notice some significant differences in the organization of participation in the group interaction. First of all, the two questioners used different methods to introduce *differences* to the group interaction: one makes a report regarding his own competency in math while the other asks a question regarding the math topic in a straightforward way. In the second episode of interaction, Qwer is a newcomer to the group who joins right at the beginning of the session. The group is still coordinating to get ready for working on a particular task of doing math. The expectation of participating, presumably already understood by the participants—also stressed by the moderator's request to **"bring Qwer up to speed"**—makes it legitimate for the newcomer to ask a question, particularly about problems of understanding the group's work in the previous session. There is little danger of interrupting or deviating the group from its workflow, as compared to the first case we analyzed. Qwer also has more time to focus on catching up to the group's work without worrying about keeping up with the current discussion on math, like Nish had to do. This perhaps helps with his understanding of the work, thus increasing his ability to construct an appropriate question.

Secondly, as shown in the data, each method results in a particular way that the subsequent participation is organized. In the first case, the self-assessment report introduces significant interactional trouble. A question only gets produced with the intervention from the moderator. It takes several turns and tremendous work for the group to finally work out the troubles among themselves and complete the question-response. At the end, the issue about the questioner's competency is raised and made explicit, which causes the questioner to be excluded from the group as a peer. In the contrasting case, there is no observable interactional trouble. An appropriate response is provided to the question, and the questioner is treated as a full-fledged member of the group in the subsequent interaction in the session.

Finally, the way the question is produced is quite different in the two cases. Nish's initial question **"the derivation of the number of squares** (is puzzling me)" lacks any indication of what he already knew. In contrast, Qwer shares with the group what he already understood through a description of the math reasoning in the problem-solving steps before posing the question. What the question could possibly be asking is made quite clear by ruling out other possible readings of it. By doing this, Qwer also demonstrates his competency at understanding the mathematical work and being a member of this peer group. The entitlements of being a peer are enacted in and as the ongoing participation. For instance, in the early interaction Qwer has with Jason, he is being responsive to Jason's effort of orienting him to the available resources in the environment, and he shows his engagement in the process. All of these allow the peer relationship to be preserved.

The Interactional Emergence of a Question

As revealed in the analyzed logs, in an online collaborative context like VMT chats, questions are not simple, well-defined queries for information, but situated moves within the group process. For instance, Nish's question about the formula goes through several steps to emerge. As a latecomer, he does not pose the question in the middle of the group's discussion of the problem. Instead, he makes a report regarding his own math ability in comparison to others in the group, which builds the context of asking a question. We have seen that the moderator solicits a question from Nish in response to the report. Nish's answer to the solicitation serves as a question to the group. The *question* is thus co-constructed through the interaction among the group, including the noticeable silence after Nish's initial report and the intervention from the moderator as a consequence. The meaning of the question is interpreted interactionally: Jason offers the history of what the group did as a perceived appropriate answer. The answer gets rejected by Nish, who subsequently reformulates the question. Reformulation of the question draws on the answer offered as well as the initial question as resources, which help eliminate other possible interpretations of its meaning. The group engages in a collaborative effort of building a response to the question. Their response is offered and considered by them as appropriate in addressing the question. However, the questioner, Nish, provides a dis-preferred reaction, treating the offered response as inadequate. The group respondents react by introducing another source of trouble, the incompetence of the questioner, and make this relevant to the group interaction. The consequence of this is that Nish is effectively shut out and the peer relationship is dissolved. In summary, a question emerges through the interactions of the group and goes through several steps; in each step, the meaning of the question is re-interpreted interactionally and its consequences are played out.

Math proposal adjacency pairs as a particular kind of adjacency pairs of interaction have been studied within the VMT Project. In particular, analysis of a "failed proposal"—in the form of a question—suggested some characteristics of successful proposals (Stahl, 2006b, pp. 445–451). Drawing on this, we have contrasted a "breakdown" example of a question-response interaction to a successful case in an attempt to pull out what a "successful question" may consist of. The analysis suggests the following characteristics for successful questions, some of which bear resemblance to those for successful proposals:

(a) *A clear question structure that elicits a response.* Making a report of one's math competency may indicate some problem of understanding, but not present a question of its own. It does not elicit a response from the group. A question on a math topic with a clear structure is more likely to elicit a response without interactional trouble.

(b) *Information on what is known by the questioner.* A question such as "**the derivation of the number of squares**" may be ambiguous as to what it is really asking for as there are multiple possible readings of it, such as the derivation by the group through a sequence of inquiry moves or the derivation of the pattern as a mathematical proof. Providing information on what the questioner already knew can help rule out some possible readings of the question, such as "**n=3 is 3+2+1 squares, n=4 is 4+3+2+1 squares … how did you get n(1+n)/2**". This may be particularly important for successful question-response interaction in a small peer group, in that such information also demonstrates the questioner's competence at being a member of the peer group.

(c) *Right timing and interactional context within the sequence of interaction.* Posing a question irrelevant to the ongoing discussion takes the risk of interrupting the group and deviating from the topic; careful work is needed to build the context for the question, and this risks failure.

(d) *Engagement in the group process.* Indication of being engaged in the group process is also helpful in that it contributes to enacting and maintaining the peer relationship. For instance, being attentive to the group's effort on catching him up demonstrates Qwer's understanding of the work the group did. It helps rule out alternative meanings of the subsequently posted question. Failing to engage in the group process like Nish does during the response construction is destructive to the peer relationship. Once the peer relationship is not maintained, the group stops the effort of addressing the question and the entitlement of asking further question on the same topic disappears.

Question-response interactions are key to pursuing group problem-solving strategies (Zhou, Zemel, & Stahl, 2008), building a joint problem space and sustaining the team discourse. Questions are ostensibly posed by participants for information seeking or help seeking by individuals. As revealed in the analyzed logs, the question-response pairs also function at the small-group level as mechanisms for managing peer relationships and organizing participation. In our case study, they can function to include—or exclude—a member. They can play an integral role in the social relations among the participants, positioning individuals as more or less competent and maintaining or adjusting peer standings.

Chapter 9
Resolving Differences of Perspective in a VMT Session

Ramon Prudencio S. Toledo

Abstract According to influential theories of learning, individual learning is most effectively furthered by the resolution of differences—whether the differences are those of cognitive conflict in the individual's mental processes or those of multiple perspectives interacting in group knowledge-building processes. This chapter investigates the methods used by virtual math teams to resolve differences of perspective having to do with the group's approach to working on a problem. A fine-grained analysis of chat interaction shows how participants engage in artful ways to negotiate or produce agreement by using each other's conclusions and appending them to their distinct, seemingly incompatible approaches. Participants negotiate which approach is in use, who is to participate in the unfolding of proffered approaches and in what order competing approaches are to be used. Participants also negotiate how solutions are to be assessed for adequacy and correctness. This interactional process of resolving differences drives the learning activity of the virtual math team by structuring the continuity of the discourse.

Keywords Negotiation · perspectives · participation · Piaget · Vygotsky · interaction analysis · difference

Learning is Driven by the Resolution of Differences

The fundamental theories of the learning sciences—going back to the classic texts of both Piaget (1990) and Vygotsky (1930/1978)—claim that learning is stimulated by an optimal level of differences among conflicting perspectives on a topic. Modern versions of learning theory refer to this claim as "cognitive conflict"—in the socio-cognitive psychological tradition focused on individual cognition (Perret-Clermont & Schubauer-Leoni, 1981)—and as the "inter-animation of perspectives"—in the socio-cultural dialogical tradition focused on collaborative small-group cognition (Wegerif, 2007).

R.P.S. Toledo (✉)
College of Information Science & Technology, Drexel University, Philadelphia, PA, USA
e-mail: ramon.toledo@drexel.edu

G. Stahl (ed.), *Studying Virtual Math Teams*, Computer-Supported Collaborative Learning Series 11, DOI 10.1007/978-1-4419-0228-3_9,
© Springer Science+Business Media, LLC 2009

While there is widespread agreement on the importance of resolving differences for stimulating learning, there has been little analysis to date of the mechanisms by which differences of approach to topics or problems are resolved. The exploration of such mechanisms requires new qualitative research. It is hard to explore scientifically the resolution of differences in the minds of individuals. However, the resolution of differences within small groups may be observable in traces of their communication and interaction. The VMT Project provides a naturalistic experimental environment that was designed and instrumented to capture the interactions of small groups of students faced with collaborative learning tasks. Moreover, this environment is an online synchronous environment—a type of learning context which has great potential for the future of education, but which is not yet adequately understood (Stahl, 2006b).

This chapter will identify excerpts from a VMT session in which multiple, conflicting approaches to problem definition and/or solution are proposed by the participating students. It will analyze these excerpts to determine the methods or mechanisms by which conflicts are resolved in the chat interactions. The findings will contribute to an understanding of the mechanisms by which differences are resolved in this case study. These findings will not only confirm that problem solving in such a context is driven by the resolution of differences or conflicts in approach, but will specify some of the ways in which such resolution takes place.

The analysis of the processes through which differences are resolved will demonstrate that the interaction of the students is driven forward (posting by posting) by the conflict between their different approaches and their attempts to resolve this conflict. A new posting accepts what was proposed by a previous posting and tries to re-situate it in the new poster's perspective. In the end, the group solves its problem as a result of such back-and-forth motion across differences.

Negotiation in Problem Solving

Participants in group problem-solving sessions engage in a number of activities such as framing the problem or problems, discussing and assessing approaches, executing these approaches and assessing their results as part of performing the activity described as a "problem-solving session." Whether the problem solving is done face-to-face or through computer-mediated communication, as long as there are multiple participants with their respective approaches, procedures and assessment methods, there will need to be some degree of negotiation. Negotiation, defined as "a discussion intended to produce agreement" or as "the activity or business of coming to an agreement" is a key activity in most group problem solving.

As a focus of research, negotiation has often been examined under theories of communication. This has certainly been the case in comparisons between face-to-face and computer-mediated negotiation in research built on theories of communication such as the media richness theory and media synchronicity theory. *Media richness theory* attempts to explain how the form and flow of information may impact understanding, especially through the reduction of uncertainty and equivocality (Daft & Lengel, 1986). It proposes that negotiation would be more difficult to conduct, the more impoverished the communication medium is. Consequently, face-to-face negotiation would be described as easier to conduct than computer-mediated negotiation performed through text messages. *Media synchronicity theory* proposes that communication effectiveness is influenced by matching the media capabilities to the needs of the fundamental communication processes, called conveyance and convergence (Dennis & Valacich, 1999). It identifies a set of five media capabilities considered important to group work because these are the capabilities an online environment would require for it to be suitable for the negotiation required for collaborative problem-solving.

Negotiation is studied under theories of learning and under the approaches to learning based on them, as negotiation is seen to be important in the interactions of groups engaged in learning. In the theory of learning called *social constructivism*, knowledge is seen to be socially co-constructed through negotiation before it can be internalized by children (Vygotsky, 1930/1978, p. 90). In the theory of *distributed cognition*, knowledge is co-constructed by interactions among people and their shared artifacts, including prominently by means of negotiation practices that result in establishing common ground for understanding (Stahl, 2006b, p. 183). A theory and approach to learning such as *situated learning* views learning in terms of changing relations within the community of practice, where knowledge is negotiated interactively and through co-construction (Lave & Wenger, 1991). In distance education, negotiation brings different people's ideas together, thus making sustained, in-depth knowledge building possible (Wegerif, 2006).

Negotiation is also studied for its role in the dynamics of small problem-solving groups within *socio-cognitive* theory (Beers, Boshuizen, & Kirschner, 2003). In such groups, important differences among participants' individual representations converge in a shared representation through negotiation. Prior to negotiating a shared representation to come to a solution, teams need to detect differences in individual representations. Two parts in negotiation are described, a process of negotiation of meaning and a process of negotiation of position.

The Mutual Impact of Computer Support and Negotiation

The field of CSCL is especially interested in negotiation in collaborative learning (Stahl, 2006b, chap. 8). The question of how computers may facilitate support for problem-solving is not only a theoretical problem but a practical one as well (Kirschner, Buckingham Shum, & Carr, 2003; Koschmann, 1996b). The literature includes not only studies on how computer support may affect negotiation but also how a group engaged in negotiation may use available computer support. Systems may consciously follow particular theories in their design. For example, designs that follow the rubrics of flexible structuring are intended to structure interactions. *Flexible structuring* operationalizes its design approach by (a) providing a restricted set of communicative acts that can be used in the interaction, without necessarily enforcing their use in given contexts, and (b) providing flexible constraints and guidance on the use of certain communicative act sequences in specific dialogue contexts (Baker & Lund, 1997).

Literature associating negotiation and problem-solving is frequently linked with the effort to find how computers may support negotiation. For example, an overview proposed by Lim and Benbasat proposes that "the use of computer support will have much to offer in terms of compensating negotiators with what they lack in conducting rational negotiations, that is, higher information-processing capabilities and capacities" (1993, p. 32). Other studies discuss negotiation in the context of how groups and individuals behave in a computer-mediated collaborative work setting. Thus group activity during which negotiation takes place may be analyzed from three perspectives; namely, (i) a group's performance in reference to other groups, (ii) each member in reference to other members of the group, (iii) the group by itself. Such a study may seek to characterize group and individual behavior in a collaborative setting through a set of attributes which would enable the identification of collaborative activity that leads to negotiation toward a shared understanding (Barros & Verdejo, 2000). Related studies show how computer-mediated communication affects group negotiation. Negotiators' performances in terms of negotiation process and outcome are affected by the communication medium; face-to-face and computer-mediated communication are compared to each other (Rhee, Pirkul, Varghese, & Barhki, 1995). Studies which focus on specific communication tools such as chat, may explore the interaction between the richness of communication (Daft & Lengel, 1986; Kock, 2001, 2004, 2005) and its impact on the recipient of the communication (Spencer & Hiltz, 2003). Conversely, groups engaged in collaborative problem-solving may use the affordances of computers in ways unforeseen by the designers of these affordances.

A Research Challenge

When problem-solving is done face-to-face by a group, participants demonstrate to other participants how they define, understand and solve the problem (Herring, 2001). Participants make visible to each other what, how and when they are thus engaged in problem solving, even if what is demonstrated is incomplete or inaccurate. Making the process visible is necessary to enable other participants to concur, disagree, modify or contribute in some way to the definition, understanding and solution of the problem. In a face-to face situation, making visible may involve both spoken word and physical gesture. When problem-solving is done online, participants see only what the computer application that they are using allows them to see. Whatever is seen, heard or read by each participant is dependent on the features of the application being used.

Though participants in a synchronous online collaborative problem-solving session make their knowledge visible in order to make it possible to collaborate, there is no guarantee that it is immediately possible to determine how participants negotiate the definition, understanding and solution of a problem they are solving. Participants may move in and out of negotiation mode seamlessly without being consciously aware that they do so. It is not even known how different their viewpoints are; what is hoped for is that after their problem-solving session, their shared output is greater than the sum of their contributed viewpoints and that they have, as a group, reached greater convergence.

To describe negotiation then means to see how participants produce agreement through the tools available to them. This entails a fine-grained analysis of the postings produced by the participants in the course of their online synchronous problem-solving session. The paucity of research which documents how negotiation is achieved in a collaborative online synchronous problem-solving session is a motivation for this exploratory study to describe negotiation as it is experienced and recognized by a problem-solving group.

In this chapter, we will be investigating negotiation in small-group online interaction. Through a detailed analysis of an excerpt from an online chat among three middle-school students, we will develop a notion of negotiation as the interactive production of agreement within a small group. Such negotiation can include the negotiation of the approach to joint problem solving, negotiation of the sequencing of multiple approaches, the negotiation of contributions to unfolding the approaches and negotiation of changing modes of participation. The analysis of negotiation in this excerpt will indicate how important negotiation is to the accomplishment of collaborative work and will note the peculiarities of such negotiation in a CSCL context.

Data and Methodology

We will describe how participants in a problem-solving session negotiate the definition, understanding and solution of the problem presented to them in the online environment. By using the actual log of an interaction, we seek to understand negotiation by seeing how it proceeds as experienced by students in a setting similar to a collaborative classroom (as opposed to a controlled laboratory). We use a method of analysis developed from conversation analysis (Sacks, 1962/1995; Sacks et al., 1974). Just as conversation analysis has been used to analyze different aspects of plea bargaining (Maynard, 1984), negotiation in the workplace (Firth, 1995) as well as the discussion and assessment of a theory in a problem-based learning group (Glenn, Koschmann, & Conlee, 1999), a method based on it can be used to analyze negotiation in chat. At face value, chat seems similar to conversation (O'Neill & Martin, 2003; Zitzen & Stein, 2004), but is different from it in important ways (van Bruggen, Kirschner, & Jochems, 2002; Vronay, Smith, & Drucker, 1999). Through this method, we describe how the chat participants initiate negotiation, recognize each other's contributions and negotiate how each other's contributions contribute to a solution, and how a solution is negotiated.

This analysis will be conducted through a description of the interaction of the participants as they conduct their negotiation in the course of their online synchronous mathematics problem solving and engage in the "members" methods for making those same activities "visibly-rational-and-reportable-for-all-practical purposes, i.e., 'accountable,' as organizations of commonplace everyday activities" (Garfinkel, 1967, p. vii).

Analysis of Logs

The excerpt we are going to look at comes from an AOL Instant Messenger (AIM) log of PoW-wow 10, conducted in the first year of the VMT Project. Prior to the session, the three participants—Mario, Alice and Fatima (*names anonymized*)—had an opportunity to look at the problem beforehand, but it is not known if any of them had actually solved the problem individually prior to the collaborative problem-solving session. The participants, who described themselves as middle-school students, knew nothing about each other. They were instructed that the moderator's role is restricted to helping them to use AIM and to post any drawings or images the participants may produce (line 011 in Log 9-1). Fig. 9.1 shows the problem as it was displayed.

Log 9-1.

010	Alice (7:01:05 PM):	Is this everyone?
011	MFPowwow (7:01:15 PM):	If you create a picture that you would like to share with your group. you can mail it to powwow or you can make a direct connection with me
012	MFPowwow (7:01:24 PM):	This is everyone tonight.
013	Alice (7:01:36 PM):	ok
014	Alice (7:02:04 PM):	so…...
015	MFPowwow (7:02:12 PM):	So you"ve all seen the problem. If you"ve got any ideas, now"s the time to start. :-)
014	Alice (7:02:29 PM):	Ok
017	Alice (7:02:38 PM):	Anyone have a pic?
018	Mario (7:02:58 PM):	Just the one with the problem statement
019	Alice (7:03:17 PM):	lol
020	Mario (7:03:25 PM):	Should we label some points?
021	Mario (7:03:56 PM):	Like, center is O
022	Alice (7:04:04 PM):	We could do that
023	Mario (7:04:21 PM):	Vertex where red line meets is, what, V?
024	Alice (7:04:38 PM):	The center?
025	Mario (7:04:47 PM):	No, down at the vertex
026	Alice (7:04:52 PM):	oh
027	Alice (7:05:00 PM):	That might help

The interaction recorded in Log 9-1 is preceded by about a minute of introductions. For the next four minutes, the participants negotiate the allocation of participation, the resources that they will use and how to approach the problem using the resources that they have. By line 027, the participants agree on who the

The Perimeter of an Octagon

Given the regular octagon below, answer the following questions:
1. What's wrong with this picture?
2. If you fix what's wrong, what's the perimeter of the octagon?

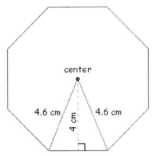

Extra: Assume that the thing you found to be wrong is actually right. What else could you change to make things right? What's the resulting perimeter of the octagon?

Fig. 9.1   The perimeter-of-an-octagon problem

participants are and the resources available to them, namely the problem statement and its accompanying picture, but they are not agreed on the approach to the problem.

The issue of who the participants are, is raised by Alice in line 010, responded to by the moderator, MFPowwow, in line 012 and acknowledged as settled in line 013. The issue of participants is important because posts whose intended recipients are unnamed or not clearly specified in some form or other, are directed to all the participants. Knowing who are the intended recipients of a post makes it possible to determine who among the participants is allocated participation. A post such as line 017, where Alice is asking whether a desired resource—a picture (stated as **"pic"**)— is available, is directed to all the participants, and any of the participants can be expected to produce a response. Mario comes forward, establishing the availability of the desired resource by stating where it is found, namely, in the problem statement.

The visibility of the indicated resource makes it possible for the participants to now make proposals regarding how the problem solving can be approached. Mario proposes labeling some points at lines 020 and 023, providing examples of how labeling can be done. The questions of lines 020, 023 and 024 perform several functions: they attempt to coordinate where the participants ought to be orienting themselves in the problem-solving process by pointing to words in the problem formulation. They also introduce labels as new resources, which can be used for a common approach to the problem. For example, both Mario and Alice use the term "center" which can be found in the diagram (Fig. 9.2) and confirm their use of the same resource.

The questions also propose candidate answers that display what the appropriate answers to the question should be. Supplying a candidate answer enables the person

Fig. 9.2 The diagram prior to
"labeling" by participants

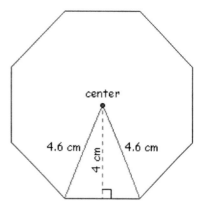

raising the question to show what an acceptable answer can be (Pomerantz, 1988). In this case, supplying candidate answers enables Mario to make Alice participate in labeling. It also enables Alice to get Mario to participate in the approach she starts when she asks, **"Anyone have a pic?"** in line 017. Through the use of candidate answers, participants are able to agree that the diagram is a resource that will be used in the problem solving.

The type of participation in the problem solving is also negotiated. In the process of agreeing that the diagram is a common resource, there is negotiation regarding how the diagram is to be used in the problem solving. The negotiation of participation includes agreeing in what order several approaches may be used. Thus in line 028 (Log 9-2), Alice proposes finding out what is wrong with the picture first. This proposal, if taken up, would expect Mario to stop labeling. However, Mario, instead of stopping, asks Alice to label a point.

Log 9-2.

028	Alice (7:05:16 PM):	Lets find out whats wrong with the pic first.
029	Mario (7:05:20 PM):	You name where the green line meets the base
030	Alice (7:05:30 PM):	B
031	Alice (7:06:19 PM):	I have an idea that might help us find whats wrong with the pic.
032	Mario (7:06:30 PM):	We could use good ol' Pythag thm to see what BV is
033	Alice (7:06:40 PM):	Lets not

After participating in the labeling, Alice repeats her presentation of an alternative to labeling. The tack that Alice takes in line 031 is different from that made in line 028. By posting that she has an idea, she is proclaiming that she has an idea that she would like to be asked about. Being asked for her idea would constitute an uptake of her proposal. She is thus continuing her attempt to convince the other participants to use her approach first, as she proposes in line 028. But this is again not taken up as Mario proposes to use the Pythagorean Theorem together with the labels B and V to find what BV is. Alice then unequivocally opposes Mario's approach and the ensuing proposal to use the Pythagorean Theorem, by posting **"Lets not"** at line 033.

By line 033, it is established that the participants are using a common resource, a labeled diagram (Fig. 9.3). While it is Alice who first brings up the possibility of using a picture as a resource by asking, **"Anyone have a pic?"** in line 017, it is Mario who initiates its labeling. By line 30 three points are labeled and all the labeling is considered complete. Subsequent postings use these labels; the chat participants use them in combinations to frame their discussions. For example, Mario proposes that the Pythagorean Theorem can be used to compute the length of BV. Through the labels, participants are able to specify which parts—initially with predefined values and later including the participant-supplied labels—of the diagram, are being referred to. Furthermore, by describing the Pythagorean theorem as **"good ol',"** Mario calls the attention of the participants to a consideration that the Pythagorean Theorem is an established method that they are familiar with. It is reasonable to claim that if the participants were labeling their own copies of the diagram, they would have had, at the end of line 30, a diagram labeled like Fig. 9.3.

Fig. 9.3 The labeled diagram

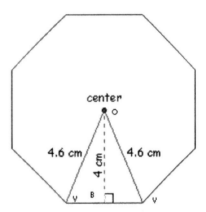

The labeling and use of the diagram is thus an interactional achievement. While the initiative for labeling is pushed forward by Mario, the participation of the other participants is critical for its acceptance, even though that acceptance may be a grudging one. This acceptance is displayed in their subsequent use of the labels.

The attainment of agreement regarding what are acceptable to the group as common resources does not mean an end to negotiation. The same resources may be used later to produce a new proposal to oppose what is being presented as a consequence of the agreement on shared resources. The outright rejection of Mario's suggestion to use the Pythagorean theorem is such an example; its position characterizes it as Alice's defensive stance. But Mario addresses the objection and continues his approach. It is noteworthy that Alice's rejection of Mario's proposal (see Log 9-3) is not based on what has been agreed about in previous postings; she bases her argument on the problem statement, **"It states that something is wrong with the pic."**

Log 9-3.

034	Mario (7:06:46 PM):	What's your idea?
035	Alice (7:07:01 PM):	It states that something is wrong with the pic.
036	Alice (7:07:08 PM):	so we can't find what BV is
037	Mario (7:07:31 PM):	Yeah, and I think if we 'found' BV, it would be something not possible

The rejectionist stance of Alice in line 033 opens up a possible range of responses. The stance can be ignored, it can also be rejected outright or it may be taken up. The latter may lead to a reorientation of the group to Alice's approach in place of wherever the group may be. When Mario posts **"What's your idea?"** in 034, it signals an uptake: asking Alice to state her position and suggesting a new orientation toward Alice's proposal. Mario's posting at line 034 comes across as a response to Alice's line 031. Mario wants to know the resource—the idea—being held back in line 031. Furthermore, it shows Mario interrupting his own presentation to seemingly favor an uptake of Alice's idea. Alice takes the turn and uses, in line 036, the same label, **"BV,"** used by Mario in line 032.

Alice now repeats, in line 035, earlier claims made at lines 028 and 031 by citing the wording of the problem. By referring to its wording, she positions herself as adopting the perspective of the problem designer and claiming what the problem designer would accept as a valid approach for solving the problem. She now states that what Mario proposes to find cannot be found based on what was said in the problem. The word **"so"** connects her present claim about the futility of finding BV to the authority of what was stated in the formulation of the problem. Lines 035 and 036 thus come across as extreme case formulations, where not finding BV has to do with the problem statement that something is **"wrong with this picture"** (Fig. 9.1) and where not finding BV is proposed as a phenomenon "in the object or objective rather than a product of the interaction or the circumstances" (Pomerantz, 1986). Furthermore, Alice uses the inclusive word **"we,"** softening a dispreferred criticism of what Mario is trying to do. The linking of the claim about BV to the wording of the problem also makes it possible for her to disagree with Mario without directly claiming that the latter is mistaken in proposing to look for BV.

The two different ways through which Alice and Mario approach the problem solving are now visible. While Mario uses labeling and builds up an argument to use the Pythagorean theorem, Alice uses the wording of the problem to argue the opposite. However, they both use the labels in orienting the participants in the problem-solving session and in their negotiating activity. An example of this takes place when Mario, in line 037, agrees with the claim of Alice by modifying his claim about BV. In response to Alice's posting that **"we can't find what BV is,"** Mario posts **"Yeah, and I think if we 'found'** BV, it would be something not possible." While his use of **"I"** qualifies his subsequent claim as an opinion, the claim opens up another way to approach the problem, which is to show that a computation of BV would result in a finding that is incompatible with known parts of the problem. Mario's post thus makes it possible for the participants not to have to choose among the competing approaches exclusively.

Alice's claim is accepted but Mario continues using his approach (see Log 9-4). He computes for BV and then makes a claim about the picture using the term **"central angle"** in line 046.

Log 9-4.

038	Mario (7:08:10 PM):	16 + BV^2 = 21.16
039	Mario (7:08:20 PM):	BV^2 = 5.16
040	Alice (7:08:23 PM):	I got it
041	Alice (7:08:29 PM):	I know whats wrong with the pic
042	Mario (7:08:31 PM):	BV = 2.27
043	Fatima (7:08:44 PM):	ok. now i'm following!
044	Mario (7:08:47 PM):	That makes the base about the same as the radius
045	Mario (7:09:01 PM):	That can't be
		Alice has left the chat room. (This is a system message.)
046	Mario (7:09:19 PM):	Central angle would be about 60 deg, that way
047	Fatima (7:09:30 PM):	yes
048	Fatima (7:09:35 PM):	i see
		Alice has entered the chat room. (This is a system message.)
049	Alice (7:10:05 PM):	Sorry
050	Alice (7:10:10 PM):	Lost connection
051	Fatima (7:10:13 PM):	what happened?
052	Fatima (7:10:15 PM):	oh
053	Fatima (7:10:26 PM):	why does that happen so often?
054	Fatima (7:10:31 PM):	nvm
055	Mario (7:10:43 PM):	Do you have what's done so far
056	Alice (7:10:51 PM):	What did you say BV was?
057	Fatima (7:11:05 PM):	2.27
058	Mario (7:11:10 PM):	With the numbers given, BV would be
059	Mario (7:11:11 PM):	yeah
060	Alice (7:11:14 PM):	I think thats wrong
061	Fatima (7:11:19 PM):	how so?
062	Alice (7:11:28 PM):	I know whats wrong with the pic
063	Mario (7:11:31 PM):	base would be twice that
064	Fatima (7:11:33 PM):	What
065	Mario (7:11:41 PM):	4.54 ish
066	Alice (7:11:45 PM):	The diagnol is not 4.6
067	Mario (7:11:51 PM):	Right
068	Fatima (7:12:02 PM):	Exactly
069	Mario (7:12:14 PM):	Otherwise, the red lines and the base are almost an equilateral triangle
070	Alice (7:12:32 PM):	I think this requires trig
071	Mario (7:12:50 PM):	So, one possible wrong thing is, this is really a hexagon
072	Alice (7:12:56 PM):	No
073	Mario (7:13:01 PM):	Right
074	Alice (7:13:09 PM):	Im talking about the triangle diagnol
075	Mario (7:13:11 PM):	Let'sd stick with octagon
076	Mario (7:13:24 PM):	So we assume 4 is right
077	Alice (7:13:32 PM):	Yes

Mario continues his approach and at line 071 points out a possible wrong thing, that the octagon (Fig. 9.5) is really a hexagon (Fig. 9.4). If the base and the radii are the same length, then the internal triangles are equilateral. Equilateral triangles have three internal angles of 60°. A regular polygon with internal angles of 60° would be six-sided (hexagonal), because the 360° around the center would be divided 360°/6=60°. The internal angles of an octagon are 360°/8 = 45°, forming triangles whose base is smaller that the two other sides. In showing the consequence of the computation of BV, Mario demonstrates that the value of BV results in a hexagon instead of an octagon and displays a finding that is incompatible with what is stated about the problem.

Fig. 9.4 Hexagon

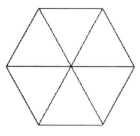

Fig. 9.5 Octagon

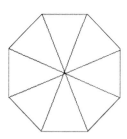

Between Mario's postings building up to the claim that the octagon may really be a hexagon, Alice repeats her claims about knowing what is wrong with the picture (lines 060 and 062) and offers the claim that the diagonal is not 4.6 (line 066). Mario's reasoning is based on the labeled dimensions of the diagram while Alice's reasoning is based on the problem statement that there is something wrong with the picture. By implication, its listed dimensions may not be correct, thus supporting her later claim that the diagonal is not 4.6. This seeming conflict between the competing approaches to the formulation is resolved when Mario accepts her claim by posting **"Right"** at line 067 and continuing his presentation by posting line 069 which incorporates her **"diagonal is not 4.6"** and his result **"4.54 ish"** in the post **"Otherwise, the red lines and the base are almost an equilateral triangle."** The acceptance of line 069 is designed to lead to the acceptance of line 071. After Alice posts **"No"** at line 072; Mario withdraws his suggestion about the inaccuracy of the shape of the figure through lines 073 and 075, where he explicitly announces an invitation to all the participants to **"stick with octagon"** that is, assume that the figure has the correct shape. This is then followed by line 076 where he asks the participants to assume that **"4 is right."** Alice's claim that **"the diagonal is not 4.6,"** is thus accepted, as that claim cannot be simultaneously true if 4 is assumed to be right.

Line 074 is an explanation attached to the **"No"** in line 72 and is an elaboration of Alice's line 070 posting about a possible use of trigonometry for the diagonal. However, It is instructive that Mario does not use Alice's self-repair in 074. Had he taken it up, another approach could have been started. But by taking up only the first part (line 072) of a two-part post (lines 072 and 074), as he does here, he is able to include the part of Alice's assertion, which can be taken as a rejection of line 071, and state an invitation to produce an approach worded in a form acceptable to her. Mario's new proposal **"to stick with octagon"** and **"assume 4 is right"** at lines 75 and 76 meets with Alice's **"yes"** at line 077, a token of agreement. The rest of the log after line 077 then shows the participants using the same approach to solve the other parts of the problem, confirming their agreement regarding both approach and participation in solving the rest of the problem after this contentious phase.

Forms of Negotiation in Chat

Negotiation in the Choice of Approach

Lines 020–030 reveal Mario and Alice trying to get the ensemble to work on the problem, with each wanting the ensemble to use their approach. Mario tries to involve the other participants in labeling the diagram (lines 020, 021, 023 and 029) to set up an approach to solving the problem at hand while Alice wants them to **"find out what's wrong with the pic first"** (line 028). By line 32, there are two proposals: Alice's yet-to-be-articulated idea (line 031) and Mario's **"good ol' Pythag thm"** (line 032). While there is no visible attempt by either Mario or Alice to make their approaches work together, both are keeping track of each other's approaches. This mutual tracking is made visible in line 036 when Alice claims, **"so we can't find what BV is"** and in line 037 when Mario agrees with Alice when he posts **"Yeah, and I think if we 'found' BV, it would be something not possible."** While both Mario and Alice appear resolved to use only their own approach as the exclusive approach which should be used by the whole group, and act accordingly, they come up with the same conclusion by using the resources that they marshal separately, present separately, but finally use cumulatively. This cumulative use is made possible by their mutual attention to each other's separate but simultaneous presentation of their own approaches. The timing of these postings also plays a part in these mutual uptakes.

Negotiation in the Choice of Sequence of Approaches

Group members may have their individual approaches to the problem. These individual approaches surface in the interaction if group members consider them relevant to the task. There is visible contention for which approach can be used first.

Mario reveals his approach first, but later, participants are made aware of another possible approach when, in line 028, Alice posts **"Lets find out whats wrong with the pic first"**—proposing that another task be done prior to the labeling being done at the present. The unequivocal opposition of Alice (made visible in line 033's **"Lets not"**) to Mario occurs after the latter proposes a claim made on the basis of the labels made prior to line 032. Alice proposes the exact opposite of the claim in line 036. There is a shift however here, because the direct claim that the group **"find out whats wrong with the pic first"** which would make Mario's approach come later, is changed to a claim about finding what's wrong with the picture, and pointing out that the results from Mario's approach would not work. Thus, by subtly dropping the demand to let the group use her approach first before labeling and using the same labels proposed by Mario, Alice is able to get Mario to stop his presentation to take up her proposal, and state a conclusion consistent with the claim being made by Alice.

While both participants try their approaches without a visible attempt to contribute to each other's approaches, both Mario and Alice remain attentive to each other's postings. For instance, we see Mario stopping to ask Alice in line 034, and in the process creating an opening for the latter to present a proposal. Alice then points to a drawing, a resource preexistent to the resource created by Mario. This technique to appeal to a preexisting resource is repeated in another section of this excerpt, in line 066, when Alice claims that **"The diagnol is not 4.6."** This posting refers to either of two red lines in the drawing (Fig. 9.2). The value 4.6 associated with the red lines is associated to the **"diagnol"** in line 066 and is made to contradict Mario's claim that it is **".54 ish."** However, similar to what happened in line 037, Mario accepts the claim and puts the claim within his own explanation. By making pauses in his own presentation, Mario is able to proceed with his approach by incorporating Alice's claims. Both proponents raise the priority of their respective approaches by invoking justifications that claim more than they initially try to prove, typically by including claims made by competing approaches. While neither Mario nor Alice is able to establish a clear priority that either of their approaches can be completely tried out first, by taking sections of each other's approaches, they come up with postings where they agree. They agree that BV cannot have a value which is consistent with known labels of the problem's diagram and that they can assume that the label "4" is right.

Negotiation in the Contribution to Unfolding a Particular Approach

While approach proponents do not seem to try to reconcile their approaches, there are attempts to elicit support from other participants. This support is solicited without a presentation of an overall goal to which the components of an approach contribute. Mario's invitation to label some points is not preceded by an explanation of how the labeling can contribute to the problem-solving; Alice's approach, which starts with a claim that there is something wrong with the picture, does not offer a workable strategy for finding out what indeed is wrong with the picture, but she does invite the others to ask her about her idea by claiming that she has an idea.

It may well be that labeling may be a way of orienting the participants. The plan to use the Pythagorean theorem is clear only after the labels have been put in. This overall goal is only gradually revealed in the unfolding of the interaction. It may well be the case that both Mario and Alice are merely exploring the problem space and do not have an explicit overall proposal that they can present to the whole ensemble. For their individual explorations to go farther, each tries to "recruit" participants to push the exploration along. This recruitment is seen in Mario's postings, which call on the participants to supply labels to parts of the diagram that Mario is indexing. Similarly, Alice brings up a proposal to find out **"whats wrong with the picture"** and then presents her idea that "we can't find what BV is." Mario agrees with Alice's idea and then proceeds to find a value of BV and concludes with line 046, which shows his approach that demonstrates **"Central angle would be about 60 deg, that way."** Mario thus contributes to Alice's method to show that there is something wrong with the picture.

The participants use each other's postings to develop a point of view which changes the direction of the initial posting, contributes to the unfolding of the other's approach and presents another picture for the consideration of the other participants. A new sense of the problem makes its appearance and becomes part of the joint meaning available to the participants.

Changing Modes of Participation and Negotiation

While participants involve other participants in the proposals that each individually puts forward, agreement is not reached by convincing other participants to adopt the proposals they advance. Agreement is achieved by including parts of claims made by others in competing proposals. Agreement is attained not by posting the result of a zero-sum approach that points out that a proposal is completely wrong, but by the appearance of a post which includes components of the other's proposal.

For example, it is instructive that Alice does not, at any point in the interaction, disagree with the computations of Mario, though she takes issue with the consequences of those computations. Neither does Mario take Alice to task for not offering any argument in favor of the claim that something is wrong with the picture. A consequence of Alice's claim is that none of the pre-defined labels can be trusted. Both Mario and Alice initially predict what they think would be the findings from their respective approaches. The **"BV"** which Alice claimed cannot be found in 036 is described by Mario as **"something not possible"** in line 037. When BV is computed, the resulting hexagon confirms Alice's claim that there is something wrong with the picture. Agreement is reached by incorporating the results of the competing approach into a conclusion of a proposal being unfolded. When these incorporations are made, there is no visible objection from the proponent of the competing approach, whose result is appropriated by the other approach. There is no objection from Alice when Mario claims that even if BV were to be found, it would be a value that is not possible. Similarly, there is no objection from Mario when Alice claims that the diagonal is not 4.6, a finding which is consistent with Mario's result that the representation is more like a hexagon than an octagon.

Member Methods for Negotiation

Participants negotiate when there are competing proposals that appear in their problem-solving interaction. As proposals are advanced, they may be accepted, rejected or ignored. Acceptance is shown in an uptake of the resources offered by the proponent of the proposal. The participants use these resources in similar or compatible ways. Acceptance thus means that the participants build on each other's postings and co-construct their framing of the problem, crafting their solution or assessing the adequacy of their proffered solution.

In the face of rejection, participants may adopt other strategies to change the allocation of participation. The spurned proponent may recycle the proposal or post an alternate message which claims to have some idea that would shed light on the group activity. However, this alternate message would require the other participants to ask the rejected proponent to reveal the idea. If this ploy works, then a counter-proposal may arise and begin another cycle of exchanges. If a proposal is ignored, its proponent may decide to go along with the other proposal, or present a new proposal, or lurk.

These member methods may not appear different from negotiation in a face-to-face setting, since acceptance, rejection or indifference can be communicated through postings as well as through talk. However, in chat acceptance, rejection or indifference may not appear immediately after the proposals to which they would be paired if the interaction were face-to-face. This makes it possible for participants who would otherwise be in an impasse to select parts of a long series of related postings that they can append to their own postings to break an impasse and thereby produce agreement. Thus we find Mario selectively appropriating the postings of Alice and including them in his own presentation. Similarly, we find Alice using the labels instigated by Mario in making her own contrary claims regarding the reliability of labels. After these appropriations, the interaction continues to another issue.

Participants recognize agreement when they post tokens of agreement in reaction to other participants' postings. Prior to these tokens of agreement, participants show that they are aware that there is some problem, that a solution has to be found, that the solution has to be implemented. The awareness of a problem is expressed in postings that supply additional resources to help frame the problem. For Mario, these additional resources are in the form of labels that eventually frame the problem as a type that can be solved using the Pythagorean theorem. For Alice, labeling is not as consequential since there is something wrong with the picture and by implication, the predefined labels are suspect. Mario proposes a solution which is based on the application of the Pythagorean theorem while Alice proposes a solution which ultimately assumes that one of the labels is not correct, and she chooses that the diagonal is not 4.6. Mario, in proposing the Pythagorean theorem, puts forward an approach that the participants are assumed to be familiar with, while Alice proposes her approach based on the problem-designer's formulation that there is something wrong with the picture.

We also note that the participants try to negotiate the order in which varying approaches may be applied to the problem at hand. Both Mario and Alice try to get the other participants to apply their approaches first. Both of them do not criticize each other's approaches and work independently of each other until such a time when either uses some resource produced by the other to advance her own approach. Thus, Alice uses the labeling "BV" that Mario first used to point out how the latter cannot produce a correct result from the latter's approach. Mario, in return, uses this claim to proceed to a computation of BV, which then produces a result, which is not directly traceable to the use of the Pythagorean theorem but rather to a set of properties associated with equilateral triangles, octagons and hexagons.

Taking these two aspects of interaction—the negotiation to agree on the approach and the negotiation to agree on the order in which the different approaches are applied—we find that the independent proposals of individual participants all fail. In spite of this, the participants agree that finding BV is either impossible or that its value would be "**something not possible**." The group participants have reached a common understanding of why this is the case. That is, they have solved the given mathematical task as a group. The group problem-solving session is then able to continue on the basis of the points thus agreed on.

If one conceives of the problem solving as the effort of individuals, then one would predict a strong likelihood that the session reviewed in this chapter would break down. Two strong-willed students brought incompatible approaches to the given task, and each vigorously resisted the approach of the other. However, through the processes of negotiation analyzed here, the differences were resolved in a productive way that led to a solution of the problem and a continuation of the interaction. The resolution of difference did not take place through a vote among preexisting personal opinions, compromise, bargaining or consensus, but through a subtle and selective building of each participant's proposals upon the uptake of the other participant's proposals. A shared framing of the problem—or a joint problem space—was co-constructed through the inter-animation of alternative perspectives on the problem. Through fine-grained analysis of the chat log, it was possible to characterize various interactional methods that were employed by the group to achieve a productive inter-animation.

The excerpt that was analyzed can be seen to have been driven forward by the interactive moves between participants, motivated by their different perspectives. From a methodological viewpoint, it is important to note that the driving force is not the individuals as agents, but the tension between them. The math solution does not arise directly from the mental representations of the individual students, but from the group effort to respond to the conflicting differences and from the interplay between the participants. Of course, the brains of each student were necessary to interpret the group meanings created in the interaction and to articulate the utterances that were posted in the chat in response to the on-going discourse, but the problem framing, the joint problem space, the solution path, the meaning making all took place at the group level in the visible, persistent chat.

What can be said about learning in this case study? If we talk about the group learning—having followed a path to that solution and having arrived at an understanding of the solution of the problem—then we can say that the group learning was driven by the process of interactively resolving the differences of proposed approaches. If, further, we assume that the individual students learned something from the experience, we can say they did so by "individuating" the group lesson, making it their own and integrating it into their personal understanding, where it can serve as a set of resources for future mathematical discourses (including internal discourses of thought). Because the effort to resolve differences in the chat discourse kept both Alice and Mario focused on the proposals of the other, it is likely that they will each internalize something of their opponent's perspective. In this sense, their individual learning will be driven by the confrontation with a perspective that conflicted with their own. Experiences like these lead to our ability to learn on our own by reading and even by thinking about perspectives that conflict with our own initial ideas. Thus, analysis of this case study seems to provide insight into grand theories of individual and collaborative learning through cognitive conflict and inter-animation of perspectives as driven by the resolution of differences.

Part III
Studying Group Discourse in Virtual Math Teams

Introduction to Part III

This Part steps back from individual case studies of group interaction methods to reflect upon larger implications of what can be seen in the VMT chats. It addresses issues of how representational practices are established across multiple chat sessions, how agency is distributed within the VMT service, how creativity in problem solving is supported by group methods of bridging across various discontinuities, how inscriptions are developed to organize mathematical patterns and how interaction in the online media systematically differs from conventional face-to-face interaction.

In raising their larger topics, the chapters of Part III provide answers to the issue of how to study group discourse in a setting like VMT. These chapters should be read for their research approaches as well as for their findings.

There are many reasons to study group discourse, and the research approach chosen should correspond to the motivation (the research questions). The VMT Project has an over-arching goal of designing a service to promote productive math discourse among students. To investigate the design of software to support online collaborative learning in the domain of school math, the VMT Project adopted a design-based research approach—a deservedly popular research strategy in the learning sciences. This involves gradually developing the software in response to frequent cycles of user trials in naturalistic settings. The approach calls for analysis of the effectiveness of the software in achieving its goals at each cycle of testing (Design-Based Research Collective, 2003). However, the approach does not specify a method of analysis. Somehow, the support for group interaction and collaborative knowledge building must be analyzed in a way that can guide design.

The VMT Project and research leading up to it are also trying to develop a theory of group cognition. This theory conceptualizes collaborative knowledge building as fundamentally consisting of group processes, largely linguistic in nature. The theory points to the field of conversation analysis as an example of insightful findings about linguistic group processes, such as the structure of turn taking in everyday conversation (Sacks et al., 1974).

For researching the nature of group cognition, the VMT Project has developed a methodology of chat interaction analysis. This supplies the missing analysis method for design-based research in the area of computer support for collaborative learning. Like conversation analysis, Project investigators want to take an ethnomethodological approach (Garfinkel, 1967) to understanding the methods that people use to collaborate online, rather than imposing categories from another theory or field on the analysis.

The VMT Project could not simply adopt conversation analysis for two major reasons:

- Conversation analysis is concerned with a very different context, one in which people are physically present to each other and are speaking and gesturing. In the VMT media, disembodied interaction takes place through text and other inscriptions.
- Conversation analysis is methodologically focused on how the participants understand what is going on. Investigating effects of design decisions imposes an external analytic perspective.

The VMT Project's development of a theory of group cognition and a methodology of chat interaction analysis in response to these issues are by no means complete. However, the chapters here make significant contributions by presenting findings related to group cognition and by showing by example approaches to studying group discourse in a setting like VMT.

Chapter 10 works out in some detail how the joint problem space (Chapter 6) is constructed over time by Team B in VMT Spring Fest 2006. It provides an analysis of the coordination of visual, narrative and symbolic group reasoning by describing methods the group develops and re-uses for creating visual representations, discussing them and then formulating symbolic expressions that capture the visualized representations (see also Chapter 7). By tracing backwards the up-take and re-use of methods, the chapter illustrates the sequentiality of the co-construction and use of the joint problem space and the temporal structure of the group's meaning making. The member methods or social practices (Chapter 4) that are seen to underlie the group's problem solving work are "bridged" across the sessions and thereby provide continuity of approach to the group effort. An ethnomethodological approach to noticing member methods at work is extended by the Hawai'i group's orientation to uptake of past utterances and practices, as well as by their concern with representational practices.

Chapter 11 discusses the relation of social institutions (like established practices) to the agency of students and groups in VMT. Chapter 10 provided a nice example of the structuration process, whereby individual actions become patterned into practices and how these practices are reproduced, for instance by different group members. They become habitual ways of acting in a given environment. Math education can be understood as the socialization of students into the culture of school math through instructional experiences in the established social practices, as well as by discovery experiences in which students are actively involved in collaborative construction of these practices. CSCL theory suggests that group agency can provide effective experiences. This chapter argues that certain characteristics of the VMT setting and the pedagogy of VMT events lend themselves to promoting the kinds of individual and group agency that promote learning through active involvement in structuration processes.

Chapter 12 describes group methods for supporting creative group agency as the process of structuration and habituation of new (for the participants) practices. These methods include collaborative referencing, remembering and bridging. These are particularly important for sustaining discourse across discontinuities. Creativity as discussed here is closely connected with the problem-solving practices and the forms of agency discussed in Chapters 10 and 11. The specific group methods analyzed here support the re-use of the representational practices and underlie the structuration processes, which are necessarily spread across relatively long time spans. Because groups have no persistent embodiment, they need to use special group methods like those presented in this chapter to establish connections across discontinuities.

Chapter 13 looks at the emergence of semiotic systems underlying the joint problem space in a chat session. Interestingly, the actors in this dyadic interaction are themselves both dyads of students who share computers. There is no apparent difference between the agency of these dyads and that of individual students, underscoring that the interpretation of chat interaction does not depend on the neural basis of thought as traditionally associated with individual brains. The two interacting dyads strongly influence each other's representational systems, while they also develop quite distinct (even contrasting) systems. These semiotic systems are inscriptional practices that related visual, narrative and symbolic elements (see Chapter 7). The analysis finds that the two interacting dyads arrived at different—though mutually compatible—representational practices corresponding to different patterns in the mathematical situation they were exploring.

Chapter 14 works out a "simplest systematics" of text chat, in analogy to the seminal work of the founders of conversation analysis regarding turn taking in informal talk. It shows how chat participants spontaneously develop group methods of communication that are appropriate to the text-based medium in contrast to verbal talk between co-present speakers. The fact that online chat participants cannot see each other not only means that they cannot rely on gaze, gesture, expression, inflection, etc. to understand each other's utterances, but also that they do not observe the production of the utterances (in contrast to the "animation" of graphical productions analyzed in Chapter 7). Text messages must, as a result of these differences, be designed and presented in ways that indicate how they are to be read. The methods associated with reading's work in text chat may be thought of as a layer below that of methods for bridging discontinuities, for math problem solving, for representing patterns and for other group habits of thought.

Chapter 10
Representational Practices in VMT

Richard Medina, Daniel D. Suthers, and Ravi Vatrapu

Abstract This chapter analyzes the interaction of three students working on mathematics problems over several days in a virtual math team. Our analysis traces out how successful collaboration in a later session was contingent upon the work of prior sessions, and shows how representational practices are important aspects of these participants' mathematical problem solving. We trace the formation, transformation and refinement of one problem-solving practice—*problem decomposition*—and three representational practices—*inscribe first solve second*, *modulate perspective* and *visualize decomposition*. The analysis is of theoretical interest because it suggests that "situated cognition" is contingent upon not only the immediate situation but also the chronologically prior resources and associated practices; shows how *inscriptions become representations* for the group through an interactive process of interpretation; and sheds light on "group cognition" as an interactional process that is not identical to individual cognition yet that draws upon a dynamic interplay of individual contributions.

Keywords Inscription · representation · shared practices · member methods

Prior work in our laboratory at the University of Hawai'i and elsewhere has examined the importance of representational resources to collaborative learning, including experimental studies testing hypotheses concerning how given notations or environments can influence learning processes (Suthers & Hundhausen, 2003; Suthers et al., 2008) and ideographic analyses of how participants make use of representational affordances (Dwyer & Suthers, 2006; Medina & Suthers, 2008). In order to broaden our understanding to a greater diversity of representations and situations, we have begun to analyze data from other sources. Sharing of data and analyses across laboratories is an important strategy for advancing our field, as exemplified by this volume. When invited to analyze data from the VMT Project, we selected for examination Team B's work in the VMT Spring Fest 2006, previously analyzed in Stahl (2007) (now expanded in Chapter 26). In this sequence of four hour-long

R. Medina (✉)
Information & Computer Sciences, University of Hawai'i, USA
e-mail: rmedina@hawaii.edu

G. Stahl (ed.), *Studying Virtual Math Teams*, Computer-Supported Collaborative Learning Series 11, DOI 10.1007/978-1-4419-0228-3_10,
© Springer Science+Business Media, LLC 2009

sessions, students address a breakdown in their understanding of how they solved a problem, making indexical references to inscriptions in a whiteboard as problem representations. The first major concern of this chapter is to understand the role of representations in these students' problem solving.

There is a convincing body of work showing that learning, problem solving and other group accomplishments are contingent upon the situation (e.g., Garfinkel, 1967; Goodwin, 2000a; Greeno, 2006b; Koschmann et al., 2007; Lave & Wenger, 1991). The second major concern of this chapter is the claim that this situated contingency is not restricted to the immediate situation or bounded at some temporal threshold, but reaches into the past at successively larger granularities. As Blumer tells us, "any instance of joint action, whether newly formed or long established, has necessarily arisen out of a background of previous actions of the participants" (Blumer, 1969, p. 20). In computer-supported collaborative learning, contingencies may extend back in time with the aid of persistent resources such as inscriptions in a workspace (Latour, 1990). Therefore, to understand the breakdown and repair of the selected VMT episode, we needed to examine participants' prior work together, and we needed to attend particularly to inscriptions in the graphical whiteboard in addition to messages in the chat board.

In the process of examining the data, we chose to focus on earlier sessions than the one including the breakdown segment analyzed by Stahl (2007). The episode analyzed by Stahl was early in the fourth session (each of the four sessions taking place on a different day, but in the same chat room). Looking back through the data, we found in the third session a remarkable event. It begins when Aznx (a self-selected pseudonym) says, **"I have an interesting way to look at this problem,"** and proceeds to describe an innovative representation of the problem that enables its decomposition into mathematically simpler expressions. Aznx's partners seem to quickly understand what he is trying to do, and indeed another participant, Bwang, supplies the actual visualization of the problem representation, using color to distinguish the components of the decomposition. Is this an instance of a brilliant insight arising whole cloth from the mind of an individual? If so, how were the others able to appropriate it so quickly? Or is the insight a product of group cognition (Stahl, 2006b)? If so, how did the group build on Aznx's comment without much apparent deliberation, quickly applying methods of problem representation and decomposition? In either case, if they understood each other so well, why was there a breakdown in the later session analyzed by Stahl (2007)?

To begin to answer these questions, we looked further back at prior sessions to identify how the insight expressed by Aznx and the group's handling of this insight were contingent upon prior interactions. We found that participants' actions in Session 3 were the continuation of prior *practices*. These practices were *joint* practices developed in the interaction of group members and shared by those members. We identified abstract problem-solving practices that were largely enacted as *representational practices*: methods for generating, manipulating and interpreting inscriptions that the group developed for handling a class of problems (Enyedy, 2005; Kozma & Russell, 2005; Roth, 2003). This chapter reports on the representational practices we identified, and the manner in which they were developed by partici-

pants and applied to generate the insights of Session 3. It then returns to some of the
theoretical issues raised above.

Background

Data

Data for this analysis was drawn from the VMT Spring Fest 2006. Groups of three
or more students and a moderator, all at different locations, convened in four separate sessions over four days to derive solutions for different algebraic geometry
problems (see Chapters 7 and 8 for excerpts from Team C). Participants interacted
using the VMT environment (Fig. 10.1), a software environment consisting of a
shared whiteboard and a chat tool with the capability of referencing the whiteboard
(see Chapter 15). They also used a wiki to post their solutions during and after each
session. These wiki pages, the software log files and a re-playable instance of the
interaction environment for all sessions served as our data sources. Our analysis
focuses on the work of team B.

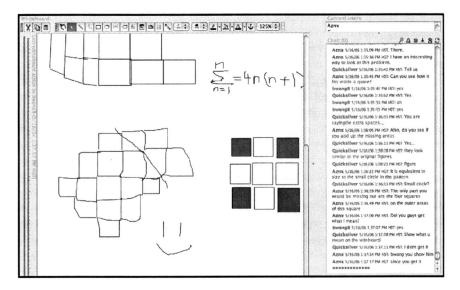

Fig. 10.1 Team B in the VMT software environment

We utilized the software logs and the re-playable version of the VMT sessions,
moving from one format to the other as needed. For example, the log maintains
the ordering of discrete events and their related information (act, actor, timestamp,
media, etc.). This is useful for recording annotations and reading participant conversations. The VMT Replayer provided a richer contextual view useful for understanding the participants' inscriptional work and its concurrent development with
the interaction in the chat tool. (Screen images in this chapter are from the Replayer.)

Method

The analysis began with identification of an episode of interest, and then worked both backwards and forwards at two granularities (termed *global* and *local* for convenience of reference) to construct accounts of the participants' interaction and accomplishments.

We began with the episode from Session 4 analyzed in Stahl (2007). In this episode, participants reference certain inscriptions available in the whiteboard, construing them as representational resources for resolving the question at hand. At the global granularity of analysis, we searched backwards to find chronologically prior episodes in which these inscriptions or related inscriptions were constructed, in order to understand how they previously functioned as representations for the participants. (Our conception of "related" expanded as the analysis progressed.) We bounded episodes by first identifying where the development of an inscription had been completed, and then worked back to where the construction and discussion of the inscription began as well as forward to the completion of discussion about the inscriptions. Episodes were first identified at the point where inscriptions were completed because this is where the inscriptions had reached the form in which they were available in future episodes. Chat interaction was as important as inscriptional activity in identifying and bounding relevant episodes, since participants' chat referenced, labeled and interpreted inscriptions in the whiteboard. This process of searching backwards for relevant prior episodes was repeated until we had identified a chain back to the first session.

Then the local granularity of analysis worked forwards within each episode to construct an account of the interaction within the episode. (Local analysis was not applied to the episode already analyzed by Stahl, 2007). This granularity was undertaken in a manner similar to conversation analysis (Heritage, 1995; Sacks, 1962/1995) as it is applied in CSCL (e.g., Koschmann et al., 2005; as well as Stahl, 2007), but attended to inscriptional acts as well as conversations in the chat tool. Discussions in the chat are often interwoven with inscriptional work in the whiteboard in a manner that distributes conversation across the two media (Suthers, 2006a) (see Chapter 7). A trace of the contributions made in each of these media at the level of speech and inscriptional acts provides a resource for understanding contingent interaction. On examination, certain events within each segment were annotated with observational notes to document relationships between individual acts. For example, we may see the reuse or introduction of inscriptional practices or linguistic references that demonstrate contingent relationships from one act to the next. During local analysis, the segment under consideration was sometimes expanded to encompass the episode of meaning making relevant to the question at hand. Issues identified locally also facilitated further global analysis of relationships between episodic frames.

In summary, we worked backwards "globally" to identify prior episodes on which a given episode's accomplishments may have been contingent; and worked forwards "locally" within each episode to identify participants' methods of meaning making with the resources available. The result is a *trace of contingencies* at two granularities that enables us to recognize patterns in the data and better understand collaborative interaction and its accomplishment in shared environments (Medina & Suthers, 2008; Suthers et al., 2007). Traces can be represented as graphs or organized as a sequentially ordered set of events. In the present analysis we relied on the latter to document interactional traces in the data.

Analysis

In this analysis we initially found a particular episode towards the end of the group project (Session 3 of 4) in which the participants co-constructed a problem representation in the whiteboard. This artifact played an indexical role in the group's interpretation of their solution discussed in Stahl (2007). Taking the construction of this artifact as a starting point, we began to document the contingent relationships between it and the interaction history.

The analyses presented in the following sections reveal that the formation, transformation and refinement of representational practices are important aspects of these participants' mathematical problem solving. The participants demonstrate four practices that are introduced, applied and adapted in ongoing group problem solving that spans four meetings. These practices are reified as inscriptions in the whiteboard, but are also enacted in linguistic interaction in the chat tool. Our analysis shows the emergence and sustaining of one problem-solving practice— *problem decomposition*—and three representational practices—*inscribe first solve second*, *modulate perspective* and *visualize decomposition*. The practices are interdependent and compositional. Each particular enactment of a practice either introduces a previously unutilized practice into the joint work or builds on a previous instantiation.

We begin with a description of an episode in Session 1 of Team B, in which the practices of *problem decomposition* and *inscribe first, solve second* are introduced into the group's work by one of the participants. We then describe a series of subsequent episodes in the next two sessions ending with our analytical entry point in Session 3 briefly discussed above. This ordering is presented to provide evidence for the historical development of representational practices in joint interaction.

Session 1: Initial Appearance of Practices

In this session participants are meeting for the first time in the collaborative environment. They settle in, ask questions about the software and begin working on their first problem. The problem description and instructions are provided on a wiki page (Fig. 10.2). The participants are instructed to derive a growth pattern, and then employ it to complete a table of incremental stages of growth in terms of number of sticks (lines) and number of squares.

Here are the first few examples of a particular pattern or sequence, which is made using sticks to form connected squares:

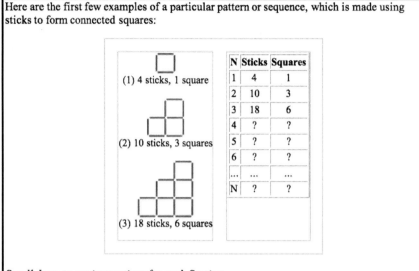

(1) 4 sticks, 1 square

(2) 10 sticks, 3 squares

(3) 18 sticks, 6 squares

N	Sticks	Squares
1	4	1
2	10	3
3	18	6
4	?	?
5	?	?
6	?	?
...	...	...
N	?	?

Scroll down to see instructions for each Session.

Session I

1. Draw the pattern for N=4, N=5, and N=6 in the whiteboard. Discuss as a group: How does the graphic pattern grow?
2. Fill in the cells of the table for sticks and squares in rows N=4, N=5, and N=6. Once you agree on these results, post them on the VMT Wiki
3. Can your group see a pattern of growth for the number of sticks and squares? When you are ready, post your ideas about the pattern of growth on the VMT Wiki.

Fig. 10.2 Instructions for Session 1

For the remainder of the discussion we will refer to the three participants using their chat handles *Aznx*, *Bwang* and *Quicksilver*. Transcripts are based on the VMT log file, which includes all actions in the software, including whiteboard edits. To preserve space, we have chosen to include only chat contributions in our transcript presentations and to provide figures as needed to display the inscriptions to be analyzed. Annotations in the right hand column of the transcript relate these inscriptions to the chat. Therefore, line numbers in the log excerpts will at times be nonconsecutive (e.g., lines 183–185 in Log 10-1 are omitted nonlinguistic actions that led to the completion of an inscription shown in Fig. 10.3).

Chronological Summary of Episode

Bwang initiates the problem solving at transcript line 182 (refer to Log 10-1 and Fig. 10.3 during this discussion) by posting, **"you can divide the thing into two parts."** He immediately begins to draw two sets of lines. One set is horizontal and

Log 10-1.

182	18:32:05	Bwang	you can divide the thing into two parts
186	18:32:10	Aznx	Let's start this thing.
206	18:32:38	Quicksilver	my computer was lagging...What are we doing?
210	18:32:49	Aznx	http://home.old.mathforum.org/SFest.html
214	18:32:58	Quicksilver	what are the lines for?

\<Bwang completes the inscription in the whiteboard (Fig. 10.3)\>

216	18:33:01	Aznx	go to view topic
219	18:33:05	Bwang	so you can see we only need to figur one out to get the total stick
222	18:33:09	Aznx	read the problem
224	18:33:32	Bwang	1+2+3+........+N+N
230	18:33:38	Bwang	times that by 2
232	18:33:40	Quicksilver	Never mind I figured it out..
237	18:34:01	Aznx	Can we collaborate this answer even more?
240	18:34:05	Aznx	To make it even simpler?
244	18:34:15	Bwang	ok
246	18:34:16	Aznx	Because I think we can.
250	18:34:50	Bwang	((1+N)*N/2+N)*2
253	18:34:58	Bwang	that's the formula, right?
258	18:35:15	Aznx	How did you come up with it?
260	18:35:16	Bwang	for total sticks
270	18:35:34	Bwang	Is a common formual
274	18:35:40	Bwang	formula
278	18:35:46	Aznx	Yeah, I know.
280	18:35:59	Bwang	and just slightly modify it to get this
292	18:36:31	Aznx	Aditya, you get this right?
315	18:37:45	Quicksilver	What does the n represent?
319	18:37:57	Bwang	the given
322	18:37:58	Bwang	N
326	18:38:02	Aznx	Yeah.
330	18:38:05	Aznx	In the problem.
341	18:38:37	Quicksilver	Oh
343	18:38:38	Bwang	The number of squares is just (1+N)*N/2
348	18:38:50	Quicksilver	We need that as well.
351	18:38:52	Gerry	I put Bwang's formula on the whiteboard

the other vertical; each set corresponds to the pattern drawn in the instruction infor-mation (Fig. 10.2), but the horizontal and vertical lines are drawn apart from each other. After completing this inscription (Fig. 10.3, top left), Bwang proceeds to explain in the chat window how the arrangement of horizontal and vertical lines can be used to derive a formula (line 219). The other two participants orient to both the inscription and the problem at lines 214 and 237.

Following the construction of the inscription, the group begins to develop a for-mula for the growth pattern. Chat postings 224 through 292 show an exchange in which Bwang and Aznx are discussing the solution and propose two formulas. Aznx then confers with Quicksilver to determine his understanding. With the assistance of the moderator at 351, the formulas initially posted in the chat tool by Bwang are inserted into the whiteboard adjacent to Bwang's inscription. After the transcript

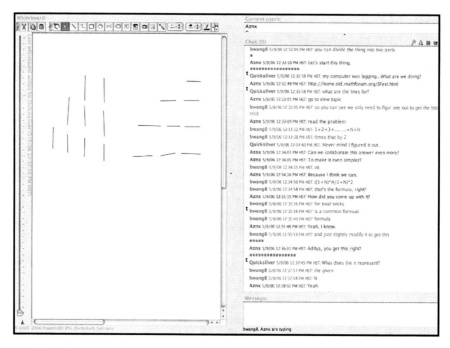

Fig. 10.3 Initiating the practice of visualizing problem decomposition

ends, the formulas are applied by the participants to complete the table, as required by the problem instructions (Fig. 10.2).

Practices Displayed

Several practices that are taken up in latter sessions make their initial appearance in this episode. Bwang has brought forward two related problem-solving strategies. The first, which we call *decompose problem,* is exemplified by his recognition that the vertical and horizontal lines (**"sticks"**) composing the geometric figure can be separated into two equal sets, so that only one set needs to be counted (lines 182, 219). The second, which we call *inscribe first, solve second,* is exemplified by his construction of an inscription before deriving the formulas for the number of **"sticks"** (250) and squares (343). This strategy is implied by the steps of the session instructions (Fig. 10.2), but is actualized by participants' actions. Bwang has also introduced a representational strategy, which we call *visualize decomposition.* His inscriptions visually decompose the structure of the geometric figure presented in the problem statement (Fig. 10.2), spatially separating horizontal and vertical lines in a manner that reflects a problem decomposition that can then be mapped to a formulaic solution. By inscribing a decomposed representation in the white board, Bwang has not only made a specific inscription available to the group, but has also made a strategy for visualizing the problem-decomposition strategy available. In subsequent sessions we see how the persistence of the whiteboard medium preserves and carries these resources forward to the future.

The three strategies are highly integrated in this episode: visualizing the decomposition in an inscription makes it easier to derive the formula from the decomposition. We will justify our identification of these strategies as *practices* by showing that the strategies are taken up in later sessions. We will justify our identification of these three practices as *distinct* practices by showing that they are sometimes enacted in different ways and combinations. For example, in this session *problem decomposition* is distinguished from *visualize decomposition* because the former is first expressed in language.

Session 2: The Practices Reappear in Different Forms

Moving now to the team's second session, we find that the participants have decided to work on a problem of their own choosing. The previous day's inscriptions remain in the whiteboard.

Summary of Episode

In this episode, Quicksilver takes the initiative and suggests working on generating a pattern for a pyramid at 1379 (refer to Log 10-2). The others agree on the idea and Quicksilver then inscribes a pyramid-shaped figure in the whiteboard (see Fig. 10.4, middle and outlined with the referencing tool). On completing the pyramid he then references the figure from the chat posting 1415, explaining that it is a **"side view"** perspective. In the ensuing discussion, the participants attempt to work out how the inscription can relate to the problem from the previous day at 1419. Participants all attempt to show how the inscription can be decomposed at 1440–1445; 1462–1464.

The exchange in the chat window concerning Quicksilver's inscription exposes an instance of the group's practice of *inscribe first, solve second*. At 1466 (Log 10-2) Aznx proposes that the group draw on the approach taken in the previous session. Bwang concurs at 1469 and further proposes aligning the current problem with specific formulas from Session 1, line 1473. Following this exchange, Quicksilver indicates that the approach the others are discussing is not compatible with his "side view." At 1493 he articulates that the others are misinterpreting the inscription. He follows this up by restating his objective at 1502 and, on Aznx's prompting at 1509, proceeds to draw a second inscription. He refers to this inscription (Fig. 10.5a) as a **"top view"** (1543) because it shows a pyramid as viewed from above. Aznx assists by adding additional lines to the drawing to complete the decomposition visualization (Fig. 10.5b). With the new inscription drawn from a different perspective, the participants begin a second round of discussion concerning the problem solution.

The **"top view"** perspective is a resource in a further exchange between Quicksilver and Aznx (1659–1760, Log 10-3) as they attempt to work out a decomposition pattern based on the new, **"top view"** inscription. The discussion results in both participants having a slightly different explanation for how the problem should

Log 10-2.

1379	19:13:18	Quicksilver	maybe a pyramind
1383	19:13:24	Bwang	yeah
1387	19:13:30	Quicksilver	although that's hard to draw
1391	19:13:35	Bwang	pryamind is good
1393	19:13:36	Aznx	Yeah, I liked that.
1395	19:13:36	Quicksilver	but we shoudl be able to managt
1398	19:13:36	Quicksilver	e
1415	19:14:25	Quicksilver	side view

<Inscription complete (Fig. 10.4)>

1419	19:14:56	Bwang	isn't this the same as yesterday problem
1423	19:15:03	Quicksilver	Really?
1430	19:15:10	Aznx	Except it's 3-D.
1433	19:15:12	Quicksilver	no it's three d
1438	19:15:16	Bwang	ok
1440	19:15:16	Aznx	So there would be more sticks
1443	19:15:19	Aznx	and blocks
1445	19:15:30	Quicksilver	and i was thinking of like 9 bricks on the bottom and 4 in the middle and 1 on top
1450	19:16:45	Aznx	So, how should we approach this?
1459	19:16:54	Aznx	What can we use that we already know?
1462	19:16:57	Quicksilver	Layer by layer shown in a chart?
1464	19:17:01	Bwang	well we can divide it into a front and a back
1466	19:17:02	Aznx	I'd suggest yesterday's problem.
1469	19:17:10	Bwang	yeah
1473	19:17:22	Bwang	using the formula from yesterday's problem
1476	19:17:32	Bwang	we can figure the front and back easily
1479	19:17:36	Quicksilver	this
1483	19:17:43	Bwang	we just need to find the center
1493	19:18:13	Quicksilver	Oh!! Wait...Your thinking of the kind of pyramid that is flat on one whole edge
1502	19:18:32	Quicksilver	I mean like a real pyramid that each layer is completely centered
1509	19:18:44	Aznx	Draw it.
1513	19:18:57	Quicksilver	i'll try
1522	19:19:24	Bwang	use the rectangle tool, it's easier
1528	19:19:32	Aznx	Yeah.
1531	19:19:33	Quicksilver	k
1539	19:19:44	Bwang	o ic
1543	19:19:49	Quicksilver	top view

<Inscription complete (Fig. 10.5a)>

be deconstructed. At issue is whether or not the top-view perspective is a three- or two-dimensional representation (1747–1760). Aznx's question, **"You want to do 3-D?"** at 1760, reveals that the two participants had a different understanding of the role of the inscription in the problem solving. Parallel to this discussion, Quicksilver inscribes a third perspective using blue and red to distinguish different levels of the pyramid (see Fig. 10.6). Quicksilver's response to Aznx's question is directed at Bwang at line 1765 in Log 10-3. Quicksilver asks Bwang for assistance in clarify-

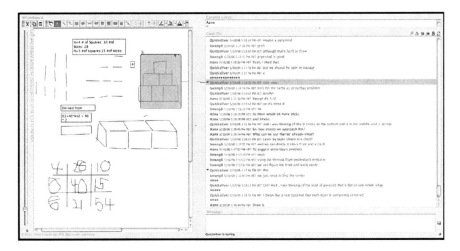

Fig. 10.4 Side view of pyramid

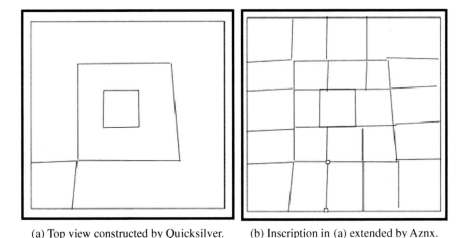

(a) Top view constructed by Quicksilver.   (b) Inscription in (a) extended by Aznx.

Fig. 10.5 Top view of pyramid

ing the group's activity. Bwang responds with a proposal to divide the layers of the pyramid into **"levels"** at 1777.

Further Development of Shared Practices

During the accomplishment of problem solving, the practices of *problem decomposition*, *inscribe first solve second*, and *visualize decomposition* are sustained in this session. These practices are enacted in multiple cycles as the participants attempt to build on their previous work. The references to the prior sessions' work in 1419, 1459 and 1473 indicate that deployment of prior accomplishments is a participants'

Log 10-3.

1659	19:23:42	Aznx	Instead of a triangular format of the sticks, we do the one you jsut made: the board format?

<Reference to top view inscription in figs. 10.5a and 10.5b>

1698	19:24:18	Quicksilver	what do u mean?
1708	19:24:42	Aznx	Look at my arrow.
1711	19:24:42	Quicksilver	ok
1715	19:24:49	Aznx	So you start off with one block.
1718	19:24:52	Quicksilver	And that's a top view right
1722	19:25:00	Aznx	Yes.
1725	19:25:04	Quicksilver	Well there's a problem

<Quicksilver begins to redraw inscription using color (Fig. 10.6, bottom left)>

1731	19:25:34	Aznx	So, the first one has 1 block.

<Quicksilver completes blue and red, top view pyramid (Fig. 10.6, bottom left)>

1735	19:25:41	Aznx	and four sticks
1739	19:25:48	Quicksilver	first block
1741	19:25:51	Aznx	The second one has 5 blocks.
1745	19:25:59	Aznx	Wait
1747	19:26:00	Quicksilver	no it is 3
1751	19:26:02	Quicksilver	d
1753	19:26:03	Aznx	You're doing it wrong.
1756	19:26:04	Quicksilver	3d
1760	19:26:12	Aznx	You want to do 3-D?
1765	19:26:27	Quicksilver	Bwang8, what are we doing?
1767	19:26:30	bwang8	?
1771	19:26:41	bwang8	you are trying to find a pattern
1777	19:26:53	bwang8	divide them up into levels
1781	19:27:01	Quicksilver	Oh.....
1784	19:27:05	Quicksilver	so that is the bottom level
1787	19:27:06	Quicksilver	I get it
1809	19:27:42	bwang8	oops
1812	19:27:45	bwang8	lol
1818	19:27:52	Quicksilver	what?
1820	19:27:55	bwang8	the last level have 9
1824	19:28:07	Quicksilver	yeah

<Quicksilver begins drawing yellow, red, blue inscription (Fig. 6)>

1831	19:28:28	bwang8	so we will just have to figure out how many sticks make up 3 by 3 blocks
1839	19:29:06	Aznx	Yes.
1843	19:29:15	Aznx	After that, we go up to Nth step.
1848	19:29:20	Quicksilver	Yes
1867	19:30:07	bwang8	ok, how do we figure that out
1871	19:30:17	bwang8	3*3 blocks
1876	19:30:26	Quicksilver	Break it down
1878	19:30:27	Aznx	I'd say look for a pattern.
1882	19:30:33	Aznx	and yes, break it down.

<Quicksilver completes yellow, red, blue inscription (Fig. 6)>

1886	19:30:40	Aznx	What other possible ways are there?
1889	19:30:44	Aznx	That we know of?
1892	19:30:52	bwang8	top, middle and bottom
1905	19:31:29	bwang8	top and bottom are 3 by 3 squares
1907	19:31:33	Quicksilver	whoops i drew it wrong
1910	19:31:36	Quicksilver	but yes

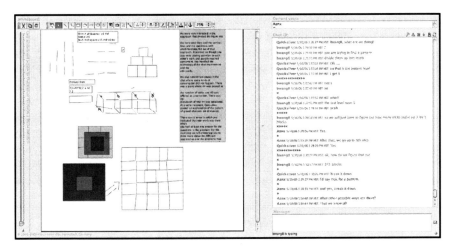

Fig. 10.6 Color used to show layers of pyramid

concern. Our analytic approach of identifying uptake of prior practices is aligned with this concern. This episode is significant because the group has established a "way of doing things" consisting of a recurring set of practices, to be affirmed in the next session.

As the participants worked out the pyramid problem they drew on their *problem decomposition* strategy from Session 1 by deconstructing the pattern into components. Quicksilver enacted the strategy *visualize decomposition* using color rather than spatial separation to visualize the layers of the pyramid. Furthermore, the *inscribe first solve second* practice recurs in this session as several inscriptions are attempted, which brings us to a new practice.

Quicksilver introduced a new practice to indicate dimensionality. He introduced a side view, and then inscribed three successive top-view perspectives of a pyramid. This *modulation of perspective* appears to enable the participants to make progress toward a solution. The side view inscription is almost identical to the original figure provided in the instructional materials (see Fig. 10.2). The difference, however, is that in the current context, the figure is a representation of a three-dimensional pyramid, not a two-dimensional triangular form. This distinction is indicated by Quicksilver at lines 1493 and 1502 in which he attempts to clarify what he sees as a misinterpretation on the part of the others. The construction of the top-view pyramid is subsequently initiated to address these different interpretations. The distinction between 2-D and 3-D nature of the inscription remains a point of concern in the ensuing discussion surrounding the top-view representation at 1747–1760. Quicksilver then begins to use color to articulate the three dimensional properties of a pyramid from a top-view perspective (Fig. 10.6).

Much of the group's work in this session seeks to coordinate the decomposition problem-solving practice with the group practice of translating the inscribed reifications into algebraic formulas (Alterman, 2007). Aligning these practices is a joint accomplishment that allows the group to progress towards a solution. An inscription can support the decomposition practice only if participants recognize that inscription as meaningful in that way. In dialogue that exposes the utility of inscriptions for problem-solving practices, we are seeing *inscriptions becoming representations.* Quicksilver introduced color into the joint work to amplify both perspective and decomposition of the pyramid at 1882 (Log 10-3 and Fig. 10.6). Bwang proposes a decomposition strategy at line 1777 (Log 10-3) that is then reified as an inscription by Quicksilver in the whiteboard at 1882. The nested yellow, red, and blue squares in Fig. 10.6 correlate to the top, middle, and bottom (1892) of the pyramid. Color is appropriated as a resource for problem-decomposition practice and as a representational tool to highlight the figure as a three-dimensional pyramid viewed from above.

Session 3: The Practices are Applied to a New Problem

The third session represents a crucial point in the group's collaborative interaction, in which they carry forward elements of their representational practices established in their prior work, applying them to a new problem. In the segment of work described next, Aznx initiates the *inscribe first, solve second* practice—producing an inscription that is then refined by Bwang, who appropriates color and perspective to display structural decomposition. These practices provide a resource for the participants as they proceed to develop the solution for the new problem. This episode shows three of the prior practices being brought to bear, in some cases applied by different individuals or using different inscriptional devices.

Summary of Session

Following a suggestion by the moderator to take up another team's solution in a different way, the participants begin working on deriving the equation for growing a diamond pattern. Team C posted this pattern and its equation on a wiki (shared by the several teams that participated in the VMT Spring Fest 2006). Figure 10.7 shows the figure and formulas posted by Team C. The Team B participants view the wiki, and begin to work out their own explanation of the pattern.

At time 19:30:38, Aznx began to inscribe Team C's figure into the whiteboard (Fig. 10.8a). On finishing the inscription, he begins reasoning about the pattern at 3911 with Quicksilver. Of concern at this early point is how the diamond pattern grows.

In the exchange presented in Log 10-4, Aznx is arguing that the pattern grows like a tessellation. Quicksilver requests explanation, and Aznx begins drawing additional squares on the top right corner of the diamond inscription (Fig. 10.8b). Building on the joint practice of using color to distinguish elements of the representation Quicksilver (3950) suggests using color to bring out the **"portion."** This portion references the component of the diamond that grows. However, Aznx does not use color but indicates the portion with a line (Fig. 10.8b). That this alternative visu-

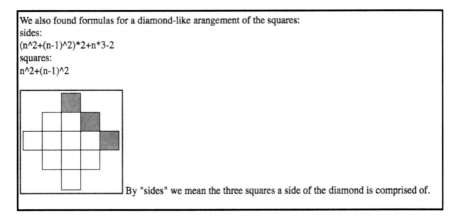

Fig. 10.7   Team C's solution in the wiki

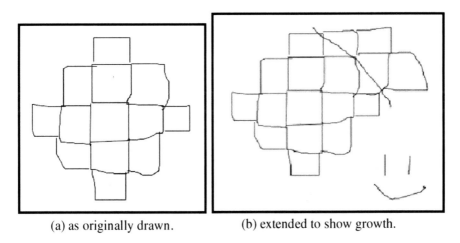

(a) as originally drawn.   (b) extended to show growth.

Fig. 10.8   Growth of a diamond pattern

alization is taken as an appropriate way to meet the request evidences the group's orientation toward *visualize decomposition* as a practice independent of the particular means of visualization.

As the interaction unfolds, Bwang initiates a transition to developing an equation for generating the growth of the diamond pattern 3971 (Log 10-5). Bwang copies Team C's equations into the chat window at 3987 and 3991 and Aznx attempts to make sense of the formulas as Quicksilver attempts to translate this reasoning to the inscription at 3996. At this moment, Aznx provides an opener into an extended explanation of how the pattern can be derived by stating, **"I have an interesting way to look at this problem"** at 4009.

At 4016 Aznx elaborates on the potential solution, noting that the diamond pattern is structurally decomposed from a square. In the ensuing exchange—4018

Log 10-4.

<Aznx draws diamond pattern, fig. 10.8a>			
3898	19:30:44	Aznx	lol, it looks horrible
3902	19:30:48	Bwang	lol
3908	19:31:01	Aznx	Ok
3911	19:31:23	Aznx	How would you grow this pattern?
3914	19:31:32	Aznx	Like a tesselation?
3917	19:31:40	Quicksilver	No
3920	19:31:45	Quicksilver	It doesn't tesselate
3927	19:31:55	Aznx	Actually it does
3932	19:31:58	Quicksilver	How?
3936	19:32:03	Aznx	Hold on
3950	19:32:11	Quicksilver	color the portion
<Aznx draws diagonal line, fig. 10.8b.>			
3959	19:32:48	Quicksilver	Besides, It grows in all directions
3962	19:32:56	Aznx	But it fits
3965	19:33:05	Aznx	You can do it on your own scratch piece of paper = P
3968	19:33:06	Bwang	ok

through 4060—Bwang and Quicksilver also engage with the explanation. Bwang indicates that he understands (4067), however Quicksilver is not as convinced. At 4075 Aznx directs Bwang to explain the idea to Quicksilver, presumably using an inscription. Bwang composes a new inscription (see Fig. 10.9, bottom right), using color to show the corners of the square that are excluded from the diamond. It is a reification of the description Aznx contributed in the previous exchange, but it also

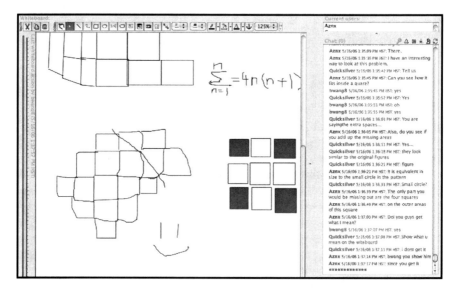

Fig. 10.9 Whiteboard at line 4096 in Log 10-5

Log 10-5.

3971	19:33:16	Bwang	lets think about the equatin
3974	19:33:22	Bwang	equation
3977	19:33:23	Quicksilver	yes
3980	19:33:30	Bwang	how did they derive it
3984	19:33:50	Aznx	There's the formula
3987	19:33:57	Bwang	(n^2+(n-1)^2)*2+n*3-2
3991	19:34:08	Bwang	n^2+(n-1)^2
3994	19:34:18	Aznx	The 3n has to do with the growing outer layer of the pattern I think.
3996	19:34:23	Quicksilver	the sides and squares
4000	19:34:55	Aznx	Right.
4005	19:35:09	Aznx	There.
4009	19:35:36	Aznx	I have an interesting way to look at this problem.
4013	19:35:42	Quicksilver	Tell us
4016	19:35:45	Aznx	Can you see how it fits inside a quare?
4018	19:35:45	Bwang	yes
4023	19:35:52	Quicksilver	Yes
4026	19:35:53	Bwang	oh
4030	19:35:55	Bwang	yes
4033	19:36:01	Quicksilver	You are sayingthe extra spaces...
4035	19:36:05	Aznx	Also, do you see if you add up the missing areas
4039	19:36:11	Quicksilver	Yes...
4043	19:36:18	Quicksilver	they look similar to the original figures
4046	19:36:21	Quicksilver	figure
4048	19:36:21	Aznx	It is equivalent in size to the small circle in the pattern
4055	19:36:33	Quicksilver	Small circle?
4057	19:36:39	Aznx	The only part you would be missing out are the four squares
4060	19:36:49	Aznx	on the outer areas of this square
4064	19:37:00	Aznx	Doi you guys get what I mean?
4067	19:37:07	Bwang	yes
4069	19:37:08	Quicksilver	Show what u mean on the witeboard
4072	19:37:11	Quicksilver	i dont get it
4075	19:37:14	Aznx	Bwang you show him
4078	19:37:17	Aznx	since you get it
4096	19:38:18	Bwang	we just have to find the whole square and minus the four corners

<Bwang completes the inscription in Fig. 10.9 (bottom right)>

draws on previously shared representational practices of using color to show how the problem can be structurally decomposed. On completing the inscription, Bwang states the solution in simple terms (4096).

Summary of Practices

The session discussed above reveals a productive group interaction. Ideas are exchanged and practices are enacted that build upon the prior interaction history of the participants. Across all the episodes we discussed, the participants applied their problem-solving and representational practices as resources in addressing different problems. For example, the practice of inscribing and then discussing a problem solution is a recurring pattern of interaction throughout the group's work. Further, for each of the above sessions, a different participant initiates the interaction by first producing an inscription that the other two subsequently orient to through the chat discourse (Bwang in Session 1, Quicksilver in Session 2 and Aznx in Session 3): the practice is shared and has been taken up by all participants. In Sessions 2 and 3 we see that the practice of *inscribe first solve second* is iteratively enacted and composed with two additional practices—*modulate perspective* and *visualize decomposition*. In Session 2, Quicksilver's use of color and perspective emerges in the joint work in support of both representational and problem-solving practices. In Session 3, Bwang appropriates color to draw out the particular decomposition previously articulated by Aznx. This is an example of the subtle ways in which the participants draw on prior work and artifacts to facilitate their current meaning-making practices.

Figure 10.10 illustrates how these interactions can be related across the sessions, participants and artifacts discussed in this analysis. The figure is composed of three layers. The top shows inscriptions and chat contributions from Bwang, the middle represents the inscriptional work and discussion contributed by Aznx, and the bottom layer shows the work of Quicksilver. Our analysis of each session is organized from left to right in the figure and suggests that practices can be formed, transformed and refined in progressive cycles of group interaction. Three practices are taken up by the participants consistently across the three sessions—inscribe first solve second, visualize decomposition, and decompose problem. A second form of visualize decomposition using color is introduced in Session 2 and reapplied in Session 3. Modulate perspective is also introduced in Session 2 and is intertwined with discussion in the chat. It is noteworthy that each of the three participants initiated a different problem-solving episode. This has provided key evidence for identifying uptake relations (Suthers, 2006a) between participants. For example, Bwang's use of color to show a diamond decomposed from a square (right side of Fig. 10.10), draws on (1) a problem decomposition strategy that he originally introduced but that was given new manifestations by his partners, (2) Quicksilver's practice of using color to visualize decomposition and (3) the prior practice of using drawings to reason about and structure algebraic formulas.

Conclusions

Stahl (2007) provides the following characterization of group cognition:

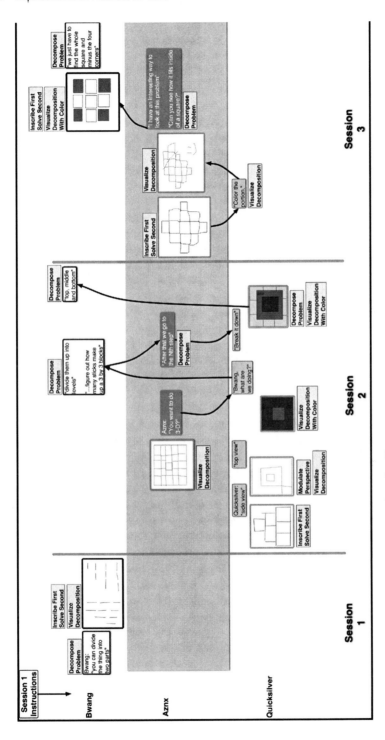

Fig. 10.10 Representational practices across people and artifacts

> Here, the term "group cognition" does not refer to some kind of mental content, but to the ability of groups to engage in linguistic processes that can produce results that would be termed "cognitive" if achieved by an individual, but that in principle cannot be reduced to mental representations of an individual or of a sum of individuals.

This description might be improved to rely less on judgments of what processes are "termed 'cognitive'"—a matter we won't pursue further here. The description can be generalized to allow for other interactive processes in addition to linguistic ones, an improvement that we must assume here to include our account of representational practices. Also, rather than the "ability" of groups to engage in such processes, it seems more consistent with Stahl's other writings to take group cognition as the processes themselves. Under this reading, the group must interact each time it "cogitates" about a given problem. One contribution of this chapter is to show that they don't do so in a vacuum, and so are not doomed to work out their methods anew each time. They can draw on their prior interactions and on the products of their interactions as resources for progressive group cognition.

Our analysis showed how uptake of prior resources enabled the development and reapplication of practices in the work of one group. It showed how the contingent nature of group accomplishments is temporally extended and is mediated by persistent inscriptions. "Immutable mobiles" (Latour, 1990) are powerful because they bring one moment's resources for interaction into another moment. The ability to re-establish mental representations can also serve this role, but they are not accessible to either other participants or us as analysts. In contrast, inscriptions that offer representational resources associated with prior practices are available to both participants and analysts in the sessions analyzed here.

Our analysis also showed that much of this group's work in mathematics involved the construction of appropriate inscriptions that support the strategy of problem decomposition and translation from inscriptions to formulas by visualizing the decomposition in an appropriate manner. In coordinating these practices, the group works towards a shared understanding of the inscriptions as representations suitable for their task. Thus, the group's practices are *representational practices* in an essential way: the inscriptions are not intrinsically representations, but become representations through the negotiated practices of participants.

This work sheds light on our questions concerning how the breakdown analyzed by Stahl (2007) could have happened in a group that seemed to be functioning so well, and the manner in which it was resolved. Stahl alludes to facilitator's doubts that participants all understood what each other were doing. Although it was not our focus in this chapter, we also see lack of convergence in the data reported here. It is conceivable that a group, "cogitating" in interaction, could produce a solution without any one person internalizing the entire solution. Whether group cognition consists of transformations of distributed representations (Hutchins, 1996) or is enacted in interaction between people (Stahl, 2006b), it is not a capability of any one person. Therefore it is not surprising that at the end not everyone is prepared to explicate the solution. Faced with the task of accounting for their work they have to re-enact some of it. Their inscriptions are still available, and their repair indexically invokes these inscriptions while also reconstructing them as representational resources.

The reapplication of prior accomplishments was a participants' concern as well as our concern as analysts, and participants' inscriptions likewise served as a resource for our own work. Organizing the analysis as a sequence of uptake relations (Suthers, 2006a) at the level of practices enriches our understanding of how locally contingent interaction unfolds over time. Interaction traces produced from uptake analysis provide a persistent resource for analytical practices—our own immutable mobiles.

Chapter 11
Student and Team Agency in VMT

Elizabeth S. Charles and Wesley Shumar

Abstract Agency is inherently a central concern for constructivist education. CSCL researchers need to think about the effectiveness of online learning environments in terms of how they encourage student groups to take active control of their learning activities. This chapter draws on the anthropological, psychological and sociological traditions and their concept of *agency* in order to consider the relationship between individual and group agency and to understand the differing constraints on interaction in classrooms and online. It then investigates agency in sessions of mathematical discourse in the VMT chat environment. Our empirical discourse analysis displays instances of significant agentic behavior and our theoretical review suggests that there are structural features to the VMT online environment that encourage agentic behavior on the part of students, individually and as a group. This has important implications for understanding learning and for designing pedagogic activities.

Keywords Epistemic agency · group agency · structuration · habitus · positioning

Computer-supported learning comes in many forms and hybrids. There is the notion of computer-supported collaborative learning (CSCL), computer-supported community-based learning (CSCBL), and so on (Shumar & Renninger, 2002). Enactments of such learning opportunities apply to students from primary school to university; they refer to formal and informal learning such as after-school and community center programs; and to online, face-to-face or blends of these. In all these forms computer tools and artifacts are used to create activities for intellectual exploration and to promote social interaction (Stahl et al., 2006). CSCL activities are designed to engage students in learning through jointly negotiating and planning how to proceed, generating questions and exploring possible problem solutions. In collaborative processes, students model and scaffold learning for each other. In short, learning in CSCL environments calls for self-directed or group-directed

E.S. Charles (✉)
Educational Researcher, Dawson College, Canada
e-mail: echarles@place.dawsoncollege.qc.ca

G. Stahl (ed.), *Studying Virtual Math Teams*, Computer-Supported Collaborative
Learning Series 11, DOI 10.1007/978-1-4419-0228-3_11,
© Springer Science+Business Media, LLC 2009

processes and is dependent on social and psychological mechanisms that support and sustain learners' willingness to collaborate and engage in productive interaction. The motivating force that drives the decision to engage with others to produce shared meaning and build common understanding (i.e., common ground or a joint problem space—see Chapter 6) can be characterized as *agency* (Greeno, 2006a; Schwartz, 1995). The primacy of agentic actions in collaborative learning is such that Scardamalia and Bereiter (Scardamalia, 2002; Scardamalia, Bereiter, & Lamon, 1994) view them as a guiding principle ("release of agency") in the design of their knowledge-building communities.

In this chapter we use the concept of agency to frame our analysis of students' collaborative participation in the VMT Project. Agency as a concept helps us understand the relationship between structural (including technological) constraints of the VMT environment and the actions of the student participants. This in turn informs our thinking about the strengths and weaknesses of these kinds of online environments for developing a sense of identity, competence[1] and self-efficacy. The aim of this chapter is to examine ways that students exhibit agency in the VMT environment. In the process, we shed light on how such actions interact with the affordances of the environment to promote learning.

While online environments like the VMT chat environment lack the bandwidth that meeting face-to-face might have, we have noted the affordances of the environment are such that they tend to support a more focused conversation around mathematical problems and objects. Further, part of the research at VMT has been to develop an environment that has a chat space, a workspace and referencing tools to make it easier for workers in the space to point things out to each other and keep track of their work (Chapter 15), overcoming some of the limitations of standard chat media. This seems to have yielded an environment that can support small groups very focused on mathematical conversation—perhaps more so than a traditional classroom with its many distractions. If this potential exists, then the question of how individuals and groups act—and act in ways that are independent of the cultural and structural forces they feel around them (agency)—is an important question in understanding learning and the development of new knowledge. Before moving forward let us briefly situate agency within the CSCL literature.

Briefly Defining Agency

Most notably, the notion of agency has been the focus of work conducted by Scardamalia and her colleagues (Scardamalia, 2000; Scardamalia & Bereiter, 1991; Scardamalia et al., 1994). In the course of observing students' use of CSILE and Knowledge Forum, she coined the term *epistemic agency* to describe the acts of

---

[1] Our definition of competence involves development in one's ability to better use resources and opportunities. This includes making full use of opportunities to practice thinking and cognitive skills (e.g., attending, selecting, monitoring) in the course of communicating with others (or self-reflecting) toward some mutually agreed purpose, such as problem solving.

initiative taken by students—very young in some cases—to present their ideas and to negotiate a fit between personal knowledge and the knowledge of others, "using contrasts to spark and sustain knowledge advancement rather than depending on others to chart that course for them" (Halewood, Reeve, & Scardamalia, 2005, p. 2). In taking on responsibility for aspects of their own learning and developing competency, students demonstrate their epistemic agency, for example setting goals, self-evaluating and doing long-range planning. Accordingly, Scardamalia (2000) views epistemic agency as one of the two major components of productive engagement. From the collaborative-learning perspective, epistemic agency implicates the students' willingness to see themselves as members of a community, hence supporting their community identity. Community identity and epistemic agency are seen as mutually constituting the students' engagement in community discourse (Brett, Nason & Woodruff, 2002), along with the development of requisite competencies. We will return to this line of reasoning below.

What is unique in our approach to agency is that we introduce communication as a component and focus on its role as the mediating device, connecting individuals and concepts on both social (group) and cognitive (individual) levels. Such ideas are similar to the thinking of scholars such as Greeno and Sfard. Greeno (2006a) talks about the distribution of agency, which might be akin to distributed cognition (Hutchins, 1996) but involves the ways in which individuals can and do contribute to collective thinking in collaborative activities—much as do group cognition analyses in this volume (e.g., Chapters 5, 26 and 28). In the process, he introduces notions of positioning, which we will discuss in more detail shortly. Sfard (2008), in her work on mathematical learning, suggests there is an intimate connection between the communication of mathematics and mathematical thinking. She refers to this unity of communication and cognition as "commognition." In a recent review of Sfard's new book, Stahl (Chapter 3) discusses how for Sfard thinking and math objects are themselves products of the discursive process. These "reifications" that get objectified and internalized by individuals come out of interaction and are re-introduced into interaction. These are critical points for us because they raise central questions about the value of online working environments like VMT and also the importance of theoretical constructs like agency.

In the following sections we elaborate on agency as a theoretical construct by looking at how it is viewed in different disciplines. As a guide to reading this chapter we suggest that those readers who prefer to dive into data before looking at the theoretical perspectives skip ahead to the data analysis sections, and return to the upcoming section afterwards.

Perspectives on Agency as a Theoretical Construct

Structure/Culture/Agency

As a particular case of the larger Western preoccupation with determinism versus free will, sociology and the social sciences since their inception have tried to think through the relationship between structure, culture and agency. One interesting perspective on the structure/culture/agency triad is the thinking of the British sociologist Giddens. For him, structure is a product of the pattern of practices in which social actors engage; structure is emergent from human activity. Different levels of structure emerge out of different forms of human practice: signification, legitimation and domination. Signification has to do with the production of meaning, legitimation has to do with the production of moral order through norms and values and domination is produced through the exercise of power (Giddens, 1979, 1984). In Giddens' view there are rules and resources. From Giddens' perspective, rules are primary and they are the things that generate resources. It is the rules that shape the pattern of interaction, and then those interactions redefine the rules in a dialectical way. For Giddens the resources produced out of this dynamic forms what is for him the structure (Porpora, 1989, 1993).

The strength of Giddens' perspective is that structures are produced by human activity, but once they exist they then work to constrain future human action. Unfortunately, there are several weaknesses in the Giddensian model. Campbell (1998) has suggested that Giddens—like much of contemporary sociology—collapses a notion of action which would be personal action with the notion of social action, actions that are oriented toward others in a particular context. While there are problems with Campbell's view too, that are too subtle to go into here, there is an important point that agency is not just patterned action but can also be action that breaks with patterns and well-defined sets of rules. A second more critical problem of Giddens is his view of structure. While structure can be defined at a micro level as the patterns, interactions and resources generated in social activity, there is a larger level of structure that has to do with the more fixed sets of relations that people find themselves in, such as social class, race, gender, geographic groupings (Porpora, 1993). These larger structural forces play an important influencing role in how individuals "play the game of life" as it were.

It is this larger notion of structure that, in the French sociologist Bourdieu's terms, produces patterns of activity. Habitual action is structured through activity of the past but is then used to structure and classify future activity as well as things in the world. By combining the dialectics used by both Bourdieu and Giddens we may be able to see a way to overcome the primacy of either structure or agency and succeed in showing how dialectically they are the product of each other. Giddens adds a further dimension to structure and that is that people are conscious of their practices and so they engage with structure in a self-conscious effort to reproduce it or change it. So there is a reflexive quality to agency. While Bourdieu is also aware of this self-consciousness, he is much more interested in the way that most human practice is habitual or semi-conscious. Bourdieu is aware of the fact that social actors often have a "strategy" for "playing the game" of life, but they are also often in his mind "shooting from the hip" (Bourdieu, 1990). This foreshadows ideas of improvisation that we will discuss shortly.

Giddens' and Bourdieu's understanding of the relationship between structure, culture and agency have proven useful for our analysis at both the level of the VMT Project itself and of the student interactions. From its beginning, the VMT Project has been a design-based development project. The practices of students using earlier generations of the chat environment influenced design decisions for future environments. The goal of the design team has been to enable future activity that students sought to engage in and to constrain activity that seemed to detract from the productive working together of the problem-solving teams. But also at the level of the activity of the participants themselves, solving a problem and interacting with the technology begins to build up a kind of small-group structure, which then carries through to the remainder of the session and may influence future work sessions of the same group. So looking at the micro interactions of structure and agency for a particular problem-solving team can help us understand how collaborative problem-solving works in this environment and how to further support team work.

Creativity/Imagination/Identity

In a major article on agency, Emirbayer and Mische (1998) offer a critique of the Giddensian and Bourdieuian position. Essentially they argue that the focus of Bourdieu and Giddens is too much on structure and the production of habitual action and not enough on the creative emancipatory potential of human agency. The conflict between Giddens and Bourdieu versus Emirbayer and Mische involves a paradox in social theory. On the one hand, social theorists have to account for the dramatic patterning of human action and the way much human behavior can be predictable. On the other hand, they must also account for the production of new culture and the process of cultural change. These two realities are difficult to contain within the same theory and theorists tend to emphasize one pole or the other. Emirbayer and Mische by implication echo Campbell's (1998) concern for the collapse of action with social action. Each of these theorists wants to preserve a space where individuals act out of their own sense of a personal meaning that is different than the forms of social action where meanings are oriented toward outsiders and one's socially-defined identity. These ideas could also be compared to those of Cobb (2004), who draws on Gee (1992) in his efforts to think about how a mathematical identity is produced by interacting in a classroom. While of course all meaning, personal or otherwise, is produced in social contexts and is by necessity socially constructed, the distinctions they are trying to maintain are important. We want to be able to make a distinction analytically between the kinds of action that yield well-worn paths of activity that are taken up by large numbers of participants and constitute rule-driven behavior and those forms of action that come from some creative space that break the patterns of activity and forge new ground. Further, following Sfard (2008) and others, since these insights will be produced dialogically and in communicative interactions we want to be able to see this creative form of agency (however rare it is) as both an achievement of individual persons and groups. And so it makes sense to see *individual agency* and *group agency* as different sides of the same coin.

Our hope then is to view agency as an act of creativity, which draws these two perspectives closer. Thus our definition of creativity does not fit with the standard psychological definition, focused on the isolated individual organism. We would argue that much of social life is constrained by cultures and structures that are both the result of larger material relations and the product of past action—both conscious and habitual—and that these constraints are something that social actors must indeed face. But, as we will discuss below, there are also creative potentials for social actors to engage with those structures in innovative ways. We feel that online services like the one the VMT Project is constructing in fact facilitate the creative and imaginative potentials when students attempt to deal with the constraints around learning math.

Holland, Lachicotte, Skinner, and Cain (1998) also make an important contribution to the discussion of agency. They weave together the notions of agency and identity—thoughts that are reminiscent of Emirbayer and Mische (1998). They describe agency as mediated by identity; in turn, identity is shaped through activity in social practice and is the principle way in which individuals come to "care about and care for what is going on around them" (p. 5). What is different in their argument is that agency and identity, as mutually constitutive aspects of human interactions, are made possible through psychosocial mechanisms, i.e., improvisations and/or imagination (the creation of *"figured worlds"*). The former are creative actions mediated by individuals' sensibilities—what we might also consider an awareness of circumstance and needs. The latter allow individuals to participate in resulting activities and develop new (or adapt/appropriate) language, signs and symbols (communication) to organize themselves and others in exploratory ways. This might also be referred to as the disposition to engage in "pretending" (Gee, 1992).

Collaboration/Communication/Competence

In addition to the discussion of collaboration and communication discussed early on, Bandura's (2001) model of agency offers a way to take the above characterizations into consideration and describe them in a developing comprehensive theory. This theory articulates a model of agency composed of four key components, which account for cognitive, affective and psychosocial characteristics: (1) intentionality, (2) forethought, (3) self-regulation and (4) self-efficacy. In this light, agency becomes a larger and more inclusive construct involving cognitive competencies included in forethought and self-regulation, e.g., selecting, planning, reasoning, monitoring progress, reflecting. In productive collaborations these four characteristics produce emergent collective actions and artifacts that describe truly jointly shared enterprises as individuals take up mutual responsibility and accountability[2] for the activity and its product (Charles & Kolodner, in revision). In this fashion, self-regulation and self-efficacy are more than cognitive acts and become socially

---

[2]This mutual sharing of responsibility and accountability might be a social form of sharing in the *cognitive load* (Sweller, van Merrienboer, & Paas, 1998) required to perform cognitive tasks such as problem solving.

and culturally driven ones as well. In fact, Bandura claims that self-efficacy promotes a "pro-social" orientation. This is consistent with Holland (1998) and her
colleagues' thoughts on caring.

Positioning

A final theoretical notion that needs to be briefly discussed is the notion of positioning. Positioning theory is a major shift away from the traditional role theories
in sociology and psychology. It is a theory that comes from a social constructionist
perspective and is very much in concert with the ways we have been trying to think
about the dialectic tensions among structure/culture/agency. The notion of positioning suggests that the social positions that individuals take up are themselves produced within the social context and not fixed in advance from outside (Davies &
Harré, 1990; Langenhove & Harré, 1999). From the position on "up takes" in a conversation, to the positions one has in an organization, to larger positions like social
class, positioning theory focuses on the ways in which these positions are socially
produced and on the dynamics of their characterizations. While radical social con-
structionism might suggest there is no larger structure and that all social relations are
completely fluid, we would not embrace such extremes of position. We would argue
that indeed some social positions that actors hold are more imposed, stable and difficult to struggle against. Further, we would argue that power relations in society are
such that individuals can be positioned against their will, and that it becomes very
difficult for them to resist that positioning. Often resistance is one of the ways that
a subordinate position is maintained. The notion of positioning has a lot in common
with the ideas of structure, culture and agency; it is an alternative way to talk about
these issues.

What is important about bringing positioning into this conversation is that it is
a dynamic way of seeing the micro-level of the structure/agency coupling being
worked out. In the VMT chats we do not have data on students' socio-economic
backgrounds or the schools they attend. This data might be interesting to capture for
future research, but it is not data that was part of the original project. So the larger
levels of structure are a bit more difficult for us to comment on. But what we can
see in the VMT chats clearly is that the interactions that students engage in are very
dynamic. In contrast to some of the thinking in role theory, roles that students find
themselves in either by being positioned by others or by their own efforts shift over
the course of even a single work session (Harré & Moghaddam, 2003). Sometimes
these shifts in position are related to insights the group makes, and so positioning
is part of the process of group cognition. Sometimes shifts in position or the ways
students find themselves positioned by others detracts from the group's ability to
make progress. So understanding the process of this micro-level positioning is an
important part of understanding group and individual forms of agency—and how
they are inextricably intertwined.

Greeno (2006a) distinguishes different types of positioning. He talks about systemic and semantic positioning. While systemic positioning refers to what might be traditional views on the topic as discussed above, semantic positioning as a construct is more cognitive in nature. It refers to the sensitivities and awareness, the choices and judgments (attending, selecting, monitoring) involved in making collective meaning, and possibly also the creative activities that emerge out of collaboration and group problem solving.

Summary

Taking all these theoretical ideas into consideration, we will now move to the analysis of VMT data in an effort to show some of the creative moments of agency and how the VMT system creates an opening for students who are constrained by the norms of classroom mathematics to really open up, think about and practice mathematics in new ways. But before doing so let us take a moment to summarize the key points in our proposition.

Agency is a product of human interaction in dealing with structural constraints. In this regard, there is a creative dimension to human agency, responsible for the production of new structures and the emergence of cultural change. This creativity may be brought about through mechanisms of improvisation and imagination, allowing for flexible social positioning and malleable sense of identity. In collaborative activities these help to develop competence to communicate and engage in discursive processes, which are paramount to knowledge-building processes, e.g., presenting ideas, building connections and refining shared artifacts (including language and meaning).

We believe it is reasonable to suggest that the notion of agency can be applied to understand learning in the socially charged context of CSCL, i.e., the creation of personal and group meanings, shared knowledge and joint ideas. In doing so, learners may break away from the structural constraints of well-worn thoughts and old habits of mind—thoughts and habits that might include traditional ideas about learning itself (i.e., teacher-lead learning), or collaboration itself, (i.e., social positioning when working with others). New environments provide new opportunities for agency because of the liberation of these old constraints and the creation of new ones.

Further, we would argue that the binary opposition between individual and group or public and private are largely false distinctions. In the Western tradition, we have had a tendency to think about cognition as primarily something that goes on in an individual's head as a private set of mental processes. Once those private processes have gone on—essentially independent of the social context—to form ideas, internal representations or mental models, the ideas may then be externalized, articulated, communicated and shared with the group or made public. But this view of cognition and communication is naïve and does not really reflect the way knowledge is developed or understood. While we do see individuals as critical to this process, we do not see a sharp separation between individual and group.

As Peirce said, all thought is dialogic. By that he meant that every private thought was the product of some former interaction and had an interlocutor in mind. Human thought is by necessity collective. The moves of particular individuals—and the strengths or weaknesses they bring to an interaction as individual participants—help form the interaction, the way knowledge is produced, the discoveries the group makes and the limitations they encounter. There is really no way to talk about individual cognition separate from group cognition. This is one piece of what Sfard (2008) implies with her notion of "commognition"—that cognition and communication cannot be separated.

VMT Data Analysis

The Research Setting

Before moving forward, we briefly describe the assigned tasks the students focused on during the featured segments. The data for this chapter comes from VMT Spring Fest 2006 (also partially analyzed in Chapters 7, 8, 10, 26). VMT Spring Fests were competitions where teams of students worked online to discuss a set of challenging, open-ended mathematical topics. The "grid world" topic for 2005 is shown in Fig. 6.2 and the "stick patterns" topic for 2006 is shown in Fig. 7.1 The team judged the most collaborative in 2006 was awarded iPods. So while the students involved seem very interested in math problem solving they also have an external incentive.

We selected Team B because of their attendance record, which allowed us to better track the progress due to individuals' agency, or lack therefore. They had four one-hour sessions working with and getting to know each other over two weeks. The full transcripts of these conversations are very long; here we look at just a couple of moments.

The teams were formed online and in general the students did not know each other or have contact with each other outside of the VMT sessions. The VMT Project is designed so that factors that are not visible in the chat room do not influence the interaction or the analysis of its record. Neither participants nor researchers know the students' real names, geographic location, gender, age, ethnicity, appearance, socio-economic status, speech accent, personality, habits, etc. In some cases, students came from the same school. According to evidence in the transcript, two students in Team B, Aznx and Quicksilver, knew each other from school; the third student, Bwang, lived in a different part of the US. From their real names, which were used occasionally in the transcript, we infer that all three are male. Because they were recruited by certain teachers, we know that they are approximately 12–14 years old. There is no evidence that they communicated about the chats outside of the environment.

In this analysis we approached the data from more of a discourse analysis perspective than a traditional conversation analysis one. While both forms of analysis look closely at text and the meanings produced therein, discourse analysis concerns itself with larger social forces such as the discursive construction of race and gender and hence may look across a wider range of utterances in a single moment of analysis. This allowed us to start with a larger chunk of the data and to develop a sense of the overall instances of agency in order to determine whether there was indeed evidence of creativity, collaboration and competence. We then identified the specific data snippets we are about to look at.

An Early Example of Agency

To start we look at Log 11-1, an excerpt from the beginning of the transcripts of Team B's first session. In establishing the structure of their working together to solve an open-ended math problem they demonstrate certain social actions, which we describe as early examples of agency; these seem to contribute to the success of their collaboration.

Log 11-1.

58	06.33.05	bwang8	so you can see we only need to figur one out to get the total stick
59	06.33.09	Aznx	read the problem
60	06.33.32	bwang8	1+2+3+........+N+N
61	06.33.38	bwang8	times that by 2
62	06.33.40	Quicksilver	Never mind I figured it out..
63	06.34.01	Aznx	Can we collaborate this answer even more?
64	06.34.05	Aznx	To make it even simpler?
65	06.34.15	bwang8	ok
66	06.34.16	Aznx	Because I think we can.
67	06.34.50	bwang8	$((1+N)*N/2+N)*2$
68	06.34.58	bwang8	that's the formula, right?
69	06.35.15	Aznx	How did you come up with it?
70	06.35.16	bwang8	for total sticks
71	06.35.34	bwang8	is a common formual
72	06.35.40	bwang8	formula
73	06.35.46	Aznx	Yeah, I know.
74	06.35.59	bwang8	and just slightly modify it to get this
75	06.36.31	Aznx	Aditya, you get this right?

Line 63, **"Can we collaborate this answer even more?"** is an agentic move because it slows down Bwang, who up to that point is acting unilaterally and moving ahead with the problem-solving task without consulting the others (lines 58, 60, 61). It takes a certain initiative to stop the flow of ongoing action and steer it toward another course. Additionally, the comment positions collaboration as a goal in the communication, and may be responsible for the spirit of collaboration we see emerging. Aznx' posting should probably be seen as taking up the moderator's earlier reminder: **"remember, you are trying to collaborate"** (occurring in line 38 of the transcript).

In line 65, Bwang accepts Aznx' proposal, **"ok"**, allowing the team to change course and begin to build a social structure framed on collaboration as a goal. This goal is confirmed in line 66, Aznx's statement—**"Because I think we can"**— which can be seen as a declaration of distributed capabilities. Alternatively, it can be viewed as a statement of the group's authority to take autonomous action. Either way, Aznx' statements demonstrate he is taking on a sense of responsibility for the goals set by Team B.

The follow up response, line 69, again displays a willingness by Aznx to take action. This comment helps build the group's common ground by asking Bwang to share his knowledge. At this early stage there is no negotiation of meaning as we see in the comment, **"(it) is a common formula"** (line 71), which is followed by **"Yeah, I know"** (line 73). In line 74, however, Bwang positions this knowledge as something malleable. In doing so, he opens it to possible future negotiation. This positioning of the concept is an agentic move because it expands the common ground and who is allowed to contribute.

Constructing and defining the rules of operation (i.e., the practices) for working together calls for a certain agency on the part of some, or all, individuals involved. The initial structure of this particular VMT chat environment emerges out of the ways these three students choose to respond to each other, their awareness of the circumstances (or lack thereof), and perhaps even the roles that they were willing to take on. In doing so, agency uses the mechanisms of positioning (Greeno, 2006a)— both systemic positioning (roles and importance of the agents and resources within the system, e.g., Aznx positions collaboration and explanation as more important than individual problem solving) and semantic positioning (meanings and significance of the practices and concepts used by the agents, e.g., Bwang positions the historic formula as malleable by the students).

Later Types of Agency

Before moving forward on this task let us take a moment to consider some important factors relating to how agency is exhibited. At one level we could say that the students in Team B took responsibility for their own learning and their developing competencies—i.e., setting goals, planning their actions, selecting cognitive strategies, monitoring and evaluating their progress in autonomous ways. As stated above they did this as both individuals and as a group. Their individual action is completely tied up with their interaction with each other such that their cognitive moves are communicative moves as well, as shown in the earlier vignette. In doing so, this team could be said to have expressed their agency and demonstrated an educationally productive use of their agency. However, what is considered agentic actions changes over time.

If we are to better understand agency and appreciate the complexity of this type of social action we also need to view agency along a continuum of significance (or consequences) of actions—small-scale to large-scale. Assessing the significance of actions, however, is dependent on context (what is the structure of the environment, its rules and its resources) and history (who participated in the action; what is the temporal nature of the structure, i.e., ongoing or time-constrained). In other words, given that all social action is situated, interpretation of such action must take into account the dimensions of context and history. Our first vignette tried to show how actions at the start-up of a group working together (time-constrained social action) might be small in scale but are nonetheless agentic because of the nature of establishing and negotiating the system's structure. Meanwhile, later actions (the upcoming vignettes) show a different type of agency (based more on creativity and competence) because of a re-constitution of established structural forces.

A Three Part Example of Agentic Movement

Below we have divided an extended set of interactions into three log segments. These are from near the end of the last of Team B's four sessions. At this point the participants' various competencies have developed significantly. When we began this analysis we tended to see Bwang as the "math student" because Bwang was very good at taking a given problem and expressing it in an equation. He had a certain math orientation and was often the first to create mathematical objects that the group later worked with. Aznx was very skilled at being creative in thinking about new problems and facilitating interaction, caring about the group as we saw above. Quicksilver was harder to get a sense of. But as we move into this final phase of work we see some significant re-positioning as each of the students engages in new forms of presentation of themselves, and there are new ways in which they react to each other. Further, much of the interaction up to this point has been an example of the kind of social action we discussed at the beginning of the chapter, where the action proceeds down a pretty clear channel and there is little disruption of the structure and the flow of action. But in this passage (Log 11-2) we will see a more significant form of agency where the "normal path" melts away in the realizations of the actors.

In lines 1512 and 1513 of Log 11-2, Axnx begins this new path through an exclamation. The **"what in the world"** and **"am I going crazy"** are utterances that reorient the participants and the reader of the transcript. Aznx sees something really big. At first it seems as if Bwang does not see the drama and suggests that Aznx not consider the corners in his analysis of the number of sticks in the shape. But quickly he sees that Aznx is concerned about something bigger. When Aznx positions himself as the leader of a new route of inquiry and positions the others as helpers in that task, Quicksilver takes up the positioning and agrees to check Aznx's work. But Bwang is more confused. He resists and also requests more information as he says, **"I don't see how you can simplify it."** This statement opens an opportunity for Aznx not only to continue to be a leader in this interaction but also to demonstrate his math competence. We have not often seen Aznx talking about math in this whole session,

Log 11-2.

1512	07.43.22	Aznx	what in the world?
1513	07.43.26	Aznx	am i going crazy?
1514	07.43.26	bwang8	don't consider the 4 cornors
1515	07.43.29	Aznx	someone check my work.
1516	07.43.36	Aznx	simplify their formula
1517	07.43.51	Quicksilver	k
1518	07.43.55	bwang8	what do you mean
1519	07.44.30	Aznx	$2(n^2+n^2-2n+1)+3n-2$
1520	07.44.34	bwang8	i don't see how you can simplify it
1521	07.44.35	Aznx	simply the formula
1522	07.44.40	Aznx	for the number of sticks
1523	07.44.45	Aznx	so that simplifies to...
1524	07.45.45	Aznx	I stil get the same.
1525	07.46.20	bwang8	how did you simplify it
1526	07.46.27	Aznx	um
1527	07.46.32	Aznx	square the n-1
1528	07.46.39	Aznx	then multiply the whole thing by 2
1529	07.46.47	Aznx	then multiply the 3 and n
1530	07.46.51	Aznx	and add it with that
1531	07.46.57	Aznx	and subtract by 2
1532	07.47.14	bwang8	quicksliver
1533	07.47.19	Quicksilver	im lost
1534	07.47.23	bwang8	did you get the same answer
1535	07.47.30	Quicksilver	no
1536	07.47.39	Aznx	i'll do it on the board
1537	07.47.44	Quicksilver	yeah
1538	07.47.53	Quicksilver	i got something totally difrent
1539	07.48.36	bwang8	so far i got $4*n^2+3*n$
1540	07.48.55	Quicksilver	indranil rite in the box
1541	07.49.17	bwang8	i mean $4n^2-n$
1542	07.49.26	Aznx	EXactly

but here he initiates a series of teaching moves, showing Bwang and Quicksilver how he reduced the formula of Team C. In lines 1527 to 1531 Aznx skillfully shows the other two how to reduce the formula. This work looks like the role that Bwang often takes in leading the math interaction. Quicksilver seems initially to have a little trouble with this work as he is coming up with a different result, but Bwang gets what Aznx got, **$4n^2-n$**, to which Aznx responds, **"Exactly."** That final response is filled with meaning as he is expecting Bwang to see something significant in that equation. It is one that they as a group earlier had proved was wrong.

The fact that the three students in Team B change roles quite dramatically was discussed in Chapter 10 from a quite different perspective. Here, we see the participants position themselves and each other interactionally to take on the roles of math explorer, explainer, questioner, checker, etc. This is a matter of individual agency within the problem-solving agency of the group. In Chapter 10, it was argued that the group developed social practices—patterns of activity that became established habits of behavior that over time became accepted and understood within the group. In this chapter's terms, these emergent practices were examples of Giddensian structuration and Bourdieuian habitus. Chapter 10's analysis of the Team B transcript (including the whiteboard inscriptions, or Latourian mobile immobiles) showed that the three students each took a turn initiating the team use of their social practices, demonstrating the extent to which these practices had truly become shared practices. Certainly within mathematics, in order to demonstrate that one has learned a skill and is competent in it, one must be able to apply the practice under appropriate circumstances in a way that is recognizable as that practice. In Log 11-2, Aznx is demonstrating his competence, which has been questionable for some time. This is a strong agentic move by him as an individual, and it drives the agency of the team toward its discovery vis a vis Team C's work.

The conversation in Log 11-2 is interesting at a number of levels. One of the things that Team B had been told they might do by the moderator's feedback after their last session was to look at Team C's solution to the diamond pattern and perhaps to work on a 3-D version of that problem. Out of that open set of instructions about what the team might do, the students may have made some normative assumptions that Team C's equations were correct, since they had been encouraged to look at them. Included in that set of assumptions were some assumptions about the role of teachers and mentors and how normal classroom activity would go. Why would a teacher (or in this case a surrogate teacher) ask you to look at someone's work if it was wrong? But in this section of the discussion Aznx has begun to show a mathematical skill he has, reducing equations, and he even takes the opportunity to teach Bwang, who up until this point has been the lead math person. In their reduction of Team C's equation they discover that it is wrong. Team C's equation simplifies to $4n^2-n$. But in their own work they had earlier arrived at this same equation and realized themselves that it did not work. Now they are realizing—thanks to Aznx's lead—that Team C was wrong too. In this interaction we see Aznx taking the lead. Quicksilver seems to be having a little trouble following, but he will catch up with the rest of the group. In this section each of the students finds themselves re-positioned by each other and by the context. This creates a level of excitement that we have not seen so far in the chat.

In this next section of the conversation in Log 11-3 the students react to their amazing discovery.

One of the reasons Aznx and the rest of the group knows the simplified equation is wrong is that Aznx tried to use it earlier in the session and the group saw that the equation did not work. Here they are each in their different ways coming to a realization about the implications of Team C's equation being wrong, as there is a kind of group "commognition" reorientation, to use Sfard's term.

While Aznx had the shocking realization in the earlier section, here Bwang is only beginning to see the repercussions of the moves that Aznx made before. And in an amusing way that both reinforces Aznx's earlier excitement and expresses his own awe, Bwang divides his **"holy moley"** between two lines—perhaps to emphasize the power...**holy**...**moley**—and then he says in line 1547 **"I think their equation was wrong."** Aznx allows Bwang to speak for the group here by announcing

Log 11-3.

1543	07.49.40	Quicksilver	yea that waht azn x got eralier
1544	07.50.00	bwang8	holy
1545	07.50.03	bwang8	moley
1546	07.50.05	Quicksilver	whyd u multiply by the two
1547	07.50.13	bwang8	i think their equation was wrong
1548	07.50.15	Aznx	It's in the equation
1549	07.50.19	Quicksilver	oh
1550	07.50.20	Aznx	Whoa dang
1551	07.50.25	Quicksilver	i missed that then
1552	07.50.25	Aznx	their equation is wrong!
1553	07.50.27	Aznx	lol
1554	07.50.28	Quicksilver	thats why i was off
1555	07.50.36	Aznx	and concidentally, that's what i got
1556	07.50.37	bwang8	because the simplified one wouln't solve the problem
1557	07.50.41	Aznx	i was thinking about the sides
1558	07.50.48	bwang8	why don't we use it on some other level
1559	07.50.52	Aznx	and thought there had to be 4n somehwere in the scenario
1560	07.50.56	bwang8	see if it works
1561	07.50.57	Quicksilver	lol
1562	07.51.00	Aznx	it doesnt
1563	07.51.01	Quicksilver	never assume
1564	07.51.05	Aznx	it doesnt work

in words what Aznx has already demonstrated he knows indirectly through expressions of affect and surprise. In the meantime Quicksilver is still a little slow to follow and in line 1546 asks **"whyd u multiply by the two."** Aznx both positions himself to help Quicksilver and then immediately follows Bwang up on his voicing the realization by stating in line 1552, **"their equation is wrong!"** The students then very collaboratively think through how they got to where they are now and also realize that the equation does not work at all.

In the last section of the conversation in Log 11-4, we will see the students attempt to engage the moderator of the session (Gerry). In these sessions the moderator is really only supposed to answer technical questions and not instruct or engage in the mathematics.

Here Aznx cannot quite believe their discovery. Bwang and Quicksilver are ready to move on and find the correct solution to the problem inspired by their discovery. But Aznx has to ask Gerry twice if they have really found something significant here. Gerry attempts to continue the low-key role of the moderator, but indirectly corroborates the group's finding in line 1593. Aznx's reply to him is appropriately subtle. Specifically in lines 1582 and 1583 Aznx shares their experience with Gerry by stating, **"Their thing doesn't work"** and **"We tried it."** The moderator indicates that he is aware of what they have been doing, which could be read as a tacit acceptance of their results. But moderation has been very low key in these chats

Log 11-4.

1578	07.52.29	Aznx	Gerry?
1579	07.52.30	bwang8	let's find out the real solution
1580	07.52.34	Quicksilver	yeah
1581	07.52.40	Gerry	What?
1582	07.52.48	Aznx	Their thing doesn't work.
1583	07.52.56	Aznx	We tried it.
1584	07.53.18	Gerry	I know you tried it. I saw.
1585	07.53.24	Quicksilver	lol
1586	07.53.32	Quicksilver	anyway
1587	07.53.32	Gerry	It does not even work for one square
1588	07.53.33	Aznx	So what do you think?
1589	07.53.40	Quicksilver	lets find the real answer
1590	07.53.43	Aznx	So their solution was wrong right?
1591	07.53.49	Aznx	Yeah, let's find it out.
1592	07.53.57	Aznx	But I want to make sure thgat it was wrong.
1593	07.53.59	Gerry	looks that way, doesn't it?
1594	07.54.07	Aznx	Yeah it does.

and so it is not clear that Gerry has supported their work. While both Bwang and Quicksilver call for finding the real solution—attempts to reposition the activity of the group—Aznx continues to resist as he seeks greater corroboration. In line 1590 Aznx directly positions Gerry as the authority by asking, **"So their solution was wrong right?"** Then to his fellow group members in 1592 Aznx makes his pursuit of Gerry very clear by saying he wants to make sure that it was wrong. It is interesting that while Bwang and Quicksilver are ready to move on, Aznx wants the voice of authority to validate their discovery. As a non-interventionist moderator, Gerry both gives Aznx what he is looking for and resists being positioned as the authority as he says in line 1593, **"looks that way, doesn't it?"** To this, Aznx replies in the same fashion in line 1594, **"Yeah it does."** We can see in Gerry's posts the effort of the moderator to have minimal impact on the way the group thinks about what they are doing as well as on how they do what they are doing. His positioning work can be seen as an effort to keep the focus on the team, positioning the team to continue to be the agent of problem solving, checking and confirming.

Discussion

Clearly, the unique features of the online chat and whiteboard tools influence the patterns of practices engaged in by the social actors in VMT, thus implicating the structure emerging from this social setting. In this case the structures produced through the interactions of the students involved act to negotiate and co-regulate the production of meaning, the norms and values of the jointly created figured world, as well as the exercise of power—what Giddens (1979) refers to as signification, legitimation and domination, respectively.

Traditionally, the structure of the classroom and the agency expressed by that structure, are transposed from other similar settings. Thus the constraints of past experiences may significantly limit what actions students take. Face-to-face classrooms can limit student expression along two major lines: First, existing structural asymmetries come to the fore such as gender, racial and class inequality. Classrooms must struggle to overcome these inequities as they are worked out in the interactions in class; as we know from the literature in education, they often fail to do so. According to Cobb and his colleagues (2004), past interactions in classrooms often form core identities where students do not feel they are good at math and they struggle against those identities that they have of themselves and the ways their identities are shared with others.

In the relatively new online chat environments, however, such structures, if they exist, are borrowed from purely social experiences (e.g., in socializing chat rooms and personal-opinion blogs). Thus in many cases the signification and legitimation are newly developing practices, and domination may not play a central role—at least not initially. Furthermore, with malleable structures there are malleable constraints, which offer greater opportunities for improvisation—the creative and unexpected taking of dialogic turns. When we think of how these adaptive structures relate to agency in collaborative activity, we see collaborative group learning in a different light.

In the examples we've given, we show that learning can be described as creative and improvised acts of agency—both individual and collective. VMT's online chat and whiteboard environment appear to free the students from the other kinds of social constraints that exist in their worlds and give them opportunities to make creative problem-solving decisions. It may also be that the types of students who are drawn to these settings are those who are more familiar and comfortable with these newer social constraints. In our example, the math topic is one that asks students to think about the relationship between the numbers of sticks one uses to make a pattern of squares and then what happens when one puts those squares into different shapes. This is a very open-ended kind of problem that might be intimidating in a typical classroom setting. But in the VMT chat the students creatively play off of one another in order to gain shared insights about the sticks and squares problem. They are able to take up a sense of agency as they play with the problem and help to define new questions to ask.

Agency requires individual and collective actions. When individuals begin to interact in coordinated or shared contexts, interdependencies are characterized by the development of mutual accountability and co-regulation—socially negotiated responsibilities, expectations and standards from which everyone is evaluated, including oneself. Interconnectedness is characterized as the development of mutual benefit—awareness of distributed capabilities, i.e., that everyone may benefit from the individual's attending and selecting, reasoning and reflections—and by the awareness of the development of a shared culture, resources and social history—ways of questioning, mathematizing and producing solutions.

In the brief examples shown, we see the interplay between individual and group. The VMT chat is a space that in some senses is liberated from the social constraints of a physical space. With virtual bodies and minds (or voices, see Chapter 24 on the interplay of polyphonic voices in VMT) students have the opportunity to play off of each other and to enjoy the creativity of that play (see Chapter 12 on group creativity in VMT). This potential for an open and free interaction encourages individuals to be agentic, and thereby encourages the group to support the individuals and stimulates students to act like mathematicians, exploring together the math worlds they project.

VMT chats like Team B's sessions create something unique and promising: an online world where students can take control, define problems, respond to each other and then explore the problems of their own making. In this way they behave more like mathematicians-in-training than like students being taught. This is not to argue that traditional forms of math instruction do not have their place as well in the future of math education or, indeed, that there is no role for adult educators. Clearly, the setting up of the math environment—topic, tools, resources—the moderation of the chats and the feedback between sessions can be seen in our data to be critical to the success of the student interactions. In addition, the positive experiences in the chats should ideally feed into integrative classroom processes before and after the chat, making connections across teams and integrating discoveries into the larger curricular picture. But the chat seems to open up a potentially transformative space in which student and small-group agency can be liberated. Within CSCL, Dillenbourg and Jermann (2006) have argued quite generally for scripting education with periods of collaboration where the student groups have full agency—bracketed by periods of teacher-led classroom activities and other periods of individual learning.

We would suggest that the VMT environment has the potential to overcome the structural constraints that one might see on social action from a Giddensian or Bourdieuian perspective. These constraints are to some extent avoided because the environment creates a collaborative space that can be defined by the participants and does not necessarily reproduce all the hierarchies or power relations in traditional school settings. Of course, it can also be argued that eventually a certain kind of social network will develop within the chat groups, based on their social interactions and potentially producing or reproducing hierarchies and power relationships. However, it is the creativity that VMT's constraints promote that is striking in our data.

The social action that is visible in the VMT data corpus shows student teams creating new structural realities for their further work together. As Giddens suggests there is a self-consciousness to this social action. The social action that is encouraged is creative and draws upon the participants' imaginations to see knowledge production as an enjoyable, stimulating activity that is accessible by ordinary people. Understanding how to harness this agentic behavior and to leverage it for scalable, sustainable learning will be a next step for this research.

Chapter 12
Group Creativity in VMT

Johann W. Sarmiento-Klapper

Abstract Understanding collective creativity is crucial for advancing the general study of human creativity as well as for guiding the design of creativity support tools for small teams and larger collectivities. In this chapter, we present a qualitative case study of collective creativity online derived from an analysis of collaborative interactions of virtual teams of students working in the field of mathematics. We examine group creative activity broadly, ranging from the micro-level co-construction of novel resources for team problem solving to the evolutionary reuse of ideas and solution strategies across teams. Our analysis focuses on describing the relationship between the dynamics of creative work present in a single collaborative episode of an online group and their evolution across time and across collectivities. Our analysis indicates that the synergy between these two types of interactions and the resulting creative engagement of the teams relies on three fundamental processes: (1) indexical referencing, (2) group remembering, and (3) bridging across discontinuities.

Keywords Bridging · interaction space · remembering · group creativity

Creativity has always been a social phenomenon. For instance, the creativity of an individual act is usually judged by the peer community based on established standards and shared histories (Csikszentmihalyi, 1988). Creation is never *ex nihilo*, but highly situated in particular contexts of activity, which are typically shaped by personal and collective histories. A famous painting by Paul Klee may be an individual masterpiece, but it is also an event in art history, an interaction with the artist's contemporaries and a product of the Bauhaus community. Philosophy from Plato onward, according to Hegel (1807/1967), has always been a "reflection of its times, grasped in concepts"—to say nothing of a 2,500 yearlong dialog.

In the networked age, creative breakthroughs are increasingly team accomplishments: the Manhattan Project, the Apollo moon landings, the analysis of a nuclear

J.W. Sarmiento-Klapper (✉)
College of Information Science & Technology, Drexel University, Philadelphia, PA, USA
e-mail: jsarmi@drexel.edu

G. Stahl (ed.), *Studying Virtual Math Teams*, Computer-Supported Collaborative
Learning Series 11, DOI 10.1007/978-1-4419-0228-3_12,
© Springer Science+Business Media, LLC 2009

accelerator experiment, the proof of Fermat's theorem, the consolidation of the European Union all involve coordinated efforts of many people. It is time to consider creativity as a group-cognitive achievement. If we are interested in promoting creativity, it may be important to understand, catalyze and support the group aspects of creativity as well as the individual psychological.

This chapter tries to explicate fundamental group phenomena that take place when a small group of students are challenged to work creatively in the domain of school mathematics as part of VMT. We do not expect to observe epoch-shattering acts of creativity here, but we hypothesize that we can see in the visible activities of interacting students some of the methods being awkwardly but explicitly worked out that experts use effortlessly and invisibly. By conducting the student discourses online, we can, moreover, easily capture for analysis a complete record of everything that is shared by the group in its collaborative work.

We assume that individual creativity involves mental efforts to pursue ideas about a problem. It may well also involve interaction with a variety of physical artifacts that are meaningful to the individual. In a setting of group creativity, this process must be extended, enunciated and shared by the group members so they can understand the problem and proposed solutions with enough commonality to work together toward a group accomplishment. As a sense-making enterprise, group creativity must co-construct group meaning that is appropriately individually interpreted by the group members (Stahl, 2006b, chap. 16). Because the effort must remain oriented to a shared task, it involves "a continued attempt to construct and maintain a shared conception of a problem" (Roschelle & Teasley, 1995, p. 70). The effort must be sustained; that is, it must overcome manifold potential discontinuities and disruptions. Group participants must be able to point to or index ideas and artifacts in the evolving problem space in ways that make sense to the others and are effective. New actions must be able to build on the past (of the group effort and of the larger culture) through group remembering situated in the present context.

If we want to support group creativity, then we have to support the building and maintaining of the joint problem space (see Chapter 6 above), the *referencing* of objects in that space, collective *remembering* of relevant histories, and *bridging* across related episodes of the group's activity. In this chapter, we explore the interactional character of referencing, remembering and bridging in small-group creative efforts through analysis of our data on virtual math teams. We consider the effectiveness of the VMT technological environment (text chat, shared whiteboard, persistent wiki, graphical referencing, social awareness) for supporting these aspects of group efforts at cognition and creativity. Both our analysis and our technological support focus on the actions between individuals, artifacts, events, sessions and groups—on inter-action more than on isolated individual actions.

Studying Group Creativity in Inter-Action

The potential of collectivities to engage in and succeed with rich explorations, discovery and innovation in various fields, has motivated many researchers, leaders and field practitioners to promote and study group creativity (e.g., Hewett, 2005;

Shneiderman et al., 2006). Half a century of research on individual creativity has clearly documented the complexity of the psychological, cultural and social processes involved in the creation of original and useful products (Mayer, 1999). When turning our attention beyond the individual creative agent, new challenges and opportunities emerge. For example, studying groups engaged in creative interactions offers us an opportunity to observe the methods employed by co-participants to conduct their explorative work together and allows us to see insight and innovation as social constructs. In fact, the emergence of digital environments that support collaborative work has opened up the opportunity for researchers to go beyond studies of "solo" action and investigate distributed systems of cognition and creativity that situate artifacts, tasks and knowing in the interactions of co-participants and activity systems over time.

In contrast to the attention that the social dimension of individual creativity has received in creativity research (e.g., Amabile, 1983; Csikszentmihalyi, 1988, 1990b; Paulus, 2003), the interactional aspects of group creativity—how groups do creative work together—have only recently begun to be explored. For example, a new conceptual model of group creativity in music and theater (Sawyer, 2003) proposes that collective creative work can be better understood as the synergy between *synchronic* interactions (i.e., in parallel and simultaneously) and *diachronic* exchanges (i.e., over long time spans and mediated indirectly through creative products). Building on this model, we attempt to explore the interdependency between synchronic and diachronic interactions, and analyze its relationship with creative work, broadly defined. In our study of mathematics collaboration online we observe collective creative work as manifested in a wide range of interactions extending from the micro-level co-construction of novel resources for problem solving to the innovative reuse and expansion of ideas and solution strategies across multiple teams.

Next, we turn our attention to describing, incrementally, three central interactional mechanisms that the VMT teams we studied engaged in and which directly relate to the creative dimension of their work. We theorize that such mechanisms are central to the synergy between single-episode collaboration and the creative work of multiple collectivities engaged together over time. In addition to describing the interactions that the virtual teams observed engage in, we also reflect on the particular aspects of the online environment used, which might promote, support or hinder synchronic and diachronic interactions.

Creative Inter-Actions in Virtual Math Teams

In the spring of 2005 and 2006, we conducted a series of pilot studies using VMT chat. In each study we formed several virtual math teams, each containing about four middle-school students selected by volunteer teachers at different schools across the USA or abroad. The teams engaged in online math discussions for four hour-long sessions over a two-week period. They were given a brief description of a novel open-ended mathematical situation and were encouraged to explore this world, create their own questions about it, and work on those questions that they found interesting. For example, the teams participating in the 2005 study (and whose work we will use to illustrate our observations about collective creativity) explored a non-Euclidian world where the concept of distance between two points in space had to be redefined. The initial task as presented to the students is displayed in Fig. 12.1. We expected this kind of task to offer a productive setting for the study of the dynamics of problem discovery and formulation, activities usually associated with creativity (Getzels & Csikszentmihalyi, 1976; Nickerson, 1999).

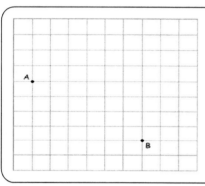

Pretend you live in a world where you can only travel on the lines of a grid. You can't cut across a block on the diagonal, for instance.

*Your group has gotten together **to figure out the math** of this place. For example, what is a question you might ask that involves points A and B?*

Fig. 12.1 Grid-world task

The analysis presented in the following sections uses the approach of ethnomethodology (Garfinkel, 1967) to examine recordings and artifacts from the team sessions in order to draw design implications for a full-scale online math discussion service. Ethnomethodology is a phenomenological approach to qualitative sociology which attempts to describe the methods that members of a culture use to accomplish what they do, such as carrying on conversations (Sacks et al., 1974), using information systems (Button, 1993; Button & Dourish, 1996; Suchman, 1987) or doing mathematics (Livingston, 1986). Ethnomethodology is based on naturalistic inquiry to inductively and holistically understand human experience in context-specific settings (Patton, 1990). Our observations come from this type of descriptive analysis applied to our entire dataset of interaction logs. We start at the micro-level of collaborative creative work and expand progressively towards more global interactional processes across collectivities and time spans. We will look at inter-actions of one virtual math team as indicative of interactions throughout the VMT data corpus.

Collaborative Referencing in a Joint Interaction Space

Our analysis of the collective interactions of virtual math teams suggests that these groups concern themselves repeatedly with the creation and development of a joint set of problem and solution *proposals* (Stahl, 2006b, chap. 21). In the VMT environment, participants use the textual and graphical resources at hand and a number of interactional methods to achieve this. These resources and the proposals for their use emerge from the collective activity of the groups themselves. References to resources evolve through a complex web of indexicals, which join them through elaboration, contrast, reframing, etc. The network of resources and utterances about them constitute the primary material of the groups' creative work. *Indexicality*, the referencing or symbolic pointing achieved through language and other means, is one of the unique aspects of group creativity which Sawyer (2003) has described in his analysis of creative collaboration in music and theater groups.

Figure 12.2 contains a passage of interaction from the last session of Team 5 in Spring Fest 2005. It illustrates the importance and complexity of collective referencing.

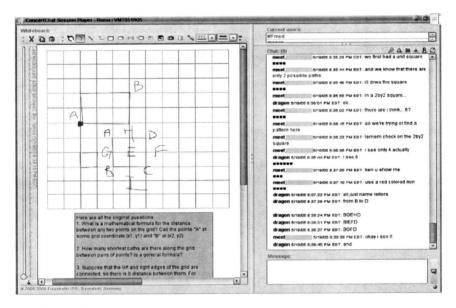

Fig. 12.2 Labeling to support reference

As can be seen in Fig. 12.2, the chat room used by the team provides a space of interaction where words, diagrams, labels, and sequences of manipulations can be used as resources for collective interaction. In this case we see on the shared whiteboard a series of textual notes with some questions that the team is investigating, a grid, and some other diagrams and labels created by the participants. Following the chat dialog in Log 12-1 (which continues from Log 6-2), we can see how the team members use a set of objects (e.g., a unit square, paths, a 2-by-2 square, etc.) and, through interaction, construct a collective web of references (e.g., "**ill draw the square**," "**there are only two possible paths**," "**from B to D**," etc.) that are determinative of how the group's joint action flows.

Log 12-1.

149	meet	we first had a unit square
150	meet	and we know there are only two possible paths
151	meet	ill draw the square
152	meet	in a 2by2 square
153	dragon	ok
154	meet	there are I think .. 6?
155	meet	so we're trying to find a pattern here
156	meet	lemme check on the 2by2 square
157	meet	I see only 4 actually
158	dragon	I see 6
159	meet	ken you show me
160	meet	use a red colored lien
161	dragon	all just name letters
162	dragon	from B to D
...		
163	dragon	BGEHD
164	dragon	BIEFD
165	dragon	BGFD
166	meet	okay I see it
167	dragon	and

This type of referential activity was widespread across all teams and sessions, although with different levels of intensity. This leads us to conjecture that the use of indexicality in combination with textual and graphical resources allowed teams: to create visualizations of strategies and ideas, to contrast multiple representations of a problem situation, to coordinate different problem-solving paths among different team members, and to reconstruct collectively past work so that it can be continued in the present moment. Indexicality seems to play a unique role in collective exploratory work when teams are engaged in active problem formulation and in the early stages of problem solving; at least this is a hypothesis that deserves further analysis.

Although the VMT collaboration environment provides some explicit supports for referencing (i.e., pointing with arrows from the chat area to the whiteboard or from one chat posting to another), the observed referencing practices extend well beyond the explicit supports provided. Our analysis points to the importance of these referential practices in creating a tightly interwoven set of resources that represents the joint interaction space. Elsewhere in this volume we have described instances of such referencing work embedded in the collaborative mathematical work of the teams (esp. Chapters 6, 7, 14, 15, 17, 20, 27). These analyses have motivated us to reconsider, as designers, the affordances in the online environment that support indexicality. Our particular interest in long-term collective engagement has resulted in a series of modifications of the VMT collaboration environment to explore and support the construction and maintenance of a sustained joint problem space. Before introducing them, we will first expand our initial characterization of the role of referencing and indexicals to consider the relationship between single-episode interactions (synchronic) and longer (diachronic) sequences of interaction.

Group Remembering with Shared Artifacts

The virtual teams involved in our studies demonstrated across their sessions a variety of methods for producing and managing relevant resources for their mathematical work. Since this work was spread over multiple sessions, they also engaged in activities related to managing their trajectory as a team. In fact, the excerpt of interaction captured in Fig. 12.2 represents a case in which the team is collectively engaged in trying to reconstruct parts of their previous session in order to initiate their current problem-solving activity. Interestingly, in this unique sequence of interaction, remembering of past activity unfolds as a collective engagement in which different team members participate dynamically. Some of the current team members were not present in the previous session, and yet they are instrumental in the reconstruction of that past and in shaping its current relevance. In the case captured in Fig. 12.2 and Log 12-1, for instance, *Meet* is engaged in remembering the work conducted in the previous session. Although he remembers that there were six shortest paths in a 2-by-2 square grid, he is only able to "see" four paths. *Dragon*, who was not part of the previous session, is able to see all six possible paths. Up to this point we could see this interaction just as a case of memory failure. However, the work in which these two participants engage in subsequently is a unique form of memory work that establishes a new method to "see" the six paths that were discovered in the last session—and to allow for that method to be more accessible and persistent so it can be shared effectively. The team creates a labeling mechanism that allows them to trace and name each path in the 2-by-2 grid (i.e., **"from B to D"** **"BGEHD," "BIEFD"**). This method is then reused for the rest of the session to explore other grid arrangements and, more importantly, to produce artifacts that can work as records of procedures, discoveries, and arguments that others can inspect, challenge, or extend. In this work, we see how indexicality also plays a central role, but we have labeled this kind of activity *group remembering* because of its particular importance to reconstructing past achievements that are relevant to present tasks.

In Fig. 12.3, the drawings, labeling, enumerated lists, tables and other inscriptions in the shared whiteboard function as "immutable mobiles" (Latour, 1990) that are shared by being persistently visible (see Chapters 7 and 10 above). The use of the whiteboard represents an interesting way of making visible the procedural reasoning behind a concept (e.g., shortest path). The fact that a newcomer can use the persistent history of the whiteboard to re-trace the team's reasoning seems to suggest a strategy for preserving complex results of problem-solving activities. However, the actual meaning of these artifacts is highly situated in the doings of the co-participants, a fact that challenges the ease of their reuse despite the availability of detailed records such as those provided by the whiteboard history. Despite these interpretational limitations, we could view the persistent artifacts created by this team as "memory" objects which, in addition to being representations of the teams' moment-to-moment joint reasoning, could also serve for their own future work and for other members of the VMT online community.

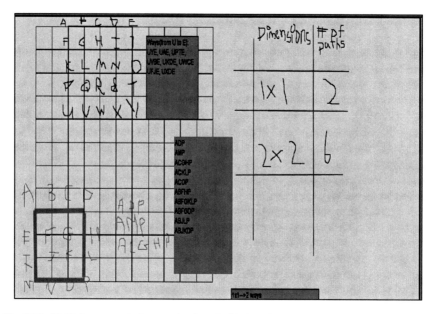

Fig. 12.3 Multiple representations on the shared whiteboard

These particular objects are constructed *in situ* as a complex mix of resources that document, represent and recall different points in the team's problem solving and, potentially, in the activities of others. As can be seen in Fig. 12.3, the two team members depicted a complex network of inter-related resources: the cases being considered, the labeling and procedural reasoning involved in identifying each path, a summary of results for each case (i.e., the list of paths expressed with letter sequences) and a general summary table of the combined results of both cases. The structure of these artifacts represents the creative work of the team but also documents the procedural aspects of such interactions in a way that can be read retrospectively to document the past, or "projectively" to open up creative new possible next activities.

Despite the fact that the problem-solving artifacts and conversations are the result of the moment-by-moment interactions of a set of participants and, as such, require a significant effort for others to reconstruct their situated meaning, they can serve as resources used to "bridge" problem-solving episodes, collectivities or even conceptual perspectives. Here, we use the term "bridging" to characterize interactional phenomena that cross over the boundaries of time, activities, collectivities or perspectives as relevant to the participants themselves. Bridging thereby can tie events at the local small-group unit of analysis to interactions at larger units of analysis (e.g., the VMT student community). Bridging may reveal linkages among group meaning-making efforts by different groups or diachronically across events in time. Bridging might play a special role in contexts where creative work and knowledge building are being pursued by collectivities.

Projecting Creative Opportunities Through Bridging

So far, we have explored two aspects of the creative dimension of the work that virtual teams engaged in as part of our studies. We have seen that the use of referencing and the configuration of indexicals are necessary elements of the "synchronic" interactions of these teams but that they can also play a central role in processes such as those that we have labeled "group remembering." As a matter of fact, we can see the central role of referencing as that of overcoming boundaries in joint activity. Deictic expressions (such as **"the one highlighted in black and dark red"**) are sometimes used to overcome gaps in perception, while temporal deictic terms (e.g., **"last time"**) can be used as part of the process of doing memory work and engaging with prior activities. In fact, in the contexts of extended sequences of collaborative knowledge work, where the membership of a team might change over time and where the trajectory of problem solving needs to be sustained over time, overcoming such boundaries might be especially challenging. We define this type of purposeful overcoming of boundaries through interaction as "bridging" work and turn our attention now to interactional strategies that virtual teams utilized to engage in these kinds of activities.

In order to investigate the dynamics of bridging we designed Spring Fest 2005 so that a number of teams worked on the same task for a series of four sequential sessions. Teams used a different virtual room for each session and had no direct access to archives of their previous interactions. Despite this apparent limitation, they demonstrated several strategies to reconstruct their sense of history and to establish the continuity of their interactions.

Analyzing several interactional episodes, we noted that teams purposefully engaged in attempts to establish continuity in collaborative problem solving as it relates to multiple sequences of work and also to the relevant work that other teams might be conducting. This type of activity involves:

(i) The recognition and use of discontinuities or boundaries as resources for interaction,

(ii) Changes in the participants' relative alignment toward each other as members of a collectivity, and

(iii) The use of particular orientations towards specific knowledge resources (e.g., the problem statement, prior findings, what someone professes to know or remember, etc.).

Bridging activity defines the interactional phenomena that cross over the boundaries of time, activities, collectivities or perspectives. It defines a set of methods through which participants deal with the discontinuities, roles and artifacts relevant to their joint activity.

As a result of our initial findings from Spring Fest 2005, we designed for Spring Fest 2006 a setting in which "bridging" could be investigated more conspicuously. We arranged for the teams to reuse the same persistent chat rooms so that they had direct access to the entire history of their conversations and their manipulations on the whiteboard across the four sessions. In addition, mentors provided explicit feedback by leaving a note on the whiteboard of each team's room in between sessions. Finally, we also provided a wiki space to allow the teams to share their explorations (e.g., formulae found, new problems suggested by their work, etc.) with other teams. The comparative analysis of these interactions provides us with more detailed confirmation of the important interrelationship between synchronic and diachronic interactions.

The reuse of the same room by teams that were much more stable in their membership over time proved effective in stimulating the constructive establishment of continuity in the creative and problem-solving activity of the teams. The feedback provided by the external mentors, however, was in several cases problematic since it re-framed past experiences in ways that seemed unfamiliar or curious to the participants themselves. In addition, the use of the wiki space provided us with a set of interesting examples of new "bridging" activity being conducted by the teams.

Through the wiki postings, teams working on the same or a similar task were made aware of the parallel work being conducted by their counterparts. In several cases, the wiki acted as an effective third workspace from which materials generated by one team could be used, validated and advanced by other teams. The authors of the postings also used them to sustain their own problem solving across the four sessions. Postings and trajectories of use in the wiki showed a structure that was very different from the conversational and interactional style of the chat room artifacts. Some postings were purposively vague and others resembled highly elaborate summaries of the teams' findings. In a few cases, postings included a narrative structure abstracted from the chat sessions (e.g., **"So in session 3, our team tried to understand Team C's formula . . ."**).

In one instance, the wiki presented evidence of cross-team asynchronous interactions: Team B found a new problem generated by Team C in addition to a possible solution. Team B proceeded to work on the problem, found a mistake in the solution formula originally reported, and proceeded to re-work the original solution and post the corrected result back to the wiki.

These findings seem to suggest the potential of explicit bridging spaces to promote continuity and to sustain creativity in problem-solving work, particularly in the context of an online community formed of multiple virtual teams with overlapping interests and activities. Naturally, the availability of bridging resources like the wiki does not by itself determine the ways participants interact over time. The fact that certain social practices were promoted (e.g., reporting to others, imitating, reflecting, etc.) influenced the way such resources were used.

Inter-Actional Dimensions of Group Creativity

When one looks closely at the interactional activity that goes into the formulation and communication of creative ideas, one sees limitations of traditional, ahistorical views of creativity. Creativity involves extended efforts to articulate, critically consider, and communicate notions that are not already part of the taken-for-granted life-world. Even when accomplished largely by an individual person, this generally involves sequences of trials with physical and/or textual artifacts (Schön, 1983). Such internal monologue generally incorporates skills learned from dialogues in dyads or small groups (Vygotsky, 1930/1978). The study of creative accomplishments in groups, where their interactions can be made visible for analysis, may provide insights about individual as well as group creativity.

Several models have been proposed to characterize features of individual creativity, such as the ability to concentrate efforts for long periods of time, to use "productive forgetting" when warranted, and to break "cognitive set" (Amabile, 1983). We expected that these individual skills could also play a role that is distinctively productive in the context of long-term collective knowledge building. In our analysis, we have seen that, in fact, some of these individual accomplishments can be characterized as fundamentally social and interactional. The virtual math teams we have studied rely for their creative work on basic interactional mechanisms such as referencing, group remembering and the bridging of discontinuities (see Chapter 6).

Recent models of group creativity (Sawyer, 2003) argue that collective creative work has to be understood as the synergy between synchronic interactions (i.e., parallel and simultaneous) and diachronic exchanges (i.e., interaction over long time spans, and mediated by ostensible products). Our analysis validates this model in the context of the creative and problem-solving work of virtual math teams and starts to provide an interactional description of some of the processes underlying these two types of interaction. This interactional description also applies to other published findings on social or collective creativity (e.g., Donmez, Rose, Stegmann, Weinberger, & Fischer, 2005; Paulus, 2003).

Because continuity in itself is important to the success of virtual teams, we have observed how participants develop a series of interactional methods to co-construct mathematical knowledge within single collaborative episodes as well as over time. The co-configuration of indexicals and the use of referencing methods allowed a collectivity to create new mathematical objects that gained their meaning through interaction and opened up new possibilities for next possible steps within a synchronous episode. Group remembering and the bridging of interactional discontinuities allowed the teams to expand the referential horizon so that the objects created by themselves or by other teams could be expanded, reconsidered, or challenged. These methods allowed the teams to evolve a sense of collectivity engaged in building new knowledge and made it possible for them to interlink their collaborative interactions with those of other teams.

Just as it has been argued that cognition should not be conceptualized solely or even predominantly as a fundamentally individual phenomenon (Stahl, 2006b), so we claim that creativity is often rooted in social interaction and that innovative creations should often be attributed to collectivities as a feature of their group cognition. Group creativity can be fostered by supporting interactional mechanisms like referencing, remembering and bridging.

Chapter 13
Inscriptions, Mathematical Ideas and Reasoning in VMT

Arthur B. Powell and F. Frank Lai

Abstract In this chapter, we trace collaborative problem solving as an interactive, layered building of meaning among learners working as a small group. Our analytic aim is to investigate how students through their inscriptive signs collaboratively build mathematical ideas, heuristics and lines of reasoning in the VMT environment.

Keywords Discourse · heuristics · reasoning · inscription · combinatorics

Similar to other computer-mediated communication systems, the VMT environment presents communicative affordances and constraints that influence users' discursive interactions. We are interested in how students use the affordances of the virtual environment—including the shared, dynamic whiteboard space, chat feature and referencing tool—as well as what mathematical ideas, heuristics and lines of reasoning are visible in their interactions. In addition, we are interested in how constraints of the system intervene in student discursive interactions.

Online communication systems present affordances and constraints to researchers, as well. VMT presents methodological challenges and opportunities to researchers interested in investigating how students exchange and interactively develop emergent mathematical ideas, heuristics and lines of reasoning. Consequently, we explore an analytic approach for inquiring into the archived interactions of students collaborating on mathematical problem solving through the online dual-interaction space. While analyses of users' online problem solving typically focus on their chat text, in the analysis that we present, for reasons that we will discuss, our analytic attention focuses almost exclusively on the evolution of participants' whiteboard inscriptions as a means to gain insight into the interactive development of their mathematical ideas, heuristics and reasoning as they solve an open-ended mathematics problem.

A.B. Powell (✉)
Urban Education, Rutgers University at Newark, USA
e-mail: powellab@andromeda.rutgers.edu

G. Stahl (ed.), *Studying Virtual Math Teams*, Computer-Supported Collaborative Learning Series 11, DOI 10.1007/978-1-4419-0228-3_13,
© Springer Science+Business Media, LLC 2009

Conceptual Framework

In this chapter, key conceptual terms include discourse, student-to-student or peer mathematical discussion, collaborative interaction, problem solving, heuristics, mathematical ideas and inscriptions. *Discourse* here refers to language (natural or symbolic; oral, gestic or inscriptive) used to carry out tasks—for example, social or intellectual—of a community. In agreement with Pirie and Schwarzenberger (1988), student-to-student or peer conversations are *mathematical discussions* when they possess the following four features: are purposeful, focused on mathematical notions, involve genuine student contributions and are interactive. We define *collaborative interaction* as individuals exchanging ideas and considering and challenging each other's ideas so as to affect one another's ideas and working together for a common purpose. In the context of the data of this study, the student-to-student, discursive collaborations involve only minimal substantive interaction with a teacher or researcher.

The term heuristics applied to human beings and machines has various uses and meanings in fields as diverse as philosophy, psychology, computer science, artificial intelligence, law and mathematics education. We construe *heuristics* to mean actions that human problem solvers perform that serve as means to advance their understanding and resolution of a problem task. We do not imply that when problem solvers implement a set of heuristics that they will necessarily advance toward a solution but only that their intent is to do so. Our sense of heuristics includes explicit and implicit general strategies such as categories outlined by Pólya (1945/1973, pp. xvi–xvii, 112–114) and others (Brown & Walter, 1983; Engle, 1997; Mason, Burton, & Stacey, 1984; Mason, 1988; Schoenfeld, 1985) and pertains to other actions such as a group of problem solvers' decision to assign subtasks to each other to later pool their outcomes to influence their progress on the larger problem at hand (Powell, 2003). Furthermore, we distinguish heuristics from *reasoning*, which we view as a broad cognitive process of building explanations for the outcome of relations, conclusions, beliefs, actions and feelings.

A paramount goal of mathematics education is to promote among learners effective problem solving. In our view, mathematics teaching strives to enhance students' ability to solve problems individually and collaboratively that they have not previously encountered. Nevertheless, the meaning of mathematical *problem solving* is neither unique nor universal. Its meaning depends on ontological and epistemological stances, and on philosophical views of mathematics and mathematics education. For the purposes of this chapter, we subscribe to how Mayer and Wittrock (1996) define problem solving and its psychological characteristics:

> Problem solving is cognitive processing directed at achieving a goal when no solution method is obvious to the problem solver (Mayer, 1992). According to this definition, problem solving has four main characteristics. First, problem solving is *cognitive*—it occurs within the problem solver's cognitive system and can be inferred indirectly from changes in the problem solver's behavior. Second, problem solving is a *process*—it involves representing and manipulating knowledge in the problem solver's cognitive system. Third, problem solving is *directed*—the problem solver's thoughts are motivated by

goals. Fourth, problem solving is *personal*—the individual knowledge and skills of the problem solver help determine the difficulty or ease with which obstacles to solutions can be overcome. (p. 47)

Coupled with these cognitive and other psychological characteristics, mathematical problem solving also has social and cultural dimensions. Some features include what a social or cultural group considers to be a mathematical problem (cf., D'Ambrosio, 2001; Powell & Frankenstein, 1997), the context in which individuals may prefer to engage in mathematical problem solving, and how problem solvers understand a given problem as well as what they consider to be adequate responses (cf., Lakatos, 1976). In instructional settings, students' problem solving are strongly influenced by teachers' representational strategies, which are constrained by cultural and social factors (Cai & Lester, 2005; Stigler & Hiebert, 1999). Moreover, with online technologies, the affordances and constraints of virtual environments provide another dimension to the social and cultural features of problem solving since "such technologies are intertwined in the practices used by humans to represent and negotiate cultural experience" (Davis, Sumara, & Luce-Kapler, 2000, p. 170) and how problem solvers think and act. Finally, the framing of abstract combinatorial concepts in the cultural context of a "pizza" problem (which is presented in the next section) also offers conceptual affordances and constraints.

In offline as well as online environments, users express objects, relations and other ideas graphically as text and as inscriptions. These are special instances of the more general semiotic category of signs. A *sign* is a human product—an utterance, gesture, or mark—by which a thought, command or wish is expressed. As Sfard notes, "in semiotics every linguistic expression, as well as every action, thought or feeling, counts as a sign" (Sfard, 2000, p. 45). A sign expresses something and, therefore, is meaningful and as such communicative, at the very least, to its producer and, perhaps, to others. Some signs are ephemeral such as unrecorded speech and gestures, while others like drawings and monuments persist. Whether ephemeral or persistent, a sign's meaning is not static; its denotation and connotation are likely to shift over time in the course of its discursive use.

As a discursive entity, a sign is a linguistic unit that can be said to contain two, associated components. de Saussure (1959) proposes that a sign is the unification of the phonic substance that we know as a "word" or *signifier* and the conceptual material that it stands for or *signified*. He conceptualizes the linguistic sign (say, the written formation) as representing both the set of noises (the pronunciation or sound image) one utters for it and the meaning (the concept or idea) one attributes to it. Examples of the written formation of a linguistic sign are "*chair*" and "*$cos^2(x)$*" — each with associated, socially constructed meanings. de Saussure observes further that a linguistic sign is arbitrary, meaning that both components are arbitrary. The signifier is arbitrary since there is no inherent link between the formation and pronunciation of a word or mathematical symbol and what it indexes. A monkey is called *o macaco* in Portuguese and *le singe* in French, and in English the animal is denoted "monkey" and not "telephone" or anything else. The arbitrariness of the signified can be understood in the sense that not every linguistic community chooses to make it salient by assigning a formation and a sound image to some aspect of the experiential world, a piece of social or perceptual reality. Consider, for example, the signifieds *cursor*, *mauve* and *zero*; they index ideas that not all linguistic communities choose to lexicalize or represent.

Signs can be considered to represent ideas. However, Sfard (2000) argues that a sign is constitutive rather than strictly representational since meaning is not only presented in the sign but also comes into existence through it. Specifically, she states,

> Mathematical discourse and its objects are *mutually constitutive*: It is the discursive activity, including its continuous production of symbols, that creates the need for mathematical objects; and these are mathematical objects (or rather the object-mediated use of symbols) that, in turn, influence the discourse and push it into new directions. (p. 47, original emphasis)

This theoretical stance on the mutually constitutive nature of meaning and sign provides a foundation for analysis of the discursive emergence of mathematical ideas, reasoning and heuristics. On the one hand, signs can represent encoded meanings that—based on previous discursive interactions—interlocutors can grasp as they decode the signs. On the other hand, through moment-to-moment discursive interactions, interlocutors can create signs and, during communicative actions, achieve shared meanings of the signs. In this sense, the sameness of meaning for interlocutors that allows for success of their communication is not something pre-existing but rather an *achievement* of the communicative act. This accomplishment may compel interlocutors to bring into existence signs to further their discourse.

Mathematical signs—objects, relations, symbols and so on—are components of mathematical discourse and are intertwined in constituting mathematical meanings. Signs exist in many different forms, and inscriptions or written signs are but one. They are produced for personal or public consumption and for an admixture of purposes: to discover, construct, investigate or communicate ideas. As mathematicians and other mathematics education researchers also emphasize (Dörfler, 2000; Lesh & Lehrer, 2000; Speiser, Walter, & Maher, 2003; Speiser, Walter, & Shull, 2002), building and discussing inscriptions are essential to building and communicating mathematical and scientific concepts. In a discussion of mathematics and science teaching, Lehrer, Schauble, Carpenter, and Penner (2000) illustrate how learners work "in a world of inscriptions, so that, over time, the natural and inscribed worlds become mutually articulated" and illustrate the importance of a "shared history of inscription" (p. 357). In mathematics, the invention, application and modification of appropriate symbols to express and extend ideas are constitutive activities in the history of mathematics (Struik, 1948/1967). Some researchers claim that mathematical meaning only exists through symbols and that symbols constitute mathematical ideas.

For researchers in mathematics education and in computer-supported collaborative learning, the arbitrariness of signifieds is a more significant point about de Saussure's observation concerning the arbitrariness of signs. The reason is that the conceptual material that a person (or a small group of people) lexicalizes—for example, with pencil and paper, with text in a chat window or with drawn objects on a shared, digital workspace—indicates to what that user attends, her insight into material reality that is external or internal to her mind. The inscriptions of individuals working online in a small group or team provide observers—who must interpret meanings constituted in the inscriptions—evidence of individual and collective thinking. The small group's inscriptions present ideas it chooses to lexicalize or symbolize. By analyzing the unfolding and use of inscriptions, researchers can understand how participants constitute their mathematical ideas, reasoning and heuristics, the meanings they attribute to their inscriptions, and how their inscriptions influence emergent meanings. As Speiser et al. (2003) underscore, what counts as mathematical in analyzing inscriptions is not the inscription itself, which are "tools or artifacts, but rather how the students have chosen to *work*" (p. 22, original emphasis) with their inscriptions. In the specific case of this study, in an online environment that offers resources for individuals to collaborate, what work they interactively accomplish with their inscriptions reveals their ideas, heuristics and reasoning.

Although some of this conceptual framework derives from psychological theories focused on individual cognition, we have tried to show how it essentially involves group and social dimensions. Moreover, it can be interpreted in group-cognitive terms applied to small groups as the creative agents of problem-solving efforts. As will be seen in the following section, the study in this chapter looked at the interactions of a pair of dyads, rather than a small group of individuals, so the active cognizing subjects were themselves cognizing groups.

Method

The data come from a class of undergraduate teacher candidates for positions in urban schools who are enrolled in a semester course—"Mathematics and Instructional Technology"—whose theme is the use of digital technologies for the teaching of mathematics in elementary schools. This data differs from the PoW-wow and Spring Fest data in many of the other chapters of this volume in that it comes from a college classroom context where the chat was part of a larger curriculum (compare Chapters 23 and 24). The second author taught this course, which was developed by the first author. During a particular class session, students worked on an open-ended problem, the Pizza Problem, interacting in chat-room teams of four through the online, collaborative VMT environment. When students enter their assigned chat room, they are presented the problem shown in Fig. 13.1.

We chose this mathematical problem for three reasons: (1) it relates to the course module, which concerned number and algebra, (2) its context is familiar to students from urban and suburban communities and (3) mathematically it affords different solution approaches, ranging from simple listing procedures to more advanced methods involving combinatorial analysis.

The Pizza Problem

A local pizza shop has asked us to help them keep track of pizza sales. Their standard "plain" pizza contains cheese with tomato sauce. A customer can then select from the following toppings to add to the whole plain pizza: peppers, sausage, mushrooms, bacon, and pepperoni.

How many different choices for pizza does a customer have?

List all the possible different selections. Find a way to convince each other that you have accounted for all possibilities.

Fig. 13.1 The pizza problem

Epistemologically, we view learning or knowledge creation as a process of conceptual change whereby individuals and groups of individuals construct new understandings of reality. Through social interactions, learners engaged with mathematics seek meaning and search for patterns, relationships and dynamics linking relationships among objects and events of their experiential world.

Our data sources are the mathematical problem and the persistent computer log of the chat-room interactions from the dual-interaction spaces that the VMT environment provides. To investigate the online, problem-solving actions of learners so as to understand how they build mathematical ideas, heuristics and reasoning, we code for instances in the data of their discursive attention to any of four markers of mathematical elements: objects, relations among objects, dynamics linking different relations and heuristics (Gattegno, 1988; Powell, 2003). In their chat text and whiteboard inscriptions, participants either communicate affirmations or interrogatives about these mathematical elements. We attend to eight different critical events that provide insight into learners' general mathematical behavior. We use both inductive and deductive codes to make sense of the data. The matrix in Table 13.1 contains deductive codes we used to flag these critical events in the chat text and whiteboard inscriptions. We also coded the data for emergent themes as related to our research questions. These include ones about interactional behaviors (II for participant initiating an interaction) and about reasoning (RC for reasoning by cases and CV for controlling variable). We will provide an example of how we coded a version of our data in Table 13.2.

Table 13.1 Matrix of event types

Subject and type of utterance or inscription	Objects	Relations among objects	Dynamics linking different relations	Heuristics
Affirmations	AO	AR	AD	AH
Interrogatives	IO	IR	ID	IH

Table 13.2 Time interval description

Example of time-interval description, interpretation, and coding of chat room (chat text and whiteboard inscriptions) data		
12:50:02–12:50:16	SOSilvestre creates an ellipse filled with the color red below the ellipse containing the textbox containing **"M/B/R."** Within this red ellipse, SOSilvestre creates a textbox and types **"P/S/R."**	SOSilvestre creates an ellipse on suzyn17's side, containing a textbox listing a pizza with pepper and two other toppings, presumably because SOSilvestre is done with her work, and wants to help out suzyn17. SOSilvestre seems to color the pizza red to have more fun with the problem. This seems to be the second attempt to collaborate since suzyn17 wrote "Plain Pizza" into the chat window. EC: (AO) SOSilvestre creates a pizza containing peppers, sausages, and pepperoni as toppings on Suzyn17's side of the whiteboard EC: (AR) By creating a pizza for Suzyn17, SOSilvestre engages in a relation among the objects on Suzyn17's side of the whiteboard. EC: (II) By creating a pizza for Suzyn17, SOSilvestre essentially initiates an interaction with Suzyn17, although the "interaction" here is not verbal. AO, AR, II
12:56:24–12:56:49	Suzyn17 types into the chat window **"WHO COLORED MY PIZZA?"** SOSilvestre types **"i did I did"**. SOSilvestre types "pizza red right?" SOSilvestre types "lol".	EC: (AO) SOSilvestre creates a pizza with peppers as the only topping on Suzyn17's side of the whiteboard. She then deletes this pizza. EC: (AR) By creating an additional pizza on Suzyn17's side of the whiteboard, SOSilvestre engages in a relation among the objects on Suzyn17's side. EC: (II) By asking **"WHO COLORED MY PIZZA?"** in the chat window, Suzyn17 attempts to initiate an interaction with SOSilvestre in the chat window around the pizza that SOSilvestre has drawn for Suzyn17. AO, AR, II
12:57:08–12:57:43	SOSilvestre adjusts the size of the ellipse containing the textbox containing **"S/M/B/R"**. suzyn17 types **"WHERE'S THE CHEESE?"** SOSilvestre colors the textbox containing **"P/S/R"** yellow. SOSilvestre types **"there it is"**.	EC: (AO) SOSilvestre colors yellow the peppers, sausages, and pepperoni pizza on suzyn17's side. AO

It is possible that an interaction receives multiple codes. We analyze the mathematical ideas and forms of reasoning that learners produce working interactively in dyads in a chat room, tracing the development of their ideas and reasoning patterns over the course of the problem-solving session.

We grouped students into teams as they arrived in the classroom. Each team consisted of four students and was assigned to a chat room. In one virtual chat room, students were grouped in dyads, each dyad at one computer. In the other chat room, three students shared a computer and one student was alone at a computer.

For this case study, we analyze data from one chat room, the one involving two dyads of students. After reviewing data of both chat rooms, using the VMT Replayer, we chose this dataset, realizing that given its paucity of chat text (compared to the wealth of whiteboard inscriptions) this chat would provide a particularly interesting analytic challenge. In what follows, we refer to the two students in each dyad collectively, using an abbreviation of the screen name of the one individual of the dyad who signed into the chat room. We refer to the first dyad as Silvestre; the participants are Sonia and Lyndsey, and they used Sonia's screen name, SOSilvestre, in the chat room. We refer to the second dyad as Suzyn; the participants are Susan and Komal, and they used Susan's screen name, suzyn17, in the chat room. In this report of our case study, although we are speaking of two dyads of students, to simplify things, we will refer to each dyad in the female singular as Silvestre and Suzyn for the sake of simplicity in our narrative. Although the dyads were co-located, they were asked to interact only through the chat room, pretending that they were located at distant sites.

In analyzing our data, we realized that the data for this particular study provided an analytic challenge that had to be overcome to make sense of the chat room interaction of the participants. Specifically, the participants hardly interacted in the chat frame of VMT and used the whiteboard almost exclusively. This meant that we had to follow the evolution of their inscriptions on the whiteboard to understand the emergence of their mathematical ideas and reasoning as they solved the Pizza Problem. To analyze the evolution of the whiteboard inscriptions, we adapted a video-data analytic technique used for qualitative investigations into the development of learners' mathematical ideas and reasoning (Powell, Francisco, & Maher, 2003). This approach allows us to view our replayed data much as we would a video recording, through four recursive stages.

Our *first* analytic move was to view attentively the data in the VMT Replayer several times at various speeds to familiarize ourselves with the real-time sequence of whiteboard actions and chat text postings. Afterwards, we discussed our sense of the data amongst ourselves. Also, as part of a professional development program for teacher candidates of secondary mathematics, we engaged undergraduate mathematics students in viewing and discussing the data.[1]

---

[1] These students are teacher candidates for teaching high school mathematics in economically impoverished, urban school districts and recipients of Robert Noyce scholarships, sponsored by the US National Science Foundation and administered through a joint project of Rutgers University, New Jersey Institute of Technology, the Newark Public Schools and the Newark Museum.

After these initial viewings of the data, our *second* analytic move was to step carefully through the data with the VMT Replayer to create an objective description of actions that transpired in the chat and whiteboard spaces. We created these descriptions for each five-minute interval.

Following the descriptions, our *third* move was to code the data deductively and inductively, while also writing analytic, interpretative notes of the problem solving and other interactive accomplishments occurring in the session. For the deductive codes, we used the markers of attention to mathematical elements indicated in Table 13.1. For the inductive coding, we inquired into the heuristics and lines of reasoning evident in the data as well as to how the participants manage affordances and constraints of the virtual environment. We present the results of our coding in the next section of this report. In Table 13.2, we present an example of a description, interpretation and coding of three intervals of the chat-room actions, each less than a minute long, in three respective columns. In the three intervals (rows of the table) Silvestre contributes to Suzyn's solution, and then Suzyn subsequently critiques this addition and induces Silvestre to make further changes. In the interpretation column, for each interval, we include rationale for our coding of a particular chunk of data. The letters, EC, which stand for "explanation of code," precedes these rationales.

Our third analytic move proceeded from our interpretations and EC rationales. We chunk the data by reorganizing them into specific categories based on the deductive and inductive codes. This allowed us further to understand the actions the team takes to make sense of the problem and the sequence of subsequent actions the participants perform to present and refine their solutions. In this stage, we also create a story line, deciding how the data informs our research question and what other interpretive frames the data suggest. The *fourth* stage of our analytic process was to compose a narrative, the report that you are reading.

Our trajectory of analytic moves is far more recursive than the linear description we have just provided. For instance, we refined and corrected the description as we coded and composed interpretations of chunks of data. In some instances, deductive and inductive coding occurred almost simultaneously.

Results

With regards to our inquiry into the cognition of the team of participants, our investigation concerns two guiding questions: (1) How do learners interactively build (externally represented) mathematical meanings by collaborating in small groups, using a computer-mediated communication system? (2) In the process, what mathematical ideas, heuristics and reasoning do they develop? These are overarching questions of our research program. The data that we analyze here represents a small, preliminary case study. We present the results along several dimensions: interaction, heuristics, mathematical ideas, mathematical reasoning. Afterward, we discuss issues that emerge from our results and conclude with implications of our case study.

The data of this case surprised us in that the team communicates sparingly with chat text and mainly through whiteboard postings. In our experience, most teams use the chat space to a much greater extent than this team does. Consequently, our analysis of the mathematical ideas and reasoning that the students engaged is not primarily based on their textual communication, but rather mainly on an examination of the evolution of their inscriptive whiteboard interactions.

Interaction

The student participants worked in dyads and the two dyads, as a team, interacted through the VMT system using two interaction spaces, the chat and the whiteboard frames. The dyads used the chat room to work through the problem, with one student of each dyad controlling the mouse and keyboard. The two dyads interacted with each other for the vast majority of the time through inscriptive postings on the whiteboard. In the nearly two hours of interaction, the students rarely used the chat frame to communicate with the other dyad.

Our analyses of the data reveal how participants use the affordances of the VMT environment, how they managed constraints they encountered in it, and what mathematical ideas, heuristics and lines of reasoning are evident in their collaborative interactions. The initial work of the online group can be read as establishing its bearings. These include how to work within the affordances and constraints of the VMT environment, how to manage the shared workspace and how to represent the object with which they will work.

Interactive Initiation of Inscriptive Phases

The two dyads of participants, collaborating in a single chat room, develop inscriptions or, more specifically, discursive objects or artifacts that serve to simultaneously represent and beget their mathematical ideas and reasoning as they build solutions to the problem. As Sfard (2000) notes, "mathematical discourse and its objects are *mutually constitutive*" (p. 47, original emphasis). While building their solutions, the development of discursive objects occurs in what we discern as phases.

Phase 1 is initiated when the dyad of participants, Silvestre, experiments with drawing ellipses, which seem to be analogous to pizza pies. The participant dyad, Suzyn, then also experiments with drawing ellipses.

Phase 2 entails labeling ellipses. Suzyn types **"Plain Pizza"** in the chat frame and uses the reference tool to link this chat statement with an ellipse on the whiteboard. Afterward, Silvestre creates a textbox in an ellipse and types **"plain T & C,"** establishing that it perhaps is more convenient to indicate a pizza and its topping such as a plain tomato and cheese pizza with a textbox superimposed onto an ellipse rather than linking a chat statement with an element—an ellipse—drawn on the whiteboard. With this action, Silvestre appears to offer an implicit proposal.

Both labeling approaches seem to be cumbersome for the participants, and in the next phase, each dyad modifies their approach.

In *phase 3*, apparently influenced by Silvestre's use of a textbox superimposed onto an ellipse, Suzyn incorporates this technique into her representation. Each ellipse that Suzyn creates is labeled with a textbox and represents a specific pizza with particular toppings. Suzyn employs this iconic representation for most of the remaining time in which she works. By this point, Silvestre and Suzyn type on separate parts of the whiteboard. Silvestre uses the left side while Suzyn uses the right side.

In their modified representations, each dyad uses the symbol, P. However, what does P represent, peppers or pepperoni? Silvestre settles the question by creating a key in which she indicates what letter represents what topping: P for peppers, S for sausage, M for mushroom, B for Bacon and R for pepperoni. In a different way, Suzyn also announces what P stands for. She creates a textbox, types **"PEPPERS"** into it and lines up in a column under this heading her three pizzas that contain P: P/B, P/S and P/M. Instead of an ellipse representing a class of pizzas, each ellipse represents a different pizza, differentiated from the others by its topping. These objects or pizzas are also similar to each other in that each contains two toppings, one of which is P, indicating that Suzyn is engaged with relations among objects. This pattern is indicative of thinking about grouping different possible pizzas by cases. In this instance, the case is two-topping pizzas with each including P as a topping. Suzyn employs this iconic representation for most of the remaining time in which she works (see Fig. 13.2).

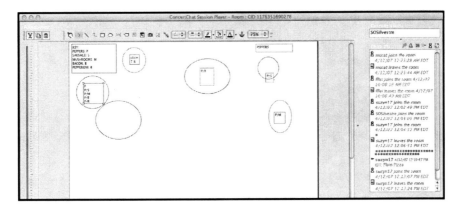

Fig. 13.2 Screenshot of phase 3

While Suzyn modified her representation, also in phase 3, Silvestre changes her notational scheme and develops a symbolic inscription. To indicate the mathematical objects with which she is working, she types **P/S**, **P/M**, **P/S** and **P/R** into a single textbox superimposed on an ellipse. Now, a single circular ellipse is not a single pizza but represents a class of pizzas. Her notation's structure appears to be the following: a single pizza has two toppings and the toppings on a pizza are separated with slashes. Her inscription also indicates a relation among the objects with which she is engaged; namely, each object is a two-topping pizza with **P** as one of its toppings. Moreover, this pattern is suggestive of a strategy by which she may intend to list different possible pizzas. In this instance, it is grouping different, possible pizzas by cases. In this case, it is two-topping pizzas with **P** as one of the two toppings (see Fig. 13.2).

Silvestre further modifies her notational scheme by removing forward slashes. Instead of using **P/M** or **P/S** to represent pizzas with peppers and mushrooms or pizzas with peppers and sausages, respectively, Silvestre uses **PM** and **PS** to represent these pizzas. In addition, she expands upon her representation and uses it to designate pizzas with more than two toppings. For instance, a pizza with sausages, bacon and pepperoni is represented by **SBR**.

In *phase 4*, Suzyn finally seems to adopt Silvestre's notational inscription to display her way of reasoning about a solution to the problem. Suzyn develops a symbolic inscription. To display her solution, she moves Silvestre's inscriptions to the bottom of the whiteboard (see Fig. 13.3, bottom center). Placing each case within a textbox, Suzyn lists and enumerates pizzas containing certain numbers of **"combinations."** She lists one pizza with **"0 Combinations"** or no toppings, five

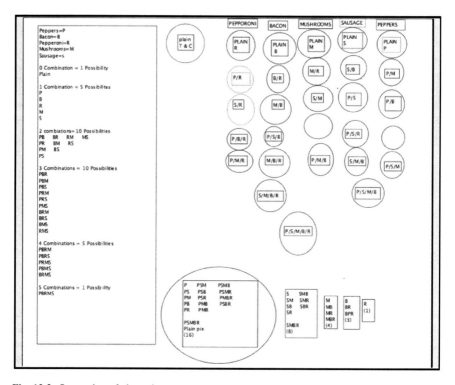

Fig. 13.3 Screenshot of phase 4

pizzas with **"1 Combination"** or one topping, ten pizzas with **"Two Combinations"** or two toppings, ten pizzas with **"Three Combinations"** or three toppings, five pizzas with **"Four Combinations"** or four toppings and one pizza with **"Five Combinations"** or five toppings. Like Silvestre, Suzyn uses combinations of letters as the objects with which she exhibits her thinking about different possible pizza pies and relationships among these possibilities, but groups her pizzas according to total number of toppings as opposed to common toppings (see Fig. 13.3, textbox on left).

Representing Objects and Engaging with Relations Among Objects

As we have seen, the groups develop two different representations for the objects with which they develop mathematical ideas and reasoning. The dyad designated by Suzyn initially uses an iconic inscription for each of their pizzas. It consists of an ellipse formed into a circle and a textbox with letters. The letters **P, S, M, B** and **R** are toppings and combinations of them are placed in a textbox atop an ellipse. Suzyn uses the two inscriptions—ellipse and a non-empty textbox—to represent a particular pizza pie.

Different from Suzyn's iconic representation, Silvestre develops a symbolic inscription. She uses combinations of letters as the objects with which she exhibits her thinking about different possible pizza pies and relationships among these possibilities. For instance, **P, S, M, B** and **R** stand for objects or pizza toppings and combinations of these letters such as **M, PS** or **SBR** designate different possible pizzas. In her semiotic system, Silvestre uses a letter or combination of letters to represent both particular toppings and pizza pies with particular toppings. That is, **P** can stand for one of the available toppings (peppers) or a one-topping pizza (of peppers). Unlike Suzyn's inscriptive system, where two distinct types of inscriptions represent toppings and pizzas with toppings, Silvestre's symbols play dual roles. Later Suzyn will appreciate the economy of this semiotic system and she will shift her notational usage.

Interestingly, although at the start of the group's problem-solving session Silvestre initiated constructing ellipses on the whiteboard and used textboxes to label an ellipse—such as when she created a **"plain T & C"** pizza—the chore or cumbersomeness of drawing and labeling within the whiteboard may have contributed to her development of another, more convenient representation. Drawing elliptical shapes and creating textboxes on the shared workspace are affordances of the system, which at the same time represent a constraint because of mechanical or motor difficulties involved in creating and coordinating these objects. This constraint may have impelled Silvestre to find a less representational, more symbolic and therefore computationally more powerful inscription.

With her inscriptive objects, Silvestre engages with relations among their objects. Just as Silvestre and Suzyn developed different representations, they also engage with different relations among the objects or pizzas. Suzyn indicates relations among her objects spatially by locating pizzas that contain a particular, common topping, like peppers, under a column head by the name of the common topping. The column headed by **"Peppers"** has four pizzas each containing peppers with one different other topping and one pizza with just peppers as its topping; the column headed by **"Sausage"** has three pizzas each containing sausage with one different other topping and one pizza with just sausages as the topping; the column headed by **"Mushroom"** has two pizzas each containing mushrooms with one different other topping and one pizza with just mushrooms as the topping; the column headed by **"Bacon"** has one pizza containing bacon with one different other topping and one pizza with just bacon as the topping; the column headed by **"Pepperoni"** has one pizza with just peppers as the topping. Each successive column had one less pizza than the one before it because it does not include the topping used in the previous column. Suzyn seems to realize this before labeling her pizzas since, as she went along, she drew just the right number of ellipses under each column heading.

Silvestre presents her perception of relationships among objects, the different possible pizzas. In turn, she considers each available topping and, in separate textboxes, lists all possible pizzas that contain it as a topping (see the five textboxes at the bottom of Fig. 13.3). That is, first, she lists all possible different pizzas containing P or peppers; second, all possible, different pizzas containing **S** or sausage, except for those that contain **P** since they were already accounted for; third, all possible, different pizzas containing **M** or mushroom, except for those that contain **P** or **S** since they have already been accounted for; fourth all possible, different pizzas containing **B**, except for those that contain **P, S** or **M** since they have already been represented, and finally, all possible, different pizzas containing **R**, except for those that contain **P, S, M** or **B** since they have already been indicated.

Engaging with Dynamics Linking Different Relations

The work of Suzyn and Silvestre evidence their engagement with dynamics linking different relations or, in other words, relations among relations. Silvestre listed, for example, pizzas containing peppers, **P**, in a textbox. This listing by itself is a relation. Ultimately, she arranged the possible pizzas containing in turn each of the five available toppings into separate textboxes. The textbox containing pepper pizzas is to the left of the textbox containing sausage pizzas, which is to the left of the textbox containing mushroom pizzas, which is to the left of the textbox containing bacon pizzas, which is to the left of the textbox containing the pepperoni pizza. Her inscriptive and spatial work indicates that Silvestre views each listing as distinct from the others. In this sense, she is also engaged with dynamics linking—by distinction—different relations.

In an analogous manner, Suzyn signals her engagement with relations among relations. She lists different possible pizzas by considering cases. In the long, rectangular textbox on the left in Fig. 13.3, Suzyn lists in turn all possible pizzas with 0 toppings, 1 topping, 2 toppings, 3 toppings, 4 toppings and 5 toppings. Each case indexes a relation and is distinct from the others. Her listing indicates Suzyn's engagement with dynamics linking different relations.

Each of the participants—Suzyn and Silvestre—considers different dynamics linking different relations. The structure of their thinking in this regard reveals different perceptions of the underlying mathematical structure of the problem. We elaborate on this in the discussion section below.

Inventing Heuristics

Both Suzyn and Silvestre seemed to invent heuristics based on the resources within the VMT environment. For example, both started off by drawing ellipses using the ellipse tool. It seems that Suzyn then realized, after using the referencing tool to label an ellipse as a plain pizza, that the textbox could be better used for this purpose. Thus, for the early part of her work session, Suzyn used ellipses labeled by textboxes to represent her pizzas. Her solution representation is iconic.

For Silvestre, the drawing of ellipses may have seemed too cumbersome. Silvestre used a symbolic method of representation. Specifically, she used the textbox tool to list pizza possibilities. Within separate textboxes, Silvestre listed pizzas containing peppers as a topping, pizzas containing sausage as a topping that have not already been listed, and so on.

Suzyn's evolution of heuristic use from iconic representation to symbolic representation may have been influenced by Silvestre's use of symbolic representation in her solution method. That Silvestre was able to list more pizzas with her method than Suzyn was able to list with her iconic representation may have influenced Suzyn to use a symbolic representation to complete her solution. Interestingly, although both Suzyn and Silvestre end up with symbolic representations, their solutions are quite different.

Reasoning About Possibilities

The work of the team and of each of the two dyads in the team exemplifies particular types of mathematical analysis: *reasoning by cases* and *reasoning by controlling variables*. The teams of Silvestre and Suzyn both begin their work by indicating possible pizzas with two toppings in which one is P, peppers. On the one hand, this line of reasoning continues to dominate the work of Suzyn throughout the session. *Suzyn reasons by cases by counting and listing pizzas with one topping, pizzas with two toppings, pizzas with three toppings and pizzas with four toppings.* Suzyn continues reasoning by cases by listing additional combinations in her textbox. She lists the combination of no toppings, a plain pizza and the combination of all toppings, a pizza containing peppers, sausages, mushrooms, bacon and pepperoni.

On the other hand, Silvestre shifts from reasoning by cases to reasoning by controlling for variables. When Silvestre creates a textbox and types in four pizzas containing peppers as a topping with the combinations of peppers and sausage, peppers and mushroom, peppers and sausage, and peppers and pepperoni, this is the first instance of reasoning by cases. Later on, *Silvestre controls for the variable P, as she lists one-, two-, three- and four-topping pizzas containing peppers.* Silvestre then creates a textbox and lists pizzas containing sausages, sausages and two other toppings, and sausages and three other toppings.

Within each textbox, Silvestre also engages in reasoning by cases. She adjusts her list of pizzas with peppers so that one-, two-, three- and four-topping pizzas all appear in separate columns. Before the adjustment, pizzas with three and four toppings appeared in the same column. In a similar fashion, Silvestre arranges her listing of pizzas containing sausage, not containing peppers, by grouping the possibilities according to the number of toppings.

Discussion

Our aims were to investigate—based on data gathered from chat-room participants' mathematical problem solving within the VMT environment—how to study chat-room participants' development of mathematical ideas and lines of reasoning, and what ideas and reasoning are evident in the data. In the following sections, we discuss the significance of the results in the light of our theoretical and cognitive perspectives.

Discourse Creating Objects and Objects Shaping Discourse

To explore, develop and communicate their mathematical ideas, the four students—acting as dyads Suzyn and Silvestre—interactively unfold an inscriptive system composed of objects as well as implicit relations among the objects and relations among the relations. After entering their assigned chat room in the VMT environment and after reading the statement of the Pizza Problem, the students experiment drawing circular ellipses and initially default to pictorial or iconic representations of pizzas. Suzyn types **"Plain Pizza"** and uses the reference tool to link this chat statement to an ellipse on the whiteboard. Immediately afterward, Silvestre creates a textbox superimposed on an ellipse and types **"plain T & C,"** which we understand to mean a plain pizza of tomato and cheese. In subsequent actions of creating objects on the whiteboard, Suzyn incorporates Silvestre's technique of drawing an ellipse and labeling it by typing into a textbox superimposed on the ellipse. Each ellipse that Suzyn creates is labeled with a textbox and represents a specific pizza with particular toppings, with each of the toppings separated by a slash. Each ellipse also represents a different pizza, differentiated from the others by its indicated toppings. Both Suzyn and Silvestre use ellipses in their representations of pizzas perhaps because representing pizzas in a pictorial manner makes the problem more personal, less abstract and easier to work with in early stages of their thinking. Their initial discourse in the chat and whiteboard spaces concerns experiments with designs for the objects on which they will work.

After Silvestre experiments with using an ellipse labeled with a textbox as a way of indicating pizzas, she changes from an iconic to a symbolic representational scheme. The chore of drawing and labeling within the VMT system may have contributed to her development of a less pictorial, more symbolic, and therefore, computationally more powerful inscription.

To indicate the mathematical objects with which they are engaged, Silvestre's initial symbolic inscription involved a list of letters and slashes—**P/S, P/M, P/S** and **P/R**—typed into a single textbox superimposed on an ellipse, indicating pizzas and their toppings. The structure of the notation appears to be the following: each group of two letters with a slash between them is a single pizza with two toppings with each topping indicated by a letter. The ellipse is not a single pizza but indexes a class of pizzas and a relation among them. The relation that it indexes seems to be all two-topping pizzas containing peppers, **P**. This pattern may suggest how Silvestre intends to list different possible pizzas, distinguishing classes of pizzas by means of ellipses.

There is an interaction between Silvestre's objects and her problem-solving strategy. The objects push her discourse in new directions. Silvestre modifies and extends her inscriptive and problem-solving strategy. She uses combinations of letters without slashes as objects to represent different possible pizza pies and relationships among these possibilities. For instance, **P, S, M, B** and **R** stand for the five different pizza toppings and combinations of these letters such as **M, PS** or **SBR** designate different possible pizzas. Silvestre uses a letter or combination of letters to represent both particular toppings and pizza pies with particular toppings. That is, **P** can stand for one of the available toppings (peppers) or a one-topping pizza (of peppers).

Silvestre's development of a more cogent and computationally powerful inscription parallels shifts in her discourse. That is, this notational scheme allows her to not only illustrate pizzas with different combinations of topping but also to engage with patterns and relationships of these combinations and to use these patterns and relationships to engage with and illustrate relations among the relations. In her final solution, she presents in five different textboxes different classes of pizzas: first, all different possible pizzas containing peppers, **P**; second, all pizzas containing sausage, **S**, but not containing peppers; and so on. Examining these textboxes makes Silvestre's strategy for listing pizzas evident. In the textbox with pizzas containing peppers, a one-topping pizza containing peppers is listed first. Then, for each two-topping combination containing peppers, peppers is listed first, followed by single-topping combinations of sausages, mushrooms, bacon, or pepperoni, listed in this order. A similar systematic strategy is followed for pizzas containing other toppings. Note that the order in which pizzas containing certain toppings are presented (pizzas containing peppers, pizzas containing sausages, pizzas containing mushrooms, pizzas containing bacon, and finally pizzas containing pepperoni) is the same as the order of the toppings presented in each textbox (Fig. 13.4).

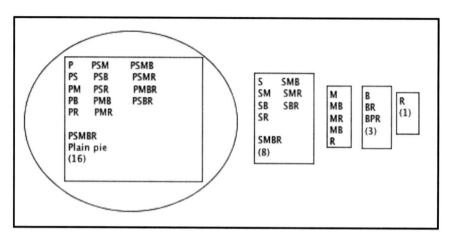

Fig. 13.4 Screenshot of Silvestre's final solution

The content of the textboxes displays particular relations among the pizzas and the different textboxes distinguish relations among these relations. This inscriptive system that Silvestre develops illustrates the theoretical point about the signs learners choose and how their signs provide an analytic window into the signified field of conceptual material or ideas with which they engage (Powell, 2003).

The team's initial and later work to create and use their mathematical objects exemplifies another theoretical point. Sfard (2000b) theorizes, "mathematical discourse and its objects are *mutually constitutive*" (p. 47, original emphasis). Through their discourse, the students in our data develop approaches to represent the objects on which they work in their solution space. They consider and modify an initial proposal for how to represent their objects—pizzas with particular toppings. Each dyad elects to work with a different representation, one iconic and the other symbolic. The emergence to these inscriptive systems usher into the discourse two directions of work toward a solution of the problem. Indeed, the process of designing objects shapes their respective solution space. Silvestre's symbolic representation supports her reasoning about the different possible pizzas as collections in which they control variables, holding **P** (peppers) fixed and listing first all possible pizzas containing **P**. Though Suzyn's iconic representation supports her reasoning—cases defined by the number of toppings—it proves cumbersome and inefficient. Toward the end of the problem-solving session, she abandons it in favor of Silvestre's symbolic representation. The iconic representation communicates the physicality of a pizza—an ellipse—and in a textbox displays its toppings. The symbolic representation—concatenated letters—simultaneously lists the toppings of a pizza and stands for the pizza itself. The meaning of the objects and the meaning presented through the objects are constituted through their use. From their discursive interactions in the two interactive spaces of VMT, the teams implicitly agree that what distinguish pizzas from one another are their toppings. Therefore, it is sufficient to list their toppings without having to draw pictures of pizzas. Through their discursive interaction the team constitutes the objects and, in turn, their objects shape and advance the discourse. This point is further evidenced in the next section.

Dyads Influencing Dyads

When Suzyn and Silvestre enter the VMT space, they both begin by drawing ellipses. Suzyn uses a chat posting of **"Plain pizza"** to link to one of her ellipses as a way of labeling it as a plain pizza. Silvestre takes one of her ellipses and places a textbox inside, and labels it **"plain T&C."** Suzyn seems to be influenced by this and subsequently uses this notational scheme to develop her solution.

While both dyads use letters to represent the pizza toppings, the letter **P** can represent either peppers or pepperoni. Silvestre settles this problem by creating a key in which she indicates what letter represents what topping: **P** for peppers, **S** for sausage, **M** for mushroom, **B** for Bacon and **R** for pepperoni. In a different way, Suzyn also announces what **P** stands for. She creates a textbox, types **"PEPPERS"** into it, and lines up in a column under this heading her three pizzas that contain **P**. After Silvestre creates this key, Suzyn appears to adopt Silvestre's notation.

Unlike Suzyn's inscriptive system, where two distinct types of inscriptions represent toppings and pizzas with toppings, Silvestre's symbols play dual roles. The economy of this semiotic system is appreciated by Suzyn and she shifts her notational usage to a symbolic notational scheme.

Throughout the session, both Suzyn and Silvestre influenced each other in various ways. In the beginning of the session, Silvestre was influenced by Suzyn to use ellipses to represent pizzas, but used textboxes instead of linked chat statements to label the ellipse. Later on, Silvestre switched to a symbolic representation of pizzas, perhaps seeing that the iconic representation was not suitable for generating large numbers of possibilities. Near the end, that Silvestre was able to list more pizzas with her method than Suzyn was able to list with her iconic representation may have influenced Suzyn to use a symbolic representation to complete her solution.

Within the session, through mutual influences the gradually shared semiotic conventions were established as a system of shared meaning underlying the on-going social practices or methods jointly available to the two dyadic participants.

Dyadic Reasoning

Interestingly, Suzyn and Silvestre engage similar reasoning processes but with different inscriptive results. They both reason by cases. Moreover, within each case, they reason by controlling variables. However, their distinct inscriptive results emerge from their differentiated cases. In her final symbolic inscription, Suzyn lists her pizzas by separating them into cases, according to the number of toppings and, within each case, controls variables. Under 0 topping pizzas, she lists a plain pizza (tomato sauce and cheese). Under 1-topping pizzas, she lists a pizza containing only peppers as a topping, then a pizza containing only bacon, followed by a pizza containing only pepperoni, then a pizza containing only mushrooms, and finally a pizza containing only sausages. Under 2-topping pizzas, she lists all pizzas containing peppers and one other topping; then all pizzas containing bacon and another topping different from peppers; then lists all pizzas containing pepperoni and another topping different from peppers or bacon; followed by all pizzas containing mushrooms and another topping different from peppers, bacon, or pepperoni. At this point, she has exhausted all of the possibilities for 2-topping pizzas. She continues to engage reasoning by cases and by controlling variables to list all her 3-, 4-, and 5-topping pizzas.

As for Silvestre, she lists her pizzas by separating them into cases of pizzas containing peppers, pizzas containing sausages but excluding those previously listed, pizzas containing mushrooms but excluding those previously listed, pizzas containing bacon but excluding those previously listed, and pizzas containing pepperoni but excluding those previously listed. Within each case, she controls variables by indicating the common topping first and followed methodically varying other toppings. For example, for pizzas containing peppers, she lists the following ones: **P, PS, PM, PB, PR, PSM, PSB, PSR, PMB, PMR, PSMB, PSMR, PMBR, PSBR**. The peppers topping is always listed first, followed by variations containing sausage, mushroom, bacon, and pepperoni always listed in that order. Afterward, she methodically lists all possible pizzas containing sausage and other toppings, not including in the list those pizzas containing sausage that were already indicated in the previous list of pizzas containing peppers. Working in this fashion, each of her cases is separated in a different textbox and within each she controls variables. Since Silvestre's cases are distinct from those of Suzyn, her inscriptive result also differs.

By the end of the session, Suzyn's thinking has progressed to the point where Silvestre was earlier. Both are now thinking beyond the idea of just generating different pizzas, but rather of producing combinations of toppings to generate patterns, and to use these patterns to ensure that they have accounted for all combinations.

Viewed as individual actors, Suzyn and Silvestre (who are themselves actually each a dyad of human students) are seen to influence each other while still maintaining different perspectives on their shared problem. Viewed as an interacting small group, they develop shared meanings, a joint problem space, common methods and accepted practices. These elements of group cognition can be seen to emerge and evolve out of the situation or activity context including the driving problem, the technical environment and the unfolding interaction.

Mathematical Significance

As a small group, Suzyn and Silvestre built sophisticated cognitive structures that can provide insight into Pascal's triangle and combinatorial analyses. From an analytical viewpoint, we find these structures to be significant since they establish cognitive foundations upon which students can build and extend their understanding of binomial structures. In Fig. 13.4, Silvestre's representation of her solution nearly mimics successive rows of Pascal's triangle. Her listing of pizzas with peppers almost represents the fourth row of Pascal's triangle (see Fig. 13.5). First, she lists a pizza with peppers, pizzas with peppers and one other topping, pizzas with peppers and two other toppings, pizzas with peppers and three other toppings and a pizza with peppers and four other toppings. The number of pizzas in each of these sub-categories is the same as one of the numbers in the fourth row of Pascal's triangle: 1 4 6 4 1. That is, there is one pizza with peppers only, four pizzas with peppers and one other topping, six pizzas with peppers and two other toppings, four pizzas with peppers and three other toppings and one pizza with peppers and four other toppings.

Zeroth row	1
First row	1 1
Second row	1 2 1
Third row	1 3 3 1
Fourth row	1 4 6 4 1
Fifth row	1 5 10 10 5 1

Fig. 13.5 The initial rows of Pascal's triangle

Combinatorially speaking, for the case of all possible pizzas containing peppers, since each pizza must have peppers as a topping, there are four remaining toppings from which to choose. Using combinatorial notation, $\binom{n}{r}$, which means the number of ways to select r items from a collection of n of them, the following are the possible pizzas containing peppers:

- Pizzas with peppers only $= \binom{4}{0} = 1$, since out of four choices of toppings none are chosen,
- Pizzas with peppers and one other topping $= \binom{4}{1} = 4$, since out of four choices of topping one is chosen,
- Pizzas with peppers and two other toppings $= \binom{4}{2} = 6$, since out of four choices of topping two are chosen,
- Pizzas with peppers and three other toppings $= \binom{4}{3} = 4$, since out of four choices of topping three are chosen and
- Pizzas with peppers and four other toppings $= \binom{4}{4} = 1$, since out of four choices of topping four are chosen.

In Silvestre's representation of all possible pizzas with peppers as a topping, she misses the pizza with peppers, bacon and pepperoni, and instead lists it as a pizza with bacon, peppers and pepperoni under her listing of pizzas with bacon as a topping (see Fig. 13.2). She also places within her listing of pizzas with peppers as a topping a plain pizza. Aside from these two inconsistencies, Silvestre's listing of pizzas with sausages as a topping, mushrooms as a topping, bacon as a topping and pepperoni as a topping represent the third, second, first and zeroth rows of Pascal's triangle, respectively, and can also be described in a combinatorial fashion as above. Finally, Silvestre's solution method represents the sum of all rows of Pascal's triangle up to the fifth row.

In contrast to Silvestre's solution method, which represents the sums of each of the first five rows of Pascal's triangle, Suzyn's solution method mimics the sixth row of Pascal's triangle: 1 5 10 10 5 1. Within a textbox, she first lists at the top a key containing abbreviations for each of the toppings, and then underneath in successive rows she lists pizzas under the following headings:

- 0 Combination = 1 Possibility (one possible pizza with no toppings)
- 1 Combination = 5 Possibilities
- 2 Combinations = 10 Possibilities
- 3 Combinations = 10 Possibilities
- 4 Combinations = 5 Possibilities and
- 5 Combinations = 1 Possibility

In our analysis of the data, we did not find evidence in the students' discourse that they were aware of Pascal's triangle or of the mathematics of binomial structures. Nevertheless, if the student sessions were to be continued over a longer period of time, students could be engaged with other problems that would provide them with opportunities to construct mathematical ideas and frameworks that underlie the rich concepts and structures of Pascal's arithmetic triangle (Edwards, 1987). In a mathematics classroom or during virtual mathematics problem-solving sessions, to promote the construction of ideas and framework, a curriculum unit could be built around a sequence of open-ended, well-designed mathematics tasks that engage teams of students with binomial structures in varied contexts. To make information on Pascal's triangle available to students as they are solving these tasks, we may do one of several things: Either an online moderator can direct students while they are in VMT to websites featuring discussions of Pascal's triangle, or a time-sensitive Wiki on Pascal's triangle may be made available to students only after they have completed a certain problem within a sequence of related problems.

In our study, the sophisticated cognitive structure that the two dyads built and made available on the shared whiteboard for each other emerged from interactional work. After the first ten minutes of nearly 120 minutes of work, the two dyads of students started to work as two separate units. In this sense, the two dyads were themselves like two entities of a single dyad. In the psychological literature on problem solving, it is commonly argued that when a dyad is engaged in solving a problem one student typically begins to solve the problem while the other listens to the ensuing solution attempt (e.g., Shirouzu, Miyake, & Masukawa, 2002). The speaker may be talking out loud while solving a problem while her partner listens. Analogously, one of our dyads presenting her solution on the whiteboard is like a speaker talking aloud about their problem-solving process. However, the data of this case study shows that instead both entities of the dyad simultaneously "talked" aloud their ensuing solution and that the non-ephemeral nature of their communication medium allowed each entity to "hear" the other while "talking" aloud their problem-solving attempt. An affordance of the virtual environment may have allowed for this simultaneous solving of the problem by both entities of the chat group. In a traditional dyad, it would be difficult for both members to solve a problem out loud while paying attention to each other as well as to their own work, because two people cannot speak at once face to face. Moreover, it is difficult to think in one way when a different way of thinking is being described aloud. In this virtual environment, perhaps because the workspace is shared, relatively large, equally visible to both dyads and communication is non-aural, it is easier for each dyad to go about problem solving individually while still paying attention to what the other dyad was doing.

As we have attempted to demonstrate, while solving the Pizza Problem, the interactional and collaborative work of Silvestre and Suzyn establishes important mathematical bases for their future action. These include ways of reasoning mathematically as well as particular combinatorial structures. Stahl (2006b) suggests that "[t]he being-there-together in a chat is temporally structured as a world of future possible activities with shared meaningful objects" (p. 115). The interactive work of the four students in the chat room that we have analyzed leaves them with tools for future collaboration. Interactively, they have built a discursive world of mathematical entities with which to engage particular combinatorial ideas and lines of reasoning. Silvestre and Suzyn experienced interacting together in the chat room, and this leaves them prepared for further collaborative mathematical actions with sets of shared, meaningful mathematical objects, relations among the objects and dynamics linking relations.

Chapter 14
Reading's Work in VMT

Alan Zemel and Murat Perit Çakir

Abstract This chapter presents a systematics of chat interaction. Online chats are advantageous sites for examining the organization of social interaction as achieved through computer-mediated communication. Chats differ from talk-in-interaction since the composition and visual inspection of text and graphical objects by any given actor is not observable by other participants. These structural constraints on the organization of interaction require that actors deploy alternative procedures for achieving what turn taking achieves in talk-in-interaction.

Keywords Co-presence · interaction · reading · CMC · text posting · indexical ground · systematics

In CSCL online chat systems like VMT, participants can engage with each other in a variety of ways. Rather than interact through emergent talk and observable embodied action, they:

- Exchange text postings through chat technology,
- Post text or graphic elements on a virtual whiteboard and/or
- Use referential tools provided by the system.

Interaction in VMT involves actors using computer hardware and software in ways that allow for the production of shared, displayed representations or virtual objects possessing various features that allow these objects to serve as the means by which participants interact. Participants are represented in various ways in VMT in terms of various conventions and practices of action identification. These representations—i.e., naming conventions and displays, avatars, authored messages, posted graphical objects, etc., as well as various changes in the appearance of objects or the state of the system—provide documentary evidence of actor presence (Zhao, 2003) and engagement with the system. It is these same resources that are put to

A. Zemel (✉)
Communication & Culture, Drexel University, Philadelphia, PA, USA
e-mail: arz27@drexel.edu

work to constitute social interaction among actors in a chat. In other words, *it is through the mediated exchange of what can be seen as locally relevant textual and graphical resources that chat participants organize and constitute their interaction*. The problem that chat participants face in task-directed chats of the sort we inspect is to coordinate their participation to collectively and collaboratively perform the task with the technical resources available in the hardware and software and with the textual and graphical resources they construct as relevant to their ongoing tasks. As it happens, this is a challenging problem that involves the management of and allocation of attention across multiple interface areas of the chat system and the ability to produce domain relevant artifacts (text messages, graphical artifacts, etc.) for inspection by others participating in the exchange of such artifacts.

Because these systems are designed in ways that allow participants to produce and inspect visual artifacts in particular ways, a natural question arises as to the nature of interaction that emerges in such environments. How do these interactions differ from talk-in-interaction? Speech exchange systems, like face-to-face conversation, telephony, video conferencing, etc., exploit and are constrained by the technical affordances of speech production. As Sacks et al. (1974) described, speech exchange systems rely on the affordances of the technology of talk to organize social interaction. The sequential organization of face-to-face conversational speech exchange is a product of the fact that actors are co-present to each other in an embodied way, which necessitates taking turns at listening and speaking. Thus actors allocate opportunities to speak and to listen in various ways such that one speaker speaks at a time and they repair problems of intelligibility that arise from mishearings, poorly produced speech and overlapping speech.

Chat environments, on the other hand, are not speech-exchange systems at all, but rather systems of interaction that involve the display and inspection of visual artifacts, including texts (Garcia & Jacobs, 1999). The sequential organization of the production of visual artifacts is both observable, available and documentable—and is something to which chat participants orient in their ongoing engagement in and through chat. However, the sequential organization of chat is not based on the same considerations that govern the sequential organization of talk-in-interaction. One obvious difference is that overlap can happen in talk but cannot happen in most kinds of chat systems. Overlap is a phenomenon of talk-in-interaction. Problems of hearability, problems related to the allocation of turns in talk, problems that provide for repair in talk-in-interaction simply do not occur in chat. Overlap does not occur in chat. Different kinds of interesting troubles with respect to the intelligibility of postings can and do occur in chat, but these have to do with sequential placement of postings and other displayed graphical artifacts. It is because of this and other differences in the technical production possibilities afforded by chat systems that we feel compelled to provide the beginnings of a simplest systematics of online chat and to describe some of the ways that interactions through online chat differ from interactions through speech.

Co-Presence

The analysis we present involves consideration of a number of foundational features that are constitutive of social interaction. According to Goodwin (2000a):

> The accomplishment of social action requires that not only the party producing an action, but also that others present, such as its addressee, be able to systematically recognize the shape and character of what is occurring. Without this it would be impossible for separate parties to recognize in common not only what is happening at the moment, but more crucially, what range of events are being projected as relevant nexts, such that an addressee can build not just another independent action, but instead a relevant coordinated next move to what someone else has just done. (p. 1491)

Not only must participants recognize what is happening, but participants must recognize "in common" what is happening. This notion strongly ties to Pollner's (1974) notion of mundane reasoning and Hanks' (2000) notion of indexical symmetry. Central to Goodwin's description are the practical achievements of presence, co-presence and the shared recognition of "what is occurring" in the scene. In other words, interaction arises when actors act in coordinated ways through mutual engagement with respect to recognizable and meaningful activities and shared-in-common and mutually recognizable orientations to (1) each other, (2) their actions and (3) features of the scene in which these activities are occurring. While Goodwin talks about coordinating contiguous actions as relevant to interaction, it is necessary to recognize that contiguity of action is not a requirement in all systems of social interaction.

In addition, social interaction requires more than reciprocal contact. Interaction requires *co-presence*. Co-presence is a condition of and for social interaction. According to Zhao:

> Copresence as mode of being with others is a form of human colocation in which individuals become "accessible, available and subject to one another" (Goffman, 1963, p. 22). More specifically, it is a set of spatio-temporal conditions in which instant two-way interactions can take place. *Instant* human interaction refers to real-time or near real-time human communication, which excludes diachronic exchanges like postal correspondence, and *two-way* human interaction refers to reciprocal or feedback-based human communication.... Copresence in this sense is thus a form of human colocation in space-time that allows for instantaneous and reciprocal human contact. (Zhao, 2003, p. 446)

Garfinkel (1967) performed an experiment to explore how people "do" co-presence. The subjects were to ask questions for which a "yes" or "no" would be an appropriate response. Respondents were presumed to have expertise in offering advice and could not be called on to account for their responses. However, in place of a presumed respondent answering, a sequence of yes-no responses were randomly constructed and offered to questioners in response to their queries. What Garfinkel observed was that the questioners were able to make sense of the responses and produce subsequent queries that oriented to the responses received. Even though, from the analyst's perspective, there was no co-present respondent, the activity and the actions of the questioners were constrained and organized in such a way that the questioner could reasonably infer a co-present respondent. We feel that Garfinkel's demonstration showed how actors worked to act as though others were co-present.

In ethnomethodological terms, *co-presence* is a gloss for the notion of a shared intersubjective world and the shared sense making and reasoning practices by which shared inferential practices manifest and sustain the reality of that intersubjective world (Pollner, 1974). In short, social interaction requires reciprocity of perspectives founded in a common life-world that allows participants to act as though each is seeing what the other is seeing despite any differences in perspective that might arise (Pollner, 1974). According to Hanks (2000, p. 7), reciprocity of perspective is "neither similarity ('sharedness'), nor congruence per se, but the idea that interactants' perspectives are opposite, complimentary parts of a single whole, with each oriented to the other." It provides the basis by which an actor can reliably act as though other actors can, to some degree, see what she sees, know what she knows, feel what she feels, etc.

> The more interactants share, the more congruent, reciprocal and transposable their perspectives, the more symmetric is the interactive field. The greater the differences that divide them, the more asymmetric the field. (Hanks, 2000, p. 8).

This reciprocity of perspectives establishes a sense of co-presence in which the experiences and perceptions of the actors in a scene become practically available to each other. The practical problem for actors engaged in online chat is quite simply to figure out how to use the visual artifacts (virtual objects and text) and the affordances of the chat system so that they and others can recognize these artifacts and their use as constitutive of social interaction in that environment.

Interaction as Reading's Work

It is clear from the data we have inspected that chat systems display an alternative organization of social interaction, one that is not based on the notions of consequential contiguity of action and turn taking in conversation. Specifically, in VMT actors may compose and post texts, develop and post graphical objects, etc., without being constrained by the actions of others precisely because the system allows it and because those actions are not witnessed or witnessable by other chat participants. In conversation, turn taking arises from just this notion that the witnessed and witnessable production of talk constrains the talk of others. The nature of these constraints are what organize action into turns, turn sequences and the like. Thus turn taking requires that an actor and the recipients of that actor's actions collaborate to allocate their participation in orderly ways to produce meaningfully contiguous actions (Schegloff, 2007). Online chats often seem unruly and disorderly (Garcia & Jacobs, 1999) precisely because there is no obvious way to achieve the same kind of orderly contiguity as can be achieved in talk-in-interaction.

In practice, the achievable orderliness of online chat interactions is produced not by the way participants collaborate to produce actions, but by readers who, through the work of "reading," are responsible for identifying the progressively sequential nature of observable online postings even though the procedures of turn-taking in a strict sense cannot apply. One oft-heard complaint about chat is that postings are often "out of turn," which causes participants to struggle with the continuity or, as Schegloff (2007) calls it, the progressivity of ongoing interaction:

> Moving from some element to a hearably-next-one with nothing intervening is the embodiment of, and the measure of, progressivity. Should something intervene between some element and what is hearable as a/the next one due—should something violate or interfere with their contiguity, whether next sound, next word, or next turn—it will be heard as qualifying the progressivity of the talk, and will be examined for its import, for what understanding should be accorded it. (p. 15)

Contiguity does not operate in chats in the same manner as in talk-in-interaction. The actions participants perform to produce text or graphical objects for display and distribution to others are not observable or available to anyone but the person performing those actions. Anyone can post a text or a graphical object at any time without regard for the actions of others. This is a feature and affordance of common chat systems. Thus, any sense of progressivity and turn organization can only be achieved *ex post facto* as the recipients' work of inspecting postings for how they could be constituted as a sequence of actions. Contiguity is problematic as a basis for establishing and recognizing the sequential organization of postings in chat. Consequently actors resort to other procedures and resources to achieve a sense of progressivity in their chats.

The constitution of sequentiality and the perceived orderliness of chat interaction is a reader's achievement in chat. The work required to make sense of textual and graphical postings is what Livingston terms *reading*. According to Livingston (1995):

> The work of reading is the work of finding the organization of that work that a text describes. The contextual clues in a text offer the grounds, from within the active participatory work of reading, for finding how those clues provide an adequate account of how the text should be read. (p. 14)

While Livingston's notion of reading is oriented to text-based materials, we would suggest that a more general notion of reading would involve the work of making sense of visual artifacts whether they are text-based, graphical, etc. Actors who are working to make sense of graphical or textual artifacts assume that these artifacts are produced, organized and displayed for inspection and to inform and instruct viewers concerning how they are to be understood. In other words, each visual artifact provides clues for how viewers are to make sense of it and, in the case of VMT, for how they are also to make sense of that artifact in relation to previously posted graphical artifacts and previous chat postings.

Interaction's Traces

The data we inspect for our analysis of social interaction in online chat consist of time-stamped chat logs of math problem solving in the VMT Project, where groups of three to five students in grades 6–11 collaborated online to solve math problems that required reflection and discussion. Each session lasted an hour and was supervised by a VMT facilitator who did not participate in problem-solving work with the other participants. The participants understood that they were to collaboratively work together to produce solutions to posted math problems. This was made evident in the way that they managed their participation in the chats.

Various software platforms were used to facilitate these sessions, including AOL's Instant Messenger (AIM) and versions of a custom VMT chat environment. AIM provides a simple chat interface where the users interact with each other by exchanging short texts. These sessions were recorded as chat transcripts with participant identifier, the time-stamp of the posting and the content posted (see Log 14.1). Note how these postings use many textual features to guide the work of reading them (words, math symbols, chat abbreviations, capitalization, ideographic conventions, etc.); these guides are available in the log traces just as they were in the live postings.

Log 14-1.

pin	(8:40:42 PM):	this is easy
pin	(8:40:46 PM):	for the 12 triangle
pin	(8:40:52 PM):	144=36+x
pin	(8:40:55 PM):	so x =////
pin	(8:40:58 PM):	....*
Avr	(8:41:03 PM):	**NOBODY DO THE MATH**
Avr	(8:41:06 PM):	**I'M DOING IT**
pin	(8:41:12 PM):	square root 108
Avr	(8:41:16 PM):	**I KNOW I KNOW**
Sup	(8:41:19 PM):	lol
Avr	(8:41:20 PM):	**LET ME DO IT**
pin	(8:42:04 PM):	be my guest
Avr	(8:42:39 PM):	**okay**

In contrast to AIM, the VMT environment provides two interactive components, namely a text-based chat and a shared whiteboard as discussed in other chapters of this volume.

One of the unique features of the VMT system is the referencing support mechanism that allows users to visually connect their chat postings either to previous chat postings or to areas on the whiteboard (see Chapter 15). VMT chat sessions are also recorded as transcripts with participant identifier, the time-stamp of the action performed and the content posted. Due to the added complexity of the whiteboard component and the referencing tool, VMT transcripts include additional types of actions, such as drawings, manipulation of an object on the board, messages indicating start/end of typing activity, referencing pointers, etc.

In an effort to tackle the practical challenges of analyzing such complex transcripts we used the VMT Replayer tool, which allows us to replay a VMT session as it unfolded in real time based on the time-stamps of actions recorded in the log file. The order of actions we observe with the Replayer as researchers exactly matches the order of actions experienced by the users. However, the temporal difference between actions we observed could differ in the order of micro-seconds from what the users had experienced due to factors such as network delays affecting the delivery of packages to clients, and the rendering performance of the user's personal computer. In other words, although we are not able to exactly reconstruct the chat from the perspective of each participant, we have a sufficiently good approximation that allows us to study the sequential unfolding of events at each session, which is crucial in making sense of the complex interactions taking place in a collaborative software environment.

Technologically-Mediated Social Interaction

Interactants in chat work with chat technology as a form of technologically mediated social interaction (Garcia & Jacobs, 1999). Technically (from the perspective of the network technology), interaction in chat-only systems is achieved as the posting of texts to the chat system for distribution to all the nodes logged into the chat server so that other participants have the opportunity to view the posted texts, read them and respond. For example, it is understood by users of chat systems that texts posted within a chat interface are made available to other participants and that other participants are to orient to these postings in their subsequently posted texts.

Even when a text is posted to which no one responds, the absence of a response may be a meaningful and consequential social action. Thus, for example, if a text is posted and no one responds, the lack of response may be treated as an accountable matter. Even if no account of a lack of response is called for, the posting and its subsequent treatment are social facts for the participants in the chat.

In chat systems with whiteboards, participants read and produce both text postings and graphical displays. Graphical artifacts posted to a whiteboard are available for other participants to view. Objects made available for inspection in the whiteboard are often treated as referential resources for and by participants in the chat. Participants in online chats with whiteboards constitute and treat each other as readers and authors of texts and graphical objects in their interactional work. (There are, of course, features of the interactional work which are oriented toward the management and use of the technology itself, which occur at individual terminals connected to the chat system and which are often times not available for inspection by other participants). The consequence of this for participants and observers of chat interactions is that the sequence, organization and textual resources of chat postings and the whiteboard positioning, manipulation and semiotic resources of graphical displays constitute the indexical ground (Hanks, 1992) by which the sense making work of chat interaction is achieved (see Chapters 6 and 7).

Typically, different areas of the user interface are devoted to whiteboard activity and chat. Participants are faced with the challenge of monitoring different areas of the interface while at times also producing text or graphical artifacts for posting and display. Participants appear to orient to the fact that simply posting a text message or a graphical artifact may not always be adequate to assure that other users will "see" it or give it the consideration that the author might hope for. Because a participant's attention may not be given to that part of the interface displaying a newly posted text or graphical artifact, the producer of a text or graphical artifact cannot be sure that any given recipient is aware of a posted text or artifact unless an explicit response to that posting is produced and displayed. While graphical displays in the whiteboard are viewable by any participant, such displays need not necessarily be designed or produced to solicit responses from others, and they are typically not treated that way (though on occasion they are). Whiteboard items are often treated as displays to which participants orient in the production of chat messages. They are treated as illustrations of conceptual objects that are available for inspection, but they are not used specifically to elicit responses from viewers. Such responses are elicited through chat postings that make reference to these items. The whiteboard postings serve to provide indexical ground for chat postings. While user-generated text postings in the chat area are oriented to, produced and treated as a way of soliciting in-kind responses from others, whiteboard postings are typically oriented to, produced and treated as ways of establishing indexical symmetry (Hanks, 1996).

Thus there are significant differences between posted text messages and other graphical artifacts made available in VMT. These differences are significant because users of VMT themselves find the differences relevant and orient to these differences in their ongoing interaction. Furthermore, designers of CSCL chat systems recognize, orient to and display the significance of these differences in the way that these systems are designed. For example, in the VMT system, chat activities occur separately from the exchange or display of visual artifacts on the whiteboard. Different technologies are deployed to handle the exchange and display of graphical and textual artifacts. Furthermore, user interfaces (viz., chat and whiteboard) are designed to reflect these differences. Therefore, as we develop this analysis, we distinguish and demonstrate the relationship between two categories of visual artifacts, i.e., text postings (or messages) to the chat interface and graphical displays on the whiteboard.

The data we examine systematically demonstrate that text exchange through chat is used as the principle method of achieving "real-time" social interaction among participants. Progressivity and the appropriate projection and production of in-kind responses in chat serve as the basis by which participants come to treat their actions as social interaction. Indexical symmetry is an achievement of both chat and whiteboard activity. While text postings accumulate and scroll out of the visual field, whiteboard content is systematically used to establish indexical symmetry; relevant artifacts and occasionally emergent content are displayed for ongoing or persistent deictic reference over the course of ongoing chat interaction. In other words, whiteboard contents are items (1) which participants add and modify to display and share their then-current state of practical reasoning and/or indexical ground with respect to the task at hand and (2) to which participants refer in their ongoing chat interaction as persistent and recoverable demonstrations of practical reasoning and/or indexical ground.

Text Postings in Chat

Recent treatments of online chat interactions have documented that chats are significantly different from face-to-face interactions. In their seminal work on online chats as interactional phenomena, Garcia and Jacobs (1998, 1999) have noted that turn taking, turn allocation and repair in chat differs significantly from the way that turn taking, turn allocation and repair are performed in face-to-face interaction. The main difference is that *online chats are not speech-exchange systems*; rather *they are text-exchange systems*. It is no wonder that turn-taking organization and repair are very different phenomena than their counterparts in face-to-face interaction because the practical achievement of sequencing actions in chat is done so differently from speech by virtue of the technology of online chat. One consequence of this is, as Garcia and Jacobs point out, that the monitoring and posting of text messages are more loosely linked to the actions of other chat participants than the monitoring and execution of conversational actions among interlocutors in face-to-face interaction. Furthermore, where violations of projected next-turn actions are treated as repairable or accountable matters in face-to-face interaction, they are routinely treated as affordances of the technology by which online chats are achieved and thus do not always warrant the production of repairs or accounts. Of course, repair happens in chats, but its organization and achievement are subject to the technical constraints that govern the posting of messages (Schönfeldt & Golato, 2003).

Text postings in chat are designed to be read by all participants in the chat. Text messages differ from speech in a number of interactionally significant ways. In most chat systems, text messages are composed "in private," i.e., only the composer can witness its production, no other chat participants see the emergent text as it is being composed[1]. Chat participants only "see" a text after it is:

- Released by its author,
- Received by the server for distribution to other chat participants and
- Displayed on recipients' computer screens.

This process of text production and distribution presents participants with significant coordination concerns as they exchange texts.

One interactionally relevant consideration of online chat is that actors cannot closely coordinate with others by monitoring what others are doing since the actual production of chat artifacts (text messages, etc.) is unavailable for examination by

---

[1] Some of the earlier chat tools offered interfaces that allow their users to witness the production of messages, such as Unix Talk and earlier versions of ICQ. However, such tools need to split the screen into multiple areas dedicated to each user so that the production process can be seen at all clients. This brings scalability and intelligibility issues of the chat taking place in the environment. Now most popular chat and IM systems employ the strategy of displaying awareness messages while the user is typing, and then display the message after the user posts the message to the server.

recipients. Problems of sequentiality and coherence become relevant to participants and are managed in the way that actors design their texts to be read and recipients come to read these texts. Therefore, chat participants face the task of producing texts to be read in ways that are designed to display their sense and to read those texts in the ways they were designed to be read, even though the actual production of postings cannot be observed.

In face-to-face interaction, actors rely on the sequential organization and production of talk, of embodied action, environmental resources, etc., for the achievement of interactional sense making. In online chat, participants only have access to posted texts that typically do not display their sequential construction, the performance of self-repairs, etc. In addition, there are no technical constraints imposed on other actors when an actor composes a text. To illustrate what this means, consider the following. In speech exchange systems, when two parties speak at the same time, hearability of the speech of either party is compromised. When two parties compose and post messages at the same time, the readability of the texts is unaffected. Thus, there is no technical incentive to manage sequentiality in text-exchange systems as there is in speech-exchange systems. This doesn't mean that actors post willy-nilly in chats. Intelligibility is an issue with respect to how actors read the texts in relation to prior postings and in relation to whatever projected subsequent postings might be possibly relevant.

One example is shown in Log 14.2. At line 318, Avr's request, **"okay can you explain how you're getting it,"** is presented in its entirety as a completed text. We don't see it's construction. This is contrasted with the work that Pin does in lines 319–323, 326 and 328, where he produces a sequence of short and grammatically linked postings that constitute, as a sequence, what readers treat as an extended posting.

Log 14-2.

318	Avr	(9:00:52 PM):	okay can you explain how you're getting it
319	pin	(9:01:29 PM):	im doing trial and error
320	pin	(9:01:31 PM):	and i know
321	pin	(9:01:32 PM):	that it is
322	pin	(9:01:36 PM):	the sides
323	pin	(9:01:39 PM):	are between
324	Avr	(9:01:41 PM):	uh huh
325	Avr	(9:01:45 PM):	I had a flash of brilliance
326	pin	(9:01:48 PM):	21
327	Avr	(9:01:48 PM):	just tell me the ratio
328	pin	(9:01:50 PM):	and 21.5

While each of Pin's postings are presented in their entirety, they are constituent elements in what is being built to be read as an extended multi-post message. By using grammatical resources and short durations between postings, Pin is able to display in the texts he is posting that they are being presented to be read as a string of connected postings. In this way, users are occasionally able to approximate the display of the sequential construction of postings.

Log 14-3.

153	azn	(8:18:27 PM):	did anyone get farther than this?
154	Ame	(8:18:35 PM):	**Because it never says which order the lengths of the segments are**
155	**lif**	**(8:18:38 PM):**	**not really, all that i know is that**
156	**lif**	**(8:18:39 PM):**	**:**
157	Ame	(8:18:39 PM):	**we have to find out**
158	Ame	(8:19:00 PM):	**I say there are six possible orders or length**
159	**Fir**	**(8:19:00 PM):**	**well i said earlier that i just used trial and error and factored it out using the number I had picked and i found that it had to be less than 4**
160	Ame	(8:19:38 PM):	**(n^2+4+4n)<9<(n^2+5n) is possible**
161	**lif**	**(8:19:53 PM):**	**(n + 2)2 < 9 + n(n + 5) and 9 < (n + 2)2 + n(n + 5) and n(n + 5) < 9 + (n + 2)2**

In Log 14.3, Lif organizes his response to Azn's query in multiple postings in such a way that the first two postings (lines 155 and 156) project the production of a longer elaboration on his findings regarding the problem at hand (line 161).

When a participant posts a text message, it may be constructed so as to be read as incomplete, projecting that a next post by that participant (not necessarily the next post in the sequence) is to be read as a continuation of the participant's current posting. This can be done using grammatical resources such as an incomplete phrase or sentence) and other lexical resources such as ellipsis, colons, etc.

An increasingly available feature incorporated into chat systems is the production of "awareness messages," which are system-generated indications of activity performed by others. In the systems we examine (VMT and AIM), various awareness messages were available. When an actor engaged in the composition of a text message, a system-generated message was displayed to all participants indicating that the actor was typing. Even though the awareness messages indicate that an actor is typing, recipients cannot know what is being typed until the text is posted to the system. On occasion, actors type and apparently erase their typing without posting.

Chat repair is organized differently than repair in talk-in-interaction. Specifically, in order to effect a repair to a posted text, another text needs to be posted indicating that it is a repair and what it is repairing. This organization of repair arises because once a text is posted to the chat system, it cannot be manipulated any further. It becomes fixed even as it is displayed.

In Log 14.4, Mcp repairs his statement in line 3 by posting two more subsequent postings. In his first posting Mcp offers a new value (line 4). His next posting (line 5) establishes the relationship between the new value and the erroneous one he previously reported, and hence accomplishes the repair.

Another feature of text postings is that they are enduring in particular ways. Once a text is posted, it becomes part of the posting history and is accessible for review.

Log 14-4.

1	mcp	(8:40:15 PM):	Oh, I see where your 18 and 10.125 are from now. I had already doubled and you waited till later. Yes, I'm with all this.
2	real	(8:40:31 PM):	I got it
3	mcp	(8:40:40 PM):	And dragging the sqrt(3) along would give exactly 156.
4	mcp	(8:40:44 PM):	15
5	mcp	(8:40:48 PM):	not 156

It is possible to scroll backward in a chat to view previous postings. Once a text has been posted, it remains available for viewing in history of the sequence of postings. This allows participants to examine previously posted texts that may have "scrolled" out of view over the course of their ongoing interaction.

The VMT chat system provides a referencing tool as an additional resource by which someone composing a text posting can link that posting to either a previously posted message or an object on the whiteboard. This tool provides actors with a graphical resource in designing their chat postings for linking the current posting to a prior one. Thus actors who compose texts and readers who read them need not only rely on lexical resources to indicate relationships between contiguous and non-contiguous postings (see Chapter 21).

The VMT referencing tool can also be used to link a current chat posting to an area of the whiteboard. It thus provides message designers with the means to make graphical indexical references in a manner that is somewhat analogous to the way gesture is occasionally deployed in face-to-face talk-in-interaction (see Chapter 17).

These are some of the features of text postings in chat. The interactional consequences of these features can be summarized as follows. By producing texts for display to other participants, actors are demonstrating their active presence by influencing and altering the state of the system by their actions. These very texts are not only produced to change the state of the system but are also produced to be read and to be responded to as meaningful by recipients. The meaningfulness of text postings derives from the work done by postings to establish a reciprocity of perspective between the text's author and its recipients. This is achieved using shared lexical, grammatical and textual resources and it is achieved by the exchange of postings which are treated as meaningful by participants. Thus text exchange in chat provides for a form of social interaction based on the production and reading of posted texts.

Graphical Artifacts

Graphical artifacts can be distinguished from text-based chat artifacts by virtue of the fact that:

- They are typically produced and displayed in a different part of the user interface of the chat system,
- They are designed for inspection by all participants but are rarely used to solicit text artifacts or other graphical artifacts from other participants and
- They call on recipients to make use of shared indexical ground and deictic practices different from those of chat for their intelligibility.

The work of producing graphical artifacts in the whiteboard involves designing and constructing artifacts to be seen and recognized in relation to ongoing chat postings and displayed whiteboard objects. This work, while similar to the work of producing for reading and reading text postings, displays certain particularities that derive from the technology of whiteboard artifact production. The technology of artifact production in the whiteboard of the VMT system involves the piece-wise production and arrangement of the constituent elements of the artifact. This is shown and analyzed in Chapter 7. The piece-wise nature of artifact production allows recipients to witness the emergent achievement of the artifact on the whiteboard.

In addition, once posted, graphical artifacts on the whiteboard can be manipulated, altered, moved, etc. Actors can position or reposition one or a collection of such constituent elements in relation to other artifacts. They can also delete items from the current whiteboard space (though they remain available by scrolling back in the whiteboard history in the VMT system). This stands in marked contrast to text postings in the chat system that cannot be manipulated or altered in any way once a text is posted.

Another feature of the VMT system is that there are awareness markers that indicate user actions in the whiteboard. These appear in the chat window as a series of colored squares. A square appears in the chat every time an action is performed and posted in the whiteboard (see Fig. 14.1). These squares are color-coded and correspond to the color assigned to users.

The sense-making apparatus invoked by the placement and display of a whiteboard artifact involves recognizing what is presented in relation to other whiteboard artifacts and to ongoing chat activity. Whiteboard artifacts become relevant to actors in a variety of ways. One use of such artifacts is to serve as an illustration of a matter that is topically relevant in chat postings. Because these artifacts are both persistent and mutable, they can serve as indexical resources that provide for symmetrical perspectives on a matter under consideration in chat. As part of an ethnomethodological study of cognitive scientists' whiteboard use during design meetings in a face-to-face setting, Suchman conjectured that "...while the whiteboard comprises an unfolding setting for the work at hand, the items on the board also index an horizon of past and future activities" (1990, p. 317). In other words, what gets done now informs the relevant actions to be performed subsequently, and what was done previously could be reproduced or reused depending on the circumstances of the ongoing activity.

Because of the mutable and persistent nature of whiteboard artifacts, it is possible for actors to add objects and arrange them. The production and placement of whiteboard artifacts allows an author to display to him/herself and other recipients the achievement of practical reasoning as the piece-wise construction of these artifacts. For instance, Fig. 14.1 shows an example where the participants move a number of individual textboxes to achieve a particular layout on the shared space. The achieved organization displays how individual items are seen and read as related pieces of a larger organization.

Additionally, practical reasoning is demonstrated by the placement and juxtaposition of these artifacts as indexical resources relevant to the ongoing interactional work of the participants. Participants coordinate their chat activities with whiteboard artifacts and also coordinate whiteboard artifacts within the field of extant artifacts using the deictic resources of the technology (reference tools, linguistic deictics embedded in the chat, etc.) and the artifacts themselves as deictic resources. For instance, Fig. 14.2 presents an example where a participant uses a recently completed drawing as a referential resource to formulate a question directed to his teammates: "so it has at least 6 triangles? / In this, for instance."

Chat postings and objects posted on the whiteboard differ in terms of the way they are used as referential resources by the participants. The content of the whiteboard is persistently available for reference and manipulation, whereas the chat content is visually available for reference for a relatively shorter period of time. This is due to the linear growth of chat content which replaces previous messages with the most recent contributions at the bottom of the chat window. Although one can make explicit references to older postings by using the scroll-bar feature, the limited size of the chat window reinforces a referential locality between postings that are visually proximal to each other. This visual locality qualifies the whiteboard as the more persistent medium as an interactional resource, although both media technically offer a persistent record of their contents through their scrollable histories.

A Systematics of Interaction in VMT

In this chapter, we have described the systematic affordances of AIM and the VMT chat systems by which actors produce and inspect various kinds of locally relevant visual artifacts as the means by which they organize their online interaction. In synchronous computer-mediated communication systems such as these, actors produce an assortment of visual artifacts—textual and graphical—to achieve co-presence and establish indexical symmetry with respect to matters of relevant concern. The work that actors do when posting graphical and textual materials is the work of creating "readable" visual artifacts that allow recipients to achieve a sense of interaction by making sense of what they see in the chat system.

When it comes to talk, co-presence and the contiguity of actions provide for turn taking as the foundational organization of talk-in-interaction (Schegloff, 2007). In chat systems of the kind we have investigated, contiguity is not a relevant or determining factor in assessing the meaning of an action. It is not about what just happened or what happens next. It is about the way that readers connect objects through reading's work to create a "thread of meaning" from the various postings available

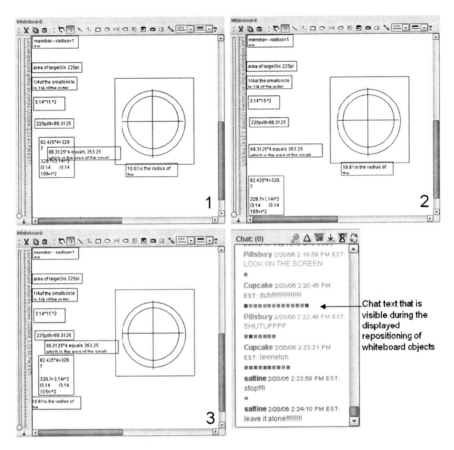

Fig. 14.1 Movement of graphical objects to do practical reasoning

for inspection. Proximity may be more relevant to the sense making required in chat systems than contiguity. Chat systems are about posting objects for visual inspection that allow readers to make connections between these posted objects based on their availability for inspection and the features they display rather than on a strict notion of their position in a sequence. This means that sequentiality is not something that has to be built based on a notion of the contiguity of actions as in talk-in-interaction. Rather, *reading's work in chat is precisely the process by which actors constitute a sequence of actions as interaction from the production and inspection of available visual artifacts.*

The specific procedures by which readers and authors constitute interaction from the production and inspection of visual artifacts in chat have been described above. In chat, participants rely on the proximity rather than the contiguity of text posting and graphical objects as a way of achieving a sense of progression in their interaction. Specific lexical, grammatical and, in the case of graphical artifacts, graphical resources are used to link postings of various sorts, to demonstrate that postings are

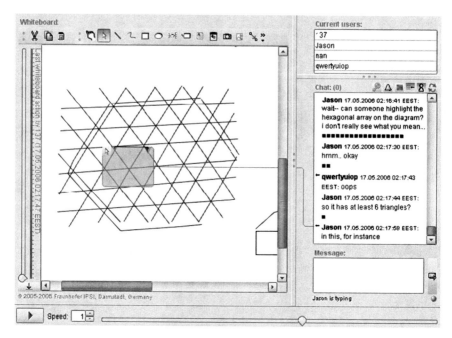

Fig. 14.2 Jason indexes an area of the whiteboard

to be seen as linked and to display what that link consists of. In addition to using reference tools in the production of chat text, when available, to regulate one's own actions and the actions of others, actors indicate with the use of ellipses and other continuation markers (short and grammatically incomplete postings, etc.) that they are producing a series of postings that are to be read as a sequence, even though the postings may not be contiguous. When producing graphical objects in the white-board, actors use proximity and its achievement by moving objects within the white-board space to indicate they are producing the composite features of what is being produced as a single object. The temporal sequence of the production of whiteboard objects is not necessarily treated as a relevant consideration in the construction of whiteboard objects, whereas the locational proximity of these objects with respect to each other may be treated as relevant.

   In chat environments, social interaction is the local achievement of reading's work, understood to be both the production and receipt of visual artifacts (both textual and graphical) that are designed to provide through their proper inspection adequate resources by which actors constitute:

- The presence of actors in the system,
- The co-presence of actors who are mutually orienting to each other and the actions they perform,
- The indexical ground of conditionally relevant objects and texts, and
- Indexical symmetry among participants with respect to these visual artifacts.

Part IV
Designing the VMT Collaboration Environment

Introduction to Part IV

In this Part, the past, present and future development of the VMT environment is considered in terms of its support for collaborative learning and mathematical discourse. Since the VMT Project proceeded through cycles of design-based research, the technical environment evolved in response to iterations of design, prototype, trial, analysis, redesign.

After an initial intervention trying small-group face-to-face collaboration on a math problem in an urban middle-school classroom, the VMT ran PoW-wows using a simple chat system (see Chapter 9). It was obvious from observations of the classroom videos and of the chat logs that mechanisms for exchanging graphical documents did not provide adequate support for visual inscriptions related to the problems being discussed. A search of open-source whiteboards and a survey of collaboration prototypes under development in North America and Europe led to the decision to use ConcertChat, with its text chat, shared whiteboard and graphical referencing tool.

Chapter 15 discusses the design rationale of the ConcertChat system, motivated largely by the need to integrate the chat with the whiteboard as a dual-interaction space. The chapter is written by the German team that designed and implemented the system. Wessner was the project manager and Mühlpfordt designed and implemented the system as part of his doctoral dissertation work. Wessner spent the summer of 2004 in Philadelphia as a visiting researcher at the VMT Project, helping to design the VMT Lobby as an extension to ConcertChat. Mühlpfordt spent the next summer at VMT, helping to adapt ConcertChat to the specific needs of the VMT Project. VMT provided a test-bed for evolving the ConcertChat software and led to it being released as open source. The integrated design of the system makes possible the kind of coordination of visual, narrative and symbolic work—distributed across the dual-interaction space of chat and whiteboard in accordance with the persistence characteristics of the different media—documented in Chapter 7.

Chapter 16 extends the discussion of integration to the modules added to ConcertChat for the VMT service. This includes the Lobby as well as wiki support. The goal is to support learning and knowledge building at the individual, small-group and community levels in an integrated way. This more extensive integration across additional interaction spaces facilitated the bridging across sessions and from the group chat to the community wiki analyzed in Chapter 6.

Chapter 17 explores the graphical referencing tool of ConcertChat through analysis of how students in a chat session enacted the affordances of the technology by coordinating their activities in the dual-interaction space using a mixture of referencing techniques. This case study illustrates the importance of the kind of support the referencing tool provides for pointing to math objects of mutual concern.

Chapter 18 reflects on the role of scripting for organizing learning activities. The VMT Spring Fests held sequences of chats: four sessions by the same team during a two-week period. Scripting took place in three ways: a topic was defined for the Spring Fest, including a phased set of activities around a mathematical problem; a facilitator was present in the chat room, equipped with a script of instructions for the student participants and trained to avoid interfering in the problem-solving work of the student team; between sessions, lengthy feedback commentaries were placed by VMT staff on the whiteboard. These three forms of scripting provided resources to help the student team direct and organize their work, without micromanaging the methods adopted by the team for achieving their aims. This can be seen as providing the basis for the group agency reported in Chapter 11 and for stimulating the group creativity discussed in Chapter 12. This chapter takes a more general look at scripting, reflecting on the concept as used in CSCL.

Chapter 19 proposes further support in the form of automated agents that provide help to the students. This chapter is somewhat speculative about possibilities for the future of VMT, that have only been prototyped in a very preliminary version. The idea is to take advantage of the computational power of the computer network that is mediating student interaction. The chapter proposes building on the success of computer tutors for math problem solving by individual students, leveraging the sophisticated linguistic analysis techniques used there. First steps in a collaboration between Carnegie Mellon University researchers and the VMT Project begin to explore the issues of scripting, agency and agent-student interaction involved in the proposed use of helpful agents.

Chapter 15
The Integration of Dual-Interaction Spaces

Martin Mühlpfordt and Martin Wessner

Abstract Dual-interaction spaces—that combine text chat with a shared graphical work area—have been developed in recent years as CSCL applications to support the synchronous construction and discussion of shared artifacts by distributed small groups of students. However, the simple juxtaposition of the two spaces raises numerous issues for users: How can objects in the shared workspace be referenced from within the chat? How can users track and comprehend all the various simultaneous activities? How can participants coordinate their multifaceted actions? We present three steps toward integration of activities across separate interaction spaces: support for deictic references, implementation of a history feature and display of social awareness information.

Keywords Dual-interaction space · deictic reference · history · social awareness

The construction, modification, annotation and arrangement of shared artifacts are key activities in many collaborative learning settings. Software systems now exist that permit synchronous coordinated manipulation of such shared artifacts even for geographically distributed users, by providing a shared graphical workspace. A shared workspace in a collaborative environment is an area of the software interface that allows a participant to construct and manipulate a graphical object so that the object and the effects of the manipulation appear in the corresponding area of the other participants' interfaces, essentially in real time. These shared workspaces may be used for creating and using external representations of knowledge (Whittaker, 2003), for collaboratively completing design tasks (Reimann & Zumbach, 2001), for working together with simulations (Jermann, 2004; Landsman & Alterman, 2003), or for solving math problems, as in VMT. The design of shared workspaces is an important topic in computer-supported collaborative learning (CSCL).

M. Mühlpfordt (✉)
Computer Science, IPSI Fraunhofer Institute, Germany
e-mail: martin.muehlpfordt@gmx.de

G. Stahl (ed.), *Studying Virtual Math Teams*, Computer-Supported Collaborative
Learning Series 11, DOI 10.1007/978-1-4419-0228-3_15,
© Springer Science+Business Media, LLC 2009

Learning at a distance requires a medium of communication. The medium can be auditory, audio-visual or text-based. For collaborative learning, textual synchronous communication with chat has two main advantages over audio and even face-to-face: For the chat poster, writing encourages a more careful planning of one's contribution; it fosters reflection on the discourse. For the recipient, the communication is persistent and available in symbolic form that "may be searched, browsed, replayed, annotated, visualized, restructured and recontextualized" (Erickson, 1999).

The combination of a shared workspace with chat makes two regions for interaction available to a group in the form of a dual-interaction space (Dillenbourg, 2005). The chat provides a medium of communication for the exchange of textual messages; the shared workspace allows for the collaborative construction and manipulation of shared artifacts that are relevant to the task at hand. In most groupware systems for synchronous distance learning, the chat and graphical workspace simply appear next to each other as two visually distinct areas of the application that are largely functionally independent of each other. This introduces a number of problems for the users (Pata & Sarapuu, 2003; Suthers et al., 2003; van Bruggen, 2003). For instance, if a group of students want to create a concept map in the shared workspace consisting of arguments pro and con and their relationships to each other, this raises the following questions:

- How can objects and relationships within the workspace be referenced from a posting in the chat area?
- How can the participants grasp and understand the relationships among each other of the activities and messages that are part of a single collaborative interaction but are distributed across the two interaction spaces? For example, how can one establish that the message, "I agree," is a response to the introduction of a particular new node in the argumentation graph?
- How can the participants coordinate their actions in the graphical workspace and in the chat with each other? For example, when and by whom should an argument introduced in the chat be added to the graphical concept map?

A better software integration of chat and workspace is needed to overcome such difficulties (Dimitracopoulou, 2005; McCarthy & Monk, 1994; Suthers, 2001). But from the perspective of software design the question, which functionalities must be provided to support the collaboration in dual-interaction spaces, remains unanswered; the claim for better integration is too general to guide the design of the learning environment. This became apparent in the workshop "Dual-interaction spaces" at CSCL 2005 in Taipei organized by Dillenbourg (2005) and the CSCL SIG of Kaleidoscope.

In this chapter we propose integration measures for three relevant aspects of the connection of chat and shared workspace:

- deictic referencing,
- coordinating simultaneous activities and
- understanding of past interactions.

These problems are analyzed in the next section. In a third section we will describe the integration measures. Then we will present experiences with ConcertChat—a collaboration tool that implements these measures and is part of the VMT environment.

For the sake of simplicity this chapter describes our development of the integration measures as a linear process starting with problem analysis that leads to certain functionalities. As we know from CSCL research, this idealized development seldom holds. Our system was developed over five years. We started with assumptions of what is needed by the users, developed first prototypes and used them in serious learning settings. The analysis of those real collaborations provided us insights into the complex nature of mediated collaborative meaning making in dual-interaction spaces. Our focus gradually shifted from an individual point of view (what is needed by a user) to a group cognition (Stahl, 2006b) perspective taking into account the creative, simultaneous, interwoven interactions among the team members.

Problems in Combined Interaction Spaces

A shared workspace can play at least two contrasting roles within a collaborative session. It can, for instance, provide the central location for the joint activity of the participants, with the chat playing a supportive role in discussing and disambiguating the activities that take place in the workspace. Conversely, the chat discourse can dominate, with the graphical workspace serving as a resource for clarification or for illustrating things that are hard to articulate in words. Which way communication is divided between the dual spaces depends upon the current task, the meta-communicative skills of the participants and the respective affordances of the two media (Dillenbourg & Traum, 2006; Pata & Sarapuu, 2003). The activities in the chat and the shared workspace are typically intimately interrelated. To the extent that the technology supports it, participants may coordinate their use of the dual spaces in creative and subtle ways (see Chapters 7 and 17).

A prominent characteristic of chat is the delay between the production of a message by its author and its presentation to others when it is complete. This has two main advantages: that the author can revise the message before sending it and that several people can be producing messages at the same time, unlike in spoken conversation (see Chapter 14). However, it also leads to the constant danger of sequential incoherence, which forces the participants to work additionally on explicitly coordinating the content and structure of their interactions (see Chapter 21). The problem is that, unlike in conversation, in chat the appearance of responses often do not immediately temporally follow the messages to which they are responding. The coherence of interaction is highly dependent upon the response structure between messages. But in the time it takes for someone to prepare and send a response to one note, a note from someone else can be posted, causing "interrupted turn adjacency" (Herring, 1999). A number of specific communication strategies may be evoked to deal with this (Fuks, Pimentel & Lucena, 2006; Lonchamp, 2006; Murray, 2000). In order to minimize the delay in responding, mistakes in syntax and wording are accepted and many abbreviations or acronyms are used (Garcia & Jacobs, 1999). Cohesive devices like explicitly naming the addressee of a contribution (Nash, 2005) are used to make references explicit.

The fact that several people can be producing messages at the same time means that the common conversational rules of turn taking (Sacks et al., 1974) do not apply. The resulting parallelism can scarcely be avoided, and must particularly be taken into account when multiple topics are discussed simultaneously.[1] This problem is eased by the fact that the flow of chat is documented in the persistent transcript, which is visible—at least for the last several postings. The chat window serves not only as the location of communications, but also as a representation of the temporal order of the messages. In contrast, the graphical workspace usually only shows the current state. All information about the actions and actors who brought about this state is ephemeral.

These problems resulting from the visual and functional juxtaposition of chat and workspace have the consequence that it is hard for users to track and specify relations of content and sequentiality between the textual contributions and the graphical activities. Specifically, there are three major problems:

Deictic references. An important means of communicative expression during collaboration with shared workspaces is deixis (Barnard, May & Salber, 1996; Clark & Wilkes-Gibbs, 1986)—the referencing of objects, relations and actions in the shared visual environment. When chat is used as the communication medium, deictic referencing is associated with high production costs and potentially also higher levels of ambiguity because gestural pointing is not possible. Purely textual descriptions of the object or of its specific position are obvious solutions, but there is no guarantee that such a description will be intelligible to others when they receive it because another user of the shared workspace may have moved or even deleted the object in the meantime.

Decontextualization of actions and messages. When collaborating in a dual-interaction space, participants interact with each other through chat messages and modifications of artifacts in the workspace. Whereas the persistent chat history represents the complete sequentiality of the discursive contributions, the same does not hold for the workspace. Both the ordering and the intermediate results of actions in the shared workspace are fleeting. This has two direct consequences. First, the necessary context for interpreting messages that reference artifacts in the workspace can quickly disappear. This defeats the important advantage of the persistent discourse history, which can support retrospective reflection. Second, the phenomenon of interrupted turn adjacency, described above, is heightened. During the time it takes for one person to respond, others can not only insert new messages but also modify referenced graphical artifacts.

---

[1] Despite the fact that this documentation is characterized by sequential incoherence, participants can apparently read and understand the chats amazingly well (Herring, 1999).

The coordination of communication and interaction. In a dual-interaction space, different participants can simultaneously be typing and posting chat messages or producing objects in the workspace. In collaboration, these various activities are interrelated: a message can announce or comment upon an action in the shared workspace and a workspace action can respond to or clarify a chat message. The awareness of the activities of the other people is a prerequisite for the construction of common ground (Dillenbourg & Traum, 2006). In chat, the chat history documents the sequence of discursive activities of the participants and the usual system messages when someone enters of leaves the room provide basic information about who is present. A series of interface features have been established to support coordination in shared workspaces (Gutwin & Greenberg, 2002), helping with turn taking and the anticipation of actions by other participants. For instance, objects that were just selected by users might be color-coded to indicate who is using them and the location of the user's mouse can be indicated (Stefik, Bobrow, Foster, Lanning & Tatar, 1987). Similarly, many chat systems display a message near the chat input area if someone is typing. However, if all these awareness techniques are combined in an environment with dual-interaction spaces, then they can overwhelm the limited attentional abilities of humans. The fleeting awareness messages scattered across the interface require users to pay constant attention to their whole screen.

Support Through Integration

People collaborating in a dual-interaction space are exposed to a series of problems that derive from the visually and functionally separated nature of the chat and workspace components. Three software mechanisms will now be presented that integrate these components with each other:

- An *explicit referencing* tool that makes possible deictic references from the chat to the workspace.
- An *integrated history* function that documents the on-going collaboration process consisting of the activities in the chat and in the shared workspace, and lets users review it.
- A visually integrated *social awareness* display that supports the perception of the simultaneous activities of the multiple participants in both areas.

To illustrate these integration measures, a shared whiteboard will be described as a common workspace for the collaborative creation of drawings, concept graphs and mind maps. See Fig. 15.1 for an example showing the most important interface elements. This screenshot shows the state of the VMT interface after the posting of a message with an explicit reference to a textbox in the shared workspace. Rtoledosj is currently working on the large textbox while Euclid is typing a chat message. The interface features for showing explicit references, the workspace history and awareness messages have been annotated.

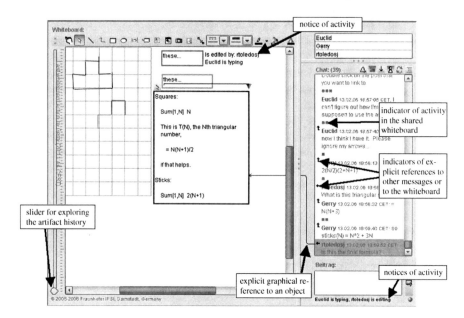

Fig. 15.1 Functionality in the VMT interface

Mechanism 1: Explicit References

The concept of explicit references addresses the difficulty of deictic referencing in the textual medium of chat (Pfister & Mühlpfordt, 2002). Pointing gestures are frequently used in face-to-face conversation (Bekker, Olson & Olson, 1995), for instance to identify objects and to clarify relationships among objects. Similarly, *explicit references* in chat allow one to associate a chat contribution with objects in the shared workspace and with other chat messages using graphical connectors. A graphical reference to a chat message can point to the whole message, a single word or some portion of the message. A reference can also point to an object or a region in the workspace. In the simplest case, one might want to point to a particular object, but in other situations to just a specific part of the object or else to a spatial constellation of several objects. So a number of different forms of referencing must be supported.

For summary statements in the chat—e.g., *"These two arguments contradict each other"*—multiple references can be made to relevant messages and objects. Just as with gestural pointing, the effective meaning of a graphical reference is given only once both the gestural and verbal messages are given. Thus, a reference can be used to clarify a "response-to-that-message" relation as well as to indicate a "related-to-this-object" relation.

The usability of an explicit referencing tool depends upon its effect on the media-dependent costs of production and reception (Clark & Brennan, 1991). In order to keep these costs low, appropriate interaction possibilities must be available for the easy production of references and for the visualization of references.

In order to maintain the chronological order of the chat history—rather than threading it—with the associated advantages for retroactive reflection, a reference is represented by a graphical arrow going from the referencing chat message to the referenced object or message. As soon as the referencing message is displayed, the accompanying reference arrow is also displayed, as illustrated in Fig. 15.1.

Mechanism 2: Artifact History

In collaboration in dual-interaction spaces, the actions in the shared workspace and the messages in the chat are but two facets of a single activity. While the chat displays a persistent history of the collaborative discourse, there is no corresponding history display for the workspace, let alone an integrated history for the whole collaboration. In technical terms, an *artifact history* of the objects in the workspace is a chronological collection of the various different versions or circumstances of the workspace resulting from the manipulations of the participants. In a shared whiteboard, every creation, movement and editing of an object changes the state of the workspace. The provision of an artifact history has two goals: to preserve the workspace context at various times and to represent its evolutionary process. The context of the workspace at the time when a chat message was being produced is important to know in order to interpret the message—particularly if the message explicitly references artifacts in the workspace. The artifact history permits the reconstruction of that context and encodes that context in the software representation of the reference. As needed, the historical context corresponding to a message of interest can be reconstructed and displayed. The other goal is to allow the normally fleeting artifact history to be replayed. The chronologically ordered developmental steps can be played back like the frames of a film, making possible reflection on the whole collaborative construction. Reflection in the group discussion is facilitated by the combination of being able to review the past developmental stages of the shared workspace and being able to point to a particular stage with an explicit reference.

Mechanism 3: Integrated Activity Awareness

The integration of *activity displays* has the goal of making it easier to be aware of the simultaneous activity of the other participants. Awareness of these activities is a prerequisite for constructing and maintaining a mutual understanding of the chat messages and the changes to the graphical artifacts—and therefore provides a necessary foundation for collaboration. In a chat environment, the chat history documents all the activities—both the individual messages and information about participant presence. This chronological documentation of activity suggests that it could serve as a representation of all activity within a dual-interaction space as well.

With chat, the process of producing a message is not directly perceivable by the other participants. The extent to which a long lasting and cognitively strenuous activity in a shared workspace is observable for the other participants depends upon the nature of the workspace and the granularity of the operations that are displayed for everyone. For instance, the editing of a textbox annotation in the shared workspace may only become visible for the others when the edit is completed. Activity awareness notifications have been established to support the coordination of activities like joint editing, so someone knows not to try to edit an object that someone else is currently editing. In a dual-interaction space, however, it is necessary to visually integrate these notices that are associated with the locations of different individual activities. If one participant wants to post a chat message in response to a contribution from another (such as responding to an annotation in the shared workspace with: "*I would say that differently*"), then she might hold off doing this if she is informed that he has just begun to make a change in the workspace that might very well serve to clarify his original contribution. Conversely, if he is informed that she is typing a chat message, he may delay his change in anticipation of a new objection. Both cases of course presume that the information about the activities is perceived. This can be supported by displaying the awareness information at the appropriate location (see Fig. 15.1).

Integrated Dual-Interaction Spaces in Use

The described integration measures are implemented in ConcertChat, an open-source dual-interaction system developed by the chapter authors and colleagues in Germany; it has been adopted and adapted in the VMT Project. A detailed case study of how deictic referencing was conducted in this context using the ConcertChat functionality in the dual-interaction space is presented in Chapter 17. Further studies of the use of ConcertChat's explicit referencing tool are reported by Mühlpfordt and Wessner (2005). These provide some evidence that the participants were able to employ effective communication strategies with the help of the explicit referencing.

For researchers, the persistence of all activities in a dual-interaction space provides the possibility of conducting fine-grained analyses of group interaction, as demonstrated in this volume. To support this, a Replayer version of ConcertChat has been developed that allows all the activities to be repeatedly reviewed, with the chat and workspace histories precisely coordinated. As mentioned in the introduction, the in-depth analysis of collaborative meaning making of groups learning together in the ConcertChat environment provided us insights in how the functionalities are used. The next three examples illustrate that.

The three examples are taken from the VMT Spring Fest 2006 (discussed in Chapters 7, 8, 10, 11 and 26). The collaborative context was set by organizing a contest: members of the most collaborative teams would win prizes. Students were recruited globally through teachers who were involved in other Math Forum activities. The teams in the excerpts consisted of students from Singapore (example 1) and from the US (Examples 2 and 3), as well as a facilitator from the Math Forum, who provided technical assistance. At the beginning of the first sessions the facilitators briefly explained the functionalities of the learning environment to the groups. Pedagogically, the topic for discussion was an open-ended exploration of geometric patterns. An initial pattern of squares formed from sticks was given. The students were to figure out the formulae for the number of squares and the number of sticks at stage N first, and then explore other patterns that they or other teams invented.

Example 1

The first example illustrates how the referencing tool is established by the group to ease deictic references. Figure 15.2 shows a screen shot of a VMT session with four participants, Amanda, Clarice, Wang and Dshia. The chat is reproduced in Log 15-1

In this interaction the group reflects on what aspects of the mathematical problem at hand they already solved. Wang asks **"so how many formulas have we come up with huh?"** and both Amanda and Clarice respond in the subsequent messages. Here the interesting response is the textual graphic from Clarice: **"<—"**. With that she textually simulates an explicit reference. In contrast to other group members, Clarice has never used ConcertChat's graphical referencing tool before, so it might be that she does not know how to create a reference with it. Wang's reply with two question marks (**"??"**) indicates a lack of understanding. Amanda, while providing

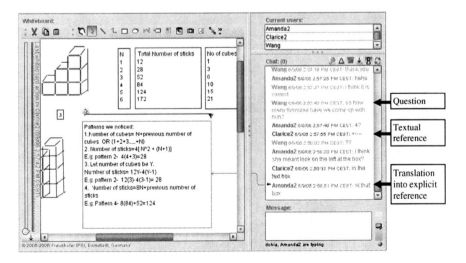

Fig. 15.2 Explicit referencing must be learned

Log 15-1.

1	Wang	thank you
2	Amanda2	haha
3	Wang	I think it is correct
4	Wang	so how many formulas have we come up with huh?
5	Amanda2	4?
6	Clarice2	<- -
7	Wang	??
8	Amanda2	I think she meant look on the left at the box?
9	Clarice2	in the text box
10	Amanda2	at that box

an interpretation (**"I think she meant look on the left at the text box?"**), also closes the message with a question mark. With her subsequent message (**"in the text box"**), Clarice again tries to establish a reference to the textbox on the shared whiteboard. Amanda finally translates this into a posting with an explicit reference to the textbox with all the collected formulas.

Example 2

While Clarice is a novice in using the referencing tool, Bwang—in the second example—uses it creatively to incorporate a formula written on the shared whiteboard into his explanation of a derived formula for the number of white squares in the rectangular pattern on the left (see Fig. 15.3). In a first step he refers to an

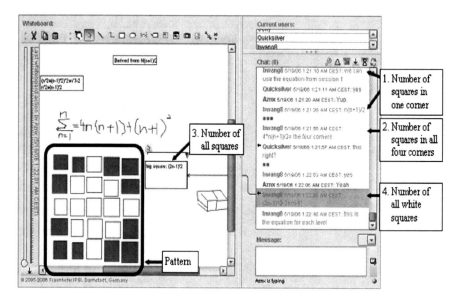

Fig. 15.3 Bwang uses an explicit reference

already found formula for the number of squares in one corner (**"we can use the equation from session 1"** and **"n(n+1)/2"**). Then in a second step he extends that to the number of squares in all four corners. This number must be subtracted from the number of all squares in the pattern. The group already found a formula for the latter number and documented that in a textbox on the whiteboard (**"big square: (2n-1)/2"**). Bwang's posting of the final formula is linked to that box. In this case, the referencing tool is used not merely for a deictic reference, but for incorporating an intermediate step in his formula derivation.

Example 3

The third example is from the same group of students (see Log 15-2 for the excerpt of the chat log) and shows that for the groups it is sometimes not trivial to choose the appropriate interaction space. In line 1516 Aznx invites the others to **"simplify**

Log 15-2.

1516	07.43.36	Aznx	simplify their formula
1517	07.43.51	Quicksilver	k
1518	07.43.55	bwang8	what do you mean
1519	07.44.30	Aznx	$2(n^2+n^2-2n+1)+3n-2$
1520	07.44.34	bwang8	i don't see how you can simplify it
1521	07.44.35	Aznx	simply the formula
1522	07.44.40	Aznx	for the number of sticks
1523	07.44.45	Aznx	so that simplifies to...
1524	07.45.45	Aznx	I stil get the same.
1525	07.46.20	bwang8	how did you simplify it
1526	07.46.27	Aznx	um
1527	07.46.32	Aznx	square the n-1
1528	07.46.39	Aznx	then multiply the whole thing by 2
1529	07.46.47	Aznx	then multiply the 3 and n
1530	07.46.51	Aznx	and add it with that
1531	07.46.57	Aznx	and subtract by 2
1532	07.47.14	bwang8	quicksliver
1533	07.47.19	Quicksilver	im lost
1534	07.47.23	bwang8	did you get the same answer
1535	07.47.30	Quicksilver	no
1536	07.47.39	Aznx	i'll do it on the board
<Aznx starts drawing on the whiteboard>			
1537	07.47.44	Quicksilver	yeah
1538	07.47.53	Quicksilver	i got something totally difrent
1539	07.48.36	bwang8	so far i got $4*n^2+3*n$
1540	07.48.55	Quicksilver	indranil rite in the box
1541	07.49.17	bwang8	i mean 4n^2-n
1542	07.49.26	Aznx	EXactly
1543	07.49.40	Quicksilver	yea that waht azn x got eralier
1544	07.50.00	bwang8	holy
1545	07.50.03	bwang8	moley
1546	07.50.05	Quicksilver	whyd u multiply by the two

their formula" (he is actually referring to a formula published by another group) and after Bwang's request (**"how did you simplify it,"** line 1525) he posts five chat messages describing the transformation of the formula. But his team members Quicksilver and Bwang seem not to understand that (**"im lost,"** line 1533). Aznx now switches to the whiteboard (**"I'll do it on the board,"** line 1536) and uses it for writing down the derivation. Figure 15.4 shows a screen shot of his final drawings. It also shows that Aznx's drawings (each drawing step is indicated by a small square in the chat history on the right side) are interwoven with chat postings, even from himself (line 1542). The interactions of the group are distributed over both interaction spaces, but highly interrelated. In line 1546 (**"whyd u multiply by the two"**) we can see how the referencing tool is used by Quicksilver for establishing referential identity.

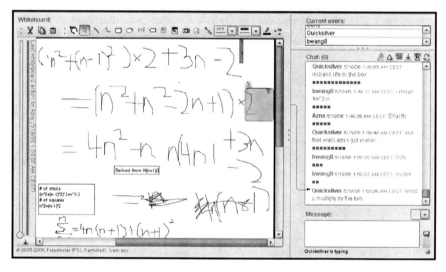

Fig. 15.4   Screen shot after message 1546

Conclusions and Future Work

The design of dual-interaction spaces for synchronous collaborative learning has to take into account the dynamic, tightly coupled and interwoven nature of the activities that are scattered across both media: the chat and the shared workspace. This demands (a) support for deictic referencing, (b) access to an integrated history and (c) integrated activity awareness. We exemplified the advantages offered by such integration measures.

Software developers like to think in modules, but when combining a shared workspace with a chat into one collaboration environment we have to think holistically about using the workspace in the context of a chat conversation and chatting in the context of working together in the workspace.

The experiences with ConcertChat to date suggest a series of further research questions:

- The storing of explicit references and the integrated representation of all activities make available additional structural and temporal information about the collaborative artifacts in the two interaction spaces. To what extent is it possible to use this information to construct a retrospective indexing, documentation or summarization of the collaboration that would facilitate future reflection or recall by the participants—for instance, when they return to the room for a subsequent session?
- An essential difference between a chat window and a shared whiteboard is the persistence of the artifacts. While a textbox in a shared whiteboard remains visible indefinitely (unless it is edited or deleted by a participant), the same is not true for chat contributions; they scroll out of sight with the appearance of the following discourse. Interesting questions arise when the additional possibility of audio communication offers a non-persistent medium. Can this supplementary mode of communication be substituted for chat to the advantage of the participants or will it be used as a secondary addition? What different communication strategies would result?
- How can the concepts of explicit referencing, integrated activity awareness and artifact history be applied to multiple interaction spaces, in which the collaboration environment provides even more than two primary workspaces?

Chapter 16
Designing a Mix of Synchronous and Asynchronous Media for VMT

Gerry Stahl

Abstract The challenges of designing computer support for education have shifted considerably in recent years, with, e.g., the rapid growth of the Web, online learning and social networking. New human–computer interaction (HCI) design approaches, methods, tools and theories are now required to analyze and understand interactions and learning of online groups. This chapter first reviews a number of issues related to the new software and pedagogy challenges. It then presents the approach of the VMT research project to address these issues by combining support for integrated synchronous and asynchronous collaboration media. The VMT system integrates a lobby, small-group chat rooms, multiple shared work spaces and community wiki pages to foster learning at the individual, small-group and community levels. The use of this system for a college HCI course is reported. The VMT Project illustrates the application of design-based research to system development, the theory of group cognition as a conceptual framework and an adaptation of chat interaction analysis for HCI design.

Keywords Educational software · human–computer interaction · user-centered design · design-based research

The Potential of Computer Support for Education

Shifting the Design Perspective on Educational Software

This chapter tries to shift the terms of debate within software design from "human–computer interaction" (HCI) to the more specific topic of *human–human* interaction and *group* learning. This is not to imply that other aspects of the broader theme of HCI are unimportant, just that the focus on group learning is one that has been largely overlooked, much to the disadvantage of the whole field of software design.

G. Stahl (✉)
College of Information Science & Technology, Drexel University, Philadelphia, PA, USA
e-mail: gerry@gerrystahl.net

G. Stahl (ed.), *Studying Virtual Math Teams*, Computer-Supported Collaborative Learning Series 11, DOI 10.1007/978-1-4419-0228-3_16,
© Springer Science+Business Media, LLC 2009

Human–computer interaction as a field has historically been oriented predominantly toward the relationship between the individual computer user and the interface of computer software. Classic HCI studies investigated the effects of different designs of desktop software upon individuals using the software. The theory of HCI was, accordingly, closely aligned with the science of individual psychology. For reasons to be discussed in this chapter, we will instead look at human–human (rather than human–computer) interaction that is mediated by computer software and by the networking of computers. The software is here seen largely as a technological communication medium, which both supports and constrains interaction among small groups of users. More precisely, the concern here is with the small-group interaction itself, that is, the group processes, rather than the interaction of one individual as such with other individuals in the group. Conceptually and methodologically, this involves a shift from the psychology of mental processes of individuals to the largely linguistic interactions of small groups.

The proposed shift is from the education of individual minds to learning within groups. The issue changes from tracing effects on students of the transfer of factual knowledge from authorized sources (teachers, textbooks, drill software) to understanding how groups learn. This new focus is sometimes termed *collaborative learning*, which includes both how groups increase knowledge and how the individuals within the groups learn concomitantly. The term *knowledge building* is perhaps preferable to either "education" or "learning." This is partially because the terms "education" and "learning" tend to be closely associated with traditional institutions of schooling and with psychological theories of individual minds. It is also due to the fact that one can observe the building of knowledge in products of group work, such as theories and documents; knowledge building can more easily be operationalized and studied. This perspective also opens new opportunities for teaching HCI, as should become evident latter in this chapter.

The History of Computer Support for Learning

Starting even before personal computers were developed and long before they were networked across the Web, a variety of educational applications of computers were proposed and to a lesser extent disseminated. In a review of instructional technology, Koschmann (1996a) identified four broad approaches for incorporating computers in educational practices, namely Computer Aided Instruction (CAI) starting in the 1960s, Intelligent Tutoring Systems (ITS) in the 1970s, Constructive Learning Environments (Logo-as-Latin) in the 1980s and Computer-Supported Collaborative Learning (CSCL) from 1995 on.

These four design paradigms were largely inspired by technological possibilities. Even in the 1960s, mainframe timesharing computers with many terminals were able to present texts to people sitting at the terminals, pose multiple-choice questions and respond based on the choice entered at their terminal. CAI applications were designed to take advantage of this automation mode. Later, tutoring systems took this a step further with a more sophisticated back-end using an AI approach to model both the domain structure (e.g., typical solution paths for a well-defined math problem) and a mental model of the student's domain knowledge (i.e., how the student was approaching the problem solution). More exploratory learning environments took advantage of subsequent 2-D graphics support and personal computer facilities for end-user programming. Finally, CSCL responded to the networking of personal computers and the spread of the Web. Each approach raised new HCI issues—or suffered from a lack of HCI analysis. The four approaches have all had limited successes and are still active in the instructional technology marketplace.

Each of the four approaches has simultaneously offered tools for classroom education and threatened the institutions of schooling. They all allow people to learn outside of school. Some have been particularly popular for home schooling and for after-school programs, as well as for industrial training workshops.

In terms of the focus of this chapter, it is important to distinguish CAI, tutoring and constructivist environments as software for individual usage *versus* CSCL as inherently for small-group usage. While the first CSCL system—CSILE (Scardamalia & Bereiter, 1996), or Knowledge Forum—has been used in classrooms around the world for a decade, most other CSCL systems are still in the research prototype stage.

The New Perspective of the Learning Sciences

Leading, or at least paralleling, the changing paradigms for learning technologies was the evolution of theories in the learning sciences (Sawyer, 2006). Moving away from the traditional educational theories of Thorndike (1914), they recreated many of the ideas of Dewey (1938/1991), supporting them with the developmental and social psychology theories of Piaget (1990) and Vygotsky (1930/1978). In particular, they increasingly recognized the socio-cultural situatedness of learning in communities-of-practice (Lave & Wenger, 1991). In this, they followed much the same path as the situated-cognition critique within AI and computer science (Winograd & Flores, 1986).

Perhaps the most important influence on the learning sciences for the focus of this chapter was the reception of Vygotsky's theory of social mediation, in particular his principle of internalization. This says that most higher functions of human thought are first learned socially, as part of interactions among people; they can later be internalized and transformed into individual mental skills (Vygotsky, 1930/1978, pp. 52–57). This principle is associated with his concept of the zone of proximal development, in which a learner can engage socially in collaborative work on a task that they would not yet have been able to accomplish on their own internally.

Vygotsky's theories—although not fully worked out in his brief lifetime—emphasize the importance of small-group interaction to the construction of meaning, representations, tools, symbolic artifacts and knowledge resources—both for the culture and for the individual. The implications of this theory have yet to be taken into account by the aims, procedures and institutions of contemporary schooling.

The Trouble with Computers in the Schools

The primary problem with how schools have adopted computers is their technology-driven view of the social role of computers. Under pressure to do something to improve schooling and to make it seem more up-to-date, politicians, administrators and parents have pushed to equip schools with computer hardware and Internet access. Of course, these are necessary, but not at all sufficient. A major problem is the lack of adequate educational software. In addition, there are needs for providing teacher training and on-site technical support. The hardware is often set up with little provision for meaningful computer-based curriculum and associated infrastructure. HCI was born to address the trouble with computers in industry. Now schools face an analogous—and overlapping—problem.

HCI was able to improve the lot of industrial software by increasing its reliability, usefulness and usability by insisting on a human-centered approach to design (Landauer, 1996). As we shall see, the problem is more complex for educational applications, involving the adoption in practice of the new learning sciences theories.

A Typical Government Study

A recent Congressional study (EETI, 2007) looked at software for reading education and for math education. Let us focus on the math software because that is a main example in this chapter. Three unnamed math applications were tested. According to the standards of the testing, the classroom use of these three applications had no significant effects on learning outcomes. From the characteristics given of the applications, it sounds like they were all examples of the CAI paradigm of drill-and-practice by isolated individual students.

There are many legitimate educational goals for which one might enlist instructional technology. As already pointed out, there are completely different approaches taken by educational software, with many different exemplars in each category. That certain software based on a 50-year-old approach may not inspire millennial children under certain conditions does not mean that software cannot be developed to be effective for educational purposes. Even CAI has its benefits for certain people trying to achieve specific goals.

The first problem in designing and assessing educational software is that one really needs to invent new and innovative approaches, based on current theories of the learning sciences. These are hard to test because one needs to develop prototypes that are robust enough to use in real classrooms over long enough periods that teachers and students can become familiar with them. Furthermore, they may require new kinds of assessments, different from those appropriate for CAI applications.

The Dim Future of the Physical University?

A critical essay in *Science* (Noam, 1995) argued against the use of computers in college education, saying that online education destroys much of the value of traditional university life. Primarily, however, the author conceived of educational software as something to be used by isolated individuals. He then saw that an education based on interaction with a computer would be missing the socializing aspects of, e.g., an undergraduate on-campus experience. However, he never considered that software can promote social contact, as can be seen not only in educational applications that incorporate discussion forums, chat, IM, wikis, websites, etc., but even more in the recent phenomena of social-networking software. Social networking, interestingly enough, is particularly popular among college undergrads. In response to Noam, one might inquire how social networking could be integrated into educational technology so that online learning would be a positive social experience, rather than an isolating, alienating one.

Computer-Supported Collaborative Learning

This is, of course, where CSCL steps in. The research field of CSCL—with its conferences, journal, book series, workshops, projects and labs—is devoted to developing ways to harness computer technology to support the rich social dimension of learning through collaboration.

The computational power of computers has the potential to provide many kinds of tools to extend human capabilities and to transform routine or complex intellectual tasks into tasks that are more interesting or feasible. With its graphic capabilities, the computer can run simulations of scientific or mathematical models and allow groups of students to explore them. With global networking, computers can put students in touch with their peers around the world, to learn each other's language and culture or to work and socialize together. The ability of computers to interact based on programmed instructions allows them to guide students through arbitrarily intricate and adaptable sequences (or scripts) of group and individual activities.

CSCL takes many approaches to mixing these potential benefits of computerization. The CSILE software was designed to allow a classroom full of students to collaboratively build scientific knowledge and theories asynchronously over periods of several weeks (Scardamalia & Bereiter, 1991). Argumentation software typically helps dyads of students to reflect on the structure of their debates and organize the logic of their thinking and persuasion (Andriessen, Baker & Suthers 2003). The VMT software is designed for groups of 2–10 to discuss mathematics in real time.

Whatever the techniques, media and domain, CSCL software is intended to foster collaborative learning and knowledge building by a group. Individuals may learn by participating, and perhaps by internalizing the experience, as Vygotsky described.

The Problem of User-Centered Groupware Design

Software for collaborative learning—like that for workplace learning and community learning—is associated with significant HCI issues, that exceed the difficulties of single-user desktop-interface and web-page design. They call for new theories, assessment tools and principles. They must centrally take into account the interactions among group participants as mediated by the software medium, and not just the interaction of an individual user to an interface. The number of possible combinations of views of the software by different participants at any given time and the variety of interactions possible explodes, making HCI analysis techniques from the 1980s inadequate. Many technical problems and many potential uses of the software are unpredictable and have to emerge from actual usage by groups of people under naturalistic conditions. This limits the utility of scenarios, mockups, walkthroughs, prototypes and lab studies as assessment tools—as essential as they may still be to specific phases of the design process.

Social Networking and Web 2.0

Despite the difficulties facing the development of effective collaborative learning technology, the potential benefits loom larger than ever. The recent increase in Internet usage, particularly by high school and college students, bodes well for the adoption of new educational technologies. In particular, the popularity of a range of social networking sites and of so-called Web 2.0 interactive technologies has already instilled a familiarity with computer-supported collaboration, its handiness and its benefits.

Designing Support for a Virtual Learning Community

Use-Centered Research

The VMT Project began by building on a successful service at the Math Forum called Problem-of-the-Week. In the original service, an interesting challenge problem in pre-algebra, algebra or geometry was posted on the Web weekly and students worked on it at home, in school or during math club. Students could submit their solutions and their analyses to get feedback. The best solution statements were posted in the Web archives.

This service had evolved over a dozen years, guided by staff and teachers who had been involved with it from the beginning. The Math Forum itself emerged out of the experience of supporting this service, by adding related services for students, teachers and mathematicians, eventually serving millions of online users. As a digital library with over a million web pages, the Math Forum site grew by archiving user problem solutions, answers to user inquiries and discussions of user groups, such as teachers—anticipating the Web 2.0 philosophy of users as contributors by more than a decade.

Presumably, most of the math problem solving in the Problem-of-the-Week was done individually. The VMT Project set out to make that a collaborative process. We took advantage of the huge popularity of text chat. We initially adopted AOL's instant messaging tool, which was already quite familiar and accessible to students. Students who came to our site were placed into small groups in an AIM chat room and given a math problem to explore. If they wanted to exchange a drawing, they could email it to us and we would post it where the group could view it.

By starting with software and procedures that were already proven in use and were familiar to the students, we finessed the design start-up issues that can bog down groupware development efforts. We were able to quickly observe students "in the wild" doing math collaboratively. By starting simply, we could allow our development process to be driven by observation of actual usage.

We had previously tried to do a face-to-face trial in a Philadelphia public school to get a feel for how collaborative math works in that kind of setting. Although informative, that effort showed how unusual collaboration in school math is and how complex it is to analyze. By contrast, our chat logs immediately revealed that students could quickly adapt to online collaborative math problem solving and that we could observe much of interest about how they accomplished that (see Chapter 9).

A Design-Based Research Process

We adapted the kind of design-based research process (Design-Based Research Collective, 2003) which has been broadly adopted in the learning sciences. This is an iterative inquiry process in which we modify the software environment, the kinds of math problems and the pedagogical script a couple of times a year. We invite students to participate in online groups in the new environments, and then we analyze the logs of their interactions to determine what was good in the service design and where improvement was needed. We thereby gradually build an understanding of chat-mediated interaction and online collaborative math problem solving.

In terms of the technology, we tried a number of commercial and open source environments, combining chat with a shared whiteboard drawing space for geometric figures. Eventually, we contracted with a research lab in Germany (Fraunhofer-IPSI) to modify their ConcertChat software for our needs. We also began to develop a portal front-end to support social networking.

The kinds of math problems evolved considerably. From well-defined challenge problems, we moved toward mathematical mini-worlds for exploration and encouraged groups to define their own math questions to investigate. Over the years, we have gathered a corpus of 1,000 student-hours of interaction logs. We developed a Replayer tool that allows us to recreate the full interaction and review it in detail.

Perhaps the most important development was at the theoretical and methodological level. We gradually developed a theory of group cognition and a methodology of chat interaction analysis, as discussed toward the end of this chapter. This resulted in about a hundred publications reporting findings of the VMT Project and analyzing it, many of them incorporated in this volume.

Supporting Joint Problem Spaces

It became increasingly clear from our analyses and from the related CSCL literature that for our students "collaboration is a coordinated, synchronous activity that is the result of a continued attempt to construct and maintain a shared conception of a problem" (Roschelle & Teasley, 1995, p. 70).

Different technologies can provide different kinds of support for the construction and maintenance of shared conceptions. For instance, chat, whiteboard and wiki have different forms of persistence for inscriptions. Student groups are very sensitive to these differences and exploit them in subtle and inventive ways. Designers cannot predict many ways that these spaces will be used without observing actual groups of interacting students trying to work out their tasks situated within specific environments.

A major issue for groups working in environments with multiple workspaces (e.g., lobby, chat stream, shared whiteboard and wiki) is how to coordinate communications in the spaces and how to shift group attention from one space to the other. Special tools can help with this. When we adopted ConcertChat, it included a referencing tool that could point from the chat to the whiteboard. We observed the power of this tool for supporting the equivalent of pointing gestures and deictic references in the disembodied online context (Chapter 7). We subsequently added wiki spaces and multiple tabs to the whiteboard, facilitating collaborative Web browsing, wiki editing, help access and viewing of the math task. Combining these spaces with the social-navigation portal and its various tools, the VMT environment has come a long way from its AOL IM starting point.

In order to orient students to the current, complex environment, we have had to develop training and help facilities as well as sometimes involving the students' teachers in providing basic training. We have also found that it is effective to engage the same groups of students across multiple sessions, making planning more complicated and fragile. Having sequences of multiple sessions brings enormous learning benefits. Not only do the students become more familiar with the affordances of the environment, but they are able to explore the mathematics more deeply and reflectively. We are able to script the sessions to gradually build understanding. We can also take advantage of the intervals between sessions to provide feedback and suggestions without interfering with the delicate group interactions.

In order to deepen and broaden our user-centered research experience, we tried out the expanded VMT environment outside of the realm of K-12 math. The next section discusses our use of the technology in a graduate-level university course. Reflexively, the course was about designing the VMT system, and encouraged the course students to use, analyze and re-design the technology.

Using the VMT Environment to Teach HCI

In Spring Quarter 2007, while we were completing our latest major software upgrade to VMT, we decided to try basing an online HCI masters-level course at Drexel on the VMT system. In our research, we were working on integrating wikis into VMT, so we decided to move the course home and the student-group websites into a wiki—away from Blackboard and HTML websites.

This gave us an opportunity to try out the new VMT lobby/chat/tabs/wiki environment in a context where we could define the course and guide the students first-hand. It turned out to be surprisingly easy to set up the entire course in a wiki, with clear instructions for the students and a clean organization of resources. Each week, the students held several online meetings with their workgroups in VMT chat rooms, where they discussed the readings and their design project assignments. They summarized their discussions in their shared whiteboards and then posted their summaries to the course wiki. We provided general feedback and guidance in the wiki as well.

The students read the whole of a newly-revised and comprehensive HCI textbook (Preece, Rogers & Sharp, 2007) as well as 18 research papers about CSCL and VMT. The textbook provided a thorough overview of the field and related background information. The papers served in place of lectures. Students maintained individual journals on the textbook chapters and reflected collaboratively on the papers. Each group posted its critiques of the papers in the wiki, where the other groups could read them and the instructor could comment on them.

The heart of the course was a group project, spanning most of the quarter, with weekly milestones requiring postings to the wiki by each group. The groups met several times a week at their convenience in VMT chat rooms to work on their group project and to discuss the readings for the week. As they discussed, they summarized their ideas on the whiteboard for posting to the wiki. That way, the whole group could draft the postings and if anyone missed a meeting they could catch up quickly without going through a long chat log.

The group project was to design an extension to the VMT software that they were using. The extension was supposed to support social networking, so that potential users of the VMT system could find others with similar skills, interests and availabilities to form groups.

The ten-week hands-on project was divided into weekly assignments, which paralleled the stages of the textbook's design model and matched the chapters and papers read the previous week:

1. An ice-breaker design project to help the students get used to working together in the environment.
2. Literature search on social networking and Web 2.0.
3. Analysis and statement of problems in social networking.
4. Establish requirements with use cases and scenarios.
5. Conceptual design (this was done individually by the students).
6. Interactive prototype and scenario.
7. Heuristic evaluation of another team's prototype.
8. Cognitive walkthrough of one's own team's prototype following a scenario.
9. Final, revised design for a new social network function in VMT.
10. In the final week, individual students submit their textbook journals and a reflection paper on their experience learning about HCI in the course.

Classroom learning is contextualized within a global horizon by situating the knowledge built by the groups within current HCI research issues. These are explicitly discussed as the student groups design and prototype solutions that apply the HCI concepts in the readings. The issues emerge mainly in the collaborative chat interactions: practice and group discussion inform each other.

The idea of collaborative peer learning through hands-on practice—which is fundamental to the course approach—is presented to the students through the syllabus document and some of the readings. The grading system stated in the syllabus shows that collaborative learning is a combination of efforts at the individual, small-group and classroom level: the grade is based on a combination of these. The assignments mix individual and small-group efforts, and the results are mostly shared at the class level.

By having the students work in the environment that they are designing for, they acquire first-person experience from a user perspective. Comprehensive histories of the interactions within the system are persistently available, so the students as designers can study their own usage of the system reflectively and analytically. It is thereby natural for the students to compare their subjective and objective analyses of the user experience. The collaborative structure of the course stimulates, encourages and supports discussion of issues of HCI and education.

The collaborative learning approach of the course is in many ways at odds with the culture at Drexel, which is traditionally an engineering school. Yet, as evidenced by the reflection papers, the students learned to appreciate the many aspects of collaborative learning in the course. Perhaps because they were mature students who knew that the work-world is increasingly organized into collaborative teams, they could understand the advantages better than undergraduates. Perhaps because they were accustomed to taking online courses in which there is no social contact, these students enjoyed the interaction with their peers.

Similarly to the schools in the EETI study discussed above, Drexel has long been committed to the visible hardware aspects of a twenty-first century education, but has not as thoroughly recognized the shifts in pedagogy that should go along with this. As the learning sciences have concluded, it is important to involve students in active, authentic, hands-on collaborative-learning experiences. Students need to take responsibility for their own learning and that of their peers. Only this way will they be prepared for the life-long learning that they will be involved in after graduation in rapidly changing high-tech fields.

Drexel was originally founded to provide educational opportunities for working-class people. One way this mission is met today is to offer online classes for people who are working fulltime. A majority of the Information School's students are now online graduate students. They typically work during the day and often have substantial family responsibilities. Many of the students in HCI courses work in computer fields and have first-hand experience with HCI issues at their work. This is a great advantage in a course, particularly when it is run collaboratively, so the experienced students can share their expertise and perspectives.

As Noam (1995) argued, colleges must redefine the benefits they offer in the contemporary educational marketplace. To some extent, this will depend upon local specifics. Perhaps a more general way colleges can promote their advantages is to emphasize social experiences through collaborative learning and other human–human interaction—including online. This applies, of course to curricula in HCI as well as to other disciplines.

The challenge is that current software support for online collaborative learning is primitive at best. There is a tremendous need for HCI work to help develop effective collaborative learning software. The help is needed at a deep level, not just superficial changes to the look-and-feel of the interface. The nature of computer-mediated human–human interaction must be understood and new media and functionality must be designed to support it.

Integrating Asynchronous and Synchronous Media in VMT

This section will describe the combination of asynchronous and synchronous media in the version of the VMT environment that was used in the HCI course as well as in the VMT Spring Fest 2007. The technological integration of the lobby, chat room and wiki should be understood as a pedagogical integration of learning at the individual, small-group and community levels.

Figure 16.1 shows an image of the VMT social networking portal in its current state. On the left are tools for defining and viewing personal profiles—in general, students in a VMT group have no knowledge about each other except for what is revealed in the chat interaction. With the functionality available in the VMT Lobby, they can define their own profiles and view profiles of each other, as well as send messages to individuals or groups in their communities. Communities are defined for various VMT constituencies, such as participants in a given Spring Fest or in

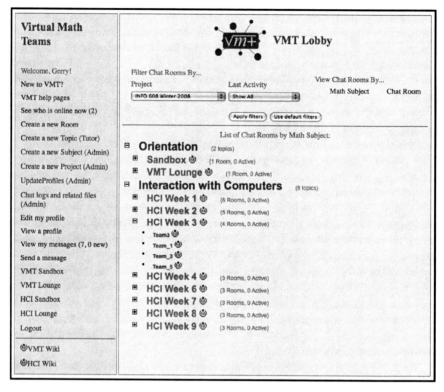

Fig. 16.1 The VMT Lobby

a given course. There is also support for defining buddies, listing favorite chat
rooms, etc. On the right is an interface for searching and browsing available chat
rooms, usually listed for a given community. For the HCI course, each group met
in a different chat room each week, to avoid overcrowding of the chat log and the
whiteboard.

Figure 16.2 shows a typical chat room, consisting of the text chat interface on
the right and the shared whiteboard on the left. Note that the user who is typing
is currently pointing to a translucent rectangle selecting part of the whiteboard, as
is a highlighted previous chat posting. The history of the whiteboard state can be
scrolled through, much like that of the chat, but unlike the chat it usually retains
inscriptions in the visible board as long as they are relevant. Here, in the HCI course,
the whiteboard is being used to collect and organize design issues for subsequent
posting to the course wiki as part of the group's weekly report.

The workspace on the left has a tabbed interface, with six default workspaces—
users can add additional spaces. The first is the old shared whiteboard, supporting
graphics and text boxes. The second is a similar shared whiteboard, intended for
preparing a summary of the week's work for automatic posting to a special wiki page
associated with this chat room. The third tab displays the topic for the course that

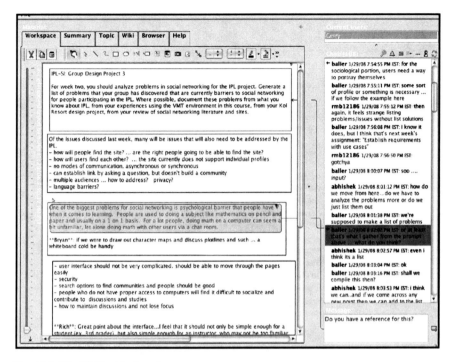

Fig. 16.2 The VMT tabbed workspace

week, stored on a wiki page by the instructor. The "wiki" tab displays a web page, using the user's default browser software. This tab initially points to the group's wiki page for their week's report. The "browser" tab uses a simplified web browser that can support the graphical referencing tool from the chat and a history scrollbar. The final tab displays wiki pages containing the VMT help manual and associated information.

Figure 16.3 shows the wiki home page for the HCI course. It points to pages describing the course and each assignment. Group assignments are all posted to linked wiki pages. The course wiki includes index pages that bring together the student assignments in various combinations and allow the instructor to post feedback that is visible to all. The student groups also rate and provide feedback to each other's previous reports.

While the chat rooms are open to all users, people rarely visit rooms other than those of their own group. So the chat rooms are basically meeting and work places for the small groups as they engage in collaborative learning. The VMT Lobby provides a portal for the individual user to browse the people and topics of the community and to select a room for group work. The wiki, on the other hand, primarily provides a community space in which the work of all groups is coordinated, commented upon and perhaps summarized.

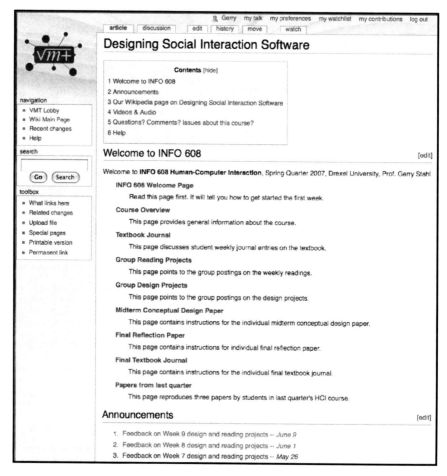

Fig. 16.3 The VMT course wiki

Figure 16.4 shows a wiki page for Spring Fest 2007, which involved probability problems. This main page for the community participating in this event provided a knowledge-building space, analogous to Wikipedia. That is, anyone in the community could add information to this catalog of knowledge about K-12 probability as well as browse the space. The space is seeded with a number of different probability problems and several strategies for solving such problems. During the Spring Fest, student groups were to each initially select a problem and try to solve it with one of the strategies. Then they would post a summary of their solution path on the wiki page linked to from the table in Fig. 16.4 for that problem and that strategy. Subsequent work would involve trying the same strategy on other problems or other strategies on the same problem, followed by comparing the results posted by other groups. The idea was that this kind of knowledge-building repository could persist and evolve through use in the future.

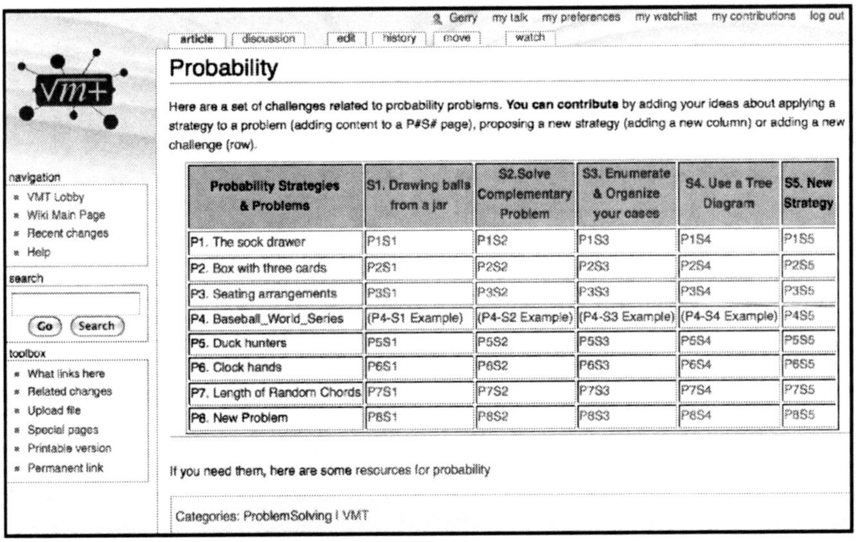
Gerry my talk my preferences my watchlist my contributions log out
article discussion edit history move watch

Probability

Here are a set of challenges related to probability problems. **You can contribute** by adding your ideas about applying a strategy to a problem (adding content to a P#S# page), proposing a new strategy (adding a new column) or adding a new challenge (row).

Probability Strategies & Problems	S1. Drawing balls from a jar	S2.Solve Complementary Problem	S3. Enumerate & Organize your cases	S4. Use a Tree Diagram	S5. New Strategy
P1. The sock drawer	P1S1	P1S2	P1S3	P1S4	P1S5
P2. Box with three cards	P2S1	P2S2	P2S3	P2S4	P2S5
P3. Seating arrangements	P3S1	P3S2	P3S3	P3S4	P3S5
P4. Baseball_World_Series	(P4-S1 Example)	(P4-S2 Example)	(P4-S3 Example)	(P4-S4 Example)	P4S5
P5. Duck hunters	P5S1	P5S2	P5S3	P5S4	P5S5
P6. Clock hands	P6S1	P6S2	P6S3	P6S4	P6S5
P7. Length of Random Chords	P7S1	P7S2	P7S3	P7S4	P7S5
P8. New Problem	P8S1	P8S2	P8S3	P8S4	P8S5

If you need them, here are some resources for probability

Categories: ProblemSolving | VMT

navigation
- VMT Lobby
- Wiki Main Page
- Recent changes
- Help

search
Go Search

toolbox
- What links here
- Related changes
- Upload file
- Special pages
- Printable version
- Permanent link

Fig. 16.4 The VMT probability wiki page

The VMT environment has come a long way from the simple AOL Instant Messaging system to the current lobby/chat/tabbed-spaces/wiki multiple interaction space. In part, this increased complexity parallels the shift from simple math exercises to open-ended explorations of math worlds, from one-shot meetings to multiple-session Fests, from problem-solving tasks to knowledge-building efforts. Along with the considerable gain in functionality come substantial increase in complexity and the potential for confusion. This has been countered by trying to extend and supplement the integration approaches of ConcertChat (see Chapter 15). The graphical referencing and the history scrollbars have been extended to the multiple tabs. New social awareness notices have been added to track which tab each group member is viewing or referencing.

Integration across modules has been important. Logins and passwords have been unified across the Lobby, chat rooms and wiki, so that logging into one automatically logs into the others. People registered in one show up in the profiles and messaging system, by their selected community. When a new chat room is created, it is categorized by a community (e.g., HCI), subject (e.g., Interaction with Computers), a topic (e.g., Week 3's assignment) and a group (e.g., Group 3). A new wiki page is generated for posting the summary from this room. The MediaWiki functionality of categories automatically associates this new page with aggregation pages for the community, subject, topic and group. The version of MathML that was developed for chat postings in ConcertChat has been implemented for the textboxes in the shared whiteboards as well as in the VMT wiki, so that math expressions copied from one of these media to another retains its formatting.

While the VMT environment has been tuned to the needs of high-school math students, it has proven effective for other collaborative activities as well. The specifically math-oriented functions—like our implementation of MathML for displaying equations and the whiteboard's stock of Euclidean shapes—play a relatively small role. The tools for integrating the multiple work spaces—like the graphical referencing from chat, the creation of wiki pages corresponding to each chat room and the automatic posting of summary text to the proper wiki page—are more important and are applicable to all knowledge domains.

Our collaborators at other locations (Singapore, Montreal, Pittsburgh, Wisconsin, Romania, Hawaii, Brazil, New Jersey) and we use the VMT environment for coordination of our design work on VMT, for collaboratively critiquing each other's research papers, for holding virtual committee meetings, for pre-teacher training and for student collaborations in other domains like physics or argumentation. Each of these different uses can work effectively in our current environment, but each also suggests new features tuned to the new application. A characteristic of design-based research as used in the VMT Project is that it makes no pretense to ever produce a final version of the software. We continue to use and evolve the VMT environment.

Chapter 17
Deictic Referencing in VMT

Gerry Stahl

Abstract Centered on a case study of a synchronous online interchange, this chapter discusses the use of the VMT graphical referencing tool in coordination with text chat to achieve a group orientation to a particular mathematical object in a shared whiteboard. Deictic referencing is seen to be a critical foundation of inter-subjective cognitive processes that index objects of shared attention. The case study suggests that cognitive tools to support group referencing can be important to supporting group alignment, intentionality and cognition in online communities such as VMT.

Keywords Graphical referencing tool · cognitive tools · deixis · epistemology · intersubjectivity · sense making

Suppose one wanted to establish a collaborative community with a certain focus, say to explore mathematics (e.g., the kind of math taught in school or accessible to interested students). How might one go about doing this? How would one invite people, where would they congregate, how would they communicate, what kinds of social practices would emerge, who would provide leadership, whence would knowledge appear? The obvious approach today is to build an online community of people who want to discuss math. Research in computer-supported collaborative learning and working (CSCL and CSCW) has taught us that this requires a well-integrated infrastructure, not just a simple cognitive tool or a generic communication medium. For instance, the following range of issues would have to be addressed: how should the software environment be designed; what kind of curriculum or domain content should be included; how are working groups to be formed; how will participants be recruited? The design of cognitive tools to support such an online collaborative community would involve many inter-related considerations, most of which are not yet well understood.

G. Stahl (✉)
College of Information Science & Technology, Drexel University, Philadelphia, PA, USA
e-mail: gerry@gerrystahl.net

G. Stahl (ed.), *Studying Virtual Math Teams*, Computer-Supported Collaborative
Learning Series 11, DOI 10.1007/978-1-4419-0228-3_17,
© Springer Science+Business Media, LLC 2009

Cognitive tools for collaborative communities are essentially different from cognitive tools for individuals. A number of publications in 2006 detail the following considerations (Dillenbourg & Traum, 2006; Jones et al., 2006; Stahl, 2006b):

- The use of cognitive tools by a collaborative community takes place through many-to-many interactions among people, not by individuals acting on their own.
- The cognition that the tools foster is inseparable from the collaboration that they support.
- The relevant cognition is the "group cognition" that is shared at the small-group unit of analysis; this is a linguistic phenomenon that takes place in discourse, rather than a psychological phenomenon that takes place in an individual's mind.
- The tools may be more like communication media than like a hand calculator—they do not simply amplify individual cognitive abilities, they make possible specific forms of group interaction.
- Rather than being relatively simple physical artifacts, tools for communities may be complex infrastructures.
- Infrastructures do not have simple, fixed affordances designed by their creators; they are fluid systems that provide opportunities that must be specified by users and enacted by them.
- The community must interpret the meanings designed into the tools, learn how to use the tools, share this understanding and form social practices or methods of use.
- Analyzing the effectiveness of these tools requires a special methodology that can analyze the methods developed by the community for taking advantage of the infrastructure to accomplish its collaborative activities.
- The community with its tools forms a complex system that cannot be modeled through simple causal relationships, because the whole is both over-determined and open-ended; the community is made possible by its infrastructure, but also interprets the meaning of its tools and adapts their affordances.

This chapter tries to respond to these considerations without having the space to present them each in depth. It reports on the effort to develop a cognitive tool for an online community of mathematics discourse. Experience—along with the preceding considerations—has shown that the design of software tools for collaborative learning must consider above all else how people will actually use the tool. Therefore, our design effort was structured as a design-based research experiment, in which a relatively simple solution is first tried out in a realistic small-scale setting. The results of actual usage are analyzed to assess what worked and what barriers were encountered. Successive re-design cycles attempt to overcome the barriers that users encountered and to evolve a tool and approach that provide increasingly effective support for a gradually emergent online community. This user-centered approach—applied to a growing community of users rather than to subjects representing an imagined "typical" individual user—focuses on the details of how the community interacts through the tool.

More specifically, we will look at a cognitive tool that was added to the infrastructural support for this community. The tool allows users to relate work in a text chat stream with work done in a shared-whiteboard drawing area. The tool draws lines from a chat message to other chat messages and/or to areas in the whiteboard. We call this tool a "graphical referencing tool" because it supports the ability of a message to reference an item already existing in the online environment by drawing a line from the message to the item. After briefly describing our research project and discussing our methodology for analyzing usage, we will present a case study of how students used the cognitive tool for referencing. Close analysis of a brief excerpt from an actual student interaction using the tool will illustrate both how complex the achievement of shared references can be and how crucial referencing can be for the group cognition that takes place. Findings of the case study will then motivate consideration of conceptual issues in understanding referencing: reflections on the epistemology and pedagogy of referencing will provide insight into issues of gesture, common ground, boundary objects and intentionality in group cognition.

An Experiment in Designing an Online Chat Community

The VMT Project is an effort to explore some of the issues posed above. In order to understand the experience of people and groups collaborating online in the VMT service, the researchers in the project look in detail at the interactions as captured in computer logs. In particular, the project is studying groups of three to six middle- or high-school students discussing mathematics in chat rooms. The logs that are collected capture what the participants see to a good approximation.

The VMT Project was designed to foster, capture and analyze instances of "group cognition." The project is set up so that every aspect of the communication can be automatically captured when student groups are active in the online community, so that the researchers have access to everything that enters into the communication and is shared by the participants. All interaction takes place online, so that it is unnecessary to videotape and transcribe. Each message is logged with the name of the user submitting it and the time of its submission. Similarly, each item placed in the shared whiteboard is tagged with the name of its creator and its creation or modification time. The chat is persistent and the history of the whiteboard can also be scrolled by participants, and later by researchers.

Although many things happen "behind the scenes" during chat sessions—such as the production of the messages, including possible repairs and retractions of message text before a message is sent, or things that the participants do but do not mention in the chat—the researcher sees everything that the participants share and all see. While the behavior of a participant may be influenced on an individual basis—such as by interactions with people outside of the chat or by the effects of various social and cultural influences—the researchers can generally infer and understand these influences to the same extent as the other participants (who typically do not know each other outside of the chats). These "external" factors (including the participants' age, gender, ethnicity, culture) only play a role in the group interaction to the extent that they are somehow brought into the discourse or "made relevant" in the chat. In cases where they play a role in the group, then, they are also available to the researchers.

In particular, the sequentiality of the chat messages and of the actions in the whiteboard is maintained so that researchers can analyze the phenomena that take place at the group level of interaction among participants. The other way in which the group interaction may be influenced from outside of activities recorded in the chat room is through general background knowledge shared by the participants, such as classroom culture, pop culture or linguistic practices. If the participants meet on the Internet and do not all come from the same school and do not share any history from outside of the VMT chats, then researchers are likely to share with the participants most of the background understanding that the participants themselves share.

This is not to say that the researchers have the same experience as the participants, but their resources for understanding the chat are quite similar to the resources that the participants had for understanding and creating the chat, despite the dramatic differences between the participant and researcher perspectives. Participants experience the chat in real time as it unfolds on their screen. They are oriented toward formulating their messages to introduce into the chat with effective timing. Researchers are engaged in analyzing and recreating what happened, rather than participating directly in it. They are oriented toward understanding why the messages were introduced when and how they were.

We want to understand how groups construct their shared experience of collaborating online. While answers to many questions in human–computer interaction have been formulated largely in terms of individual psychology, questions of collaborative experience require consideration of the group as the unit of analysis. Naturally, groups include individuals as contributors and interpreters of content, but the group interactions have structures and elements of their own that call for different analytic approaches. In particular, the solving of math problems in the chat environment gets accomplished collaboratively, interactionally. That is, the cognitive work is done by the group.

We call this accomplishment *group cognition*—a form of distributed cognition that may involve advanced levels of cognition like mathematical problem solving and that is visible in the group discourse, where it takes place. It is possible to conduct informative analyses of chats at the group unit of analysis, without asking about the individuals—e.g., their motivations, internal reflections, unexpressed feelings, intelligence, skills, etc.—beyond their participation in the group interaction. Of course, there are also intriguing questions about the interplay between group cognition and individual cognition, but we will not be considering those here.

The VMT Project is studying how small groups of students do mathematics collaboratively in online chat environments. We are particularly interested in the new *methods* that the chat members must develop to conduct their interactions in an environment that presents new affordances for interaction. "Member methods"

(Garfinkel, 1967) are interactional patterns that participants in a community adopt to structure and give meaning to their activities. A paradigmatic example of member methods is the set of conventions used by speakers in face-to-face conversation to take turns talking (Sacks et al., 1974). The use of such methods is generally taken-for-granted by the community and provides the social order, meaning and account-ability of their activities. Taken together, these member methods define a group culture, a shared set of ways for people interacting to make sense together of their common world. The methods adopted by VMT participants are subtly responsive to the chat medium, the pedagogical setting, the social atmosphere and the intellectual resources that are available to them. These methods help define the nature of the collaborative experience for the small groups that develop and adopt them. Through the use of these methods, the groups construct their collaborative experience. The chat takes on a flow of interrelated ideas for the group, analogous to an individual's stream of consciousness. The referential structure of this flow provides a basis for the group's experience of intersubjectivity and of a shared world.

As designers of educational chat environments, we are particularly interested in how small groups of students construct their interactions in chat media that have different technical features. How do the students learn about the meanings that designers embedded in the environment and how do they negotiate the methods that they adopt to turn technological possibilities into practical means for mediating their interactions? Ultimately, how can we design with students the technologies, pedagogies and communities that will result in desirable collaborative experiences for them? Our response to the question of how cognitive tools mediate collabora-tive communities is to point to the methods that interactive small groups within the community spontaneously co-construct to carry out their activities using the tools.

To explore this complex topic within the confines of this chapter, we will look at a brief excerpt of one dyad of students within an online small group using the affordances of the technological environment of the VMT Project at one point in its development. Specifically, we look at how the students reference a particular math object in the virtual environment. We will see a number of methods being used within a 16-line excerpt. We will also mention other methods that we have observed students employing for referencing in similar chat sessions.

Technology for Referencing in a Chat Environment

In our design-based research at the VMT Project, we started by conducting chats in a variety of commercially available environments, including AOL Instant Messenger, Babylon, WebCT, Blackboard. Based on these early investigations, we concluded that we needed to include a shared whiteboard for drawing geometric figures and for persistently displaying notes. We also found a need to minimize "chat confusion" by supporting explicit referencing of response threads. We decided to adopt and adapt ConcertChat, a research chat environment with special referencing tools. By collaborating with the software developers, our educational researchers have been able to successively try out versions of the environment with groups of students and to gradually modify the environment in response to what we find by analyzing the chat logs.

The ConcertChat environment allows for a variety of referencing methods in math chats:

Referencing the Whiteboard from a Posting

When someone types a new chat message, they can select and point to a rectangular area in the whiteboard. When that message appears in the chat as the last posting or as a selected posting, a bold line appears connecting the text to the area of the drawing (see Fig. 17.1). The image has been modified to show graphical references from chat lines 1, 5, 10 and 12 to the whiteboard. The drawing from the whiteboard has been duplicated in the margin twice to accommodate this; of course, only the reference from a single selected chat line would actually appear at any given time.

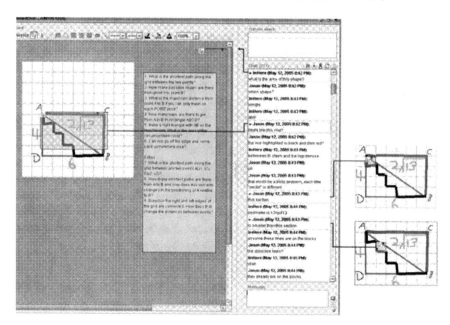

Fig. 17.1 Screen view of referencing

Referencing Between Postings

A chat message can point to one or more earlier textual postings with a bold connecting line, like whiteboard references. ConcertChat includes a threaded view of the chat postings that, based on the explicit references between postings, displays them like a typical threaded discussion with responses indented under the posting that they reference.

Referencing a Recent Drawing

The shared whiteboard allows chat participants to create drawings. As new objects are added to the drawing by participants, an implicit form of referencing occurs. Participants typically refer with a deictic term in their textual chat to a new addition to the drawing, whose recent appearance for the group makes it salient.

Linguistic Referencing

Of course, one can also make all the usual verbal references to an object on the whiteboard or posting in the chat stream: using deictic terms (*that, it, his, then*); quoting part of an earlier posting; or citing the author of a previous posting.

In May 2005, we conducted VMT Spring Fest 2005, a series of chats using ConcertChat. We formed five virtual math teams, each containing about four middle-school students selected by teachers at different schools across the USA. The teams engaged in online math discussions for four hour-long sessions over a two-week period. They were given a brief description of a non-traditional geometry environment: a grid-world where one could only move along the lines of a grid (Krause, 1986). The students were encouraged to come up with their own questions about the grid-world, such as questions about shortest paths between points A and B in this world.

The chats were each facilitated by a member of our research project team. The facilitator welcomed students to the chat, pointed them toward the task, briefly demonstrated the graphical referencing tool and then kept generally quiet until it was time to end the session. We then analyzed the resultant chat logs in order to draw design implications for revising the tools and the service.

An Analysis of a Case of Referencing

The chat log excerpt visible in Fig. 17.1 is reproduced in Log 17-1 (with line numbers added to enable referencing in this chapter). In this interactional sequence, two students discuss parts of a drawing that has already been constructed in the shared whiteboard by the larger group to which they belong. The group had created the drawing as part of discussions about shortest paths between points A and B in a grid-world. In particular, a red triangle, ABD, was drawn with sides of length 4, 6 and $2\sqrt{13}$. A thick black staircase line was drawn as a path on the grid from A to B. In this excerpt, the students propose a math problem involving this drawing.

Log 17-1.

1	ImH:	what is the area of this shape? [REF TO WB]
2	Jas:	which shape?
3	ImH:	woops
4	ImH:	ahh!
5	Jas:	kinda like this one? [REF TO WB]
6	Jas:	the one highlighted in black and dark red?
7	ImH:	between th stairs and the hypotenuse
8	Jas:	oh
9	Jas:	that would be a tricky problem, each little "sector" is different
10	Jas:	this section [REF TO WB]]
11	ImH:	perimeter is 12root3
12	Jas:	is smaller than this section [REF TO WB]
13	ImH:	assume those lines are on the blocks
14	Jas:	the staircase lines?
15	ImH:	yea
16	Jas:	they already are on the blocks

The message in line 1 of the chat excerpt makes a bid at proposing a mathematical question for the group to consider: "**What is the area of this shape?**" This is accompanied by a graphical reference to the whiteboard. The reference does not indicate a specific area—apparently ImH did not completely succeed in properly using this new referencing tool. Line 2 raises the question, "**Which shape?**" pointing out the incompleteness of the previous message's reference. The proposal bid in line 1 calls for a proposal response, such as an attempt to answer the question. However, the question was incompletely formed because its reference was unclear, so it received a call for clarification as its immediate response. Lines 3 and 4 display a recognition and agreement of the incomplete and problematic character of the referencing.

Lines 5 and 6 offer a repair of line 1's problem. First, line 5 roughs in the area that may have been intended by the incomplete reference. It includes a complete graphical reference that points to a rectangular area that includes most of the upper area of rectangle ACBD in the drawing. The graphical referencing tool only allows the selection of rectangular areas, so line 5 cannot precisely specify a more complicated shape. The text in line 5 ("**kinda like this one?**") not only acknowledges the approximate nature of its own referencing, but also acknowledges that it may not be a proper repair of line 1 and accordingly requests confirmation from the author of line 1. At the same time, the **like** reflects that this act of referencing is providing a model of what line 1 could have done. Peer instruction in the use of the software is taking place among the students as they share their growing understanding of the new chat environment.

Line 5 is accompanied by line 6, which provides a textual reference or specification for the same area that line 5 pointed to: the one highlighted in black (the staircase line) and dark red (lines AC and CB). The inexact nature of the graphical reference required that it be supplemented by this more precise textual reference. Note how the sequence of indexical attempts in lines 1, 2, 5 and 6 successively focuses shared attention on a more and more well-defined geometric object. This is an interactive achievement of the group. The reference was not a simple act of an individual. Rather, it was accomplished through an extended interaction between ImH and Jas, observed by others and situated among the math objects constructed by the whole group of students in the chat room.

Lines 5 and 6 were presented as questions calling for confirmation by ImH. Clarification follows in line 7 from ImH: "**between the stairs and the hypotenuse.**" Line 8's "**Oh**" signals mutual understanding of the evolving reference and the establishment of an agreed upon boundary object (Star, 1989) for carrying on the mathematical investigation incompletely proposed in line 1. Now that the act of referencing has been successfully completed by the group, the group can use the referenced area as a mathematical object whose definition or meaning is intersubjectively understood. Viewed at the individual unit of analysis, the referenced area can serve as a boundary object shared among the interpretive perspectives of the interacting individuals. In other words, it becomes part of the joint problem space shared by the students. The referencing interaction established or grounded this. Note, however, that what took place was not an aligning of pre-existing individual opinions— as the theory of common ground is often taken to imply—but a group process of co-constructing a shared reference through a complex interaction involving many resources and social moves.

Now that a complete reference has been constructed to a math object that is well enough specified for the practical purposes of carrying on the chat, Jas launches into the problem solving by raising an issue that must first be dealt with. Line 9 says that calculating the area now under consideration is tricky. The tricky part is that the area includes certain little "**sectors**" whose shapes and areas are nonstandard. Line 9 textually references "**each little 'sector'.**" **Little** refers to subparts of the target area. **Each** indicates that there are several such sub-parts and **sector**, put in scare quotes, is proposed as a name/description of these hard-to-refer-to sub-parts.

Clarification of the reference to sectors is continued by lines 10 and 12. These lines compare two sectors, demonstrating that they are different by showing that one is smaller than the other. Lines 10 and 12 reference two different sectors, both with the same textual, deictic description: **this section**. It is possible to use the identical description twice here because the text is accompanied by graphical references that distinguish the two sectors. Line 10 points to the small grid square inside of rectangle ACBD in the upper left-hand corner adjacent to point A. Line 12 points to the next grid down the hypotenuse (see Fig. 17.1). Because of the roughness of the graphical reference tool, lines 10 and 12 can only indicate the squares of the grid, not the precise odd-shaped sectors that are of concern in the group discourse. On the other hand, the textual clause, **this section** has been given the meaning of the odd-shaped sub-areas of the area "**between the stairs and the hypotenuse,**" although it cannot differentiate easily among the different sections. The carefully constructed combination of graphical and textual referencing accomplished in lines 10 and 12 was needed to reference the precise geometric objects. The combination of the two textual lines, with their two contrasting graphical references, joined into one split sentence was necessary to contrast the two sectors and to make visible the tricky circumstance. In this way, the discourse succeeded in constituting the complicated geometric sectors despite the limitations of the tool on its own and of textual description by itself.

Line 13 responds to the tricky issue by treating it as a non-essential consequence of inaccurate drawing. By proposing that the group "**assume those lines are on the blocks**," this posting treats the difference among the sectors as due to the inaccuracy of the drawing of the thick black staircase line in not precisely following the grid lines. Physical drawings are necessarily rough approximations to idealized mathematical objects in geometry. Lines drawn with a mouse on a computer screen tend to be particularly rough representations. The implication of line 13 is that the tricky issue is due to the inaccurate appearance of the lines, but that the faults of the physical drawing do not carry mathematical weight and can be stipulated away. But line 14 questions this move. It first makes sure that line 13's reference to **those lines** was a reference to **the staircase lines** that form part of the perimeter of the target area and of its different-sized sectors. When line 15 confirms that line 13 indeed referenced the staircase lines, line 16 responds that "**they already are on the blocks**"—in other words, the tricky situation was not due to inaccuracies in the drawing but the staircase lines were indeed already *taken as* following the grid for all practical purposes. The problem was still seen to be a tricky one once the mathematical object was clearly referenced and specified.

We see here that referencing can be a complex process in online mathematical discourse. In a face-to-face setting, the participants could have pointed to details of the drawing, could have gesturally described shapes, could have traced outlines or shaded in areas either graphically or through gestures with ease. Conversationally, they could have interrupted each other to reach faster mutual orientation and understanding. Online, the interaction is more tightly constrained and burdensome due to the restricted nature of the affordances of the software environment. On the other hand, we have seen that middle-school students who are new to the graphical tools of ConcertChat, as well as to online collaborative mathematics, can call upon familiar resources of textual language, drawing, pointing and school mathematics to construct interaction methods that are seen to be amazingly sophisticated, efficient, creative and effective when analyzed in some detail.

Methods of Making Referential Sense

We have here only been able to look at what took place in a single effort to reference a mathematical object. In the series of chats that this effort was taken from, we observed groups of students engaging in a variety of other referencing methods within this version of ConcertChat. (See Chapter 15 for additional usages of the referencing tool.) Common methods in our chats included the following:

- Graphical references to previous messages were sometimes used to make salient a message from relatively far back in the chat. Without the graphical referencing functionality, this would have required a lengthy textual explanation justifying change of topic and quoting or describing the previous message.

- Some students used graphical references to previous messages to specify a recipient for their new posting. If a student wanted to address a question to a particular student rather than to the group as a whole, he or she would accompany the question with a graphical reference to a recent posting by that student. (This was a use of graphical referencing not at all anticipated by the software tool designers or VMT researchers.)
- It is common in chat for someone to spread a single contribution over two or more postings (e.g., lines 10 and 12). In conversation, people often retain their turn at talk by indicating that they are not finished in various ways, such as saying "ummm." In generic chat systems, people often end the first part of their contribution with an ellipsis (. . .) to indicate that they will continue in a next posting. In ConcertChat, students sometimes graphically referenced their first posting while typing their second. Then the two parts would still be tied together even if someone else's posting (like line 11) appeared in the meantime.
- Similarly, students graphically referenced their own previous posting when repairing a mistake made in it. The reference indicates that the new posting is to replace the flawed one.
- In chat, where the flow of topics is not as constrained as in conversation, it is possible for multiple threads of discussion to be interwoven. For instance, line 11 starts to discuss perimeter while area is still being discussed. Graphical references are used to tie together contributions to the same thread. For instance, line 12 might have referenced line 10 graphically.
- The graphical referencing tool is treated as one of many available referencing resources. Deictic terms are frequently used—sometimes in conjunction with graphical referencing (e.g., line 5).
- In textual chat, as in spoken conversation, sequential proximity is a primary connection. By default, a posting is a response to the immediately preceding post. Chat confusion arises because sequentiality is unpredictable in chat; people generally respond to the most recent posting that they see when they start to type, but by the time their response is posted other postings may intervene. Interestingly, the recency of drawings may function as a similar default reference. Students frequently refer to a line that was just added to the whiteboard as **that line** without needing to create a graphical reference to it.
- Of course, purely textual references are also widely used to point to postings, people, groups, drawings, abstractions and math objects.

The many forms of referencing in chat tie together the verbal and graphical contributions of individual participants into a tightly woven network of shared meaning. Each posting is connected in multiple ways—explicit and implicit—to the flow of the shared chat. The connections are highly directional, granting a strong temporality to the chat experience (hard to fully appreciate from a static log).

The being-there-together in a chat is temporally structured as a world of future possible activities with shared meaningful objects. The possibilities for collaborative action are made available by the social, pedagogical and technical context (world, situation, activity structure, network of relevant significance) (Heidegger,

1927/1996, §18). While the shared context is opened up, enacted and made salient by the group in its chat, aspects of the discourse context appear as designed, established or institutionalized in advance. They confront the participants as a world filled with meanings, priorities, resources and possibilities for action. It is a world whose features, meanings and co-inhabitants are initially largely unknown.

We are interested in providing cognitive tools to help groups of students navigate worlds of online collaborative mathematical discourse. We want to support their efforts to build collaborative knowledge. Since the Greeks and especially following Descartes, the issue of how people can know has been called "epistemology." We have seen in our case study that methods of referencing can play an important role in grounding the construction of shared knowledge in an environment like VMT. Conceptually, referencing can be seen as a key to the question of how groups can know, i.e., construct collaborative knowledge.

Epistemology of Referencing

Referencing is a primary means for humans to establish joint attention and to make shared meaning within a (physical or virtual) world in which they find themselves together. Vygotsky, in a particularly rich passage, described the interactional origin of pointing as an example of how gestures become meaningful artifacts for individual minds through social interaction:

> A good example of this process may be found in the development of pointing. Initially [e.g., for an infant], this gesture is nothing more than an unsuccessful attempt to grasp something, a movement aimed at a certain object which designates forthcoming activity. . . . When the mother comes to the child's aid and realizes this movement indicates something, the situation changes fundamentally. Pointing becomes a gesture for others. The child's unsuccessful attempt engenders a reaction not from the object he seeks but from another person. Consequently, *the primary meaning* of that unsuccessful grasping movement *is established by others*. . . . The grasping movement changes to the act of pointing. As a result of this change, the movement itself is then physically simplified, and what results is the form of pointing that we may call a true gesture. (Vygotsky, 1930/1978, p. 56, italics added)

The pointing gesture is perhaps the most fundamental form of deictic referencing. In its origin where the infant begins to be socialized into a shared world, the meaning of the gesture emerges interactionally as the participants orient to the same object and recognize that they are doing so jointly. This fundamental act of collaborative existence simultaneously comes to be symbolized for them by the pointing gesture, which is practiced, repeated and abstracted by them together over time and thereby established as meaningful. The mother and infant become an organic small group, caring for shared objects by being-in-the-world-together and understanding as collaborative practice the symbolic meaning of the physical gesture as a referencing artifact.

In grasping, the infant's being-in-the-world is intentionally directed at the object; the existence of the pointing infant is a being-at-the-object (Husserl, 1929/1960). When the mother joins the infant by transforming his individual grasp into a joint engagement with the object, the intentionality of the infant's grasp becomes intersubjective intentionality, constituting the infant and mother as being-there-together-at-the-object (Heidegger, 1927/1996, §26). For Husserl, consciousness is always consciousness-of-something. Human consciousness is intentional in the sense that the conscious subject intends an object, so that the subject as consciousness is at the object. Heidegger transformed this idealist conception into an embedded analysis of human being-there as being involved in the world. Heidegger's analysis builds up to the brink of a foundational social philosophy of being-there-together, but then retreats to an individualistic concern with the authentic self (Nancy, 2000; Stahl, 1975a). Vygotsky points the way to a fully social foundation, interpreting Marx' social *praxis* in social-psychological terms, such as in the intersubjective interaction of the infant-mother bonding.

Epistemology as a philosophic matter is a consequence of the Platonic and Cartesian separation of mind and meaning from the physical existence of objects in the world. The "problem of epistemology" is the question of how the mind can know facts—how one can bridge the absolute gulf that Plato (340 BC/1941) and Descartes (1633/1999) drew between the mental and the physical. Vygotsky's social philosophy overcomes this problem by showing how interactions among people achieve shared involvement in the world. In Descartes' system, there was no way to put together the mother's understanding, the infant's understanding, the physical grasp and the symbolic meaning of pointing. In Vygotsky's analysis, the interaction between mother and infant creates the shared meaningfulness of the pointing grasp as an intersubjectively achieved unity. There is no longer any reason to ask such questions as where is the meaning of the gesture, how does the mother know the infant's intention or whether there is common ground. *These are pseudo-problems caused by trying to reduce a social phenomenon at the group unit of analysis to issues at an individual unit of analysis.* These philosophical issues are intimately related to issues of empirical methodology. They imply that certain matters should be analyzed as group phenomena and not reduced to individual psychic acts or mental representations.

As researchers, we can empirically observe new referencing gestures being created within interactions among collaborating people, particularly when their interaction is taking place via a new medium that they must learn how to use. In the analysis above, a chat posting—"**What is the area of this shape?**"—constitutes the participants in the chat as a group by designating them as the intended collective recipient and as the expected respondent to the question (Lerner, 1993). The group is the intended agent who will work out the mathematics of the proposal to compute the area. Simultaneously, by referencing a mathematical object ("**this shape**"), the posting constitutes the group as a being-there-together-at-the-object—at an object that is constituted, identified, referenced and made meaningful by the group interaction. We saw how both these aspects of being a group necessitated considerable interactional work by the participants. Before the elicited answer about area could be given in response to the question, the group had to negotiate what it as a group took the object to be. Also, it required a number of actions for group participants to co-construct the shared object and their being-there-together-at-the-object.

In attempting to do this, they constituted themselves as a group and they established referential gestures and terms that took on the shared meaning of intending the new math object.

The interactional work of the group involved making use of the resources of the environment that mediated their interaction. This is particularly noticeable in online interaction. Vygotsky's infant and mother could use fingers, gaze, touch, voice. Online participants are restricted to exchanging textual postings and to using features of the mediating software. The chat participants must explicitly formulate through text, drawings or graphical references actions that can be observed by their fellow group members. These actions are also available to researchers retroactively.

The textual interactions in the chat excerpt as the cognitive actions of the group are in intimate contact with the details of the drawing as the physical intentional object. For instance, as we saw above, in the interchange in lines 13–16 the group attention is focused at a particularly interesting and ambiguous drawn line. Group methods of proceeding often involve *adjacency or uptake pairs*, sequences of utterances by different people that construct group meaning and social order through their paired unity. The meaning is constituted at the group unit of analysis by means of the interaction of the pair of utterances, not as a presumed pre-interactional meaning in the heads of individuals. Line 13 is a bid at opening up a math proposal adjacency pair (Stahl, 2006b, chap. 21): it offers a new step for mathematical discussion and elicits an uptake response from the rest of the group. Line 16 is the elicited response that takes up the bid with a kind of repair. It indicates that the proposed assumption is unnecessary and thereby attempts to re-establish a shared understanding of the situation. Lines 14 and 15 form a question/answer adjacency pair inserted in the middle of the proposal pair in order to make sure that the group really is together at the same detail of their shared math object.

The issue that is worked out by the group as they look carefully at the drawing together illustrates the subtlety of abstract mathematical thinking that the group is engaged in as a group. The issue involves the lines that were drawn with the whiteboard's rough cognitive tools for drawing and whether or not these lines coincide with lines of the grid (i.e., if the group should "**assume those lines are on the blocks**"). The issue is not one that is resolved by a close analysis of the actual pixels on the screen. Rather, it is a conceptual question of the meaning of those lines for the group: What do they mean in the drawing and how should they be taken by the group in its math discourse? In being together at the lines, the group makes sense of the meaning of the lines. There is no separation of fact and meaning here—or, if there is, the group interaction engages in meaning-making processes that fluidly overcome the gulf. This is particularly important in math discourse, where rough sketches are used to represent (mean and reference) abstract objects. Maintaining a shared understanding by a group of students working in a mathematical context like this is a subtle and intricate matter. The group must negotiate whether they are talking about the rough physical lines or the abstract mathematical lines they represent, and must jointly establish the working relationship of representation between them, as is done in the interaction of lines 13 and 16.

As designers of online education, we are interested in understanding how students collaboratively create new communicative gestures or interactional methods, including ways of referencing objects for joint consideration. More generally, an interactional understanding of referencing and meaning making leads to a theory of group cognition—rather than individual cognition based on mental representations—as a basis for studying collaborative learning. All the technical terms like *cognition, intentionality, reference, sense making, temporality* and *learning* needed to articulate a theory of group cognition must be re-conceptualized at the group unit of analysis. In some cases, the nature of these phenomena are actually easier to see at the group level, where participants have to make things visible to each other in order to coordinate their actions as group activities, as was the case with referencing in the excerpt discussed above.

Pedagogy of Referencing Math Objects

Our case study suggests that cognitive tools for referencing can be important supports for group cognition and collaborative knowledge building, particularly in a setting of computer-supported collaborative mathematics.

In the investigation reported here, we tried to encourage relatively open-ended explorations of mathematical inquiry by online teams of math students. We presented them with a non-traditional form of geometry in which notions like distance, area or shortest-path have to be renegotiated—i.e., the meanings of these terms must be jointly constructed anew. While trains of inquiry can go in many directions, in a collaborative effort each step of the path may be clarified and shared. New math objects emerge and develop out of the discourse, including both geometric figures (the tricky area) and terminology ("**distance along the grid**").

In this study, the analysis of a snippet of a group cognitive process in a concrete empirical case has suggested the centrality of joint referencing to collaboration. This may serve as an additional clarification of what is meant by defining collaboration as "a continued attempt to construct and maintain a shared conception of a problem . . .. an emergent, socially-negotiated set of knowledge elements that constitute a Joint Problem Space" (Roschelle & Teasley, 1995, p. 70) and what goes into actually doing such a thing. The persistent whiteboard serves as a "group external memory" that plays a useful role in grounding shared understanding at the scale of analysis of CSCL problem solving (Dillenbourg & Traum, 2006, p. 122f), in contrast to Clark and Brennan's (1991) psycholinguistic level. The intertwining uses of the dual workspaces of whiteboard and chat mirror the intertwining of content space and problem space that is characteristic of collaborative learning (Barron, 2003, p. 310). Given the complexity resulting from dual spaces—whether split for work vs. reflection (Fischer, Nakakoji, Ostwald, Stahl & Sumner, 1998; Schön, 1983) or transitory vs. persistent (Dillenbourg & Traum, 2006, p. 143f)—and the concomitant substantially increased burden of coordination within the group, we can clearly see the importance of cognitive tool support for referencing from one space to the other (see Chapters 7 and 15).

Referencing in mathematical worlds has its own domain-specific characteristics and priorities. Widespread conceptions of math learning as the memorization of "math facts" or the mastery of formulaic algorithmic solutions are oriented to the routine application of arithmetic rather than to the creative process that inspires mathematicians (Lockhart, 2008). The history of mathematics as a branch of scientific inquiry and knowledge building is a systematic unfolding of new domains through the shared construction of new math objects, like complex numbers, fractals, curved spaces. To share these created math objects as boundary objects within their discourse community, mathematicians have had to define new vocabularies, symbols and representations for referencing objects that do not exist as such in the physical world. Referencing such abstractions presents special cognitive challenges.

People who do not understand mathematical references can scarcely be expected to share the wonder and excitement that mathematicians feel who can see what is being referenced (Lakoff & Núñez, 2000). It is likely that much of the general population simply does not share the understanding of what is referenced in most mathematical proofs and discussions. Since our goal is to increase mathematical appreciation and participation through opportunities for online math discourse, we are keen to support shared referencing in our environments with effective cognitive tools.

Chapter 18
Scripting Group Processes in VMT

Gerry Stahl

Abstract The concept of scripts has considerable appeal as addressing or at least naming an urgent issue in CSCL: how to use the promise of networked computers to guide groups of students to engage in desirable and successful collaborative learning. However, the concept of scripts is often applied inconsistently or founded on problematic theoretical grounds. Reconceptualizing scripts as situated resources rather than implementable plans for action is therefore undertaken here to align the concept with current socio-cultural thought. Studying how such a resource is made sense of in detailed interactions is then recommended for studying how scripts can be designed to guide situated collaboration.

Keywords Scripts · scripting · resources · group cognition

As any attempt at designing CSCL must be, the VMT Project is concerned with ways of embedding group interaction in larger pedagogical activities. In the CSCL research community, this concern is increasingly discussed in terms of "scripting." This is exemplified by the publication of Fischer, Mandl, Haake & Kollar (2006) in the Springer CSCL book series and the flash theme on scripting (Kobbe et al., 2007) in the CSCL journal.

The term *script* encapsulates many connotations. This grants it the power to bring diverse topics together to cross-fertilize each other, as has been done in the Springer edited book. At the same time, the term's overloaded meanings threaten to dull its focus and emasculate its power; if it conjures up different visions for each reader, the term loses its power to build *shared* meaning. This chapter will reflect on the discussion of scripting in the CSCL community by trying to highlight its central claims, trace its historical roots and clarify its foundations.

We will proceed by commenting on the senses of the term *script* that can be associated with several of the theoretical sources repeatedly referenced in the scripting book: Schank and Abelson (1977), Vygotsky (1930/1978), Suchman (1987) and

G. Stahl (✉)
College of Information Science & Technology, Drexel University, Philadelphia, PA, USA
e-mail: gerry@gerrystahl.net

G. Stahl (ed.), *Studying Virtual Math Teams*, Computer-Supported Collaborative
Learning Series 11, DOI 10.1007/978-1-4419-0228-3_18,
© Springer Science+Business Media, LLC 2009

Schwartz (1995). In reviewing this history, the chapter will define a view of scripts that may differ from the term's commonly understood sense. It will then conclude by revisiting central claims of the scripting book in terms of this refined view.

Scripts as Cognitive Models

The script metaphor has its commonsense roots in the theater. Actors follow a script, which defines the narrative context, roles, actions and outcomes of a play, movie or television drama. Although the public idolizes the actors and remains ignorant of the script designers, the real agency lies in the script, not in the pretty faces who mouth it. The play's intelligence is that of the author, put into word and onto paper, reified and made persistent so that it can control the action that may later take place on camera, in the author's absence, for the benefit of a projected audience at yet another time and place.

Pop sociology would have us all playing socially defined roles. Somehow, conventions of our culture define what everyone (present company perhaps excluded) does, says and thinks. When we enter a restaurant, we supposedly slip into the customer role and interact with the person in the waitress role according to a well-defined script.

This is not quite the sense of script that Schank and Abelson's *Scripts, Plans, Goals and Understanding* (1977) originally proposed. In their pioneering contribution to artificial intelligence (AI) and cognitive science, they were exploring a computational model of how people understand stories. They proposed that people organize their memories of how events like visits to restaurants proceed by constructing data structures that represent knowledge of generalized events and connections among events, like causal relations. This theory of scripts is quite complex, attempting to incorporate much domain knowledge as well as linguistic structure. It is specifically designed to account for our ability to make sense of stories by speculating about mental representations of commonsense knowledge that allow us to fill in the implicit relationships between consecutive narrative utterances.

Written in the heyday of rationalist AI research, Schank and Abelson's concept of scripts assumed that human minds worked like computer programs, accessing data structures and drawing long sequences of logical conclusions. Motivated by toy problems like analyzing artificially simple narratives about restaurant visits, such theories have not stood up well to subsequent reflection, especially when people try to extend the theory beyond its original restricted domain of understanding stories to human activity more generally.

The restaurant script, with its necessarily large collection of associated variations, sub-scripts and related scripts might help one to analyze restaurant visits in stereotyped television plots or in boring visits to the local diner. But these are not necessarily events worth writing about. A story needs to have an element of novelty or interest—precisely something that goes outside of the generalized script. And every actual restaurant visit involves situated human interactions that spontaneously improvise around the assumed roles with personality, humor and humanity.

There is also the theoretical question of whether we really walk around with these huge, detailed, logically organized data structures covering all our common-sense, social and personal knowledge. It may be more reasonable to imagine that we *construct* on the spot generalized versions of something like restaurant scripts as spontaneous resources for thinking about specific stories or events as they confront us. This is not the way computers were programmed to organize knowledge in the 1970s, but it seems plausible given the way stories are actually told to people, at least in face-to-face situations. A story is designed by the teller to interact with the audience (Livingston, 1995). The teller continually adjusts the telling to form a desired interaction with the recipient of the story. Through subtleties of gaze, intonation, body position, facial expression, gesture, rhythm and word choice, the narrator and the recipients maintain an intimate alignment that ensures moment by moment that the story is actually being shared. Assumptions of what each other hold to be generalized patterns of, for instance, restaurant behaviors, may play significant roles in this dance of shared meaning making.

Scripts as Social Resources

The notion that we should look at the details of interactions among people in groups rather than speculating about mental representations in individual minds in order to understand human knowledge was developed in Vygotsky's *Mind in Society* (1930/1978). Inspired by a deep grasp of Marx's (1867/1976) social philosophy around the time of the Russian revolution, Vygotsky argued on theoretical and empirical grounds that what is distinctive about the way that people learn is the construction of new skills in interactions with others within cultural contexts: "Human learning presupposes a specific social nature and a process by which children grow into the intellectual life of those around them" (p. 88).

Vygotsky's concept of the zone of proximal development distinguishes a person's intellectual abilities when working alone from those when collaborating with others. The fact that learners have significantly higher skill levels when working in dyads or small groups suggests that intellectual development generally takes place during interactions with others. Vygotsky was able to show with controlled experiments that children could accomplish tasks with external memory aids and with collaboration that they could not do on their own. Older subjects could achieve these tasks on their own, suggesting that they had somehow internalized the intersubjective or environmental aids in the intervening years. Vygotsky was not able to study the detailed interactions whereby collaboration and external artifacts were used, let alone observe directly the mechanisms of internalization. However, his visionary—if sketchy—theories inspired the emphasis on collaborative learning in socio-cultural contexts within CSCL.

Vygotsky's theory of learning suggests that scripts not be taken as models of mental representations of individual learners, but be used for structuring social environments to foster collaborative interactions that can engender intersubjective knowledge building.

Scripts as Computer-Based Resources

A methodology for studying the moment-to-moment interactions of dyads and small groups engaged in collaborative problem solving—with computer support—is motivated, described and illustrated in Suchman's *Plans and Situated Actions* (1987). The use of video analysis based on principles of ethnomethodology (Garfinkel, 1967) as practiced by conversation analysis (Sacks, 1962/1995), allows Suchman to propose an approach that she explicitly contrasts with the AI approach of Schank and Abelson: "Instead of looking for a structure that is invariant across situations, we look for the processes whereby particular, uniquely constituted circumstances are systematically interpreted so as to render meaning shared and action accountably rational. Structure, on this view, is an emergent property of situated action" (p. 67). For instance, structures of meaning, goals, roles or turn taking in conversation are not pre-existing structures, but are constructed interactively by the on-going discourse itself (Garfinkel & Sacks, 1970; Sacks et al., 1974).

For Suchman, plans such as the scripts of Schank and Abelson are not rigid blueprints for action that are simply implemented as stated, but are flexible resources that people construct, interpret, adapt and use in their specific, situated acts of making sense. People's commonsense understandings of their plans may be similar to the AI view, but if one studies closely the role that plans play in actual activities—such as accomplishing office tasks—one gets a different view. In Vygotsky's (1930/1978, e.g., p. 28f) analysis, planning skills evolved out of resources for interpersonal interaction. Young children simply act and then may retroactively give a name to their action (e.g., to a drawing they did, when prompted for a description). Later, they verbalize actions to be taken: at first in an attempt to control another person's behavior (e.g., their caretaker), and subsequently to control their own future behavior. In such ways, verbalizations of action (plans) can function either before or after the actions as ways of making shared sense of the actions.

In Suchman's ethnomethodological terms, plans are resources that may be used to prepare for and guide up-coming actions or to give an accounting of on-going or completed actions (i.e., they are often retroactive rationalizations). Under this analysis, *plans are not causal agents of the action*, but are possible useful accompaniments to the action that play (at least originally) a largely *interpersonal* role rather than an individual mental function. The social functioning of verbal plans (or their silently internalized derivatives in thought) is hidden in the taken-for-granted everyday functioning of human existence, and plans are then conceptualized based on their adult, conscious appearances. Commonsense folk theories—and the rationalist abstractions of these theories in AI—project plans into mental representations that cause planned action.

Suchman studies the use of a computer-based help system for a sophisticated copying machine. The help system defines an AI-type script that was designed on assumptions about mental models of scripts in users' heads controlling their actions. Suchman documents the failure of this approach by showing how dyads of users negotiate their understandings of various problematic states of their copying tasks through interactively trying to make sense of various resources in their environment, including messages from the copier, their shared discourse, verbalizations of their goals, generalizations of past experiences and attempts at various actions.

The fundamental problem, as Suchman points out, is an asymmetry in the data that the copier computer has about the on-going work context and what the users understand about the situation. This asymmetry is closely related to the fact that people do not make sense of their activities according to generalized scripts. Rather, they make use of an unconstrained set of resources that they make relevant in their environment. Perhaps most importantly, they engage in subtle processes of problem solving to overcome breakdowns in the kinds of anticipated normal patterns of events that might be captured in scripts and plans. Such problem solving is critical to success because breakdowns are ubiquitous. Analysis of the discourse of dyads or small groups engaging in situated problem solving can reveal how people actually make use of available resources and where they get stuck trying to follow computer scripts. The detailed collaborative procedures captured on video and comprehended through intensive and repeated study are rarely what designers of computer-based scripts might have planned for.

The copier help system is a script that provides computer support for small groups to collaboratively learn how to use the copier. It is an instance of scripting for CSCL. It mediates the users' collaborative actions and their meaning making. It poses the central practical tension that gnaws at the enterprise of CSCL:

(a) Collaborative learning is achieved under unique circumstances whose significance is interactively constructed by the learners and cannot be predicted.
(b) Computer support attempts to define a specific context and to direct the meaning-making process in order to (i) guide the learning toward pedagogical goals and (ii) provide a real-time model of the learners' state that can steer the delivery of computational resources.

Based on her theoretical, methodological and empirical study, Suchman recommends (p. 181) that computer support compensate for its limitations by: (1) extending its access to the actions and circumstances of the user; (2) clarifying for the user the limits of the computer's access to the users' rich interactional resources; and (3) providing a wider array of alternative resources, particularly to help the users respond to unforeseen breakdowns. These recommendations should be implemented based on careful empirical study of a given application, along the lines of Suchman's video analysis of copier usage. Only this way will designers discover: (1) the relevant factors of the use situation; (2) the way that the user treats the computer as an interaction partner; and (3) the kinds of breakdowns that can occur and the resources that users take advantage of to make sense of and overcome the breakdowns.

Scripting Group Cognition

It is not easy to study the details of how people use situational resources to construct shared meaning in computer-mediated learning tasks. In particular, it is hard to delineate what is accomplished by individuals and what is best analyzed at the small-group unit of analysis. Hardest of all, perhaps, is to describe how individual and group cognition—once distinguished—work symbiotically. Schwartz' *The Emergence of Abstract Representations in Dyad Problem Solving* (1995) takes some steps in this direction.

Schwartz scripts three controlled experiments—one in a lab with video camera and two in classrooms—that compare individuals and dyads working on the same science problems. In order to get at the problem-solving process, Schwartz looks at the intermediate problem representations that the students construct, rather than at their final solutions. He finds that although there is little significant difference between individuals and dyads in their final solutions, the groups construct more abstract representations. Schwartz concludes from this that the group-level cognitive processes are qualitatively different from the cognitive processes of the isolated individuals: "Group cognitions sometimes yield a product that is not easily ascribed to the cognitions that similar individuals have working alone. In particular, groups have a tendency to construct representations that are more abstract than individuals' representations" (p. 322).

In the first experiment, where the activities were captured on video, Schwartz was able to see how the dyads were forced to construct collaborative representations, to negotiate their meaning and to overcome breakdowns in shared understanding. These unique, situated, unpredictable interactions and verbalizations produced and made visible joint articulations of the structures of the objects in the scientific problem, leading to insights into the final solution. Because of their interactive work in overcoming the additional hardships introduced by having to negotiate and maintain shared understandings between two people who started with independent ideas, the dyads performed significantly better than would be predicted based on combining the best individual performances of the dyad members.

Unfortunately, the other two experiments were not videotaped and therefore the interactions of the dyad members could not be analyzed. Consequently, Schwartz was largely reduced to speculation that if the interactions could be studied they would show that the processes of overcoming breakdowns in maintaining mutual knowledge fostered the joint construction of abstract graphical and verbal representations that were useful for problem solving:

> I suspect that interactional studies would find numerous forms of negotiation depending on the individuals' knowledge and the affordances of the task at hand. ... Although the process and products of representational negotiation may take numerous forms, I believe that careful attention to the conditions preceding a period of representational negotiation will reveal strong evidence for the important role of mutual-knowledge problems in the co-construction of representations. (p. 348)

Scripts for Framing Collaborative Interactions

The preceding quick review of Schank and Abelson, Vygotsky, Suchman and Schwartz has attempted to reconceptualize the concept of scripts as situated resources rather than implementable plans for action so as to align the concept with current socio-cultural thought. It has recommended the micro-analysis of how such resources are made sense of in small group interactions in order to guide the design of scripts based on actual examples of the kinds of situated action for which the scripts are intended.

Dillenbourg and Jermann (2006) display a healthy recognition of the nature of scripts as flexible resources. They take the concept of script not as a cognitive model of how people actually decide what to do, but rather as a design metaphor for finding the delicate balance between too little computer control to be helpful and too much control to allow for flexible group interactions.

Interestingly, they finesse the problem of constraining group interaction by confining scripting to the individual or whole-class activities that precede and that follow the core small-group collaborative activities. They define CSCL scripts to be instructional sequences that prepare for and then reflect upon, but do not interfere with peer interactions. Adopting Schwartz' conclusion that the power of collaborative learning comes from the effort necessary for the group to build a shared understanding, Dillenbourg and Jermann use scripts to set up situations in which groups will be forced to construct group meanings—their SWISH model. The meaning-making phase itself is then left unconstrained, for it is too fragile, complex and unpredictable to be supported by a script that is written in advance.

Dillenbourg and Jermann's chapter is clearly a synthetic presentation, based on extensive experience using scripts in real learning contexts. It would be nice to see some of the detailed interactions that were observed during the experimentation as examples that motivate the principles enumerated in that chapter. Presumably, page limitations for the chapter prohibited that, and one must go back to their earlier individual studies for such examples.

Scripts for Learning and for Life

Carmien, Kollar, Fischer & Fischer (2006) call for a distributed cognition perspective to account for the interplay of mental and environmental phenomena. While this is an important move, the details of the particular theory developed are also decisive. The preceding discussion has argued for building more on Vygotsky and Suchman than on Schank and Abelson in defining an approach to distributed cognition or group cognition. Rather than starting from a theory of individual cognition and then supplementing it to build a "person-plus" theory, it has invoked Vygotsky's theory in which individual cognition is a social-cognition-minus product of internalization processes. In place of adopting a view of scripts as controlling data structures, it has recommended Suchman's conception of situated resources.

Vygotsky's and Suchman's alternative approaches could be used to account for the design, study and analysis of tools for living and tools for learning. Computational tools mediate between people, for instance between a cognitively disabled person and their caregiver or a group of students and their teacher. The tool can be viewed as an externalization of the caregiver's or the teacher's guidance. The users must learn how to use the tool, and they may or may not be able to internalize its guidance to varying degrees.

Carmien et al. cite Suchman and recognize the dangers of technology-driven design. Careful study—such as that done by Suchman—at a detailed level of interactional granularity would be needed to analyze the specific processes of internalization and externalization and to design the tools for a successful fit to the situated meaning-making interactions through which the tool is put into service. This would also ensure that the users' situated needs drive design.

The discussion of scripting in the scripting book poses central issues for theory building, assessment methodology and design practices in scripting CSCL. However, it also presents the danger of encouraging the design of educational technologies and pedagogical interventions based on infirm conceptual ground unless the notion of scripting is located within an adequate theory of group cognition, as suggested by Vygotsky, Suchman and Schwartz.

Chapter 19
Helping Agents in VMT

Yue Cui, Rohit Kumar, Sourish Chaudhuri, Gahgene Gweon, and Carolyn Penstein Rosé

Abstract In this chapter we describe ongoing work towards enabling dynamic support for collaborative learning in the Virtual Math Teams (VMT) environment using state-of-the-art language technologies such as text classification and dialogue agents. The key research goal of our long-term partnership is to experimentally learn broadly applicable principles for supporting effective collaborative problem solving by using these technologies to elicit behavior such as reflection, help seeking, and help provision, which are productive for student learning in diverse groups. Our work so far has yielded an integrated system that makes technology for dynamic collaborative learning support—which has proved effective in earlier lab and class-room studies—available for experimental use within the "wild" VMT environment.

Keywords Dialog agents · dynamic support · helping behavior · cognitive tutors · TagHelper · Basilica

Introduction

We are in the beginning stages of a long-term partnership, the goal of which is to enhance participation and learning in the Virtual Math Teams (VMT) online math service by designing, developing, implementing, testing, refining and deploying computer-based tools to support facilitation and collaborative learning in this lightly-staffed service. This project brings together the Drexel VMT Project—with the Math Forum's long track record and infrastructure for hosting and facilitating collaborative math problem-solving experiences in "the wild"—and the Carnegie Mellon team—with expertise developing effective, state-of-the-art language technologies—to pursue the potential to create a new, more dynamic form of computer-supported collaborative learning than what has been possible in VMT until now. In addition to complementary technologies provided within the scope

C. P. Rosé (✉)
School of Computer Science, Carnegie Mellon University, 5000 Forbes Avenue, Pittsburg, PA 15213, USA
e-mail: cprose@cs.cmu.edu

G. Stahl (ed.), *Studying Virtual Math Teams*, Computer-Supported Collaborative Learning Series 11, DOI 10.1007/978-1-4419-0228-3_19,
© Springer Science+Business Media, LLC 2009

of this strategic partnership, insights from complementary methodologies come together in a powerful way. In this chapter, we describe our progress to date, both in terms of technological development and new insights gained from a "full circle" methodology, which takes insights from naturalistic observations, confirmed and refined through experimental lab studies, implemented within a technical infrastructure, and finally provided for future cycles combining naturalistic observations in the wild and refinement in controlled settings.

In the VMT environment, collaboration is currently supported with a combination of script-based support and human moderation. The script-based structuring is stage-based. Students typically work in small groups on the same problem over three or four sessions. In the first session, they work out solutions to the problem. In between the first and second sessions, students receive feedback on their solutions from human moderators. In the second session, students discuss the feedback they received on their respective solutions and step carefully through alternative correct solutions. In that session and the subsequent session, they also discuss additional possible ways of looking at the problem including variations on that problem in order to take a step back and learn larger mathematics principles that apply to classes of problems rather than individual problems. Although the problem provides the opportunity to investigate multiple possible solutions and to engage in deep mathematical reasoning, VMT researchers have found from analysis of chat logs where students have worked together that students tend to jump to finding one solution that works rather than taking the opportunity to search for alternative solutions. Prior work comparing students working with well defined versus non-specific problem-solving goals supports the belief that students can benefit from exploring multiple solutions, when those alternative solution paths provide opportunities to learn different concepts (see Chapter 10 for an example of re-use of problem-solving methods). Thus, there is reason to believe this typical pattern of narrowing to a single solution prematurely is counter-productive for learning. To address this and other issues, the moderator plays an important role in stimulating conversation between students, encouraging knowledge sharing and probing beyond a single acceptable solution.

While support from human moderators is extremely valuable to students, it is a rare commodity. Currently, only a tiny fraction of the approximately one million visitors to the Math Forum site each month have the opportunity to benefit from this expert-facilitated group-learning experience. Thus, our long-term goal is to greatly expand this capacity by using technology to support collaboration in this environment in two main ways, both of which leverage our prior research on automatic collaborative process analysis (Donmez et al., 2005; Rosé et al., 2008; Wang & Rosé, 2007). The first approach is to deploy *conversational agents* to offer fully automated support. As in our previous investigations in other collaborative environments, agents in VMT would participate in the student conversation. Automatic analysis of the collaborative-learning process can be used to detect when a conversational agent should intervene in a conversation. Another direction we plan to pursue is to use the automatic analysis of the conversation to *construct reports* that inform human facilitators of which groups are most in need of support (Joshi & Rosé, 2007;

Kang, Chaudhuri, Joshi & Rosé, 2008; Rosé et al., 2007). In this chapter, we focus primarily on the first approach.

The key research goal in the long term is to optimize a design and implementation for dynamic feedback in support of collaborative problem solving that will maximize the pedagogical effectiveness of the collaboration by eliciting behavior that is productive for student learning in collaborative contexts, including but not limited to the VMT environment. Towards this end, we have conducted a series of investigations across multiple age groups and multiple domains related to the design, implementation and evaluation of conversational agents that play a supportive role in collaborative-learning interactions (Chaudhuri et al., 2008; Gweon, Rosé, Zaiss & Carey, 2006; Kumar, Rosé, Wang, Joshi & Robinson, 2007; Wang et al., 2007). We are working towards supporting collaboration in a dynamic way that is responsive to what is happening in the collaboration rather than operating in a "one size fits all" fashion, which is the case with state-of-the-art static forms of support such as assigning students to roles (Strijbos, 2004), providing prompts during collaboration (Weinberger, 2003), designing structured interfaces (e.g., with buttons associated with typical "conversation openings") (Baker & Lund, 1997), guiding learners with instructions to structure their collaboration (Webb & Farivar, 1999), or even various forms of training in collaboration (Rummel, Spada & Hauser, 2006). Our investigations thus far have been in lab and classroom studies. The far less controlled VMT environment provides a more challenging environment in which to test the generality and robustness of our prior findings, while at the same time providing a context where successful technology for supporting collaborative-learning interactions can reach a broad spectrum of students in need of support in their mathematics education.

While there has been much work evaluating a wide range of conversational agents for supporting individual learning with technology (Kumar, Rosé, Aleven, Iglesias & Robinson, 2006; Rosé et al., 2001; Rosé & Torrey, 2005; Rosé & Van-Lehn, 2005; VanLehn et al., 2007), a similar effort in *collaborative* contexts is just beginning. We have observed in our recent research that working collaboratively may change the way students conceptualize a learning task and similarly how they respond to feedback (Wang and Rosé, 2007; Wang et al., 2007). For example, Wang and Rosé found that students approached an idea-generation task more broadly when they worked in pairs rather than as individuals, in particular behaving in a way that indicated more of a fluid boundary between tasks, whereas students who worked individually focused more narrowly on one task at a time. Correspondingly, students who worked in pairs with feedback showed even more evidence of a connection between tasks, where individuals with feedback during idea generation simply intensified their success within their original narrow focus. This difference in how students responded to feedback when they worked individually and in pairs tells us that before we will be able to effectively support collaborative learning—with tutorial dialogue technology (Gweon et al., 2005; Jordan, Hall, Ringenberg, Cui & Rosé, 2007; Rosé et al., 2001) in particular as well as intelligent tutoring technology more generally—it will be essential to re-evaluate established approaches that have proven effective for individual learning now in collaborative contexts, and we have begun to engage in such comparisons (Gweon, Rosé, Albright & Cui, 2007; Kumar, Rosé et al., 2007).

Our initial investigations using dialogue agent technology as collaborative learning support have been tremendously successful (Chaudhuri et al., 2008; Kumar, Gweon, Joshi, Cui & Rosé, 2007; Wang et al., 2007), suggesting that the presence of dialogue agents in the conversation increase learning of human participants as much (Kumar, Gweon et al., 2007) or more (Wang et al., 2007) than the human collaborators do.

We begin this chapter by describing our research methodology, which benefits from a combination of qualitative investigations conducted by Drexel's VMT team with insights from experimental studies and quantitative discourse analysis from our Carnegie Mellon team. Next, we describe our investigations of helping behavior, which are still in progress, but which have already suggested directions for dynamic support in the VMT environment. We will then describe our current integration between the technology for dynamic collaborative-learning support and the VMT environment, which we have now piloted with college-aged students in both math and thermodynamics (Chaudhuri et al., 2008). We will conclude with plans for future work.

Full-Circle Methodology: Complementary Insights from Complementary Contexts

In recent years, the CSCL community has grown in its openness to mixed methods and has made progress towards bridging a wide spectrum of methodological approaches from qualitative, ethnographic-style investigations to highly controlled, highly quantitative approaches. In that spirit, we leverage a broad spectrum of methodologies, ranging from high-internal-validity studies in the lab and in the classroom, with pre/post-test designs, to high-external-validity investigations in the "wild" VMT environment, where the same analyses of observable collaborative behavior are possible even with naturalistic, non-controlled observation, but experimental designs are less practical and must be administered with caution because of the way imposing too much control may interfere with the natural working of the community.

As an illustration of our full-circle, mixed-methods approach, we offer an example of how our informal collaboration to date is already yielding synergistic findings. This investigation provided the data for the quantitative investigation of math helping behavior discussed later in the chapter. Because our ultimate goal is to achieve success in the "wild" VMT environment, we begin with insights gained from an ethnomethodological analysis of chat logs collected in the VMT environment (see Chapter 5). In one notable chat session, the VMT team observed a group of students that was successful at solving problems collaboratively that none of them were capable of solving alone. On close inspection of the chat logs, a student who at first appeared as "the class clown" emerged as a tone setter in the analysis, putting his team mates at ease, and allowing them to forge ahead as a group to solve a particularly challenging problem. From this analysis, a hypothesis emerges that interventions that inject humor in a collaborative-learning setting may act as a "social lubricant," and thereby may increase success in collaborative problem solving. The Carnegie Mellon team has tested this hypothesis experimentally in a classroom study in which students worked in pairs in a collaborative problem-solving environment that shares some common simple functionality with the VMT environment. We refer to this study as the Social Prompts study (Kumar, Rosé et al., 2007).

Experimental Infrastructure

The Social Prompts study was run as a classroom study with middle school students learning fraction arithmetic using a simple collaborative problem-solving environment (see Fig. 19.1), which was a precursor to the integrated version of the VMT environment discussed later in the chapter. Although this study took place in a school computer lab, students worked in pairs, communicating only through text chat.

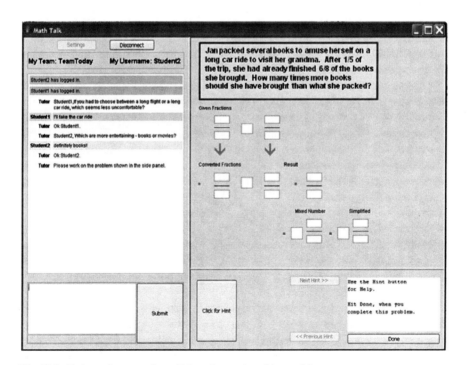

Fig. 19.1 Early environment for collaborative math problem solving

The interface in Fig. 19.1 has two panels. On the left is a chat interface, which allows students to interact with each other as well as with conversational agents that are triggered at different occasions during the problem-solving session to offer support to the collaborating pairs. The panel on the right is the problem-solving interface, which allows students to work collaboratively on a given problem. In this case the interface in the right panel was built using the Cognitive Tutor Authoring Tools (CTAT) (Aleven, Sewall, McLaren & Koedinger, 2006). The problem-solving panel has a problem layout and a hint button. The hint button triggers support built into the environment. The hint messages are displayed in the chat window. Both panels of the interface maintain a common state across both the participants at all times, creating a shared experience for the student dyad. All actions performed by a student in either of the panels are immediately communicated and reflected on the interface of the other student. This integrated shared experience of problem solving is unique to this interface in contrast to systems used in our earlier experiments where a similar collaborative environment was used to manage the shared-problem-solving interaction (Gweon et al., 2007; Gweon et al., 2006).

Experiment and Results

The purpose of the experiment was to test the facilitative effect of off-task, social conversation on collaborative problem solving. Our hypothesis was that in a condition in which this form of social interaction was encouraged, students would work together better, offering each other more help, and thus benefiting more from the collaboration.

The experimental procedure extended over 4 school days, with the experimental manipulation taking place during days two (i.e., lab day 1) and three (i.e., lab day 2). The fourth day of the experiment was separated from the third day of the experiment by a weekend. Teams remained stable throughout the experiment. The students were instructed that the teams would compete for a small prize at the end of the study based on how much they learned and how many problems they were able to solve together correctly. The second and third days were lab days in which the students worked with their partner. Each lab session lasted for 45 minutes. At the end of each lab period, the students took a short quiz, which lasted about 10 minutes. At the end of the second lab day only, students additionally filled out a short questionnaire to assess their perceived help received, perceived help offered, and perceived benefit of the collaboration. On the fourth experiment day, which was two days after the last lab day, they took a posttest, which was used for the purpose of assessing retention of the material.

In the experimental condition of the Social Prompts study, before a problem is displayed in the shared problem-solving space, a tutor agent first asks each student what we refer to as a social question. For example, the agent may first ask student 1 **"Student 1, if you had to choose between a long flight or a long car ride, which seems more uncomfortable?"** The student indicates that a car ride would be preferable. Then the tutor agent may ask, "**Student 2, which are more entertaining—books or movies?**" The student may respond that books are more amusing. These two pieces of information are then used to fill in slots in a template that is used to generate personalized wording for the math problem. In particular, the resulting story problem says, "**Jan packed several books to amuse herself on a long car ride to visit her grandma. After 1/5 of the trip, she had already finished 6/8 of the books she brought. How many times more books should she have brought than what she packed?**" The lighthearted nature of the word problem was meant to inject a note of humor into the conversation, and possibly spark off-task discussion, because the focus of the questions was on personal preferences of the students rather than strictly on math. In order to control for content and presentation of the math content across conditions, we used exactly the same problem templates in the control condition, but rather than presenting the social questions to the students, we randomly selected answers to the social questions "behind the scenes." Thus, students in both conditions worked through the same distribution of problems.

The results of the Social Prompts study provided some evidence in support of the hypothesis that emerged from observations in the VMT environment. We began our analysis by investigating the socially-oriented variables measured by means of a questionnaire, which we designed as a subjective assessment of perceived problem solving competence of self and partner, perceived benefit, perceived help received and perceived help provided. Each of 8 questions included on the questionnaire consisted of a statement such as "**The other student depended on me for information or help to solve problems.**" and a 5 point scale ranging from 1 (labeled "strongly disagree") to 5 ("strongly agree"). For perceived benefit and perceived confidence, scores were high on average (about 4 out of 5) in both conditions, with no significant difference between conditions. However, with perceived help offered as well as perceived help received, there were significant differences between conditions (see Table 19.1). Students in the experimental condition rated themselves and their partner significantly higher on offering help than in the control condition. Interestingly, there is more evidence of requesting help in the control-condition chat logs. However, these requests were frequently ignored.

Table 19.1 Questionnaire results

	Control	Experimental
Perceived self competence	4.2 (0.56)	4.1 (0.23)
Perceived partner competence	4.3 (0.62)	3.9 (0.49)
Perceived benefit of collaboration	4.5 (0.74)	4.4 (0.70)
Perceived help received	1.8 (1.3)	3.3 (0.69)
Perceived help provided	1.8 (1.1)	3.1 (1.1)

The learning-gains analysis is consistent with the pattern observed on the questionnaire, and offers some weak evidence in favor of the experimental condition on learning. The trend was consistently in favor of the experimental condition across tests and across units of material on the test. The strongest effect we see is on lab day 2 where students in the experimental condition gained marginally more on interpretation problems (p = 0.06, effect size 0.55 standard deviations). The student chat logs contain rich data on how the collaborative problem-solving process transpired.

We also conducted a qualitative analysis of the conversational data recorded in the chat logs in order to illuminate the findings from the test and questionnaire data discussed above. Overall, we observed that students were more competitive in the control condition. Insults like "**looser**," "**you stink**" or "**stupid**" occurred frequently in the control condition, but never in the experimental condition. Instead, in the experimental condition we observe light-hearted teasing. Furthermore, students referred to themselves as a group more frequently in the experimental condition. More details of the analysis of the chat logs are presented in the next section.

The full-circle methodology that we follow begins with ethnographic observations from interactions in the VMT environment. These observations lead to hypotheses that can be tested in high-internal-validity environments such as lab and classroom studies. These studies help us to confirm causal connections between actions and subsequent effects, between which we observe a correlation in our earlier ethnographic analyses. Discovered causal connections can then form the basis for the design of full-scale interventions, which can be prototyped and tested in the VMT environment. These investigations can eventually serve both as a test of the generality and robustness of findings from the lab and classroom studies as well as a source of new insights, forming the basis for new hypotheses that can be tested in further cycles—although only a large-scale controlled study evaluating the full intervention, such as we plan in the future, can provide definitive evidence of its effectiveness.

Analysis of Helping Behavior

Many of the benefits of collaborative learning are experienced through the discussions that students have in these contexts, so much of our work is focused on the dynamics of those conversations. For decades, a wide range of social and cognitive benefits have been extensively documented in connection with collaborative learning, which is mediated by conversational processes. The exchange of help is one valuable aspect of this process. Because of the importance of these conversational processes, in our evaluation of the design of conversational agents for supporting collaborative learning we must consider both the learning that occurs when individuals interact with these agents in the midst of the collaboration (i.e., learning from individual direct interaction with the agents) and learning that is mediated by the effects of the agents on the group interaction between the students. A formal analysis of helping behavior in our collected chat logs allows us to do that.

Theoretical Foundation

The help that students offer one another in the midst of collaborative learning ranges from unintentional help provided as a byproduct of other processes, to help offered with full intentionality. Beginning with unintentional help, based on Piaget's (1985) foundational work, one can argue that a major cognitive benefit of collaborative learning is that when students bring differing perspectives to a problem-solving situation, the interaction triggers consideration of questions and ideas that might not have occurred to the students individually. This stimulus could help them to identify gaps in their understanding, which they would then be in a position to address. This type of cognitive conflict has the potential to lead to productive shifts in student understanding.

Related to this notion of cognitive conflict, other benefits of collaborative learning focus on the consequences of engaging in intentional teaching behaviors, especially the articulation of deep explanations (Webb, Nemer & Zuniga, 2002). Other work in the CSCL community demonstrates that interventions that enhance argumentative knowledge construction, in which students are encouraged to make their differences in opinion explicit in collaborative discussion, enhances the acquisition of multi-perspective knowledge (Fischer, Bruhn, Gräsel & Mandl, 2002). Furthermore, based on Vygotsky's seminal work and his concept of the zone of proximal development (Vygotsky, 1930/1978), we know that when students who have different strengths and weaknesses work together, they can provide scaffolding for each other that allows them to solve problems that would be just beyond their reach if they were working alone. This makes it possible for them to participate in a wider range of hands-on learning experiences.

While the cognitive benefits of collaborative learning are valuable, they are not the only positive effect of collaborative learning. In fact the social benefits of collaborative learning may be even more valuable for fostering a productive classroom environment. These are obviously strongly related to the social interaction between students, which could be greatly enhanced by conversational interactions. By encouraging a sense of positive interdependence among students—where students see themselves both as offering help and as receiving needed help from others—collaborative learning has been used as a form of social engineering for addressing conflict in multi-ethnic, inner-city classrooms (Slavin, 1980). Some examples of documented social benefits of successful collaborative learning interactions include: increases in acceptance and liking of others from different backgrounds, identification with and commitment to participation in a learning community, improvements in motivation and aptitude towards long-term learning.

The social benefits of collaborative learning are closely connected with the Vygotskian foundations of collaborative learning because the positive interdependence that is fostered through collaborative learning is related to the exchange of support, or scaffolding, that students offer each other. Our own research has affirmed this connection. For example, in a previous study where we used a dynamic support intervention to encourage helping behavior, we observed anecdotal evidence that the manipulation increased helping behavior, and we observed a significant positive learning effect in the condition where we observed the increase in helping behavior (Gweon et al., 2006). In a subsequent study where we manipulated the availability of help from the problem-solving environment, we observed a significant positive correlation between the frequency of help offered and learning by the help provider (Gweon et al., 2006). In the same study, we observed that students perceived more benefit and learned more in the condition where they offered more help. Below we demonstrate through an analysis of the chat logs from the Social Prompts study introduced earlier that the presence of social dialogue agents that show an interest in the personal preferences of participants not only created a more positive atmosphere between students and increased the perception of both help offered and help received, but also increased the concentration of actual verbal help exchanged per problem. As noted, the manipulation resulted in a marginal increase in learning on the second lab day of the study. All of these studies offer evidence of the value of helping behavior, consistent with what would be predicted by the theoretical foundations for collaborative learning put forward by Piaget, Vygotsky and others.

Simple Coding Scheme for Helping Behavior

In order to investigate whether students in the experimental condition actually offered each other more help in the Social Prompts study, we coded the chat logs from each lab day with a coding scheme developed in our previous work (Gweon et al., 2007). In order to make the sometimes cryptic statements of students clearer during our analysis, and also to provide an objective reference point for segmenting the dialogue into meaningful units, we merged the log-file data recorded by the problem-solving interface with the chat logs recorded from the chat window using time stamps for alignment. We then segmented the conversational data into episodes using the log files from the tutoring software as an objective guide. Each episode was meant to include conversation pertaining to a single problem-solving step as reified by the structured problem-solving interface. Between problems, conversation related to a single social prompt counted as one episode, and conversation related to one cognitive support agent also counted as one episode. All entries in the log files recorded by the tutoring software refer to the step in the action it is associated with as well as any hints or other feedback provided by the tutoring software. Note that steps where no conversation occurred did not have any episode associated with them in our analysis.

The simple coding scheme consisted of five mutually exclusive categories: (R) Requests Received, (P) Help Provision, (N) No Response, (C) Can't Help and (D) Deny Help. Along with the "other" category, which indicates that a contribution does not contain either help seeking or help providing behavior, these codes can be taken to be exhaustive.

The first type of conversational action we coded was Request Received (R). Help requests are conversational contributions such as asking for help on problem solving, asking an explicit question about the domain content, and expressing confusion or frustration. Not all questions were coded as Requests Received. For example, there were frequent episodes where students discussed coordination issues such as whether the other student wanted to go next, or if it was their turn, and these questions were not coded as help requests for the purpose of addressing our research questions.

Adjacent to each coded Request Received, in the column associated with the partner student, we coded four types of responses. Help Provisions (P) are actions that attempt to provide support or substantive information related to the other student's request, regardless of the quality of this information. These actions are attempts to move toward resolving the problem. Can't Help statements (C) are responses where the other student indicates that he or she cannot provide help because he or she doesn't know what to do either. Deny Help (D) statements are where the other student responds in such a way that it is clear that he or she knows the answer but refuses to stop to help the other student. For example, "**Ask** [the teacher], **I understand it**" or "**Hold on** [and the other student proceeds to solve the problem and never comes back to answer the original question]" are type D statements. And finally, No Responses (N) are statements where the other student ignores help requests completely. Each chat log was coded separately by two coders, who then met and resolved all conflicts. Note that often where Requests Received are not met with a verbal Help Provision, the students are still able to collaboratively or independently work out an answer to their questions, at least at the level of moving forward with the problem solving. In some cases, however, the students seem to move forward through guessing.

Log 19-1 shows two example episodes where a Request Received is met with a Help Provision:

Log 19-1.

Student 1: What operation do we do?
<Student 2 tries multiplication and gets negative feedback from the
  problem-solving environment>
<Student 2 tries divide and gets positive feedback from the problem-solving
  environment>
Student 2: We divide. Now look at the problem, what is the other fraction we
  must divide by?

Student 1: What do we put on top of the fraction?
Student 2: Did you find a common denominator?
<Student 1 correctly finds the common denominator>

In Log 19-2 are two example episodes where a Request Received is met with a Can't Help response. In the second example, the student who requested help eventually figured out what to do on his own.

Log 19-2.

Student 1: Why 16?
Student 2: I don't know.

Student 1: I need help.
Student 2: Same
Student 1: 23/2
Student 2: What's 23/2?
Student 1: 11.5

Log 19-3 provides two example episodes where a Request Received is met with a Deny Help response. In the first case, the student who asked for help was able to figure out the answer by guessing.

Log 19-3.

Student 1: I don't get it
Student 2: hold on
<Then Student 1 tried something and got negative feedback from the problem-solving environment>
<Finally Student 1 tried something else, which was correct, and got positive feedback from the problem-solving environment>

Student 1: I don't know what to do
Student 2: click on the help button

Two example episodes where a Request Received is met with No Response are given in Log 19-4. In both cases the students seem to find the answer by guessing.

Log 19-4.

Student 1: I don't get it
<Student 2 tries something and gets negative feedback from the problem-solving environment>
<Student 2 tries something else and gets negative feedback from the problem-solving environment>
<Student 2 clicks on the help button>
<Student 1 tries something that is correct and gets positive feedback from the problem-solving environment>

Student 1: ?
<Student 2 tries something and gets negative feedback from the environment>
<Student 1 tries something, which is correct, and gets positive feedback from the environment>

The results from our coding of the corpus are displayed in Table 19.2. First, we see that there are a significantly larger total number of episodes on the transcripts from the Experimental condition. Recall that all episodes contain some

Table 19.2 Results from corpus analysis

	Experimental (Day 1)	Experimental (Day 2)	Control (Day 1)	Control (Day 2)
Total Episodes	47.1 (8.2)	61.3 (12.3)	33.8 (17.9)	49.1 (26.9)
Social Prompt Episodes	24.1 (9.9)	33.7 (16.2)	0 (0)	0 (0)
Solicited Help Episodes (P)	0.79 (1.6)	0.36 (1.1)	1 (1.3)	1.4 (2.9)
Unsolicited Help Episodes	*1.7 (2.1)*	*3.2 (6.0)*	*2.1 (3.2)*	*1.9 (3.2)*
Unanswered Help Requests (C+R+N)	2.4 (2.7)	1.4 (1.9)	2.2 (1.9)	1.4 (1.4)
Non-Help Episodes	19.9 (5.6)	35.8(9.3)	30.6 (16.3)	46.3 (25.1)

conversation. Steps where no conversation occurred do not count in our total number of episodes. The larger number of episodes in the Experimental condition is primarily due to the fact that episodes in which social prompts were given to students only occurred in the Experimental condition, and two of these occurred between every problem solved during the Experimental condition.

Looking at the totals in Table 19.2, our finding regarding the average number of Help Provisions was that—contrary to what we might suspect based on the questionnaire data—there was no significant difference between conditions, although there was a non-significant trend for fewer verbal Help Provisions to be given in the Experimental condition. The number of Requests Received met with no verbal form of help was not different between conditions. However, there were significantly more non-help related conversational episodes in the control-condition transcripts. Furthermore, there were significantly more help episodes per problem in the Experimental condition $F(1,15) = 16.8$, $p < 0.001$, effect size 1 s.d. Thus, the students in the control condition may have perceived less help behavior because there was a lower proportion of helping behavior, both on a per problem basis (in terms of total amount of help per problem) as well as on an overall basis (in terms of proportion of conversational episodes altogether that were help related).

Ultimately it became clear to us that limiting our scope to verbal help was not adequate. As we examined both the verbal and non-verbal behavior of students, we began to see that sometimes where it appeared from the chat behavior that an explicit help request went unanswered, we saw behavior from the other student in the problem-solving logs that suggested that the student's intention was indeed to offer help, however not verbally. Thus, our recent work, discussed in the next section, has focused on characterizing help more broadly. Ultimately, we believe our efforts to monitor and support helping behavior in the VMT environment will need to account for both verbal and non-verbal behavior of students (e.g., through the VMT's whiteboard).

Extended Coding Scheme for Verbal and Nonverbal Helping Behavior

We are at the beginning stages of developing a coding scheme that captures both verbal and non-verbal helping behavior. This is a tricky analysis problem since from the non-verbal problem solving behavior we see it is often difficult to distinguish a case where a student is offering assistance non-verbally, from a case where a student is simply taking over the problem solving, and moving ahead without the partner.

From the collaborative problem-solving environment discussed earlier, log-files were generated that combined time-stamped records of each attempt to fill in a problem-solving step, along with who contributed that step and whether the contribution was correct or not, as well as time-stamped records of every contribution to the chat interface. We used the problem-solving behavior as an objective guide for segmenting the log-files into units for analysis. We used the problem-solving step as our unit of analysis. So all of the attempts to fill in a step counted together as one unit along with any chat contributions that were submitted during that time. Because the step was our unit of analysis, rather than coding each helping action as we had done in our earlier coding scheme, we coded each segment for what was the most explicit helping behavior, if any, we observed for each participant. Thus, at most we would assign one Request Received code and one Help Provision code per student, per segment. In what follows, we will describe the multi-step coding process.

The first step in the coding process is to mark for each step which student eventually entered the correct answer. This is used in the process of interpreting non-verbal help. We say that a non-verbal help request is initiated whenever the same student has contributed two unsuccessful attempts for the same step. The first time this condition is true within a step, the student who is responsible for contributing that step is said to have non-verbally requested help by demonstrating a lack of ability. A code is then assigned that indicates how that help request was resolved, i.e., whether the student who initiated the help request was able to eventually contribute the right answer for the step without any intervention, either verbally or non-verbally from the other student, or whether the other student was the one who contributed the correct answer for the step, or whether the first student eventually contributed the right answer after receiving some form of help from his partner.

One interesting finding from this analysis was that between the experimental and control conditions of the Social Prompt study there were no significant differences in raw number of help requests, or number of help requests where the other student completed the step. However, between the experimental and control conditions there were marginally more cases in the experimental condition where a student requested help, received help from his partner, and then was able to complete the step himself using that help (p = 0.07).

Virtual Math Teams with Adaptive Support

In our recent work, we have integrated our technology for automatic analysis of the collaborative-learning process with our technology for supporting conversational interactions with computer agents into a single unified framework, which we refer to as Basilica. Conceptually, this framework allows monitoring conversational interactions as they unfold, which allows it to track behaviors such as argumentation, helping and explanation. Based on this analysis, conversational agents that are capable of engaging students in discussion on a variety of topics can be triggered. The purpose of this integrated framework is to make it possible to easily integrate these technologies with a wide range of collaborative environments. For example, we have recently integrated Basilica with the massively multi-player on-line environment called Second Life (Weusijana, Kumar & Rosé, 2008).

Example Interactions in the Integrated VMT-Basilica Environment

We have just begun to collect pilot data with the integrated VMT-Basilica environment using the types of open-ended math problems that are characteristic of prior investigations in the VMT environment. Here we describe our small pilot investigation in the math domain. A larger, experimental study in the thermodynamics domain is described elsewhere (Chaudhuri et al., 2008).

Fig. 19.2 displays the interface for the integrated VMT-Basilica environment. It is identical to the original VMT environment, except that chat agents can participate along with a group of human students in the chat. (Note "Tutor" in the list of Current users and as the second poster in Fig. 19.2.) On the whiteboard is displayed the problem statement the students are working on. Below it is a drawing one of the students has pasted on in order to share it with his partner. The goal of the exercise is for students to understand that they can use a binary search strategy to solve the problem of finding a heavier weighted coin among a set of other coins that all weigh the same as each other.

In Log 19-5, we see that the students first think together about a strategy for approaching the problem.

After a short time, the tutor agent jumps in with a hint that the students then take up and use in their problem solving (see Log 19-6, from Fig. 19.2).

Student 1 has worked out a solution based on the tutor's hint and then pasted it onto the whiteboard. This is indicated on Fig. 19.2 with a small square in the chat following Student 1's "hm. . ." (see Log 19-5). When Student 2 clicks on this square, an arrow appears that points to what Student 1 has pasted onto the whiteboard. However, Student 2 is not able to fully understand Student 1's drawing (see Log 19-7).

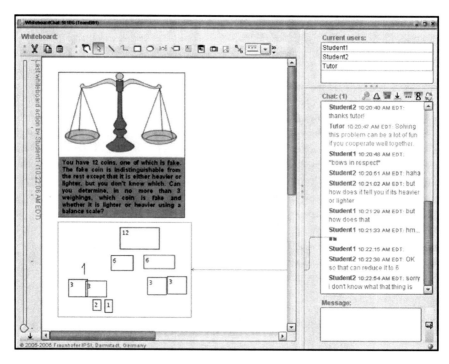

Fig. 19.2 Integrated version of the VMT environment

Log 19-5.

Student2: i was thinking what if you weighted them all out
Student2: and then took an average
Student2: but i guess you cant do that
Student2: because we cant know the weight
Student1: i was thinking of weighing them all, then weigh one (and hope it's not fake XP)
Student2: haha

Log 19-6.

Tutor: HINT: If you split a group of coins into half and they weigh equal, then that whole set doesn't contain the fake coin. It must be in the other set from the previous weighing. This also tells you whether the fake coin is heavier or lighter.
Student2: oh!
Student2: thanks tutor
Tutor: Solving this problem can be a lot of fun if you cooperate well together.
Student1: *bows in respect*
Student2: haha

Log 19-7.

Student2: but how does it tell you if its heavier or lighter
Student1: but how does that....
Student1: hm...
Student2: ok so that can reduce it to 6
Student2: sorry i dont know what that thing is
Student2: once we know its in one group of 6

After Student 2 has expressed confusion, Student 1 jumps in with a further explanation of the hint that originally had come from the Tutor agent (Log 19-8).

Log 19-8.

Student1: hm...so you recommend...first splitting the whole thing into groups of 3
Student2: yeah
Student1: then weighing two groups of 3 against each other
Student1: if they're equal, we use this as a benchmark against another group

---

The students were then able to move on from there to solve the problem. In addition to individual hints, the tutor agent is also able to engage students in multi-turn directed lines of reasoning, as in our previous investigations (Chaudhuri et al., 2008; Kumar, Gweon et al., 2007).

Technical Description: The Basilica Framework

Based on our experiences with designing and engineering collaborative-learning systems that involve integrating the state of the art in text classification and conversational-agent technology, we recognized the need for a framework that facilitates such integration. In this section, we describe our continuing work to develop such a framework. Initial specification of the desiderata of our framework included reusability of component technologies, compatibility with other platforms, and the ability to provide flexibility to system designers to select from a wide range of existing components and then to synchronize, prioritize and coordinate them as desired in a convenient way.

While we continue to make further improvements to the framework to better achieve these specifications, in its current form the Basilica framework is an event-driven framework that enables development of conversational agents by using two basic components, referred to as Actors and Filters. These components communicate using Events. The Actor component, as the name suggests, displays behavior. Filters, on the other hand, observe behavior. Behavior and data are encapsulated into Events. For example if an Actor component generates a text message to be shared by the other participants in the conversational interface, it broadcasts a *TextMessageEvent*. Similarly, if a human logs into the conversational interface, a *LogInEvent* is sent to all relevant filters.

The Basilica framework implements a set of abstract software classes, which correspond to components, events and other supporting elements of the framework like channel independent communication, logging and process management. Along with these abstract classes, the Basilica framework now has a growing set of reusable Actors, Filters and Events that can be used to rapidly build custom conversational agents.

Supporting procedural behavior in an event-based framework like Basilica brings together two very different approaches of generating conversational behavior within the same framework. With this integration, we can view the conversational task as a space of graphs. Each graph represents a procedural behavior and graphs are triggered by events. The traversal of each graph, once it is triggered, is guided by the control strategy of the behavior associated with the graph. This has implications for the amount of effort involved in developing conversational applications of very different scales. In a procedural framework, the task may be represented by a simple graph or a quite complex graph. However if the task is designed appropriately, by using Basilica a complex graph can be divided into several smaller graphs, allowing distributed development with fewer dependencies and higher possibility of reuse of behavior. The event-driven approach adopted by Basilica has further advantages for building multi-modal conversational applications. This is particularly relevant if the different human participants engage in the conversation through different media like text, speech, short message service (SMS), gesture, etc. The programmatic approach to authoring taken by Basilica enables easier integration with devices and software for which a conversational interface has been developed.

A Basilica component can be defined on the basis of the events it observes and the operations it performs when it observes each of those events. These operations may include updating its beliefs, accessing its resources and generating events. Building a conversational agent under this framework is essentially an exercise in instantiating the desired actors and filters from a library of reusable components and establishing communication links, called Connections, between them. The exercise involves ensuring that all components are well connected to receive events they require. In some cases the exercise may involve creating new actors and/or filters to generate or observe some new behavior.

Figure 19.3 shows the design of Basilica within the integrated VMT-Basilica environment. Each Basilica component is represented by a polygon with three sections. The bottom section is marked with an out-pointing arrow on its left side and the text in that box is right aligned. The events generated by the component are listed in this box. The middle section is marked with an in-pointing arrow on its right side and text in this box is left aligned. The events received by the component are listed in this box. The name of the component is written in the top section. The shape of the top box determines the type of component it represents. An Actor component is drawn as a parallelogram and a Filter component is drawn as a rectangle. An "x" sign is placed in the corresponding box if a component does not receive or send any event.

In this integrated environment, the Basilica agent communicates with a VMT chat room (maintained by the ConcertChat server) using the *PresenceActor* and the

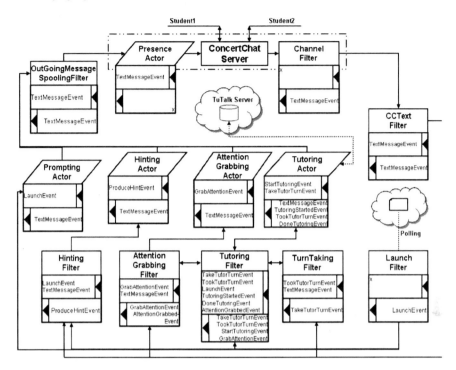

Fig. 19.3 Configuration of Basilica

ChannelFilter. The *PresenceActor* exhibits agent behavior like tutor turns, login and
logout in the chat room while the *ChannelFilter* observes similar behavior by the
students. All incoming text messages are encapsulated as *TextMessageEvent* and
routed to all Filters that need it through the *CCTextFilter*. On the output end, all
outgoing messages are spooled through the *OutGoingMessageSpoolingFilter*.

There are four specific behaviors exhibited by the agent. These behaviors are distributed across four actors in the design. The *PromptingActor* prompts students at
different times to inform them about the time left and also to give them certain motivating prompts at fixed time-points during the exercise. The *HintingActor* presents
hints to the students to help them cover concepts that they have not yet discussed but
which may be helpful in improving their design. The *HintingActor* works with the
HintingFilter, which continuously monitors the students' conversation to evaluate
which of the key concepts have been least discussed in the student conversations.
Depending on that, the *HintingFilter* triggers the *HintingActor* to produce an appropriate hint at fixed time-points during the exercise. A hint is produced only once,
and it is not reused during the exercise for the same students.

The *AttentionGrabbingActor* and the *TutoringActor* work together along with
the *AttentionGrabbingFilter*, *TutoringFilter* and *TurnTakingFilter* to initiate and
complete the instructional dialog session. At fixed time intervals during the exercise,
the agent interacts with the students about certain concepts relevant for the exercise.

Before an instructional dialog begins, to grab the student's attention, the tutor produces an *AttentionGrabbing* prompt. An example of an *AttentionGrabbing* prompt is "**Now might be a good time for some reflection**." The strategy to produce an *AttentionGrabbing* prompt is motivated from our past experience with building conversational support in a collaborative-learning environment. Students tend not to notice the tutor's instructional turn in between their turns, and the tutor never gains the floor in the conversation. We think that an *AttentionGrabbing* prompt may be successful at getting the tutor the floor in a text-based conversational environment.

Current Directions

In this chapter we have described our vision for enhancing the quality of support offered to students in the VMT environment. We began by discussing our mixed-methods approach to studying this problem and iteratively developing an evidence-based design. We have discussed our findings and continued explorations related to helping behavior as well as describing the current integrated environment that we have developed.

A major direction of our current work is to continue with our analysis of helping behavior. Ultimately, we would like to use TagHelper tools (Rosé et al., 2008) to automate this analysis, so that helping behavior in the VMT environment can be tracked and supported.

Part V
Representing Group Interaction in VMT

Introduction to Part V

This Part addresses a core issue for the analysis of online text chat: how to represent the structure of the interaction. In particular, as noted in several chapters, the reconstruction of the implicit response structure is a necessary, but tricky, initial step in making sense of a chat log. The response structure is known as the *threading* of the postings as they take up or reference previous postings. Response structure is particularly important for interaction analysis because it tracks the pairing of utterances in functional-adjacency or uptake pairs, or the way in which particular utterances take up the possibilities offered by previous utterances. It corrects for the appearance of postings that appear in the midst of functional pairs as a result of the simultaneous and unobserved production of chat postings.

Another generic way of analyzing relationships among postings is *coding*, i.e., assigning a category from a coding scheme to each posting in order to differentiate kinds of posts and to compare numbers of different kinds of postings. This method is not bothered by the arbitrary order of posting appearances because coding typically treats each posting in isolation. Coding has been quite popular in CSCL studies, because it allows researchers to make quantitative comparisons between different data sets in terms of their code distributions. However, the analyses in this volume are generally quite concerned with the sequentiality of postings and the implications of this for group processes as interactions across postings.

These chapters look at group interaction in VMT by means of the threading analysis and coding of the chat postings. They *represent* the group interaction structurally though diagrams of the threading and coding.

Chapter 20 reports early work in the VMT Project attempting to understand patterns of interaction in PoW-wow chats by means of thread analysis. Through an analysis of ten hour-long chats, it looks at patterns of interactions, from the fine-grained structure of responses to statistical patterns of typical responses of one type of utterance to another. This introduces work on threading in the VMT Project.

Chapter 21 looks at the oft-cited phenomenon of chat confusion. In particular, it studies the use of the VMT environment by the authors of this volume as they conducted chats about first drafts of the book's chapters. The chapter investigates the effectiveness of the VMT environment's graphical referencing in dealing with problems of chat confusion—at least in the hands of adults experienced in its use.

This study was conducted independently by a research group that has extensively investigated chat confusion.

Chapter 22 discusses the major coding effort within the VMT Project, an attempt to develop a general coding scheme for analysis of VMT chats. The goal was to produce a coding scheme based on general interests within the Project that could guide exploration of the data corpus; this is in contrast to most coding efforts, which are designed to test a specific hypothesis. During the first summer of the project, the coding scheme was developed through a major effort to code ten complete PoW-wow logs. In the fall, statistical analyses of the coding of the ten logs was conducted. A number of issues with the results of this coding and analysis process led to a shift of VMT analysis efforts away from coding and toward conversation-analysis-inspired approaches.

Chapter 23 tells the story of the shift from coding to chat interaction analysis. It first investigates a puzzling result from a statistical analysis of the coding discussed in Chapter 22 and solves the puzzle through a conversation analysis of two different kinds of framings of the chats related to the difference in experimental design but not reducible to it. The analysis of expository and exploratory sequences segues into a proposal to code "longer sequences" as defined by the chat participants themselves in their interaction. Graphical representations of the interweaving of these topical sequences and the statistical analysis of their patterns provides insights into the comparison among chats that differs from the findings of traditional coding and counting.

Chapter 24 proposes to represent chats in terms of their two-dimensional polyphonic connections. An individual student's perspective or "voice" forms a longitudinal trajectory—or melody—during a chat. At any given moment along this melody, multiple participants may be interacting with each other, producing a harmony across voices. The metaphor of polyphony drives this chapter to propose methods for analyzing and representing the interconnections among chat postings.

Chapter 25 provides yet another representation of group interaction in VMT. In this case, it is junior college students in Singapore working on different kinds of relatively advanced math problems. The types of problems are designed to promote different kinds of interactions and to have different learning consequences. The graphical representation of the chat flow highlights pivotal postings and the stages of discussion that they initiate. In addition, the student participants are interviewed about their perceptions concerning pivotal postings and references, as a source for triangulating researcher analyses.

Chapter 20
Thread-Based Analysis of Patterns in VMT

Murat Perit Çakir, Fatos Xhafa, and Nan Zhou

Abstract In this chapter we present a thread-based approach for analyzing synchronous collaborative math problem-solving activities. Threading information is shown to be an important resource for analyzing collaborative activities, especially for conducting sequential analysis of interaction among participants of a small group. We propose a computational model based on thread information, which allows us to identify patterns of interaction and their sequential organization in computer-supported collaborative environments like VMT. This approach enables us to understand important features of collaborative math problem solving in a chat environment and to envisage several useful implications for educational and design purposes.

Keywords Sequential organization · threading · problem-solving patterns

The analysis of fine-grained patterns of interaction in small groups is important for understanding collaborative learning (Stahl, 2006b). In distance education, collaborative learning is generally supported by asynchronous threaded discussion forums and by synchronous chat rooms. Techniques of interaction analysis can be borrowed from the science of conversation analysis (CA), adapting it for the differences between face-to-face conversation and online discussion or chat. CA has emphasized the centrality of turn-taking conventions and of the use of adjacency pairs (such as question-answer or offer-response interaction patterns). In informal conversation, a given posting normally responds to the previous posting. In threaded discussion, the response relationships are made explicit by a note poster, and are displayed graphically. The situation in chat is more complicated, and tends to create confusions for both participants and analysts.

In this chapter, we present a simple mathematical model of possible response structures in chat, discuss a program for representing those structures graphically and for manipulating them, and enumerate several insights into the structure

M.P. Çakir (✉)
College of Information Science & Technology, Drexel University, Philadelphia, PA, USA
e-mail: mpc48@drexel.edu

G. Stahl (ed.), *Studying Virtual Math Teams*, Computer-Supported Collaborative Learning Series 11, DOI 10.1007/978-1-4419-0228-3_20,
© Springer Science+Business Media, LLC 2009

of chat interactions that are facilitated by this model and tool. In particular, we show that fine-grained patterns of collaborative interaction in chat can be revealed through statistical analysis of the output from our tool. These patterns are related to social, communicative and problem-solving interactions that are fundamental to collaborative-learning group behavior.

CSCL research has mainly focused on analyzing content information. Earlier efforts aimed at identifying interaction patterns in chat environments—such as Soller and Lesgold (2003)—were based on the ordering of postings generated by the system. A naïve sequential analysis solely based on the observed ordering of postings without any claim about their threading might be misleading due to artificial turn orderings produced by the quasi-synchronous chat medium (Garcia & Jacobs, 1998), particularly in groups larger than two or three (O'Neill & Martin, 2003).

In recent years, we have seen increasing attention to thread information, although most of this research is focused on asynchronous settings (King & Mayall, 2001; Popolov, Callaghan & Luker, 2000; Smith, Cadiz & Burkhalter, 2000; Tay, Hooi & Chee, 2002; Venolia & Neustaedter, 2003). Jeong (2003) and Kanselaar et al. (2003), for instance, use sequential analysis to examine group interaction in asynchronous threaded discussion. In order to do a similar analysis of chat logs, one has to first take into account the more complex implicit linking structures of text chat.

Our approach makes use of the thread information of the collaboration session to construct a graph that represents the flow of interaction, with each node in the graph denoting the content that includes the complete information from a posting in the recorded transcript. By traversing the graph, we mine the most frequently occurring dyad and triad structures, which are analyzed more closely to identify the patterns of collaboration and sequential organization of interaction in such online settings. The proposed thread-based sequential analysis is robust and scalable, and thus can be applied to study synchronous or asynchronous collaboration in different contexts.

The rest of the chapter is organized as follows: The next section introduces the context of the research and the coding scheme on which the thread-based sequential analysis is based. The following section states the research questions we want to investigate. Then we introduce our approach. Finally, we present interesting findings and discuss them to address our research questions and to envisage several useful implications for educational and design purposes.

Context of the Research

The VMT Project and Data Collection

The VMT Project began with an experiment called *PoW-wow*, which extended the Math Forum's "*Problem of the Week (PoW)*" service. Groups of 3–5 students in grades 6–11 collaborate online synchronously to solve math problems that require reflection and discussion. We used the popular AOL Instant Messenger (AIM) software to conduct the experiment, in which each student group is assigned to a chat room. Each session lasts about 60–90 minutes. The PoW-wow sessions are recorded as chat logs (transcripts) with the handle name (the nickname of the participant who made the posting), the timestamp of the posting, and the content posted (see Table 20.1). The analysis conducted in this chapter is based on six of these sessions. In three of the six sessions the math problem was announced at the beginning of the session, whereas in the rest the problem was posted on the Math Forum's website in advance.

Table 20.1 Description of the coded chat logs

PoW-wow session number	Facilitator	Members	Number of postings	PoW name	Announced before?
1	MUR	PIN, GOR, REA, MCP	334	Finding CE	No
2a	GER	AVR, PIN, SUP, OFF	724	Equilateral Triangle Areas	No
2b	MUR	MCP, AH3, REA	204	Equilateral Triangle Areas	No
9	POW	EEF, AME, AZN, LIF, FIR	715	Making Triangles	Yes
10	MFP	AME, FIR, MCP	582	The Perimeter of an Octagon	Yes
18	MFP	AME, KON, KIL, ROB	488	A Tangent Square and Circle	Yes

Coding Scheme

Both quantitative and qualitative approaches are employed in the VMT Project to analyze the transcripts in order to understand the interaction that takes place during collaboration within this setting. A coding scheme has been developed in the VMT Project to quantitatively analyze the sequential organization of interactions recorded in a chat log (see Chapter 22). The unit of analysis is defined as a posting that is produced by a participant at a certain point of time and displayed as a single posting in the transcript.

The coding scheme includes nine distinct dimensions, each of which is designed to capture a certain type of information from a different perspective. They can be grouped into two main categories: one is to capture the content of the session whereas another is to keep track of the threading of the discussion, that is, how the postings are linked together. Among the content-based dimensions, conversation and problem solving are two of the most important, which code the conversational and problem-solving content of the postings. Related to these two dimensions are the conversation thread and the problem-solving thread, which provide the linking between postings, and thus introduce the relational structure of the data. The conversation thread also links fragmented sentences that span multiple postings. The problem-solving thread aims to capture the relationship between postings that relate to each other by means of their mathematical content or problem-solving moves (see Log 20-1 from PoW-wow 2a).

Each dimension has a number of subcategories. The coding is done manually by three trained coders independently, after strict training assuring a satisfactory reliability. This chapter is based on four dimensions only: the conversation thread, conversation dimension, problem-solving thread and problem-solving dimension.

Research Questions

In this exploratory study we address the following research questions:

- *Research Question 1:* What patterns of interaction are frequently observed in a synchronous, collaborative math problem-solving environment?
- *Research Question 2:* How can patterns of interaction be used to identify: (a) each member's level of participation; (b) the distribution of contributions among participants; and (c) whether participants are organized into subgroups through the discussion?
- *Research Question 3:* What are the most frequent patterns related to the main activities of the math problem solving? How do these patterns sequentially relate to each other?
- *Research Question 4:* What are the (most frequent) minimal building blocks observed during "local" interaction? How are these local structures sequentially related to each other, yielding larger interactional structures?

The Computational Model

We have developed software to analyze significant features of online chat logs. The logs must first be coded manually, to specify both the local threading connections and the content categories as in Log 20-1. When a spreadsheet file containing the coded transcript is given as input, the program generates two graph-based internal representations of the interactions, depending on the conversation and problem-solving thread dimensions respectively. In this representation each posting is treated as a node object, containing a list of references pointing to other nodes according to the corresponding thread. Moreover, each node includes additional information about the corresponding posting, such as the original statement, the author of the posting, its timestamp and the codes assigned in other dimensions. This representation makes it possible to study various kinds of *sequential patterns*. Here sequential patterns refer to a set of postings that are linked according to the thread, either based on the authorship information or on the conversational and/or problem-solving content of each posting as captured by the codes.

Log 20-1.

Line Number	Handle	Statement	Time	Conversation Thread	Conversation	Problem Solving	Problem Solving
45	AVR	Okay, I think we should start with the formula for the area of a triangle	8:21:46		Offer		
46	SUP	ok	8:22:17	45	Follow	45	Strategy
47	AVR	A = 1/2bh	8:22:28		Offer	45	Perform
48	AVR	I believe	8:22:31	47	Extension	47	
49	PIN	yes	8:22:35	47	Setup	47	
50	PIN	i concure	8:22:37	49	Agree	19	Check
51	PIN	Concur*	8:22:39	50	Repair Typing		
52	AVR	then find the area of each triangle	8:22:42		Offer	45	Strategy
53	AVR	oh, wait	8:22:54		Regulation		
54	SUP	the base and heigth are 9 and 12 right?	8:23:03		Request		Orientation
55	AVR	no	8:23:11	54	Setup	54	
56	SUP	o	8:23:16		No Code		
57	AVR	that's two separate triangles	8:23:16	88	Critique	55	Reflect
58	SUP	ooo	8:23:19	55	Setup	55	
59	SUP	ok	8:23:20	58	Follow	58	

After building a graph representation, the model performs traversals over these structures to identify frequently occurring sub-structures within each graph, where each sub-structure corresponds to a sequential pattern of interaction. Sequential patterns that have different features in terms of their size, shape and configuration type are studied. In a generic format, dyads of type C_i–C_j, and triads of type C_i–C_j–C_k where $i<j<k$ are examined in an effort to get information about the local organization of interaction. In this representation C_i stands for a variable that can be replaced by a code or by author information. The ordering given by $i<j<k$ refers to the ordering of nodes by means of their relative positions in the transcript. It should be noted that a posting represented by C_j can only be linked to previous postings, say C_i where $i<j$. (This restricts the threading to a directed acyclical graph.) In this notation the size of a pattern refers to the number of nodes involved in the pattern (e.g., the size is 2 in the case of C_i–C_j). Initially the size is limited to dyads and triads since they are more likely to be observed in a chat environment involving three to five participants. Nonetheless, the model can capture patterns of arbitrary size whenever necessary. The shape of the pattern refers to the different combinations in which the nodes are related to each other. For instance, in the case of a triad like C_i–C_j–C_k there are two possible type configurations: (a) if C_i is linked to C_j and C_j is linked to C_k , then we refer to this structure as *chain* type; (b) if C_i is linked to C_j and C_i is also linked to Ck, then we refer to this structure as *star* type. The dyadic and triadic patterns identified this way reveal information about the local organization of interaction. Thus, these patterns can be considered as the fundamental building blocks of a group's discussion, whose combination would give us further insights into the sequential unfolding of the whole interaction.

The type of the configuration is determined by the information represented by each variable C_i. In a display of the threading, a variable C_i can be replaced by the author name, the conversation code, the problem-solving code, or a combination of conversation and problem-solving codes. This flexibility makes it possible to visualize and analyze patterns that link postings by means of their authors and the codes they receive from the conversational or problem-solving dimensions.

As shown in Table 20.1, the maximum number of chat lines contained in a transcript in our data repository is about 700 lines, and we analyzed a corpus containing 6 such transcripts for this exploratory study. Thus, in this chapter the emphasis is given to ways of revealing relevant patterns of collaborative interaction from a given data set. Nonetheless, we take care of efficiency issues while performing the data-mining task. Moreover, there exist efficient algorithms designed for mining frequent substructures in large graphs (Inokuchi, Washio & Motodam, 2000; Kuramochi, 2001; Zaki, 2002), which can be used to extend our model to process larger data sets.

Results and Discussion

In this section we show how the computational model presented in this work enables us to shed light on the research questions listed above.

Local Interaction Patterns

In order to identify the most frequent local interaction patterns of size 2 and 3, our model performs traversals of corresponding lengths and counts the number of observed dyads and triads. The model can classify these patterns in terms of their contributors, in terms of conversation or problem-solving codes, or by considering different combinations of these attributes (e.g., patterns of author-conversation pairs). The model outputs a dyad percentage matrix for each session in which the (i,j)th entry corresponds to the probability that C_i is followed by C_j during that session. For example, a probability matrix for dyads based on conversation codes is shown in Table 20.2.

Table 20.2 Conversation dyads

Powwow_2a conversation dyads percentage matrix	State	Offer	Reqest	Regulation	Repair typing	Response	Follow	Elaboration	Exension	Setup	Agree	Disagree	Critique	Explain	No code
State	0	0	0	0	0	6	0	0	4	1	0	0	0	0	0
Offer	0	0	0	0	0	0	2	1	3	1	1	0	0	0	0
Reqest	0	0	0	0	0	7	0	0	3	1	0	0	0	1	0
Regulation	0	0	0	0	0	4	0	0	1	0	0	0	0	0	0
Repair Typing	0	0	0	0	0	0	0	0	0	0	0	0	0	0	0
Response	0	0	0	0	0	5	0	0	1	1	0	0	0	0	0
Follow	0	0	0	0	0	0	0	0	0	0	0	0	0	0	0
Elaboration	0	0	0	0	0	0	0	0	0	0	0	0	0	0	0
Exension	0	0	0	0	0	0	0	0	0	0	0	0	0	0	0
Setup	1	3	2	2	0	7	1	1	3	0	1	0	0	0	0
Agree	0	0	0	0	0	0	0	0	0	0	0	0	0	0	0
Disagree	0	0	0	0	0	0	0	0	0	0	0	0	0	0	0
Critique	0	0	0	0	0	0	0	1	0	0	0	0	0	0	0
Explain	0	0	0	0	0	0	0	0	0	0	0	0	0	0	0
No code	0	0	0	0	0	0	0	0	0	0	0	0	0	0	0

The %s are computed over all pairs

In addition to this, a row-based probability matrix is computed to depict the local percentage of any dyad C_i–C_j among all dyads beginning with C_i. Table 20.3 shows a row-based percentage matrix for the conversation dyads. Similarly, the model also computes a list of triads and their frequencies for each session.

Table 20.3 Row based distribution of conversation dyads

Powwow_2a conversation dyads_ row percentage matrix	State	Offer	Reqest	Regulation	Repair typing	Response	Follow	Elaboration	Exension	Setup	Agree	Disagree	Critique	Explain	No code
State	0	0	0	1	1	45	0	0	35	9	3	0	1	0	0
Offer	0	0	0	0	4	2	23	15	26	8	10	4	4	0	0
Reqest	0	0	3	3	1	43	0	0	22	8	1	4	0	11	0
Regulation	0	4	8	4	4	60	0	0	16	4	0	0	0	0	0
Repair Typing	0	0	0	0	0	0	0	0	0	0	0	100	0	0	0
Response	0	0	5	0	2	55	0	0	14	17	0	0	2	0	0
Follow	0	0	0	0	0	33	0	0	50	0	0	0	16	0	0
Elaboration	0	12	0	0	25	0	0	12	12	0	25	0	12	0	0
Exension	0	50	0	0	0	0	0	0	0	0	0	50	0	0	0
Setup	4	11	9	7	0	27	6	6	11	2	3	2	2	0	0
Agree	0	0	0	0	20	40	0	0	20	20	0	0	0	0	0
Disagree	0	0	0	0	0	0	20	0	20	40	0	20	0	0	0
Critique	0	0	6	6	0	20	20	26	6	13	0	0	0	0	0
Explain	0	0	11	0	0	22	22	0	33	0	0	0	11	0	0
No code	0	0	0	0	0	0	0	0	0	0	0	0	0	0	0

The %s are computed separately for each row

Frequent Conversational Patterns

For the conversational dyads, we observed that there are a significant number of zero-valued entries on all six percentage matrices. This fact indicates that there are strong causal relationships between certain pairs of conversation codes. For instance, the event that an *Agree* statement is followed by an *Offer* statement is very unlikely due to the fact that the *Agree-Offer* pair has a zero value in all 6 matrices. By the same token, non-zero valued entries corresponding to a pair C_i–C_j suggests which C_i variables are likely to be followed by a reply of some sort. Moreover, C_j variables indicate the most likely replies that a conversational action C_i will get. This motivated us to call the most frequent C_i-C_j pairs *source-sink* pairs, where the source C_i most likely solicits the action C_j as the next immediate reply.

The most frequent conversational dyads in our sample turned out to be *Request-Response* (16%, 7%, 9%, 9%, 10%, 8% for the 6 PoW-wows respectively), *Response-Response* (12%, 5%, 2%, 4%, 10%, 11%) and *State-Response* (8%, 6%, 4%, 2%, 5%, 16%) pairs. In our coding scheme conversational codes *State, Respond, Request* are assigned to those statements that belong to a general discussion, while codes such as *Offer, Elaboration, Follow, Agree, Critique* and *Explain* are assigned to statements that are specifically related to the problem-solving task. Thus, the computations show that a significant portion of the conversation is devoted to topics that are not specifically about math problem solving.

In addition to this, dyads of type *Setup-X* (8%, 14%, 12%, 2%, 3%, 4%) and *X-Extension* (14%, 15%, 9%, 7%, 9%, 6%) are also among the most frequent conversational dyads. In compliance with their definitions, *Setup* and *Extension* codes are used for linking fragmented statements of a single author that span multiple chat lines. In these cases the fragmented parts make sense only if they are considered together as a single statement. Thus, only one of the fragments is assigned a code reflecting the conversational action of the whole statement, and the rest of the fragments are tied to that special fragment by using *Setup* and *Extension* codes. The frequent occurrence of *Setup-X* and *X-Extension* dyads shows that some participants prefer to interact by posting fragmented statements during chat. The high percentage of fragmented statements strongly affects the distribution of other types of dyadic patterns. Therefore, a "pruning" option is included in our model to combine these fragmented statements into a single node to reveal other source-sink relationships.

Handle Patterns

Frequent dyadic and triadic patterns based on author information can be informative for making assessments about each participant's level and type of participation. For instance, Table 20.4 contrasts the author-dyad percentages of two groups—Pow2a and Pow2b, hereafter, group A and B, respectively—that worked on the same math problem. In both matrices an entry *(i,j)* corresponds to the percentage of the event that the postings of participant *i* were conversationally related to the postings of participant *j* during the session. For the non-pruned matrices, entries on the diagonal show us the percentage that the same participant either extended or elaborated his/her own statement. For the pruned matrices the "noise" introduced by the fragmented statements is reduced by considering them together as a single unit. In the pruned case diagonal entries correspond to elaboration statements following a statement of the same participant.

The most striking difference between the two groups, after pruning, is the difference between the percentage values on the diagonal: 10% for group A and 30% for group B. The percentages of most frequent triad patterns show a similar behavior. The percentage of triads having the same author on all 3 nodes (e.g., AVR-AVR-AVR) is 15% for group A, and 42% for group B. The pattern we see in group B is called an elaboration, where a member takes an extended turn. The pattern in group A indicates group exploration, where the members collaborate to co-construct knowledge and where turns rarely extend over multiple pruned nodes.

Patterns that contain the same author name on all their nodes are important indicators of individual activity, which typically occurs when a group member sends repeated postings without referring to any other group member. We call this *elaboration*, where one member of the group explains his/her ideas. The high percentage of these patterns can be considered as a sign of separate threads in ongoing discussion, which is the case for group B. Moreover, there is anti-symmetry between MCP's responses to REA's comments (23%) versus REA's responses to MCP's comments (14%). This shows that REA attended less to MCP's comments than MCP to REA's messages. In contrast, we observe a more balanced behavior of group *exploration* in group A, especially between AVR-PIN (17%, 18%) and AVR-SUP (13%, 13%). Another interesting pattern for group A is that the balance with respect

Table 20.4 Handle dyads for Pow2a and Pow2b

Pow 2a %	SYS	PIN	OFF	SUP	AVR	GER
SYS	0	0	0	0	0	0
PIN	0	11	1	2	11	0
OFF	0	0	3	0	1	0
SUP	0	3	0	10	9	0
AVR	0	11	1	9	16	0
GER	0	0	1	0	1	0

(pruned) Pow 2a %	SYS	PIN	OFF	SUP	AVR	GER
SYS	0	0	0	0	0	0
PIN	0	4	1	3	18	0
OFF	0	0	0	0	2	0
SUP	0	6	1	0	13	0
AVR	0	17	1	13	6	1
GER	0	1	1	0	1	0

Pow 2b %	SYS	MCP	AH3	REA	MUR
SYS	0	0	0	0	0
MCP	0	17	0	10	8
AH3	0	1	6	2	0
REA	0	18	2	20	3
MUR	0	2	1	1	3

(pruned) Pow 2b %	SYS	MCP	AH3	REA	MUR
SYS	0	0	0	0	0
MCP	0	14	0	14	10
AH3	0	1	1	3	0
REA	0	23	3	15	4
MUR	0	3	1	1	1

SYS refers to system messages. GER and MUR are facilitators of the groups.

to AVR does not exist between the pair SUP-PIN. This suggests that AVR was the dominant figure in group A, who frequently attended to the other two members of the group. To sum up, this kind of analysis points out similar results concerning roles and prominent actors as addressed by other social-network-analysis techniques. (Chapter 23 discusses the distinction between elaboration and exploration patterns.)

Dyadic and triadic patterns can also be useful in determining which member was most influential in initiating discussion during the session. For a participant i, the sum of row percentages (i,j) where $i \neq j$ can be used as a metric to see who had more initiative as compared to other members. The metric can be improved further by considering the percent of triads initiated by user i. For instance, in group A the row percentages are 31%, 22%, 20% and 2% for AVR, PIN, SUP and OFF respectively and the percentage of triads initiated by each of them is 41%, 29%, 20% and 7%. These numbers show that AVR had a significant impact in initiating conversation.

In addition to this, a similar metric for the columns can be considered for measuring the level of attention a participant exhibited by posting follow-up messages to other group members.

Problem-Solving Patterns

A similar analysis of dyadic and triadic patterns can be used for making assessments about the local organization of a group's problem-solving actions. The problem-solving data produced by our model for groups A and B will be used to aid the following discussion in this section. Table 20.5 displays both groups' percentage matrices for problem-solving dyads.

Table 20.5 Problem-solving dyads for Pow2a and Pow2b

Pow2a Pbsol_dyads %_matrix	Orientation	Strategy	Tactic	Perform	Check	Restate	Summarize	Reflect	Result
Orientation	1	0	3	0	2	1	0	1	0
Strategy	0	1	0	1	0	0	0	2	0
Tactic	0	0	3	2	4	3	0	7	2
Perform	0	0	0	4	4	0	0	0	1
Check	0	0	0	0	6	0	0	0	0
Restate	0	0	0	0	2	0	0	2	0
Summarize	0	0	0	0	0	0	0	0	0
Reflect	1	0	3	0	7	3	0	9	1
Result	0	0	0	1	8	1	0	2	0

Pow2a Pbsol_dyads row_% matrix	Orientation	Strategy	Tactic	Perform	Check	Restate	Summarize	Reflect	Result
Orientation	12	0	37	0	25	12	0	12	0
Strategy	0	25	0	25	0	0	0	50	0
Tactic	0	0	15	10	20	15	0	30	10
Perform	0	0	0	44	44	0	0	0	11
Check	0	0	0	0	100	0	0	0	0
Restate	0	0	0	0	50	0	0	50	0
Summarize	0	0	0	0	0	0	0	0	0
Reflect	4	0	13	0	27	13	0	36	4
Result	0	0	0	9	63	9	0	18	0

Pow2b Pbsol_dyads %_matrix	Orientation	Strategy	Tactic	Perform	Check	Restate	Summarize	Reflect	Result
Orientation	2	0	1	5	0	0	0	0	1
Strategy	0	0	0	1	0	0	0	0	1
Tactic	0	0	0	6	0	0	0	2	1
Perform	0	0	0	12	10	3	0	3	8
Check	0	0	0	1	0	0	0	6	0
Restate	0	0	0	0	0	0	0	0	0
Summarize	0	0	0	0	0	0	0	0	0
Reflect	0	0	0	0	0	0	0	5	0
Result	1	1	2	10	3	1	0	0	3

Pow2b Pbsol dyads row_% matrix	Orientation	Strategy	Tactic	Perform	Check	Restate	Summarize	Reflect	Result
Orientation	25	0	12	50	0	0	0	0	12
Strategy	0	0	0	50	0	0	0	0	50
Tactic	0	0	0	62	0	0	0	25	12
Perform	0	0	0	32	25	9	0	9	22
Check	0	0	0	16	0	0	0	83	0
Restate	0	0	0	0	0	0	0	0	0
Summarize	0	0	0	0	0	0	0	0	0
Reflect	0	0	0	0	0	0	0	100	0
Result	5	5	10	42	15	5	0	0	15

Before making any comparisons between these groups, we briefly introduce how the coding categories are related to math problem-solving *activities*. In this context a problem-solving activity refers to a set of successive math problem-solving actions. In our coding scheme, *Orientation*, *Tactic* and *Strategy* codes refer to the elements of a certain kind of activity in which the group engages in understanding the problem statement and/or proposes strategies for approaching it. Next, a combination of *Perform* and *Result* codes signal actions that relate to an execution activity in which previously proposed ideas are applied to the problem. *Summary* and *Restate* codes arise when the group is in the process of helping a group member to catch up with the rest of the group and/or producing a reformulation of the problem at hand. Further, *Check* and *Reflect* codes capture moves where group members reflect on the validity of an overall strategy or on the correctness of a specific calculation; they do not form an activity by themselves, but are interposed among the activities described before.

Given this description, we use the percentage matrices (see Table 20.5) to identify what percent of the overall problem-solving effort is devoted to each activity. For instance, the sum of percentage values of the sub-matrix induced by the columns and rows of *Orientation, Tactic, Strategy, Check* and *Reflect* codes takes up 28% of the problem-solving actions performed by the group A, whereas this value is only 5% for group B. This indicates that group A put more effort in developing strategies for solving the problem. When we consider the sub-matrix induced by *Perform, Result, Check* and *Reflect*, the corresponding values are 21% for group A and 50% for group B. This signals that group B spent more time on executing problem-solving steps. Finally, the values of the corresponding sub-matrix induced by *Restate, Summarize, Check* and *Reflect* codes adds up to 7% for group A and 0% for B, which hints at a change in orientation of group A's problem-solving activity. The remaining percentage values excluded by the sub-matrices belong to transition actions in between different activities.

Maximal Patterns

The percentage values presented in the previous section indicate that groups A and B exhibited significantly different local organizations in terms of their problem-solving activities. In order to make stronger claims about the differences at a global level, one needs to consider the unfolding of these local events through the whole discussion. Thus, analyzing the sequential unfolding of local patterns is another interesting focus of investigation, which will ultimately yield a "global" picture of a group's collaborative problem-solving activity. For instance, given the operational descriptions of problem-solving activities above, we observed the following sequence of local patterns in group A. First, the group engaged in a problem-orientation activity in which they identified a relevant sub-problem to work on. Then, they performed an execution activity on the agreed strategy by making numerical calculations to solve their sub-problem. Following this discussion, they engaged in a reflective activity in which they tried to relate the solution of the sub-problem to the general problem. During their reflection they realized they made a mistake in a formula they used earlier. At that point the session ended, and the group failed to produce the correct answer to their problem. On the other hand, the members of group B individually solved the problem at the beginning of the session without specifying a group strategy. They spent most of the remaining discussion revealing their solution steps to each other.

In this work we have shown how thread information can be used to identify the most frequent patterns of interaction with respect to various different criteria. In particular, we have discussed how these patterns can be used for making assessments about the organization of interaction in terms of each participant's level of participation, the conversational structure of discussion, as well as the problem-solving activities performed by the group. Our computations are based on an automated program that accepts a coded chat transcript as input, and performs all necessary computations in an efficient way.

Chapter 21
Studying Response-Structure Confusion in VMT

Hugo Fuks and Mariano Pimentel

Abstract Online text chat has great potential for allowing small groups of people in school or at work to build knowledge and understanding together. However, chat participants often post in parallel, making it difficult to follow the conversational flow and to identify who is talking to whom about what. The loosely ordered succession of turns contributes to "response-structure confusion." Parallel posting results in overlap of different topics; as a wave of discussion swells, another washes over it, causing ambiguity of linguistic references. Some chat environments implement tools to reduce the confusion. This paper presents an investigation into the effect of a graphical referencing tool for combating response-structure confusion. The paper documents the problem in a classroom setting and demonstrates the tool's effectiveness in a research lab.

Keywords Chat response structure · chat analysis method · chat tools

Communication across networked computers allows people to work and learn together despite being geographically distributed. In particular, text chat supports small groups to communicate by typing short messages synchronously. This has the potential to pool the creativity and understanding of several individuals to build knowledge through group interaction. Unfortunately, posting texts in parallel tends to intersperse threads of discussion and cause confusion concerning the references among postings, which are essential for making sense.

If several people are posting in parallel and some are contributing to a wave of ideas on one topic while others are discussing other topics, the various waves will crash into each other, interfere and cause confusion. In face-to-face conversation, thanks to conversational conventions of turn taking, texts are connected sequentially and linearly by explicit and implicit references to each other. In text chat, these references may be inadequate and require special mechanisms or extensive repair interactions.

H. Fuks (✉)
Informatics, Pontifical Catholic University of Rio de Janeiro, Brazil
e-mail: hugo@inf.puc-rio.br

G. Stahl (ed.), *Studying Virtual Math Teams*, Computer-Supported Collaborative Learning Series 11, DOI 10.1007/978-1-4419-0228-3_21,
© Springer Science+Business Media, LLC 2009

One mechanism for avoiding chat confusion was pioneered in ConcertChat (Chapter 15) and explored in the VMT Project (Chapter 17). The mechanism allowed chat participants to connect their postings to previous chat postings or other items by means of an arrow representing an explicit reference. In order to assess the effectiveness of this mechanism in reducing text chat, this chapter reviews the use of the mechanism in a set of VMT chats. This set involved the VMT staff, researchers and colleagues in a series of weekly chats about their academic papers on the project. These chats involved the largest groups of users in the VMT data corpus, making them particularly interesting for observing chat confusion from interference of messages posted in parallel.

Chat Excitement and Confusion

Chat tools are increasingly being used in education, particularly as distance learning spreads (Fuks et al., 2006). Conversation mediated by the synchronous chat tool is typically informal, providing a space for emotions and decreasing the feeling of impersonality. The situation in which several people communicate at the same time makes it possible for a learner to better perceive herself as part of the group, minimizing the feeling of isolation that is notoriously identified as one of the main causes of disappointment in distance courses. The lively exchange of messages among participants and the de-emphasis of expositive content lead to the displacement of the teacher as a controlling authority, who directs all discourse and assesses all knowledge. This creates opportunities for new forms of teaching and learning that represent alternatives to traditional instructional classroom models. These characteristics make learners regard chat sessions as interesting activities in online courses (Pimentel, Fuks & Lucena, 2003).

Unfortunately, chat conversation also has some characteristics that make it difficult to follow. This well-known problem has been variously referred to in the literature as "chat confusion," "chaotic flow of conversation," "mutual interactional incoherence" or "lack of coherence and understanding" (Cornelius & Boos, 2003; Garcia & Jacobs, 1999; Herring, 1999; McGrath, 1990; O'Neill & Martin, 2003; Pimentel, Fuks & Lucena, 2005; Pimentel et al., 2003; Thirunarayanan, 2000).

Participants in educational chat sessions frequently mention chat confusion. Interviewees typically complain about: the large number of participants typing at the same time; message overload; and parallel conversations. The mixing of messages on different topics causes participants to experience co-text loss (Pimentel et al., 2003). Then confusion moves in; learners report that a high level of attention is required to follow the conversation and that they feel disorientated, anguished, anxious and tired.

Chat conversation is particularly difficult to follow for beginner chatters. Over time chatters develop strategies that enable them to follow the conversation, such as: focusing on the messages addressed to oneself, on those from people with whom the chatter prefers to talk, and on those from the moderator; trying to pay attention to one subject at a time; and trying not to repeat what others have already said. These strategies point to the fact that over time users acquire experience and learn how to better interact, rendering the confusion less disturbing. On the other hand, these participation strategies also make it evident that there is an added effort that could be avoided if the confusion did not occur in the first place. Ideally, chatters should feel excitement and interest without also feeling disorientation, anguish, anxiety and fatigue.

Response-Structure Confusion

This section discusses the phenomenon of response-structure confusion: its causes, its manifestation and mechanisms that could reduce it. We will consider in this section examples of chat sessions that originate from the 20 iteractions of an online course entitled Information Technology Applied to Education (ITAE) (Fuks, Gerosa & Lucena, 2002). Analyses of logs of the ITAE 2000.1 edition (1st semester of 2000), which used the typical chat tool of the AulaNet LMS (Fuks, 2000; Fuks & Assis, 2001; Lucena, Fuks, Raposo, Gerosa & Pimentel, 2007) are presented. In these chat sessions, hour-long educational debates were conducted with 9 participants, discussing the subjects studied during that week in the ITAE course (Gerosa, Fuks & Lucena, 2003).

Causes

From text that is "linear" and "well organized," as generally is the case in books, articles and magazine texts, one expects threading, concatenation, sequencing of information and cohesion (Halliday & Hasan, 1976; Herring, 1999; Sacks et al., 1974). Although a given text may be more than a mere chain of enunciations, it is this chaining that provides for a more legible text. Unlike linear and well-organized text, text from a chat session is non-linear. The majority of the messages are not related to the immediately preceding message. The high degree of non-linearity in a chat conversation is considered the main cause of response-structure confusion.

In order to characterize the non-linearity of a chat session it is necessary to identify the conversational sequences, as exemplified in Log 21-1. There is linearity when a message is related to the previous message. Log 21-1 is non-linear because message 4 is related to a message located three rows prior to it.

Log 21-1.

Line	Nick	Message
1	Pablo	I want to begin by asking you to comment about the observation I made about the Aulanet being or not being groupware.
2	Marcelo	Pablo, is there any doubt?
3	Pablo	If there are no doubts, let's go on to another point.
4	Geraldo	In my opinion, the aulaNET is groupware given that its objectiveis to facilitate communication, cooperation and coordination among people.

The degree of linearity of a chat text is defined here as the percentage of messages related to the previous message. The degree of non-linearity of a chat session is its complement. As exemplified in Fig. 21.1, a chat session has a high degree of non-linearity. This graph shows the distribution of relation distances in a chat debate (ITAE 2000.1, debate #1, 9 participants, 256 messages). Relation distance is the difference in position between related messages. Linearity takes place when the relation distance is equal to 1, as illustrated by the chaining between messages 2 to 1 and 3 to 2 of Log 21-1. Non-linearity takes place when the relation distance is higher than 1, as illustrated by the chaining of message 4 to message 1, presenting a distance equal to 3.

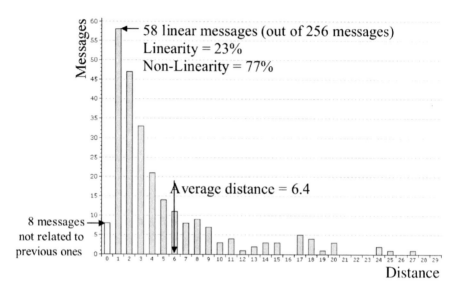

Fig. 21.1 Relation-distance distribution

Moreover, in a chat conversation, even the discussion of subjects is non-linear. According to the diagram presented in Fig. 21.2, based on the subject analysis of the same chat session, it can be seen that different subjects are discussed in parallel.

If each subject started after the end of the previous one, there would be subject linearity. However, what generally occurs is that different subjects are discussed at the same time, in parallel and alternately, as illustrated by the data presented in Fig. 21.3 and Fig. 21.4. In Fig. 21.3, on average 2 subjects are being discussed in parallel. In Fig. 21.4, subject alternation takes place every 2.8 messages on average (91 changes in 256 messages).

Unlike what occurs in a linear text, subjects in a chat conversation behave like waves. Participants start to discuss a subject—represented as a wave—which gains momentum until it reaches a peak, and then it tapers down until a new subject wave predominates, displacing the previous one. These waves are illustrated by the

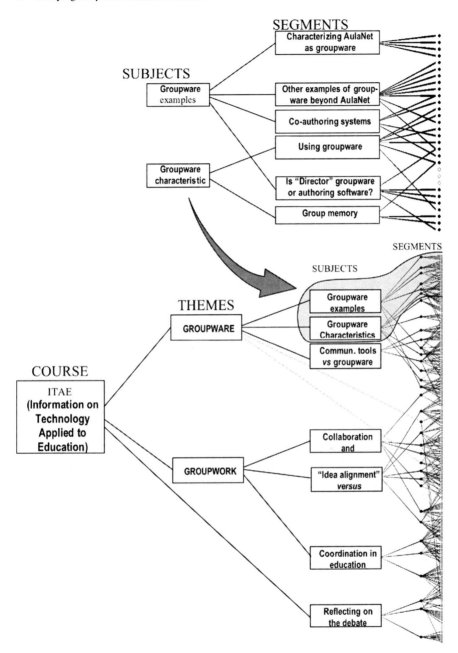

Fig. 21.2   Subject distribution (first 30 messages in detail above)

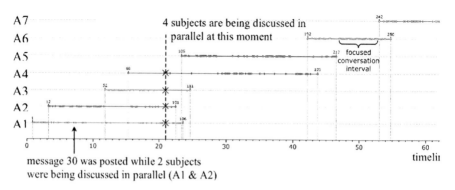

Fig. 21.3 Subjects in parallel

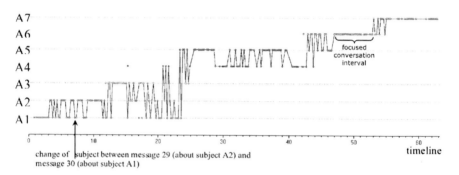

Fig. 21.4 Subject alternation

diagram presented in Fig. 21.5. As the subjects are discussed in parallel and alternately, there is a confluence of waves.

The representation of subjects as waves helps to visualize the parallelism of a chat conversation. Although on one hand subjects are being discussed in parallel, on the other hand it can be observed that a subject prevails for a while, as illustrated in Fig. 21.6.

Despite our focus here, we do not claim that non-linearity is the only cause of confusion in chat conversation. There are other known problems: lack of links among people and what they say; lack of visibility of turns-in-progress; flooding, overloading and gusting (sudden pouring) of messages; lack of useful recordings and social context; anonymity and flaming; and various other problems (Fuks et al., 2006; Oikarinen & Reed, 1993; Smith et al., 2000; Viegas & Donath, 1999).

Manifestation

Response-structure confusion is the difficulty in identifying to which previous message each chat message is responding. Eventually, a participant may manifest her

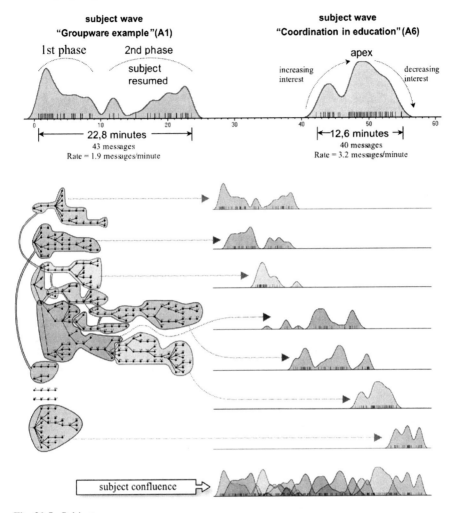

Fig. 21.5   Subject waves

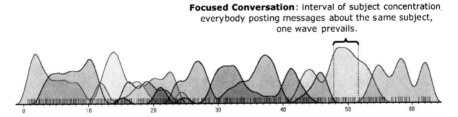

Fig. 21.6   Concentration and confluence

confusion in the conversation by posting a message where she states her discomfort in following the conversation, or asks for the sender to confirm or disambiguate her inference. Another way to identify the manifestation of confusion is when the chatter wrongly infers a chaining and another chatter clarifies the misunderstanding. Messages 31 and 167 from Log 21-2 are manifestations of confusion.

Log 21-2.

Line	Nick	Message
→ 30	Liane	I believe that it is just the contrary,that group ware can help in the authoring process since it can facilitate the communication process among members of a team
31	Homero	Contrary to what, Liane, I'm lost
...		...
→166	Liane	I agree...
167	Marcelo	with what, Liane?

Counting the incidents that could be identified as manifestations of response-structure confusion is a very rough way of measuring the problem. The manifestations seem to indicate only the tip of the iceberg—not every doubt or confusion is textually acknowledged by the participants.

Chat Tool Mechanisms

Chat threading mechanisms have the potential for reducing confusion. Most chat tools do not have a mechanism for establishing references among messages. A few tools such as ThreadedChat (Smith et al., 2000), HiperDialog (Pimentel, 2002) and MuViChat (Holmer, Lukosch & Kunz, 2008) structure the discourse in a tree, forcing chatters to indicate always to which previous messages their current message is an answer as in forums (Gerosa et al., 2003).

ConcertChat (see Chapter 15)—which was adopted and adapted in VMT—offers a mechanism for referencing messages that is optional. It is a hybrid solution between the chat systems without referencing and the chat systems where all messages are chained. The aim of this chapter is to investigate confusion given the VMT environment's graphical referencing mechanism.

Response-Structure Analysis Method

In this section, the strategies developed to analyze chat sessions are introduced. In order to exemplify the response-structure analysis method, first the corpus of analysis of this work is presented.

Corpus of Analysis

The chat sessions analyzed in this section took place through the VMT chat environment. The purpose of the sessions was to discuss papers prepared for the Chat Analysis Workshop at CSCL 2007. These papers comprise early drafts for this volume. Table 21.1 presents a synthesis of the sessions' data.

Table 21.1   Data from the VMT chat-analysis workshop

Session	Day/ Month	Number of messages in the log	Number of discussion messages	Number of participants	Chapter in book	Elapsed time of discussion
Nan Paper	21/05	510	199	11	8	1 h 14 min
Ramon Paper	23/05	388	261	11	9	1 h 11 min
Murat Paper	25/05	311	111	7	7	0 h 42 min
Johann Paper	29/05	478	249	9	6	1 h 24 min
Stefan Paper	30/05	424	311	11	24	1 h 19 min
Chee-Kit Paper	01/06	349	203	10	25	1 h 36 min
Liz Paper	04/06	341	265	8	11	1 h 17 min
Carolyn Paper	06/06	435	284	11	19	1 h 09 min
Alan Paper	08/06	416	314	10	14	1 h 19 min
Terry Paper	11/06	304	180	7	27	1 h 19 min
Dan Paper	18/06	287	208	6	10	1 h 22 min
Arthur Paper	20/06	141	69	4	13	0 h 27 min
Average	-	365	221	8.8		1 h 11 min

These chat sessions took place in the two months preceding the CSCL 2007 workshop. They comprised a total of 12 sessions. On average, in each session 365 messages were exchanged, 221 of them being identified as discussion messages. The discussion part of the chat sessions took an average of 1 hour and 11 minutes. Including the papers' authors and co-authors, an average of 9 people associated with the VMT Project joined in the discussion session. Their objective was to discuss ways to enhance their papers.

Discussion Messages

The first step of the response-structure analysis method is to isolate the messages that are relevant for the analysis, classifying log messages in types, namely: system messages, pre-discussion messages, discussion messages and post-discussion messages. This typology is shown in Log 21-3, using the data from the session on Nan's paper. System messages announce the participants who are joining or leaving the chat session. Pre-discussion messages are exchanged before the "real thing" starts and include all sorts of greetings; the same is true for post-discussion messages at the end of the session, where participants say good-bye. Discussion messages deal with the subject being discussed, including coordination messages and jokes. The data analyzed in the next sections only considers the discussion messages.

As exemplified by Log 21-3, even after trying to start the discussion by posting messages 80 and 81, participants might continue sending pre-discussion posts

Log 21-3.

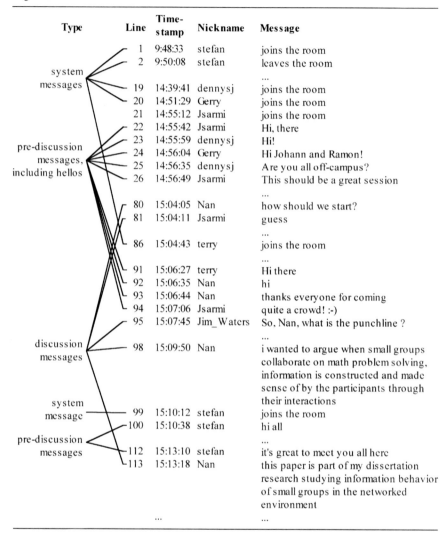

Type	Line	Time-stamp	Nickname	Message
system messages	1	9:48:33	stefan	joins the room
	2	9:50:08	stefan	leaves the room
				...
	19	14:39:41	dennysj	joins the room
	20	14:51:29	Gerry	joins the room
	21	14:55:12	Jsarmi	joins the room
pre-discussion messages, including hellos	22	14:55:42	Jsarmi	Hi, there
	23	14:55:59	dennysj	Hi!
	24	14:56:04	Gerry	Hi Johann and Ramon!
	25	14:56:35	dennysj	Are you all off-campus?
	26	14:56:49	Jsarmi	This should be a great session
				...
	80	15:04:05	Nan	how should we start?
	81	15:04:11	Jsarmi	guess
				...
	86	15:04:43	terry	joins the room
				...
	91	15:06:27	terry	Hi there
	92	15:06:35	Nan	hi
	93	15:06:44	Nan	thanks everyone for coming
	94	15:07:06	Jsarmi	quite a crowd! :-)
	95	15:07:45	Jim_Waters	So, Nan, what is the punchline ?
				...
discussion messages	98	15:09:50	Nan	i wanted to argue when small groups collaborate on math problem solving, information is constructed and made sense of by the participants through their interactions
system message	99	15:10:12	stefan	joins the room
	100	15:10:38	stefan	hi all
pre-discussion messages				...
	112	15:13:10	stefan	it's great to meet you all here
	113	15:13:18	Nan	this paper is part of my dissertation research studying information behavior of small groups in the networked environment
		...		...

like messages 91–94. There is also a late chatter who automatically generates a system message (99) and then greets the group (100). In Nan's session, the discussion started on message 80, falling back to a pre-discussion phase that lasted until message 113. From then on all participants engaged in the discussion.

Referencing Messages: Explicit and Inferred

After isolating the discussion messages, the next step is to get the response structure. For each message, we identified which previous message it takes up. This establishes a chain (not necessarily sequential) of messages. VMT chat offers a referencing mechanism that allows chatters to explicitly reference a previous message. However, given that the use of this mechanism is optional, there are non-referenced messages in the log, leaving the job of inferring references to the reader or analyst. The strategies described below help the reader to infer these references. The mapping of all the response structure of a chat session is necessary in order to carry on with the confusion investigation.

In Log 21-4 from the chat on Stefan's paper, solid arrows represent the explicit references established by the chatters, while the dotted arrows represent the references inferred by the reader. For example, in message 65 Stefan uses the referencing mechanism to link his message to message 58 in response to Nan's questioning. On the other hand, message 59 posted by Wes also refers to Nan's message 58, but given that Wes made no use of the referencing mechanism, the relation had to be inferred by the reader from the content of Wes' message, which began by explicitly addressing Nan.

The reader should consider the following strategies in order to infer references among messages: recency analysis, cohesion analysis, turns and conversational sequences analysis, subject analysis, context analysis and coherence analysis (Pimentel & Sampaio, 2001).

Recency Analysis

Usually chatters tend to answer more recent messages. Normally, most messages are related to messages posted not longer than 2 minutes earlier; they rarely answer messages 5 minutes old (Pimentel, 2002). On the other hand, a regular chatter needs some time to read a message and type a response: it might take 30 seconds to enter a turn (Vronay et al., 1999). Therefore, it is quite improbable that a paragraph-long message is related to a previous message that is just 10 seconds old. These recency patterns guide the reader in trying to infer the referencing of a message to messages posted in the previous time interval ranging from 10 seconds to 5 minutes. For example, the reader should not consider message 59 when trying to infer message 60's referencing, for it was posted only 1 second before. He should also refrain from considering messages before message 33, itself older than 5 minutes. It is probably the case that message 60 is related to messages within the 54–58 scope given their recency.

Cohesion Analysis

Looking for grammatical and lexical links between messages is another strategy that should be pursued by the reader. Cohesive devices are employed by chatters when preparing messages. In Log 21-5, the expression **"the idea of voices"** that appears in message 58 is repeated in message 65, constituting a lexical cohesion (Halliday & Hasan, 1976) that helps the reader to infer a referencing between them.

Log 21-4.

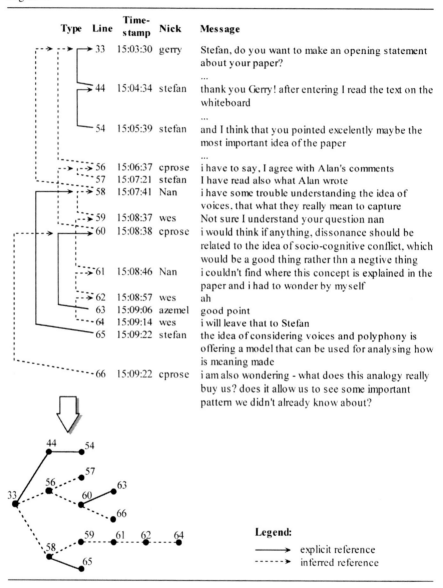

Type	Line	Time-stamp	Nick	Message
	33	15:03:30	gerry	Stefan, do you want to make an opening statement about your paper? ...
	44	15:04:34	stefan	thank you Gerry! after entering I read the text on the whiteboard ...
	54	15:05:39	stefan	and I think that you pointed excelently maybe the most important idea of the paper ...
	56	15:06:37	cprose	i have to say, I agree with Alan's comments
	57	15:07:21	stefan	I have read also what Alan wrote
	58	15:07:41	Nan	i have some trouble understanding the idea of voices, that what they really mean to capture
	59	15:08:37	wes	Not sure I understand your question nan
	60	15:08:38	cprose	i would think if anything, dissonance should be related to the idea of socio-cognitive conflict, which would be a good thing rather thn a negtive thing
	61	15:08:46	Nan	i couldn't find where this concept is explained in the paper and i had to wonder by myself
	62	15:08:57	wes	ah
	63	15:09:06	azemel	good point
	64	15:09:14	wes	i will leave that to Stefan
	65	15:09:22	stefan	the idea of considering voices and polyphony is offering a model that can be used for analysing how is meaning made
	66	15:09:22	cprose	i am also wondering - what does this analogy really buy us? does it allow us to see some important pattern we didn't already know about?

Legend:

⟶ explicit reference

------➤ inferred reference

Log 21-5.

58	15:07:41	Nan	i have some trouble understanding the idea of voices, that what they really mean to capture
65	15:09:22	stefan	the idea of considering voices and polyphony is offering a model that can be used for analysing how is meaning made

Turns and Conversational Sequences Analysis

In the basic dialog model, interlocutors wait for their turn to speak (Sacks et al., 1974). In a face-to-face conversation going on between more than two persons, a common conversation coordination mechanism is to look to the person to whom the answer is addressed. When many persons are chatting, it is common to write in the responding message the addressee's name (handle or nickname), as exemplified in Log 21-6.

Log 21-6.

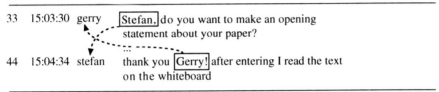

33	15:03:30	gerry	Stefan, do you want to make an opening statement about your paper?
44	15:04:34	stefan	thank you Gerry! after entering I read the text on the whiteboard

Another way to infer the reference between messages is to identify conversational sequences (adjacency pairs) where one turn or message leads to another, like: question → answer; invitation → acceptance or refusal; greeting → greeting; challenge → justification etc. In the example presented in Log 21-6, it is expected that after Gerry offers the floor to Stefan to open the discussion, Stefan will react to it by posting a message.

It is likely in a chat conversation that the sequence of messages exchanged between two chatters will be separated by unrelated messages. The more active participants there are the more likely this is to occur. The reader should look for a previous sequence of messages from the same pair of chatters, as exemplified in Log 21-7, which shows an example of a two-person dialog embedded within a many-persons chat.

Log 21-7.

58	15:07:41	Nan	i have some trouble understanding the idea of voices, that what they really mean to capture
59	15:08:37	wes	Not sure I understand your question nan
			...
61	15:08:46	Nan	i couldn't find where this concept is explained in the paper and i had to wonder by my self
62	15:08:57	wes	ah

Monologs are also quite common in chats: the same chatter sends message after message fostering a "long turn" like the one in Log 21-8. This is a consequence of message recency, for it might be better to post 2 or 3 short messages than take the time to write a long elaborate message and risk that the chat context will change substantially in the meantime. Therefore, the reader should also look to the same chatter's previous messages in order to infer references.

Log 21-8.

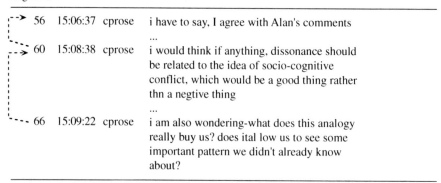

	56	15:06:37	cprose	i have to say, I agree with Alan's comments
				...
	60	15:08:38	cprose	i would think if anything, dissonance should be related to the idea of socio-cognitive conflict, which would be a good thing rather thn a negtive thing
				...
	66	15:09:22	cprose	i am also wondering-what does this analogy really buy us? does ital low us to see some important pattern we didn't already know about?

Log 21-9.

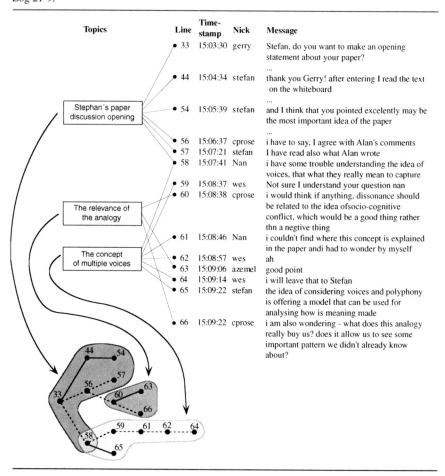

Topics	Line	Time-stamp	Nick	Message
	33	15:03:30	gerry	Stefan, do you want to make an opening statement about your paper?
				...
	44	15:04:34	stefan	thank you Gerry! after entering I read the text on the whiteboard
Stephan's paper discussion opening				...
	54	15:05:39	stefan	and I think that you pointed excelently may be the most important idea of the paper
				...
	56	15:06:37	cprose	i have to say, I agree with Alan's comments
	57	15:07:21	stefan	I have read also what Alan wrote
	58	15:07:41	Nan	i have some trouble understanding the idea of voices, that what they really mean to capture
	59	15:08:37	wes	Not sure I understand your question nan
The relevance of the analogy	60	15:08:38	cprose	i would think if anything, dissonance should be related to the idea ofsocio-cognitive conflict, which would be a good thing rather thn a negtive thing
	61	15:08:46	Nan	i couldn't find where this concept is explained in the paper andi had to wonder by myself
The concept of multiple voices	62	15:08:57	wes	ah
	63	15:09:06	azemel	good point
	64	15:09:14	wes	i will leave that to Stefan
	65	15:09:22	stefan	the idea of considering voices and polyphony is offering a model that can be used for analysing how is meaning made
	66	15:09:22	cprose	i am also wondering - what does this analogy really buy us? does it allow us to see some important pattern we didn't already know about?

Subject Analysis

Normally, when answering a message, chatters stick to the same subject or write something related to it. During a conversation, a subject unfolds until it is finished, abandoned or drifts off into a different subject. In Log 21-9 it is possible to identify groups of messages related to the same subject. The reader should consider messages dealing with the same subject when looking for references.

Context Analysis

In order to infer references, sometimes the reader has to make use of information that is not within the log. VMT offers a whiteboard where chatters can pose and share information related to the session, but which does not appear typed in the chat. Eventually, this information makes its way into the chat conversation—as is the case of messages 44, 54, 56 and 57 in Log 21-9, where chatters discuss Gerry's and Alan's whiteboard comments. This contextual information helps the reader in inferring references.

Coherence Analysis

In order to infer references among messages, coherence has to be investigated: the reader should question whether a message makes sense as being a response to another one. The conversation is expected to make sense, unfolding in a sound way. Consistency, relevance, linguistic elements, etc., should be considered when looking for coherence.

All these strategies help the reader to infer references among messages. Nevertheless, sometimes this inference is blurred by ambiguity causing the occurrence of response-structure confusion.

Data Analysis

In this section, the data are analyzed in order to investigate response-structure confusion, and particularly to check whether the use of the referencing mechanism implemented in VMT reduces confusion. The first step is to characterize how the mechanism was used based on its frequency of use. Next, a study of the profiles of different users regarding their use of the referencing mechanism is presented: some chatters establish references systematically in all the messages they write, while others almost never make use of the mechanism. Finally, a study of the occurrence of response-structure confusion is presented, indicating that there was confusion even with the use of the referencing mechanism in the VMT environment.

The Frequency of Use of the Referencing Mechanism

Table 21.2 synthesizes the data obtained from the chat sessions of the corpus under investigation regarding the use of the graphical referencing mechanism implemented in VMT.

Table 21.2 Referencing data

Discussion session	Number of discussion messages	Number of messages with explicit reference	Number of explicit references to text fragment	Number of messages with explicit reference to workspace	Number of messages with several explicit references
Nan Paper	199	115 (58%)	3	2	4
Ramon Paper	261	128 (49%)	6	1	2
Murat Paper	111	41 (37%)	2	2	3
Johann Paper	249	131 (53%)	19	1	2
Stefan Paper	311	166 (53%)	10	0	1
CheeKit Paper	203	136 (67%)	11	0	2
Liz Paper	265	136 (51%)	5	0	0
Carolyn Paper	284	56 (41%)	0	1	3
Alan Paper	314	151 (48%)	13	1	2
Terry Paper	180	104 (58%)	4	1	1
Dan Paper	208	111 (53%)	9	0	0
Arthur Paper	69	42 (61%)	4	0	1
Average	221	110 (50%)	7.2	0.75	1.75

The *referencing mechanism was used in half of the messages* (see column "Number of messages with explicit reference" of Table 21.2—this is the type of reference represented graphically by solid lines in Log 21-4). This 50% average indicates that the referencing mechanism was widely used. From the logs' analysis, it can be verified that the references between messages were established almost error-free, as in Logs 21-1–21-9 presented thus far. Log 21-10 from Nan's paper's session shows a counter-example: in message 340 the chatter established the reference erroneously and alerted peers about that error in the subsequent message.

Log 21-10.

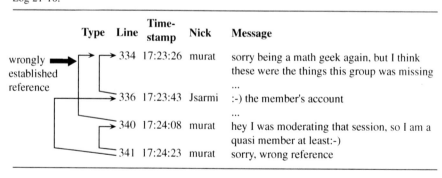

	Type	Line	Time-stamp	Nick	Message
wrongly established reference		334	17:23:26	murat	sorry being a math geek again, but I think these were the things this group was missing
					...
		336	17:23:43	Jsarmi	:-) the member's account
					...
		340	17:24:08	murat	hey I was moderating that session, so I am a quasi member at least:-)
		341	17:24:23	murat	sorry, wrong reference

The referencing mechanism is so useful for chatters that in many cases the reference established among the messages becomes an inalienable part of the discourse, i.e., the reference is used as a means of expression. For example, message 63 of Log 21-11 is better understood taking into consideration the reference established by Azemel to message 60. Had the reference not been established the message would

have to be elaborated in a different way, something like: **"cprose: good point"** citing the name of the sender of the message being replied to; or **"good point about
dissonance"** introducing cohesion devices.

Log 21-11.

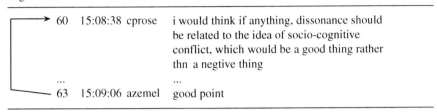

From these data, one concludes that the referencing mechanism is implemented
in such a way that it leads to correct usage, and that it is a desirable one because it
was incorporated as a means of expression. The non-establishment of references in
the other half of the messages seems to be a consequence of the chatters' expression
styles rather than of some problem with using the mechanism (see next section on
chatter profiles).

In the VMT system, it is possible to *reference a specific selection of text* within
a previous posting by highlighting that section when pointing to it. Regarding the
use of the referencing mechanism for citing a text fragment in the body of another
message, it was used on average in 7% of the established references—see column
"Number of explicit references to text fragment" of Table 21.2. Logs 21-12 and
21-13 illustrate this way of referencing. In Log 21-12 from the session on Johann's
paper, the following posting fragment is highlighted: **"making time reference is
not particularly interesting."** In Log 21-13 from Ramon's paper, the single words
"requires" and **"Negotiation"** are referenced.

Log 21-12.

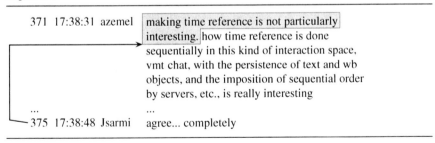

An average of 7% is considerable: it characterizes neither intensive nor low use.
However, when analyzing the citation-references, one can conclude that some were
established as a result of errors in using the referencing mechanism: the objective
was to establish the reference for the whole message, but in the referencing mechanics by mistake some random part of the message was selected. These malformed
citations are exemplified in Log 21-14 (Johann's paper) and Log 21-15 (Nan's
paper).

Log 21-13.

---

189 15:41:23 dennysj Argumentation, I think, requires opposing

viewpoints. Negotiation may result in merging

or even grafting together non-opposing but

different positions.

...   ...

193 16:41:57 Jsarmi but this two things are different

Log 21-14.

---

150 16:33:50 murat   I know how hard it is to incorporate graphical

stuff to analysis, but it is really a vital resource

151 15:34:02 azemel indeed

Log 21-15.

---

248 15:57:39 dennysj You want to make the case that this is GROUP

information behavior in contrast to

INDIVIDUAL infomration behavior?

...   ...

252 15:58:43 Jsarmi   right, so one thing that I think that will take

your paper further (besides the ideas about

theory already presented) is to actually name

some methods, show more instances and then

see if you can ask more questions about them

From these data and its analyses, one concludes that the citation referencing is desirable and useful for chatters, as it was used properly and frequently. However, the mechanics of citation referencing occasionally leads chatters to committing mistakes.

Regarding *referencing to the workspace*—see column "Number of messages with explicit reference to the workspace" of Table 21.2—this mechanism was used no more than twice per session. This apparent low use of the mechanism is not an indication of its uselessness. It was observed that the mechanism was correctly and continuously used throughout the sessions—it enables the integration between the chat conversation and the workspace objects. The sessions analyzed here were not math problem-solving sessions, as is typically the case for which the VMT system with whiteboard was designed. These were discussions of papers that were not displayed in the system, and the whiteboard was only minimally used.

The possibility of establishing *multiple references originating from a single message*, such as in message 341 of Log 21-10 and as in message 193 of Log 21-13, was used in less than 1% of the messages—see column "Number of messages with several explicit references" of Table 21.2. The very low use of this mechanism and the decrease in its application throughout the chat sessions indicate that referencing multiple messages is not normally useful (or well understood, or easy to accomplish). Establishing a single reference per message seems to be enough in a chat conversation. It is not clear whether the very low use justifies the increase in the complexity of the user interface and of the conversation structure.

Chatters' Profiles Regarding Referencing

Given that the use of VMT's referencing mechanism is optional, it is possible to identify different profiles regarding referencing. It is striking that some participants use it with full intensity while others practically do not use it at all.

In Table 21.3, the percentage of messages with explicit references is presented. Three types of chatters were identified:

- *Intensive*: establish references in most of their messages;
- *Occasional*: establish references in some of their messages;
- *Low*: rarely establish references in their messages.

It is not a matter of learning how to use the mechanism—if that were the case, then the infrequent initial use of the mechanism by a few chatters would be understood as a consequence of their lack of experience with the tool and would be expected to increase over time. However, chatters tend to keep the same pattern of referencing usage throughout several chat sessions, indicating that this is an individual expression style.

Establishing references is a question of profile. Occasional and low users choose to reference in specific situations, like when they anticipate ambiguity, want to discuss an old message or need to be explicit about some previous message. In Log 21-16 (from Stephan's paper session) there is a fragment where chatters were discussing these referencing situations.

A distinguished feature of VMT's referencing mechanism is that it suits different types of chatters. Some prefer not to use it at all and are probably happy enough to have messages showing just in chronological order with no other apparent structure. Others rather need to establish references in order to clearly express themselves and find comfort in tree-like structures forced by threading tools. VMT's referencing mechanism does not force any single expression style, suiting everybody.

The Manifestation of Response-Structure Confusion

Unlike previous research (Pimentel et al., 2003; Smith et al., 2000), in this chapter there is no comparison of conditions with and without a referencing mechanism. Here, the aim is not to prove that such a mechanism reduces confusion, but to check whether confusion takes place even when VMT's referencing mechanism is being used.

It is reasonable to believe that there is less chance of having confusion when using VMT's referencing mechanism compared to when using other chat tools that

Table 21.3 Chatter profiles

| Discussion session | Chatter profile on referencing mechanism (explicit references/total postings) | | | | | | | | | | | | Non-counted participants: those who only participated in 1 or 2 sessions |
| | intensive user | | | | | occasional user | | | | low user | | | |
	Dennysj	Stefan	Jim	Jsarmi	Murat	Nan	Gerry	Weiqin	Wes	Azemel	Terry	Cprose	
Nan / Paper	94% (17/18)	78% (7/9)	35% (6/17)	86% (18/21)	93% (13/14)	52% (43/82)	50% (10/20)	–	–	–	0% (0/7)	–	Frank: 9% (0/5) Liz: 33% (1/3) Powel: 0% (0/3)
Ramon / Paper	91% (40/44)	86% (12/14)	79% (15/19)	77% (20/26)	70% (7/10)	57% (13/23)	32% (7/22)	–	38% (3/8)	19% (10/54)	6% (1/16)	0% (0/25)	–
Murat / Paper	50% (3/6)	–	63% (5/8)	–	57% (13/23)	29% (6/21)	25% (5/20)	–	–	26% (6/23)	30% (3/10)	–	–
Johann / Paper	100% (11/11)	100% (1/1)	64% (9/14)	73% (62/85)	78% (14/18)	31% (4/13)	47% (7/15)	–	–	26% (22/85)	14% (1/7)	–	–
Stefan / Paper	100% (15/15)	81% (42/52)	93% (14/15)	80% (12/15)	64% (9/14)	50% (5/10)	61% (22/36)	–	41% (13/32)	43% (26/61)	33% (4/12)	8% (4/49)	–
CheeKit / Paper	89% (8/9)	100% (4/4)	79% (23/29)	87% (20/23)	82% (9/11)	–	54% (14/26)	–	90% (9/10)	–	14% (1/7)	–	Chee: 43%(10/23) Wee: 62%(38/61)
Liz / Paper	60% (3/5)	–	100% (9/9)	73% (27/37)	78% (18/23)	46% (6/13)	45% (25/56)	–	38% (37/97)	–	–	–	Liz: 44% (11/25)

Table 21.3 (continued)

| Discussion session | Chatter profile on referencing mechanism (explicit references/total postings) | | | | | | | | | | | | Non-counted participants: those who only participated in 1 or 2 sessions |
| | intensive user | | | | | occasional user | | | | low user | | | |
	Dennysj	Stefan	Jim	Jsarmi	Murat	Nan	Gerry	Weiqin	Wes	Azemel	Terry	Cprose	
Carolyn Paper	83% (10/12)	100% (1/1)	100% (13/13)	–	77% (10/13)	41% (7/17)	17% (2/12)	45% (9/20)	17% (1/6)	0% (0/9)	–	1% (2/180)	Mjkhoo: 100% (1/1)
Alan Paper	86% (6/7)	40% (2/5)	85% (17/20)	68% (26/38)	63% (17/27)	44% (15/34)	83% (5/6)	35% (4/11)	35% (8/23)	36% (51/143)	–	–	–
Terry Paper	83% (5/6)	80% (4/5)	95% (20/21)	–	85% (29/34)	43% (3/7)	40% (18/45)	–	–	–	40% (25/62)	–	–
Dan Paper	–	89% (17/19)	–	–	–	–	48% (22/46)	33% (2/6)	–	46% (23/50)	57% (4/7)	–	Suthers: 54% (43/80)
Arthur Paper	58% (7/12)	64% (9/14)	–	–	84% (16/19)	–	42% (10/24)	–	–	–	–	–	–
Average	86% (11/13)	80% (10/12)	79% (13/17)	76% (26/35)	75% (14/19)	46% (11/24)	45% (12/27)	41% (5/12)	40% (12/29)	32% (20/61)	30% (5/16)	2% (0/85)	–

Log 21-16.

Line	Time-stamp	Nick	Message
219	16:42:24	stefan	what I observed was that the explicit links (the ConcertChat refences) are different from the implicit ones
221	16:42:59	stefan	that means mayve that the participants felt to make explicit something that was not obviously related
223	16:43:10	Jsarmi	and they serve many purposes as we discovered, not just say: . posting X is about posting Y
225	16:44:31	Jim_Waters	Having read a loy of threaded discussions I would be cautious about such a conclusion
229	16:45:11	Nan	i thought participants usually thought of the need before they actually made the reference
231	16:45:38	Jim_Waters	i.e this is sometimes just a matter of personal style, some prefer to make their responses more concrete and others assume that peers will know what they are referring to
236	16:47:16	Jim_Waters	Yes, but how they choose to express is a matter of style
238	16:47:29	dennysj	If there is a sign of misunderstanding later, then it wil be clear that the assumption had not been correct.
239	16:47:47	Nan	it may be
240	16:48:11	Jim_Waters	yes but by then its too late :-)
243	16:48:39	dennysj	But not too late to be clarified or repaired in a subsequent posting.
244	16:48:42	cprose	i agree about the style comment

do not let chatters establish references between messages because a reader does not have to infer the main reference of messages whose authors establish the link.

However, it is unreasonable to believe that just by using the VMT tool no confusion will take place—particularly given that the use of the referencing mechanism is optional. When the reference is not established by the author, the reader has to infer what previous message is being answered. Moreover, when the reader does not pay attention to the established reference or when it is wrongly established, it may give way to confusion.

As a matter of fact, some evidences of confusion were found in the VMT corpus. For example, in Log 21-17 (on Stephan's paper), after CPRose declared in message 267 **"i don't understand denny's question above,"** Dennysj could not identify which of his messages above was being cited and manifested confusion in message 270: **"Which question?"** Faced with Dennysj's manifestation, CPRose used the referencing mechanism in messages 274 and 276 in order to point to Dennysj's cited message. Then, Dennysj's confusion is gone, and in message 283 he posts an explanation regarding the message that CPRose had not understood.

Had no confusion been manifested in Log 21-17, four messages—270, 274, 276 and 283—would not have been posted. These messages were needed to restore understanding in spite of disturbing the conversation flow and not developing the subject. This is probably what moved Gerry to post message 277: **"Let's get back to Stefan's paper."**

The confusion shown in Log 21-17 might have taken place because CPRose wrongly thought that Dennysj's message 260 was associated to one of her messages. However, Dennysj's message was referencing Terry's message 252, and in spite of it, CPRose answers Dennysj in message 262 as if he was talking to her. A few moments later the coin finally drops and in message 267 she says, **"then i don't understand denny's question above."**

The process of identifying an occurrence of confusion is not an exact one, and being subject to interpretation makes it difficult to state how many of them took

Log 21-17.

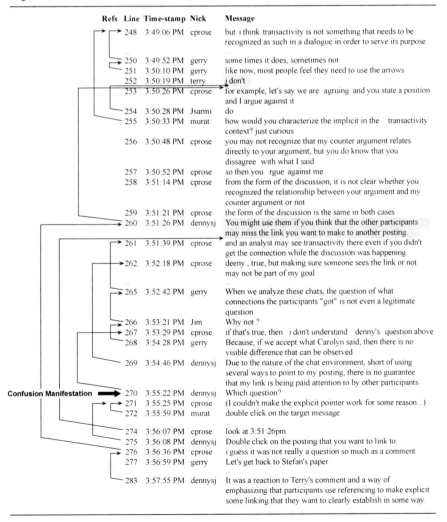

Refs	Line	Time-stamp	Nick	Message
	248	3:49:06 PM	cprose	but i think transactivity is not something that needs to be recognized as such in a dialogue in order to serve its purpose
	250	3:49:52 PM	gerry	some times it does, sometimes not
	251	3:50:10 PM	gerry	like now, most people feel they need to use the arrows
	252	3:50:19 PM	terry	i don't
	253	3:50:26 PM	cprose	for example, let's say we are agruing and you state a position and I argue against it
	254	3:50:28 PM	Jsarmi	do
	255	3:50:33 PM	murat	how would you characterize the implicit in the transactivity context? just curious
	256	3:50:48 PM	cprose	you may not recognize that my counter argument relates directly to your argument, but you do know that you dissagree with what I said
	257	3:50:52 PM	cprose	so then you rgue against me
	258	3:51:14 PM	cprose	from the form of the discussion, it is not clear whether you recognized the relationship between your argument and my counter argument or not
	259	3:51:21 PM	cprose	the form of the discussion is the same in both cases
	260	3:51:26 PM	dennysj	You might use them if you think that the other participants may miss the link you want to make to another posting
	261	3:51:39 PM	cprose	and an analyst may see transactivity there even if you didn't get the connection while the discussion was happening
	262	3:52:18 PM	cprose	deeny , true, but making sure someone sees the link or not may not be part of my goal
	265	3:52:42 PM	gerry	When we analyze these chats, the question of what connections the participants "got" is not even a legitimate question
	266	3:53:21 PM	Jim	Why not ?
	267	3:53:29 PM	cprose	if that's true, then i don't understand denny's question above
	268	3:54:28 PM	gerry	Because, if we accept what Carolyn said, then there is no visible difference that can be observed
	269	3:54:46 PM	dennysj	Due to the nature of the chat environment, short of using several ways to point to my posting, there is no guarantee that my link is being paid attention to by other participants.
Confusion Manifestation ➡	270	3:55:22 PM	dennysj	Which question?
	271	3:55:25 PM	cprose	(I couldn't make the explicit pointer work for some reason...)
	272	3:55:59 PM	murat	double click on the target message
	274	3:56:07 PM	cprose	look at 3:51:26pm
	275	3:56:08 PM	dennysj	Double click on the posting that you want to link to.
	276	3:56:36 PM	cprose	i guess it was not really a question so much as a comment
	277	3:56:59 PM	gerry	Let's get back to Stefan's paper
	283	3:57:55 PM	dennysj	It was a reaction to Terry's comment and a way of emphasizing that participants use referencing to make explicit some linking that they want to clearly establish in some way.

place. For example, as is illustrated in Log 21-18 (on Ramon's paper), message
240—**"which term? 'common ground'?"**—is not a confusion manifestation, but
really an expression of amazement caused by the **"dump the term"** proposal in
message 239. Although messages 240 in Log 21-18 and message 270 in Log 21-17
are similar, the latter is a manifestation of confusion while the former is not.

Log 21-18.

Line	Time-stamp	Nick	Message
237	16:52:02	dennysj	I referred to the term 'common ground' because it is used in the literature but I have not been able to see an actual specification of it.
...			
239	16:52:16	azemel	then dump the term
240	16:53:08	dennysj	which term? 'common ground'?

Only a few cases of response-structure confusion manifestation were identified
in this corpus of analysis, probably due to the use of VMT's referencing mechanism.
Nevertheless, one has to consider that these chatters are researchers in chat analysis
and for that reason were more experienced than most people in following a chat
conversation. Most were also quite experienced in using the referencing mechanism.
Perhaps, having other people as chatters, more confusion manifestations might take
place given that VMT cannot prevent them from occurring by offering a mechanism
for its reduction.

Conclusion

In this chapter the response-structure confusion problem was presented. This problem derives from the difficulty in identifying which previous message is being taken
up by a message in a chat conversation. When participants are unable to infer the
unfolding of a conversation, have doubts regarding which previous message is being
answered, or wrongly infer a referencing between messages, then co-text loss takes
place. This problem is quite relevant when the chat session is for learning, for working or for supporting the enactment of some group dynamics that requires precise
understanding of the chat conversation.

Response-structure confusion stems from the high non-linearity of chat conversation: most messages do not refer to the preceding one and the subjects that are being
discussed are not chained linearly. In a chat session, different subjects are discussed
at the same time, in parallel and alternately, fostering a confluence of subject waves.
These chat characteristics bring confusion to the conversation, making it especially
difficult to follow by novice chatters.

In order to properly follow the conversation, the reader has to infer the response structure. In this chapter the main strategies to help inferring this structure were presented. However, even for advanced chatters it is sometimes ambiguous and difficult to find out which previous message is currently being answered. For that reason, some chat tools offer mechanisms to let a chatter indicate the message to which they are responding.

VMT's referencing mechanism was investigated in this chapter. Based on evidence from the VMT workshop corpus it is clear that the referencing mechanism was used considerably and was quite useful, especially for chatters who systematically used it in almost all or in many of their messages (intensive and occasional user profile). Even chatters who rarely used the mechanism (low-user profile), sometimes felt like using it for returning to a subject originated in a far-away message, or for avoiding ambiguity and its potential for co-text loss. For example, CPRose, although being a typical non-user, felt the need of referencing after the confusion manifested in Log 21-19.

Log 21-19.

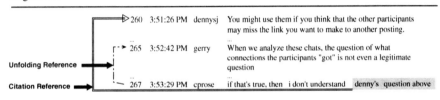

The possibility in VMT of establishing references to multiple messages did not appear to be very useful to indicate conversation structure. Establishing a single reference per message seems to be enough for the unfolding of a chat conversation. However, chatters sometimes feel like citing messages and pointing to objects on the workspace making the multiple-referencing capability a desirable one. It might be interesting to have a way to differentiate the unfolding (**"that's"**) and citing (**"above"**) references as illustrated in Log 21-19.

When a participant explicitly indicates a reference, it lessens the chance of causing a co-text loss related to that reference. On the other hand, establishing the graphical reference is time consuming, makes the conversation somehow more formal, introduces undesirable hand movements, and is not prized by all chatters. Unlike threaded chat tools where all messages have to be in a thread, or chat tools that do not support graphical referencing, VMT's referencing mechanism is optional. Being optional, the mechanism suits a variety of chatters' profiles, even the typical non-user that scarcely deems it necessary. This way, it has the potential to reduce confusion without imposing itself by forcing chatters to always explicitly indicate their references.

Chapter 22
A Multidimensional Coding Scheme for VMT

Jan-Willem Strijbos

Abstract In CSCL research, collaboration through chat has primarily been studied in dyadic settings. In VMT's larger groups it becomes harder to specify procedures for coding postings because the interactions are more complicated and ambiguous. This chapter discusses four issues that emerged during the development of a multidimensional coding procedure for small-group chat communication: (a) the unit of analysis and unit fragmentation, (b) the reconstruction of the response structure, (c) determining reliability without overestimation, and (d) the validity of constructs inspired by diverse theoretical-methodological stances. Threading, i.e., connections between analysis units, proved essential to handle unit fragmentation, to reconstruct the response structure and for reliability of coding. In addition, a risk for reliability overestimation is illustrated. Implications for reliability, validity and analysis methodology in CSCL are discussed.

Keywords Unit of analysis · response structure · reliability · validity · coding scheme · methodology

Coding of communication processes (content analysis) to determine effects of computer-supported collaborative learning (CSCL) has become a common research practice (Barron, 2003; Fischer & Mandl, 2005; Webb & Mastergeorge, 2003). In the past decade, research on CSCL has opened new theoretical, technical and pedagogical avenues of research. Comparatively less attention has, however, been directed to methodological issues associated with coding (Strijbos, Kirschner & Martens, 2004).

Early attempts to analyze communication in computer-supported environments focused on counting messages to determine students' participation, and on mean number of words as an indicator for the quality of messages. Later, methods like "thread-length" analysis and "social network analysis" expanded this surface-level

J.W. Strijbos (✉)
Institute of Education and Child Studies, Centre for the Study of Learning and Instruction,
Leiden University, The Netherlands
e-mail: jwstrijbos@fsw.leidenuniv.nl

G. Stahl (ed.), *Studying Virtual Math Teams*, Computer-Supported Collaborative
Learning Series 11, DOI 10.1007/978-1-4419-0228-3_22,
© Springer Science+Business Media, LLC 2009

repertoire. Now the CSCL research community agrees that surface methods can provide a useful initial orientation, but believes that more detailed analysis is needed to understand the underlying mechanisms of group interaction.

Content analysis is widely applied in collaborative learning research (Barron, 2003; Gunawardena, Lowe & Anderson, 1997; Schellens & Valcke, 2005; Strijbos, Martens, Prins & Jochems, 2006; Weinberger & Fischer, 2006). Communication is segmented into analysis units (utterances), coded and their frequencies used for comparisons and/or statistical testing. Increasingly, collaborative learning studies are moving to a mixed-method strategy (Barron, 2003; Hmelo-Silver, 2003; Strijbos, 2004) and new techniques are being combined with known ones, such as multilevel modeling of content analysis data (Chiu & Khoo, 2003; Cress, 2008).

At present, however, the number of studies reporting on the specifics of an analysis method in detail is limited. With respect to content analysis this is highlighted by how many citations still reference Chi (1997), whose article was until recently the most cited article regarding the methodological issues involved. Within the CSCL community an academic discourse is gradually developing on issues such as analysis scheme construction, comparability and re-use (De Wever, Schellens, Valcke & Van Keer, 2006), unit of analysis (Strijbos et al., 2006) and specific processes like argumentative knowledge construction (Weinberger & Fischer, 2006)—but many issues remain.

Background

This chapter reports on an attempt to use coding under circumstances that may be typical in CSCL research, but where coding has not generally been applied. The reported work with the coding scheme was conducted at the end of the first year of the VMT Project.

The theory behind our research focuses on group processes and the meaning making that takes place in them, as elaborated by Stahl (2006b) and Stahl, Koschmann & Suthers (2006). The theory recommends ethnomethodologically-informed conversation analysis as the most appropriate analysis methodology, but we wanted to try to apply a coding approach as well. Coding is most frequently used to compare research groups under controlled experimental conditions with well-defined dependent variables; we wanted to use coding to help us explore initial data where we did not yet have explicit hypotheses. Coding is often used in cases of face-to-face talk (e.g., in a classroom) or between communicating dyads; we were interested in online text-based synchronous interaction within small groups of three to five students. Educational and psychological research using coding generally takes utterances or actions of individuals as the unit of analysis; we wanted to focus on the small group as the unit of agency and identify group processes. In undertaking our inquiry into the use of coding under these circumstances, we strove for both reliability and validity.

We wanted to understand what was happening in the chats along a number of dimensions. We wanted insights that would help us to develop the environment and the pedagogical approach. In particular, we were interested in how students communicated, interacted and collaborated. We were also interested in how they engaged in math problem solving as a group. So we drew upon coding schemes from the research literature that addressed these dimensions while developing the VMT coding scheme. In this chapter, we take a close look at both reliability and validity of the coding scheme.

VMT Coding Scheme

The VMT coding scheme can be characterized as a multidimensional coding scheme. Multidimensional coding schemes are not a novelty in CSCL research, but they are often not explicitly defined. Henri (1992) distinguishes five dimensions: participation, social, interactive, cognitive and meta-cognitive. Fischer, Bruhn, Gräsel & Mandl, (2002) define two dimensions: the content and function of utterances (speech acts). Finally, Weinberger and Fischer (2006) use four dimensions: participation, epistemic, argument and social. These studies assign a single code to an utterance, or they code multiple dimensions that differ in the unitization grain size (i.e., message, theme, utterance, sentence, etc.).

The first step in the development of the coding scheme was to determine the unit of analysis; its granularity can affect accuracy of coding (Strijbos et al., 2006). We decided to use the chat line as the unit of analysis mainly because it is defined by the user. It allowed us to avoid segmentation issues based on our (researcher) view. We empirically saw that the chat users tended to only *do* one thing in a given chat line. Exceptions requiring a separate segmentation procedure were rare and too insubstantial to affect coding. We decided to code the entire log, including automatic system-generated entries. In contrast to other multidimensional coding schemes unitization is the same for all dimensions: a chat line receives either a code or no code in each dimension—this allows for combinations of dimensions and expands the analytical scope.

We decided to separate communicative and problem-solving processes and conceptualized these as independent dimensions. Our initial scheme consisted of the conversational thread (who replies to whom), the conversation dimension based on Beers, Boshuizen, Kirschner and Gijselaers (2005), Fischer et al. (2002) and Hmelo-Silver (2003), the social dimension based on Renninger and Farra (2003) and Strijbos, Martens, Jochems and Broers, (2004), the problem-solving dimension based on Jonassen and Kwon (2001) and Polya (1945/1973), the math-move dimension based on Sfard and McClain (2003) and the support dimension (system entries and moderator utterances).

Then we spent the summer trying to apply these codes to ten chats that we had logged in Spring 2004. Naturally, we wanted our coding to be reliable, so we checked on our inter-rater reliability as we went along. Problems in capturing what was taking place of interest in the chats and in reaching reliability led us to gradually evolve our dimensions. As the dimensions became more complicated with sub-codes, it became clear that some of them should be split into new dimensions.

Table 22.1 VMT coding steps (italic signals addition during calibration)

Step 1	Step 2	Step 3	*Step 4*	Step 5
C-thread	Conversation	Social	*PS-thread*	Problem Solving
Reply to U_i	No code	Identity self	*Connect to U_i*	Orientation
	State	Identity other		Strategy
	Offer	Interest		*Tactic*
	Request	Risk-taking		Perform
	Regulate	Resource		*Result*
	Repair typing	Norms		Check
	Respond, *more general than the codes below that are tied to problem solving*:	Home		*Corroborate/ counter*
	Follow	School		*Clarify*
	Elaborate	Collaborate group		Reflect
	Extend	Collaborate individual		*Restate*
	Setup	Sustain climate		Summarize
	Agree	Greet		
	Disagree			
	Critique			
	Explain			

We ended with the dimensions in Table 22.1, and the additions during calibration trials have been italicized (the math move and support dimension are not discussed in the remainder of this chapter and therefore not shown).

It turned out that it was important to conduct the coding of the different dimensions in a certain order, and to agree on the coding of one dimension before moving on to consider others. In particular, determining the threading of chat in small groups is fundamental to understanding the interaction. For the participants, confusion about the threading of responses by other participants can be a significant task and source of problems (see Chapter 21). For researchers, the determination of conversational threading is the first step necessary for analysis (see Chapter 20). Agreement on the threading by the coders establishes a basic interpretation of the interaction. Then, individual utterances can be assigned to codes in a reliable way. In addition, we were interested in the math problem solving. So we also determined the threading of math argumentation, which sometimes diverged from the conversational threading, often by referring further back to previous statements of math resources that were now being made relevant. Determining the problem-solving threading required an understanding of the math being done by the students, and often involved bringing math expertise into the coding process.

In this chapter, we focus on four issues that emerged in our attempt to apply a coding scheme in preliminary stages of CSCL research:

(a) We tried to use the natural unit of the chat posting as our *unit for coding*. This rarely led to problems with multiple contents being incorporated in a single posting, but rather with a single expressive act being spread over multiple postings.

(b) The reconstruction of the chat's *response structure* was an important step in analyzing a chat. We developed a conversation thread and a problem-solving thread to represent the response structure.

(c) The goal of acceptable reliability drove the evolution of the coding scheme. The calculation of *reliability* itself had to be adjusted to avoid over-estimation for sparsely coded dimensions.

(d) Irrespective of reliability we wanted to take advantage of the diverse theoretical-methodological stances within the VMT research team that best reflected behaviors of collective interest (*validity*).

Unit Fragmentation and Response Structure Reconstruction

We started with the calibration of the conversation dimension and combined this with threading in a single analysis step, but quickly discovered that *threading* actually consisted of two issues namely *unit fragmentation* and *reconstruction of the response structure*. Unit fragmentation refers to fragmented utterances by a single author spanning multiple chat lines. These fragments make sense only if considered together as a single utterance. Usually, one of these fragments is assigned a conversational code revealing the conversational action of the whole statement, and the remaining fragments are tied to the special fragment by using "setup" and "extension" codes. This reduces double coding. Log 22-1 provides an example of both codes: line 155 is an extension to 154 and together they are a "request" and line 156 is a setup to line 158 forming a "regulation".

CSCL research on chat technology previously mainly focused on dyadic interaction (e.g., research on argumentation; Andriessen, Baker & Suthers, 2003), which poses few difficulties to determine who responds to whom. In contrast, the VMT's small-group chat transcripts revealed that the chain of utterances was problematic. A discussion forum uses a threaded format that automatically inserts a response to a message as a subordinate object in a tree structure, and in a similar vein, a prefix is added to the subject header of an e-mail reply. Current chat technology has no such indicators identifying the chain of utterances. Moreover, while there is no confusion about the intended recipient in a dyadic setting (the other actor), students in small groups often communicate simultaneously, making it easy to loose track of to whom they should respond. Coding small-group conversation in a chat required the reconstruction of the response structure as shown in Log 22-1.

Delay between utterances proved to be important. For example, lines 157 and 158 fully overlap (no delay) and the delay between lines 166 and 167 of 16 seconds reveals that the short utterance of 167 is more likely to be connected to 166 than 164. Our reasoning is that it takes only a few seconds to type and submit this utterance,

Log 22-1.

Line	Time	Delay	Name	Utterance	T1	T2	T3	TA
154	7:28:03	0:15	AME	How about you fir				
155	7:28:35	0:32	AME	Do you agree	154		154	154
156	7:28:50	0:15	AME	nvm				
157	7:28:55	0:05	MCP	I used cos(22.5) instead of .924. Got 4.2498ish	151	153	153	153
158	7:28:55	0:00	AME	lets go on	156	156	156	156
159	7:29:16	0:21	AME	Its close enough	157	157	157	157
160	7:29:22	0:06	AME	How about 4.25?			157	157
161	7:29:53	0:31	MCP	I guess use 4.6^ - 4.25^ to get BV^2	160	160		160
162	7:30:03	0:10	AME	ya	161	161	161	161
163	7:30:05	0:02	MCP	Then 16*that, again		161	161	161
164	7:31:03	0:58	AME	I got 1.76 or so			161	
165	7:31:09	0:06	MCP	yes	164	164	164	164
166	7:31:28	0:19	AME	So the perimeter should be 28.16		164	164	164
167	7:31:44	0:16	FIR	ye!	166	164	166	166
168	7:31:51	0:07	FIR	*YES!	167	167	167	167

Note. T1 = Thread coder 1, T2 = Thread coder 2, T3 = Thread coder 3, TA = Agreed after discussion.

and if line 167 was intended as a response to line 164 this utterance would have appeared before or simultaneous with line 166.

Connecting utterances to handle unit fragmentation and to reconstruct the response structure is performed simultaneously, and referred to as *threading*. The threading is performed separately from the conversational coding, including assignment of extension and setup, because not all spanned utterance connections concern fragmentation. There is one infrequent exception of a spanned utterance in the shape of three fragments coded as "explain/critique" + "elaborate" + "extension", but this emphasizes that coding of extend and setup should be performed separately. In other words, threading only reconstructs connections between the user-defined chat lines that form (a) a fragment of a spanned utterance or (b) a response to a previous utterance, but the nature of the chat line is decided during coding and not during threading. It also highlights that coders should be familiar with the codes to ensure that they know which lines should be considered for threading because the conversational code depends on whether or not a thread is assigned.

Calibration trials for the problem-solving dimension revealed a similar need for the reconstruction of a problem-solving thread—to follow the co-construction of ideas and flow of problem-solving acts (e.g., proposing a strategy or performing a solution step)—prior to the coding of problem solving.

Calibration trials showed that threading is of utmost importance for the analysis of chat-based small-group problem solving and should be assigned prior to the (conversational) coding. In the next section we will discuss the reliability for threading and coding of three dimensions in detail, as their calculation presented additional methodological issues—more specifically the risk for reliability overestimation. In line with Strijbos et al. (2006) we address reliability stability by presenting two trials, each covering about 10% of the data.

Reliability of Threading, Coding and Reliability Overestimation

Reliability of Threading

Threading is already a deep interpretation of the data and therefore a reliability statistic should be determined. The calculation of *threading reconstruction* reliability proved complicated, because coders can assign a thread indicator to a chat line or not, assign an indicator to the same chat line or to a different chat line. As a result, only a proportion agreement can be computed. We used three coders (author and two research assistants) and computed two indices for all possible coder dyads:

- For the assignment of a thread or not by both coders (% thread);
- For the assignment of the same thread whenever both assigned a thread (% same).

Table 22.2 presents the results for both reliability trials for each pair of coders. The first trial (R1) consisted of 500 chat lines and the second trial (R2) consisted of 449 chat lines. The top of Table 22.2 presents the results for the conversational thread and the bottom the results for the problem-solving thread.

Table 22.2 The proportion agreement indices

| | Conversational thread | | | |
| | R1 | | R2 | |
Pair	% thread	% same	% thread	% same
1–2	0.832	0.731	0.835	0.712
1–3	0.778	0.727	0.824	0.749
2–3	0.750	0.687	0.832	0.730
	Problem-solving thread			
	R1		R2	
Pair	% thread	% same	% thread	% same
1–2	0.756	0.928	0.942	0.983
1–3	0.805	0.879	0.909	0.967
2–3	0.753	0.890	0.880	0.935

A threshold for the proportion agreement reliability of segmentation does not exist in CSCL research (De Wever et al., 2006; Rourke, Anderson, Garrison &

Archer, 2001b), nor in the field of content analysis (Neuendorf, 2002; Riffe, Lacy & Fico, 1998). Given the various perspectives in the literature, a range of 0.70–0.80 for proportion agreement can serve as the criterion value. Combined results for the conversational thread reveal that, on average, both coders assign a thread in 80.7% of all cases. Overall, 72.2% of the thread assignments are the same. These combined results show that the reliability of conversational threading is actually quite stable and fits the 0.70–0.80 range.

The results of both reliability trials reveal for the problem-solving thread that, on average, in 87% of all the instances both coders assigned a thread. Of all threading assignments by either coder 91.5% are the same. These results show that the reliability of problem-solving threading exceeds the 0.70–0.80 range. It should be noted that the problem-solving thread is very often the same as the conversation thread, so the reliability indices are automatically higher. The R2 selection also contained fewer problem-solving utterances than R1, so the problem-solving thread is more similar to the conversational thread and thus the reliability is higher. Since the reliability of problem-solving threading depends on the number of utterances that actually contain problem-solving content, it will fluctuate between transcripts. Therefore, the first trial should be regarded as a satisfactory lower bound: 77.1% for thread assignment and 89.9% for same thread assignment.

Reliability of Three Coding Dimensions and Reliability Overestimation

Given the impact of the conversational and problem-solving threads during the calibration sessions, codes were added or changed, definitions adjusted, prototypical examples added, and rules to handle exceptions established. Nine calibration trials were conducted prior to the reliability trials.

We used three coders (author and two research assistants) and adopted a stratified coding approach for each reliability trial: the coders first individually assigned the conversation threads, followed by a discussion to construct an agreed upon conversational thread, after which each coder independently coded the conversational and social dimension. Next, coders first individually assigned the problem-solving thread before a discussion was held to construct an agreed upon problem-solving thread, followed by assigning the problem-solving codes. Between both reliability trials, minor changes were made in the wording of a definition or adjusting a rule. The final version of the coding scheme included 40 code definitions (with examples of actual data samples) in 5 dimensions (not counting the mathematical and system-support dimensions) (see Table 22.1). Mastery of the coding procedure is laborious; some dimensions take about twenty hours of training and discussion with an experienced coder.

In contrast to our initial conceptualization of the dimensions as being independent we have been thus far unable to avoid ties between some of the conversational codes and the problem-solving dimension. Coding qualitatively different processes, social versus problem-solving, using the same data corpus was problematic—especially involving "elaborate," "explain" and "critique" codes. The implications of ties for the validity of the coding scheme will be discussed in the section on validity.

Calculating the reliability for the conversation, social and problem-solving dimensions proved to be less straightforward than expected. Each chat line receives a conversation code and can have either one or no code for any other dimension, but not all chat lines are eligible to receive a particular code. The social and problem-solving dimensions only apply to a portion of all of the chat lines, and the pool of valid units will fluctuate between different pairs of coders. When not all units are eligible to receive a code we should decide how we handle units coded by only one coder or none in the reliability computation:

(a) Include only units coded by both coders (exclude units with missing values);
(b) Categorize missing values as "no code" and include this code;
(c) Categorize missing values and non-coded units as "no code" and include this code.

For possibilities (a) and (c) we calculated three reliability indices as suggested by De Wever et al. (2006): proportion agreement (%), Cohen's kappa (κ) and Krippendorff's alpha (α) for each dimension and each pair of coders.

Although proportion agreement is still often used, it is insufficient to serve as an indicator for reliability because it does not correct for chance agreement, and we report this solely for comparison. Kappa is computed because this is the most widely used statistic that corrects for agreement by chance. However, recent publications revealed that kappa behaves strangely, i.e., the kappa for two coders with a radically different distribution of frequencies over categories will be higher than for coders with a similar distribution (Artstein & Poesio, 2005; Krippendorff, 2004). Alpha does not suffer from this statistical artifact, so it should be preferred. We retain kappa for comparison because alpha is not widely used in CSCL or educational research.

Option (b) was only computed for kappa and alpha. To determine whether the reliability is sufficient the 0.70–0.80 range is mostly used as criterion for proportion agreement. Perspectives in the literature on a criterion value for kappa differ, but in our opinion these criteria—intermediate, strict and lenient—apply best: below 0.45 "poor", 0.45–0.59 "fair", 0.60–0.74 "good" and 0.75 and above "excellent" (De Wever et al., 2006; Landis & Koch, 1977; Neuendorf, 2002). We apply the same criteria to alpha. Table 22.3 shows the reliability results for the conversation, social and problem-solving dimension. We will first discuss the pair-wise comparisons for the social and problem-solving dimension.

When only those units coded by both coders are included in the computation—κ_1 and α_1—the reliability is consistently higher than proportion agreement, which is expected because κ_1 and α_1 do not treat all units coded by only one coder as disagreement. It should be noted that alpha allows including missing values in the

Table 22.3 Proportion agreement, kappa and alpha

Conversation dimension

Pair	R1 ($U = 500$) %	κ	α	R2 ($U = 449$) %	κ	α
1–2	0.750	0.723	0.704	0.735	0.703	0.702
1–3	0.644	0.583	0.600	0.724	0.687	0.686
2–3	0.692	0.663	0.654	0.724	0.689	0.681
3 coders			0.653			0.689

Note. % = percentage agreement, κ = Cohen's kappa, α = Krippendorff's alpha, κ_1 = kappa with missing excluded, α_1 = alpha with missing excluded, κ_2 = kappa with missing as disagreement, α_2 = alpha with missing as disagreement, analysis units in italics, $\%_A$, κ_A, and α_A = percentage, kappa and alpha when all units are included.

Social dimension

R1

Pair	%	Missing excluded κ_1	α_1	Missing as "no code" κ_2	α_2	Missing and no-code units included ($U = 500$) $\%_A$	κ_A	α_A
1–2	0.550	0.835	0.850	0.464	0.430	0.812	0.651	0.641
	208	*127*	*208*	*208*	*208*			
1–3	0.495	0.793	0.771	0.382	0.372	0.788	0.594	0.593
	218	*129*	*218*	*218*	*218*			
2–3	0.529	0.798	0.831	0.413	0.439	0.824	0.637	0.656
	185	*115*	*185*	*185*	*185*			
3 coders		0.787		0.462				0.629
		225		*225*				

R2

Pair	%	Missing excluded κ_1	α_1	Missing as "no code" κ_2	α_2	Missing and no-code units included ($U = 449$) $\%_A$	κ_A	α_A
1–2	0.646	0.748	0.733	0.565	0.550	0.857	0.755	0.733
	176	*140*	*176*	*176*	*176*			
1–3	0.543	0.737	0.733	0.444	0.412	0.835	0.669	0.649
	163	*107*	*163*	*163*	*163*			
2–3	0.506	0.730	0.739	0.407	0.367	0.820	0.634	0.609
	174	*106*	*174*	*174*	*174*			
3 coders		0.735		0.480				0.668
		182		*182*				

Note. % = percentage agreement, κ = Cohen's kappa, α = Krippendorff's alpha, κ_1 = kappa with missing excluded, α_1 = alpha with missing excluded, κ_2 = kappa with missing as disagreement, α_2 = alpha with missing as disagreement, analysis units in italics, $\%_A$, κ_A, and α_A = percentage, kappa and alpha when all units are included.

Table 22.3 (continued)

Problem-solving dimension

R1

Pair	Missing excluded %	κ₁	α₁	Missing as "no code" κ₂	α₂	Missing and no-code units included (U = 500) %_A	κ_A	α_A
1–2	0.469	0.631	0.628	0.382	0.385	0.821	0.622	0.613
	178	*127*	*178*	*178*	*178*			
1–3	0.351	0.564	0.543	0.229	0.242	0.782	0.514	0.504
	172	*97*	*172*	*172*	*172*			
2–3	0.439	0.542	0.520	0.339	0.340	0.834	0.618	0.608
	148	*106*	*148*	*148*	*148*			
3 coders			0.563		0.370			0.576
			181		*181*			

R2

Pair	Missing excluded %	κ₁	α₁	Missing as "no code" κ₂	α₂	Missing and no-code units included (U = 449) %_A	κ_A	α_A
1–2	0.657	0.674	0.666	0.588	0.576	0.864	0.766	0.762
	178	*158*	*178*	*178*	*178*			
1–3	0.553	0.649	0.662	0.484	0.464	0.804	0.675	0.665
	195	*147*	*195*	*195*	*195*			
2–3	0.556	0.576	0.654	0.485	0.469	0.815	0.688	0.667
	190	*146*	*190*	*190*	*190*			
3 coders			0.650		0.523			0.699
			196		*196*			

Note. % = percentage agreement, κ = Cohen's kappa, α = Krippendorff's alpha, κ₁ = kappa with missing excluded, α₁ = alpha with missing excluded, κ₂ = kappa with missing as disagreement, α₂ = alpha with missing as disagreement, analysis units in italics, %_A, κ_A, and α_A = percentage, kappa and alpha when all units are included.

data matrix, however units coded by only one coder are ignored in the final computation. So, although it seems that more units are included there is computationally no difference with the case where these units are excluded (Table 22-3 shows the number of units that appear to be used for the computation for α_1, although they are in reality the same as for κ_1).

When the missing values for units that were coded by only one coder are categorized "no code" and this "extra" code is included in the computation—κ_2 and α_2—reliability drops. This is stronger for the social dimension as compared to the problem-solving dimension, and is caused by the number of missing values; more missing values lead to a stronger downward correction when these are treated as disagreement. Alpha and kappa have similar values, but differ slightly (caused by the different distribution of frequencies over categories).

When the missing values and all units that were not coded by both coders are included and categorized as "no code"—$\%_A$, κ_A and α_A—proportion agreement is consistently higher, α_A is higher than α_2 for the social and problem-solving dimension but is lower than α_1 for the social dimension and equal to α_1 for the problem-solving dimension. The same pattern is visible for the three kappa indices.

Since proportion agreement does not correct for chance agreement and kappa suffers from a statistical artifact, alpha is preferred. Excluding missing values in the computation neglects a source of disagreement and inflates reliability, so α_1 is not adequate. Including all units that were not coded by both coders appears appealing and consistent but treats those units that are conceptually not eligible to receive a code as agreement. So, α_A also inflates reliability and is not adequate. Including only those units coded by either coder, categorizing missing values as "no code", is the strictest computation. Thus, α_2 should be preferred although this statistic is a slight underestimation of the possible "eligible" units—because it ignores the ambiguous units that both coders considered but did not code—but this is favored given the substantial overestimation if missing values are excluded or all non-coded units are included.

The pair-wise comparisons provide insight into the performance of particular coders, but if more than two coders are available this should be preferred. We had three coders and alpha is suited to compute reliability for more than two coders (although Fleiss kappa can also correct for multiple coders, it applies only to nominal data; alpha can also be used for ordinal, interval and ratio data). Again, α_2 is preferred over α_1 and α_A for the case of three coders, and appears the best approximation for the reliability for the social and problem-solving dimension.

Considering the reliability statistics for three coders, alpha for the conversation dimension can be considered "good" for both trails, 0.653 for R1 and 0.689 for R2. The alpha for the social dimension can be considered "fair" for both trials, 0.462 for R1 and 0.480 for R2. The alpha for the problem solving dimension is "poor" for R1 (0.370) and "fair" for R2 (0.523).

Validity of the VMT Coding Scheme

Although the methodological debate in CSCL research has intensified over the past decade (Strijbos & Fischer, 2007), it is apparent that regarding content analysis the issue of reliability has received much more attention than validity and generalizability. Rourke and Anderson (2004) convincingly argued that content analysis should be regarded as a form of testing and measurement and stressed the importance of validity, especially when the analysis moves from description to making inferences. Their approach to validity in content analysis is modeled on Messick's (1989, 1995) aspects of construct validity. Rourke and Anderson (2004) describe five steps for developing a theoretically valid protocol:

(a) Identifying the purpose of the coded data (content aspect),
(b) Identifying behaviors that represent the construct (substantial aspect),
(c) Reviewing the codes and indicators (structural aspect),
(d) Holding preliminary try-outs and
(e) Developing guidelines for administration, scoring and interpretation of the coding scheme.

We will first briefly discuss the development of the VMT coding scheme with respect to these five steps and elaborate on design decisions made, followed by some empirical evidence for validity. Finally, Messick's generalizability aspect and external aspect will be briefly discussed in view of the current state of content analysis literature in CSCL.

Identifying the Purpose of the Coded Data

As briefly stated in the background section, we were interested in understanding what was happening in the chats—how students communicated, interacted and collaborated—to obtain insights that would help us to develop the environment and the pedagogical approach. Thus, the purpose of the VMT coding scheme was to describe collaborative processes of small groups solving a mathematical problem via chat, rather than drawing inferences (or stated differently, hypothesis generation rather than hypothesis testing).

Identifying Behaviors that Represent the Construct

Our dimensions of interest—conversation, social and problem solving—are latent constructs and inferred from observable behaviors (utterances). Construct validity draws on the connection between theory and method. This requires careful operationalization of behaviors to avoid construct under-representation and construct-irrelevant variance (Messick, 1989, 1995). Or in other words, that the coding scheme "neither leaves out behaviors that should be included, nor includes behaviors that should be left out" (Rourke & Anderson, 2004, p. 9).

Given the exploratory focus and descriptive purpose of coding we adopted a broad perspective on processes of interest. While developing the VMT coding scheme we relied on diverse theoretical-methodological stances within the research team, i.e., quantitative content analysis and qualitative approaches such as conversation analysis and ethnographic perspectives (e.g., grounded theory). We wanted to take advantage of these different viewpoints to construct a coding scheme that best reflected behaviors that we were collectively interested in. The codes of the scheme are based on literature study (published coding schemes) and transcript observations. They reflect the different theoretical approaches: speech act (e.g., "offer", "agree" and "disagree"), conversation analysis (e.g., "repair typing") and grounded theory (e.g., "follow" and "sustain social climate").

With its combined theoretical-methodological perspective the coding scheme can be regarded as an example of hybrid analysis methodologies called for by Suthers (2005a). As the development of hybrid methodologies induces theoretical boundary-crossing, the question arises whether internal validity (relevant behaviors by participants from a single theoretical perspective) takes precedence over the substantial aspect of validity (relevant behaviors by participants from a combination of theoretical perspectives). In other words, a combination of theoretical perspectives appears more susceptible to construct-irrelevant variance, whereas a single theoretical perspective appears more susceptible to construct under-representation. In our view, hybrid analysis methodologies are well suited for hypothesis generation and descriptive analyses. Although we acknowledge the risk of construct-irrelevant variance, they do not automatically result in bias invalidating the outcomes of exploratory analyses, but can reveal new possible ways to describe the data.

Reviewing the Codes and Indicators

A provisional coding scheme was constructed by a researcher experienced in content analysis (author). The coding scheme was then discussed with three senior VMT researchers with diverse theoretical-methodological backgrounds: conversation analysis, ethnography and mathematical problem solving. We conducted three discussion rounds where codes and indicators were added and deleted, while trying to balance the diverse perspectives on interaction analysis and the behaviors of interest. In between discussions we applied the codes to transcript excerpts (individually and in pairs) moving back and forth between the codes, definitions, indicators, the data and reasoning about it. The experiences were discussed in the following meeting and the codes adapted accordingly. The coding scheme evolved from each utterance receiving a single code to a coding scheme in which each utterance receives more than one code—but each of them in a separate dimension.

The tension between the theoretical-methodological stances was reflected strongest in the discussion on the number of codes and the degree of specificity needed to describe behaviors of interest. The debate focused on the desire for a parsimonious set of codes versus inclusion of all relevant—even if infrequent—behaviors. A point in case are the codes "school" and "home". They are relevant from an interactional point of view because VMT participants only met online and references to their school or home context can be indicative for the social climate in the group, but their infrequent occurrence makes these codes more suited for descriptive analyses rather than statistical inferences.

Interestingly, the issue of the number of codes has so far not been explicitly addressed in leading publications on content analysis and in CSCL research. Obviously a set rule for the number of codes does not make much sense, but there are several aspects that can guide this decision: level of detail required, theory-driven versus a data-driven focus (or in other words researcher codes versus participant codes), cognitive demand of coding (a large amount of codes is cognitively more demanding and increases the risk of errors due to fatigue), and representativeness of the behavior of interest. Given these issues we initially decided to limit the number of codes in each dimension to a maximum of 12. Only the conversation dimension was further expanded to 15 codes during calibration.

Finally, there were utterances that could not be assigned to any of the codes. Often "no code" is used to handle the utterances that do not appear to fit any of the codes in the coding scheme. Ideally this should be no more than 20% of all utterances, since it directly questions whether the coding scheme actually measures the behaviors of interest. We only used "no code" in the conversation dimension. The number of utterances that we assigned this code was well below 20%. As discussed in the section on reliability, we did not include this code in the social and problem-solving dimensions as this would result in reliability overestimation due to sparse coding in these dimensions.

Holding Preliminary Try-Outs

Calibration trials (or preliminary try-outs) should be based on a large enough number of observations in different groups, and/or different research conditions. In our case we made sure that each trial consisted of material from two different groups to prevent tuning the coding scheme to a single group. This practice makes the codes more universally applicable and improves reliability (consistency across different groups) and validity (identifying the same behavior in different groups). In general, several trials are required and about 10% of the data (depending on the frequency of behaviors and the number of codes) should be used in each trial to ensure that the sample is representative and behavior of interest actually occurs.

We conducted nine calibration trials to refine the set of codes constructed during the conceptual phase. During the first six trials the experienced content analysis researcher and two research assistants focused on the calibration of codes in the conversation and social dimension: adapting definitions, adding examples and adding rules to code ambiguous utterances. We discovered that conversational threading had to be reconstructed prior to coding the conversation dimension. In contrast to our conceptualization of the dimensions as being independent we had to allow ties between some of the conversational codes and the problem-solving dimension. Coding qualitatively different processes, social versus problem-solving, using the same data corpus was problematic. Usually a small amount of any given VMT chat falls into the social dimension, so in most chats utterances tied to problem-solving would also belong to the problem-solving dimension regardless of ties since most of the chat would be task-focused (i.e., solving the mathematical problem). Nevertheless, there will be instances where utterances in the social dimension are in fact technically of a more specific nature in a communicative sense than a mere "response" (this code was introduced to cover utterances not tied to problem-solving). The decision to allow for ties reflects our primary interest, that is, the mathematical problem solving. Nevertheless, we acknowledge that a stronger separation would have been preferred.

In trials seven to nine we focused on the problem-solving dimension and brought in three additional experts from the Math Forum team to assist with coding of mathematical problem solving. We concluded that a problem-solving thread had to be constructed prior to coding. An overview of possible solutions and strategies proved to be indispensable for coding problem solving. Yet, although we were able to identify problem-solving we had to concede that mathematical operations were too diverse and uncommon to achieve valid and reliable codes.

Developing Guidelines for Administration, Scoring and Interpretation of the Coding Scheme

In line with prior published coding schemes, we encountered ambiguous utterances that could be assigned several codes within a dimension. Ambiguous utterances are generally handled by establishing a set of rules. The number of rules should be limited as a need for many rules directly questions whether codes represent the behavior of interest (Beers, Boshuizen, Kirschner & Gijselares, 2007). During the calibration trials we gradually accumulated rules to assist coding of ambiguous utterances. Two examples of rules for the conversation dimension are shown in Fig. 22.1

If an utterance is phrased as a question it is in general coded as a request. Sometimes a question mark is lacking, and it can be useful to use the preceding lines to determine the code. Exceptions:

- Although the use of a question mark may be guiding in assigning a "request," this can be misleading as occasionally utterances may be phrased as a question, when in fact they may be an "offer" in disguise, such as *"We need to calculate the height, right?"* In these cases the utterance is coded as an offer.
- If an utterance is framed as a question, but a specific responding conversational category applies to the content—often the content is a critique or regulate —the utterance is not coded as a request, but as critique or regulate.
- An utterance that consists only of a question mark is still coded as a "request" (? is a chat convention).

If the content of an utterance that has been coded as an "offer" or "elaborate" is phrased as a conclusion or the concluding step of a problem solving sequence, utterances following such an utterance—that contain *"Yes "*—are coded as agree. If the utterance that contains *"Yes "* is threaded to a solution step—which is not the final concluding step or utterance —this utterance is coded as "follow."

Fig. 22.1 Sample rules for conversation codes

We conducted two reliability trials. In each trial we used three coders (author and two research assistants). The first trial revealed an acceptable reliability for the conversation dimension, but the social and problem-solving dimensions needed to be refined and minor changes were made in the wording of a definition or adjusting a rule. The second trial revealed that the reliability for the social and problem-solving dimension improved, and reliability for the conversation dimension proved to be stable. An example of a coded transcript excerpt is shown in Log 22-2 (compare qualitative analysis of the same log in Chapter 9).

Log 22-2.

Line	Name	Utterance	Time	Delay	Ct	C	S	PSt	PS
32	AME	I have an idea that might help us find whats wrong with the pic.	06:19	00:49		s	is		
33	MCP	We could use good ol' Pythag thm to see what BV is	06:30	00:11		o	cg		s
34	AME	Lets not	06:40	00:10	33	d	cg	33	rf
35	MCP	What's your idea?	06:46	00:06	32	rq	ci	32	
36	AME	It states that something is wrong with the pic.	07:01	00:15	35	e		35	o
37	AME	so we can't find what BV is	07:08	00:07	36	el	cg	36	t
38	MCP	Yeah, and I think if we 'found' BV, it would be something not possible.	07:31	00:23	37	o	cg	37	t
39	MCP	16 + BV^2 = 21.16	08:10	00:39		o		33	p
40	MCP	BV^2 = 5.16	08:20	00:10	39	el		39	p
41	AME	I got it	08:23	00:03		se			
42	AME	I know whats wrong with the pic	08:29	00:06	41	s	is		
43	MCP	BV = 2.27	08:31	00:02	39	el		39	r
44	FIR	ok. now i'm following!	08:44	00:13	39	f	ci	39	

Note. Conversational thread (Ct), conversational dimension (C), social dimension (S), problem-solving thread (PSt) and problem-solving dimension (PS).

Empirical Evidence for Validity

In the end, the value of the coding scheme depends on whether the coding scheme is able to reveal the behaviors of interest. Empirical evidence for validity relates to Messick's (1989, 1995) consequential aspect of validity.

The purpose of the coding scheme was to describe collaborative processes of small groups solving a mathematical problem via chat. Once we had reliable coding of ten chat logs, we looked for statistical patterns. It turned out that the chats almost fell into two sets depending upon whether the students had seen the math problems in advance of their chats or not. However, there were two anomalous chats that fell into the wrong sets. The use of codes brought this anomaly to our attention, but could not explain it. Using conversation analysis, we saw a difference in interaction patterns that we termed expository versus exploratory (see Chapter 23).

Furthermore, the development of the VMT coding scheme and diversity of theoretical-methodological stances within the research team motivated the attempt to integrate the two seemingly disparate approaches: conversation analysis and coding. By using conversation analysis to construct a coding scheme—segmentation and codes based on the participants' view—statistical analyses revealed qualitative differences between chats in terms of activities that group members engaged in (e.g., socializing and problem solving), without violating the analytical requirements of either approach (see Chapter 23 again).

Finally, the VMT team investigated the expression and role of multiple voices in small-group chat communication (see Chapter 24). Evidence of multiple voices and differential social position with a corpus of chats could be expressed by the statistics of personal pronouns usage: *"I"* and *"me"* (appears in coding scheme as "collaboration individual") were used more often than *"we"* and *"us"* (appears as "collaboration group" code); the second person addressing (*"you"*) was well represented.

Nevertheless, even if analysis outcomes provide evidence that are deemed "valid", we should not forget that these outcomes are directly tied to what we "constructed" as an adequate representation of what might exist. Thus, however much our codes reflect a certain theory or perspective; we cannot assume that our representation fully covers the construct. At best a coding scheme reflects a more or less accurate approximation of what we intend to measure.

Generalizability

Regarding content analysis in collaborative learning research, Messick's (1989, 1995) generalizability and external aspect are least addressed. Generalizability information is gathered through the re-use of a coding scheme in diverse contexts and knowledge domains, with diverse research populations and documenting whether similar behavioral patterns emerge.

Thus far, generalizability information has been accumulated for the Gunawardena et al. (1997) coding scheme (see De Wever et al., 2006), the Rainbow scheme (see Baker, Andriessen, Lund, Van Amelsvoort & Quignard, 2007) and the

Webb and Mastergeorge (2003) coding scheme (see Oortwijn, Boekaerts, Vedder & Strijbos, 2008). However, these examples account for a small fraction of coding schemes that have been developed and applied in collaborative learning research.

When judging generalizability information the source for variation should be kept in mind, i.e., different groups, different contexts and/or different domains. Furthermore, re-use of a coding scheme invariably leads to minor changes (e.g., adapting a definition, adding examples) or major changes (e.g., adding or deleting a code(s) or dimension)—tuning the coding scheme to the specific nature of the data collected or the research context (e.g., historical argumentation has features distinct from mathematical problem solving). The subsequent implications for reliability and validity should be addressed and carefully documented to foster re-use and accumulate validity evidence.

The external aspect has, thus far, only been addressed by Schellens and Valcke (2005), who coded the same data corpus with two coding schemes (Gunawardena et al., 1997; Veerman & Veldhuis-Diermanse, 2001) purportedly measuring the same construct. Irrespective of similarities there were differences as well, and there was evidence for convergent validity as "results confirm the theoretical mapping between phase 3 and 5 in the model of Veerman and phase 1 and phase 3 in the model of Gunawardena" (p. 972), but also divergent validity as other phases produced less similar results. In this respect it would be challenging—for example in the domain of argumentation in CSCL—to code argumentative knowledge construction in the same data corpus using both the Rainbow framework (Baker et al., 2007) and the Weinberger and Fischer (2006) framework.

Discussion

CSCL research using chat technology has focused primarily on dyads. The VMT Project investigates chat-based small-group problem solving. During the development of a multidimensional coding scheme to analyze interactions in these groups, four issues emerged that have strong implications for content-analysis methodology and practice in general and chat communication in particular.

The first methodological issue concerns unit fragmentation. We chose the chat posting as the unit of analysis because this is defined by the user, but frequently an utterance spanned across several chat lines makes sense only when considered as a whole. Consequently, connections (the conversation-threading dimension) between these units were required prior to coding, and two codes were added to the conversation dimension to mark these fragments (setup and extension).

The second issue concerns the need to reconstruct the response structure. Whereas in a dyadic chat the intended recipient is always the other partner, it is not easy to determine this in a larger group. Similarly to fragmentation, the connection between chat lines forming a chain of problem-solving responses needs to be reconstructed prior to coding of the conversation dimension. Furthermore, the delay between chat line postings proved to be relevant to determining this response structure. Also, a threading coder must be familiar with the conversational codes. Assignment of both conversational and problem-solving threading connections is performed simultaneously and termed "threading." This represents a deep interpretation of what is going on in the chat. Aggregating all coding divergence would result in very low reliabilities, so agreement on threading prior to coding is necessary.

The third methodological issue concerns reliability calculation. We conducted two trials and computed the reliability for both types of threading. Reliability for the conversation and problem-solving threading could only be expressed as a proportion agreement, but this proved to be sufficiently reliable. Calculation of reliability for the social and problem-solving dimension was problematic: not all chat lines are valid analysis units for these dimensions and can lead to overestimation of their reliability. The extent of overestimation was shown by calculating reliability for the case where (a) only units coded by both coders are included (missing values are excluded), (b) missing values are categorized as "no code" and included in the computation and (c) missing values and non-coded units are categorized as "no code" and included in the computation. We computed and compared three reliability indices and concluded that excluding missing values and including all non-coded units lead to over-estimation. Including missing values as a "no code" is the strictest computation and a slight underestimation of the reliability. In our opinion a slight underestimation should be favored given a substantial overestimation if units with missing values are excluded or all non-coded units are included. If available the use of more than two coders is preferred, and the valid pool of units should be reported (see e.g., Hurme & Järvelä, 2005, p. 6). We included proportion agreement and Cohen's kappa for comparison, although both statistics are problematic. Overall, coding reliability—Krippendorff's alpha for three coders—ranged "poor" to "good" in the first trial and "fair" to "good" in the second trail. Conducting more than one reliability trial helped to determine the impact of refinements (rewording definitions and changes to rules) and to assess reliability stability.

The fourth methodological issue concerns validity. Reliability is only one aspect of a coding scheme—addressing the extent to which the coding can be reproduced— and it should not be mistaken for validity. The VMT coding is explorative and draws on prior studies with content analysis, conversation analysis and ethnographic perspectives, which may have introduced some imbalance. Most codes are based on prior studies, but several codes emerged from working with the data. We spent considerable effort to establish the dimensions' independence, but were unable to achieve that. In principle this was due to codes such as explain, critique and elaborate that are historically connected to problem-solving rather than social issues. In reporting on an early stage in the VMT iterative, evolutionary design-based research of the VMT Project, we are not claiming that our coding scheme is the ultimate solution. It provided a starting point, based on our knowledge of existing coding schemes, some modification based on our research interests and on an inductive, grounded-research approach taken during the development and refinement of the scheme. We would certainly use a different set of codes now, based on our evolving understanding of the VMT student experience.

We found that students working in our chat environment developed methods of interacting that were not adequately captured—let alone explained—by codes adopted from the work of researchers investigating other media or from a priori theories of interaction. For instance, we determined that "math proposal adjacency pairs" often play a distinctive driving role in our math chats (Stahl, 2006e). Ethnomethodologically-informed design-based research needs to grasp the methods that participants creatively invent in response to innovative learning situations and technologies; they cannot simply reduce everything to instances of codes of actions generalized from past studies.

Finally, we are particularly interested in group cognition taking place at the group unit of analysis, while coding schemes generally focus on the individual. For instance, we look at problem solving by the group as a whole. Our coding scheme tried to capture group phenomena like proposal bid-and-uptake or interaction question-and-answer by coding these as sequences of individual contributions (e.g., offer followed by response). The format of chat logs and the traditions of coding practice misled us to fragment group interactions into individual contributions. We turned to conversation analysis to allow us to look at paired interactions and longer sequences as atomic elements of chats.

As the VMT environment evolved and incorporated a shared whiteboard, graphical referencing, math symbols and other functionality, even our multidimensional coding of utterances could not capture the increasingly complex and innovative interactions (e.g., in Chapter 7). To understand the unique behaviors as students adapt to the new environment—custom technology, pedagogical guidance, open-ended math worlds—we need to look closely at the design of unique group interactions, and not simply code them with pre-existing codes, no matter how multidimensional and reliable. While general codes can be applied to many of these phenomena, they do not capture what is new, as required for design-based research. Reducing the chat to a sequence of codes that are general enough to be applied reliably can eliminate the content and details that are of particular interest (Stahl, 2006b, Chap. 10). This is a paradox of reliable and valid coding efforts in exploratory CSCL research.

Chapter 23
Combining Coding and Conversation Analysis of VMT Chats

Alan Zemel, Fatos Xhafa, and Murat Perit Çakir

Abstract This chapter considers the relationship between statistical analysis of coding based on theoretical schemes and conversation analysis of VMT participants' structuring of their chats. It describes how a statistical test on a hypothesis regarding collaboration in VMT showed an unexpected result, whose understanding required the use of qualitative methods. The phenomenon behind the puzzling result was identified using conversation analysis. The chapter explores an approach to coding based on analysis of how sequences of discussion of different topics are defined interactionally by chat participants as accomplishments of their postings. A form of "mixed methods" is proposed using codes for the different sequences and displaying the ordering of these longer sequences of interaction or compiling statistics of these codes.

Keywords Statistical analysis · conversation analysis · expository participation · explanatory participation · long sequences · probability transition tables

The analysis of the use of software by groups is particularly problematic. Most methods of human-computer interaction were developed for single-user systems and are not applicable to computer mediation of group interaction. A common approach to analyzing the use of groupware is to compare statistical measures of usage across conditions or cases. However, this can be criticized for not investigating and taking into account qualitative differences that may be crucial to understanding the quantitative differences. While there is a widespread feeling that fields like CSCL and CSCW need to take a multidisciplinary approach incorporating a variety of analytic methods, it is difficult to see how quantitative and qualitative approaches built on fundamentally incompatible theoretical foundations can be synthesized. This chapter reports a case in which a quantitative finding motivated a qualitative analysis to explain the significance of the statistical results. This experience suggested to us a

A. Zemel (✉)
Communication & Culture, Drexel University, Philadelphia, PA, USA
e-mail: arz27@drsexel.edu

G. Stahl (ed.), *Studying Virtual Math Teams*, Computer-Supported Collaborative Learning Series 11, DOI 10.1007/978-1-4419-0228-3_23,
© Springer Science+Business Media, LLC 2009

novel approach to combining the two: using qualitative analysis to derive the coding scheme for quantitative analysis.

In the VMT Project, we have investigated online problem solving from a variety of analytical and methodological perspectives. In our first year, we developed a coding scheme and applied it to logs of online chats among actors participating in math problem solving (Chapter 22). The coded logs were intended to provide a basis for quantitative analysis of the chats. While we were still investigating the coding approach, we also became interested in conversation analytic methods as a way of describing the procedures participants use to make sense of their ongoing activity. Conversation analysis (CA) and statistical analysis (SA) are uneasy partners in the analytic enterprise. These two orientations to analysis derive from very different perspectives on the role of the analyst and the kinds of assumptions that can be made with respect to the data and its interpretation.

In *statistical analysis*, hypotheses are put forward and tested. Coding schemes are devised that are designed to facilitate the testing of these hypotheses and statistical methods are applied to the coded data. In this approach, it is the analyst's perspective that is privileged. The analyst:

- Proposes the hypotheses,
- Produces the coding scheme to capture the relevant data from an experiment designed specifically to allow for testing of the hypothesis, and
- Assesses and interprets the statistical results (Mason, Gunst & Hess, 2003).

Statistical analysis of data gathered from online collaborative learning experiments plays a central role in many CSCL studies (e.g., Avouris & Margaritis, 2002; Daradoumis, Martínez & Xhafa, 2004; Dillenbourg et al., 1996; Strijbos, 2004). A whole range of statistical methods—from descriptive statistics to multilevel and other sophisticated methods—have been used to analyze the underlying features (variables) of the collaborative activity that takes place in a small group.

Conversation analysis, on the other hand, is an analytical methodology that attempts to describe the actions of participants in terms of the relevancies demonstrated by participants through their interaction (Pomerantz & Fehr, 1991; Psathas, 1995; ten Have, 1999). Actions are analyzed as situated within a stream of ongoing action and as sequentially organized. Furthermore, conversation analysts presume that actors design their action to fit the particular circumstances in which they are accomplished—and which they thereby reproduce, extend and help constitute.

The differences between SA and CA are consequential. For statistical analysts, validity and reliability are significant concerns (see Chapter 22). However, these are not concerns for conversation analysts because CA has a different view of the nature of the data. For SA, the analysis of data is to be conducted through what statisticians consider to be objective procedures that control for subjectivity and bias. In contrast, CA takes the data as already meaningful in the eyes of the participants and therefore open to being understood by analysts (who share membership in the social and linguistic cultures of the participants). Conversation analysts are concerned with providing adequate descriptions of the sense-making procedures used by participants as they interact. Where statistical analysts want to discover frequently observed regularities in interactions, conversation analysts are concerned with how specific actions were made relevant by prior actions and how a current action makes relevant subsequent actions over the course of a particular sequence of actions. For conversation analysts, it is sufficient that the participants in a particular interaction treat their ongoing actions as sensible. The conversation analyst's task is to describe these sequences of actions as sense-making procedures. SA assumes a causal model of behavior and tries to confirm predictive statistical patterns, whereas CA looks for non-deterministic social methods that people use as interacting agents.

While these two types of analysis—statistical and conversational—may seem incompatible, it turns out there are circumstances in which they can be mutually informative (Heritage & Roth, 1995). In this chapter, we describe a situation in which a puzzling statistical result was made intelligible by conversation analytic investigation. This is a novel approach to analyze the organization of the interaction in collaborative math problem-solving activities in online chats. Indeed, existing approaches in the literature treat quantitative and qualitative methods separately, often relegating the qualitative to pre-scientific exploration or post-scientific speculation. Our results show the strength of using a combined approach. Specifically, by using a quantitative approach, we detected an unexpected result in a hypothesis test. This made further investigation necessary. The qualitative method of CA enabled us to identify the phenomenon that produced the unexpected result in the SA hypothesis test.

The Statistical Analysis

We took the six chats discussed in Chapter 20 (see Table 20.1, reproduced as Table 23.1). In each chat, a group of 3–5 students in grades 6–11 collaborate online synchronously to solve math problems that require reflection and discussion using AOL's Instant Messenger software. We coded each chat using the scheme discussed in Chapter 20 and analyzed in greater detail in Chapter 22. The coding scheme includes nine distinct dimensions, each of which is designed to capture a certain type of information from a different perspective. The coding scheme was synthesized from research in CSCL, adapted through trial with VMT data (as described in Chapter 22). Two dimensions coded the threading (see Chapter 20) in order to unpack the response structure—which might otherwise lead to confusion in analyzing the flow of interaction (see Chapter 21). The other dimensions were intended to capture the content of the session. This chapter considers only the content-based dimensions: conversation, problem solving, social reference, math moves and system support.

Table 23.1 Description of the coded chat logs

PoW-wow session Number	Facilitator	Members	Number of postings	PoW name	Announced before?
1	MUR	PIN, GOR, REA, MCP	334	Finding CE	No
2a	GER	AVR, PIN, SUP, OFF	724	Equilateral Triangle Areas	No
2b	MUR	MCP, AH3, REA	204	Equilateral Triangle Areas	No
9	POW	EEF, AME, AZN, LIF, FIR	715	Making Triangles	Yes
10	MFP	AME, FIR, MCP	582	The Perimeter of an Octagon	Yes
18	MFP	AME, KOH, KIL, ROB	488	A Tangent Square and Circle	Yes

Recall that the sample of six chats is made up of three in which the math problem was announced at the beginning of the session, whereas in the rest the problem was posted on the Math Forum's web site in advance. It should be noted, however, that announcing the math problem in advance doesn't necessarily mean that the participants of the chat already solved the problem in advance.

To see what we could learn from statistical analysis after putting in a major effort in developing the coding scheme and coding six full chats, we looked for statistical differences between the chats by students who knew the problem before working together ("known") versus the chats by students who did not ("not").

Our first objective was to test whether there is any significant effect of the "known/not" criterion on the sample of the six chats ("PoW-wows"). To this end, we started by computing, through descriptive statistics, the distribution of frequencies in different dimensions (conversation, social reference, problem solving, math move and system support) for the six PoW-wows; we used Means and ANOVA to test the existence of significant differences due to the known/not criterion. The study showed that there was no such effect, at the usual confidence level of 95% (in fact, significance in differences, that is significant pairs, were not noticed even at a 90% confidence level). The fact that there is no clear effect of the criteria known/not prompts us to conclude that the classification of the sample of PoW-wows into groups according to the known/not criterion is not relevant. We could also observe this by computing the box-plot representation of the variables under study (see Fig. 23.1).

Given the above finding, we refined the statistical analysis by looking at the correlation between vectors of values of the six PoW-wows—we continued to group by "known in advance"/"not known in advance" just for visual effect. By computing similarities between the PoW-wows we could see which PoW-wows are similar to each other and which are different from each other. We computed the correlations (Pearson correlations) in the proximity matrix shown in Table 23.2.

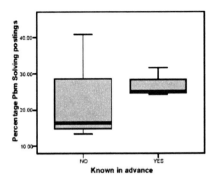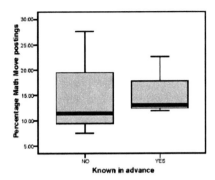

Fig. 23.1 Box-plots of problem-solving and math-move dimensions

Table 23.2 Pearson correlation of vector values of 6 PoW-wows

	Pow1: Not	Pow2a: Not	Pow2b: Not	Pow9: Known	Pow10: Known	Pow18: Known
Pow1: Not	1.000	0.756	−0.452	0.567	0.108	−0.197
Pow2a: Not	0.756	1.000	−0.219	0.912	0.603	0.067
Pow2b: Not	−0.452	−0.219	1.000	0.202	0.620	−0.956
Pow9: Known	0.567	0.912	0.202	1.000	0.867	−0.470
Pow10: Known	0.108	0.603	0.620	0.867	1.000	0.791
Pow18: Known	−0.197	0.067	0.956	0.470	0.791	1.000

From Table 23.2 we observe the following:

- Pow2b (Not) is negatively correlated to the other two PoW-wows of the Not group (Pow1 and Pow2a) and positively correlated to the PoW-wows of the Known group (Pow9, Pow10, Pow18). Moreover, significant correlations of Pow2b (Not) with Pow10 (Known) and Pow18 (Known) are observed and a non-significant correlation with Pow9 (Known).
- There is a significant positive correlation of Pow9 with Pow1 and Pow2a of the Not group. In pair-wise terms, Pow9 is more correlated to the PoW-wows of the Not group than to the PoW-wows of its own Known group.
- There are some pairs of PoW-wows positively and strongly correlated, namely (Pow2a, Pow9) and (Pow2b, Pow18) which suggest taking a closer study of the possible common features of these PoW-wows.

The previous observations on the correlations between PoW-wows from different groups not only support the claim that there is no significant effect of the known/not criterion, but also shed light on the reason why these two groups are not really separated. Indeed, the negative correlation of Pow2b with the PoW-wows of the

Not group shows that its place is not in the Not group. Even more, its positive correlation with the PoW-wows of the Known group indicates that this PoW-wow is better grouped with the PoW-wows of the Known group.

In our next step, we decided to exclude the system-support dimension from the analysis; indeed, this dimension is less relevant in the context of the interaction analysis, and could have introduced some noise in the analysis. We ran the statistical computations again by re-computing the correlations in the proximity matrix shown in Table 23.3.

Table 23.3 Pearson correlations with system support excluded

	Pow1: Not	Pow2a: Not	Pow2b: Not	Pow9: Known	Pow10: Known	Pow18: Known
Pow1: Not	1.000	0.999	−0.427	0.868	0.376	−0.145
Pow2a: Not	0.999	1.000	−0.396	0.884	0.407	−0.112
Pow2b: Not	−0.427	−0.396	1.000	0.080	0.678	−0.957
Pow9: Known	0.868	0.884	0.080	1.000	0.787	−0.366
Pow10: Known	0.376	0.407	0.678	0.787	1.000	0.862
Pow18: Known	−0.145	−0.112	0.957	0.366	0.862	1.000

By excluding the system-support dimension, we observe a clear effect on the correlations, namely:

- On the one hand, an increased negative correlation of Pow2b (Not) with the other PoW-wows of its group (Pow1 and Pow2a) is now observed. Notice also that the correlation between Pow1 and Pow2a is almost a perfect correlation. On the other hand, an increased positive correlation of Pow2b (Not) with the PoW-wows of the other group (Pow9, Pow10, Pow18) is observed. Interestingly, Pow2b is now less correlated to Pow9 (Known).
- An increased positive correlation of Pow9 with the PoW-wows of the Not group (Pow1 and Pow2a) is now observed. Moreover, we observe a decrease in its correlation with Pow10 and Pow18.
- Finally, Pow18 is now negatively correlated to both Pow1 and Pow2a.

We repeated the above computations by standardizing the variable values by z-score, as shown in Table 23.4.

Table 23.4 Proximity matrix

	Pow1: C1	Pow2a: C1	Pow2b: C2	Pow9: C1	Pow10: C2	Pow18: C2
Pow1: C1	1.000	0.987	−0.999	0.869	−0.921	−0.993
Pow2a: C1	0.987	1.000	−0.977	0.778	−0.845	−0.999
Pow2b: C2	−0.999	−0.977	1.000	−0.894	0.939	0.986
Pow9: C1	0.869	0.778	−0.894	1.000	−0.993	−0.808
Pow10: C2	−0.921	−0.845	0.939	−0.993	1.000	0.870
Pow18: C2	−0.993	−0.999	0.986	−0.808	0.870	1.000

According to the statistical computations indicated in Table 23.4, the PoW-wows fall into the following two clusters:

- Cluster 1: Pow1, Pow2a, Pow9
- Cluster 2: Pow2b, Pow10, Pow18

By re-computing the box-plot representation of this new clustering we can observe the significant separation between variables under study for the two groups (see Fig. 23.2).

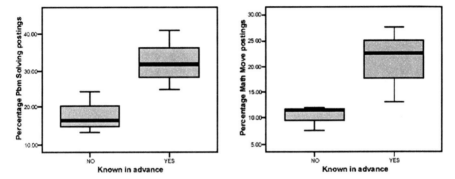

Fig. 23.2 Box-plots of problem-solving and math-move dimensions

In other words, we expected the chat logs to be clustered based on the idea that in some chats, participants had access to the problem prior to their participation in the chat, while in other chats, participants had no access to the problem. However, the statistical analysis demonstrated that the clustering of chats was organized according to some other basis. At this point, we determined to conduct a qualitative approach to identify the reasons for this alternative organization of the online chats.

The Conversation Analysis

To discover possible reasons for the failure of our initial hypothesis that the six PoW-wows would fall into two clusters based on the Known/Not criterion, we re-examined the chats using CA. We decided to see if we could find a difference in participation frameworks organized by the students in the two clusters. For this approach, we examined logs of the online chats to identify participants' perspectives on their own actions, with an eye to describing their actions as sense-making procedures by which they distinctively organized their interactions and their participations in the chats.

The work of conversation analysis involves close inspection of interactional data. In conventional face-to-face interaction, this involves inspecting video and audio recordings of interaction (including non-verbal glances, gestures, facial expressions and bodily orientations, as well as verbal hesitations, repeats, silences, intonation, etc.). When it comes to online chats, the data inspected are just the textual logs of the chats, which display the text postings of participants, the participant's handle (login name) and the time stamp associated with each posting.

The object of inquiry in conversation analysis is not exclusively conversation per se, but rather talk and social interaction. Thus, as Ten Have describes it, "CA's interest is with the local production of [social] order and with 'members' methods' for doing so" (1999, p.19). As Psathas writes,

> Conversation analysis studies the order/organization/orderliness of social action, particularly those social actions that are located in everyday interaction, in discursive practices, in the sayings/tellings/doings of members of society. (Psathas, 1995, p. 2)

Using the methods of CA, we began to notice that the organization of social order in these chats could be differentiated according to the way that participants oriented to the production of problem solutions. In particular, we noticed that, in some circumstances, participants reported on work they had already completed, whether it was work done prior to the chat or work done offline and without the participation of others in the production of that work during a chat. This organization of participation we have termed "expository" participation. On the other hand, we noticed that there were circumstances in which participants engaged each other (as a group) both in the investigation of the problem and in the production of possible solutions. This organization of participation we termed "exploratory" participation.

Expository participation in the chats we examined involved one actor producing a report as an extended narrative of an activity performed by that actor. Such reporting is designed to project recipient participation in terms of the production of assessments of the report or the reported work. Recipients of that report have not participated in the work being reported. The report is designed and presented either as an already achieved understanding of the problem in terms of a candidate solution or as steps anyone with appropriate understanding of the problem might take to produce a solution.

One version of expository participation is where one actor first announces that a solution has been achieved and then, upon prompting from recipients, proceeds to tell recipients what the solution is and how he or she produced the candidate solution. For example, in the chat excerpt from Pow2b reproduced in Log 23-1, the student named AH3 reports: "**I think I have the solution!**" This calls upon the recipients of this message (the other students in the math team) to solicit the result. REA asks "**what**" the solution is that AH3 found. To this solicitation, AH3 offers, "**The solution is sqrt(74)**." Announcing a result makes it relevant for recipients to ask for an explanation. REA then asks "**how**" AH3 arrived at that solution. Explanations might be offered in ways that describe the production of the solution as having been already achieved by the actor reporting the result, as in, "**First I did ... and then I computed ... which equals ...**" Another way to produce an explanation involves the circumstance where an actor describes how a competent person would go about solving the problem, as in "**First you do ... then you compute ... which equals ...**" In this regard, these approaches to the exposition of a problem's solution is much like the telling of a story (see, e.g., Sacks, 1962/1995). AH3's exposition, consisting of a series of seven uninterrupted postings (34–40) points his teammates to a formula given on a Math Forum site as a resource needed for understanding his solution to the problem. In school math, the whole trick of solving a problem is often selecting the standard formula to apply. The expository character of the chat consists of exchanges like announcement/solicitation, solicitation/report, report/question, question/explanation, which drive the group interaction, along with extended turns being granted to the expositor without undue interruption from the rest of the group.

Log 23-1.

24	AH3	I think I have the solution!
25	REA	what
26	MCP	I guess 15
27	REA	k
28	MCP	I think it's like the Pythagorean idea, applying to triangles.
29	AH3	sqrt(5^2 + 7^2) = sqrt(74)
30	MCP	Yes, 30-60-90 is needed fact
31	AH3	The solution is sqrt(74)
32	REA	how
33	MCP	7?
34	AH3	Go to...
35	AH3	http://mathforum.org/dr.math/faq/formulas/faq.triangle.html
36	AH3	Under scalene triangle, the formula for the area of any triangle is...
37	AH3	K = a^2 * sin(B) * sin(C)/[2 sin (A)]
38	AH3	Why is that smiley their
39	AH3	K = a^2 * sin(B)* sin(C)/[2 sin (A)]
40	AH3	Where a = an edgelength of an isosceles triangle

An expository report is a way that an actor constitutes a problem as solvable. This characterization can be supported because there is evidence in the transcripts that actors themselves orient to these reports in just this way. For example, the actor producing the report treats the problem as having already been solved and thereby constitutes a participation framework in which he or she acts in the manner of an instructor, explaining what is already known by the instructor to an audience that presumably does not yet know. Constituting such a participation framework is a delicate business in the conduct of these chats—partially because within a peer group it positions the explainer as an authority and the others as lacking knowledge. To do so, actors often draw upon the resources of news reporting by indicating they have something newsworthy to report, i.e., the solution to the problem. In other words, it is not that they possess knowledge that makes them superior, but that they have discovered something and are just pointing it out to others. The actor reporting the solution designs his or her report in a way that allows the recipients of the report to "discover" for themselves in the report how the problem can be seen as solvable and solved. Thus, e.g., AH3 just points the others to a resource that is available to all and allows them to work out the solution themselves to compare with the result that AH3 had discovered in the same way.

Exploratory participation, on the other hand, is a more explicitly egalitarian peer process. It involves group participation patterns in which actors interact so as to constitute, in and as their chat, an understanding of a problem in terms of the conjoint (group) production of possible organizations of mathematical activity from which a solution could be achieved. In such circumstances, actors use the resources afforded them by their interaction to constitute the math problem and their understanding of that problem as an emergent sequence of possible and/or achieved math activities designed to produce what may come to be subsequently recognizable and treated as a solution to the problem. If expository participation is a form of "news" reporting, then the distinguishing feature of exploratory participation is that the actors themselves are constituting the "news" as their ongoing interaction rather than reporting it and receiving the report.

Actors engage in exploration by identifying and offering candidate formulations of the problem and possible solutions by constituting and drawing on resources, which are distributed among participants and which are made available by actors' participation in the chat. Like expository participation, the work of exploratory participation also constitutes the problem in terms of its solution, but with exploratory participation neither the solution nor the problem itself are treated as settled matters by participants. Exploratory interactions involve putting forward proposals for consideration and assessment, negotiating ways of formulating the problem in terms of different solution strategies, soliciting resources, candidate solutions, versions of the problem and so on from other participants. Thus the work of exploration often involves articulating alternative provisional versions of the problem in terms of the development, presentation and assessment of possible knowables, as well as alternative possible solutions for the purpose of identifying a problem participants can work on. This is shown in Log 23-2, excerpted from Pow10.

Log 23-2.

47	GOR	what's the question
48	PIN	how long is CE
49	PIN	well isnt AB proportional to DE
50	REA	maybe
51	GOR	what's the question
52	REA	are the two similar
53	REA	and how
54	PIN	maybe by Angle Angle
55	PIN	angle C by reflexive
56	MUR	please refer to http://mathforum.org/pow/vmt/feb1204/ problem.html for the question GOR.
57	PIN	and then angle A is congruent to angle D
58	REA	hold up
59	PIN	becuase corresponding angles congruent?
60	PIN	if lines are parallel, corresponding angles are congruent
61	REA	true
62	GOR	what's BC

Log 23-2 (countinued)

63	PIN	doesnt say
64	PIN	well look, we know the 2 triangles are similar
65	PIN	lets see if we can do anything from that
66	REA	lte's say y is DC
67	REA	and x is CE
68	REA	so if similar ; 5/8= y/AC= x/BC
69	REA	it is proportional
70	PIN	yep
71	GOR	there's two variables
72	REA	yes there is
73	GOR	so what are we going to do now
74	REA	That means 2 or more equations
75	PIN	ya
76		<GOR has left the room.>
77	REA	PIN
78	PIN	ya
79	REA	I have the idea of solving the question
80	PIN	what ya thinkin?
81	REA	If we some how get angle b congruent to angle c. Then triangle DCE is isosceles
82	REA	so if DE is 5
83	REA	then CE has to be five
84	REA	This could include sin, cos, and tan
85	PIN	im thinking that we have to use the other info they gave us
86	PIN	abotu the bisector
87	PIN	some how
88	PIN	cuz then why else would they put it?

In this segment, actors are producing what they themselves take to be incremental displays of both the problem and candidate solution steps as proposals to be taken up and assessed by others for how they might contribute to the production of a solution. In such circumstances, participants' postings constitute their epistemic stance with respect to the material presented. Epistemic stance displays the participants' orientation to the "truth" value of the propositions being put forward. Actors often use explicit markers like "**I think that** ...," or "**It could be that** ...," etc., as a way of producing mitigated or less that fully committed positions concerning their degree of certainty with respect to propositions they put forward in interaction. However, explicit markers are not always required, especially if the participation of recipients of a proposition is organized in ways that make them responsible, at least in part, for determining the appropriate epistemic stance to take with respect to the posting.

In this example, GOR is a latecomer to the interaction and is soliciting a version of the problem from participants (lines 47 and 51). The moderator, MUR, refers this participant to an online location where the problem statement can be found. In the meantime, PIN and REA engage in an exploration of possible approaches to the solution to the problem (lines 48–50; lines 52–61; lines 64–75). At line 79 REA announces that she might have a solution strategy. This was put forward as a possibility for consideration and assessment, not as an account of previously achieved accomplishment. This description is produced specifically to display to PIN that (a) the status of REA's candidate solution is less than certain (Kärkkäinen, 2003; Pomerantz, 1984), and (b) that PIN is called on to assess the epistemic status of the proposal. PIN's response at lines 85–88 suggests that some of the information provided in the problem statement constitutes a resource that must be considered and incorporated into any solution approach they might derive. The mere fact of the presence of the information in the problem description in the first place provides for its relevance as part of the solution. This contrasts with an expository approach where the speaker would not propose but rather would *report on* a solution step in a way that did not require the participation of others in the interaction to affirm the certainty with which it is presented. Actors' participation and the way they constitute their propositions in the ongoing interaction are thus fundamentally different between expository and exploratory organizations of interaction.

It is important to note that expository and exploratory work may be done during the same chat. Furthermore, expository participation requires that the expositor did the work of producing a solution "offline," i.e., without the participation of other actors in the chat. One of the affordances of chat is that such "offline" activities are possible even as a chat is occurring. Participants only have access to the messages that are posted. An actor's work with a pencil and a pad of paper beside his or her computer is not available to others unless and until it is posted in the chat system for others to inspect and assess.

Solving the Puzzle

By examining the PoW-wow chats, we were able to see that there were qualitatively significant differences in the way participation was organized. Despite the fact that actors in Pow2b had not seen the problem in advance of their chat, they did their work "offline" during the chat and displayed an expository organization of participation—in common with Pow10 and Pow18. Despite the fact that the actors in Pow9 had access to the problem in advance of the chat, they displayed an exploratory organization of participation—in common with Pow1 and Pow2a. Thus, using CA, we were able to identify the same correlation among the PoW-wows discovered by the statistical analysis. Moreover, whereas the clustering of the PoW-wows flew in the face of the statistical hypothesis, the conversation analysis provided a clear explanation of the clustering in terms of the organization of participation in the chats.

Once we solved the puzzle that emerged from the statistical analysis, we considered whether or not our coding scheme could have been used to identify these different organizations of participation—through a different analysis. We decided that it would not have been possible. The primary reason for this decision was that the existing coding scheme treated the individual posts as the primary units of analysis. Codes applied to individual chat postings could not be used to characterize larger sequences of postings. This made it impossible to analytically identify the organization of participation, understood as a relation among groupings of posted chat messages.

While an alternative coding scheme defined at a different unit of analysis might have made an analysis of exploratory vs. expository organization possible, it would have raised a logical problem of consistency: that the use of coding schemes is generally conducted in ways that lend themselves to finding things for which there are codes. That is, to distinguish exploratory from expository chats, we would have to design codes for characteristic features of these chat forms. We concluded that if we want to understand how participants organize their participation—if we want to understand a sequence of actions from the participants' perspectives—then the coding scheme would need to capture these perspectives rather than a preconceived (a priori) perspective or interest of the researcher.

While we found coding problematic from a CA perspective, we recognized the need for quantitative measures for certain kinds of important claims that we would like to be able to make. According to Heritage and Roth (1995) practitioners of CA have often made informal distributional claims with respect to observed interactional phenomena—e.g., that certain methods of accomplishing interactional tasks are typical, at least within specific linguistic communities. However, questions about the typicality or distribution of certain features of interactions of a particular type can ultimately only be measured quantitatively. We need a way to classify (code) interactions (at some appropriate unit of analysis) so that they can be counted and compared to similar counts from contrasting sets of interactions. In such cases, questions arise as to the appropriate way to code data such that the requirements of valid statistical and quantitative analysis can be met without violating the requirements of preserving the participants' perspectives on the sequential organization that they create in their unfolding action. In order to determine whether our qualitative results provide an adequate explanation across multiple cases, we need to re-specify a coding scheme that derives from the perspective of the participants, as observed in our logs (for further discussion, see Heritage & Roth, 1995; Kaplan, 1964).

As explained in the remainder of this chapter, we have begun to explore an approach to coding, based on the ways that interactants organize themselves and their interaction into recognizable activities. This approach uses CA methods to identify closings and openings of action sequences, by which participants organize their activities into "long sequences" (Sacks, 1962/1995) of identifiable action types. For example, we have begun to identify sequences in which math problem-solving activities are being conducted, as distinct from various other kinds of non-math social interaction. In this way, we are developing a coding scheme that preserves actors' orientations, concerns, relevancies and their sequential organization of the ongoing interaction. This proposed approach to coding makes possible the comparison of different instances of social interaction in ways that preserve the participants' organization of interaction and exploit that local organization as a source of insight into the ways we come to treat action sequences as sequences of particular sorts.

A CA Approach to Coding

In conducting inquiry into matters of collaboration, learning and instruction, the analyst is confronted with a range of methodological and assumptive commitments that shape the nature of the research performed and the kinds of claims that can be sustained by that research. In examining the early VMT chats, we considered how best to begin asking relevant questions from a CA perspective. For example, we were concerned with questions such as, "What are the chat participants *doing* in these chats?" "Are their chats collaborative and, if so, *what* makes their chats collaborative?" "How do these students *organize* their interactions?" "How do these students *do* math in an online environment?" "Are there similarities and differences in the way these chats are *done*?" The rest of this chapter represents our effort to conduct an analysis based on assumptions from the CA perspective about human action, social interaction, collaboration and communication.

In this research, we have begun to develop a CA-informed alternative to classical SA coding. Our approach is based on ethnomethodological assumptions regarding sense making, action and the competence of participants. The main difference between the two approaches consists in the definition of the "unit of analysis": while in the SA approach the unit of analysis is chosen by the analyst (usually a unit of fixed length or a posting), in the CA approach it is identified according to the participants' perspective within the interactional situation.

Since postings are authored and contributed by each participant, one can argue that selecting individual postings as the unit of analysis is not an arbitrary choice imposed by the researcher on the data. Indeed, at first glance this seems to be a natural choice, which is compatible with the participants' perspective. However, the arbitrariness of this choice becomes clear when one thinks about the interactional work that each posting is designed to accomplish in chat. The quasi-synchronous nature of the environment and the fact that one needs to type his/her contributions encourages participants to interact with each other in particular ways in a chat environment. Participants are pressed to quickly submit multiple short texts in order to post their contributions at relevant points. Due to this characteristic of the chat interface, it is often the case that only a combination of postings constitutes a coherent turn or activity. More importantly, an individual post is essentially situated within the larger context, in which it must be understood as a response to previous activities or at least to the possibilities opened up by them. It must also be seen as a solicitation of responses and follow-ups, or at least as a text designed to be understood by other participants, who may be expected to then express their comprehension or lack thereof. Thus, as far as an analytical effort that aims to study the organization of collaborative activities in a chat environment is concerned, considering a single posting as the unit of analysis without making any claim about its relationship to other activities would be a premature choice.

We used CA methods to identify how the chat participants themselves organized their interaction into "long sequences" (Sacks, 1962/1995) or, as we call them, "chunks" of activity. The VMT research team engaged in numerous data sessions to identify those locations in the chat where new activities were initiated and where ongoing activities were suspended or brought to some kind of closure. In so doing, we were able to identify activity sequences to which the participants themselves visibly oriented. An activity sequence in this sense is a set of postings that are highly connected in terms of their response structure and that work together to accomplish some coherent activity that can be observed (by the participants and the analysts) in the design of the postings as the focus of the postings. For instance, the explicit and implicit indexical references of the postings tie the individual postings together as contributions to the activity. We then assigned labels to these activity sequences based on the way the participants themselves oriented to, conducted and regulated their actions in these activity sequences. In so doing, we were able to identify how participants themselves managed the sequential organization of their math problem-solving chats. We were also able to apply our labeling schemes across the six different chats discussed in the beginning of this chapter (see Table 23.1), making it possible for us to begin to compare how these chats were organized.

We base our approach on the presumption that the sequential organization of the interaction is the basis by which participants and observers alike make sense of the online collaborative activity of a small group of participants. We call this approach "participant-centered analysis." The basic idea is that the perspective of the participants and the work they do to make sense of their own actions provides the ground for organizing their interactional work into coherent long sequences or chunks of activity. By incorporating participants' perspectives and trying to get a sense of the organization of their activity in terms of the ways they themselves achieve that organization, we hope to demonstrate that it is possible to begin to do quantitative analysis in ways that do not elevate the analyst or privilege the analyst's perspective over the perspectives of the participants. We firmly hold that the sense and coherence of interaction is locally produced for and by the participants in that interaction. This suggests that the analyst's role is not to impose an external sense-making structure based on some theoretical interests of the analyst on observed activity but to allow the participants' own sense-making work to become evident and to allow that sense-making work to reveal itself in the coherent ways that ongoing action is organized and produced.

Though our approach differs substantially from the classical SA approaches, there are some similarities such as the use of labeling/codes and a sort of multilevel approach. It is worth mentioning here that ours is a top-down approach, starting from "high"-level activities in which the participants engaged, to the most detailed levels of interaction shown/found in the data—beyond the level of the posting to individual lexical, syntactical and indexical features. In contrast, in classical coding the multilevel approach is done in a bottom-up fashion (from a single posting to groups of postings representing "activities"), in order to look at the distributions of the codes, and consider aggregations and vector representations derived from these values to do hypothesis testing and comparisons. Because our CA approach takes this top-down view, we do not *reconstruct* the activities—as it is done in the classical SA approach—but use the organization of activities achieved by the participants themselves as a way of conducting analysis. Although there are some SA studies that focus on the sequential relationships between codes to make claims about the type of the ongoing activity at certain episodes (e.g., whether a given episode is an effective knowledge-sharing episode), they usually assume a simple linear ordering of short sequences of postings (e.g., Soller & Lesgold, 2003).

Long Sequences

While most CA research examines very short sequences of interaction (such as adjacency pairs and their elaborations), long sequences have also been matters of concern for conversation analysts. Sacks (1962/1995) devoted a lecture to long sequences and remarked:

> A basic sort of investigation is that of long sequences as a coherent matter as compared to simply studying utterance by utterance, a long sequence which you then have as an in-some-way connected series of small fragments. And such investigation is, if it's going to develop at all, at a rather primitive stage—leaving aside obvious sorts of things where you're dealing with relatively game-like situations or other sorts of known, pre-organized matters. The sequences we're dealing with are not pre-organized. (Vol. II, p. 355)

As Sacks noted, conversation analysts have developed an extensive body of research regarding the observable regularities, those "series of small fragments" that are produced in the conversations they constitute. But the issue of long sequences, packages or chunks is of a different order. Sacks recognized that chunks were not simply assemblies of smaller sequences:

> Certain aspects of the work you might do on a small sequence won't do you any good in trying to package longer sequences. Indeed, they might be misguiding in that you would figure that you've dealt with some pair in some fashion, and even in a sequential fashion, and thereby not see the potentiality for building a larger package for which the way you had studied the smaller sequence didn't have much bearing, or had only some relatively intricate bearing. (Vol. II, p. 354)

In fact, the classical object of conversation analytic interest, i.e., the conversation, is actually a gloss for a kind of long sequence of social interaction involving something like informal talk, i.e., multi-turn, multi-participant interactions that are not pre-organized, that are composed of sequences of talk, gesture and other forms of embodied action, and that are built to be and treated as coherent by the participants who produce them (Schegloff, 1990). Recent work has also begun to investigate features of other kinds of long sequences like the medical interview (Maynard, 2003), negotiations (Firth, 1995), talk at work (Boden, 1995; Suchman, 1987) and different organizations of institutional discourse (Drew & Heritage, 1993). These studies all treat long sequences as locally situated and contingent achievements that are organized and produced in ways that allow participants to treat their participation in them as participation in ongoing and contingently coherent activity.

Among the regularities observed and studied by conversation analysts are the ways that long sequences begin and end. For example, participants in conversations engage in recognizable boundary-producing activities to which participants orient and by which participants initiate conversations and bring them to a close. These are referred to in the literature as *openings* and *closings* (Schegloff & Sacks, 1973; Schegloff, 1968). These kinds of activities are also used within conversations as ways that participants display to each other that some activity in which they had been engaged is completed or suspended and another is starting. As such, they serve to mark something like boundaries between long sequences in an ongoing interaction and allow participants a wide range of opportunities to manage, regulate and build their interaction to become coherent stretches of lengthy activities.

Upon close examination of the VMT PoW-wow chat transcripts, it became apparent that the participants themselves were orienting to and organizing their participation in the chats in terms of long sequences of interaction that extended beyond conventional conversation analytic notions of the turn and the adjacency pair (Schegloff, 1990). Participants organized their interaction into longer sequences, sequences that were coherent by virtue of their sequential organization, by virtue of the fact that "participants are oriented to finding coherence'if they can'" (p. 73). According to Schegloff, the coherence of these long sequences is a structural feature of the way they are opened, expanded and closed.

As a practical analytical matter, we began with the following noticings in order to identify these longer sequences in the chats. First, the chats were of finite duration; they had identifiable beginnings and endings, which the participants themselves performed and to which they oriented as relevant in the conduct of their chat. In addition, participants appeared to organize their interaction into long sequences in which they attended to the math problem, worked out problems associated with the distribution of geometric figures to other chat participants, dealt with problems associated with the chat technology itself, and engaged each other with respect to matters other than the math problem they were discussing.

These noticings led us to consider how we might be able to distinguish among these long sequences or chunks of activity across a number of different chats to see what, if any, similarities or differences there might be in the way that chats were organized by the participants themselves. To achieve this, we first elected to use CA methods to identify actions such as openings and closings of various sorts that indicated participants were initiating, suspending and/or closing a sequence or chunk of activity. This allowed us to identify coherent long sequences of activity based on participants' own methods of organizing their activities. We then created a participant-centered coding scheme by assigning labels to the chunks of activity we identified, producing what effectively might be termed a data dictionary. Finally, we were able to develop visual representations of these chunks of activity and draw certain conclusions based on this participant-centered coding scheme.

Identifying Long Sequence Boundaries

The approach we are developing in this research is a form of participant-centered analysis (PCA). PCA involves identifying and working with those features of social interaction that the participants find relevant and to which the participants orient in their ongoing participation in the social interaction. To do this, we inspected six transcripts of the VMT PoW-wow chats in detail using CA methods to identify how the participants in the activity had organized their activity. One way we did this is to identify openings and closings by which participants either (1) bring one activity to a close and initiate another activity or (2) suspend an ongoing activity and initiate a new activity. In Log 23-3 from Pow2M (referred to as Pow2b earlier), we see two such transitions. One begins at lines 10 and 11, and the other begins at lines 21–23.

Log 23-3.

5	MUR	Hi. Thanks for participating in our PoW-Wow. For privacy reasons, we're asking that you don't share any personal information about yourself, such as your name, age, or where you live.
6	MUR	Let's go around and have everyone share a greeting with the group. I'll start by saying that I'm really looking forward to seeing you talk about math tonight!
7	AH3	Hello everyone
8	REA	Hi
9	MCP	Hi! Last time was fun, and I look forward to this - -
10	REA	I remember you MCP
11	MUR	OK, here are four guidelines that we'll use tonight.
12	MUR	1. During the session, share ideas about how to solve the problem.
13	MUR	2. Feel free to ask about anything that seems unclear.
14	MUR	3. If you all think the problem is solved please make sure everyone in the group understands the explanation for the answer.
15	MUR	4. I'm here if you have any technical problems or questions, but I won't help with the math.
16	MUR	Here's the problem that you'll be working on tonight:
17	REA	where is the problem
18	MUR	If two equilateral triangles have edgelengths of 9 cubits and 12 cubits, what's the edgelength of the equilateral triangle whose area is equal to the sum of the areas of the other two?
19	MUR	You can also read the problem at http://mathforum.org/pow/vmt/feb2604/problem.html
20	MUR	Good luck:-)
21	MUR	By the way, if you create a picture that you would like to share with your group, there are instructions on the problem page about how to do that.
22	MCP	Probably a straight area compute. B4 I do it, I want to guess, ok?
23	REA	Have any of you guys learend of the 30-60-90 concept
24	AH3	I think I have the solution!
25	REA	what
26	MCP	I guess 15
27	REA	k

Upon examining this fragment of the transcript, it became evident that the posting at line 11 was designed to do two things: initiate a new activity and close down the prior activity. In particular, the use of the particle "**OK**" in line 11 is specifically designed to indicate both an opening and a closing (Beach, 1993; Condon, 2001). In this usage, "**OK**" is a transition marker designed to indicate that a new (and as yet unspecified) activity is about to be initiated. In so doing, it also serves to bring to a close the prior interaction.

Another transitional moment occurred at lines 21–23. In particular, line 22 displays uptake by a student of the problem identified in the previous set of instructions and marks the close of the sequence of instructions for doing the problem (lines 11–21), which are provided by the facilitator, MUR. This uptake is affirmed by REA's subsequent post (line 23), in which he addresses a problem-relevant question to other participants. Thus, for our purposes, we did not consider the "content" of MUR's posted messages in lines 11–21 to identify it as a long sequence or "chunk of activity." What makes this segment a chunk is the fact that it has a discernable opening produced and taken up by the participants and a discernable closing, which is also produced and taken up by the participants.

One of the features of chats is that strict adherence to conversational turn taking is problematic for participants (see Chapter 21). Thus, it is often the case that a person produces a post that is in response to some prior post other than the immediately prior post. This is an artifact of chat technology, which makes it possible for two different activity sequences to be "interleaved," as Log 23-4 from Pow1 demonstrates.

Log 23-4.

81	REA	If we some how get angle b congruent to angle c. Then triangle DCE is isoceles
82	REA	so if DE is 5
83	REA	then CE has to be five
84	REA	This could include sin, cos, and tan
85	PIN	im thinking that we have to use the other info they gave us
86	PIN	abotu the bisector
87	PIN	some how
88	PIN	cuz then why else would they put it?
89	REA	two ideas
90	MUR	We have a new participant who wants to join you. Do you mind?
91	PIN	fine w/ me
92	REA	tnope
93	REA	nope
94		<MCP has entered the room>
95	REA	never mind about the two ideas
96	PIN	k
97	MUR	Hi MCP. Could you guys help MCP to catch up?
98	PIN	sure
99	REA	k
100	MCP	I just read the prob and got a diagram.

Prior to line 90, student participants had been working on finding a solution to the math problem on which they were working in this chat. In lines 85–88, PIN had problematized "**the other info**" made available in the problem in a particular way. PIN's remarks were designed to make questionable to and for other student participants what could serve as an adequate account for the availability of that "**other**" information in the first place. REA responded to PIN's solicitation of an account with a prefatory posting at line 89 that indicated that a subsequent expansion of what those "**two ideas**" were would be forthcoming as a next set of postings from REA.

One of the features of this chat is that work on the math problem was done by students. The facilitator served only to regulate certain aspects of their interaction (i.e., introduce newcomers to the chat) and attend to technical questions (i.e., methods for disseminating drawings of the problem to chat participants). So, when the facilitator announced that there was another participant who wanted to join the chat at line 90, the very appearance of a post from the facilitator indicated that something other than the problem-solving work the students had been engaged in was about to begin. MUR's posting at line 90 calls on participants to suspend their ongoing work on the problem and to indicate their willingness to accept a newcomer to the chat. PIN and REA indicated their willingness in lines 91 through 93.

Line 94 is a system-generated message indicating that the new participant, MCP, had entered the chat room. At this point, REA posts a message, the sense of which is derived from the problem-solving work they were doing immediately prior to MUR's intervention at line 90. Specifically, REA proposes to close the prior discussion of reasons for the additional (and as yet apparently unused) information provided in the problem statement at line 95. PIN accepts this proposal at line 96, bringing to a close (at least for the moment) any further consideration of the problem. This is followed almost immediately (after one second) by a greeting from MUR and by MUR's request that the other students bring MCP current with their work on the problem. Thus, we see that interleaved in MUR's opening intervention is work done by student participants that is relevant to closing the problem-solving work in which they had been engaged prior to the intervention.

The Data Dictionary and Long Sequences

The preceding instances serve as examples of the way that CA methods were applied to identify boundaries between long sequences. The next step was to apply these methods to the six chat transcripts and to identify those postings belonging to each of the long sequences that formed the chat. We derived a set of descriptive labels for the long sequences, which served as a provisional data dictionary for this first level of long sequence analysis. These are shown in Table 23.5.

The labels we applied to the sequences were designed as provisional and defeasible shorthand descriptions of the activity performed in the sequence. Other descriptors are certainly possible, but these seemed to be adequate for our purpose of

Table 23.5 Data dictionary

Code	Explanation
STARTCHAT	STARTING THE CHAT
FACLn	FACILITATOR GIVES INSTRUCTIONS, NUMBER n
PBn	PROBLEM-SOLVING SEQUENCE, NUMBER n
PICn	SEQUENCE INVOLVING POSTING OF PICTURES, NUMBER n
CATCHn	PARTICIPANTS WORK TO ALLOW ANOTHER TO CATCH UP WITH THE WORK THAT HAS BEEN DONE, NUMBER n
SOCn	SOCIALIZING SEQUENCE, NUMBER n
SERVICEn	SEQUENCE CONCERNING MATHFORUM SERVICES, NUMBER n
ENDCHATn	SEQUENCE TO END CHAT, NUMBER n
LOSTn	STUDENTS DEALING WITH PARTICIPANT WHO IS LOST, NUMBER n
ASKHELPn	STUDENTS REQUEST MATH HELP FROM FACILITATOR, NUMBER n
NEWMEM	NEW MEMBER JOINS THE CHAT
QUIT	STUDENT QUITS FROM CHAT
TECH_PBn	ADDRESSING A TECHNICAL PROBLEM WITH THE CHAT, NUMBER n
PAUSE	PARTICIPANT TEMPORARILY SUSPENDS PARTICIPATION IN THE CHAT
SYSMESSAGE	MESSAGE PRODUCED BY CHAT SYSTEM
SYSBREAK	TECHNICAL BREAKDOWN OF CHAT SYSTEM
CH_GP_STATn	CHECKING THAT ALL PARTICIPANTS UNDERSTAND WHAT IS GOING ON, NUMBER n
CH_W_FACn	SEEKING ASSESSMENT OF RESULTS FROM FACILITATOR, NUMBER n
PB_W_FACn	DOING PROBLEM-SOLVING WITH THE FACILITATOR, NUMBER n
RES	PARTICIPANT PRODUCES ACCOUNT OF ACTION

characterizing sequences in terms of what the participants were doing in them. Each long sequence is often composed of smaller sequences, which may be quite long in their own right. For example, doing problem solving involves a number of activities, all of which were grouped together to form our problem-solving sequences.

Graphical and Statistical Analyses

We distinguished our sequences according to the way that participants themselves brought them to a close or temporarily suspended their participation in them and initiated activities that were not related to the work done in that sequence. This allowed us to produce graphical representations of the chats, which showed the sequential organization of the chats in terms of the long sequences of which they were composed. These are shown in Figs. 23.3 through 23.8. A number of interesting results emerged from the various descriptive statistics available for these chats. For

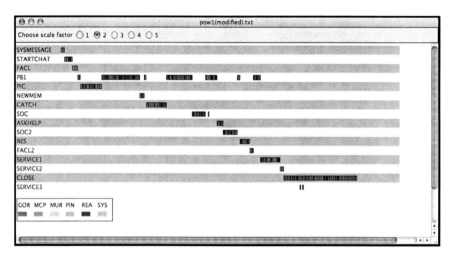

Fig. 23.3 Pow1

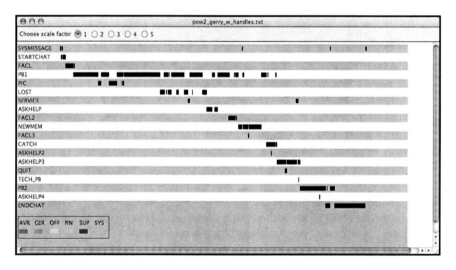

Fig. 23.4 Pow2G (referred to as Pow2A earlier)

example, it is evident from these graphs (rows labeled PB1, PB2, PB3 or PB4) that participants in collaborative problem-solving chats spend a considerable amount of time actually engaged in problem-solving activities.

Individual participants are listed with color codes in the figures (as in Pow1, Fig. 23.3). If the chats were lengthy (as in Pow2G, Fig. 23.4), a scale factor was used to condense the display, which merged individual contributions, making it impossible to represent with colors the participation in the sequences we identified.

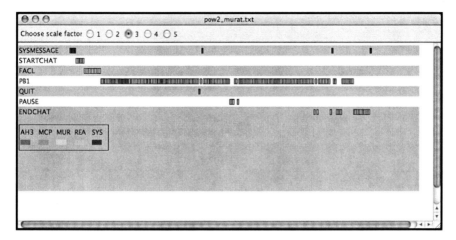

Fig. 23.5 Pow2M (referred to as Pow2b earlier)

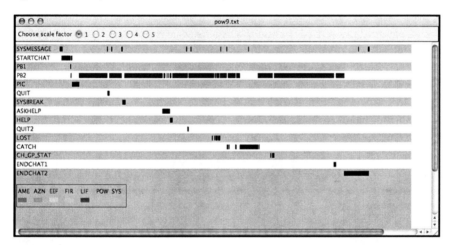

Fig. 23.6 Pow9

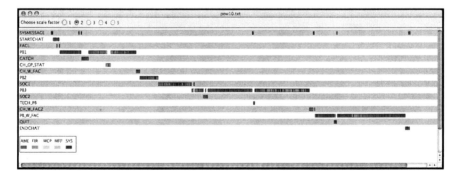

Fig. 23.7 Pow10

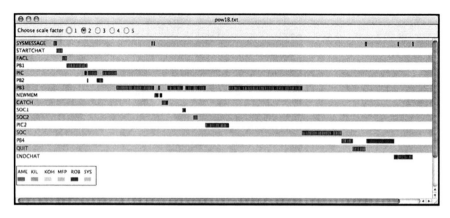

Fig. 23.8 Pow18

The feature of the chats that emerges from an inspection of Figs. 23.3 through 23.8—that postings related to problem solving were the most prevalent in each of the chats—is confirmed by the coding statistics shown in Table 23.6:

As can be seen in the PB row, on average, problem solving accounted for slightly over half of the postings in the chats (ranging from 30% to 77%). While this may

Table 23.6 Frequency of postings in each activity by PoW-wow

		Powwow						
		Powwow 01 (%)	Powwow 02G (%)	Powwow 02 M (%)	Powwow 09 (%)	Powwow 10 (%)	Powwow 18 (%)	Total (%)
LONGSEQ	ASKHELP		9.4		2.4			2.8
	CATCH	8.1	2.9		6.4	1.9	1.6	3.7
	CH_CP_STA				0.7	1.2		0.4
	CH_W_FAC					2.2		0.4
	ENDCHAT	23.7	11.3	8.9	8.4	1.0	4.9	8.8
	FACL	3.0	5.3	5.4		0.3	1.2	2.2
	LOST		5.7		1.3			1.6
	NEWMEM		6.8				1.6	1.9
	PAUSE			2.0				0.1
	PB	29.7	50.6	76.8	71.6	53.5	57.7	56.7
	PB_W_FAC					24.6		4.7
	PIC	6.6	4.0		2.2		13.3	4.3
	QUIT		0.4	0.5	0.8	0.5	3.5	1.0
	SERVICE	6.6	1.1					1.0
	SOC	16.2				10.7	12.3	5.8
	STARTCHAT	2.7	1.2	3.0	2.9	1.5	1.6	2.0
	SYSBREAK				0.8			0.2
	SYSMESSAG	3.3	1.1	3.4	2.4	2.1	2.1	2.1
	TECH_PB		0.1			0.3		0.1
Total		100.0	100.0	100.0	100.0	100.0	100.0	100.0

not seem terribly surprising, it is nonetheless quantitative confirmation that the participants themselves oriented to their participation in the chats heavily in terms of problem solving.

Another feature of collaborative problem-solving chats is that student participants were able to organize their chat interaction in ways that allowed them to engage in multiple, concurrently performed activities. It has been claimed that one of the affordances of chat technology is precisely that participants can and do engage in multiple, concurrent activities (Garcia & Jacobs, 1999; O'Neill & Martin, 2003). As the transcripts and Figs. 23.3 through 23.8 demonstrate, participants were able to do more than one thing at a time in a number of different ways. For example, actors were capable of suspending their engagement in problem solving over multiple postings to take up a next activity and then return to problem solving where they had left off. Also, they were capable of posting messages in one activity while inserting postings related to a different activity in the stream of current-activity postings.

Among the research questions we asked was the question regarding how similar the different PoW-wows were. We constructed a similarity matrix displaying Pearson correlation coefficients based on the distribution of postings across the categories we had discovered. This is shown in Table 23.7.

Table 23.7 Similarity matrix with all variables

Proximity Matrix					
Correlation between Vectors of Values					
	1:P01	2:P02G	3:P02M	4:P09	5.P10	6:P18
1:P01	1.000	0.736	0.731	0.741	0.630	0.779
2:P02G	0.736	1.000	0.965	0.968	0.814	0.918
3:P02M	0.731	0.965	1.000	0.991	0.877	0.948
4:P09	0.741	0.968	0.991	1.000	0.874	0.952
5.P10	0.630	0.814	0.877	0.874	1.000	0.866
6:P18	0.779	0.918	0.948	0.952	0.866	1.000

As the figures indicate, these chats are all quite similar. Again, this is not a surprising result in that the students self-selected to participate in these chats with the understanding that they were going to be doing math problem solving.

We then asked, how similar these chats are with respect to the distribution of postings in non-problem-solving activities. When the problem-solving category was removed, the correlations in Table 23.8 emerged when run with the following variables, ASKHELP, CATCH, CH_GP_ST, CH_W_FAC, ENDCHAT, FACL, LOST, NEWMEM, PAUSE, PIC, QUIT, SERVICE, SOC, STARTCHAT, SYSBREAK, SYSMESSAGE, and TECH_PB.

The idea here was to see how similar chats were with respect to the organization of non-problem-solving activities. As we can see, Pow10 shows small negative correlations to Pow2G, Pow2M and Pow9. The rest show positive but relatively small correlations with other PoW-wows, suggesting that there are similarities in

Table 23.8 Similarity matrix without problem solving

	Proximity Matrix					
	Correlation between Vectors of Values					
	1:P01	2:P02G	3:P02M	4:P09	5:P10	5:P18
1:P01	1.000	0.376	0.559	0.638	0.493	0.582
2:P02G	0.376	1.000	0.479	0.550	−0.272	0.061
3:P02M	0.559	0.479	1.000	0.547	−0.66	0.038
4:P09	0.638	0.550	0.547	1.000	−0.050	0.149
5:P10	0.493	0.272	−0.066	−0.050	1.000	0.557
6:P18	0.582	0.061	0.038	0.149	0.557	1.000

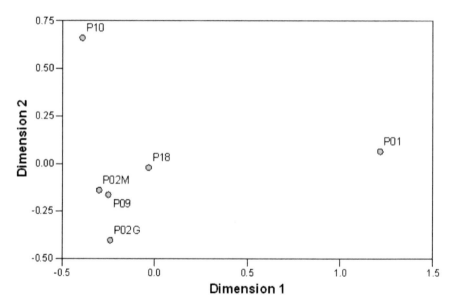

Fig. 23.9 Multidimensional scaling analysis of proximity matrix

the ways that participants deal with circumstantial contingencies that arise during their chats, but also that there are issues to be investigated with respect to the differences in the kinds of contingencies that arise during these problem-solving chats.

We then did a multidimensional analysis based on the proximity matrices we calculated. Fig. 23.9 gives us a graphical representation derived from the similarity matrix in Table 23.9. It appears that the data cluster into three groups:

Table 23.9 Similarity matrix

Proximities						
	P01	P02G	P02M	P09	P10	P18
P01						
P02G	0.293					
P02M	0.260	0.927				
P09	0.308	0.936	1.000			
P10	0.000	0.510	0.683	0.675		
P18	0.412	0.798	0.881	0.892	0.654	

Goodness of Fit	
Stress and fit Measures	
Narmalized Raw Stress	0.00191
Stress-I	0.04367[a]
Stress-II	0.07998[a]
S-Stress	0.00341[b]
Dispersion Accounted For (D.A.F.)	0.99809
Tucker's Coefficient of Congruence	0.99905

PROXSCAL minimizes Normalized Raw Stress.
[a]Optimal scaling factor = 1.002.
[b]Optimal scaling factor = 0.999.

- Cluster 1, which consists of Pow2M, Pow2G, Pow18 and Pow9,
- Cluster 2, which consists of Pow1, and
- Cluster 3, which consists of Pow10.

Some of this cluster pattern may be accounted for by the following. In the first cluster there is usually a main problem-solving activity that is interleaved with other sorts of activities, but the main activity is usually sustained. In Pow 1 there are not many activities that are interleaved with the problem-solving activity. The activities unfold in a linear way without interleaving with each other. Finally, Pow 1 lies somewhere in between these two clusters. Except the PB2, CATCH, SOC and PB3 chunks (which add up to almost half of the whole session), the remaining chunks unfold in a linear way without much interleaving. Clearly, further investigation is required to account for the basis for this clustering.

We understand that, from a statistical perspective, we do not have conclusive results. But we do have suggestive results. We see that there are differences in the chats, at least initially in terms of the distribution of activities in which student participants are engaged. Furthermore, we see that there are also interesting structural similarities. For example, Figs. 23.3 through 23.8 show that participants are capable of engaging in sustained problem-solving work while dealing with the interactional contingencies that emerge over the course of their chats.

Probability Transition Tables

There are a number of areas we wish to explore further as this research evolves. First of all, we have adopted a top-down approach based on the way that participants themselves organize their activities. This is to be distinguished from the CA work that Heritage and Roth (1995) have done, which uses the ways that participants constitute question-response pairs in presidential news conferences as a basis for doing statistical analysis. Essentially what Heritage and Roth did was to look at an activity in which the predominant organization of interaction involved asking questions and offering responses to those questions. We are doing something different. We are looking at a chat among multiple student participants who engage in a variety of different kinds of activity over the course of their chats. We begin by identifying the way the students themselves have organized their interaction in terms of activities to which they were oriented.

As a next step, we want to use CA methods to further characterize the constituent features of these activities. In other words, we are asking questions like, "How are problem-solving activities built?" and "From what kinds of more finely grained activity types are these problem-solving activities built by the participants?" This will allow us to discover the different ways that students *do* problem solving, in terms of how their activity emerges over the course of these chats.

Another area of significant interest is to use the coding scheme we are developing to capture the sequential organization of problem-solving chats. We have begun to develop conditional probability tables (see Tables 23.10–23.12) that we hope will allow us to model ways that problem-solving chats are likely to unfold.

Table 23.10 Pow2G probability transition table

	CATCH (%)	END (%)	FACL (%)	HELP (%)	LOST (%)	NEW (%)	PB (%)	PIC (%)
CATCH	80,95	0,00	0,00	9,52	0,00	0,00	9,52	0,00
END	0,00	97,62	0,00	0,00	0,00	0,00	2,38	0,00
FACL	0,00	0,00	81,58	0,00	0,00	2,63	15,79	0,00
HELP	1,47	0,00	0,00	85,29	0,00	0,00	5,88	0,00
LOST	0,00	0,00	0,00	2,44	73,17	0,00	21,95	0,00
NEW	0,00	0,00	2,00	0,00	0,00	92,00	5,00	0,00
PB	0,82	0,82	1,37	0,55	3,01	0,82	91,53	1,09
PIC	0,00	0,00	0,00	0,00	0,00	0,00	13,79	86,21
QUIT	0,00	0,00	0,00	66,67	0,00	0,00	0,00	0,00
SERV	0,00	0,00	0,00	25,00	0,00	0,00	12,50	0,00
START	0,00	0,00	7,69	0,00	0,00	0,00	0,00	0,00
T_PB	0,00	0,00	0,00	100,00	0,00	0,00	0,00	0,00
Total	2,91	11,77	5,26	9,42	5,68	6,98	50,69	4,02

As we do more refined analyses of long activity sequences within the chats, we expect to be able to develop conditional probability tables that describe how such activities as problem-solving or help-seeking activities unfold. While this is not possible at this stage of our research, we feel that with additional work over a larger

Table 23.11   Pow2M probability transition table

	ENDCHAT (%)	FACL (%)	PAUSE (%)	PB (%)	QUIT (%)	STARTCHAT (%)
ENDCHAT	77,78	0,00	0,00	22,22	0,00	0,00
FACT	0,00	90,91	0,00	9,09	0,00	0,00
PAUSE	0,00	0,00	50,00	50,00	0,00	0,00
PB	3,23	0,00	1,29	94,19	1,29	0,00
QUIT	0,00	0,00	0,00	100,00	0,00	0,00
STARTCHAT	0,00	10,00	0,00	0,00	0,00	90,00
Total	9,50	5,50	2,00	77,50	1,00	4,50

Table 23.12   Pow18 probability transition table

	CATCH (%)	ENDCHAT (%)	FACL (%)	NEWMEN (%)	PB (%)	PIC (%)	QUIT (%)	SOC (%)	STARTCHAT
CATCH	87,50	0,00	0,00	0,00	12,50	0,00	0,00	0,00	0,00
ENDCHAT	0,00	100,00	0,00	0,00	0,00	0,00	0,00	0,00	0,00
FACL	0,00	0,00	83,33	0,00	16,67	0,00	0,00	0,00	0,00
NEWMAN	10,00	0,00	0,00	70,00	20,00	0,00	0,00	0,00	0,00
PB	0,00	0,36	0,00	1,07	94,64	1,79	0,36	1,79	0,00
PIC	0,00	0,00	0,00	0,00	7,69	92,31	0,00	0,00	0,00
QUIT	0,00	0,00	0,00	0,00	5,26	0,00	94,74	0,00	0,00
SOC	0,00	0,00	0,00	0,00	8,20	0,00	0,00	91,80	0,00
STARTCHAT	0,00	0,00	8,33	0,00	0,00	0,00	0,00	0,00	91,67
Total	1,65	5,35	1,23	2,06	57,61	13,37	3,91	12,55	2,26

sample of chats, one would be able to begin to observe the structural organization of problem-solving chats as interactional phenomena and social facts.

Mixing Methods

One of the most important features of the work we have done here is to demonstrate that very different analytical methodologies can be used together to tackle interesting problems. The key here was to recognize that conversation analysis could be used effectively to provide a coding scheme, based on the interactional relevancies of the participants whose actions were of interest in the study, which could be used effectively to do comparative statistical analysis of the data. Statistical studies often treat anomalies in the data and in findings as random occurrences. Occasionally they are. But rather than assume the status of such anomalies, we took the approach that our initial analyst-based coding scheme might have been responsible for such anomalies. By working to produce a coding scheme based on the demonstrated relevancies of the participants in the interactions under examination, we were able to resolve the anomalies and achieve insights into the data that would have otherwise gone unnoticed.

There are many advocates for mixed-methods studies. We are among them. However, we hold to the position that mixing methods can only be done effectively when analysts give careful consideration to the assumptions governing the organization of all methods deployed, making sure that no method violates the assumptions governing the use of another method. In our examination of the literature, we have found that conversation analysis has not yet managed to develop methods for examining long sequences. On the other hand, statistical analysis is often used to test analysts' hypotheses without regard for the inherent organization of interaction based on participants' practices. However, together, CA and SA can be used to explore the structural and sequential organization of participants' own actions over long sequences and across distinct interactional occurrences in ways that respect the inherent orderliness of the data while allowing for generalization beyond specific instances.

Chapter 24
Polyphonic Inter-Animation of Voices in VMT

Stefan Trausan-Matu and Traian Rebedea

Abstract This chapter introduces a theoretical framework for analyzing collaborative problem solving in chats, based on the concept of polyphony and Bakhtin's theory of dialog. Polyphony, a notion taken from music theory, may be considered as a general model for interaction and creativity by a group of people ("voices," in an extended sense) following patterns of counterpoint. As Bakhtin emphasized, polyphony may occur in texts; we will show that it can occur in problem-solving chat texts. One of the features of polyphonic music is its potential development of complex architectures starting from a given theme. Polyphonic structuring of dialogs may transform the interaction into a "thinking device": Different voices jointly construct a melody (story or solution), sometimes adopting different positions and then generating, identifying or solving dissonances (unsound, rickety stories or solutions). Polyphony consists of several "horizontal," longitudinal melody lines that are "vertically," transversally integrated. Similarly, in chats, the continuations of utterances are tied together over time providing a melodic line. Simultaneously, they are coordinated with the utterances of others, maintaining the integration toward unity across various themes and variations that sometimes can introduce differences. This chapter also proposes software tools for the visualization of the polyphonic weaving in chats. These tools identify and visualize the explicit and implicit links among utterances, and may determine or visualize the contributions of each participant in a chat.

Keywords Bakhtin · polyphony · voice · dialog · reference

This chapter introduces a theoretical framework, a method and a visualization tool for analyzing CSCL chats, based on the ideas of polyphonic inter-animation introduced by Bakhtin (1981, 1984a). As in the dialog theory of Bakhtin, we extend the polyphonic musical model for analyzing language-based interactions, in our case, transcripts of text chats for collaborative learning. Although Bakhtin's ideas are

S. Trausan-Matu (✉)
Computer Science, Politehnica University of Bucharest, Romania
e-mail: stefan.trausan@cs.pub.ro

G. Stahl (ed.), *Studying Virtual Math Teams*, Computer-Supported Collaborative
Learning Series 11, DOI 10.1007/978-1-4419-0228-3_24,
© Springer Science+Business Media, LLC 2009

quite well known and considered as a theoretical starting point in the CSCL community (Koschmann, 1999b; Stahl, 2006b; Wegerif, 2006), there are no elaborations that propose how to use his theory in practice. The analysis method we introduce is inspired from the ideas of counterpoint, which is the theory and methodology used in music for composing and analyzing pieces for multiple instruments or voices. Our theory and method was used for the implementation of a system to analyze and visualize polyphonic threading in chats, proposing an evaluation of the contributions of the participants. This polyphonic perspective shed new light on the dialogic nature of discourse in human language and in problem solving in general. It could also have consequences for the design of collaborative-learning environments.

In polyphony, a number of melodic lines (or "voices," in an extended, non-acoustical perspective, as we will discuss later) jointly construct a harmonious musical piece, generating variations on one or several themes. Dissonances should be avoided and resolved, even if several themes (melodies) or theme variations are played simultaneously, and even if sometimes the voices situate themselves in opposing positions.

Bakhtin considers that multiple voices are present in texts, and sometimes (e.g., in Dostoevsky's novels) they constitute a polyphonic framework (Bakhtin, 1984a). Extrapolating this idea, we observe that inter-animation of voices following polyphonic patterns can be identified in dialogs generally, and in chats in particular. A polyphonic collaboration involves several participants who play several themes and their variations in a game of sequential succession and differing positions. The existence of different voices introduces "dissonances," unsound, rickety stories or solutions. This polyphonic game may eventually facilitate knowledge building through the tension of their opposition and the pressure to resolve the difference (see Chapter 9).

Polyphony, in our view, may be taken as a model of collaboration, in which several participants ("voices") invent, discuss and elaborate ideas—often eventually achieving coherence even if "centrifugal" forces, divergences or differences arise temporarily. In fact, as in physics, centrifugal forces or differences determine a reaction of centripetal forces that act towards increasing unity. Bakhtin identified this centrifugal/centripetal phenomenon in the discourse of novels (Bakhtin, 1981). From a polyphonic point of view, these forces manifest themselves in two dimensions: longitudinal and vertical (melody and harmony).

The above ideas are exemplified in this chapter with chat excerpts for collaborative learning in two domains: mathematics problem solving—investigated in the VMT Project—and human–computer interaction—studied at the Computer Science Department of Bucharest "Politehnica" University. Inter-animation patterns were discovered in the above-mentioned two dimensions: longitudinal (chronologically sequential) and transversal (effectively simultaneous). They move in both dimensions between two opposite trends: unity and difference. Moreover, we consider that even individual thinking can be analyzed as an implicit collaborative (dialogic) process that involves multiple voices. However, actual collaborations in small groups of different personalities illustrate more explicitly the dialogic process.

The chapter continues with a section that discusses the role of discourse in learning and that introduces the dialogic theory of Bakhtin and polyphony. The following section is dedicated to the presentation and exemplification of the novel polyphonic theoretical model and analysis method of CSCL chats, starting from counterpoint and Bakhtin's ideas. Inter-animation patterns are identified and classified along the longitudinal-vertical and unity-difference dimensions in chats. Software tools that support the identification and visualization of the polyphonic architecture, allowing the analysis of inter-animation and even assessing individual contributions are presented in the fourth section.

Discourse, Dialog and Polyphony

The Role of Discourse in Learning

The assessment of learning achievement in a given domain is often based on evaluating the amount of knowledge acquired by the student, as in question-answering examinations. However, in other cases as in mathematics and other disciplines needing problem-solving abilities and/or creativity, this approach is not adequate. Instead, successful discourse building (e.g., constructing a reasoning chain or writing an essay linking a series of ideas) is required for evaluation. Because discourse is an artifact achieved in communication, discourse-building abilities benefit from social, collaborative learning.

The above two approaches correspond to the contrast between socio-cognitive and socio-cultural theories or between the Intelligent Tutoring System and CSCL paradigms (Koschmann, 1999b; Stahl, 2006b). The socio-cultural theory of learning is based on Vygotsky, and has had an increasing influence as the limitations of the knowledge acquisition model become recognized. As Hicks noted, "Learning occurs as the co-construction (or reconstruction) of social meanings from within the parameters of emergent, socially negotiated and discursive activity" (Hicks, 1996, p. 136, quoted by Koschmann, 1999). Sfard (2000a) remarked, "Rather than speaking about 'acquisition of knowledge,' many people prefer to view learning as *becoming a participant in a certain discourse.*"

Links and Threads

As we have seen above, discourse is a central concept in learning. There are many definitions for discourse, the majority stating that it is characterized by structures beyond a sentence or utterance. One definition that captures ideas present in several others says also: "its main concepts are cohesion—the features that bind sentences to each other grammatically and lexically—and coherence—which is the notional and logical unity of a text" (Newmark, 1988). Therefore, for studying discourse, we could analyze links and threads (connecting sentences or utterances) providing cohesion and coherence.

In the chat from which an excerpt is presented in Fig. 24.1, students at a Human–Computer Interaction course had to discuss facilities and tools for a collaborative environment. The students used the VMT chat environment, which allows the users to explicitly link an utterance to the one it continues or replies to (see Chapter 15). These explicit links are represented in the left part of Fig. 24.1 by curly arrows.

Nr	Ref	Time	User	Text
17		10.26.25	tim	You discussed about a topic separation
18	15	10.26.37	adrian	First of all, the reply method is cumbersome
	17	10.26.50	john	yes.. because we did not like the way the topics were presented in concert chat
0	18	10.26.56	john	yes !!
	20	10.27.04	john	i hate double-clicking!
	20	10.27.18	tim	and how can we find topics ?
	18	10.27.26	adrian	What bothers me is the linear presentation of the discussin
	23	10.27.43	john	Yep
2	18	10.27.46	adrian	and double-clicking too
26		10.27.54	tim	You mean i want something like a chat forum ? D
27	14	10.27.58	john	and the reply to facility is supposed to help you
28	8	10.28.15	adrian	i'd like a tree presentation more
29	18	10.28.38	adrian	or maybe multiple chat columns, for each chat sub-thread
30	27	10.28.58	john	but it is really difficult to use in real-time, because there are so many topics discussed which intertwine each other
31	28	10.29.18	john	i subscribe to the tree like presentation form
32	P 70	10.29.20	adrian	yes, that's why a clear separation of topics is needed
33	31	10.29.47	adrian	this is easy to implement, no problem here :)
34	30	10.29.49	tim	You need also a clever visual representation
35	30	10.30.05	tim	you'll need also a clever visual interface
36		10.30.22	tim	Who decides the topics ?
37	33	10.30.33	john	i suppose you are refering to the visual representation, right ?
38	37	10.30.45	john	What i would like is a clever way to separate the topics :)
39	38	10.30.59	john	not just doing ot myself, manually
40	37	10.31.00	adrian	Yeah
41	39	10.31.44	adrian	When you start a new thread (a new message, non-related to other message), the app can assume a new topic
42	39	10.31.46	john	i would like the application to be able to detect w topic change all by itself

Fig. 24.1. Two types of links in the chat.

In addition to the explicit references, a second type of link may be identified in any text, including chats. It is the case of implicit references among words or phrases. The simplest case of such implicit links is between repeated words, represented in Fig. 24.1 by straight lines. In general, these implicit links may be very complex, relating, for example, semantic arguments.

An interesting thing is that the implicit and explicit links are usually different (e.g., in 21 of the 24 cases in Fig. 24.1). This phenomenon might be explained by the fact that the participants probably only felt the need to include an explicit link when an implicit one was not present or obvious. This observation introduces the idea that repetition (e.g., of words or phrases) is a strong interaction pattern that is perceived as such by the participants—as evidenced by the fact that they do not feel the need to introduce explicit links when repetitions of words are present.

Implicit and explicit links form threads. In the case of implicit links between repeated words, this fact is obvious (see Fig. 24.1). Threading occurs also for explicit references, indicated by the users, as is seen in Fig. 24.2.

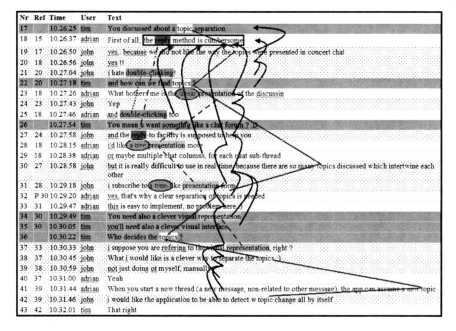

Nr	Ref	Time	User	Text
17		10.26.25	tim	You discussed about a topic separation
18	15	10.26.37	adrian	First of all, the reply method is cumbersome
19	17	10.26.50	john	yes.. because we did not like the way the topics were presented in concert chat
20	18	10.26.56	john	yes !!
21	20	10.27.04	john	i hate double-clicking!
22	20	10.27.18	tim	and how can we find topics ?
23	18	10.27.26	adrian	What bothers me is the linear presentation of the discussin
24	23	10.27.43	john	Yep
25	18	10.27.46	adrian	and double-clicking too
26		10.27.54	tim	You mean u want something like a chat forum ? :D
27	24	10.27.58	john	and the reply to facility is supposed to help you
28	18	10.28.15	adrian	i'd like a tree presentation more
29	18	10.28.38	adrian	or maybe multiple chat columns, for each chat sub-thread
30	27	10.28.58	john	but it is really difficult to use in real time because there are so many topics discussed which intertwine each other
31	28	10.29.18	john	i subscribe to a tree-like presentation form
32	P 30	10.29.20	adrian	yes, that's why a clear separation of topics is needed
33	31	10.29.47	adrian	this is easy to implement, no problem here
34	30	10.29.49	tim	You need also a clever visual representation
35	30	10.30.05	tim	you'll need also a clever visual interface
36		10.30.22	tim	Who decides the topics ?
37	33	10.30.33	john	i suppose you are refering to the visual representation, right ?
38	37	10.30.45	john	What i would like is a clever way to separate the topics ;)
39	38	10.30.59	john	not just doing ot myself, manually
40	37	10.31.00	adrian	Yeah
41	39	10.31.44	adrian	When you start a new thread (a new message, non-related to other message), the app can assume a new topic
42	39	10.31.46	john	i would like the application to be able to detect w topic change all by itself
43	42	10.32.01	tim	That right

Fig. 24.2. Multiple parallel threads.

All these threads—in addition to their intrinsic longitudinal nature—due to their co-presence at the same time influence each other, inter-animating in different ways, as we will see later. For example, Fig. 24.3 represents a part of the inter-animation process among the three students in the development of the threads of implicit links in Fig. 24.1 and 24.2. Time flows from left to right and the same representation of the themes (texture and types of lines) is used. In addition to the sequential dimension of theme development, the same figure also represents (with curly arrows) three interactions between themes, which may be considered as transversal interaction patterns (two divergent and one convergent).

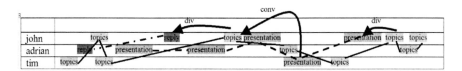

Fig. 24.3. The longitudinal-transversal dimensions.

During the chat, each of the participants introduces new variations on the theme of the chat or iterates an already uttered theme variation. For example, in Fig. 24.3, three theme variations are emphasized: "**replying**," the "**topics**" in a collaborative chat and ways of "**presentation**." Threads may be easily discovered from the obvious repetition pattern of these words.

Similarly to a musical piece, the chats for CSCL have a main theme, a topic that is, for example, the problem to be solved or the product to be designed by the students. This theme generates threads of discussion containing interactions that may be identified and classified according to classes of interaction patterns. These threads contain variations (sub-topics) of the theme, analogous to musical variations. One fundamental issue in polyphony is the presence of several participants (or "voices") uttering ("singing") in a unitary way in a given moment. Among the participants, brief dissonances may appear, but these are "solved" and a unity is obtained.

Dialogism and Discourse

Bakhtin considered that, "Any true understanding is dialogic in nature" (Voloshinov, 1973). From his perspective, any discourse may be seen as an intertwining of at least two threads belonging to dialoguing voices. Even if we consider an essay, a novel or even a scientific paper, discourse should be viewed as implying not only the voice of the author. For example, the potential listener also has an important role: The author constructs a thread of ideas, a narrative. Meanwhile, parallel to it, she must take into account the potential flaws of her discourse, the potential questions or replies; she must see it as an utterance that can be disputed by the listener. In this idea, discourse in a novel is similar to dialog in conversation and to polyphony in music, where different voices inter-animate each other.

Voices

The "voice" concept in Bakhtin's work is central and complex. In the context of a dialog, we understand by a *voice* not the acoustical, physical, vocal expression of a given participant in a dialog but, rather, a distinct position, an utterance, an event or a recurrent series of events of emitting utterances that are heard, remembered, discussed and have influence on the utterances emitted by the other voices. In music, for example, a voice is not fixed to an instrument; the same instrument may play several voices, and different instruments may take the position of a given voice, simultaneously or sequentially.

A voice may be seen as a distinctive position in a group, a person or a group of people who have uttered something, with effects on the subsequent utterances. For example, in Fig. 24.1, the voice of John from utterance number 21 is taken up by Adrian, at 25. Moreover, a voice has some particularities; it may have a personality, goals, beliefs, desires and emotions. Consequently, a dialog among several voices is not a dialog among impersonal entities. From another point of view, a voice may become a theme or may contribute to a theme of the discussion.

Polyphony

Discursive voices sometimes weave a polyphonic texture—a feature that Bakhtin admired so much in Dostoevsky's novels. Bakhtin characterized them as "a plurality of independent and unmerged voices and consciousnesses" (Bakhtin, 1984a).

Polyphony, a concept taken from music, may be considered as a general model for interaction and creativity in a group of human "voices" following counterpoint rules. As Bakhtin emphasized, it may occur also in texts and, as we will show in this chapter, in problem-solving chats. One of the features of polyphonic music is its development of complex architectures starting from a given theme; polyphonic structuring of dialogs may transform them into a "thinking device."

Polyphony is not only a randomly overlapped set of voices. It also has musicality; it is in fact one of the most complex types of musical compositions, exemplified by the sophisticated contrapuntal fugues of Johann Sebastian Bach.

> When there is *more than one independent melodic line happening at the same time* in a piece of music, we say that the music is contrapuntal. The independent melodic lines are called counterpoint. The music that is made up of counterpoint can also be called polyphony, or one can say that the music is polyphonic or speak of the polyphonic texture of the music. (Polyphony, 2005)

In polyphonic music, the melodic, linear dimension does not, in general, disturb the transversal harmony. Even if differential dissonances may appear for a while, they are usually quickly resolved and the unity of the musical piece is restored. This makes a kind of game, which drives (for example, in Bach's fugues) the inter-animation of the participant voices. The main theme is introduced by one voice, reformulated by others, even contradicted sometimes (e.g., inverted) but all the voices keep a vertical harmony in their diversity, resolving the brief dissonances. The inter-animation is generated by the different conflicting personalities or ideas of the participants. Sometimes the conflicts derive from serious causes (e.g., different approaches for solving a problem), but other times, they derive from pure ludic, playful, carnivalesque (Bakhtin, 1984b) reasons. Dissonances usually appear but they are soon resolved, restoring the global unity.

In each dialogue, similarly to polyphonic music, there are one or more themes, which are debated by the participant voices. Each theme is introduced by a voice and developed by it or by the others. Several themes may be present at the same time in the dialogue, influencing each other.

Starting from Bakhtin's ideas, we extend the polyphonic, dialogic perspective to collaborative learning. Therefore, we will describe how polyphony may arise in collaborative learning and we will propose ways of analyzing and supporting it in learning environments.

We will use in our further analyses the term "voice" instead of "participant" because it is more general, as mentioned above. In the polyphonic framework for analyzing chats, voice is a central concept, being the point that contrasts with the counterpoint. It is not fixed to a person, but, rather, is a position, an idea, a proposal.

The Polyphony of Collaborative-Learning Chats

Computer and communication technologies offer new possibilities for collaboration, by allowing virtual classroom group interaction. New types of artifacts, like hypertext, the World Wide Web, instant messenger chats or discussion forums are changing the classical learning scenarios. In addition to traditional sheets of paper or blackboards for drawing diagrams and writing formulas and sequences of problem-solving steps, computer animations, simulations, chat logs or even virtual participants in the dialog (artificial agents) may now be used for collaboration. It is extremely important to analyze the particularities of discourse in this new context, to identify interaction patterns, and to design supporting software tools. A good example is the fact that in chats we can use a multiply threaded discourse much more easily than in face-to-face conversations.

In order to develop a theoretical background and the associated supporting tools for CSCL chats, we have started from the musical polyphony model and we have looked for analogous structuring in collaborative-learning chats. Next, we have searched for classes of interaction patterns that resemble musical counterpoint rules that are used in composing polyphonic music. Eventually, we have designed and developed tools that would facilitate the analysis from the polyphonic theory.

The analysis and the experiments were performed in two cases: mathematics problem solving and the design of human–computer interfaces. The first case involved students using several different versions of the VMT environment. The language they used was English. The experiments in the second case were performed with college seniors at the Politehnica University of Bucharest (PUB). The students were in a computer science course and they chatted in the VMT environment either in English (as a second language) or in Romanian. All the chat groups had from 3 to 5 participants. The Polyphony system, developed at PUB was used for analyzing the polyphonic structure of all the chats.

Collaborative Solving of Mathematics Problem

Let us consider the following problem from Chapter 5:

> Three years ago, men made up two out of every three Internet users in America. Today the ratio of male to female users is about 1 to 1. In that time the number of American females using the Internet has grown by 30,000,000, while the number of males who use the Internet has grown by 100%. By how much has the total Internet-user population increased in America in the past three years? (A) 50,000,000 (B) 60,000,000 (C) 80,000,000 (D) 100,000,000 (E) 200,000,000

This problem was one of a set of eleven problems that were used for an experiment. A group of students had to solve these problems, initially individually, and subsequently collaboratively, using a chat instant messaging system. The above problem was one of the two that were not solved individually by any student but it was successfully solved collaboratively.

Consider Log 24-1, which includes the main utterances that contributed to the finding of the solution of the problem:

Log 24-1.

350	4:31:55	Mic	how do we do this..
351	4:31:59	Mic	without knowing the total number
352	4:32:01	Mic	of internet users?
.....			
357	4:32:23	Dan	it all comes from the 30000000
358	4:32:23	Mic	did u get something for 10?
359	4:32:26	Dan	we already know
360	4:32:44	Mic	30000000 is the number of increase in american females
361	4:33:00	Mic	and since the ratio of male to female
362	4:33:02	Mic	is 1 to 1
363	4:33:09	Mic	that's all i got to give. Someone finish it
364	4:33:10	Mic	Haha
365	4:33:18	Cosi	Haha you jackass
366	4:33:20	Mic	Haha
367	4:33:21	Dan	Hahaha
368	4:33:26	Mic	u all thought i was gonna figure it out didn't
369	4:33:27	Mic	U
370	4:33:28	Mic	huh?
371	4:33:28	Hal	it would be 60,000,000
372	4:33:30	Mic	Hal
373	4:33:31	Mic	its all u
374	4:33:33	Mic	See
375	4:33:34	Mic	i helped
376	4:33:54	Cosi	ok, so what's 11 – just guess on 10
....			
..			
386	4:34:45	Mic	lets get back to 5
387	4:34:47	Cosi	i think it's more than 60,00000
388	4:34:57	Mic	way to complicate things
389	4:35:03	Cosi	Haha sorry
390	4:35:05	Mic	life was good until you said that
391	4:35:07	Mic	:(
392	4:35:18	Cosi	they cant get higher equally and even out to a 1 to 1 ratio
393	4:35:27	Cosi	oh, no wait, less than that
394	4:35:32	Cosi	50000000
395	4:35:34	Cosi	yeah, it's that
396	4:35:36	Cosi	im pretty sure
397	4:35:37	Mic	Haha
398	4:35:38	Mic	how?
399	4:35:57	Cosi	because the women pop had to grow more than the men in order to even out
400	4:36:07	Cosi	so the men cant be equal (30)
401	4:36:11	Mic	oh wow...
402	4:36:16	Mic	i totally skipped the first sentencwe
403	4:36:16	Cosi	Therefore, the 50,000,000 is the only workable answer
404	4:36:19	Dan	very smart
405	4:36:21	Cosi	Damn im good

Discourse begins with Dan's idea of starting from the 30,000,000 number specified in the problem statement (line 357). It continues with Mic, who seems to start a reasoning path (lines 360–362) by writing typical fragments of mathematical problem-solving speech genre containing the typical phrase "... **and since** ..." After just three lines, unexpectedly, the reasoning path ends abruptly and Mic states that his discourse is a buffoonery (lines 363–364, 366 and 368–370), taking a "carnavalesque" (Bakhtin, 1984b) direction. This fact is explicitly remarked upon by the utterances of Cosi (line 365) and Dan (line 367). However, even being a pastiche, the "voice" of Mic in his fake discourse fragment has an echo in the succeeding utterances, being continued by Hal, who extrapolates the 1:1 ratio from the present (as stated in the problem) to the whole 3 years, advancing 60,000,000 as a solution (line 371).

Mic continues his buffoonery (lines 372–375), claiming that he helped Hal to find the supposed solution. After a while, Cosi's utterance "**i think it's more than 60,00000**" appears as an opposing position, a critique, an intuition of something wrong, of some kind of an "unsuccessful story" or some "dissonant" chord. Nevertheless, after about a minute, she realizes that her own supposition is wrong because the ratio cannot be 1:1 or bigger. This idea drives her to choosing the solution 50,000,000, the single value of the multiple choice answers less than 60,000,000.

We can say that the collaborative discourse enabled Cosi to solve the problem. She didn't solve it in the first phase, when they had to solve it individually. However, when she listened to the discourse proposing a solution (correct in the case of Dan's beginning proposal, fake by Mic and wrong by Hal), she felt the need to take on a different position and she eventually succeeded in solving the problem. Therefore, the discourse acted as a tool, as an artifact that enabled Cosi to find the correct answer. Moreover, we may say that the building of the solution contains the voices of the other participants. They inter-animate, weaving together variations of the starting theme (the problem to be solved), as in a polyphonic musical piece.

Another, no less important feature is the "carnavalesque" character of utterances that eventually gave rise to the solution. The role of carnavalesque utterances was discussed in detail in Bakhtin (1984b).

Polyphonic Structuring in Chat Conversations for Problem Solving

As we have seen in many chapters of this volume, discourse in collaborative problem-solving chats has an obvious sequential, longitudinal, time-driven structure in which the speakers/listeners (readers/writers) are permanently situated and in which they emit their utterances in a threaded manner, having, ideally, a unitary character, oriented toward finding the solution. In parallel with this linear threading dimension, in problem-solving chats the participants also situate themselves in transversal relationships that often adopt critical, differential positions. For example, in the chat excerpt considered in the preceding section, Dan's theme was continued by Mic's buffoonery, continued itself by Hal and then contradicted by a first theme of Cosi's that was subsequently reversed into its opposite.

In this longitudinal-transversal space, voices partake in a unity-difference— or centripetal-centrifugal (Bakhtin, 1981)—dynamic and display various inter-animation patterns. This phenomenon is not specific solely to chats. It also appears in polyphonic music:

> The deconstructivist attack—according to which only the difference between difference and unity *as an emphatic difference* (and not as a return to unity) can act as the basis of a differential theory (which dialectic merely claims to be)—is the methodical point of departure for the distinction between polyphony and non-polyphony. (Mahnkopf, 2002)

Interactions of voices towards the unity and difference dimensions were identified in all chats we have analyzed. Some of these interactions may be abstracted in classes of *inter-animation patterns* in which an utterance by one voice triggers an utterance by another voice. In the next section, patterns of inter-animation are identified along the unity-difference dimension. The subsequent section will discuss how these interactions weave into a polyphonic structure.

Inter-Animation Patterns

When somebody listens to Bach's fugues or other classical music works, one remarks how several themes and their variations are exposed, developed and re-exposed by several instruments. Moreover, these themes and their variations seem to inter-animate each other; even the term musical "fugue" expresses the idea that several voices are "running" and "chasing" each other. The soundscape becomes a playful ground for creativity; for example, a particular type of polyphonic musical piece is called an "invention."

Bakhtin used the musical metaphor for language, considering that "the voices of others become woven into what we say, write and think" (Koschmann, 1999b). Therefore, for analyzing CSCL chats, we investigate how voices are woven in discourse, how themes and voices inter-animate in a polyphonic way. This is important not only for understanding how meaning is created, but also for trying to design tools for support and evaluation.

Specific inter-animation patterns may be identified along each of the unity and difference dimensions in a chat. In CSCL, each of these patterns may be used for automatic abstraction of useful data, either for the participants in a chat, or for teachers for evaluation purposes. Such an application, using natural language processing, is presented in the end of this chapter.

Unity Inter-Animation Patterns

Unity-pursuing patterns are characterized by a trend towards continuity and achieving coherence in the chat. A first such class of patterns are *adjacency pairs* (Sacks et al., 1974), containing couples of logically succeeding utterances like question–answer. The first utterance in an adjacency pair normally requires (in a coherent dialog) the emitting of the second utterance. Examples of adjacency pairs are utterances 398 and 399 in Log 24-1, or utterances 68–69, 71–72, 73–74, 76–77 in Log 24-2:

Log 24-2.

68	mathisfun	see angle alpha?
69	Bob123	yes
70	Bob123	what about it?
71	mathisfun	is that 60 degrees?
72	Bob123	yes
73	mathisfun	can u use the degree, 2 length to find the last length of a triangle?
74	Bob123	i don't get what you're saying
75	mathisfun	the two arrow pointed lengths and the angle can find the length A
76	Bob123	by what?
77	mathisfun	the two sides and the degree

Question–answer adjacency pairs are important in learning because they force the students to participate, to face questions, to answer and, implicitly, to reason and understand the discussed problems.

Other kinds of adjacency pairs may be identified, for example, greeting–greeting (19–20, 21–22 in Log 24-3):

Log 24-3.

19	john:	hi all
20	Dan:	hi john
21	mary:	happy birthday, john!
22	john:	Thanks mary!

In CSCL, specific adjacency pairs have been identified. For example, Stahl (2006b, chap. 21) identified *math proposal adjacency pairs*, with the structure:

1. An individual makes a proposal to the group for the group's work.
2. Another member of the group accepts or rejects the proposal.

A second kind of unity inter-animation pattern is *repetition*, which plays an important role in creating coherence in a discourse. Repetition generally involves a larger number of utterances than an adjacency pair. Tannen (1989) considers that repetitions may be seen as a kind of rhythm making, with a main role of enhancing the involvement of the participants in a dialogue. Of course, repetition and rhythm are features with strong links with music, enforcing our analogy. Log 24-4 (which is a transcript of a face-to-face conversation, taken from Stahl (2006b, p. 250)) exemplifies these ideas:

Log 24-4.

1:21:53	Teacher	And you don't have anything like that there?
1:21:56	Steven	I don't think so
1:21:57	Jamie	Not with the same engine
1:21:58	Steven	⌈No
	Jamie	⌊Not with the same
1:21:59	Teacher	With the same engine … but with a different (0.1) … nose cone?=
1:22:01	Chuck	⌈=the same=
	Jamie	⌊=Yeah,
1:22:02	Chuck	These are both (0.8) the same thing
1:22:04	Teacher	Aw ⌈right
1:22:05	Brent	⌊This one's different

Socialization or jokes are also a way of creating unity. For example, many times participants in chats feel the need to joke, probably for establishing a closer relation with the other participants, perhaps in order to establish a group flow state (Csikszentmihalyi, 1990a). In fact, in all the chats we examined there is always a preliminary socialization phase.

Another interaction pattern is *cumulative talk* (Mercer, 2000) or, in Sacks' words, *collaborative utterances* (Sacks, 1962/1995). In such a situation, several participants jointly utter a sentence, like a single person. Log 24-5 shows a collaborative utterance co-constructed by three people completing each other's contribution (Sacks, 1962/1995, p 144–145):

Log 24-5.

1	Joe	(cough) We were in an automobile discussion,
2	Henry	discussing the psychological motives for
3	Mel	drag racing on the streets

A second example of cumulative talk is the inter-animation of Mathpudding and Mathman in a VMT problem-solving chat (Log 24-6):

Log 24-6.

117	ModeratorSf	could you guys tell templar what's going on?
118	mathpudding	we're experimenting with circles
119	mathman	and finding as many possible relations as we can

The last unity inter-animation pattern we will discuss here is *convergence*, which is an utterance that links two discussion threads having different topics. For example, in Fig. 24.1, the utterance 34 links the discussion thread on "(re)presentation" with the one on "topic." Convergence is an extremely important pattern, considered by Roschelle (1996) the crux of collaboration. It is the single transversal pattern among the previous, longitudinal ones.

Difference Inter-Animation Patterns

Difference patterns are inherent to chat conversations. Disputes or negotiations are inter-animated by differences and opposing positions. Difference making has a crucial role in chats for collaborative learning, a role that may be best understood from a polyphonic, musical perspective. The possibilities of contemplating (listening, reading) from a critical position the ideas (melodies) of other people and entering into negotiation and argumentation (polyphony of voices) enhance problem solving and enable learning through a trial-and-error process. Such processes also appear in individual learning (we can say that thinking also includes multiple inner voices), but the presence of multiple participants enhances both the possibility of developing multiple threads and, meanwhile, of identifying differences. The inter-animation of the multiple perspectives of the participants, their opposition as a result of contemplation, the presence of a third opinion in cases of conflict, and sometimes the synthesis it brings are better aids to success than a multi-voiced discourse performed by an individual (as inner thinking), where there is inherently much less conflict.

Several classes of difference inter-animation patterns may be identified. There are simple, obvious differential utterances that dismiss an assertion (Log 24-7):

Log 24-7.

371	4:33:28	Hal	it would be 60,000,000
.....			
387	4:34:47	Cosi	i think it's more than 60,00000

There might be difference making that not only disapproves an assertion but also proposes a development (Log 24-8):

Log 24-8.

392	4:35:18	Cosi	they cant get higher equally and even out to a 1 to 1 ratio

Sometimes, the participants even explicitly state that they found a difference and describe it (Log 24-9):

Log 24-9.

1	P4nzer	agree with me so far?
2	Tricavl	yes, but i did the same thing
3	Tricavl	the difference was the place of the space :).
4	petry_g	and the number of moves :)

Another example of this last type of difference making is Log 24-4 used above for the exemplification of repetitions. It ends with an extremely important difference making, which, in fact, is the moment of finding the solution (Stahl, 2006b). Actually, we could say that learning is achieved in many situations by understanding significant differences.

Evidence that participants make their own (internalize, individualize) differential position is also provided by the statistics of personal pronoun usage in chat sessions. For example, in a corpus of chats recorded in May 2005, "**I**" was used 727 times, much more than the usage of "**we**," with 472 occurrences. First person "**me**" was used 84 times comparing to "**us**," used only 34 times. However, the second person addressing is very well represented by 947 uses of "**you**."

Automatic Analysis and Graphical Representation

The polyphony-based theoretical framework presented above may be used for developing automated analysis and visualization tools for examining chats from different points of view. As previously discussed, we consider a *voice* as a particular position, which may be taken by one or more *persons* when they emit an *utterance*, which has *explicit* and *implicit* links or *influences* on the other voices. In the implementation of our analysis tool, we start from the utterances in the dialog, we identify themes by detecting recurrent concepts and, in addition to explicit links, stated by the referencing facility of VMT, we try to find implicit links, reflecting voices' influences. These implicit links are detected by searching for instances of the possible interaction patterns discussed above. Eventually, we try to measure the influence of each participant in the chat, considering the "strength" of their voices (positions, uttered utterances) on the subsequent utterances, according to the existing links. Computational linguistics techniques are used for the identification of the themes and of implicit links among utterances.

Identification of Chat Themes

Chat themes are identified using text-mining techniques. The first step in finding the chat subjects is to strip the text of irrelevant words (stop-words), text emoticons — like ":)" or ":**P**"—special abbreviations used while chatting (e.g., "**brb**," "**np**" and "**thx**") and other words considered irrelevant at this stage.

The next step is the tokenization of the chat text. Recurrent tokens and their synonyms are considered as candidate concepts in the analysis. Synonyms are retrieved from the WordNet lexical ontology (http://wordnet.princeton.edu). If a concept is not found on WordNet, mistypes are searched. If successful, the synonyms of the suggested word will be retrieved. If no suggestions are found, the word is considered as being specific to the analyzed chat and the human analyst is asked for details. In this way, the analyst can tag the part of speech for each word and can add synonyms. All this information is saved into a cache, so the analyst will not be prompted twice for the same word.

The last stage for identifying the chat topics consists of a unification of the candidate concepts discovered in the chat. This is done by using the synonym list for every concept: if a concept in the chat appears in the list of synonyms of another concept, then the two concepts' synonym lists are joined. At this point, the frequency of the resulting concept is the added frequencies of the two unified concepts. This process continues until there are no more concepts to be unified. At this point, the list of resulting concepts is taken as the list of topics for the chat conversation, ordered by their frequency.

In addition to the above method, used for determining the chat topics, there is an alternate technique we used to infer them by using a surface analysis technique of the conversation. Observing that new topics are generally introduced into a conversation using some standard expressions such as "**let's talk about email**" or "**what about wikis**," we can construct a simple and efficient method for deducing the topics in a conversation by searching for the moment when they are first mentioned.

A list of patterns of ways of introducing topics in a conversation can be manually edited. If an utterance matches any one of the patterns, it means that the utterance introduces a new topic. A pattern consists of a number of words that must be identified in the utterance and a key word that is associated to the new topic of the conversation (e.g., "**let's talk about** <topic>" or "**what about** <topic>"). The process of identifying a pattern in an utterance is done using the synset for each word that has already been extracted from WordNet.

The implemented system has an interface (see Fig. 24.4) that lists the topics sorted according to their number of occurrences in the chat. This interface also displays the utterances of the chat associated with the topics they include and with information about the detected interaction patterns (e.g., adjacency pairs). It also contains some parameters that can be tuned for obtaining the best analysis.

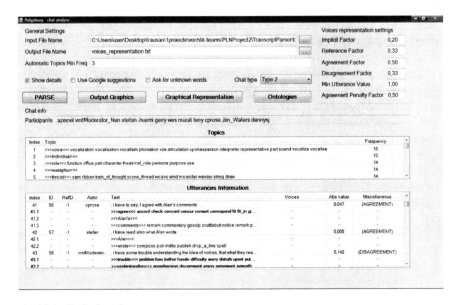

Fig. 24.4. Topic detection screen.

The topics of the chat may also be detected as the connected components in the chat graph described in the next section. All the details of an utterance in the chat—the content of the utterance, the implicit and explicit references and other details—can be visualized by clicking the rectangle representing the utterance in the chat graph.

Discovering Implicit Links in an Utterance

As we have previously discussed, in a log of a VMT conversation two types of links among utterances may be identified. There are explicit links, stated by participants by means of the VMT referencing tool. In addition to these, many implicit links may be identified, as was exemplified in Fig. 24.1.

We consider that each chat utterance may have a certain influence in the development of the conversation; it can become a chat voice. Each utterance may contain the influence of at least one other, alien voice, for example that to whom it refers, as an answer to a question, an elaboration, a disagreement, etc. By transitivity, voices may accumulate during a conversation. The emitter of the utterance implicitly can note the presence of alien voices in his utterance, when he explicitly refers to a previous utterance with the VMT referencing tool.

Because users are generally in a hurry or they don't consider it necessary, many of the utterances do not have any explicit references. Thus, it is necessary to find a method for discovering the implicit references in an utterance. The method proposed here is similar to the one presented above for determining the introduction of new chat topics, based on text mining techniques (Manning & Schutze, 1999) and patterns. The system uses another list of patterns that consists of a set of words (expressions) and a local subject called the referred word. If an utterance matches one of the patterns, it is first determined what word in the utterance is the referred word (e.g., "**I don't agree with your assessment**"). Then, a search for this word is performed, in a predetermined number of the most recent previous utterances. If such a word is found in one of these utterances, then an implicit relationship is defined between the two lines, the current utterance referring to the identified utterance. In addition, two other empirical methods were implemented.

A graphical representation of chats was designed to facilitate an analysis based on the polyphony theory of Bakhtin and to permit the best visualization of the conversation. For each participant in the chat, there is a separate horizontal line in the representation and each utterance is placed in the line corresponding to the issuer of that utterance, taking into account its positioning in the original chat file—using the timeline as an horizontal axis (see Fig. 24.5). Each utterance is represented as a rectangular node having a horizontal length proportional with the textual length of the utterance. The distance between two different utterances is proportional to the time between the utterances (Trausan-Matu, Rebedea, Dragan & Alexandru, 2007).

The explicit references between utterances are depicted using blue connecting lines while the implicit references (deduced using the method described in Trausan-

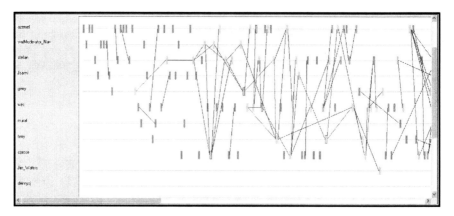

Fig. 24.5. Graphical visualization of the discussion threads.

Matu et al., 2007) are represented using red lines. The utterances that introduce a new topic in the conversation are represented with a red margin.

The graphical representation of the chat has a scaling factor that permits an overview of the chat, as in Fig. 24.6, as well as an attentive observation of the details in a conversation (as in Fig. 24.5).

(a)

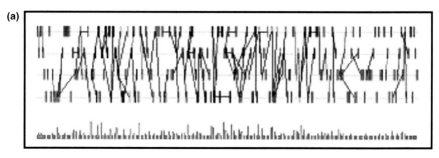

(b)

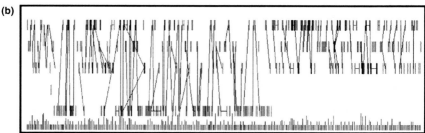

Fig. 24.6. A conversation with (a) equal and (b) non-equal participation.

Viewing the whole conversation graph gives an idea of the global participation of the learners. For example, in Fig. 24.6a, all the participants make about an equal number of contributions. This is not the case in Fig. 24.6b, where one participant has almost no participation and another student leaves early in the chat session.

At the bottom of the graphical representation of the conversation (see Fig. 24.7), after the line corresponding to the last participant in the chat, there is a special area that represents the importance (strength) of each utterance, considered as a chat voice, in the conversation (Trausan-Matu et al., 2007). The height of the rectangle corresponding to each utterance is proportional with the strength of that utterance (or voice). The details about how this measure is computed are presented in the next section.

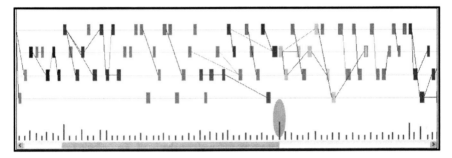

Fig. 24.7. A fragment of the conversation from Log 24–10.

Assessing the Contributions of the Learners in the Conversation

One of the most important goals in any collaborative-learning process is the assessment of the contribution of each learner. For CSCL using chat conversations, in order to determine the contributions of the participants, a graphical representation of the contribution was implemented starting from the polyphonic theory and the analysis method. The evaluation of the contributions of each learner considers the degree to which they have influenced the conversation. In terms of our polyphonic model, we evaluate to what degree they have emitted strong utterances that influenced the following discussion, or, in other words, to what degree the utterance became a strong voice.

An utterance is considered strong if it influences the continuation of the conversation. The contribution of each participant is computed by accumulating the strengths of the utterances they emitted.

The automatic analysis considers the inter-animation patterns in the chat. It uses several criteria such as the presence in the chat of questions, agreement, disagreement or explicit and implicit referencing. The diagram is generated using a series of parameters like: implicit and explicit reference factors, bonuses for agreement, penalties for disagreement, minimum value for a chat utterance, penalty factors for utterances that agree or disagree with previous ones because the current utterances have less originality than the first ones. In addition, the strength of a voice (of an utterance) depends on the strength of the utterances that refer to it. If an utterance is referenced by other utterances that are considered important, obviously that utterance also becomes important.

By using this method of computing their importance, the utterances that have started an important conversation within the chat, as well as those that began new topics or marked the passage between topics, are more easily emphasized. If the explicit relationships were always used and the implicit ones could be correctly determined in as high a number as possible, then this method of calculating the contribution of a participant would be considered successful (Trausan-Matu et al., 2007).

During the first step of the graph generation, the importance value of each utterance is computed by relating it to an abstract utterance that is built from the most important concepts in the conversation (the themes). When constructing this utterance, we take into account only the concepts whose frequency of appearance is above a given threshold. Then all the utterances in the chat are scaled in the interval 0–100, by comparing each utterance with the abstract utterance. The comparison is done using the synonym sets of each word contained in the utterance. Thus, this process uses only the horizontal relations from WordNet. An utterance with a score of 0 contains no words from the concepts in the abstract utterance and an utterance with a score of 100 contains all the concepts from the abstract utterance.

Log 24-10 contains a sequence of utterances where the participants collaborate intensively (it may be considered as a "collaborative moment" (Stahl, 2006b)), a fact revealed from the relations graph (Fig. 24.7) and from the large number of explicit and implicit relations interconnecting utterances 122 through 136.

From Fig. 24.7, we can see that the highest strength (the highest rectangle below the utterances) has the voice of RaduDumitrescu at the utterance nr. 122 (an oval shadow was manually added for emphasizing it). This fact is also observable by the large number of relations following utterance 122 (see Log 24-10) and in the change of the amount of contribution of RaduDumitrescu, in Fig. 24.7.

The graph that shows the contributions of every participant (in Fig. 24.8) contains on the x-axis the utterances in the chat and on the y-axis the value computed for each participant in the conversation, for his/her cumulative contribution. This value is computed by summing the numerical values corresponding to the strengths of the utterances that the participant has uttered up to the position on the x-axis. Accordingly, for each utterance, at least the value of one user contribution is modified—the value for the user that issued that utterance.

Conclusion

In all of the chats from the CSCL experiments we have analyzed, the interactions are structured in a polyphonic manner. Discourse in chats implies an inter-animation of multiple voices along two dimensions, the sequential utterance threading and the transversal one, similar to polyphonic music. In addition, another dichotomy, the unity-difference (or centrifugal-centripetal, (Bakhtin, 1981)) opposition may also be

Log 24-10.

122	RaduDumitrescu	also the application allows the user to describe the topic of the meeting
123	Alexrosiu	yes, and furthermore, several topics should be defined Reference to message No. 122
124	Alexei	yes, that would also help an automatic application to parse the ch Reference to part of the message No: 122
125	RaduDumitrescu	so everybody must know what are the meeting is all about
126	Alexrosiu	maybe even some users could be waned if they are offtopic... but this is a rather sci-fi feature, i guess :) Reference to message No. 124
127	RaduDumitrescu	and at the end the application should specify if all the topics were covered.... what do you think? Reference to message No. 123
128	Alexei	yes, i agree, but I think it can be done if the user is going too "offtopic" Reference to part of the message No: 126
129	Alexei	yes, maybe some percentage of coverage... Reference to part of the message No: 127
130	Alexrosiu	Correct Reference to message No. 127
131	Dorin	this feature implies a rather advanced natural language processing engine, though Reference to message No. 128
132	Alexei	so, about the reminders - when a user leaves the conference for some reason, he should be reminded about the missed parts of the conversion Reference to part of the message No: 121
133	Alexrosiu	maybe some kind of reminders should be set for future conferences... meaning that all people invited to the conference should be reminded to attend
134	Alexei	a problem that i've also noticed here is the rather unsynchronized way of talking
135	Alexrosiu	well, this would be solved by using the tree view i was talking about earlier Reference to message No. 134
136	RaduDumitrescu	i think the users can check the topics, no need for natural language processing Reference to message No. 131

observed. Adjacency pairs, repetitions, collaborative utterances, socialization and convergent inter-animation patterns contribute to the unity-directed dimension at diverse discourse levels.

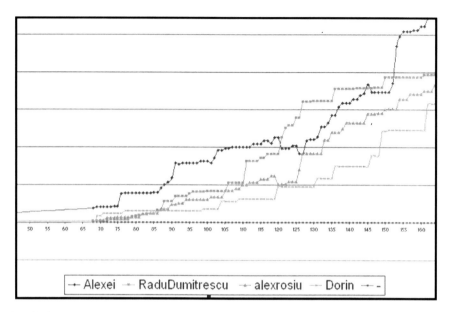

Fig. 24.8. The evolution of the contribution of the participants in the chat.

The second, differential dimension could be better understood if we consider discourse as an artifact that—taking into account that every participant in collaborative activities has a distinct personality—is a source of a critical, differential attitude. Even if individual, inner discourse may be multi-voiced, difference and critique are empowered in collaborative contexts, in a community of different personalities.

A consequence of the unity-differential perspective for the design of CSCL environments is that they must facilitate inter-animation not only on the unity dimension through threading, but also along the transversal, differential, critical dimension. Tools that can assist in this category should be able to provide abstractions of the discourse and recommendations, in order to facilitate differential position taking. They should also allow the participants to emphasize the different proposed themes and to relate them in threads, polyphonically.

Wegerif advocates the use of a dialogic framework for teaching thinking skills by stressing inter-animation: "meaning-making requires the inter-animation of more than one perspective" (Wegerif, 2006). He proposes that "questions like 'What do you think?' and 'Why do you think that?' in the right place can have a profound effect on learning" (Wegerif, 2007). However, he does not develop the polyphonic feature of inter-animation.

Starting from the theory of dialog, an application was implemented that may be used for inspecting what is going on and for measuring the degree to which learners are involved in a forum discussion or a chat conversation. The effective contribution of each participant to the inter-animation process may be measured. The application visualizes the strengths of the voices of the participants in chat conversations, following Bakhtin's ideas. Diagrammatic representations are used for viewing the influence of a given speaker and of the comparative evolution of the contribution of the learners. The visualization application described here can be further extended to consider more aspects related to the polyphonic, contrapuntal features of chat conversations.

Chapter 25
A Model for Analyzing Math Knowledge Building in VMT

Juan Dee Wee and Chee-Kit Looi

Abstract This work describes a methodology for analyzing the social construction of mathematical knowledge within a chat environment like VMT. It proposes a model for representing the flow of discourse by linking contributions based on information uptake. A framework for analysis using the model is designed to represent: (1) the co-construction and manipulation of mathematical representations and artifacts such as symbols, concepts, math formulas and linguistic expressions; (2) segmentations that identify critical boundaries during chat interactions; (3) meaning-making paths intertwining through series of uptakes; (4) pivotal moments during interactions influencing the direction of the discourse and (5) elements of the model for educators to apply in understanding the learning of mathematics by groups. The long-term goal behind this research is to develop a structure for analyzing online collaborative math learning. More specifically, this methodology seeks to contribute to a holistic approach to understanding the process of meaning-making embedded in interactions among chat postings. We discuss this methodology in the context of data collected in VMT from small groups of junior-college students solving mathematics problems using three different types of problem design.

Keywords Meaning making · up-take · segmentation · pivotal contributions · Collaborative Interaction Model · problem design · individual uptake descriptor table

Participants in chat sessions in settings like the VMT environment learn as an indirect result of having to keep up their end of conversation. This process prompts learners to construct meaning, relate experiences and construct knowledge (Baker, Jensen & Kolb, 2002). Participants have to think of a response to what they have

J.D. Wee (✉)
Learning Sciences, Nanyang Technological University, Singapore
e-mail: vmtchat@gmail.com

G. Stahl (ed.), *Studying Virtual Math Teams*, Computer-Supported Collaborative Learning Series 11, DOI 10.1007/978-1-4419-0228-3_25, © Springer Science+Business Media, LLC 2009

heard. Their reasoning process leading to their response requires analysis of what they have heard for an extraction of something meaningful, and then relating this meaning to resources from past experiences (Schank, 2002). Collaboration requires conversation, in which participants work in groups to socially negotiate a shared understanding of the approaches they use to accomplish tasks (Jonassen, Peck & Wilson, 1999).

Networked computers offer many opportunities to introduce conversation in an online environment in order to support the building of collaborative knowledge. People who are geographically apart can access chat software through a network of computers connected through a server to communicate and co-construct knowledge. In quasi-synchronous chat environments, the generation of communication occurs when textual and graphical inscriptions are interpreted by one or more participants, who subsequently construct new representations in the chat medium. This social construction process involves interpretation of another person's understanding and reflection upon this understanding in a cultural sense that is similar to the other's (Bruner, 1995). Here, the understanding is situated in the context of creation (Brown, Collins & Duguid, 1989) and externalized in the form of representations afforded by the chat environment. When the conversation content is seen rather than heard, the methods participants use to facilitate their conversation are clearly dependent on the medium in which interaction takes place. This context must be taken into account by researchers trying to interpret and understand the meaningful interaction among participants.

Our research explores patterns in chat transcripts to look for instances of inter-subjective cognitive activity distributed across participants and their manipulations of representations. We interpret this activity from both the researcher's and participant's perspectives. We build on the work of social network analysis (Scott, 1991; Wasserman & Faust, 1992), information uptake (Suthers, 2006b), group cognition (Stahl, 2006b) and interaction analysis (Jordan & Henderson, 1995) to propose a model for analyzing small groups of collaboration in quasi-synchronous chat environments like VMT.

Our work adopts the concept of information uptake (Suthers, 2006a, 2006b) to understand group cognition in small group problem solving (Stahl, 2006b). We propose a *Collaborative Interaction Model* (CIM) to provide a structural view of the uptakes. By linking contributions together in a diagrammatic model, we provide a representation to support deeper analysis of the way an individual's contribution is influenced by the uptake or interpretation of another participant's contribution. Using this model, we identify the construct of a *pivotal contribution* as one that is central to the group's knowledge-building or problem-solving process, and the construct of a *stage transition* that shifts direction in the discourse. A sequence of postings forms the elemental cell of interactional meaning making. Subsequent sections will explain the development of the proposed model, using chat segments to examine how participants construct knowledge and mediate shared understanding in the VMT chat environment.

Organization of the Chapter

This chapter is organized with the following sections:

- A review of common methodologies to analyze online conversation.
- An overview of the VMT learning environment and of the context and background of the usage of the environment for collecting our data.
- Three types of mathematical problem designs that we deployed in the environment.
- Samples of transcripts using the problem designs, constructed from the replay of the chats.
- The proposed analysis model and the underlying assumptions for using the model.
- The process followed for constructing analyses using the model, and the key features of the model.
- Further implications and features of the model, as well as its broader applicability to students and educators.

Research Methods for Analyzing Online Conversations

Various studies have suggested methods to analyze online conversations (asynchronous and synchronous environments) from the perspective of the researcher. Garcia and Jacobs (1999) proposed using the methodology of *conversation analysis* (Goodwin & Heritage, 1990; Sacks et al., 1974) to study interactions taking place in online chat environments with video capture of participants' computer screens during chat sessions. They argued that for some research questions, the use of single-point logs to analyze interaction transcripts did not sufficiently capture external interaction processes such as the behaviors of participants when using the computer to transmit information (Rintel, Mulholland & Pittam, 2001). Their research was further developed by O'Neill and Martin (2003) through the illustration of how repairing problematic postings by participants could be easily managed and how the timing of chat postings may disrupt conversational coherence. The characteristic of a chat environment makes it challenging to identify appropriately the referential relationships among postings. Hence, it is important for researchers when doing analysis to take into account the disruptive nature of "quasi-synchronous" chat environments, i.e., online environments in which the gradual production of utterances cannot be observed by others. Unlike in face-to-face (F2F) communication, in quasi-synchronous chat it is difficult for participants to observe how postings are taken up by subsequent postings because there are no visual, auditory or kinesthetic cues indicating when someone decides to enter into the conversation (Murphy & Collins, 1997; Siemieniuch & Sinclair, 1994). As such, the analysis of methods used by participants to communicate F2F may not be appropriate in analyzing communication in a quasi-synchronous environment. One must engage in some form of content analysis to examine computer-mediated communication transcripts (Chen & Looi, 2007).

Content analysis—involving coding messages and counting the number of individual postings with given codes—is of limited use for studying interactions between messages and for analyzing the group processes resulting from such interactions (Jeong, 2003). This is an area in which traditional experimental studies often focused too much on quantitative measures of classifications of isolated utterances, ignoring the sequential structure of the discourse (Stahl, 2002b; Suthers, 2006b).

Sequential analysis uses transitional state diagrams to illustrate the transitional probabilities between coded event categories. The categories are agreed upon by coders (with inter-rater reliability measured by Cohen's Kappa coefficient), and assigned using the grounded theory approach (Jeong, 2003).

Other types of analysis include the use of constructed *message maps* to illustrate the flow of an online discussion (Levin, Kim & Riel, 1990) and the use of an idea within a message as the unit of analysis (Henri, 1992), reinforcing the idea that the unit of analysis could possibly encompass an entire message constructed by an individual at a certain time during the discourse (Gunawardena et al., 1997; Rourke, Anderson, Garrison & Archer, 2001a). The selection of the unit of analysis is based on the situation in which it is used (De Wever et al., 2006) and the granularity of the content to be analyzed (Chi, 1997).

Suthers (2005b) proposed examining patterns of *information uptake* for the analysis of intersubjective meaning-making, beginning with the identification of uptake acts in which one participant takes up another participant's contribution and acts on it. The basis of intersubjective meaning-making is the process of communication requiring participants to establish a common ground, building from this common ground through adjustment and development in understanding (Rogoff, 1997).

The analysis of online conversations is typically a task done by researchers pouring over data collected on the conversations. As discussed above, there is the additional ambiguity posed by non-adjacency of uptakes. In our work, we perform the analysis of information uptakes from the researcher's perspective, but in addition we explore the interpretations of uptakes by asking the participants to provide their own perspectives on which specific utterance or action they were responding to when they responded, and why. We recognize that the use of post-event analysis faces similar interactional troubles to face-to-face survey interviews (Hammersley, 2003; Lee & Roth, 2003; Suchman & Jordan, 1990); we consider the data from participants' interpretations as another data source to triangulate interpretations of the discourse with that of the researcher's interpretations. Situations where uptake information might be missed by researchers are identified, hence increasing the reliability of the identification of uptake relationships between postings.

The Chat Environment and its Participants

The design of a learning environment should allow students to articulate their understanding because students learn best when they are able to express what they have learned (Sawyer, 2006). The quasi-synchronous chat environment of VMT allows students to articulate their thinking and to collaborate to solve math problems. We used the VMT system with a target group of students (ages 17–18 years) from a junior college in Singapore (Stahl, Wee & Looi, 2007). They have a basic foundation in mathematics and are among the top 20% of their cohort in terms of academic ability. The students have received sufficient mathematical training that the level of mathematical background knowledge assumed in any problem used was compatible with their expertise. The transcripts in this chapter are extracted from samples of interactions of different online teams from this group of students. (We have slightly modified some of the wording within the textual postings for readability by an international audience.)

Mathematical Problem Designs

Three mathematical problem designs were used to construct problems for use with the VMT environment in the Singapore junior college. The problems are designed to complement the existing school curriculum, where students solve traditional close-ended (CE) math problems individually during lectures and tutorials (Stahl et al., 2007). The first type is known as the *open-ended* (OE) problem design, where there is more than one possible solution to the problem. The second type, called the *conceptual approach* (CA) problem design, focuses on the use of strategies to solve the problem rather than emphasizing the solution itself. This design provides the opportunity for students to articulate their interpretation of the problem as well as sharing methods of approaching the problem. The third type adopts the *guided collaborative critique* (GCC) problem design (Wee, 2007a), where students are guided through a proposed situation (including the problem solution) and through a critique of identified common conceptual errors.

Open-Ended Problem Design (OE)

Open-ended problems were designed to encourage students to reason mathematically about their problem-solving steps. OE designs lead to many possible answers. However, such designs are often perceived as not very useful in preparing students for standardized tests and examinations. There is a need to construct problems that not only prepare students academically for examinations but also strengthen their mathematical reasoning in the process. Figure 25.1 shows an OE problem that was used.

Diagrams 1, 2, 3 and 4 show four graphical plots. Select one plot that contains a function. Illustrate using mathematical proofs or otherwise, why the graphical plot selected is a function.

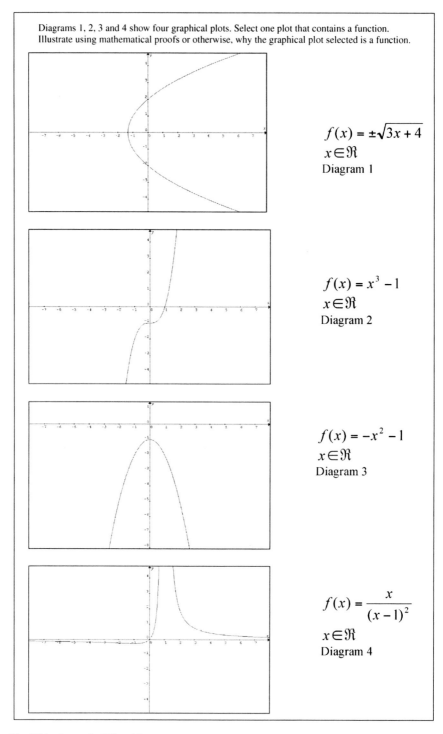

$$f(x) = \pm\sqrt{3x + 4}$$
$$x \in \Re$$
Diagram 1

$$f(x) = x^3 - 1$$
$$x \in \Re$$
Diagram 2

$$f(x) = -x^2 - 1$$
$$x \in \Re$$
Diagram 3

$$f(x) = \frac{x}{(x-1)^2}$$
$$x \in \Re$$
Diagram 4

Fig. 25.1 A sample OE problem

> (a) Identify any graphical plot that is not a function. Illustrate using mathematical proofs or otherwise, why the graphical plot selected is not a function.
>
> (b) Using the result obtained in part (a), restrict the domain of $f(x)$ such that $f^{-1}(x)$ exists.
>
> (c) Find the domain and range of $f^{-1}(x)$
>
> (d) Given that $g(x) = 2x+1$, $x \in (a,b)$ and using the $f(x)$ obtained in part (b), find suitable values for a and b such that $g(f(x))$ exists.

Fig. 25.1 (continued)

Traditional Closed-Ended Problem/Conceptual Approach (CA) Problem Design

Initial versions of VMT problems used the traditional close-ended (CE) problem design. Such designs were adopted from textbooks where students were tasked to read a given problem and apply standard procedures to find the unique correct solution. However, the implementation of CE problem design in the chat environment was not effective in promoting quality mathematical reasoning between participants. One drawback of the CE problem design is that students tried to just type expressions, with limited mathematical reasoning. This prompted us to develop the CA problem design. The CA problem design gives students the opportunity to discuss the rationale or purpose of the approaches they take to solve the problem, thus developing their mathematical reasoning rather than simply presenting the solution itself. One advantage offered by the CA problem design is that students are given the opportunity to explore collaboratively mathematical concepts encountered when solving mathematical problems individually during class. Figure 25.2 shows a CA problem we used.

> The functions f and g are defined by $f : x \rightarrow 4x^2 + 3$, $g : x \rightarrow 3 + e^{-2x}$, $x \in \Re$.
> With the aid of the graph $y = f(x)$, explain why f is a 1-1 function. Find
> (i) $f^{-1}(x)$, and
> (ii) $f^{-1}g(x)$, giving the domain of each function.
> Read the problem and collaboratively discuss the rationale for the mathematical concepts behind what is a 1-1 function with respect to $f(x)$, understanding that $R_f = D_{f^{-1}}$ where $f^{-1}(x)$ is the reflection of $f(x)$ about $y = x$ and understanding the relationship between the two domains, $D_{f^{-1}g(x)}$ and $D_{g(x)}$.

Fig. 25.2 A sample CA problem

Guided Collaborative Critique (GCC) Problem Design

The latest VMT problem design type, *Guided Collaborative Critique* (GCC) (Wee, 2007b), is constructed using a hybrid design that combines the merits of both CE and OE problem designs. The problem is first constructed using a CE design, but an erroneous solution is proposed for it. (The example analyzed in Chapter 9 is also of this type.) The choice of using the CE problem design to construct the problem is to familiarize students with examination-oriented questions while enabling them to evaluate, critique and repair the given erroneous worked-out solutions based on the OE problem design. The term "guided" refers to a sequence of structured steps in place to aid students in the analysis of the problem. The term "collaborative" empha-sizes use of dialogue in the group problem-solving process to construct knowledge. The term "critique" is associated with the group's ability to locate errors embed-ded in the proposed (but erroneous) solution and collaboratively build arguments to substantiate their identification of the errors and defend the validity of the proposed repair. In the context of this research, an error is defined as a representation identi-fied as mathematically inappropriate in the "proposed solution." Students not only collaboratively explore mathematical concepts learned in class, but also reason out the feasibility of their application in various GCC problems.

Embedded in the worked-out solution in the GCC problem in Fig. 25.3 are three common errors found in student assignments. The first error requires the student to identify the common term as 3 and not 3^{-1} when factoring the term $(1 + \frac{x}{3})^{-2}$. The second error is designed for students to realize that the expansion is only valid when $|x| < 3$ and not $|x| > 3$. The third error is the most complex of the three, requiring students to understand the need to take into account the $(-1)^r$ term when simplifying $\frac{(-2)(-3)(-4)...(-2-r+1)}{r!} 3^{-r-2} x^r$. The students were required to collaboratively work within their group to locate the three errors in the proposed solution and discuss ways to repair the errors.

VMT Interaction Transcript

The VMT Replayer tool is a VCR-like interface used to reproduce the session so that it unfolds on the screen the same way that it did for the students. The VMT Replayer tool plays back the entire session, capturing the moment-by-moment inter-action between the students as they post messages in the chat line and manipulate artifacts on the shared whiteboard. The interaction is also available to researchers as a log in the form of a spreadsheet, which is handy for analysis. Log 25-1 shows the interaction transcript of three participants (Lincoln, William and Smith) solving the OE designed math problem. Log 25-2 shows the interaction transcript of three other participants (Mason, Charles and Kenneth) solving a CA designed math problem. Log 25-3 shows the interaction transcript of three participants (Wane, Yvonne and Tyler) solving a GCC designed math problem. The first column shows the time that an utterance was posted or a graphic drawn. The second column shows the name of

Expand $(3+x)^{-2}$ as a series of ascending powers of x, up to and including the term in x^3, expressing the coefficients in their simplest form. State the range of values of x for which the expansion is valid. Find also the coefficient of x^{25} in the form $\frac{k}{3^m}$ where k and m are constants to be found.

Proposed solution:

$$(3+x)^{-2} = 3\left(1+\frac{x}{3}\right)^{-2}$$

$$= 3\left[1+(-2)\left(\frac{x}{3}\right)+\frac{(-2)(-3)}{2!}\left(\frac{x}{3}\right)^2+\frac{(-2)(-3)(-4)}{3!}\left(\frac{x}{3}\right)^3+\cdots\right]$$

$$= 3-2x+x^2-\frac{4}{9}x^3+\cdots$$

Expansion is valid for $\left|\frac{x}{3}\right|>1 \Rightarrow |x|>3$.

The general term is

$$(3)\frac{(-2)(-3)(-4)\cdots(-2-r+1)}{r!}\left(\frac{x}{3}\right)^r$$

$$= \frac{(2)(3)(4)\cdots(r+1)}{r!}3^{-r+1}x^r$$

$$= \frac{r!(r+1)}{r!}3^{-r1+}x^r$$

$$= (r+1)3^{-r+1}x^r$$

Identify the faults in the proposed solution and suggest repairs to fix it.

Fig. 25.3 A sample GCC problem

the participant. The third column shows the message posted by the participant in the VMT chat room. The message can take the form of text posted in the chat line or an artifact constructed on the shared whiteboard. The fourth column shows a contribution number assigned during analysis (we will come back to discussing the purpose of contribution numbers in a later section) and the action performed by the participant. The action performed is (by default) that the participants are typing into the chat line, unless otherwise indicated. Other possible actions include drawing on the shared whiteboard and using the referencing tool to link to another posting or artifact. Subsequent sections will illustrate how the interaction transcripts are used in the construction of the proposed chat interaction analysis model. Note that the first step in construction has already been performed in the following logs by assigning contribution numbers to individual postings or sets of sequential postings that form a single interactional move by one participant.

Log 25-1.

Time	Name	Message	Contribution
10:27:34	Lincoln	for qn E, the range of F is the domain of G	C86
10:27:44	William	Ya	C87
10:28:22	Smith	i thought domain of gf(x) equals to domain of f?	C88
10:28:27	Lincoln	so it 0 to -ve infinity	C89
10:29:12	Lincoln	no, that is for gf to exist first	C90
10:29:25	Lincoln	to prove that gf can happen	
10:29:58	Lincoln	then domain of gf is equal to the domain of f	
10:31:28	William	den wat is the range	C91
10:32:37	William	i think range is -2 to infinity	
10:32:38	Lincoln	no is the domain of f	C92
10:32:50	William	ooh	C93
10:32:54	Lincoln	that is the domain of gf	C94
10:33:01	Smith	to prove, gf does exist, range of f must be a subset of domain of g	C95
10:33:18	Lincoln	yah that is wat i am trying to say	C96
10:33:25	William	so wat the range of g	C97
10:33:40	Lincoln	sorry if i write the word equal just now, it is subset	C98
10:33:46	Smith	we r using diag 1 u know guys?	C99
10:33:54	William	ya	C100
10:34:11	William	so whats the range	
10:34:42	Lincoln	i thought is the domain of f that is the domain of g	C101
10:35:07	William	wat qn we doing	C102
10:35:13	Lincoln	it is the domain lah	C103
10:35:26	Lincoln	E wat	
10:35:26	William	Domain is all negative real values a is 0 b is -infinity	C104 [ref to WB]
10:36:18	William	ok the ahs is up	
10:36:25	Smith	we must first make diag a 1-1 function	C105
10:36:40	Smith	we take the top throw the bottom.	
10:37:02	Smith	range of f is a subset of domain of g, so we take the highest possible range of diagram 1 lo	
10:37:07	Lincoln	u are talking about question e right?	C106
10:37:19	Smith	yup	C107
10:37:21	William	ya	C108 Ref to C106
10:37:31	Lincoln	that will be infinite	C109
10:37:38	William	we take the bottom	C110 Ref to C108
10:38:05	Smith	take the top better	C111
10:38:16	Lincoln	i will take the top	C112
10:38:29	Lincoln	more comfortable	
10:38:36	William	ok	C113
10:38:44	Smith	so, a=0 b= +ve infinity	C114
10:38:44	William	b is infinity	C115 [Amend WB]

Log 25-2.

Time	Name	Message	Contribution
7:35:26	Mason	lets start	C1
7:35:46	Charles	so we need to draw the f	C2
7:36:35	Charles	hw to draw here	
7:36:40	Kenneth	draw the graph y=f(x), then use horizontal line to prove is 1-1	C3
7:36:41	Mason	then take a horizontal line test	C4
7:37:00	Mason	u dun have to solve the problem. Just say how u gonna solve it	C5
7:37:09	Kenneth	okay	C6
7:37:27	Charles	then Range of f inverse = domain of f	C7
7:37:54	Charles	Domain of f inverse=range f	
7:38:01	Kenneth	Yar	C8
7:38:07	Kenneth	then (i) done	
7:38:34	Charles	for f inverse g(x)	C9
7:38:42	Kenneth	domain of g = domain of f inverse g	C10
7:39:05	Charles	its the subset	C11
7:39:12	Mason	I think you have to test on the range of g and see if it fits the domain of f-1	C12
7:39:21	Kenneth	ops	C13
7:39:42	Mason	ken	C14
7:39:49	Kenneth	?	C15
7:39:53	Mason	dun draw such conclusion	C16
7:40:07	Kenneth	must test	C17
7:40:15	Mason	like domain of g=domain of f inverse g	C18
7:40:22	Mason	How u know?	
7:40:15	Charles	Domain of f inverse g(x)=Domain of g correct?	C19
7:40:22	Charles	then we can solve	C20
7:41:05	Kenneth	formula of composite functions lol	C21/Ref to C18
7:41:26	Kenneth	coz domain of f inverse g cannot exceed domain of g	C22/Ref to C18
7:41:32	Mason	oh	C23
7:41:37	Mason	then i wrong	
7:41:38	Mason	sorry	
7:42:27	Kenneth	No need to actually work out? so we state method le	C24
7:42:45	Mason	en	C25
7:42:43	Kenneth	?	C26
7:42:45	Mason	1st one settle	C27
7:42:49	Mason	move on	

Log 25-3.

Time	Name	Message	Contribution
4:15:03	Wane	i cant remember the method for finding the coefficient	C1
4:15:08	Yvonne	yea	C2
4:15:16	Wane	do u remember tt formula we learnt in secondary school?	C3
4:15:18	Tyler	it's a binomial series	C4
4:15:28	Yvonne	same... but there is one mistake ler	C5
4:15:32	Tyler	use the binomial formula	C6
4:15:42	Wane	the more than sign	C7
4:15:43	Tyler	yeah step by step	C8
4:15:52	Yvonne	i not sure cause it's power to -2	C9
4:15:58	Wane	the first part is correct	C10
4:15:06	Yvonne	can enlighten me?	C11
4:16:16	Yvonne	no.... that first part is wrong ler	C12
4:16:19	Wane	then the modules x more than 3 is wrong	C13
4:16:23	Wane	it should be less than	
4:16:25	Tyler	first take out the 3	C14
4:16:33	Yvonne	when he take out constant, it will not be 3	C15
4:16:49	Yvonne	cos it's 3^-2	
4:16:52	Tyler	yeah. coz there is a a power to -2	C16
4:17:15	Yvonne	but the rest of the steps i'm not very sure	C17
4:17:18	Tyler	so the second line is not correct	C18
4:17:28	Tyler	$3\left(1+\frac{x}{3}\right)^{-2}$	C19/Shared
Whiteboard / "3" outside the bracket is circled			
4:17:39	Yvonne	$3\left[1+(-2)\left(\frac{x}{3}\right)+\frac{(-2)(-3)}{2!}\left(\frac{x}{3}\right)^2 \right.$ $\left. +\frac{(-2)(-3)(-4)}{3!}\left(\frac{x}{3}\right)^3+\cdots\right]$	C20/Shared
Whiteboard / "3" outside the bracket is circled			
4:17:40	Tyler	see I circle it .right?	C21
4:17:44	Wane	that 3 is correct	C22
4:17:54	Yvonne	y?	C23
4:18:10	Tyler	no . that3 should also to the power to 3	C24
4:18:23	Yvonne	-2	C25/Ref to C23
4:18:42	Tyler	sorry.	C26
4:18:45	Wane	the formula is (a+ bx) power n	C27
4:19:12	Yvonne	the person took out the common factor	C28
4:19:26	Wane	Tyler is correct	C29
4:19:28	Wane	i over look it	
4:19:32	Tyler	but should take out the a.	C30/Ref to C26

Log 25-3. (continued)

Time	Name	Message	Contribution
4:19:51	Yvonne	ok.... for the next part... did your spot any error?	C31
4:19:52	Tyler	coz -2 is a negative value	C32
4:19:54	Wane	the formula is a power n (1+ bx/a) ower n	C33
4:20:06	Tyler	so it cant use Wane's formula	C34/Ref to C28
4:20:21	Wane	what?????	C35
4:20:34	Yvonne	i don't get it	C36
4:20:35	Wane	hold on	C37
4:20:35	Wane	wait	
4:21:16	Tyler	i mean if the power is a negative value. it should use(1+ax) to power of n	C38
4:21:42	Yvonne	ya... that's why they took out the common factor	C39
4:21:44	Tyler	see?	C40
4:21:53	Tyler	yes	C41
4:22:11	Wane	tts what i was saying	C42
4:22:27	Yvonne	ok	C43
4:22:41	Tyler	so move to the next line	C44

Collaborative Interaction Model

The analysis of interaction transcripts is complex and time consuming. Our proposed model—called the Collaborative Interaction Model (CIM)—is designed to analyze relationships among contributions (graphical and textual postings). There is a high probability that the postings may appear in an order that obscures their response structure. It is not possible to shrink the time window for searching relations of relevance to adjacent contributions in order to reduce the complexity of analysis caused by this, because there is always a chance that any past contribution could be taken up again. Focusing the analysis on the relationship between adjacent postings is therefore in general insufficient for understanding relationships between the postings in a quasi-synchronous chat.

In CIM, chat postings are analyzed line by line; postings belonging to the same interactional unit are grouped together as a contribution and assigned a single contribution number. Contributions belonging to the various participants are represented by differently shaped nodes. The interaction betweens contributions are mapped using arrows to illustrate uptake relationships (Suthers, 2006a).

Jordan and Henderson (1995) pointed out that all events (in this case the occurrences in the discourse) of any duration are *segmented* in some way. They argued that researchers would be keen to understand the transition process of interaction between segments (known as *stages* in the CIM). The CIM model adapts the concept of segmentation to trace the development of knowledge construction across stage boundaries. Segmentation is constructed initially using the researcher's interpretations of the interaction transcript. This is then triangulated with the participant's interpretations, hence increasing the reliability of interpretations.

The CIM traces the development of knowledge construction in an online collaborative environment by mapping the interaction between participants (linking of contributions by uptake arrows) throughout the discourse. The model is applicable for a group of 3–5 persons. The object with a contribution number is known as a *node* in the CIM. The concept of contribution will be elaborated below. Each node shape (rectangle, oval or hexagon) represents one of the participants. Nodes represent contributions constructed. The model does not directly address design issues. It does not analyze the design of the software or compare it to other designs. The model is intended to help understand how learners interpret and build on each other's representations. It is used to trace emerging paths of knowledge construction. The CIM is a methodology that describes how groups collaborate in an online environment. This descriptive method could help instructional designers review different ways of improving tested collaborative interface designs.

Constructing the CIM

Chat postings (including constructions on the shared whiteboard) are coded into contributions (numbered in Logs 25-1, 25-2 and 25-3). The contributions are then mapped and linked to form the CIM (see Figs. 25.4 and 25.5). The concept of uptake is defined as a situation in which a participant references or manipulates content in previous contributions (Suthers, 2006b), either their own or someone else's. Uptakes

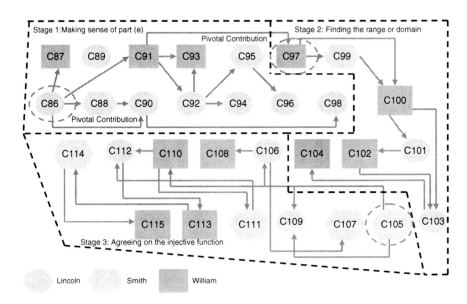

Fig. 25.4 CIM before triangulation with IUDT

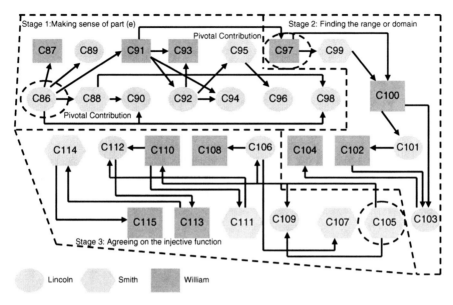

Fig. 25.5 CIM after triangulation with IUDT

are indicated by arrows linking contributions in the CIM. The construction of this network of arrows takes place through two phases. The first phase occurs when the CIM is constructed based on the researcher's interpretation (see Fig. 25.4 and Log 25-1). Figure 25.4 shows a segment of a three-person team Collaborative Interaction Model. Researchers discuss their interpretations of the interaction transcripts during data sessions. The second phase (see Fig. 25.5) occurs when the CIM is triangulated with post-mortem interpretations made by the participants using a tool that we call the Individual Uptake Descriptor Table (IUDT).

Coding of a Contribution

Chat postings and whiteboard artifacts are coded in sequential order to form contributions, logical units from the participant's perspective. Sequential order is defined by the order of postings. A participant may type in a representation in the chat and then manipulate some artifacts on the shared whiteboard. When coding a hybrid interaction like this, the researcher has to take into account all the actions in sequential order. Assigning a logical contribution number is based on the researcher's interpretation of how participants defined the logical unit of their interactions. Each contribution is assigned a contribution number in the interaction transcript. In the CIM, participants are represented by differently shaped nodes. For example, in Fig. 25.4, rectangles represent William's contributions, ovals represent Lincoln's contributions and hexagons represent Smith's contributions. Each node has a contribution number which represents a posting by a participant in the interaction transcript (Log 25-1).

Stages in the CIM

A *stage transition* is defined to occur when there is a shift of direction in the discourse. Events in temporal and spatial orientation can be segmented in various ways (Jordan & Henderson, 1995; Kendon, 1985); participants negotiate across segment boundaries. The boundaries are known as stages in the CIM, negotiated by two types of transitions: abrupt and seamless. An abrupt transition is defined as a sudden change due to a new proposal. Seamless means that the transition is smooth (e.g., participants have agreed to move on to a next stage). Figure 25.6 shows the CIM constructed from the GCC problem design (see Fig. 25.3). It consists of six stages with three abrupt transitions and two smooth transitions. When no member takes up a prior contribution, the stage transition may be abrupt. For example, the transitions from stage 1 to 2, stage 2 to 3 and stage 3 to 4 are abrupt. The last contribution of each stage was not taken up by any member of the group. It will be useful for researchers to analyze why such contributions are not taken up. Unlike stage transitions mentioned earlier, the transition from stage 4 to 5 and stage 5 to 6 arise from pivotal contributions where the transition process is not abrupt.

Stage Transition

Interaction analysis classifies events of any duration to be segmented in some way. An event has an internal structure that is recognized and maintained by the participants. A transition from one segment (or stage) to another occurs once the segment reaches its boundary. The next segment is of a different "character." The notation

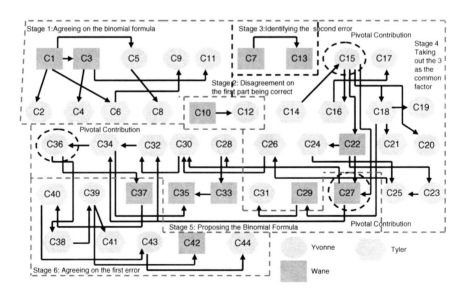

Fig. 25.6 Stages in the Collaborative Interaction Model

of "character" is similar to what we called "direction," where the direction of each stage consists of contributions aligned by coherence. Some of the possible ways in which a stage transition can occur are illustrated in Fig. 25.6.

Consider the stage transition from stage 1 to 2. Yvonne takes up Tyler's **"it's a binomial series"** [C6] with **"i not sure cause it's power to -2"** [C9]. Wane proposed that **"the first part is correct"** [C10], stating a different direction to the conversation between Yvonne and Tyler, who were discussing the validity of the secondary school binomial formula. This caused an abrupt stage transition. Yvonne takes up Wane's proposal "the first part is correct" [C10] but rejects the claim by stating **"no.... that first part is wrong ler"**[1] [C12], informing Wane that there is a mistake in the first part of the proposed solution. Again there is an abrupt stage transition from stage 2 to 3, as Wane ignores Yvonne's proposal [C12] and continues with **"then the modules x more than 3 is wrong"** [C13]. Tyler proposed **"first take out the 3"** [C14].

Tyler's Individual Uptake Descriptor Table (IUDT) mentions that the question was reviewed and that he realized an error occurred when 3 was taken out of the term $3\left(1 + \frac{x}{3}\right)^{-2}$. Wane's [C13] mentioned the second error while Tyler's [C14] mentioned the first error, leading to an abrupt stage transition from stage 3 to 4.

Stage transitions may also occur when participants propose a significant contribution resulting in a shift of direction in the discourse. For example, Yvonne's [C15] **"when he take out constant, it will not be 3, cos it's 3^-2"** is selected as a pivotal contribution due to the implication resulting from its construction. [C15] was taken up by Wane who rejected Yvonne's claim and counter proposed, **"that 3 is correct"** [C22]. [C15] was also taken up by Tyler who agreed with Yvonne's [C15], **"yeah. coz there is a a power to -2"** [C16] and **"so the second line is not correct"** [C18], explaining to Wane that there is indeed an error and concurrently agreeing with Yvonne. The construction of [C15] enables the participants to take up and manipulate [C15] constructively through argumentation and agreement, forming a basis for knowledge construction. Wane's contribution, **"the formula is (a+ bx) power n"** [C27], is selected as a pivotal contribution as well as the contribution nearest to the boundary between stage 4 and 5 because the formula **"(a+ bx) power n"** does not appear to be coherent with the direction of stage 4, which focuses on having the power -2 assigned to 3 when it is taken out of the term $3\left(1 + \frac{x}{3}\right)^{-2}$. The above two cases illustrate a smooth transition arising from a pivotal contribution, where participants readily take up and manipulate this significant contribution, and thereby take the discourse in another direction.

Stage Reversal

A *stage reversal* occurs when participants revert to an earlier direction in the discourse. In a similar sense, the probability of an occurrence of a stage reversal is

---

[1] The expression, *ler*, is an emphatic term derived from Chinese and commonly used by Singapore students.

dependent on the group's motivation in returning to issues discussed in the previous stage. The accuracy of the knowledge constructed in the earlier stages may also result in a stage reversal applied in later chat segments. A stage reversal could have occurred when participants require knowledge constructed in previous stages to solve tasks in the current stage. Researchers should analyze how group interaction results in a stage reversal. Figure 25.5 shows that stage 1 shares a similar direction to that of stage 4. Both directions (stages 1 and 4) focused on making sense of an error found in the term $3\left(1 + \frac{x}{3}\right)^{-2}$. In stage 4, Tyler's **"first take out the 3"** [C14] appears to be coherent with **"i not sure cause it's power to -2"** [C9] by Yvonne, where both contributions mentioned the first error.

Uptake of Contributions

Our study refines the notation of uptake (Suthers, 2006b) as not just building on another group member's contribution, but also interpreting that existing contribution based on the new contribution. The manipulation of contributions involves not only the action of working on the contribution, but also the interpretation that motivates the action. By identifying the rationale of interpretations, researchers can understand the objective of the manipulation leading to the new contribution. Through this identification, researchers are able to identify how group members interpret other interpretations (their own or others'), and understand the purpose of their manipulation and why this manipulation is essential to construct a new contribution. In the CIM, the uptake is represented by the arrow linking two contributions. Uptake is a function of the following variables: (1) Participants must interpret contributions that are related somehow to their prior understanding, making a connection between a prior understanding and the current interpretation in order to construct a new understanding. (2) Prior understanding is achieved from previous contributions or knowledge constructed prior to the discourse. Uptakes resulting in knowledge constructed from previous contributions form the basis of interpretation, but knowledge constructed prior to the discourse such as previous encounters with similar types of problem also contribute actively to the interpretation. (3) Language and cultural representations are mutually dependent and they form the vehicle of communication in the discourse. Language and cultural representations are embedded in the contribution, forming part of the interaction and affording a meaning-making process somewhat different from that of another group of a different cultural and language background. Uptakes encompass not only information related to the tasks, but also the language and culture of the participant.

Pivotal Contributions

A significant contribution known as a *pivotal contribution* shifts the emergence of meaning-making patterns into new stages. The concept of stages simplifies the analysis of different knowledge construction patterns in the discourse. Figure 25.7 shows

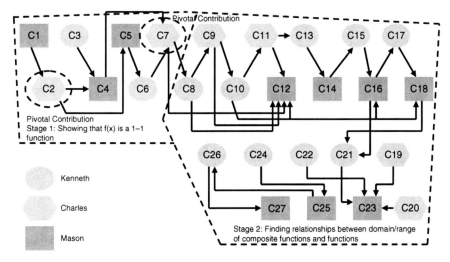

Fig. 25.7 Collaborative Interaction Model (Mason, Charles and Kenneth)

the CIM with two stages (see Log 25-2). The first stage shows how the participants attempt to show that the function $f(x)$ is one-to-one. The second stage shows how participants use the mathematical definitions to establish relationships between the range/domain of $f(x)$ and that of the composite function. Contribution [C2] in Fig. 25.7 and Log 25-2 was selected as a pivotal contribution because it steers the discourse into the direction of showing $f(x)$ as a one-to-one function. Contribution [C7] was also identified as a pivotal contribution, shifting the group's focus from showing $f(x)$ as a one-to-one function to using knowledge of composite functions to find the range/domain of $f(x)$.

The emergence of meaning-making patterns leading to the construction of the pivotal contribution and patterns of knowledge construction diverging from the pivotal contribution form the basis for analyzing how shared meaning-making is achieved at a group level, rather than at an individual level—i.e., across multiple contributions by multiple group members.

Individual Uptake Descriptor Table (IUDT)

Postings in a quasi-synchronous chat environment may arrive out of sequence and this makes it challenging for researchers to identify accurately the uptake relationships among postings. The CIM is designed to increase the reliability of identifying uptake relationships through the use of *individual uptake descriptor tables* (IUDTs). Figure 25.5 shows three uptake arrows ([C86] to [C98], [C88] to [C98] and [C91] to [C94]) not identified by researchers before the triangulation process with IUDTs. The IUDT (see Table 25.1) consists of three columns; "Each chat line you typed," "Whose and what chat lines did you see that made you type the chat line?" and

Table 25.1 Lincoln's individual uptake descriptor table

Each chat line you typed.	Whose and what chat lines did you see that made you type the chat line?	What were your other thoughts?
61 **No the domain of F**	William: **I think range is -2 to infinity**	**Wrong answer given by William**
62 **That the domain of GF**	William: **I think range is -2 to infinity**	
63 **Sorry if I write the word equal just now when I suppose to write subset**. [C98]	Lincoln:**For qn E, the range of F is the domain of G** [C86] Smith: **I thought domain of GF equals to the domain of F**. [C88]	**I make a typing error**.

"What were your other thoughts?" The IUDT is to be constructed within 24 hours of the chat session. The first column indicates the chat lines typed by the participants. The second column shows the representations the participants were interpreting prior to the construction of the chat posting. The representations could be the participant's own or other participants'. The third column indicates the rationale behind the construction of the chat posting.

Let's take the following case where researchers missed an information uptake relationship. Table 25.1 shows a segment of Lincoln's IUDT. Before Lincoln constructed the posting, **"Sorry if I write the word equal just now when I suppose to write subset"** [C98], Lincoln was interpreting his previous posting, **"For qn E, the range of F is the domain of G"** [C86] and Smith's posting, **"I thought domain of GF equals to the domain of F"** [C88]. Without Lincoln's IUDT, researchers would merely be guessing at what led to the construction of [C98]. Referring to Log 25-1, researchers would have attempted to locate **"equal"** in earlier postings, to match Lincoln's apology that **"equal"** was mentioned when it was supposed to be **"subset"** [C98]. The most recent posting where Lincoln mentioned "equal" is found in **"then domain of gf is equal to the domain of f"** [C90]—which was mathematically correct, causing a confusion as to why Lincoln apologized. When reviewing Lincoln's IUDT,the term **"equal"** [C98] was referring to **"the range of F is the domain of G"** [C86] as a mistake. The mathematical condition for a composite function $gf(x)$ to exist is that the range of $f(x)$ is a subset of the domain of $g(x)$. Lincoln was also attempting to address Smith's confusion, **"I thought domain of GF equals to the domain of F"** [C88], of his posting, **"For qn E, the range of F is the domain of G"** [C86], by correcting it to a **"subset"** [C98].

The use of IUDTs faces many of the same interactional troubles as face-to-face survey interviews (Hammersley, 2003; Lee & Roth, 2003; Suchman & Jordan, 1990). In a group of three chat participants, the researchers asked each of them to complete an IUDT individually, and then triangulated their own (researchers') interpretations together with each of the chat participant's. In addition, a focus group was formed to further probe conflicting interpretations as a group. As in the discussion of the IUDT in Table 25.1, the participant's perspectives provided the researchers with opportunities to identify missed interpretations, thereby increasing the reliability of the representation of uptake relationships between interactions.

Discussion

Collaborative learning analysis is the fundamental motivation for the development of the CIM. The model provides a systematic approach to analyze contributions in quasi-synchronous chat environments. The following describes the characteristics of the CIM.

Generality of the CIM

The CIM is designed to analyze quasi-synchronous interaction transcripts across various disciplines. We have applied the model to three different math problem designs. In ongoing research, more interaction transcripts will be analyzed using the CIM, further exploring the generality of the CIM.

Triangulation of Interpretations

The construction of the CIM was based on several data sessions conducted to analyze the interaction transcripts. The data were analyzed from the researchers' perspective and triangulated with the participants' individual uptake descriptor tables (IUDTs). The IUDTs were constructed from the participants' perspectives within 24 hours of the chat session and served to assist researchers in triangulating interpretations of the interaction transcript after data sessions. Subsequent research will explore issues related to the development of the CIM using our methods with the objective of seeking objectivity and validity in the construction process.

Unit of Analysis

The CIM proposes uptakes as the unit of analysis. The *IUDT* is designed to help researchers understand the motivations for the construction of the uptake from the participants' perspectives. This is insufficient to understand the group knowledge construction process, since the *IUDT* is designed to capture information from an individual perspective. Further analysis of the relationships among uptakes is required for researchers to understand the moment-to-moment interaction between participants before any conclusion on group knowledge construction can be drawn.

Stages

The CIM divides groups of contributions into stages. The concept of stages relates the analysis of the discourse to its respective directions. Each stage represents a different direction in the discourse and a change of stage indicates a shift of direction.

The construction of meaning is embedded in the interactions. The segmentation process, where contributions are clustered into different stages, allows researchers to explore the negotiation process directed by the group in a particular area during problem solving.

Pivotal Contribution

This study was implemented using three different types of problem design: Open-Ended (OE), Conceptual Approach (*CA*) and Guided Collaborative Critique (*GCC*). The chat interaction of these three problem designs was analyzed using the CIM. It identified "pivotal moments," known as pivotal contributions,which exerted major effects on the outcome of the discourse. Pivotal contributions are currently identified from the researchers' perspective. Ongoing work attempts to triangulate pivotal contributions from the researchers' perspective with pivotal contributions from the participants' perspective.

Level of Analysis

The CIM model provides a framework for analysis of textual contributions at both the micro level and the macro level for appropriate understanding of the ways group meaning making is achieved. The CIM captures the moment-to-moment interaction between participants through the analysis of uptakes at the micro level. The segmentation of the flow of knowledge construction by stages and pivotal contributions is intended to inform the understanding of group cognition and functionality at the macro level.

Problem Design

The CIM is primarily designed to map out interactions in the quasi-synchronous VMT environment. A good problem design should promote effective mathematical conceptual discourse. For example, the use of the *GCC* problem design promotes awareness of common conceptual errors in specific math problems. Through discussion of such errors, students will become prepared to encounter such errors in similar future problems. Educators can use the CIM to provide feedback to students during a post chat session. For example, representations of stages can be used to explain how students negotiate mathematical concepts during problem solving, or pivotal contributions can be used to acknowledge a student's contribution of a useful math proposal.

Educator's Tool

The CIM can also assist teachers in understanding interaction transcripts (how students interpret and manipulate mathematical representations in the stages) and in reflecting on their teaching. The analysis can help groups of teachers devise alternative approaches to teach a given topic. In Fig. 25.3, stage 1 shows that there is a possible confusion in using binomial formulas as taught in secondary school when students reach junior college (refer to Log 25-3). Teachers can clarify this concept to the students by differentiating between positive n and negative n powers. Teachers may also explicitly distinguish what is taught in secondary school from what is taught in junior college to avoid conceptual confusion in preparation for related lessons.

Conclusion

This research proposes an approach that builds on the concepts of information uptakes to understand group cognition in small-group problem solving. It provides a structural view to the uptakes, with arrows in the model linking contributions representing uptakes. The linking of contributions affords a deeper analysis of the way one individual's contribution is influenced by its uptake or interpretation by another participant's contribution. From the model, we distill the notion of a pivotal contribution as one that is central to the group's knowledge-building or problem-solving process. A sequence of postings forms the elemental cell of interactional meaning making. Shared meaning is constructed across several postings of more than one participant, and the unit of meaning making is the interaction itself, which is a group accomplishment. In subsequent research we will further elaborate the coding framework of the CIM to more fully operationalize the key ideas discussed in this chapter.

Three different mathematical problem designs were adopted in the construction of VMT problems: the open-ended (OE), the conceptual approach (CA) and the guided collaborative critique (GCC) problem designs. Through the constructed CIM models, we would like to further explore whether different problem types engender different types of meaning-making paths, and investigate how and why.

A further contribution of our work is the exploration of triangulation of data, including the interpretation of uptakes by the participants themselves, individually and as a focus group. In the transcripts we looked at, we shared some incidents where uptake information was first missed by researchers. When participants suggested them later, the researchers did re-consider their analysis. We will continue to explore these methods as a way of increasing the reliability of identifying uptake relationships between interactions, and of drawing more accurate CIMs.

Part VI
Conceptualizing Group Cognition in VMT

Introduction to Part VI

This Part wraps up the volume by reviewing its approaches to studying the nature and structure of interaction in virtual math teams. It conceptualizes the view of group cognition that has emerged in the previous Parts and reflects on how to study it further.

Chapter 26 expands on the approaches in Part V to response-structure analysis, seeing the implicit and explicit references among postings as part of a more complex *referential network*. In this view, everything is taken as a potential resource for the discourse, an object that can be referenced from the next chat posting. This includes elements of inscriptions on the whiteboard, points in the math topic statement, clauses in previous postings, icons on the computer interface, math concepts/techniques/theorems brought in from classroom experiences, bits of pop culture, and so on. The referential network is related to notions of joint problem space (Chapter 6), common ground (Chapter 7), indexical ground (Chapter 14). The approach in this chapter brings the author's life-long research full circle, explicating the Heideggerian notion of the situation as a network of significance, but doing so in the social context of intersubjectivity (Stahl, 1975a). It revisits the dialectic of tacit and explicit knowledge (Stahl, 1993a) by combining implicit and explicit references in the knowledge-building process. And it expands the theory of group meaning and individual interpretation (Stahl, 2006b, ch. 16) as it combines contributions designed by individuals into a shared network. By illustrating with a brief excerpt the complexity of the referential structure in a VMT chat, the chapter problematizes the notion that chat utterances can be objectively categorized and coded without the larger discourse being first subjected to rigorous fine-grained interaction analysis to determine its response and referential structure.

Chapter 27 argues that the analyses conducted in the VMT Project—and extensively represented in this volume—have many characteristics of *critical ethnography*. It develops its concept of critical ethnography with an example of its applicability to software design, a summary of its roots in critical social theory and a review of its history of successive generations of thought in anthropology. The tie to the VMT Project is made in terms of three key phenomena: temporality, objectivity and intersubjectivity. These phenomena were theorized by critical ethnographers. They were also central to analyses of VMT data. Chapter 6 analyzed several bridging mechanisms as ways for groups to establish a *temporal* dimension at the heart of the joint problem space. Chapter 7 explored in detail how virtual teams co-constructed math *objects* through the coordination of their work across multiple media. Chapter 8 presented an analysis of the construction of questioning in a group as a process of establishing *intersubjectivity*—not only by sharing each other's understanding of the answer to the question, but even by building the intersubjective meaning of the questioning. The critical thrust of the VMT Project's ethnographic investigation of online student groups takes the form of design-based research, which aims to support a new educational social practice.

Chapter 28 concludes the volume with a trio of summaries addressing the central goals of the VMT Project. It construes these in terms of their relevance for a needed new science of group cognition:

- *How to design a service for virtual math teams.* The design-based approach driven by a preliminary theory of group cognition and supported by a tentative methodology of chat interaction analysis entails establishing a collaboration environment instrumented for appropriate data collection. This chapter describes the design rationale for the VMT environment and service from the often-conflicting constraints of the pedagogical desiderata and the research criteria of the VMT Project. The operation of the VMT service creates and records a data corpus for the rigorous study of group cognition.
- *How to analyze a chat log from a setting like VMT.* Analysis of the reference structure among postings is crucial. This can be aided by various representations of the data. Collaborative analysis by researchers in data sessions provides for intersubjective reliability. The description of social practices that contribute to cognition at the group unit of analysis is a primary goal. This section describes how data are analyzed within the VMT Project and discusses how chat interaction analysis meets the criteria for scientific study.
- *How group cognition may take place in a setting like VMT.* Although group processes are composed of contributions that come from individuals and that must be interpreted—read and responded to—by individuals, these processes are distinct from and should not be reduced to individual-mental phenomena. A variety of such group-cognitive processes have been presented in this volume. This section argues for the need for a new science of group cognition modeled on the VMT Project and leading to a theoretical conceptualization of group phenomena associated with collaborative learning, problem solving and knowledge building.

As documented in this volume, the VMT Project has made progress on its original central goals and has provided a variety of suggestive preliminary explorations for a science of group cognition:

- Although the VMT environment was designed as a testbed for design-based research, it provides a basic platform and approach for an on-going service at the Math Forum. The service can now be extended to integrate with local school curriculum or to form groups of students from across the world to discuss math together. It demonstrates the effective design of software to support group cognition and to generate a data corpus of group interaction.

- The findings in the previous chapters indicate that math problem solving, knowledge building and other cognitive processes occur distinctively on the individual, small-group and community levels. Although these processes are intimately intertwined, it can be productive to isolate group-cognitive phenomena without reducing them to contributions by individuals. This yields a research methodology different from psychological approaches that rely on mental constructs and from sociological small-group studies that model group variables and non-cognitive group processes; it describes how the groups themselves accomplish cognitive tasks and how their group processes can be studied.

- The volume responds implicitly to a common criticism of group cognition theory, namely that the group has no on-going identity, no brain-based mind that can retain knowledge and learn. Various chapters have described how virtual math teams have bridged discontinuities in their existence between chat sessions and how they sustain a joint problem space by taking advantage of the persistence of digital media to encapsulate traces of their cognitive achievements in math artifacts inscribed in specific combinations of those media. Although the group phenomena may be short lived, they mediate individual and social phenomena that persist, as well as producing artifacts that objectify their accomplishments.

It is the hope of the authors of this volume that the chapters here will open new vistas of practical math education, research methodology and group cognition theory.

Chapter 26
Meaning Making in VMT

Gerry Stahl

Abstract Meaning making is central to the interactions that take place in CSCL settings. The collaborative construction of shared meaning is a complex process that has not previously been analyzed in detail despite the fact that it is often acknowledged as being the distinguishing element in CSCL. Here, a three-minute excerpt from a discussion among three students is considered in some detail. The students are reflecting on their analysis of mathematical patterns in a synchronous online environment with text chat and a shared whiteboard. A complex network of references is identified from the chat postings to each other and to resources in the discourse situation. The group's meaning making in the chat is a function of constructing this shared referential network. The analysis suggests a number of conditions and preconditions of such interaction. These are necessary for achieving the potential of CSCL as the accomplishment of high-order cognitive tasks by small groups of learners. An understanding of the conditions and preconditions of the small-group meaning-making process may aid in the design and analysis of CSCL activities, as well as in the development of a science of group cognition.

Keywords Meaning making · group cognition · network of reference · conditions and preconditions · intersubjectivity

The Centrality of Meaning Making in CSCL

The vision of CSCL is that networked computers can bring learners together in new ways and that shared digital environments can foster interactions that produce new understandings for the groups and their participants. Accordingly, the uniqueness of CSCL pedagogical and technological designs consists in their techniques for

G. Stahl (✉)
College of Information Science & Technology, Drexel University, Philadelphia, PA, USA
e-mail: gerry@gerrystahl.net

G. Stahl (ed.), *Studying Virtual Math Teams*, Computer-Supported Collaborative
Learning Series 11, DOI 10.1007/978-1-4419-0228-3_26,
© Springer Science+Business Media, LLC 2009

supporting group interactions that can solve problems, gain insights, build knowledge. To guide design, CSCL theory needs to explicate the processes by which groups accomplish these cognitive tasks and to specify the preconditions for such interactions to take place.

In the formative days of the history of CSCL (see Stahl et al., 2006), collaboration was defined as "a process by which individuals negotiate and share meanings relevant to the problem-solving task at hand... a coordinated, synchronous activity that is the result of a continued attempt to construct and maintain a shared conception of a problem" (Roschelle & Teasley, 1995, p. 70). The study of collaboration so defined suggests a shift away from the psychology of the individual to the small group as the unit of analysis. It suggests a process-oriented focus on the socially-constructed properties of small-group interaction: "Empirical studies have more recently started to focus less on establishing *parameters* for effective collaboration and more on trying to understand the *role* that such variables play in mediating interaction" (Dillenbourg et al., 1996, p. 189, emphasis added). These re-definitions of the object of research differentiate *an approach to CSCL interested in group cognition* from the orientations of educational-psychology studies of individual learning in settings of cooperation and/or distance learning.

CSCL has been defined explicitly in terms of the analysis of *meaning making*. A keynote at CSCL 2002 proposed: "CSCL is a field of study centrally concerned with meaning and the practices of meaning making in the context of joint activity, and the ways in which these practices are mediated through designed artifacts" (Koschmann, 2002, p. 18). Recently, this approach has been re-conceptualized as studying the "practices of understanding" (Koschmann & Zemel, 2006). At the CSCL 2005 conference, a research agenda for the field was proposed in terms of "intersubjective meaning making" (Suthers, 2006b). This emphasis has a two-fold implication. It suggests that empirical studies investigate the processes of meaning making that take place in the studied settings. In addition, in theoretical terms, it implies that we should be analyzing the nature of shared meaning and the structures of small-group meaning-making processes in general.

For all the talk about meaning making, there has been little empirical analysis of how meaning is actually constructed in small-group interactions. It is generally assumed that meaning is created and shared through processes of interaction, communication and coordination. However, the nature of these processes is taken for granted. Even a special journal issue on "Meaning Making" presents alternative analyses of a particular interaction recording and reflects on the methodologies used, but never explicitly discusses what is meant by the term "meaning making" (Koschmann, 1999a). Similarly, a recent book devoted to the topic of *Meaning in Mathematics Education* concludes, "various aspects of communication which may affect the construction of meaning are discussed. On the other hand, the problem of the construction of meaning itself is not really tackled" (Kilpatrick et al., 2005, p. 137).

For some time, I have been trying to work out structures of collaborative meaning making. At ICLS 2000, I presented a model of collaborative knowledge building

(Stahl, 2006b, chap. 9), followed at CSCL 2002 with a theoretical framework for CSCL (Stahl, 2006b, chap. 11). In an extended analysis of building collaborative knowing illustrated with my SimRocket data, I presented elements of a social theory of CSCL centered on meaning making (Stahl, 2006b, chap. 15). I subsequently distinguished between *interpretation* from individual perspectives and *meaning* as shared and embodied in artifacts in the world in my CSCL 2003 paper (Stahl, 2006b, chap. 16). At CSCL 2005, I argued that groups can think, that they can have cognitive agency (Stahl, 2006b, chap. 19). My book on *Group Cognition* develops this notion that small groups of learners—particularly with the support of carefully crafted digital environments—have the potential to achieve cognitive accomplishments, such as mathematical problem solving. Here, the term "group cognition" does not refer to some kind of mental content ("group mind"). It refers to the fact that groups can engage in linguistic (and other interactional) processes, which can produce results that are comparable to results that are commonly called "cognitive" when achieved by an individual, but that in principle cannot be reduced to mental representations of one individual or of a sum of individuals. Thus, the theory of group cognition is similar to theories of distributed cognition, but here the emphasis is more on the interaction between people than on the mediation of individual cognition by artifacts, and the cognitive accomplishments are high-order tasks like creative math problem solving rather than routine symbol manipulations, as even in Hutchins (1996).

The VMT Project has been investigating specific structures of meaning-making practices, analyzing online interactions among math students. For instance, we characterized "math-proposal adjacency pairs" (Stahl, 2006e), looked at how a group could solve a math problem that none of its members could solve (Chapter 5), and investigated how students used a referencing tool in our environment (Chapter 17). We try to closely analyze brief interactions in well-documented case studies to determine the social practices or methods that groups use to accomplish their meaning making. Thereby, we seek to determine structures of small-group cognitive processes. We believe that the foundation of CSCL as a unique field of study is the investigation of the meaning-making processes that take place in online collaborative settings. The analysis of intersubjective meaning making or group cognition is not the whole story; one can, of course, also analyze individual learning and other psychological phenomena or larger activity structures and communities-of-practice, but we believe the processes of small-group interaction are of particular centrality to CSCL.

A Case of Group Cognition

Although meaning and related topics like grounding have been debated for millennia, they have usually been discussed using examples that were made up by the authors to seem like natural, commonsensical interactions or using data generated under laboratory conditions. To study interaction "in the wild" or with examples that occurred in real-life situations is a new and important approach that we can borrow from ethnography (Hutchins, 1996) and ethnomethodology (Garfinkel, 1967). However, finding cases of interaction that are relevant to CSCL research interests cannot be left up to chance. CSCL research aims to inform technological and pedagogical design. Therefore, cycles of design-based research are often appropriate. One must put students in situations where they are motivated to pursue certain kinds of tasks in particular kinds of environments. The situations must be instrumented to capture an adequate record of the interactions that take place.

In this chapter, we will observe meaning making in a brief excerpt from the VMT Spring Fest 2006. The collaborative context was set by organizing a contest: members of the most collaborative teams would win prizes. Students were recruited globally through teachers who were involved in other Math Forum activities. The team in the excerpt consisted of two students who apparently went to the same school and one from another time zone in the US, as well as a facilitator from the Math Forum, who provided technical assistance—this is all that either the students or the facilitator knew about each other. Pedagogically, the topic for discussion was an open-ended exploration of geometric patterns. An initial pattern of squares formed from sticks was given. The students were to figure out the formulae for the number of squares and the number of sticks at stage N first, and then explore other patterns that they or other teams invented (see Fig. 7.1 in Chapter 7).

Each team in Spring Fest 2006 met for four sessions over a two-week period. Each session lasted a little over an hour. At the end of each session, the teams posted their findings on a wiki for the other teams to read. Between sessions, the facilitators posted feedback to the teams on their whiteboards. The feedback generally acknowledged the team's accomplishments and suggested next steps. In the case considered here, the team was particularly encouraged to explain what they had done because it was not clear to the facilitators from the interactions that the team members always understood what the group was doing.

Pattern problems are commonly used in teaching the concepts of beginning algebra. The research literature on this shows that explaining solution paths is generally particularly difficult for students (Moss & Beatty, 2006). By pressing the students to explain their work in the wiki posting—and to prepare for this in their chat interaction—we encouraged the creation of data that allows us to see something of how a group of students made sense of their mathematical problem solving and where they had difficulty in conducting group practices leading to personal and mutual understanding.

Records of the sessions are available in the form of textual logs and the VMT Replayer. For instance, the chat message selected in Fig. 26.1 appears as line 1424 in Log 26-1. Note the graphical reference from this posting to a formula on the whiteboard. The chat and whiteboard record can be replayed at any speed and stepped through. Virtually all aspects of the group interaction including everything that the participants knew about each other's actions were captured and are available for analysis in the Replayer.

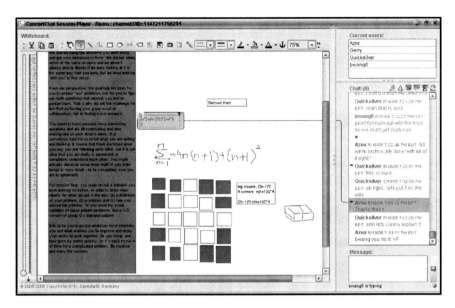

Fig. 26.1 View of VMT environment during the excerpt

Log 26-1.

line	participant	chat posting	time	delay
1393	Quicksilver	(a) was define the problem, (b) was the solution which we got...	07.29.46	
1394	bwang8	we calculated the # of square if the diamond makes a perfect square	07.29.48	2
1395	Aznx	We can define the problem.	07.29.48	0
1396	Aznx	We got the solutions.	07.29.55	7
1397	Quicksilver	yes	07.30.12	17
1398	Quicksilver	the added corners	07.30.16	4
1399	Aznx	But I'm not sure how to explain how we got to the solutions, although it makes prefect sense to me.	07.30.18	2
1400	Quicksilver	to make a square	07.30.19	1
1401	Aznx	I'm just not sure how to explain it.	07.30.24	5
1402	Quicksilver	and we found those were triangular numbers	07.30.25	1
1403	Aznx	Well, I can explain the second formula.	07.30.32	7
1404	Quicksilver	lets go step by step	07.30.35	3
1405	Quicksilver	NO!	07.30.37	2
1406	Quicksilver	we don't know hte second formula	07.30.42	5

line	participant	chat posting	time	delay
1407	Aznx	It was done through the method of finsing the pattern of triangular #s.	07.30.45	3
1408	Aznx	Yes we do.	07.30.50	5
1409	Quicksilver	?	07.30.55	5
1410	Aznx	Suppose their second formula is our third.	07.30.56	1
1411	Quicksilver	That was taem c's tho	07.31.06	10
1412	Aznx	No.	07.31.12	6
1413	Aznx	They didn't do.	07.31.16	4
1414	Aznx	The nuumber of squares	07.31.20	4
1415	Quicksilver	ohj!	07.31.25	5
1416	Aznx	or the find the big square	07.31.26	1
1417	Quicksilver	that formula	07.31.27	1
1418	Quicksilver	i thot u meant the other one	07.31.31	4
1419	Quicksilver	yeah that is ours	07.31.36	5
1420	bwang8	point formula out with the tools so we don't get confused	07.32.37	61
1421	Aznx	So we're technically done with all of it right?	07.32.49	12
1422	Quicksilver	this is ours	07.32.51	2
1423	Quicksilver	all right...lets put it on the wiki	07.32.58	7
1424	Aznx	That is theirs.	07.33.02	4
1425	Quicksilver	adn lets clearly explain it	07.33.05	3
1426	Aznx	bwang you do it. = P	07.33.11	6

Analysis of the Meaning Making

At first glance, the excerpt in Log 26-1 seems hard to follow. In fact, that is why the VMT research group started to look at this segment in its data sessions. The postings themselves express lack of clarity (e.g., line 1410), inability to explain what is going on (line 1401) and confusion about what is being discussed (line 1418). In addition, it is hard to understand how the postings hang together, how the participants are responding to each other and making sense together. It is often informative to focus on such excerpts. When the taken-for-granted flow of conversation breaks down—seemingly for the participants as well as for the researchers—the nature and structure of the interaction is likely to be made explicit and available for analysis. For instance, in my SimRocket excerpt (Stahl, 2006b, chap. 12), the students' shared understanding of the facilitator's reference broke down, and they had to work hard to make the reference successively more explicit until everyone saw it the same way. Similarly, the analysis of deictic referencing in the VMT environment (Stahl, 2006d) looked at how students combined available resources to define a math object that was not at first clear and that required considerable work to establish agreement on what was being referenced. In the excerpt in this paper, the meaning-making process is displayed by the participants as problematic for them—presenting an analytic opportunity for us as researchers to observe characteristics of meaning making rendered visible in their announced breakdown and explicit repair.

Breakdown and repair of shared understanding is a common pattern in collaborative small group interactions. In our corpus of about 1,000 student-hours of online collaborative problem solving, it is frequently a driving force (as discussed in Stahl, 2006e). It becomes apparent to the participants that they are not understanding each other or do not know what references are pointing to. The participants gradually make more explicit what they mean or the object of their references, using various available resources in their environment or their communication media. Eventually, each participant acknowledges that they understand the others, at least well enough to continue what they were doing before they paused to repair their mutual confusion. Thus, the nature of collaborative processes work to align individual interpretations to a gradually shared meaning that is itself co-constructed in this process. In this way, "group cognition" is not something that exists somewhere outside of the interaction, but is a gradually emerging accomplishment of the group discourse itself (Stahl, 2006b). It is also important to note that the collaborative meaning-making process that produces the shared group meaning tends to produce in parallel individual interpretations of this meaning. Accordingly, when the individual participants later leave the group, the understandings of the group accomplishment may remain available to the individuals and can be re-introduced by them and re-situated in subsequent group interactions (see Chapter 6 and Chapter 10 for examples of bridging across sessions).

In our present excerpt, the students are responding to the feedback in the large text box in Fig. 26.1. Here the facilitators wrote, **"For session four, you could revisit a pattern you were working on before, in order to state more clearly for other groups in the wiki (a) a definition of your problem, (b) a solution and (c) how you solved the problem."** We can see that the students are oriented to this feedback because line 1393 translates it from a suggestion by the facilitators to the students (**"you"**) into a summary by the students of what they (**"we"**) should do. The students are hesitant to post a statement of how they solved the problem on the wiki for others—including, of course, for the facilitators who will be judging whether they are one of the most collaborative teams and deserving of a prize. So in line 1394, they begin to go over their solution path together. But lines 1395 and 1396 do not continue this review; they return to line 1393 to agree that they accomplished parts (a) and (b). It is ambiguous what line 1397 is responding to. The line is continued (by the same participant) in line 1398. To understand this new line requires recalling how the students solved the pattern problem in a previous session.

Look at the large diagram in Fig. 26.1. The white (empty) squares form a diamond pattern of width 5 squares. The red (filled) squares fill in a large square encompassing the diamond, by adding 4 corners each composed of 3 red squares. One can compute the number of squares that it takes to form a diamond pattern by first easily computing the number of squares in the large encompassing square and then subtracting the number of squares in the 4 corners. This was the strategy used by the group in a previous session. If we now look at the sequence of postings by

Quicksilver, we see that they make sense as a response to Bwang's posting. Quicksilver is taking up Bwang's description, recalling that the square was formed by adding the "*corners*" and then further specifying the strategy as treating the number of squares in a corner as being part of a "*triangular number*" sequence. Meanwhile, Aznx's postings in lines 1395, 1396, 1399 and 1401 seem to form an independent sequence of statements, focusing on the problem of step (c) from the feedback, explaining how the problem was solved. If we follow the sequences of different students, they seem to be working in parallel, with Aznx despairing of explaining the group solution path even while Bwang and Quicksilver are reviewing it.

As is well known, chat technology results in confusion because the turn-taking rules of face-to-face conversation do not apply in chat (Chapter 14). Participants type in parallel and the results of their typing do not necessarily immediately follow the posting that they are responding to. When more than two people are chatting, this can produce confusion for the participants and for researchers (Chapters 14, 20 and 21). Moreover, in an attempt to prevent postings from becoming too separated from their logical predecessors, people rush to post, often dividing their messages into several short postings and introducing many shortcuts, abbreviations, typos, mistakes and imprecision. Technological responses to this problem have been explored (e.g., Fuks et al., 2006). Analytically, it is important to begin a study of a chat record by reconstructing the threading and uptake structure of the chat log. Threading specifies what posting follows (responds to or takes up) what and when the structure diverges into parallel or unrelated threads (Chapter 20). The threading or uptake structure indicates which specific elements of a posting, gesture, reference, drawing action, etc. are building upon previous elements (Suthers, 2006a).

While Aznx (in lines 1395, 1396, 1399, 1401, 1403) and Quicksilver (in lines 1397, 1398, 1400, 1402) seem to be following their own independent threads, there are also increasing signs of interaction between these threads. While one is complaining that he (or she) does not know how to explain their solution path, the other is demonstrating a way of systematically explaining, or at least enumerating, the path. Aznx' **"Well, I can explain the second formula"** (line 1403) delimits his previous general statement that he could not explain their solution. Now he is stating that he can explain part of the solution—possibly the part that Quicksilver (line 1402) has just characterized as finding that the pattern of the corners followed the pattern of **"triangular numbers"** (from Pascal's triangle, which is relevant to many pattern problems). So line 1403 reacts to Quicksilver's 1402 as well as continuing from Aznx' own 1401. Similarly, while Aznx' 1407 sounds like a simple continuation of his seemingly private reflection in 1399, 1401 and 1403, it quotes Quicksilver's parallel line 1402. Line 1407 transforms 1402's **"found"** into **"finsing"** (**"finding"**) and its **"triangular numbers"** into **"triangular #s."**

In chat, postings frequently continue a train of meaning making from the same participant as well as responding to a recent posting by another participant, thereby potentially contributing to *intersubjective* meaning making (or polyphony according to Chapter 24). We will see below an example of face-to-face collaboration where four students pursue their own trains of thought in whispered self-talk that is intentionally loud enough that the four can follow each other's work while doing "their own." This keeps them aligned and allows them to help each other, maintaining a joint problem space and producing a group product.

We have already seen that new postings do not only relate to previous postings. They also reference things outside of the immediate chat discourse. For instance, line 1393 made reference to the feedback displayed in the text box in the shared whiteboard. It did this partially by quoting an excerpt from the feedback and partially by transforming it from the facilitator perspective to the participants' perspective. Line 1402 referred to Pascal's triangle by using the phrase "**triangular numbers**" that the students had used before. Line 1403 refers to "**the second formula.**" The referent for this phrase is not obvious to the engaged participants or to us as retrospective analysts. Quicksilver says "**No**" in line 1405. This seems to be a response to line 1403 about the second formula, with 1404 being a response to 1401 and to the general problem of preparing an explanation for the wiki.

When references become unclear to some members of the discourse, it may be necessary to repair the breakdown in mutual understanding. A lot of important interaction in collaborative activities consists in such repair, clarifying the references by making them more explicit so that each participant comes to understand them well enough to continue the discourse (Koschmann & LeBaron, 2003). Clark's contribution theory of grounding (Clark & Brennan, 1991) describes how this takes place among dyads in face-to-face informal conversation, illustrated with made-up examples. For online small groups using text chat in real examples of knowledge building, such as explaining math problem solving, the repair may be more complicated (Dillenbourg & Traum, 2006).

Quicksilver's "**No**" is followed by, "**we don't know the second formula.**" The phrase, "**second formula**" in line 1406 here is not referencing the same thing as "**second formula**" in line 1403, as indicated by the question mark in line 1409. In fact, it takes two and a half minutes and 21 postings (1403–1424) to reach the point where the discourse can go on. The confusion gets translated by line 1410 into which formula is this team's and which was Team C's solution that this team found on the public wiki. Aznx tries to clarify (lines 1413–1416) that the formula he is concerned with could not be Team C's because Team C did not calculate the number of squares using the encompassing big square (they only proposed a formula for the number of sticks). Quicksilver describes his confusion, but the conversation does not continue; there is a one-minute silence, which is embarrassingly long in chat.

The silence is broken by Bwang's suggestion in line 1420 to use the graphical referencing tool that is part of the VMT environment. As they wrap up the discussion, Quicksilver points to one formula ("**ours**") in the whiteboard (line 1422) and Aznx to the other ("**theirs**") (line 1424). This resolution of the confusion through the use of the available technology was thus accomplished by all three of them, using the referencing tool to point to objects in the whiteboard in coordination with labeling them with the terms "**ours**" and "**theirs**" in the chat. In parallel with this, the students propose to move on to post on the wiki: Aznx suggests that they may be finished preparing the explanation (line 1421). Quicksilver agrees, "**all right, let's put it on the wiki and let's clearly explain it**" (lines 1423, 1425). Finally, Aznx concludes the preparations by saying, "**Bwang, you do it**" (line 1426).

Ambiguity of the Interaction

We can follow the discussion taking place in the excerpt now better than at first sight. Not only do we have some sense of its structure and flow, but we see how it is embedded in the situation of the preceding interactions, the tasks that are driving the discourse forward, the items in the whiteboard and other available resources (wiki postings by other teams, math knowledge, etc.). We had to conduct a preliminary analysis of the meaning-making process in terms of the interactional threading, the uptake of one posting by a subsequent one, the continuity of postings by individual participants, the subsidiary discussions to repair confusions, the references to various resources and the repeated citation of terms or phrases. Only then could we look more deeply into the interaction or investigate specific research questions.

If we wanted to classify individual chat postings according to some coding scheme (as in Chapters 22 and 23) in order to compare our excerpt to other interaction records, we would have had to do such a preliminary analysis to know what the brief, elliptical chat postings meant. CSCL is a human science and the analysis of its data requires an understanding of the *meaning* that things had for the participants. One cannot code a posting like "**No!**" as a mathematical proposal, a repair of understanding, an argumentative move or an off-topic comment without having a sense of the meaning of what the participants were doing linguistically and interactionally. Of course, if a chat posting just says, "**Hi**," then even a simple algorithm can code it as Greeting, Social or Off-Topic with high reliability. However, we have found that the most interesting interactions are challenging for experienced researchers and likely to inspire divergent but productive analyses.

So far, our analysis of the excerpt is quite preliminary. There is still a lot of ambiguity about what is going on. Line 1396/1399 remains quite intriguing: "**We got the solutions. But I'm not sure how to explain how we got to the solutions, although it makes perfect sense to me.**" If the solutions make perfect sense to Aznx, why does he feel that he cannot explain how they got the solutions? As noted above, this points to a fundamental problem in mathematics education. Students are trained to compute solutions, but they have difficulty articulating explanations. Some educational theories point to explanation as the core of "deep understanding" (Moss & Beatty, 2006). Proponents of collaborative learning point to the importance of opportunities to explain math thinking to others as being important even for the development of one's own higher-order learning skills (Wegerif, 2006).

We may still wonder what the significance is of the fact that Aznx seems ready to post an explanation at line 1421 despite his repeated disclaimer at line 1401. Does line 1421 signal that the ensuing interaction is being taken as an adequate account or is the fact that things made perfect sense to Aznx now taken as adequate although it was not previously? Aznx does say in line 1403 that he can explain "**the second formula**." Does this entail that all that is needed is such an explanation of the second formula? Note that Aznx's line 1421 says, "**So we're technically done with all of it, right?**" What does the "**So**" respond to as an uptake? What has suddenly made the group ready to post an explanation? This line follows the extended effort to overcome the confusion of referencing, and it is hard to trace the "**So**" back to some clear point that it is building on. Furthermore, what is the significance of the hedge, "**technically**"? In fact, it is not even clear what "**it**" refers to. Is Aznx just saying they are done with the repair, rather than with the whole explanation? Line 1423/1425 with its "**all right**" response seems to take line 1421 as saying that the group is ready to post their solution. It then proceeds to propose the logical next step, "**let's put it on the wiki. . .. And let's clearly explain it.**" Aznx no longer resists, yet in line 1426 he proposes that Bwang do the posting. In previous sessions, Aznx has requested that Bwang do the wiki postings, using precisely the same wording. Bwang has done previous wiki postings for the group. In this way, Aznx' statements leave ambiguous whether or not he still expresses doubt about his ability to explain the group's solution path and the extent to which he indicates understanding that path.

It not only remains ambiguous how much Aznx can explain, but also what exactly he was referring to as "**the second formula**." The repair of confusion shifted from distinguishing the second from the third formula to distinguishing Team C's formula from Team B's. Quicksilver and Aznx clearly pointed to two different text boxes in the whiteboard containing formulae as "**ours**" and "**theirs**." However, the text box called "ours" contained three formulae: for the big square, for the 4 corners and for the diamond pattern as the difference. Did Aznx originally mean that he could only explain the second of these three—which was based on the formula for triangular numbers? Did Quicksilver's mention of triangular numbers in line 1402 and more general review of their solution path help Aznx to feel that they could put together an explanation of how all the formulae fit together? The discourse in this excerpt does not seem to provide complete answers to some of these questions. While careful analysis of small-group discourse often reveals much about the problem-solving work of the group and its members, many other issues remain ambiguous, missing and even contradictory. The group did its work without resolving or explicating all of the issues that researchers may want to know about.

Resources in the Network of Reference

We have seen that an understanding of the intersubjective meaning-making process of a small group in a text-chat environment involves paying attention to an intricate web of connections among the items in the interaction record and items from the context that are made relevant in the discourse. There is a *threading* of the flow, with a particular posting following up on a preceding one (that may not be immediately adjacent in the chat log) and opening the possibility of certain kinds of postings to follow. There is *up-take* of one phrase or action by another, carrying the work of the group ahead. There are often important *continuities* from one posting of a particular individual to the same person's subsequent postings. Various sorts of communication problems can arise—from typos to confusion—and *repairs* can be initiated to overcome the problems. Lines of chat can *reference* items outside the chat, such as whiteboard drawings, formulae learned in the past or notions raised earlier. Terms and phrases in a posting can serve as *citations* of previous statements, making the former meanings once more present and relevant. Later in the chapter we will draw arrows on a record of the chat excerpt to indicate several dozen of these connections of threading, uptake, continuity, repair, reference and citation. The postings can be separated into columns by poster to reflect continuity (see Stahl, 2006e, p. 100), and a column added for referenced items external to the immediate discourse. The intricate web of arrows will indicate how interwoven the postings are and how the postings of the different participants are tied together, creating an overall flow to the group discourse.

Meaning making proceeds through the weaving of different forms of referencing. As Valsiner and van der Veer (2000) put it,

> We come to knowledge by taking part in collective activities that evolve over time, and where language and material artifacts function as collective structural resources.

We can distinguish a variety of kinds of resources that function in the excerpt that we have considered. The students take part in collective activities that evolve over four hours of online interaction. In the online context, textual and graphical artifacts contribute as resources in the web of meaning that is co-constructed by the group and shared by its members.

The resources available in face-to-face settings are not available online in the same format, but many of them have online analogues. When we conducted a pilot study for the VMT Project in a face-to-face collaborative math classroom, we observed four girls sitting around a table and working in closely-coordinated parallel work (Fig. 26.2). The students were physically distinct and we could observe the embodiment of their individual behavior. The girls were obviously friends who knew each other well; they maintained close visual and auditory coordination by looking at each other's papers and by talking aloud about their work. Their quiet

Fig. 26.2 Collaborative math in a classroom

self-talk was a way of letting the others know what they were doing without requiring responses, a subtle form of polyphonic communication (Chapter 24). Their body language, positioning and gesturing communicated their progress on the math tasks—or lack of progress. Gestures to their own and each other's work papers were used extensively, both to communicate and to coordinate turn taking.

We can distinguish various kinds of resources in the face-to-face case:

- *Lexical definitions*. The words the students speak and hear to describe their work and their understanding may be mumbled, may interfere with other words or sounds and may be altered as they are produced. They incorporate modes of expression typical of the students' cultural background.
- *Environmental resources*. There are many physical artifacts scattered about the work area: pencils, papers, rulers, scissors, calculator, watches.
- *Intentional continuities*. The bodies of the students persist as visible embodiments of their identity throughout the session.
- *Topical responses*. The students engage in conversational turn taking to organize their verbal interaction.
- *Contextual relevancies*. They share the visual and physical environment of the classroom and their table.
- *Indexical frames*. They make heavy use of glance and gesture to index resources in their shared environment, including the inscriptions on their individual pieces of paper.

These kinds of resources have their equivalents online, although they take different forms there:

- *Lexical definitions*. The postings the students type and read in the chat window to describe their work and their understanding and the iconic drawings they create in the whiteboard are posted after they have been carefully typed or crafted. They tend to be more explicit, elliptical and ambiguous. They use cultural conventions of instant messaging.
- *Environmental resources*. There are many tools and affordances available in the VMT environment. The students gradually learn to make use of these and to share ways of using them.
- *Intentional continuities*. The successive chat postings of a given individual participant are identified with a specific chat handle or name and timestamp. Identification of whiteboard actions are less obvious.
- *Topical responses*. The students engage in implicitly-threaded chat postings to organize their verbal interaction, often through proposals and responses. They sometimes use the graphical referencing tool to clarify threading response structure.
- *Contextual relevancies*. They share the software environment of the VMT interface, which reflects most of what is seen in the interfaces of the other participants. The text and graphics are visually persistent for a while.
- *Indexical frames*. The textual sequentiality establishes most of the indexical framing. Students have more trouble indexing resources online, and sometimes have to engage in chat discussions to try to straighten out referential problems.

We can see these different kinds of resources at work in the excerpt reproduced in Log 26-1.

Lexical Definitions

Meaning is most commonly associated with dictionary definitions of words. While this is a commonsensical view of meaning, in fact the definitions of words encapsulate a wealth of resources. Language can be theoretically construed as a vast cultural repository of sedimented experiences, skills, lessons and resources. In local interactions like Team B's sessions, new jargon and shared understandings of specific verbal constructs are co-constructed and shared. Drawings and arrangements of inscriptions in the whiteboard provide visual images for the meaning of words and symbolic expressions in the chat or in whiteboard textboxes.

As Chapter 24 discussed, repetition of words can be used to build "polyphonic" structures in which a term used by one participant at one point is picked up by another later on, and perhaps additional times. The repetition of a significant word often serves to create a reference back to the earlier occurrence(s).

Of course, there are also terms in the language whose very function is to make references. Often terms like deictic reference words carry no other semantics. For instance, line 1424 in Log 26-1 has little content beyond its dual references: "**That is theirs**." Part of a complicated sorting out of references, Aznx's posting verbally references a particular symbolic expression on the whiteboard and associates it with Team C. The referencing is done purely linguistically with the use of deictic terms and the formal (syntactic) meaning of the posting consists of the combining (with the copula "is") of the two references. The meaning content (semantics) of such a posting is completely dependent upon the situatedness of the posting, including the whiteboard inscriptions and the community of VMT teams.

Environmental Resources

The group enacts or co-constructs the resources and affordances of its environment through the ways that it references and makes use of them. In the VMT sessions, the environment includes not only the technological medium with its interface, but also the presented problem and the social setting. The session was arranged by the students' teachers with the anticipation of prizes for the best collaborators. So, although it took place outside of school, using home computers, it had ties to schooling and through the Math Forum sponsorship and facilitators to school mathematics. The specific problem, carefully worded by Math Forum staff, and the feedback between online sessions posted in the whiteboard by VMT staff provided strong direction to the interaction. The students made reference to wording and ideas from the topic and from the feedback. They explored and took advantage of many of the affordances of the VMT interface and media. The software environment included the chat with its options and tools, the whiteboard with its options and tools, the graphical referencing tool, the wiki, various social awareness features and the VMT lobby.

An example of the student reference to the pointing tool is given in line 1420 of Log 26-1. Bwang says, "**point formula out with the tools so we don't get confused.**" This comes after a struggle by Aznx and Quicksilver to clarify their references to formulae in whiteboard textboxes and a 60-second silence during which no one takes any visible action. Bwang is pointing to the affordance of the available tool for clarifying confused references. His suggestion is effectively taken up by the others to co-construct a clarifying reference.

Intentional Continuities

Each chat posting is associated with the name (handle) of the poster. Readers of postings pay considerable attention to this handle. A new posting is closely associated with the history of previous postings under the same handle. The co-presence of participants to each other is primarily mediated by the association of each posting with its poster's handle. Just as people in face-to-face situations attribute human intentionality to active human bodies that provide a visible persistent identity of speakers, so users in text chat situations attribute human intentionality and interactional presence to the sequence of postings associated with a given handle.

In the VMT interface, above the chat messages window there is a list of people (handles) who are currently logged into the chat room. Social awareness messages about who is typing, who is editing a textbox, who entered or exited the room or who placed an object in the whiteboard also reference the handles of participants, connecting all these activities to a unique actor. The work discussed in Chapter 19 about software agents being introduced into the VMT environment assigns a handle to the software agents and lists the agents in the list of participants logged in as well as announcing when agents "are typing" or when they enter and leave the room.

Issues of intentionality gain in ambiguity in an online environment like VMT where the indicators of agency are designed and indirect. Sometimes students wonder if the VMT mentor in a chat room is a software agent, because he/she/it may have an unusual handle, may not be very interactive and may suddenly produce long pronouncements that sound highly scripted. When viewing a chat in the VMT Replayer, you may not be able to tell if it is being generated live or if the students disappeared years ago. Although the meaning of the "interaction" must exist exclusively in the text, drawings, visual appearances and animated sequentiality of the displayed digital record, we interpret it in terms of the intentionality of virtually co-present human agents. It actually takes considerable training for an analyst to interpret the meaning as a referential network among visual and linguistic resources rather than as "expressions" of mental representations.

In analyzing a chat log, it may be useful to provide a visual representation of participation and individual continuity by linking successive postings of individuals, as in Fig. 26.3.

line	participant	chat posting	time	delay
1393	Quicksilver	(a) was define the problem, (b) was the solution which we got...	07.29.46	
1394	bwang8	we calculated the # of square if the diamond makes a perfect square	07.29.48	2
1395	Aznx	We can define the problem.	07.29.48	0
1396	Aznx	We got the solutions.	07.29.55	7
1397	Quicksilver	yea	07.30.12	17
1398	Quicksilver	the added corners	07.30.16	4
1399	Aznx	But I'm not sure how to explain how we got to the solutions, although it makes perfect sense to me.	07.30.18	2
1400	Quicksilver	to make a square	07.30.19	1
1401	Aznx	I'm just not sure how to explain it.	07.30.24	5
1402	Quicksilver	and we found those were triangular numbers	07.30.25	1
1403	Aznx	Well, I can explain the second formula.	07.30.32	7
1404	Quicksilver	lets go step by step	07.30.35	3
1405	Quicksilver	NO!	07.30.37	2
1406	Quicksilver	we don't know his second formula	07.30.42	5
1407	Aznx	It was done through the method of finding the pattern of triangular #s.	07.30.45	3
1408	Aznx	Yes we do.	07.30.50	5
1409	Quicksilver	?	07.30.55	5
1410	Aznx	Suppose their second formula is our third.	07.30.56	1
1411	Quicksilver	That was team c's tho.	07.31.06	10
1412	Aznx	No.	07.31.12	6
1413	Aznx	They didn't do	07.31.16	4
1414	Aznx	The number of squares	07.31.20	4
1415	Quicksilver	oh!	07.31.25	5
1416	Aznx	or the find the big square	07.31.26	1
1417	Quicksilver	that formula	07.31.27	1
1418	Quicksilver	i thot u meant the other one	07.31.31	4
1419	Quicksilver	yeah that is ours	07.31.36	5
1420	bwang8	point formula out with the tools so we don't get confused	07.32.37	61
1421	Aznx	So we're technically done with all of it right?	07.32.49	12
1422	Quicksilver	this is ours	07.32.51	2
1423	Quicksilver	all right...lets put it on the wiki	07.32.58	7
1424	Aznx	That is theirs	07.33.02	4
1425	Quicksilver	adn lets clearly explain it	07.33.05	3
1426	Aznx	bwang you do it. =P	07.33.11	6

Fig. 26.3 The threading of Aznx's postings

Topical Responses

The most obvious type of referencing in chat is the threaded response to a recent previous posting on a given topic. This is the equivalent of adjacency pairs in conversational talk (see Chapter 14). In face-to-face conversation within a dyad, when one person raises a question or makes a proposal, the other person is expected to provide an answer to the question or to accept the proposal. Of course, there are many possible variations for a response, like asking a clarification question or countering with an alternative proposal. The question/answer or proposal/acceptance response pair can be interrupted by a secondary sequence of interaction, for instance to repair a problem in understanding the initial question or proposal. The secondary interaction may consist of a response pair itself—and it may be interrupted, and so on recursively. But eventually, the pairs tend to get closed.

In chat, because the gradual production of the original question, proposal, etc. is not observable, other participants in the chat may simultaneously be producing their own greetings, repairs, questions or proposals. They may also still be responding by producing answers to previously posted questions. Especially when more than two participants are active, the response pair structure becomes confused. Nevertheless, there is still an underlying pairing of posts responding to each other with expectations similar to those in talk. People reading the chat must put more effort into untangling the threading of the structure of the responses. In Fig. 26.4, each

line	Azar	Quicksilver	bwang8	reference
1393		(a) was define the problem, (b) was the solution which we got...		feedback text-box on whiteboard
1394			we calculated the # of square if the diamond	drawing of diamond with red corners on whiteboard
1395	We can define the problem			
1396	We got the solutions.			
1397		yes		
1398		the added corners		
1399	But I'm not sure how to explain how we got to the solutions,			
1400		to make a square		
1401	I'm just not sure how to explain it.			
1402		and we found those were triangular numbers		a previous discussion of "triangular" numbers
1403	Well, I can explain the second			
1404		lets go step by step		formula for # of sticks
1405		NO		
1406		I don't know hte second		
1407	It was done through the method of finsing the pattern of tri			
1408	Yes we do.			
1409		?		
1410	Suppose their second formula is our third.			
1411		That was taem c's tho		Team C wiki page
1412	No.			
1413	They didn't do.			
1414	The nuumber of squares			
1415		ohh!		
1416	or the find the big square			
1417		that formula		
1418		i thot u meant the other one		
1419		yeah that is ours		
1420			point formula out with the tools so we don't get confused	the VMT referencing tool
1421	So we're technically done with all of it right?			
1422		this is ours		big square: (2n-1)^2 corners: n(n-1)/2*4 (2n-1)^2 - n(n-1)/2*4
1423		all right .lets put it on the wiki		the wiki pages n^2 - (n-1)^2 * 2 - n*3 -2
1424	That is theirs.			
1425		adn lets clearly explain it		

Fig. 26.4 The response structure

participant's postings have been displayed in a separate column, with a common sequential time line running down. The response structure has been indicated with arrows. The overall visual pattern of the arrows provides a sense of the flow of the group interaction.

Contextual Relevancies

The con-text—literally, what is given with the text—of text chat is co-constructed by the participants through their postings which make reference to objects and thereby make them relevant to the discourse. Often, the chat includes implicit references to people, events or artifacts. This incorporates them into the chat context. Sometimes they are referred to by some form of citation or by repetition of words. In Fig. 26.5, references that establish contextual relevancies from previous chat postings or whiteboard inscriptions are indicated.

Indexical Frames

The discourse creates and maintains a referential system in which indexicals and deictic terms are resolved. Words like *you, now, this, his, it* or *then* rely for their

line	Acns	Quicksilver	bwang5	reference
1393		(a) was that the problem, b) was the solution which we got...		feedback text-box on whiteboard
1394			we calculated the # of square if the diamond	drawing of diamond with red corners on whiteboard
1395	We can define problem,			
1396	We got the solution.			
1397		yes		
1398		the added corners		
1399	But I'm not sure how to explain how we got to the solutions,			
1400		to make a square		
1401	I'm just not sure how to explain it.			
1402		...and those were triangular numbers		a previous discussion of "triangular" numbers
1403	Well, I can explain the second			
1404		lets go step by step		formula for # of sticks
1405		NO!		
1406		we don't know hte second		
1407	It was done through the method of finsing the pattern of triangular			
1408	Yes we do.			
1409		?		
1410	Suppose their second formula is our third.			
1411		That was taem c's tho		Team C wiki page
1412	No.			
1413	They didn't do.			
1414	The nuumber of squares			
1415		ohj!		
1416	or the find the big square			
1417		that formula		
1418		i think i meant the other one		
1419		yeah that is ours		
1420			point formula out with the tools so we don't get confused	the VMT referencing tool
1421	So we're technically done with all of it right?			
1422		this is ours		big square: (2n-1)^2 4 corners: n(n-1)/2*4 (2n-1)^2 - n(n-1)/2*4
1423		all right...lets put it on the wiki		the wiki pages
1424	That is theirs.			n^2 + (n-1)^2 * 2 * n*3 -2
1425		adn lets clearly explain it		
1426	bwang you do it. =P			

Fig. 26.5 References to contextual relevancies

meaning on the specific situation in which they are used. Their role is to index or point to agents, artifacts or events within the discourse context. They help to weave that context in which references gain their situated significance. For instance, the reference of *me* or *you* depends upon who is speaking (or typing) and who is being addressed (or reading). Verb tenses—*is, was, had been, will be*— are also relative to the speaker (poster) and the speaker's perspective. The use of these terms in the chat co-constructs an indexical space (see Chapter 7), which helps future similar terms to be resolved consistently. By referring to events in past, present and future tenses, participants indicate a temporal dimension in which those events and possible related other events are ordered. Fig. 26.6 indicates some of the indexical references in the excerpt.

Although this chapter has distinguished several kinds of referential structures and has displayed them in different diagrams to guide the reader in seeing them in the log excerpt, they all function together to make meaning. Fig. 26.7 displays the references that were identified in the preceding diagrams together. When one reads a chat—either in real-time as a participant in the chat or retrospectively as an analyst, one must at least implicitly gain a sense of this complex of references in order to understand the meaning that is created in the chat. In chats like that recorded in Log 26-1, some of those references are hard to clarify, both for the participants and for analysts. Some may have gotten so confused in the interplay of the interaction that they must be considered ultimately ambiguous, at least in certain aspects.

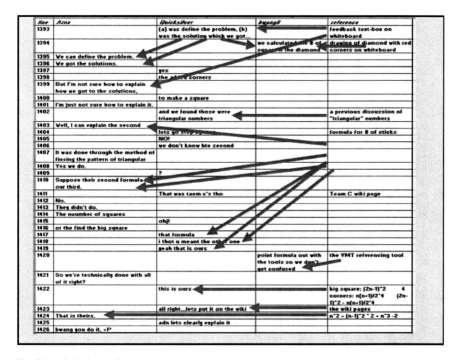

line	Azns	Quicksilver	bwang6	reference
1393		(a) was define the problem, (b) was the solution which we got...		feedback text-box on whiteboard
1394			we calculated # of squares in the diamond	drawing of diamond with red corners on whiteboard
1395	We can define the problem.			
1396	We got the solutions.			
1397		yes		
1398		the added corners		
1399	But I'm not sure how to explain how we got to the solutions,			
1400		to make a square		
1401	I'm just not sure how to explain it.			
1402		and we found those were triangular numbers		a previous discussion of "triangular" numbers
1403	Well, I can explain the second			
1404		lets go step by		formula for # of sticks
1405		NO!		
1406		we don't know hte second		
1407	It was done through the method of finsing the pattern of triangular			
1408	Yes we do.			
1409		?		
1410	Suppose their second formula our third.			
1411		That was taem c's tho		Team C wiki page
1412	No.			
1413	They didn't do.			
1414	The nuumber of squares			
1415		ohj!		
1416	or the find the big sqaure			
1417		that formula		
1418		i thot u meant the other one		
1419		yeah that is ours		
1420			point formula out with the tools so we don't get confused	the VMT referencing tool
1421	So we're technically done with all of it right?			
1422		this is ours		big square: (2n-1)^2 4 corners: n(n-1)/2*4 (2n-1)^2 - n(n-1)/2*4
1423		all right...lets put it on the wiki		the wiki pages
1424	That is theirs.			n^2 + (n-1)^2 * 2 + n^3 -2
1425		adn lets clearly explain it		
1426	bwang you do it. =P			

Fig. 26.6 Indexical references

Methods of Intersubjective Meaning Making

The meaning of the interaction is co-constructed through the building of a web of contributions and consists in the implicit network of references. The point is not to reify this network as the answer to the question, *what* is meaning, but to see it as a way of understanding *how* meaning is co-constructed, i.e., how people *make sense* together.

There are many methods that members of a group, community-of-practice or culture employ to accomplish meaning-making moves in small-group interactions. In face-to-face interactions, certain typical "adjacency pairs" (like question/answer or greeting/response) form common "member methods" (Garfinkel, 1967). In chat, the two postings that belong to an adjacency pair may not be directly adjacent, but they retain the basic structure of forming a meaningful interaction through their combination. In looking at collaborative problem-solving extracts in VMT logs, I defined a typical pattern of "math-proposal adjacency pairs" (Stahl, 2006e). Here, one participant proposes an approach for the group to take to a problem or current sub-problem and someone else must either accept or decline the proposal on behalf of the group. If it is declined, then some kind of argument or alternative proposal is expected. If the proposal is accepted, then the group can continue working on the proposal, often by considering a follow-up proposal pair. There are a number of conditions that must be met by a proposal for it to be successful. These involve its timing and

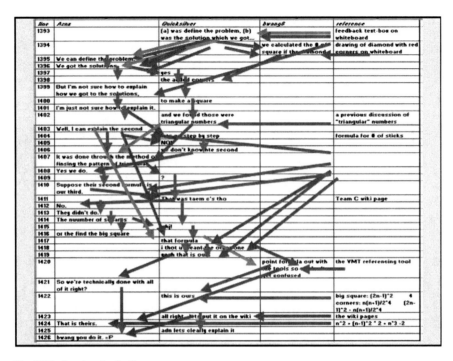

Fig. 26.7 A network of references

relevance in the flow of the discourse. A bid at a proposal that does not satisfy these conditions is likely to fail to be taken up as a proposal. The bid/acceptance pair may be temporarily interrupted by clarification questions or repairs to the bid's formulation. These, in turn, can lead to discussions of indeterminate length. Math proposal response pairs provide a social order for discussions of mathematical problems in small groups.

In the excerpt of Log 26-1, the students are no longer solving a math problem, but reflecting on their solution, trying to recall the steps that they went through and to explain how they solved it in a way that will be meaningful for an audience of their peers (the other teams who read the wiki) and their facilitators (who provide feedback and judge the winning teams). Here, there is a similar process of making proposals and responding to them, but the proposals are formulated more as declarative statements that recall past actions and the responses are rather oblique. In addition, Quicksilver and Aznx tend to continue their presentations in multiple postings, creating parallel threads. While there is an underlying social order that makes this excerpt meaningful, as we have seen it takes some analysis to uncover this relatively complicated and ambiguous order.

Furthermore, the order was made complicated by the overlapping of different temporalities. The students were not simply conducting their own math problem-solving inquiry, they were recalling sequences of action from their previous sessions and from Team C's work. In an effort to organize and judge their explanations in the present, they repeatedly recalled, reviewed and rehearsed past sequences of math moves for future documentation on the wiki. The meaning-making process as seen here may deal with complicated temporal relationships and, in the process, weave intricate new temporal webs, including parallel meaning-making flows.

Even in this brief excerpt, we have seen many member methods or social practices that the participants use to co-construct meaning. Mostly, they respond to each other, making suggestions and posing questions. In addition, they work on repairing problems, such as the confusion about references to formulae. In resolving the confusion, they called upon the referencing tool in the VMT environment. This was the equivalent for the online context of pointing with a physical gesture when face-to-face. Different media provide different affordances and impose different constraints. In new media like this specific chat environment, participants have to be creative in adapting traditional meaning-making methods or inventing new ones. Students may be very inventive and this may impose extra effort on analysts who want to study the meaning-making processes and practices in innovative settings.

The foregoing analysis of meaning making in the excerpt is purely preliminary. A fuller analysis would depend upon one's research interests and specific questions. The excerpt would have to be understood within its larger context, including: the four full sessions (see Chapter 10), which are being reflected on here; the feedback from the facilitators, as it developed in response to the different sessions and based on the original task instructions; the various postings to the whiteboard and to the wiki; and even some of the work of the other teams. But perhaps this preliminary analysis is enough to indicate some of the methods of meaning making that take place in CSCL settings like the VMT sessions. There are phenomena observable at many granularities of analysis. The interactions among brief sequences of postings such as those in Log 26-1 may be considered the cell-form or elements of the meaning making that underlies computer-supported collaborative learning.

Preconditions for Cognitive Processes by Groups

Now that we have a general sense of how meaning making takes place in CSCL (its *conditions*), what are the implications for design? What do we need to consider when attempting to support effective meaning making in CSCL? One approach to this question is to consider the logical and practical *preconditions* for students to get together and engage in joint meaning making to accomplish group cognitive tasks. In philosophical terms, this is to specify the preconditions for the possibility of group cognition.

Based on our empirical experiences in the VMT Project, here is a tentative list of some necessary—though not sufficient—preconditions for small groups of students to collaborate on math problems and other high-order cognitive tasks. The particular number, order and description of these preconditions is, of course, open to debate, extension and refinement. Nevertheless, it may be helpful to consider them when organizing CSCL environments and activities. Here are some preconditions (with parenthetical examples from the analyzed excerpt):

- *Opening of interaction space.* There must be a "world" in which people can come together and interact. The world must provide a network of meanings and possibilities for action. This situation defines deictic (Hanks, 1992), semiotic and semantic relations (a virtual world, such as those created in the VMT Project).
- *Object of activity.* There must be a reason for interacting, a goal to work for, a topic to discuss, a problem to solve or an outcome to reach (the math topic and motivating context).
- *Shared intentionality.* It must be possible for participants to orient in common to objects, to focus their comments and activities on the same items, to "be-there-together" at a topic of joint concern, to "construct and maintain a shared conception of a problem" (e.g., the students' focus on the same formulae and tasks).
- *Intersubjectivity.* Participants must be willing and able to interact with others as peers. They must recognize others as active subjects with their own agency and be willing to relate to them as such (human co-presence).
- *Historical interpretive horizon.* Meanings of artifacts, words, domain concepts, etc. evolve through history and local pasts. Participants must have lived histories that overlap enough to share understandings of historically evolved meanings (the term "triangular numbers" brought in from classroom background experience).
- *Shared background culture.* Participants must share a language, a set of member methods, a vast tacit background knowledge of domain information and of ways of being human (including how to "do" math).
- *Member methods for social order.* Participants inherit and are socialized into an endless variety of member methods for conducting interaction and creating social order. However, small groups must also constantly adapt and enact methods to meet unique situations and innovative technologies. New methods must be fluidly negotiated and adopted for shared use in situ (such as pointing from a chat message).
- *Designed affordances of infrastructure.* The technological features of a CSCL medium define many features of the world which is opened up for interaction. These features are enacted by the participants to provide affordances for their activities. The enacted affordances are often quite different from the features imagined by the designers and can only be discovered through analysis of actual usage (e.g., the pointing tool).
- *Dialogic inter-animation of perspectives.* A key source of creativity, meaning making, problem-solving vitality—but also ambiguity—is the interaction of participants with essentially different interpretive perspectives (Wegerif, 2006). The power of CSCL is largely dependent upon its ability to bring different perspectives together effectively (Bwang's math skills, Aznx' questioning, Quicksilver's recall).
- *Creation and interpretation of group meaning.* The meaning-making process discussed in this paper lies at the core of computer-supported collaborative learning. It must be supported by CSCL environments (pointing).
- *Group-regulation and group meta-cognition.* Small groups of learners working on wicked problems that have no fixed solution path must have methods for

proposing, negotiating, discussing, adopting and reflecting upon their path of inquiry. Methods of explaining their work are part of this. Scripting and other forms of scaffolding may help groups develop skills of self-regulation (feedback about reflection on what to post to the wiki).

- *Individual learning and interpretation.* The establishment of shared group meanings takes place through interactive processes like those we have noticed in this paper, involving the contribution of proposal bids by individual participants and the interpretation of meanings from individual perspectives (Stahl, 2006b, chap. 16). Individual learning may result indirectly from the group cognitive processes that establish understanding by all participants (the wiki posting done by Bwang later).

- *Motivation and engagement.* Small groups and communities-of-practice determine their own interests and involvements through the particulars of what they work on and how they approach it. Individuals tend to become caught up in the group process through their contributions and participations in the interactions. Small-group processes appeal to the social inclinations of people, although they can also engender fears and pressures. In groups of several participants, the interactions can become quite complex, and engagement by different individuals in different activities may ebb and flow (Bwang kept quiet, but entered strategically).

Chapter 27
Critical Ethnography in the VMT Project

Terrence W. Epperson

Abstract The approach of the VMT Project has usually been described as design-based research in the learning sciences. However, it can also be understood as ethnography, using a micro-ethnographic style of interaction analysis to study the construction of social order in the exotic culture of virtual math teams. This chapter reviews the history of critical ethnography (CE) to describe the orientation and concerns of a stream of social science theorizing that seems particularly relevant to the work of the VMT research team. CE adopted the ideas of critical social theory and philosophy from Kant to Habermas. It passed through two distinct generations of thought. After reviewing this history, the chapter focuses on three key phenomena that are characteristic of CE analysis: temporalizing, objectification and intersubjectivity. It then suggests that these phenomena are also significant within the VMT analysis (e.g., Chapters 6, 7, 8), where they receive detailed analysis of empirical data. The VMT Project can be seen as a productive extension of CE work in a contemporary social setting.

Keywords Critical ethnography · critical social theory · critical philosophy · intersubjectivity · temporality · objectification

Although "ethnographic" research is frequently cited or conducted in CSCL, there is little consensus in this literature about what distinguishes ethnographic analysis from other forms of research. While the term ethnography can be used in a methodological sense to designate any form of unstructured observation, a survey of recent anthropological ethnography reveals profound transformations that challenge classic conceptions of ethnographic practice. The social constructionist tradition of "critical ethnography" (CE) is particularly relevant for CSCL practitioners because of its critique of scientism and concomitant focus on intersubjectivity. Within CSCL and more generally in the learning sciences, scientistic assumptions that fundamental aspects of reality and ideas are given rather than developed by human and social

T.W. Epperson (✉)
Social Sciences Librarian, The College of New Jersey, Ewing, USA
e-mail: epperson@tcnj.edu

G. Stahl (ed.), *Studying Virtual Math Teams*, Computer-Supported Collaborative Learning Series 11, DOI 10.1007/978-1-4419-0228-3_27,
© Springer Science+Business Media, LLC 2009

activities has been thoroughly critiqued by constructivism. Specifically, the emphasis on intersubjectivity as a foundation for the nature of the social world is by definition relevant to CSCL, concerned with collaboration and collaborative learning.

This chapter aims to describe a form of ethnography that corresponds in many ways with the work of the VMT Project. This form has come to be known as *critical ethnography*. CE grew out of critical social theory as developed in the Frankfurt school of social research, including Horkheimer, Adorno, Marcuse and Habermas. The chapter will briefly review the development of CE through two distinct generations of thought that were enunciated before and after 1986, respectively. It will then look more closely at the CE analysis of three social phenomena. These phenomena have also been analyzed in the VMT Project.

The VMT Project—through its fine-grained analyses and emphasis on issues such as temporality, objectification and intersubjectivity—not only embodies many of the tenets of CE, but can be seen as an effort to adopt and advance the CE research agenda.

Exemplary Ethnography

It is difficult to formulate a helpful description of CE or even of ethnography in a sentence of two. It may be useful to first become familiar with a prototypical example. Forsythe's book (2001), *Studying Those Who Study Us: An Anthropologist in the World of Artificial Intelligence*, provides an excellent introduction to the concerns and challenges of critical ethnography.

Of particular interest is her account of a project to build a natural-language patient-education system for migraine sufferers, which would elicit a patient's symptoms and medical history and use that information to present individually tailored information about diagnosis and treatment. Her fieldwork included observation of visits in neurology, interviews with physicians and patients, and extended formal interviews with migraine sufferers. Forsythe was simultaneously conducting ethnographic analysis *of* and *for* the design project. However, as the project progressed she found it increasingly difficult to reconcile the roles of participant and observer because of the epistemological and practical tensions between the "relativist understandings of ethnographic data" and "the positivist expectations and procedures of normal system building." Despite compilation of a rich body of ethnographic data about migraines and a shared intention to incorporate anthropological insights into an innovative system design, the resulting software prototype "reflected much less ethnographic input than we had originally envisioned" (p. 98).

Forsythe demonstrates how the software designers' cultural and disciplinary assumptions were embedded in every stage of development. Rather than await compilation of ethnographic research, developers performed their own knowledge acquisition, interviewing a single neurologist about issues like treatment strategies and the use and side effects of different migraine drugs. The neurologist also provided a model dialog of a typical doctor-patient encounter, wherein both participants speak in unambiguous declarative sentences and the distinction between questions and answers is quite clear. The model dialog also assumed that all communication is verbal and context-independent. However, Forsythe found that patients' speech was often rambling and repetitive and unintelligible in the absence of nonverbal and contextual cues (pp. 154–55). When the time came to "add in" the results of the ethnographic analysis, fundamental contradictions were revealed. The perspective of the neurologist, which privileged the knowledge and categories of formal medicine, was incorporated into the basic design of the system. This perspective conflicted with the ethnographic findings, which saw the patients' and the physicians' perspectives as being different, but equally valid (pp. 105–107).

Forsythe's work provides an excellent example of the potentially holistic nature of ethnographic research. Her reflexive awareness of positionality eschews any pretensions of impartiality and neutrality; rather, she argues for a stance of epistemological awareness. Because she observes people whose status and power are generally greater than her own, Forsythe's work also exemplifies what Nader (1972) calls "studying up," the antithesis of traditional colonialist anthropology. Instead of "going native" to elicit and uncritically reproduce the perspectives of her informants (be they migraine sufferers or neurologists), she believes the ethnographer's method should be a continual "stepping in and stepping out" of the field situation (2001, pp. 71–72). Ethnography is predicated on the creative tension inherent in the oxymoron "participant observation." The researcher must balance the cultural immersion required for meaningful participation with the critical distance required for observation and analysis.

Yet, Forsythe also demonstrates how difficult it is to incorporate foundational, critical ethnographic insights into system designs, particularly when there are substantial, often unrecognized, epistemological differences between the worldviews of system designers and social scientists. Bader and Nyce offer a comparably pessimistic assessment: "The difficulty is that knowledge about the social construction of reality is not the kind of knowledge the development community values, can do much with, or seems to be much interested in" (1998, p. 6). They conclude: "There is, we believe, a demonstrable, fundamental gap between the knowledge the development community values and that which cultural analysis yields. Much of what goes on in social life developers and programmers simply do not see as having any relevance for their work" (p. 10).

However, as a field of inquiry explicitly concerned with the collaborative social construction of knowledge, CSCL has an obligation to seize the opportunity the larger software development community has thus far eschewed. The VMT Project has embraced this opportunity, addressing many of the concerns raised by Forsythe's analysis.

Classic and Critical Ethnography

This section will discuss how fundamental elements of critical ethnography are grounded in the continental critical theory tradition and, in turn, are embodied in the VMT Project. First, a brief (and highly selective) overview of contemporary ethnography will demonstrate both the wide variety of current research approaches and the extent to which CE concerns have been incorporated into mainstream theory and practice in anthropology and cognate disciplines.

In a chapter entitled "Erosion of Classic Norms," Rosaldo critiques the "classic period" of ethnography which he dates to the period 1921–1971 (1993, pp. 25–45). Classic period ethnographers, especially in Great Britain, typically worked within the French sociological tradition of Durkheim, where culture and society were analyzed as objective systems that "determined individual personalities and consciousness." Not surprisingly, the classic mode of analysis was predicated upon "a detached observer using a neutral language to study a unified world of brute facts" (Rosaldo, 1993, pp. xviii, 32). The inherent positivism of classic ethnography also presupposed a series of inviolate Cartesian dichotomies such as fact/value, subject/object, mind/body, individual/society and self/other.

According to Rosaldo, a range of social, political and intellectual transformations have transformed classic modes of ethnographic analysis since the late 1960s, "leaving the field of anthropology in a creative crisis of reorientation and renewal" (1993, p. 28). Some of these issues will be examined in greater detail below, but for the moment Table 27.1—selectively compiled from a wide variety of sources— presents an overview of some of the major issues addressed by CE.

Several of these transformations are particularly relevant to the fields of ethnomethodology (EM) and conversation analysis (CA). For example, Button critiques the shortcomings of "classical ethnography," making a distinction between "scenic" fieldwork "that merely describes and codifies what relevant persons do in

Table 27.1 Schematic comparison of classic and critical ethnography

Classic ethnography	Critical ethnography
Positivist, scientistic method	Reflexive, critical (Clifford & Marcus, 1986; Marcus, 1999b; Scholte, 1972)
Exotic, bounded field site	Studying at home, studying up (Nader, 1972), multi-sited research (Marcus, 1995), cyberspace (Hakken, 1999, 2003; Teli, Pisanu & Hakken, 2007)
Cartesian dichotomies	Embodied knowledge, unity of consciousness and activity (Kaptelinin & Nardi, 2006)
Interrogation, extraction	Dialog, collaboration (Tedlock, 1986)
Neutrality, detachment	Political engagement (Smith, 1999), circumstantial activism (Marcus, 1999a)
Elicitation, analysis of un-interpreted facts	Everyone's an analyst (Garfinkel, 1967, 2002)
Common sense as resource	Commonsense as topic (Forsythe, 1999, 2001)
Fact/value dichotomy	Unity of theory and practice (Lave, 1991)
Objective reality is "out there"	Social construction of reality (Hacking, 1999)
Context as container	Context as construct (Nardi, 1996)
Disembodied scientific objectivity	Feminist objectivity, situated action and knowledge (Haraway, 1991; Nader, 1996; Suchman, 2007)
Participant observation	Observation of participation (Nader, 1996; Tedlock, 1991)

the workplace" and ethnography that explicates "members' knowledge—what people have to know to do work, and how that knowledge is deployed in the ordering and organization of work" (Button, 2000, p. 319). Similarly, Goodwin and Heritage demonstrate how "CA transcends the traditional disciplinary boundaries of social anthropology by providing a perspective within which language, culture, and social organization can be analyzed not as separate subfields but as integrated elements of coherent courses of action" (1990, p. 301). Finally, classic ethnography's aspiration to "holism" dictated a preference for isolated, bounded field sites where all aspects of a culture (e.g., ritual, subsistence, kinship) could be analyzed. In CE, this is supplanted by a "truly holistic framework ... that captures the interactional and discursive constitution of human relations and social organization" regardless of context (Streeck & Mehus, 2005, p. 399).

Critical Theory: From Kant to Habermas

Much of the research in CSCL can be situated within a social-constructivist tradition grounded in continental critical theory. This tradition rejects the empiricist assumption of objective, pre-existing facts and can be characterized by three basic theses:

> (1) The *ontological* thesis that what appears to be 'natural' is in reality an effect of social processes and practices; (2) the *epistemological* thesis that knowledge of social phenomena is itself socially produced; and (3) the *methodological* thesis that the investigation of the social construction of reality must take priority over all other methodic procedures. (Sandywell, 2008, p. 96, emphasis added)

Both critical ethnography and the theory of group cognition explicitly draw upon the history of critical philosophy, as illustrated in Fig. 14-1 of (Stahl, 2006b, p. 289). The term "critical" first arose in Kant's *Critique of Pure Reason*, where it signified the drawing of the limits of the topic under study. Synthesizing the previously prevailing philosophies of rationalism and empiricism, Kant undertook a "Copernican revolution," arguing that the world is not "given" to us as objective empirical data, but is constituted as causally connected and arrayed in space and time thanks to our minds, which constitute it as so ordered (Kant, 1787/1999). Hegel's critical dialectics radically extended the argument to show how mind itself has developed historically and culturally (Hegel, 1807/1967). Dialectical thinkers since Hegel have critiqued various phenomena and disciplines by tracing their historical development. Thus, Marx demonstrated that capitalism, its products and its social relations are not fixed, universal and necessary, but are products of specific developments and can be further transformed (Marx, 1867/1976). Whereas empiricist theories of science hold that observers, data, facts, concepts, etc. are fixed aspects of a given reality, critical theories reflect on how these entities have been constituted through social processes.

Critical social theory became an explicit topic in the writings of the Frankfurt School of Social Theory (Held, 1980). Horkheimer began by defining the approach, based on the traditions of Kant and Hegel. Adorno expanded it, applying it to cultural criticism, sociology, philosophy, music and aesthetics. Other twentieth century

philosophic approaches have also adopted a critical stance toward reality. In phenomenology, Husserl conducted a thorough-going critique of psychologism and its
conception of transcendental mind. Schutz (1967) situated Husserl's view in a social
context, and Heidegger rejected the view of a detached mind, describing how we
are active beings in a world into which we are thrown as burdened with a past,
but one whose meanings are structured by our current cares and future orientations (Heidegger, 1927/1996). Even Anglo-American philosophy is largely based
in Wittgenstein's (1953) critique of the view of language espoused by logical positivism. All these philosophical influences have been incorporated into the theory of
group cognition.

As a student of both Horkheimer and Adorno, Habermas represents the "second
generation" of the Frankfurt School, and his work—particularly *On the Logic of
the Social Sciences* (Habermas, 1967/1988) and *Knowledge and Human Interests*
(Habermas, 1965/1971)—provided a foundation for the development of CE during
the late 1960 s and early 1970 s. Habermas drew "a parallel between critical theory's
critique of positivism and Marx's critique of idealism" (Outhwaite, 1994, p. 26). In
Knowledge and Human Interests, Habermas described his undertaking as "a historically oriented attempt to reconstruct the prehistory of modern positivism with the
systematic intention of analyzing the connections between knowledge and human
interests" (1965/1971, p. vii). Although Habermas' work can be situated within the
Frankfurt School's general critique of positivism, it bears repeating that his specific
interest was in reconstructing "the *prehistory* of modern positivism," in understanding positivism's conditions of possibility. He found that: "Positivism stands or falls
with the principle of scientism, that is, that the meaning of knowledge is defined
by what the sciences do and can thus be adequately explicated through the methodological analysis of scientific procedures" (1965/1971, p. 67).

Turning specifically to the social sciences, Habermas notes that "the concept of
value freedom (or ethical neutrality)" is reflected in an epistemological "severance
of knowledge from interest." This dichotomy "is represented in logic by the distinction between descriptive and prescriptive statements, which makes grammatically
obligatory the filtering out of merely emotive from cognitive contents" (1965/1971,
p. 303). The "illusion of objectivism," the belief in "a self-subsistent world of facts
structured in a law-like manner," provides the basis for the "restricted, scientistic consciousness of the sciences" which can only be challenged "by demonstrating what it conceals: the connection between knowledge and interest" (1965/1971,
pp. 69, 316). However, positivism has so effectively repressed older philosophical
traditions and permeated the self-understanding of the sciences that

> the illusion of objectivism can no longer be dispelled by a return to Kant but only
> immanently—by forcing methodology to carry out a process of self-reflection in terms of its
> own problems. . . . It can no longer be effectively overcome from without, from the position
> of a repurified epistemology, but only by a methodology that transcends its own boundaries.
> (1965/1971, p. 69)

In other words, the pervasive influence of positivism can no longer be directly
challenged through philosophical critique, but only through actual disciplinary

praxis (practice) that "transcends its own boundaries." This is the challenge taken up by early critical ethnographers, and is reflected today in the transformative research of the VMT Project.

Critical Ethnography

Because the term "critical ethnography" is currently used in a wide variety of theoretical and disciplinary settings, it is difficult to provide a concise, encompassing definition. Instead, we will take an historical approach, examining CE's origins in continental critical theory and highlighting elements of particular relevance for CSCL practitioners. In subsequent sections, we will show how elements of CE are embodied in the VMT Project and discuss how VMT advances the CE research agenda.

We can speak of two "generations," of CE, the first initiated by the publication of *Reinventing Anthropology* (Hymes, 1972) and the second by the publication of *Writing Culture: The Poetics and Politics of Ethnography* (Clifford & Marcus, 1986), although, as we shall see, a few scholars have remained consistently influential through both generations. This generational distinction is essential because the seminal early works have been overlain by, and incorporated into a subsequent generation of "critical" ethnographic perspectives that are grounded in a variety of disciplinary perspectives, particularly post-modernist literary criticism. Although these second-generation perspectives built upon, or emerged in opposition to, the foundational works, the "presentist" orientation of the recent scholarship obscures these connections and the aspects of CE of greatest potential relevance to CSCL are not readily accessible (Bunzl, 2005, p. 192).

The First Generation (c. 1968–1986)

An important precondition for the emergence of CE was the contestation of the meaning of "ethnography." Fabian (1990b) notes an implicit method/theory dichotomy within the anthropological tradition in the distinction between *ethnography* (literally "description of peoples"), and *ethnology* as a comparative, theoretical, synthesizing enterprise. By the late 1950s the dichotomy between ethnography (which had become synonymous with empirical research and data collection) and theory was being challenged by a generation of "new ethnography" practitioners. According to Fabian, "the old opposition between theory and ethnography was abolished and ethnography itself was declared a theoretical enterprise" (1990b, p. 760).

In "History, Language and Anthropology"—certainly one of CE's foundational documents—Fabian discusses the shortcomings of "scientistic social research" revealed by his empirical research on Jamaa, a charismatic religious movement in the Congo (1971; reprinted in Fabian, 1991b). In a later monograph he reflected:

> The phenomena I was interested in offered little in the way of outwardly observable behavior, of traits that could be mapped or counted, in short, of the kind of "hard data" that, properly collected, classified, and analyzed, are said to produce ethnographic knowledge. Probably, working with an illusive religious movement that refused to be approached in any other way but talk, in and on their own terms, was decisive in shaping my convictions. (Fabian, 1990b, p. 4)

Fabian's dissatisfaction with the limitations of his "Weberian-Parsonian" doctoral training at the University of Chicago and his anxieties arising from a "failure to find the sort of hard social 'facts' which my training in 'scientific' sociology had let me to expect," forced him to explore more dialectical analytical approaches (1971, p. 23; 1991a, p. 183). Realizing that the "positivist-pragmatist approach" is intellectually mired "in the period of pre-Kantian metaphysics," he turned to the work of Marx, Habermas and the linguists von Humboldt and Hymes. However, he also realized that the quandaries he was facing could not be resolved through philosophical or theoretical discourse alone, but only through anthropological praxis. In explaining the motivation for his publication, Fabian noted that it was Habermas who

> pointed out that it would be unrealistic to cite social science before the court of Kant's critique of reason; a reform must come from within, from, as I understand him, a confrontation with the epistemological problems of today's social research. To attempt, or at least to approximate, such radical critique from within is the intention of this paper. (Fabian, 1971, p. 21)

In his struggle to develop a non-positivist theoretical approach that maintained standards of objectivity and addressed the issue of intersubjectivity, Fabian developed a language-centered approach predicated on two theses:

(1) In anthropological investigations, objectivity lies neither in the logical consistency of a theory, nor in the giveness of data, but in the foundation (*Begründung*) of human *intersubjectivity*.
(2) *Objectivity* in anthropological investigations is attained by entering a context of communicative interaction through the one medium which represents *and* constitutes such a context: *language*. (1971, p. 25, 27)

As we will see, the connection between objectivity and intersubjectivity was to become a continuing theme of Fabian's research.

In language that resonated with contemporaneous work in ethnomethodology, Fabian noted that, for the positivist social scientist, social facts consist of observed regularities revealing a "reality behind" the observed data. Citing Hegel and Marx, Fabian proposed a radical counter proposition, "that the particulars of observation are not just contingent indicators of an underlying necessary reality. They are not seen as 'cases of' but as *results of a process* in which a totality realizes itself" (Fabian, 1971, p. 26).

Scholte, in his contribution to *Reinventing Anthropology* (Scholte, 1972) and elsewhere, offered a similar critique. Again citing Habermas, he wrote that "scientism ... is finally and radically being challenged on political, normative, philosophical, and even anthropological grounds" and he thus advocated creation of "a reflective, critical, and emancipatory anthropology" (1971, p. 781). "Critical anthropology," according to Scholte, "seeks to transcend the naïve dualism of subject and object ... The communicative and constitutive relation between self and other is considered the absolute foundation of anthropological praxis" (1978a).

The only way "scientism" could overcome its inherent limitations would be "to embark on a self-reflexive and self-critical course, that is, one which would emancipate it from its own paradigmatic stance." However, such a course is precluded by "the widely held assumption that there is, and should be, a discontinuity between experience and reality, between the investigator and the object investigated" (Scholte, 1972, p. 435). Taking an explicitly anthropological perspective, he also wrote that scientism is "ethnocentric in presuming that the canons of scientific reason and technical application are objective and universal. In fact, they are neither" (Scholte, 1978b, p. 178). In a move that presaged future developments in ethnomethodology, Scholte also suggested that Garfinkel's "claims for action may be applicable to scientific activity as well," that a paradigm's sense of its own facticity, objectivity, accountability, and communality, "is to be treated as a contingent accomplishment of socially organized common practices. In short, they are not given, but accomplished" (citing Garfinkel, 1972, p. 323; Scholte, 1978a, pp. 8–9).

Finally, we should note Nader's essay, *Up the Anthropologist—Perspectives Gained From Studying Up* (1972). Nader suggested that traditional ethnographic research depended upon power relations that favored the anthropologist and she exhorted anthropologists to "study up," to explore situations where they are *less* powerful than the people or institutions being analyzed: "What if, in reinventing anthropology, anthropologists were to study the colonizers rather than the colonized, the culture of power rather than the culture of the powerless, the culture of affluence rather than the culture of poverty?" (1972, p. 289). She also challenged the "mystique about participant observation," noting that this form of research had unexamined theoretical consequences and "weighed heavily in the decisions as to where anthropologists study: we prefer residential situations, whether the residence is in a primitive village or a modern hospital" (1972, p. 306). Nader's work prodded anthropology toward transcendence of its colonialist origins and opened a space where non-traditional research methods and venues could be considered valid ethnographic research, ranging from "microethnography" (Streeck & Mehus, 2005) through "multi-sited" and "world systems" ethnography (Marcus, 1995). The anthropology of education (Hamann, 2003) and cyberspace (Hakken, 1999, 2003; Teli et al., 2007) owe her particular debts of gratitude.

Writing two decades after the publication of *Language, History and Anthropology*, Fabian was hesitant to revisit the early critique of positivism and scientism. However, he insisted that "moral perplexities," "political impasses" and "paradoxes regarding the nature of anthropological knowledge" should still be examined in epistemological terms (Fabian, 1991b, p. 190). Fabian's admonition notwithstanding, a review of these early critiques enhances our understanding of the divergent strands of second generation CE. According to Roscoe, "modern critical anthropology" went awry "in failing to follow a lead laid down by its radical forbearers," particularly Scholte, in their careful distinction between "science" and "scientism." In collapsing science into positivism, "the scientistically inclined have trapped incautious critics into accepting at face value their claim that the positivist program is science." However, the objective of the first-generation critical anthropologists "was not to reject a science of society but to place it within a humane rather than a scientistic framework" (Roscoe, 1995, p. 501). The spirit of first generation CE is preserved and nourished by the continuing publication of the journals *Critique of Anthropology* and *Dialectical Anthropology*, founded in 1974 and 1975, respectively.

The Second Generation (c. 1986–present)

The onset of second generation CE can be defined by the publication of *Writing Culture* (Clifford & Marcus, 1986). Co-edited by a non-anthropologist (Clifford), the volume was self-consciously "post-disciplinary" in its shift away from "anthropology" per se toward conceptions of "ethnography" and "culture" that were situated within larger debates in Cultural Studies. However, according to Bunzel, the innovative and transformative character of *Writing Culture* should not be overstated:

> Having incorporated the epistemological, political, and textual reorientations engendered by the crisis of anthropology, the volume thus stood at the beginning of anthropology's transdisciplinary turn—a turn that reinvented the discipline through the deliberate erasure of what had come to be seen as its compromised history. (2005, p. 192)

In addition to analyzing ethnography as a method of social science research, the "literary turn" (Evans, 2007; Handelman, 1994) initiated by *Writing Culture* also fostered examination of "ethnography" as a genre of social science text as well as experimentation with non-realist literary forms of ethnographic writing. Fabian acknowledges that the focus on ethnographic authority prompted by the "postmodern turn" provides a "much more sophisticated view of the literary means in the production of ethnographic knowledge [adding] another dimension to the critique of anthropology." However, he argues that some "recent celebrations of the anthropological muse" have confused "*diagnosis* (of anthropology being constituted as a literary practice) with *therapy* (the claim that literature will save anthropology)," concluding, "seeking oblivion in the embraces of literary theory or philosophy of science cannot be the way to go for critical anthropology" (1991a, pp. 92, 94, emphasis added).

The expansive conception of ethnography exemplified by *Writing Culture* is also celebrated by Rosaldo, who argues that "ethnography has been cultural anthropology's most significant contribution to knowledge," representing "an emergent interdisciplinary phenomenon" (1993, pp. 38–39). Although the unmooring of ethnography from anthropology has fostered creative, and often critical, ethnographic research in a wide variety of disciplines and settings, there are potential perils. The decontextualization of ethnography, coupled with the historical "erasure" represented by second generation CE, means that well-intentioned attempts to infuse ethnography with critical perspectives are often conducted in isolation from historical and contemporary debates within anthropology, debates about what Fabian calls "the very 'conditions of possibility' of producing ethnographic knowledge in communicative, interactive, and dialogical rather than positivistic ways" (Fabian, 1991a,

p. 187). Elsewhere, Fabian optimistically reflected on the influence of *Writing Culture* and similar second generation CE works: "The critique of misplaced scientism in anthropology has been a good thing, a hard-fought victory over a collusion of theories of knowledge, conventions of representation, and the practice of Western imperialism." Now that "interpretative and hermeneutic approaches" had demonstrated "viable alternatives to positivism," Fabian felt it was time to take "critical anthropology" to "a new level" (1990b, p. xiii).

Fabian's innovative monograph *Power and Performance: Ethnographic Explorations Through Proverbial Wisdom and Theater in Shaba (1990a)* exemplifies his own attempts to incorporate insights from the "literary turn" in ethnographic writing and take critical anthropology to a "new level." The ethnography was born in Zaire when Fabian heard a local proverb, spoken only in French, "*Le pouvoir se mange entire*" ("power is eaten whole"). Consultation with friends and colleagues revealed that, while everyone seemed to know the proverb, there were no analogous proverbs in Swahili or any other local African languages. Fabian's inquiries inspired a local theater troupe to write and produce a play based upon—and named after—the proverb. The play was eventually filmed and broadcast on national television. Fabian observed and recorded every stage of the project, and his monograph includes extensive transcriptions (in both original Swahili and English translation) of various rehearsals and the final production.

Fabian makes a distinction between "informing" and "performing," stating that most "theories of ethnographic knowledge are built on models of information transfer, of transmission of (somehow preexisting) messages via signs, symbols, or codes." While these models may be descriptively useful, they are "epistemologically ... deficient because they fail to account for historically contingent creation of information *in and through the events* in which messages are said to be transmitted" (Fabian, 1990a, p. 11). Furthermore, many realms of information cannot "simply be called up and expressed in discursive statements" by ethnographic interlocutors. "This sort of information can be represented—made present—only through action, enactment, or performance" (1990a, p. 6). A performance does not "simply enact a preexisting text. Performance *is* the text in the moment of its actualization (in a story told, in a conversation carried on, but also in a book read)." Rather than being a questioner eliciting information, Fabian suggests that the ethnographer "be a provider of occasions, a catalyst in the weakest sense, and a producer (in analogy to a theatrical producer) in the strongest." Borrowing a phrase from Turner, Fabian is suggesting that the ethnographer play the role of "ethnodramaturge" (see Turner's essay in Ruby, 1982).

Temporalizing, Objectification, Intersubjectivity in CE

Three concerns emerging from the CE tradition are of particular relevance for the VMT Project: temporalizing, objectification and intersubjectivity. This section briefly discusses these three topics in CE before turning to the corresponding VMT analyses.

Temporalizing

Anthropologists have traditionally addressed the issue of socio-cultural time through a wide variety of topics, such as "time-reckoning, calendric patterns, cultural constructions of the past, [and] time as a medium of strategy or control." In her review essay, Munn advocates a conception of "'temporalization' that views time as a symbolic process continually being produced in everyday practices" (1992, p. 116). One of the most radical and influential anthropological examinations of time is Fabian's *Time and the Other: How Anthropology Makes its Object* (published in 1983, reissued in 2002). It stands at the transition between first and second generation CE (Bunzl, 2002; Fabian, 2002) and was an important precursor to *Writing Culture* (Clifford & Marcus, 1986).

Time and the Other examines the connections between practices of temporal distancing in anthropological writing and the creation of the anthropological "Other." Fabian uses the term *coevalness* to characterize intersubjective sharing of historic time and space. According to Bunzl, "Fabian deploys the designation 'coevalness' in order to merge into one Anglicized term the German notion of '*Gleichzeitigkeit*,' a phenomenological category that denotes both contemporaneity and synchronicity/simultaneity." The skilled ethnographer establishes an intersubjective, coeval relationship with her interlocutors during the course of fieldwork. However, the conventions of classic anthropological writing, particularly the suppression of the autobiographical voice and the use of the "ethnographic present" trope, result in a "denial of coevalness," which Fabian characterizes as the *allochronism* of anthropology. Allochronism is a necessary precondition for—and an inevitable manifestation of—scientistic ethnography's belief in distanced neutrality and "objectivity" (Fabian, 2002, pp. 1–35).

Of particular relevance for the VMT Project is Fabian's analysis of *intersubjective time*, which is grounded in the phenomenological insight "that social interaction presupposes intersubjectivity, which in turn is inconceivable without assuming that the participants involved are coeval, i.e. share the same Time" (2002, p. 30). The conception of intersubjective time reflects an

> emphasis on the communicative nature of human action and interaction. As soon as culture is no longer primarily conceived as a set of rules to be enacted by individual members of distinct groups, but as the specific way in which actors create and produce beliefs, values, and other means of social life, it has to be recognized that Time is a constitutive dimension of social reality ... not just a measure, of human activity. (2002, p. 24)

However, intersubjective time is not the inevitable result of spatial and temporal proximity between individuals. Fabian stresses, "for human communication to occur, coevalness has to be *created*. Communication is, ultimately, about creating shared Time" (2002, emphasis in original, p. 31). Writing in 1983, Fabian noted "an increased recognition of intersubjectivity in such new disciplines as ethnomethodology and the ethnography of speaking." However, the dominant model of human communication was still predicated upon the assumption of temporal distancing between participants:

At least, I believe this is implied in the widely accepted distinctions between sender, message, and receiver. Leaving aside the problem of the message (and the code), these models project, between sender and receiver, a temporal distance (or slope). Otherwise, communication could not be conceptualized as the *transfer* of information. (Fabian, 2002, p. 31)

In his recent essay *Language and Time*, Fabian notes that his "growing awareness of our ways with time" has sustained his interest in the convergence between "pragmatically oriented approaches in linguistics and language-oriented views of anthropology" (2007, p. 33). Describing his "point of departure" as "a philosophical position that is materialist and dialectical," he realizes his interests are shared only by "those to whom relating language and time is an empirical, hence a practical, and an epistemological problem. 'Epistemological' means related to, accounting for, and justifying practices of knowledge production" (2007, p. 37). His examination of the connection between time and language is predicated upon a critique of linguistic formalism, "the kind of linguistics that requires the elimination of time." This atemporality can be traced to Saussure's absolute dichotomy between language as the system of *langue* (synchronic) and language as spoken *parole* (diachronic). However, Fabian counters by citing literary critic Jameson:

> Once you have begun by separating diachronic from synchronic ... You can never really put them back together again. If the opposition in the long run proves to be a false or misleading one, then the only way to suppress it is by throwing the entire discussion on a higher dialectical plane. (Fabian, 2007, p. 34; quoting Jameson, 1972, p. 18)

Since language-centered research is based upon the production and analysis of textual empirical data, Fabian also examines the connections between knowledge production, the creation of shared time, and the use of texts:

> Epistemologically this means that what we have said earlier about presence must include memory in the sense that texts become evidence through being re-cognized as relevant. There are no texts "as such"; every text exists in a context of other texts and our ability to recognize such context presupposes remembrance of a past. Put more concretely: current practices of speaking or "languaging" are always rehearsals of earlier practices. (2007, p. 38)

Despite its excellent, though brief, discussions of intersubjective time, Fabian's *Time and the Other* was primarily about the allochronism of anthropological writing, about the *denial* of coevalness. Similarly, his later work contains tantalizing hints for empirical research on the interrelations between shared time, history, language and texts, but we find only limited application. Therefore, the VMT Project can be seen as not only embracing but also advancing the research concerns of CE through fine-grained analysis of the *creation* of coevalness during interactions between members of virtual math teams.

Objectification

Returning to reflect upon the phenomenon of objectification in his 1971 essay *History, Language, and Anthropology*, Fabian in 2001 wrote: "One thing is clearer to me now than it was at the time. The decisive difference between the positivist conception of objectivity and the alternative I was struggling to formulate involved a

theory of *objectification*" (2001, p. 15). In a footnote to this passage, he grapples
with the concept of objectification:

> I am neither able nor willing to give this term a clear axiomatic definition. What it desig-
> nates is a problem I am struggling with: the notion of objectivity as applied to knowledge
> of "things historical and cultural" needs to be developed in terms of a theory of *Vergegen-*
> *ständlichung*, that is, of the making of all those things that can become the objects of—in
> the case we are discussing here—ethnographic knowledge. (2001, p. 208)

Positivism, because it claimed that social scientific knowledge was based on the
study of preexisting facts that could be studied like natural objects, "needed no theory of the constitution of objects." However, the language-based view of ethnographic knowledge Fabian was struggling to articulate was "based on what is intersubjectively and communicatively produced," and therefore "had to include a theory
of objectification capable of specifying what in communicative interaction becomes
an object and thereby the basis of objective knowledge" (2001, p. 15).

The complex and nuanced use of the term *objectification* has been taken up
within the learning sciences, and specifically math education by Sfard in her theory
of how math objects are constructed in math history and in math learning. According
to Sfard, the process of objectification involves "two tightly related, but not inseparable discursive moves: *reification*, which consists in substituting talk about actions
with talk about objects, and *alienation*, which consists in presenting phenomena in
an impersonal way, as if they were occurring of themselves, without the participation of human beings" (2008, p. 44). For example, the statement "He *cannot cope*
with even the simplest arithmetic problems in spite of years of instruction." might
be reified as "He *has a learning disability*" (2008, p. 44). Once reified, the "alleged
products of the mind's actions may undergo the final objectification by being fully
dissociated, or *alienated* from the actor . . . by such discursive means as the use of
the passive voice or the employment of the given noun in the role of grammatical subject." Even a simple mathematical statement like "two plus three make five"
eliminates the human subject, effectively disguising "the fact that numbers are discursive constructs and, as such, are human-made rather than given" (2008, p. 50).

Sfard continues by discussing both the "gains" of objectification, particularly
in mathematics discourse, and the "traps" of objectification, particularly in "discourse on thinking." Objectification increases both the communicative and practical
effectiveness of mathematical discourse. For example, it is the objectification of
complex discursive sequences that allows us to see $(86 + 37)$ and (123) as equivalent and interchangeable numerical expressions. Similarly, a symbolic expression
such as $(3 + 4 = 7)$ is actually "a shortcut for a rather lengthy story about our own
discursive actions of counting. As a result of objectification, the meta-discursive
nature of this proposition remains invisible." The problem occurs when "all, the
objects—discursive (words, expressions) and extra-discursive (independently existing material objects)—seem to belong to the same ontological category of 'things
in the world,' with their mutual relations being similarly 'objective' and mind independent." Sfard characterizes this situation as *ontological collapse*, which can result
in (a) illusory dilemmas, (b) false dichotomies and/or (c) consequential omissions
(2008, pp. 51–57).

The reason all of this matters is that children who are first learning about math have not yet objectified these discursive processes. They therefore have trouble, for example, seeing ten marbles and ten coins as "the same number." However, once "mathematists" begin to objectify these discursive processes, numbers become discourse-independent entities. The subsequent invisibility of the objectification process is reflected in mainstream math education, where "numbers are self-sustained entities existing in the world along with humans and animals." Piaget's "expression 'child's contact with numbers' further implies that when a child is born, the numbers are already out there in the world waiting to be discovered along with stars, trees, and other material objects" (Sfard, 2005, p. 285).

In her most recent work, Sfard offers an extended analysis of the discursive construction of math objects (2008, pp. 163–194). In Chapter 4, Stahl related Sfard's work to the issue of "deep learning" in mathematics:

> One must be able to unpack or de-construct the processes that are reified as the object. To be able to write an equation—e.g., during a test in school, where the particular equation is indicated—is not enough. One must to some extent be able to re-create or derive the equation from a concrete situation and to display alternative visual realizations, such as graphs, formulas, special cases and tables of the equation. There is not a single definition of the equation's meaning, but a network of interrelated realizations. (2008a, p. 363)

Thus, deep learning in mathematics is not the acquisition of knowledge, but rather "participation in co-construction of realizations" through discursive social processes.

Fabian's ongoing struggles to link: (1) a non-empiricist conception of objectivity, (2) intersubjectivity, and (3) a theory of objectification all have deep resonances with the VMT Project. In fact, Sfard's work on the discursive construction of math objects, coupled with VMT's fine-grained analyses of math discourse represent a productive embodiment and extension of CE concerns.

Intersubjectivity

Turning to the third element of CE that is particularly relevant to the VMT Project, *intersubjectivity* involves social phenomena, which are not simply mental (individual psychological) or physical objects, but have been co-constructed by sets of people and are shared within dyads, small groups, communities or cultures. It can briefly be characterized as:

> some set of relations, meanings, structures, practices, experiences, or phenomena evident in human life that cannot be reduced to or comprehended entirely in terms of either subjectivity (concerning psychological states of individual actors) or objectivity (concerning brute empirical facts about the objective world). (Zurn, 2008, p. 116)

We can begin our extended discussion of intersubjectivity by juxtaposing two seemingly disparate studies presented by Goodwin. The first analyzes the communication skills of an elderly man with severe aphasia (1995, 2004), while in the second study we watch as a student archaeologist learns an essential component of her craft, the delineation and documentation of soil features encountered during an excavation (Goodwin, 1994; 2000b). The point in both cases is how the aphasic man's communication and the archaeologist's categorizations are intersubjectively achieved.

Chil, a close relative of Goodwin, was a 65-year-old attorney when he suffered a massive stroke in the left hemisphere of his brain that left him paralyzed on the right side of his body. The stroke also resulted in severe aphasia, an almost complete loss of the ability to produce meaningful language. At the time of Goodwin's study thirteen years after the stroke, Chil had a vocabulary consisting of only three words: *yes, no,*and *and.* However, Goodwin's video-assisted analysis revealed that the man has "a wider communicative repertoire than his limited vocabulary would indicate." While not perfect, his ability to understand what others were saying was quite good and he was able to utilize the sequential organization of conversation, his social and material environment, and the communicative resources and actions of his interlocutors to enhance his communicative abilities. He could also use gesture and prosody to display affect and project "a range of subtly differentiated stances toward talk and other events" (2004, p. 152). For example, a single *no* had a structurally different meaning than the three-unit *no, no, no*, and the prosody of a longer string could help refine its meaning.

In the episode presented, Chil is asked a question about whether he had ever been "in a big earthquake." The sequential positioning of the question and Chil's response makes this a "second story" that draws on the structure and narrative content of an earlier account. After a few incorrect attempts to interpret his gestures, Chil's wife begins an account that he shapes, elaborates, and corrects through his gestures and limited vocabulary. Goodwin stresses that this is not merely a narrative requested by Chil and then related by his wife. Although this is a "shared story," he remains the primary author. When his wife takes the narrative in a direction other that the one he intended, Chil is able to display his disagreement and redirect her telling.

Chil's use of gestures, coupled with the work performed by his interlocutors to correctly understand the gestures, is particularly intriguing. Rather than representing "a single underlying psychological process," gesture and talk are "structurally different kinds of sign system." For fluent speakers, "talk and gesture ... mutually inform each other and indeed are deeply parasitic on each other. Gesture achieves its typical transparent intelligibility through the way it is embedded within a larger ecology of meaning-making practices." The "intrinsic multimodality of human language use" is typically not noticed in everyday interactions. However, in this case the mutually-informing relationship between talk and gesture is absent, necessitating "a reallocation of participant roles within this ecology of sign systems, with an interlocutor rather than the gesturer/speaker providing the language necessary to explicate the gesture" (Goodwin, 2004, p. 160). Chil's ability to shape the actions of others through gestures and other interventions requires:

> the active collaboration of others, who must engage and work with his signs in ways that extend well beyond simply decoding conventionalized meanings. Fortunately, the sequential organization of interaction provides an architecture for the accomplishment of

this intersubjectivity.... Chil and his interlocutor can check and negotiate their provisional understandings through a collaborative process of meaning making. (Goodwin, 2004, p. 162)

Although the case of Chil, with his three-word vocabulary, would seem to be an extreme example inapplicable to the analysis of "fluent" conversation, Goodwin notes than these are differences of degree rather than kind. All conversationalists draw upon and tie into what has been said by other parties, transforming prior talk to suit their own projects, and storytelling in fluent conversation is typically a collaborative activity rather than a monologue. This is also an extreme manifestation of Vygotsky's "zone of proximal development," wherein a participant in a conversation "goes beyond his or her abilities as an individual by using resources provided by others" (2004, p. 155). The extreme nature of Chil's case gives us an enhanced appreciation of the "architecture of intersubjectivity" that characterizes all human interactions. This example challenges the view that linguistic competence is based exclusively upon psychological or neurological structures lodged within individual minds, or that conversations can be analyzed merely as exchanges between discrete individuals.

Turning to our second example, Goodwin analyses how archaeological features are delineated and documented (Goodwin, 1994) and how Munsell color charts are used to differentiate and describe soil colors (Goodwin, 2000b). He examines three specific practices: *coding, highlighting*, and *producing and articulating material representations*, through which practitioners "build and contest *professional vision*, which consists of socially organized ways of seeing and understanding events that are answerable to the distinctive interests of a particular social group" (1994, p. 606).

Coding schemes are one of the systematic practices used to transform the world into categories and events that are relevant to professional practice. Specifically, the

encounter between a coding scheme (i.e., Munsell color classification) and the world is a key locus for scientific practice, the place where the multifaceted complexity of "nature" is transformed into the phenomenal categories that make up the work environment of a scientific discipline. It is precisely here that nature is transformed into culture. (1994, p. 608)

Here, nature is *objectified*. The use of coding schemes requires active physical, perceptual and cognitive work, but also organizes and structures perception of the world: "Insofar as the coding scheme establishes an orientation toward the world, it constitutes a structure of intentionality whose proper locus is not an isolated Cartesian mind but a much larger organizational system" (1994, p. 609).

The practice of highlighting is used in complex perceptual fields to make distinctions between figure and ground, between what is relevant and important for the purpose at hand and what can be dismissed as "noise." Goodwin's example is the delineation of post molds (features that indicate where structural posts once stood) based upon very subtle differences in soil color and texture. The ability to make these delineations is one of the most important skills a novice archaeologist needs to acquire. Borrowing a phrase from Garfinkel (1967), Goodwin describes the "documentary method of interpretation" whereby "the category 'post mold' provides a texture of intelligibility that unifies disparate patches of color into a coherent object. These patches of color in turn provide evidence for the existence in this patch of dirt of an instance of the object proposed by the category" (1994, p. 610).

Goodwin discusses the importance of graphic representations as embodied practice, using the example of a novice archaeologist (Sue) working with her professor (Ann) to draw a profile that depicts the soil layers and cultural features visible in the vertical face of an excavation. Drawing a profile is not just an isolated, individual skill: "The ability to build and interpret a material cognitive artifact, such as an archaeological map, is embedded within a web of socially articulated discourse" (1994, p. 262). Describing graphic representations as "a central locus for the analysis of professional practice," Godwin notes that they do not mirror spoken language, but rather "complement it, using the distinctive characteristics of the material world to organize phenomena in ways that spoken language cannot." Fine-grained video analysis was used to capture complex situated interactions as Ann guides Sue in the proper delineation and measurement of soil features. According to Goodwin,

> growth in intersubjectivity occurs as domains of ignorance that prevent the successful accomplishment of collaborative action are revealed and transformed into practical knowledge—a way of seeing that is sufficient to complete the job at hand—in a way that allows Sue to understand what Ann is asking her to do and make an appropriate, competent response to her request. (1994, p. 614)

However, in this situation "the relevant unit for the analysis of the intersubjectivity" is not Sue and Ann "as isolated entities," but rather

> archaeology as a profession, a community of competent practitioners, most of whom have never met each other but nonetheless expect each other to be able to see and categorize the world in ways that are relevant to the work, tools, and artifacts that constitute their profession. (1994, p. 615)

Upon reflection, we see that Goodwin's two studies are perhaps not so disparate after all. The issue of intersubjectivity was central to both cases: For Chil, contextual resources and the sequential organization of interaction provided an "architecture of intersubjectivity" that allowed his interlocutors to understand him much better than would be indicated by his extremely limited vocabulary. Although his case was extreme, it serves as a reminder that linguistic competence is never lodged merely within the skull of a discrete individual. In the case of Sue, the student archaeologist, we saw that establishment of intersubjectivity was integral to becoming a full-fledged member of her community of practice (Lave, 1991). Finally, both case-studies drew our attention to the multi-modality of human communication. In Chil's case the mutually-informing relationship between talk and gesture was severed, forcing his interlocutors to frequently decode his gestures in the absence of complementary speech. In the training of the novice archaeologist we saw the importance of graphic representation as a mode of communication that complements, but does not mirror, speaking. In fact the ability to construct graphic representations and to coordinate between textual, graphic, and spoken modes of communication will be essential for Sue's development as an archaeologist.

Temporalizing, Objectification and Intersubjectivity in VMT

In the following subsections, we will briefly explore how the critical ethnography issues of temporalizing, objectification and intersubjectivity are manifested in the VMT Project.

Temporalizing the Problem Space

In the preceding section, we stated that Fabian advocated a "materialist and dialectical" philosophical stance to understanding the interrelations between language and time. However, he also noted that this approach would be of interest only to researchers who see this relationship as "an empirical, hence a practical, and an epistemological problem." In this context, epistemological means "accounting for, and justifying practices of knowledge production" (2007, p. 37).

In Chapter 6 of this volume, Sarmiento implicitly responds to the challenge, providing a fine-grained analysis of the practices of knowledge production employed by small groups of VMT students engaged in collaborative problem solving over multiple sessions. He is particularly interested in understanding group construction and maintenance of a joint problem space (JPS). He describes the JPS "as a metaphor for the social order that is established in small-group problem-solving interactions," and traces the development of the concept from the individualist conception of problem spaces in information-processing research to more sophisticated conceptions that capture complexities of collaborative problem solving. Within the learning sciences today, collaborative activity is often conceived as occurring within a joint problem space, where successful collaboration requires integration of "a *content space* pertaining to the problem being solved and a *relational space* pertaining to the ways that participants relate to each other." Not surprisingly, construction and maintenance of a JPS "*represents the central interactive challenge of effective collaborative knowledge building and learning.*"

Construction and maintenance of a JPS is complex enough in brief, single-episode collaborations; however, it becomes even more challenging when the collaborative activity is dispersed over time in multiple episodes and across multiple collectivities, as is generally the case in naturalistic, "real world" settings. In this chapter Sarmiento is particularly interested in understanding how co-participants "bridge" between multiple, discontinuous collaborative episodes over time, particularly when there are changes in group composition. He found that bridging activities included: "(a) narrating or *reporting* past doings as resources for constructing a new task, (b) *remembering* collectively and (c) *managing* the history of the team." Given the importance and ubiquity of these bridging activities, it is suggested that the two-dimensional model of the JPS: (1) managing participation (relational) and (2) knowledge artifacts and actions (content) be expanded to include a third dimension: "the temporal and sequential unfolding of activity" (see Fig. 6.4). The temporal and sequential dimensions of collaborative activity are particularly apparent in Log 6-2, an episode that built upon and extended a previous session, but which also included members not present in the earlier encounter. At first glance, it might appear that one group member (Meets) was solely responsible for remembering prior activities and bringing newcomers up-to-date. However, closer examination of the transcript reveals, "The activity of remembering unfolds as a collective engagement in which different team members participate." In fact, there is a fascinating segment where Meets was unable to "see" how an aspect of their earlier problem solving was accomplished, and Drago—who did not participate in the earlier episode—was able to contribute an essential element to the construction of the collective memory.

Although it was not presented in these terms, in Logs 6-1 and 6-2 we are witnessing what Fabian, in *Time and the Other*, calls the creation of *coevalness*, or "intersubjective time." Recall that for Fabian, time "is not just a measure of human activity," but rather "a constitutive dimension of social reality." However, coevalness does not just happen; shared time has to be *created*, and intersubjectivity is impossible without it. The notion of coevalness also implicitly challenges the dominant "information transfer" model of human communication, which is predicated upon the assumption of "temporal distancing" between participants and clear "distinctions between sender, message and receiver." Chapter 6 provides an analysis of the connections between knowledge production, collective memory and the production and use of texts. For Fabian, "there are no texts 'as such'; every text exists in a context of other texts and our ability to recognize such context presupposes remembrance of a past."

While *Time and the Other* was primarily about the *denial* of coevalness in classic ethnographic writing, Fabian's work also provides a framework for understanding the *creation* of intersubjectively shared time, and the VMT research provides an ideal opportunity for fine-grained understandings of how shared time is created. The work presented in Chapter 6 uncovers how intersubjective time is co-constructed as a temporal dimension of the joint problem space, i.e., the social order established by the group of students. In their bridging activities of reporting, remembering and managing their work, the virtual math team discursively constructs their past, present and future events as intersubjectively available, ordered and meaningful. It labels the events with temporal markers such as tensed verbs and it locates the events within an indexical network of significance (see Chapter 26 also), which has a temporal dimensionality.

Objectification of Math Artifacts

We saw above Fabian struggling to formulate and articulate what he tentatively called a theory of *objectification* "capable of specifying what in communicative interaction becomes an object and thereby the basis of objective knowledge." He noted that the positivist social scientist has no need for a "theory of the constitution of objects" since knowledge is supposedly based on the study of pre-existing facts (including "social facts") that can be studied like natural objects. While not phrased in precisely these terms, Çakir's Chapter 7 reports on a fine-grained examination of processes of objectification or, in other words, the collaborative construction of math objects by VMT students. Çakir analyzes how three non-co-located middle-school students construct and coordinate whiteboard inscriptions, chat postings, mathematical expressions and other elements of virtual math team activities.

As previously noted, Sfard (2008) discusses the "gains" and "traps" of objectification, noting that all math objects—from basic numbers up through advanced theorems and proofs—are objectifications of complex discursive processes. This objectification process provides an essential foundation for all mathematical discourse. The problem, however, is that once objectification occurs, the socially constructed nature of the math object can become invisible to mathematists and analysts alike. This invisibility is reflected, for example in mainstream math education's tacit assumption that "numbers are already out there in the world waiting to be discovered [by the young child] along with stars, trees and other material objects." Although the social construction of math objects is a theme that can be found throughout this volume, Chapter 7 provides a particularly compelling analysis of the complexly "sedimented" nature of these semiotic objects (see also Chapter 3). In the extended example we see the three students constructing and narrating a complex math object that they eventually refer to as a *hexagonal array* while they work to define and solve their own math problem (see especially Log 7-3 and Figs. 7.6 and 7.7). Çakir's analysis carefully avoids a literal, empiricist understanding of math object, noting that the students' term "hexagonal array does not simply refer to a readily available whiteboard illustration. Instead it is used as a *gloss* to talk about an imagined pattern that grows infinitely and takes the shape illustrated on the whiteboard only at a particular stage."

Çakir's analysis also focuses on the different affordances of the two interaction spaces (text chat and whiteboard), showing how the students coordinate these two modes of communication. For example, in Fig. 7.7 we see Jason coordinating between text chat and the whiteboard illustration, using the referencing tool to link a specific chat posting with a highlighted segment of the hexagonal array. In this illustration, we see the result of a sequence of at least three separate actions: posting the chat text, highlighting a portion of the array and using the arrow to link the two items. Çakir notes the complexity of coordination between the two interaction spaces: "a participant cannot narrate his/her whiteboard actions with simultaneous chat postings as can be done with talk in a face-to-face setting." This observation recalls Goodwin's analysis of the aphasic communication skills of Chil. Goodwin noted that talk and gesture do not represent "a single underlying psychological process," but are, rather, "structurally different kinds of sign systems." Nevertheless, the "intrinsic multimodality of human language use" is typically not noticed in everyday interactions. In Chil's case, however, "the mutually-informing relationship between talk and gesture is absent," and his interlocutors must work collaboratively with Chil, and with each other, to make out his meaning. This is possible only because the "sequential organization of interaction provides an architecture for the accomplishment of this intersubjectivity."

As it happens, the unfamiliar nature of the VMT dual interaction spaces (text and graphics) helps us notice structurally different kinds of sign systems and understand how the students use the sequential organization of interaction as a sense-making resource. In this exotic virtual world, where the normal methods of coordinating gesture and talk are not available, people can be seen to be collaboratively employing innovative methods to create objects and discuss them. Chapter 7 is able to follow in detail the processes by which the group of budding mathematists objectifies the math object, *hexagonal array*. In this analysis, we see that the object is, in fact, quite different from physical objects in the world. It incorporates the lessons of visual reasoning with illustrative diagrams, narrative reasoning that follows the growth of hexagonal line patterns and symbolic reasoning that captures relationships in symbolic equations. The rich phenomena that the students explored and shared are encapsulated and sedimented in the term *hexagon* and the corresponding equation. While this objectification provides a convenient gloss for their discourse, it also alienates the original experiences, making it difficult for newcomers to appreciate the mathematical understanding incorporated in the new math object.

Intersubjectivity of Questioning

A fundamental, if implicit, theme that unites CE is the issue of how (or even, if) genuinely intersubjective understandings can be accomplished across barriers of difference, particularly power differences. However, all human interactions are characterized by some form of difference, which may or may not be made relevant during the course of an interaction. This is particularly true in teaching/learning and apprenticeship contexts, which, by definition, are predicated upon differential skill and knowledge. In a compilation of ethnographic studies that included examinations of apprenticeship among Mayan midwives, Liberian tailors, US navy quartermasters, US butchers, and "non-drinking alcoholics," Lave and Wenger (1991) began to challenge metaphors of "knowledge acquisition" and "knowledge transfer" with a model of "learning-as-participation" (see also Sfard, 2008, pp. 76–80). In this model, beginning practitioners learn by participating in existing communities of practice. In the beginning, the novice's participation will be quite peripheral to the activities of the community, but will become less peripheral over time. Because the apprentice's activities are sanctioned by the community, Lave and Wenger characterize this model of learning as "legitimate peripheral participation." We saw a nice example in the collaborative work of Sue, the student archaeologist, and her professor, Ann. Goodwin noted that "growth in intersubjectivity occurs as domains of ignorance that prevent the successful accomplishment of collaborative action [in this case, drawing an archaeological unit profile] are revealed and transformed into practical knowledge." Goodwin also noted that, ultimately, "the relevant unit for the analysis of the intersubjectivity" in this example is not Sue and Ann "as isolated entities," but rather "archaeology as a profession, a community of competent practitioners."

While the participationist model of learning is compelling, it is yet to be seen how this is accomplished at the small-group level of interaction. In Chapter 8, Zhou examines interactionally delicate situations where group participants are purportedly peers (at least in age and school level) but there are marked differences in competences relevant to their task. Her interest is in understanding how (or if) these disparities in competence are made relevant, negotiated, and addressed. In her first example, Nish joins as the interaction is well underway. He presents a self-oriented report indicating a lack of understanding about what is happening (Log 8-1). Because Nish's report came at an interactionally awkward moment (as group members were engaged in an unrelated task) and because Nish gave dispreferred responses indicating that he found answers to his initial query inadequate, all group members were forced to do additional interactional work. In Logs 8-3 and 8-4, we see what Zhou calls "situated expertise" as other group members work collaboratively to address Nish's questions. In Log 8-4 line 146, Nish is presented with a formula as part of the response to his continuing queries. Zhou notes:

> In their response to Nish's question, the three participants treat the formula n(n+1)/2 as something already existing that has been "*incorporated*" (in Jason's words) into the construction of their problem solution. By offering this as established knowledge, they assume this knowledge is available and accessible to all, including the questioner.

Although it is not presented in these terms, it is clear that, for the original three participants, the formula is an objectification of earlier discursive "realizations" (Sfard, 2008, see also Chapter 3, above) (presumably in their math classrooms), so it can be presented as a self-evident, pre-existing "thing" rather than as a result of earlier work. For Nish, who had not experienced this formula in class, the formula is certainly not a self-explanatory math object.

In her last example (Logs 8-8 and 8-9), Zhou presents an example where a new member, Qwer, joins the same group and asks a similar question. However, in this instance, the newcomer was able to phrase his question in a manner that displayed his general math competency, thereby demonstrating the legitimacy of his/her participation, no matter how peripheral.

The analysis of Chapter 8 shows that a question is not a simple expression of an individual's mental contents, but is co-constructed in the group discourse as an intersubjectively significant action. The statement of the question may be stretched across several minutes and many chat postings. The initial postings of Nish and Qwer were only opening bids to develop something that could be developed into a question, could be intersubjectively understood and accepted as a question within the context of the group discourse and could elicit an appropriate and adequate answer. The initial bid could easily fail and be ignored, misunderstood or rejected. It only becomes a meaningful activity in terms of how it is taken up by the group, developed, framed, discussed and answered. As Chapter 8 shows, the intersubjective process of asking a question is not a simple comparison of pre-existing mental models of some matter to establish "common ground" through agreement of individual opinions (Clark & Brennan, 1991), but involves a co-construction within the group's discourse, work situation, interpersonal relations, history and indexical network. Successful questioning in a virtual math team illustrates the establishment of intersubjectivity.

VMT as a CE Approach to CSCL

Although not initially framed as a traditional ethnographic research project, the VMT Project has its ethnographic influences. One of the three principal investigators of the project, Shumar, is an anthropologist and has co-contributed Chapter 11, which takes an ethnographic view of agency and frames it in sociological terms. In addition, the project's design-based approach to research is inherently ethnographic. Also, the VMT team has been influenced by anthropologists who are important within CSCL, HCI and the learning sciences (e.g., Suchman, Lave, Nardi). As we have seen, VMT certainly exemplifies a critical ethnographic approach to CSCL and, in turn, also has the potential to address and advance many aspects of the CE research agenda.

From our comparisons between "classic" and "critical" ethnography we see profound transformations in ethnographic research and writing, transformations that resonate quite strongly with the VMT Project. First generation CE emerged primarily from continental critical theory, particularly social constructivism and Habermas' critique of scientism. However, first generation critical ethnographers (particularly Fabian and Scholte) also agreed with Habermas' realization that scientism could not be challenged merely through philosophical and theoretical disputation, but must be confronted through anthropological praxis that "transcends its own boundaries."

With the onset of second generation CE, Fabian could celebrate the hard-fought victory resulting from the "critique of misplaced scientism in anthropology," noting that this critique had been implicitly incorporated into second-generation CE. With its primary emphasis on group cognition and intersubjective understanding, VMT also embodies a profound, if implicit, critique of scientism in social research. However, the victory celebrated by Fabian was certainly not final or ubiquitous. In particular, the push for "science-based" educational research represents what Maxwell calls "reemergent scientism" (2004a, 2004b).

Fabian (1990a) embodied his interest in taking critical anthropology to a new level by making an important distinction between "informing" and "performing" models of ethnographic knowledge. Rather than eliciting "information" by interrogating ethnographic "informants," Fabian played the role of "ethnodramaturge," the provider of occasions for performances through which cultural knowledge could be interactively created and expressed. He also departed from standard ethnographic practice by presenting detailed transcripts of the events upon which his analysis was based. It might seem like a bit of a stretch to characterize the moderator of a VMT chat session as an ethnodramaturge, but this research proceeds not by surveying or interviewing middle-school students for retrospective accounts of their collaborative cognitive processes, but by setting the stage for collaborative performances by young mathematists—staying out of the way as much as possible, and meticulously recording and analyzing the results. In accordance with Fabian's CE approach, these recorded interactions "are not just contingent indicators of an underlying necessary reality" but rather embody the "*results of a process* in which a totality realizes itself." The VMT data sets are also archived in a form that will allow subsequent researchers to do their own analyses.

For readers accustomed to the classic image of the lone ethnographer who sets off for the most remote, bounded and "untouched" locale available to conduct detached, "objective" social scientific research, VMT will seem like a very non-ethnographic project indeed. However, as we have seen, the successive generations of CE have profoundly transformed ethnographic practice and writing. Rather than affecting a pose of detached neutrality and non-intervention, VMT research can be characterized as "design-based research" (Barab & Squire, 2004) or perhaps "critical design ethnography" (Barab, Thomas, Dodge, Squire & Newell, 2004), where the ongoing actions and interventions of the researchers become part of the research process. Several researchers represented in this volume have presented their work as "micro-ethnography." While classic ethnography's aspiration to "holism" dictated a preference for isolated, bounded field sites where all aspects of a culture (e.g., ritual, subsistence, kinship) could be analyzed and integrated, micro-ethnography represents a very different conception of holism, one "that captures the interactional and discursive constitution of human relations" without abstracting "interaction from its material foundations and historical contexts," providing "an encompassing and complex understanding of what Lukacs (1971) called the 'totality' of social facts" (Streeck & Mehus, 2005, p. 399). Although we do not find prominent explicit linkages between the two research traditions, this characterization of the VMT Project resonates very nicely with the image of CE we have developed here.

Recall that Bader and Nyce (1998) offered a rather pessimistic assessment of the value placed on ethnographic research: "The difficulty is that knowledge about the social construction of reality is not the kind of knowledge the development community values, can do much with, or seems to be much interested in." However, as we have seen, this is precisely the type of knowledge the VMT team—as the software developers of an online math discourse environment—values, knows what to do with, and is, indeed, very interested in.

As design-based research, the VMT Project explicitly aims to study the (critical) "conditions of the possibility" (see Chapter 26) of a form of learning that does not yet exist, but that could emerge based on existing technological and social conditions. It is significant that the Director of the VMT Project studied critical theory for three years in Heidelberg and Frankfurt during the late 60s and early 70s and took courses from Fabian at Northwestern University during the early 70s. His philosophy dissertation and writings from that period tried to synthesize in a mutually critical manner the social theory of Marx and Adorno with the anti-positivist philosophy of Heidegger (see Stahl, 1975a, b; 1976). In his subsequent AI dissertation, he applied this perspective to software design methodology (Stahl, 1993a). The current volume—particularly in the concluding Chapter 28—envisions a critical science of group cognition that overcomes reductionist influences in CSCL research that he has critiqued at least since (Stahl, 2002b). The VMT Project—with its focus on group cognition—has deep roots in critical ethnography and its philosophical influences, as well as in the more apparent post-cognitivist traditions like ethnomethodology, distributed cognition, activity theory, situated theory, actor-network theory and phenomenology.

Chapter 28
Toward a Science of Group Cognition

Gerry Stahl

Abstract Studying virtual math teams involves explorations along multiple dimensions: (a) designing a testbed to support interaction within teams, (b) analyzing how math is discussed within this setting and (c) describing how the teams achieve their cognitive tasks. Previous chapters have shown in various ways how virtual math teams co-construct their shared worlds of math discourse. This concluding chapter discusses how the VMT Project designed an environment in which this could take place and be studied; it reviews how the project approached the rigorous study of what took place in these virtual worlds; and it reflects on the nature of group cognition as an object for scientific investigation. In this way, the present volume prepares the way for a science of group cognition, a systematic description of the processes at the group level of analysis that may contribute to problem solving, knowledge building and other cognitive tasks undertaken by small groups collaborating synchronously over networked computers.

Keywords Group cognition · science · testbed · interaction analysis · theory

The preceding studies of virtual math teams may serve as preliminary explorations for a science of group cognition. The individual chapters were written by different people under various circumstances and their collection here is not intended to present a systematic theory. Rather, they provide varied investigations and models for diverse approaches to analyzing synchronous online problem-solving efforts by small groups of students. In this chapter, we step back and reflect on the implications of these studies. One feeling that reading this book may leave the reader with is the sense that a new, theoretically motivated and methodologically coherent science of group cognition is needed. Much of the best research in CSCL, the learning sciences and foundational theories has been touched on—at least in passing—and found to be off the mark for studying what is unique to small-group knowledge-building

G. Stahl (✉)
College of Information Science & Technology, Drexel University, Philadelphia, PA, USA
e-mail: gerry@gerrystahl.net

G. Stahl (ed.), *Studying Virtual Math Teams*, Computer-Supported Collaborative
Learning Series 11, DOI 10.1007/978-1-4419-0228-3_28,
© Springer Science+Business Media, LLC 2009

interactions. It focuses either on the actions of the individuals in the group or on the influences of the surrounding community, not on the small group's own distinctive processes. What is needed is a science of group interaction focused on the group level of description to complement psychological theories of individuals and social theories of communities.

Preparing for a new science requires three major undertakings:

(a) The domain of the science must not only be defined, it must be explored and captured in the form of a data corpus.
(b) Methods for analyzing the data must be selected, adapted, refined and mastered.
(c) Analytic findings must be organized in terms of a framework of theoretical conceptualizations.

After discussing the need for a new science of group cognition, this chapter indicates how the VMT Project approached these tasks by:

(a) Creating the Virtual Math Teams service, in which small groups of students engage in problem-solving work in mathematics,
(b) Conducting chat interaction analysis of a number of case studies from the data recorded in that service and
(c) Reflecting (largely in the chapters of this volume) on what took place in the small-group interactions.

The focus on small groups was originally motivated by the realization that CSCL was fundamentally different from other domains of the learning sciences in that it took as its subject matter *collaborative* learning, that is, what takes place when small groups of students engage together in cognitive activities like problem solving or knowledge building (Koschmann, 1996a; Stahl, 2006b, chap. 11). In terms of its theoretical framework, CSCL is strongly oriented toward Vygotsky (1930/1978), who stressed that learning and other higher psychological processes originally take place socially, intersubjectively. Piaget (1985), too, pointed to inter-subject processes like conflicting perspectives as a fundamental driver for cognitive development. Despite this powerful insight, Vygotsky, Piaget and their followers generally maintain a psychological focus on the individual mind in their empirical studies and do not systematically investigate the intersubjective phenomena of small-group interaction.

A science of group cognition would aim to unpack what happens at the small-group unit of analysis. Thus, it might be particularly relevant for CSCL, but not directly applicable to other forms of learning, where the individual or the community level predominates. As a science of the group, it would not be a competing alternative to existing theories of learning and cognition, to the extent that they focus either on the individual or the community or that they reduce group phenomena to these other levels of description. CSCL has a different object.

In the specific domain of mathematics, it is clear that professional mathematicians today engage in significant collaborative efforts, sometimes involving hundreds of mathematicians in the derivation of a single proof. However, the collaborative nature of knowledge building at either the professional or student level is not well studied or documented. Studies of collaboration that have been undertaken in math classes overwhelmingly look at the work of dyads. Dyads have their own distinctive dynamic, in which the roles of the two participants maintain strong cognitive identities. A general finding of these studies is that one of the two students will often do most of the mathematical work and then explain it to the other (Cobb, 1995). This may be a useful cooperative arrangement for developing math skills, but it is quite different from the collaborative group cognition that can take place in groups of three or more students. In contrast to much of the CSCL literature, the study of virtual math teams aimed to develop a concrete demonstration of how small groups can mediate the interplay between individual and community, producing individual expertise in domains of culturally established mathematics as a result of group discourse.

More generally, in the chapters of this volume and of *Group Cognition* (Stahl, 2006b), we have reviewed some of the research literature on small-group learning, on small-group processes and on collaborative mathematics. We have noticed that small-group learning studies generally look for quantitative correlations among variables—such as the effect of group size on measures of participation—rather than trying to observe group knowledge-building processes. Studies of small-group processes from psychology, sociology and other social sciences also tend to focus on non-cognitive aspects of group process or else attribute all cognition to the individual minds rather than to group processes. There are some notable exceptions; in particular, we viewed (Barron, 2000, 2003; Cohen et al., 2002; Sawyer, 2003; Schwartz, 1995) as important preliminary studies for a science of group cognition.

Even theories that seem quite relevant to our concerns, like distributed cognition (Hutchins, 1996), actor-network theory (Latour, 2007), situated cognition (Lave & Wenger, 1991), ethnomethodology (Garfinkel, 1967) and activity theory (Engeström, 1987) adopt a different focus, generally on interaction of individuals with artifacts rather than with other people. In particular, recent commentaries on situated cognition (Robbins & Aydede, 2009) and distributed cognition (Adams & Aizawa, 2008) frame the issues at the individual level, even reducing all cognitive phenomena to neural phenomena. At the other extreme, social theories focus on community phenomena like division of labor, apprenticeship training, linguistic structure, laboratory organization. For all its insight into small group interaction and its analysis, ethnomethodology maintains a sociological perspective. Similarly, even when activity theory addresses the study of teams—in the most detail in Chapter 6 of Engeström (2008)—it is mostly concerned with the group's situation in the larger industrial and historic context; rather than analyzing how groups interactionally build knowledge, it paraphrases dialog that deals politically with organizational management issues. These theories provide valuable insights into group cognition, but none of them thematizes the small-group level as a domain of scientific study. As sciences, these are sciences of the individual or of the society, not of the collaborative group.

Each of the three levels of description is populated with a different set of phenomena and processes. For instance, in the chats we analyze, *individuals* interpret recent postings and design new postings in response, the *group* constructs, maintains and repairs a joint problem space and the *community* evolves its shared methods of social organization. The description of the individual level is the province of psychology; that of the community is the realm of sociology or anthropology; *the small-group level has no corresponding science.*

A science of group cognition would take its irreducible position between the psychological sciences of the individual and the social sciences of the community— much as biology analyzes phenomena that are influenced by both chemicals and organisms without being reducible to either. The science of group cognition would fill a lacuna in the multi-disciplinary work of the learning sciences. This science would not be primarily oriented toward the "low level" processes of groups, such as mechanical or rote behaviors, but would be concerned with the accomplishment of creative intellectual tasks. Intellectual teamwork, knowledge work and knowledge-building activities would be prototypical objects of study. The focus would be on group cognition.

The bifurcation of the human sciences into individual and societal creates an irreconcilable opposition between individual creative freedom and restrictive social institutions. A science of group cognition would flesh out the concept of structuration, demonstrating with detailed analyses of empirical data how group interactions can mediate between individual behavior and social practices (Chapter 11).

The term *group cognition* does not signify an object or phenomenon to analyze like brain functions or social institutions. It is a proposal for a new science or focus within the learning sciences. It hypothesizes:

> When small groups engage in collaborative problem solving or knowledge building, there are distinctive processes of interest at the individual, small-group and community levels of analysis, which interact strongly with each other. The science of group cognition is the study of the processes at the small-group level.

Processes at the small-group level are not necessarily reducible to processes of individual minds, nor do they imply the existence of some sort of group mind. Rather, they may take place through the weaving of semantic and indexical references within a group discourse. The indexical field (Hanks, 1992) or joint problem space (Chapter 6) co-constructed through the sequential interaction of a group (Chapter 7) has the requisite complexity to constitute an irreducible cognitive act in its own right. Cognitive science broadened the definition of "cognition" beyond an activity of human minds in order to include artificial intelligence of computers. What counts as cognitive is now a matter of computational complexity. Anything that can compute well enough to play chess or prove theorems can be a cognitive agent—whether they are a person, computer or collaborative small group (Stahl, 2006b, chap. 19).

The science of group cognition is a human science, like critical ethnography. It is not a predictive science like chemistry, nor a predominantly quantitative one like physics. It deals with human meanings in unique situations, necessarily relying upon interpretive case studies and descriptions of inter-personal processes.

Such a science is timely and relevant, as indicated by the rise of the CSCL field. The 21st century will increasingly rely on small groups—due to networked computers providing the new means of group intellectual production, with the power to overcome the limitations of the individual mind (Fischer & Ostwald, 2005). The dominance of the individual in production and in science was part of a larger epochal trend, as seen in the growth of monotheism, rationalist philosophy, the ideology of the individual, capitalist competitive economics and the role of the individual worker's labor-power. The traditional pre-capitalist social formations of tribe and family were systematically broken down by the nature and functioning of mobile capital in modern societies. Now, forces of instantaneous communication, globalization and ecological crisis seem to be bringing about a transformation of that historic trend, resulting in the rising prominence of the small group as an important mediator between the isolated individual and an increasingly abstract society. The small group is becoming an effective new form in the social relations of intellectual production.

By visiting the exotic world of virtual math teams—like critical ethnographers conducting fieldwork—we have been able to investigate largely unexplored territories of people learning collaboratively, working cooperatively, interacting virtually and achieving cognitive tasks within small groups. There, we have tried new approaches to designing experimental test-beds for research, to analyzing interaction at the group unit of analysis and to theorizing group cognition as a foundational mode of mastering the shared virtual worlds.

We can now return to our everyday world with new eyes. Here, we can see how small groups operate and how cognitive tasks can be accomplished collaboratively. At least in some VMT excerpts, we see the power of collaborative math problem solving and the depth of math learning that can take place in synchronous online environments. We may also note more clearly how our physical individual activities and our community lives are rapidly being infused with virtual media and are being organized into team efforts. Our glimpses of life in the parallel VMT universe can guide us as we seek ways to overcome the limitations of practices that were learned or institutionalized long ago and as we design alternative visions of possible futures.

Having motivated the development of a science of group cognition as future work, let us see how the VMT Project may have begun to prepare the way. We start with how the futuristic VMT world of online collaboration was constructed as an object of study.

Designing a Shared World for Math Discourse

Before undertaking a study of virtual math teams, one might well ask about the desirability of math teams as such, even face-to-face. While there is considerable research literature about the social and socially situated nature of mathematics, there are few studies of collaborative learning of math. Math is a historically evolving aspect of the broader culture and is disseminated through typical socialization processes. For instance, fundamental skills of counting and measurement are instilled in early childhood, basic arithmetic is instructed in school and advanced math research takes place through academic channels. It is clear that math skills are dependent upon the various social contexts in which they may operate, such as during school tests (Lockhart, 2008), on grocery shopping trips (Lave, 1988) or in engineering work (Hall & Stevens, 1995). Socio-cultural theory recognizes the central role of discourse, perspectives and explanation to others in the development of math mastery. However, one can still ask, what empirical evidence is there for the efficacy of collaborative learning of mathematics?

To provide a baseline for understanding virtual math teams, the VMT Project began with a pilot study of face-to-face math teams in a traditional school setting. We carried out a one-class-period intervention in an urban middle school, as discussed briefly in Chapter 26. We asked teams of four students to produce a single piece of paper representing their group solution to a math task. We recorded the work of a particular group of four girls (pictured in Fig. 26.2 in Chapter 26), using a high-end mike, a fixed video camera and researcher notes. Rather than working together on a single piece of paper, the students each worked on their own, always maintaining a close parallelism to their work through a rich verbal and gestural communication. In the end, the group had to select one student's paper to submit for the group. They selected the work of the girl they considered smart. Although the four students coordinated their work closely and built on one another, and although they all came away from the experience with an understanding of the group accomplishment, they attributed the origin of their accomplishment to individuals who they judged as more or less "smart," rather than as effective collaborators.

The face-to-face experience was difficult to analyze. Despite our having focused high-quality equipment on the one group, we ended up with a recording of their interaction that was incomplete. We had to carefully transcribe their talk—which was not always hearable—including indications of emphasis and measurements of pauses. The facial expressions, gestures and bodily postures of the four students were not always visible to the single camera. In addition, the team was immersed in a noisy and busy classroom, with the teacher circulating and advising different teams; it was impossible to know about all the external influences on the team's work. Moreover, the four students seemed to be close friends, so they had a lot of history together that influenced their understanding of each other in ways that were not available to the researchers.

The first step in the online phase of our design-based research process was to start simply and see what issues came up. We had seen in the face-to-face case that there were problems with (a) recording and transcribing the verbal interaction, (b) capturing the visual interaction and (c) knowing about all the influences on the interaction. We decided to form groups of students who did not know each other and who only interacted through text chat. We used AIM, AOL's Instant Messaging system, which was freely available and was already familiar to many students. We included a researcher or Math Forum staff person in the chat room with each small group of students. The facilitator told the students their math task, dealt with any technical difficulties, posted drawings from the students on a web page where they could be seen by all the students, notified the group when the session was over and saved an automatically generated log of the chat. In this way, we obtained a complete and objective log of the interaction, captured everything that the students shared visually and excluded any unknown influences from affecting the interaction.

The issue of including everything affecting the interaction is a subtle issue. Of course, the interaction is influenced by the life histories, personalities, previous knowledge and physical environment of each student. A student may have windows other than AIM open on the computer, including Internet browsers with math resources. A student may be working out math problems on a piece of paper next to the computer. Or, a student may leave the computer for some time to eat, listen to music, talk on the phone, and so on without telling anyone in the chat. So, we do not have information about everything involved in a particular student's online experience. We do not even know the student's gender or age. We do not know if the student is shy or attractive, speaks with an accent or stutters. We do not know if the student usually gets good grades or likes math. We do not know what the student is thinking or feeling. We only know that the students are in an approximate age group and academic level—because we recruited them through teachers. However, the VMT Project is only concerned with analyzing the interaction at the *group unit of analysis*. Notice that the things that are unknown to us as researchers are also unknown to the student group as a whole. The students do not know specifics about each other's background or activities—except to the extent that these specifics are brought into the chat. If they are mentioned or referenced in the chat, then we can be aware of them to the same extent as are the other students.

The desire to generate a complete record for analysis of everything that was involved in a team's interaction often conflicted with the exploration of technology and service design options. For instance, we avoided speech-based interaction (VOIP, Skype, WIMBA) and support for individual work (e.g., whiteboards for individual students to sketch ideas privately). We tried to form teams that did not include people who knew each other or who could interact outside of the VMT environment.

In addition to personal influences, the chat is responsive to linguistic and cultural matters. Of course, both students and researchers must know English to understand the chats. In particular, forms of English that have evolved with cell-phone texting have introduced abbreviations, symbols and emoticons into the chat language. The linguistic subculture of teenagers also shows up in the VMT chats. An interdisciplinary team of researchers comes in handy for interpreting the chats. In our case, the research team brought in experience with online youth lingo based on their backgrounds as Math Forum staff, teachers or parents.

More important for interpreting the VMT chats than linguistic variations is the language of mathematics. In following the arguments or presentations of the students, it is often necessary to reconstruct the mathematical references, manipulations and connections that underlie the postings. Sometimes the postings of one student presuppose one mathematical approach and those of another presuppose a different approach. To sort these out and understand conflicts and misunderstandings that arise among the students, a research team must be conversant with the mathematics. As argued in Chapter 26, the postings operate within complex networks of meaning, combining a variety of kinds of implicit and explicit references. To understand them requires research teams capable of comprehending those references, whether linguistic, mathematical, cultural or internal to the chat history.

For instance, in Chapter 9 one must understand the underlying math to see how the two different proposed approaches build off each other. In Chapter 25, the junior-college-level math and the Singapore slang create problems of interpretation for many researchers. The VMT research team and its collaborators brought considerable understanding of school math to the analyses.

The early AIM chats used simple math problems, taken from standardized math tests and Math Forum Problems-of-the-Week. The comparison of individual and group work in Chapter 5 used problems from a standardized multiple-choice college-admissions test. These problems had unique correct answers. While these provided a good starting point for our research, they were not well suited for collaborative knowledge building. Discourse around them was often confined to seeing who thought they knew the answer and then checking for correctness. For the VMT Spring Fests in 2005, 2006 and 2007, we moved to more involved math topics that could inspire several hours of joint inquiry.

Even with straight-forward geometry problems—like that in Chapter 9—it became clear that students needed the ability to create, share and modify drawings within the VMT chat environment. We determined that we needed an object-oriented draw program, where geometric objects could be manipulated (unlike a pixel-based paint program). We contracted with the developers of ConcertChat to use and extend their text chat and shared whiteboard system, which is now available in Open Source. This system included the graphical referencing tool (analyzed in Chapter 17) as well as social awareness and history features (described in Chapter 15). In order to help students find desirable chat rooms and to preserve team findings for all to see, we developed the VMT Lobby and integrated a Wiki with the Lobby and chat rooms (see Chapter 16). Gradually, the technology and the math topics became much more complicated in response to the needs that were revealed when we analyzed the trials of the simpler versions of the VMT service. As the system matured, other research groups began to use it for their own trials, with their own math topics, procedures, analytic methods or even new technical features. These groups included researchers from Singapore (Chapter 25), Rutgers (Chapter 13), Hawai`i (Chapter 10), Romania (Chapter 24) and Carnegie-Mellon (Chapter 19).

The evidence for the adequacy of a testbed for design-based research lies in the success of the analyses to reveal how the prototyped environment is working at each iteration and to provide ideas based on problems encountered by users to drive the design further. Therefore, we now turn to the analyses of interaction in the virtual math teams to see if the testbed produced adequate data for understanding group cognition in this context.

Analyzing Student Interaction

The approach to chat interaction analysis that emerged in the VMT Project will be discussed in this section in terms of a number of issues (which correspond to general issues of most research methodologies, as indicated in parentheses).

Group Cognition in a Virtual Math Team (Research Question)

Learning is not a simplistic memorization or storage of facts or propositions, as traditional folk theories had it. The term *learning* is a gloss for a broad range of phenomena, including: the development of tacit skills, the ability to see things differently, access to resources for problem solving, the discursive facility to articulate in a new vocabulary, the power to explain, being able to produce arguments or the making of new connections among prior understandings. We can distinguish these phenomena as taking place within individual minds, small-group interactions or communities of practice. The analysis of learning phenomena at these various levels of analysis requires different research methodologies, appropriate to corresponding research questions. The VMT Project was intended to explore the phenomena of group cognition and accordingly pursued the research question:

> How does learning take place in small groups, specifically in small groups of students discussing math in a text-based online environment? What are the distinctive mechanisms or processes that take place at the small-group level of description when the group is engaged in problem-solving or knowledge-building tasks?

While learning phenomena at the other levels of analysis are important and interact strongly with the group level, we have tried to isolate and make visible the small-group phenomena and generate a corpus of data for which the analysis of the group-level interactions can be distinguished from the effects of the individual and community levels.

The methods used to gather and analyze one's data should be appropriate to one's research question. To support such research, one must generate and collect data that are adequate for the selected kinds of analysis. Because we are interested in the group processes that take place in virtual math teams, we had to form teams that could meet together online. In the Spring Fests, they had to be able to come back together in the same teams on four occasions. The VMT environment had to be instrumented to record all messages and activities that were visible to the whole team in a way that could be played back by the analysts. The math problems and the feedback to the teams had to be designed to encourage the kinds of math discussions that would demonstrate processes of group cognition, such as formulating questions and proposals, coordinating drawings and textual narratives, checking proposed symbolic solutions, reviewing the team's work and so on. A sense of these desirable group activities and the skill of designing problems to encourage them had to develop gradually through the design-based research iterations. Fortunately, the Math Forum staff's 15 years of prior experience was relevant and useful for this.

Non-laboratory Experimental Design (Validity)

Of course, to isolate the small-group phenomena we do not literally isolate our subject groups from individuals and communities. The groups consist of students, who are individuals and who make individual contributions to the group discourse based on their individual readings of the discourse. In addition, the groups exist and operate within community and social contexts, drawing upon the language and practices of their math courses and of their teen and online subcultures. These are essential features of a real-world context and we would not wish to exclude them even to the extent possible by confining the interaction to a controlled laboratory setting. We want the students to feel that they are in a natural setting, interacting with peers. We do not try to restrict their use of language in any way (e.g., by providing standardized prompts for chat postings or scripting their interactions with each other—except in rare cases like the experiments in Chapter 19).

We are designing a service that can be used by students and others under a broad array of scenarios: integrated with school class work, as extra-curricular activities, as group experiences for home-schooled students, as cross-national team adventures or simply as opportunities (in a largely math-phobic world) to discuss mathematics. To get a sense of how such activities might work, we have to explore interactions in naturalistic settings, where the students feel like they are engaged in such activities rather than being laboratory subjects.

Data Collection at the Group Level of Description (Unit of Analysis)

Take the network of references in Fig. 26.7 as an image of meaning making at the group level. One could almost say that the figure consists entirely of contributions from individuals (the chat postings and whiteboard drawings) and resources from the math community; that everything exists on either the individual or community level, not on the group level. Yet, what is important in the figure is the network of densely interwoven references, rather than the objects that are connected by them. This network exists at the group level. It mediates the individual and the community by forming the joint problem space, indexical ground, referential network or situation within which meanings, significant objects and temporal relations are intersubjectively co-constructed. On the individual level, these shared group meanings are interpreted and influence the articulation of subsequent postings and actions. On the community level, the meanings may contribute to a continually evolving culture through structuration processes (see Chapter 11). The VMT Project is oriented toward the processes at the group unit of analysis, which build upon, connect and mediate the individual and community phenomena.

Elements from the individual and community levels only affect the group level if they are referenced in the team's interaction. Therefore, we do not need to gather data about the students or their communities other than what appears in the interaction record. We do not engage in surveys or interviews of the students or their teachers. For one thing, the design of the VMT Project prohibits access to these sources of data, because the students are only available during the chat sessions. External sources of data would be of great interest for other research questions having to do with individual learning or cultural changes, but for our research question, they are unnecessary and might even form a distraction or skew our analysis because they might cause our readings of the postings to be influenced by information that the group had not had.

Our focus on the group determines the questions that we pose to our data. Our data consists largely of messages in chat logs. It would be possible to ask many questions while analyzing these messages. One could, for instance, ask what categories they belong to in a coding scheme (see Chapters 22 and 23, where we asked this question, but where the categories related to group interaction). One could also ask if the message demonstrates creativity, leadership or agency by the individual who typed the message (see Chapters 11 and 12, where we transformed these questions to look at group creativity, group positioning and group agency). When looking at a posting, one could ask what the person might have been thinking or feeling when typing it. Of course, we have no way of knowing this beyond what is said in the posting and through the way that it is designed within the ongoing interaction. The fact that we have never seen the students face-to-face and know nothing about them except what they post, may help us to avoid unfounded speculation about their mental states. At the other extreme, we also have no evidence for speculating about cultural matters of larger communities, such as teen texting culture or the community of school math practices. We can really only legitimately analyze how the particular virtual math team is interacting.

By moving to the disembodied virtual realm of group cognition in virtual math teams, it is easier for us to abandon the positivist metaphors of the mechanistic worldview. Not only is it clear that the virtual group does not exist in the form of a physical object with a persistent memory akin to a computer storage unit, but even the individual students lack physical presence. All that exists when we observe the replayed chats are the traces of a discourse that took place years ago. Metaphors that might come naturally to an observer of live teamwork in a classroom—student personalities, the group, learning, etc.—no longer seem fundamental. What exist immediately are the textual, graphical and symbolic inscriptions. These are significant fragments, whose meaning derives from the multi-layered references to each other and to the events, artifacts and agents of concern in the group discourse. This meaning is as fresh now as when the discourse originated, and can still be read off the traces by an analyst, much as by the original participants. This shows that the meanings shared by the groups are not dependent upon mental states of the individual students—although the students may have had interpretations of those meaning in mind external to the shared experience. The form of our data reinforces our focus on the level of the shared group meaning making as an interactive phenomenon rather than a psychological one.

Instrumentation and Data Formats (Objectivity)

It was noted above that when one videotapes small-group interactions a number of practical problems arise. Our data on the face-to-face classroom collaboration ran into issues of (a) recording and transcribing the verbal interaction, (b) capturing the visual interaction and (c) knowing about all the influences on the interaction. The data was in effect already partially interpreted by our selective placement of the microphone and fixed camera. It was further interpreted by our transcription of the talk and was restricted by our limited access to facial expressions and bodily gestures. Much happened in the classroom influencing the student team, which we could not record.

The online setting of the VMT sessions eliminated many of these problems. As already described, everything that influences the group as a whole is captured in the automatic computer log of the session. This includes all the postings and whiteboard activity, along with their precise timing. They are captured at the same granularity as they are presented to the students. Chat postings appear as complete messages, defined by the author pressing the Enter button. Whiteboard textboxes appear as complete, when the author clicks outside of the textbox. Whiteboard graphics appear gradually, as each graphical element is positioned by the author. Computer-generated social-awareness messages (when people enter or exit the chat room, begin or end typing, move a graphical object, etc.) are also accurately recorded. The precision of the log recording is assured because it consists of the original actions (as implemented by the computer software) with their timestamps. The original display to the students is generated from the same data that is used by the VMT Replayer. There is no selectivity or interpretation imposed by the analysts in the preparation of the full session record.

Figure 8.1 shows how the record of a session can be viewed by analysts in the VMT Replayer. The Replayer is simply an extended version of the Java applet that serves as the chat/whiteboard room in the VMT environment. The reproduced chat room is separated by a thin line at the bottom from a VCR-like interface for replaying the session. The session can be replayed in real time or at any integral multiple of this speed. It can be started and stopped at any point. An analyst can drag the pointer along the timeline to scroll both the whiteboard history and the chat history in coordination. One can also step through the recorded actions, including all the awareness messages.

In addition, spreadsheet logs can be automatically generated. Options for these include: spreading the chat postings across the page in a different column for each student, incorporating social awareness messages, incorporating graphical references and incorporating graphical object actions. These spreadsheets were used for generating many of the logs used in this book, including those in Chapter 26 with the columns for different students.

The data analyzed in the VMT Project is recorded with complete objectivity. There is no selectivity involved in the data generation, recording or collecting process. Furthermore, the complete recording can be made available to other researchers as a basis for their reviews of our analyses or the conducting of their own analyses. For instance, there have been multiple published analyses of the set of ten PoW-wow sessions discussed in Chapters 9, 20, 22 and 23. In addition, Chapter 10 began from the analysis in Chapter 26 and took it in another direction, following the somewhat different research questions, theories and methods of a different research group. While collaborative sessions are each unique and in principle impossible to reproduce, it is quite possible to reproduce the unfolding of a given session from the persistent, comprehensive and replayable record.

Collaborative Data Sessions (Reliability)

Interpretation of data in the VMT Project first begins with an attempt to describe what is happening in a chat session. We usually start this process with a data session involving six to twelve researchers. A typical data session is initiated by a researcher who is interested in having a particular segment of a session log discussed by the group. Generally, the segment seems to be both confusing and interesting in terms of a particular research question. For instance, the segment in Chapter 26 contains the intriguing line 1396/1399 (Log 26-1), Axnx: **"We got the solutions. But I'm not sure how to explain how we got to the solutions, although it makes perfect sense to me."** If the solutions make perfect sense to Aznx, why does he feel that he cannot explain how they got the solutions? The data session about this data might raise many of the points that were written up subsequently in the more systematic narrative that eventually became Chapter 26.

For our data sessions, we sit around a circle of tables and project an image of the VMT Replayer onto a screen visible to everyone. Most of us have laptop computers displaying the same Replayer, so that we can scan back and forth in the segment privately to explore details of the interaction that we may want to bring to the attention of the group (see Fig. 28.1). We might start by playing the segment once or twice in real time to get a feel for how it unfolds. Then we typically go back to the beginning and discuss each line of the chat sequentially in some detail.

The interpretation of a given chat line becomes a deeply collaborative process. Generally, one person will make a first stab at proposing a hypothesis about the

Fig. 28.1 A VMT data session

work that line is doing in the logged discourse. Others will respond with suggested refinements or alternatives to the proposal. The group may then engage in exploration of the timing of chat posts, references back to previous postings or events, etc. Eventually the data analysis will move on to consider how the student group took up the posting. An interesting interpretation may require the analysts to return to earlier ground and revise their tentative previous understandings.

The boundaries of a segment must be considered as an important part of the analysis, as discussed in Chapter 23. When does the interaction of interest really get started and when is it resolved? Often, increasingly deep analysis drives the starting point back as we realize that earlier occurrences were relevant. For the authors of Chapter 10, for instance, the analysis of the couple-minute excerpt in Chapter 26 required consideration of the entire four-hour set of student meetings leading up to that excerpt.

The analysis in Chapter 26 reflects typical preliminary analytic concerns. It is necessary to clarify the referential structure of the chat postings and how they relate to events in the whiteboard or to the comings and goings of participants. As explained in Chapter 14, the threading of the chat postings provides the primary structure of the online, text-based discourse in much the same way that turn taking provides the core structure of spoken informal conversation. That is why most of the chapters in Part V of this book represent the group interaction largely in terms of the threading structure. Because of the overlap in the typing of chat postings, it is sometimes tricky to figure out who is responding to what. Looking at the timestamps of posts and even at the timestamps of awareness messages about who is typing can provide evidence about what was visible when a posting was being typed. This can often suggest that a given post could or could not have been responding to a specific other post, although it is sometimes impossible to determine. When it is hard for the analyst to know the threading, it may have also been hard for most of the chat participants (other than the typist) to know; this may result in signs of trouble or misunderstandings in the subsequent chat.

The test of *correctness* of chat interaction analysis is not a matter of what was in individuals' minds, but of how postings function in the interaction. Most of the multi-layered referencing pictured in Chapter 26 takes place without conscious awareness by the participants, who are experts at semantic, syntactic and pragmatic referencing and can design utterances in response to local resources without formulating explicit plans (Suchman, 2007). Thus, inspection of participants' memories would not reveal causes. Of course, participants could retroactively tell stories about why they posted what they did, but these stories would be based upon their current (not original) interpretations using their linguistic competence and upon their response to their current (not original) situation, including their sense of what the person interviewing them wants to hear. Thus, interpretations by the participants are not in principle privileged over those of the analyst and others with the relevant interpretive competence (Gadamer, 1960/1988). The conscious memories that a participant may have of the interaction are, according to Vygotsky's theory, just more interaction—but this time sub-vocal self-talk; if they were brought into the analysis, they would be in need of interpretation just as much as the original discourse.

Since our research question involves the group as the unit of analysis, we do not raise questions in the data session about what one student or another may have been doing, thinking or feeling as an individual. Rather, we ask what a given posting is doing interactionally within the group process, how it responds to and takes up other posts and what opportunities it opens for future posts. We look at how a post is situated in the sequential structure of the group discourse, in the evolving group order and in the team's meaning making. What is this posting doing here and now in the referential network? Why is it "designed to be read" (according to Chapter 14) in just this way? How else could it have been phrased and why would that not have achieved the same effect in the group discourse?

We also look at how a given posting *positions* both the author and the readers in certain ways (see Chapter 11). We do not attribute constant personalities or fixed roles to the individuals, but rather look at how the group is organized through the details of the discourse. Perhaps directing a question toward another student will temporarily bestow upon her a form of *situated expertise* (Chapter 8) such that she is expected to provide an extended sequence of *expository* postings (see Chapter 23).

The discussion during a data session can be quite unorderly. Different people see different possible understandings of the log and propose alternative analyses. Generally, discussion of a particular posting continues until a consensus is tentatively established or someone agrees to look into the matter further and come back next week with an analysis. Notes are often taken on the data session's findings, but the productive result of the discussion most often occurs when one researcher is inspired to write about it in a conference paper or dissertation section. When ideas are taken up this way, the author will usually bring the more developed analysis back for a subsequent data session and circulate the paper.

In coding analysis, it is conventional to train two people to code some of the same log units and to compare their results to produce an inter-rater reliability measure (see Chapter 22). In our chat interaction analysis, we do not pretend that the log can be unproblematically partitioned into distinct units, which can be uniquely assigned to a small number of unambiguous codes. Rather, most interesting group discourse segments have a complex network of interwoven references. The final figure in Chapter 26 only starts to convey the level of complexity involved. The analysis of such log segments requires a sophisticated human understanding of semantics, interpersonal dynamics, mathematics, argumentation and so on. Much is ultimately ambiguous and can be comprehended in multiple ways—sometimes the chat participants were intentionally ambiguous. At the same time, it is quite possible for analysts to make mistakes and to propose analyses that can be shown to be in error. To maintain a reasonable level of reliability of our analyses, we make heavy use of data sessions. This ensures that a number of experienced researchers agree on the analyses that emerge from the data sessions. In addition, we try to provide logs—or even the entire session data with the Replayer—in our papers so that readers of our analyses can judge for themselves the interpretations that are necessarily part of chat analysis.

Describing Group Practices (Generalizability)

The research question that drives the VMT Project is: What are the distinctive mechanisms or processes that take place at the small-group level of description when the group is engaged in problem-solving or knowledge-building tasks? Therefore, we are interested in describing the inter-personal practices of the groups that interact in the VMT environment. There are, of course, many models and theories in the learning sciences describing the psychological practices of *individuals* involved in learning. At the opposite extreme, Lave and Wenger's (1991) theory of situated learning describes social practices of *communities* of practice, whereby a community renews itself by moving newcomers into increasingly central forms of legitimate peripheral participation. However, there are few descriptions specifically of how *small groups* engage in learning practices.

Vygotsky (1930/1978) argued that learning takes place inter-subjectively (in dyads or groups) before it takes place intra-subjectively (by individuals). For instance, in his analysis of the infant and mother (p. 56), he outlines the process through which an infant's unsuccessful grasping at some object becomes established by the mother-child dyad as a pointing at the object (see Chapter 17). This social practice of pointing subsequently becomes ritualized by the dyad (LeBaron & Streeck, 2000) and then mediated and "internalized" by the infant as a pointing gesture. The pointing gesture—as a foundational form of deictic reference—is a skill of the young child, which he can use for selecting objects in his world and learning about them. The gesture is understood by his mother because it was inter-subjectively established with her. In this prototypical example, Vygotsky describes learning as an inter-subjective or small-group practice of a dyad.

While we can imagine that Vygotsky's description is based on a concrete interaction of a specific infant and mother in a particular time and place, the pointing gesture that he analyzed is ubiquitous in human culture. In this sense, the analysis of a unique interaction can provide a generalizable finding. The science of ethnomethodology (the study of the methods used by people) (Garfinkel, 1967) is based on the fact that people in a given culture share a vast repertoire of social practices for accomplishing their mundane tasks. It is only because we share and understand this stock of practices that we can so quickly interpret each other's verbal and gestural actions, even in novel variations under unfamiliar circumstances.

Chapter 10 described three group practices that the team working on the sticks and squares pattern developed: inscribe first solve second, modulate perspective and visualize decomposition. In their analysis, these methods were deeply situated in the specifics of their particular interaction. However, Chapter 7 described similar methods arising from another team working on another math problem. Although the interactions of the two teams were each unique and non-replicable, they both involved a small group of students working in the VMT environment and coordinating their activities in the graphical whiteboard and the textual chat. The analysis of unique case studies can result in the description of group practices that are generalizable (Maxwell, 2004a). The methods developed in specific situated encounters are likely to be typical of a broad range of cases under similar conditions.

In our data sessions, we find the same kinds of moves occurring in case after case that we analyze. On the one hand, group practices are extremely sensitive to changes in the environment, such as differences in features and affordances of the communication media. On the other hand, groups of people tend to adapt widespread methods of social interaction to changing circumstances in similar ways—to support general human and social needs. Group practices are not arbitrary, but draw on rich cultural stocks of shared behavior and adapt the outward appearances in order to maintain the underlying structure under different conditions.

By describing the structure of group practices in detailed case studies, we can characterize general methods of group behavior, group learning or group cognition. Findings from analyses of case studies can lead to the proposal of theoretical categories, conceptualizations, structures or principles—in short, to a science of group interaction.

Conceptualizing Group Interaction

As discussed in the beginning of this chapter, students in virtual math teams are active as individuals, as group participants and as community members. They each engage in their own, private *individual* activities, such as reading, interpreting, reflecting upon and typing chat messages. Their typed messages also function as *group* actions, contributing to the on-going problem solving of the team. Viewed as *community* events, the chats participate in the socialization process of the society, through which the students become increasingly skilled members of the community of mathematically literate citizens. For instance, the students in Spring Fest 2006 were motivated as *individuals* to be successful participants in the contest. Their *teams* were motivated to successfully accomplish the problem-solving tasks. As young members of *society*, they were motivated to advance to acceptance as adult members of their community.

A thesis of the theory of group cognition is, "Small groups are the engines of knowledge building. The knowing that groups build up in manifold forms is what becomes internalized by their members as individual learning and externalized in their communities as certifiable knowledge" (Stahl, 2006b, p. 16). Despite their centrality, small groups have not been theorized or studied extensively.

Some small-group literature has been produced from either the methodological perspective of psychology or that of sociology, primarily since World War II. Traumatized by the mass-culture horrors of fascism and by extreme forms of mentalist pseudo-science, these predominantly behaviorist studies focused on the negative aspects of "group think" and caricatured the notion of "group mind"—which had a well-respected history before the rise of positivism (Wegner, 1986).

More recent theories like distributed cognition, situated action or activity theory actually conduct case studies of small-group interaction, but they do not theorize the small group as their unit of analysis and therefore they do not produce descriptions of small-group practices as such. Even Hutchins (1996), in studying distributed cognition in the wild, does not thematize the interpersonal interactions, but focuses on the cognitive unit of analysis, simply broadening it to include the external computational and physical representational artifacts that an individual worker uses. Furthermore, the cognitive accomplishments he studies are routine, well scripted procedures that do not involve creative solutions to ill-structured problems; the coordination of the navigational team is fixed by naval protocol, not co-constructed through the interaction.

The VMT studies provide a model for describing the small-group practices as distinct from individual and community processes. They look at rich interactions in groups larger than dyads, where individual identities play a smaller role. They analyze group efforts in high-order cognition such as mathematical problem solving and reflection on their problem-solving trajectory. They investigate groups that meet exclusively online, where the familiar visual, physical and aural modes of communication are unavailable, and where communication is mediated by designed technological environments. A number of findings are prominent in these analyses.

We shall review two findings here: One is that much group work is sustained and driven forward by *proposals* and responses to them. Another is that group interactions form a *social order*, which can often be characterized in terms of a temporal dimension, a joint problem space and an interaction space.

Proposal-Driven Sustained Group Activity

Careful review of many VMT logs shows that group interaction in these sessions is driven forward and sustained by various kinds of proposals. One of the first findings of the VMT Project was the role of "*math proposal adjacency pairs*" (Stahl, 2006b, chap. 21 esp. pp. 442–456). These are simply a form of proposal adjacency pairs as found in informal face-to-face conversation, except that they deal with mathematical matters and they are only "adjacent" once their timing has been adjusted for threading. Technically, they might better be termed "math proposal response pairs," except that the term "adjacency" brings in the valuable theoretical contribution from conversation analysis. Chapter 17 analyzes an example of a math proposal—"**What is the area of this shape?**"—which leads into considerable group work to clarify the deictic reference involved in the proposal. The clarification work brings in several mathematical issues. The chapter goes on to consider how proposals orient the group to a common topic (e.g., the area of the shape) and thereby establish a basis for *intersubjectivity*.

Chapter 6 discusses how math proposals can bridge across discontinuities between sessions or even between teams to bring in mathematical content for consideration in the current chat. Chapter 7 considers rich examples of math proposals being formulated primarily visually in the whiteboard. Chapter 8 treats questioning as a form of proposal making. Asking for a math term to be defined, a symbol to be explained or an expression to be checked is a form of proposing math work to be undertaken. Chapter 9 explores what happens when two conflicting proposals are made, how they often build off each other and how productive learning can result from the inter-animation of the perspectives implied by the proposals.

A proposal is not a solitary speech act. It involves minimally two acts: a bid and a response. Chapter 8 showed in some detail that a question is only gradually formulated as people respond to an original opening bid and thereby define the question as an activity taken up in a certain way by the group. Proposals generally, and math proposals more specifically, also have this structure:

- Someone posts a chat message or engages in some other activity that is designed to be read as a math proposal bid.
- This begins to identify a math object as a potential focus of future group work.
- It is also designed to create possible responses, such as acceptances of a proposal for math work by the group.
- A second actor may respond to the bid as a proposal bid and accept it on behalf of the group, meaning that the group should work on it.
- The responder can alternatively reject the proposal on behalf of the group.
- The responder or additional group members can delay acceptance by posing a clarification question, for instance.
- Many other options and further steps are possible.

Through the proposal co-construction process, the group work becomes "object-oriented." The group orients to some mathematical object. Early in a session, the object may be based on a phrase from the task set for the group by the organizers of the VMT session. Later, it may be explicated by the group members in terms of visual representations or graphical objects in the whiteboard or symbolic math expressions in the chat. As group work continues through a series of many linked proposals, the math object to which the group orients may be a growing tree of multiple realizations of a math concept like *grid-world path*, *stair-step pattern*, *diamond pattern* or *hexagonal array*. The making of math proposals can be a mechanism for the *objectification* of a math object.

The idea that group activity is strongly "object-oriented" is an important principle of activity theory (Engeström & Toiviainen, 2009; Kaptelinin & Nardi, 2006). It stresses the task-driven nature of group work. In the occupational settings that activity theory generally studies, activities often aim to accomplish a goal that has been established in advance as the purpose of the group. By highlighting the role of proposals as important means of structuring group interaction, the VMT studies of learning settings reveal a key interactional mechanism by means of which groups co-construct their own work goals in concrete detail.

Student groups in VMT sessions are highly responsive to the tasks that are pre-defined before they enter the chat room. These tasks are stated for them in various ways—on special web pages and/or by the moderator in chat—and the students clearly orient to them. However, one of the first things that the student group does is to discuss the task they will pursue. This is often put in the form of a posting like, **"OK, let's figure out**...." This is a proposal for what the group should work on next. It is selective of some feature of a broader task that was given to the group. As a proposal, it elicits a response from the rest of the group. The response further develops the proposed task. By highlighting the structure of the proposal, the analyses of the VMT Project show how the group itself accomplishes object orientation as an interactional achievement of the group. The object of a group's work is not given in advance and fixed for all time. Nor is it defined only at the level of a goal for the whole session. It is worked out and continually refined by the group interaction, even if it references texts and motivations from outside the group discourse. Furthermore, objects that orient the group work are proposed for small sequences of interaction as well as for the session-long sequences, as each new proposal is taken up.

The proposal structure introduces a temporal structure. A proposal often puts forward a task for the group to take on in the (near) future, possibly as a next step in its work. Sometimes—like at the end of a session that will be followed by another session of the same team—a proposal will plan for a future session. By its nature, a proposal bid creates possible next actions for the group, such as accepting, rejecting, questioning or ignoring the bid. In turn, the second part of the math proposal pair references back to the first part, which by now exists in the interaction past. It may well also reference events further back in the team's past, such as work already done or decisions previously made. The proposal as a whole, as it unfolds over potentially many actions, is always situated firmly in the present network of references. Thus, the proposal process contributes to establishing the temporal dimension of the group's work, with references to future, past and present events.

The proposals also serve to structure the temporal flow of the group interaction into episodes. They often define coherent sequences of discussion on the proposed topic, with openings and closings of the sequence as discussed in Chapter 23. An episode of discussion on a given topic will typically be opened by a proposal bid, which begins to define the object of discussion. Chapter 25 calls such proposals "pivotal contributions." A protracted discussion may be closed by a new proposal that changes topic. Proposals operate on multiple scales: there may be a proposal about the object for a whole session, with proposals for large episodes of discussion within the session and proposals for detailed steps in the work. This provides a multi-layered temporal structure that can be analyzed at various granularities.

The chat representations developed in Chapters 20, 21, 23, 24, 25 and 26 all display aspects of this proposal-response structure. Such representations can be an important part of a science. As these and other chapters argue, the response structure, uptakes, adjacency pairs, sequences, etc. are central to an analysis of a chat interaction. This theme is familiar in the broader literature on chat as well. The diversity of representations proposed (each with their rationale) indicates that this is a problematic issue as well as an important one for a future science of group cognition.

Similarly, many CSCL researchers try to develop and apply coding schemes to analyze chats. Chapters 13, 22, 23 and 25 are concerned with coding and its basis in theories of interaction. A science of group cognition will have to take a stand on coding and on the appropriateness of specific coding schemes to interaction analysis.

The temptation to develop automated software (Erkens & Janssen, 2008; Rosé et al., 2008) to construct graphical representations of the response structure and to categorize utterances may ironically serve to highlight the issues involved in making simplistic assumptions about the objective nature of the response structure and of the utterance character. A threading or uptake graph may make it look like postings exist with measurable attributes and fixed relationships, like the objects of Newtonian mechanics, with their precise location, mass and velocity. However, chat messages are more analogous to quantum particles, with their indeterministic and probabilistic characteristics. Whether a posting is a math proposal, a question or a joke (as in Chapter 5) depends on how an interpretive, thread-producing "reading" (Chapter 14) of it not only construes its uptake by subsequent postings, but also how it situates that posting in relation to previous postings. A particular posting may reference past and current artifacts, event and agents, but it also projects relevant "nexts" or responses or uptakes by opening a field of possibilities. This is more complicated and less well-defined than implied by a static diagram of nodes and links, however useful such a diagram may be to support visual reasoning about specific issues involving the flow of a chat. It may make more sense to treat postings as *mediating agents* in Latour's (2007) sense, as an alternative to metaphors from mechanistic theories of causation.

Proposal structures in VMT data can be more complicated than traditional analyses of adjacency pairs in studies of talk-in-interaction. Most case studies inspired by conversation analysis look at short sequences like a single adjacency pair or a pair that is temporarily interrupted by clarifications or repairs. The Spring Fests allow analysis of longer sequences, such as the analysis of a series of episodes in Chapter 7 or the retrospective review of four entire sessions in Chapter 10. In these, one sees mechanisms by means of which the work of a group is integrated into a layered temporal unity—which Chapter 24 characterizes as polyphonic. The study of proposal mechanisms may lead to the identification of social structure in groups.

The Social Order of Group Cognition

The temporal structure is one dimension of the social order that a collaborative small group co-constructs of, by and for its interaction. Proposals are but one interactive mechanism for establishing the social order that supports the achievement of group cognition. Near the beginning of this book, in Chapter 6, the notion of a joint problem space was discussed. By looking at bridging methods in longer sequences and across temporal and other discontinuities, the research summarized in that chapter was able to demonstrate the importance of the temporal dimension in addition to the content and relational dimensions that had been proposed by previous related research (see the triangle image in Figure 6.4). This suggests three dimensions to the social order established by virtual math teams and other small groups engaged in group cognition:

- The *temporal dimension* of ordered events.
- The *problem space* of shared knowledge artifacts.
- The *interaction space* of positioned actors.

The first dimension of social order, the *temporal dimension*, was just discussed in terms of the ways in which proposal interactions are themselves temporally structured, with references to possible next responses, past resources and the current situation. As analyzed in Chapter 26, the temporal dimension is also woven as part of the referential network of meaning that is built up through the group discourse. In particular, temporal indexicals (like *then*) and verb tenses establish the indexical ground of deictic reference (Hanks, 1992), which is part of the shared meaning structure that makes sense of references to events and locates them within their temporal ordering (see Chapters 6, 7 and 10).

In discourses about math, the second dimension, the *problem space*, is traditionally conceived of within the cognitivist tradition (Newell & Simon, 1972) as a mental representation of mathematical relationships (see Chapter 6). The analysis of the work of virtual math teams (e.g., Chapter 7) shows that the group works out a shared notion of the math object, for instance by constructing visualizations in the whiteboard and instructing the group members to see them in a certain way. There is often a coordinated movement back and forth between visual, narrative and symbolic reasoning that gradually objectifies the math object into a rich, interconnected, meaningful multiplicity of significances and realizations. The representation of the object for the group does not lie hidden in individual minds like the data structure of an artificial intelligence software system. It consists of a network of visible inscriptions in the visual interface of the VMT environment, tied together into a meaningful whole by the set of carefully crafted references within the group interaction. The object exists as an *artifact*, a physical object that is meaningful (Stahl, 2006b, chap. 16). However, in the case of math objects that are the result of extensive group work, there is not a single identifiable artifact; the math object consists of a "tree of multiple realizations" (Sfard, 2008) united by the group discourse and only imperfectly objectified in a single phrase or symbol.

In particular, once the rich experience of the group interaction that built the math artifact is summarized or sedimented into a single sign and passed on to others who were not involved in the original experience (e.g., late-comers or newcomers), the full meaning of the artifact is hard to come by. This is the problem of math education. For new individuals to build anything like a mental representation of a math artifact, they need to go through a process like that which Vygotsky termed *internalization*. Either they need to experience a group process like those that occur in virtual math teams or they need to simulate such a process on their own. One often sees math students sketching visual reasoning diagrams on paper, playing around with symbolisms and talking to themselves as though they were acting out the parts of a complete team. The path to math comprehension seems to require the practices of group problem solving, which experienced experts have learned to individuate and to conduct as individuals, imagining the visualizations and speaking the discourse sub-vocally.

The third dimension of social order is the *interaction space* of intersubjective relations. This has been analyzed in Chapters 6 and 11 in terms of *positioning*. In the VMT environment, there is no power hierarchy or other system of roles among the students. (The adult mentor who may be in the chat room with the students is, of course, an authority figure, but tends to play a minimal role in the session and rarely enters into the math work or interactions among the team. The mentor is positioned as being outside of the team, often by the mentor's own postings.) Researchers often discuss collaboration in terms of roles (Strijbos, Martens et al., 2004). They even advocate scripting or assigning fixed roles to students to make sure that certain functions of group process are carried out—such as leading the discussion, watching the time allotted for the session, summarizing the group accomplishments, monitoring the active participation of all members, controlling turn taking. In contrast to such an imposed approach, an analysis in terms of positioning views roles as fluidly changing, based on details of the group discourse.

Perhaps the clearest examples arise from questioning. When one student asks another what some term means or how a result was derived, the questioner may be positioned as lacking knowledge and the addressee as having *situated expertise*. What this means is that the first student cedes the second the floor. The first student will refrain from posting anything for awhile and will expect the other group members to do likewise while the second student—the temporary expert for purposes of this question—will be expected to post a series of expository messages responding to the question (see Chapter 23 for a description of this kind of expository discourse). As Chapter 8 showed, questions are carefully designed to engage in positioning moves and other interpersonal work. Through methods like questioning and displays of individual knowledge, group members co-construct the intersubjective fabric of the group, often starting from a condition where there are no differentiations.

The three dimensions of the social order associated with group cognition correspond closely to the three key phenomena highlighted in Chapter 27: temporalizing, objectification and intersubjectivity. Temporalizing takes place from the bridging across discontinuities of the *temporal dimension* in longer segments of discourse, down to the individual posting that indexes the past and opens possible future nexts from its current situatedness. Objectification proceeds in the joint *problem space* as knowledge artifacts are elaborated in visual, narrative and symbolic forms of the discourse. Intersubjectivity is established, maintained and repaired as objects, events and agents are positioned within the *interaction space's* indexical field of semantic, syntactic, pragmatic, historical, cultural, physical and mathematical references.

Within the practice of the VMT Project, the methodology of our chat interaction analysis and the theory of group cognition, the phenomena of temporalizing, objectification and intersubjectivity are treated as fluid developmental products of human interaction, rather than as fixed givens. These are themes within a broad theoretical tradition, which was discussed in the previous chapter as "critical ethnography" during the past 40 years. As mentioned there, the tradition has its roots two centuries earlier in Kant's *Critique of Pure Reason* (1787/1999).

Critique of Group Reason

Kant was situated in the heyday of two conflicting perspectives: empiricism and rationalism. In his creative attempt to resolve the cognitive conflict in the philosophical community of his day, Kant argued that the empirical world is not simply given in fixed form, but that human reason is not unlimited in its powers either. The mind works with the data given it by its senses, but it constitutes the objects in the world by imposing a spatial, temporal and causal structure on these data. In modern terms, we would say that people construct the nature of the physical world from their perceptual sense data. Among the constructed, co-constructed or socially constructed aspects of the world are: lived temporality (the sense we have of the flow of time as a sequence of related events, as opposed to a measured passing of homogeneous time), artifacts (humanly formed physical objects, which have meanings shared within a community) and intersubjectivity (the case that we live in a shared world, which we all understand in basically the same way).

Typically, the meanings of the world that are socially constructed are only shared within a given culture. Therefore, it is natural that ethnographers or anthropologists, who study different cultures, would be interested in how temporalizing, objectification and intersubjectivity work in different cultures. Similarly, the VMT research team should be interested in how these work in the particular culture of virtual math teams. We might not originally have thought to look for these phenomena, but it is not surprising that they would show up in our analyses. Although we are studying small groups rather than the cultures of large communities, these phenomena seem to have their analogues at the unit of analysis of the individual, small group and community—whether the community-of-practice or the linguistic-community or the geographic-community.

The concern of critical ethnographers with combating scientism was an important methodological move to allow them to see the world as socially constructed. By *scientism*, they meant the ideological commitment to a pre-given empiricist world. Trends like behaviorism thereby returned to a pre-Kantian worldview. They reserved the claim of being "real science" to their own approach, dismissing alternative analyses of reality. For ethnographers, who were oriented toward the different views of reality in different cultures, this was counter-intuitive. Furthermore, the scientistic ideology meant that the status quo was the only possible way for things to be. In general, for social scientists who wanted to explore possible improvements to social conditions, this was unacceptable.

Already for Kant, the term *critique* meant more than just viewing the world as socially constructed. To critique something was to lay bare its "conditions of possibility," that is, its logical structure and preconditions. A particularly clear example of this kind of critique—and the example that led to Horkheimer and Adorno's critical theory of society—is Marx' critique of political economy. Marx (1867/1976) rebuffed the ideologists of the early stages of capitalism in England by investigating the historical conditions that made the development of capitalism possible. He studied the shifts in work from the agricultural fields to home-based piecework and then to urban factories, as well as the shifts in population from the countryside to the industrial centers. He also analyzed the drive for capital accumulation that led to cyclical crises, the exploitation of workers that led to the reserve army of the unemployed and the incentive of technological advantage that led to the industrial revolution. Marx showed that capitalism was not an ahistorical social formation, but the result of a specific historical development. An important consequence of this analysis was to suggest that a post-capitalist social form could develop out of the current capitalist form and overcome its undesirable features.

Chapter 26—on meaning making in an excerpt from a VMT chat—concluded by trying to specify the preconditions for the possibility of group cognition. The goal of the VMT Project analyses is to help design an online environment to support an ongoing service of virtual math teams, so that many students globally can experience what students like Aznx, Quicksilver and Bwang did in the session discussed in Chapter 26. This is a critical undertaking in many senses of the word. It is an attempt to go beyond the forms of math education fettered by outmoded institutions of the industrial age, and open up possibilities offered by online technologies, theories of math as discourse and visions of education as group cognition.

To accomplish this, we may need a research community dedicated to collaboratively developing a science of group cognition. The studies in this volume may suggest some starting points for accomplishing that in small groups of researchers working together polyphonically around the world.

Notes

The Virtual Math Teams Project was supported in part by the following grants from the US National Science Foundation:

- "Catalyzing & Nurturing Online Workgroups to Power Virtual Learning Communities." Award REC 0325447. IERI Program. PI: Gerry Stahl; co-PIs: Stephen Weimar and Wesley Shumar.
- "Collaboration Services for the Math Forum Digital Library." Award DUE 0333493. NSDL Services Program. PI: Gerry Stahl; co-PIs: Stephen Weimar and Wesley Shumar.
- "Engaged Learning in Online Communities." Award SBE-0518477. Science of Learning Center Catalyst Program. PI: Gerry Stahl; co-PIs: Sharon J. Derry (Wisconsin); K. Ann Renninger (Swarthmore); Mary R. Marlino (UCAR); Daniel D. Suthers (Hawaii).
- "Exploring Adaptive Support for Virtual Math Teams." Award DRL 0723580. REESE-SGER Program. PI: Carolyn Rosé (CMU); consultant: Gerry Stahl.

Chapter 1

Adapted from Stahl (2008b).

Chapter 2

Adapted from Stahl & Zhou (2006). *Bridge* article and photo of the VMT team by Susan Haine, October 2008.

Chapter 3

Adapted from Stahl (2008a).

Chapter 4

Adapted from Stahl (2009b).

Chapter 5

Adapted from Stahl (2006a). The analysis in this chapter is indebted to chat analysis data sessions at the VMT Project, led by Alan Zemel, and comments from Stephen Weimar and Martin Wessner.

Chapter 6

Adapted from Sarmiento and Stahl (2008a), which was nominated for best student paper of the conference. This chapter is closely related to Sarmiento-Klapper (2009).

Chapter 7

Adapted from Çakir et al. (2009). This chapter is closely related to Çakir (2009).

Chapter 8

Written for this volume. The author acknowledges the influence of Alan Zemel in particular for helping her to develop the analysis of her data. This chapter is closely related to Zhou (2009).

Chapter 9

Written for this volume.

Chapter 10

Written for this volume. Data for this analysis was drawn from the VMT Spring Fest 2006 project, and was provided courtesy of the VMT Project. The analysis was influenced by prior collaboration with Nathan Dwyer and Gerry Stahl.

Chapter 11

Written for this volume.

Chapter 12

Adapted from Sarmiento and Stahl (2008b).

Chapter 13

Written for this volume.

Chapter 14

Adapted from Zemel, Shumar, and Çakir (2007) and Zemel and Çakir (2007).

Chapter 15

Adapted from Mühlpfordt (2006). ConcertChat was developed at the Fraunhofer Institute IPSI in Darmstadt, Germany. Involved in the development were, among others, Axel Guicking, Torsten Holmer, Friederike Jödick, Martin Mühlpfordt, Christian Stab, Martin Wessner, Bo Xiao. Translated from the German by Gerry Stahl.

Chapter 16

Adapted from Stahl (2008c).

Chapter 17

Adapted from Stahl (2006d).

Chapter 18

Adapted from Stahl (2006c).

Chapter 19

Written for this volume. The authors gratefully acknowledge the VMT team for their collaboration and support in this work. They believe their own research has benefited tremendously from this partnership, both in terms of results jointly achieved, as well as through what they have learned through discussions along the way. This work was funded in part through NSF REESE-SGER Number 0723580, IERI REC-043779 and REC 0723580 as well as ONR Cognitive and Neural Sciences Division, Grant number N000140510043. TagHelper tools is freely available for download from http://www.cs.cmu.edu/~cprose/TagHelper.html

Chapter 20

Adapted from Çakir, Xhafa, Zhou, & Stahl (2005).

Chapter 21

Written for this volume. This work was funded in part through grants to Hugo Fuks from the CNPq National Research Council n° 301917/2005-1 and from the FAPERJ project "Cientistas do Nosso Estado."

Chapter 22

Adapted from Strijbos and Stahl (2007).

Chapter 23

Adapted from Zemel, Xhafa, and Çakir (2007) and Zemel, Xhafa, and Stahl (2005).

Chapter 24

Written for this volume. The authors wish to express their appreciation to the members and collaborators of the VMT Project, whose voices are present in different ways in the chapter. A special mention should be made of the students of the Computer Science Department of the Bucharest "Politehnica" University, who participated in experiments proposing useful ideas and especially to Alexandru Dragan and Catalin Alexandru, who contributed to the design and implementation of the application. The research presented here has been partially supported by a Fulbright fellowship to Stefan Trausan-Matu to visit the VMT Project for six months, and by the Romanian CNCSIS K-Teams Research Project.

Chapter 25

Written for this volume.

Chapter 26

Adapted from Stahl (2007). The analysis of the excerpt began in several of the VMT team's collaborative data sessions. Detailed documentation of the VMT session that is excerpted here is available at: mathforum.org/wiki/VMT?VMTGroupB. The idea of preconditions of possibility for interaction was suggested by Rupert Wegerif in a discussion at Intermedia in Oslo. The theoretical and methodological focus on joint meaning making has prospered through interactions with Tim Koschmann and Dan Suthers, most recently in invited workshops on group cognition at Freiburg and Tübingen. The version published in the CSCL 2007 proceedings has been extended based on the conference presentation and a data session of the VMT team on 12/2/2008 with visitors Fei-Ching Chen, Terry Epperson and Tim Koschmann.

Chapter 27

Written for this volume. Photo of the VMT data session by Susan Haine, October 2008.

Chapter 28

Adapted from Stahl (2009a).

References

Adams, F., & Aizawa, K. (2008). *The bounds of cognition*. Malden, MA: Blackwell.

Aleven, V., Sewall, J., McLaren, B. M., & Koedinger, K. R. (2006). *Rapid authoring of intelligent tutors for real-world and experimental use*. Paper presented at the 6th IEEE International Conference on Advanced Learning Technologies (ICALT 2006), Proceedings pp. 847–851.

Alterman, R. (2007). Representation, interaction, and intersubjectivity. *Cognitive Science, 31*(5), 815–841.

Amabile, T. M. (1983). *The social psychology of creativity*. New York: Springer-Verlag.

Andriessen, J., Baker, M., & Suthers, D. (Eds.). (2003). *Arguing to learn: Confronting cognitions in computer-supported collaborative learning environments* (Computer-supported collaborative learning book series, Vol. 1.). Dordrecht, Netherlands: Kluwer Academic Publishers.

Arrow, H., Poole, M. S., Henry, K. B., Wheelan, S., & Moreland, R. (2004). Time, change, and development: The temporal perspective on groups. *Small Group Research, 35*(1), 73–105.

Artstein, R., & Poesio, M. (2005). *Kappa3 = alpha (or beta) (NLE technical note 05-1)*. University of Essex: Natural Language Engineering and Web Applications Group.

Avouris, K., & Margaritis, F. (2002). A tool to support interaction and collaboration analysis of learning activity. In G. Stahl (Ed.), *Computer support for collaborative learning: Foundations for a CSCL community. Proceedings of CSCL 2002*. Boulder, CO: Lawrence Erlbaum Associates.

Avouris, N., Dimitracopoulou, A., & Komis, V. (2003). On analysis of collaborative problem solving: An object-oriented approach. *Computers in Human Behavior, 19*, 147–167.

Bader, G., & Nyce, J. M. (1998). When only the self is real: Theory and practice in the development community. *Journal of Computer Documentation, 22*(1), 5–10.

Baker, A., Jensen, P. J., & Kolb, D. A. (2002). *Conversational learning: An experiential approach to knowledge creation*. Westport, Connecticut: Quorum Books.

Baker, M., Andriessen, J., Lund, K., Van Amelsvoort, M., & Quignard, M. (2007). Rainbow: A framework for analysing computer-mediated pedagogical debates. *International Journal of Computer-Supported Collaborative Learning, 2*, 315–357.

Baker, M., Hansen, T., Joiner, R., & Traum, D. (1999). The role of grounding in collaborative learning tasks. In P. Dillenbourg (Ed.), *Collaborative learning: Cognitive and computational approaches* (pp. 31–63). Oxford, UK: Pergamon.

Baker, M., & Lund, K. (1997). Promoting reflective interactions in a CSCL environment. *Journal of Computer Assisted Learning, 13*, 175–193.

Bakhtin, M. (1981). *The dialogic imagination: Four essays*. Austin University of Texas Press.

Bakhtin, M. (1984a). *Problems of Dostoevsky's poetics* (C. Emerson, Trans.). Minneapolis, MN: University of Minnesota Press.

Bakhtin, M. (1984b). *Rabelais and his world* (H. Iswolsky, Trans.). Bloomington, IN: Indiana University Press.

Bakhtin, M. (1986a). *Speech genres and other late essays* (V. McGee, Trans.). Austin, TX: University of Texas Press.

Bakhtin, M. M. (1986b). The problem of speech genres (V. McGee, Trans.). In C. Emerson & M. Holquist (Eds.), *Speech genres and other late essays* (pp. 60–102). Austin, TX: University of Texas Press.

Bales, R. F. (1953). The equilibrium problem in small groups. In T. Parsons, R. F. Bales, & E. A. Shils (Eds.), *Working papers in the theory of action* (pp. 111–161). New York: Free Press.

Bandura, A. (2001). Social-cognitive theory: An agentic perspective. *Annual Review of Psychology, 52*, 1–26.

Barab, S., & Squire, K. (2004). Design-based research: Putting a stake in the ground. *Journal of the Learning Sciences, 13*(1), 1–14.

Barab, S., Thomas, M. K., Dodge, T., Squire, K., & Newell, M. (2004). Critical design ethnography: Designing for change. *Anthropology & Education Quarterly, 35*(2), 254–268.

Barnard, P., May, J., & Salber, D. (1996). Deixis and points of view in media spaces: An empirical gesture. *Behaviour and Information Technology, 15*(1), 37–50.

Barron, B. (2000). Achieving coordination in collaborative problem-solving groups. *Journal of the Learning Sciences, 9*(4), 403–436.

Barron, B. (2003). When smart groups fail. *The Journal of the Learning Sciences, 12*(3), 307–359.

Barros, B., & Verdejo, M. F. (2000). Analysing student interaction processes in order to improve collaboration. The degree approach. *International Journal of Artificial Intelligence in Education, 11*, 221–241.

Beach, W. A. (1993). Transitional regulations for 'casual' "okay" usages. *Journal of Pragmatics, 19*(4), 325–352.

Beers, P. J., Boshuizen, H. P. A., Kirschner, P. A., & Gijselaers, W. (2005). Computer support for knowledge construction in collaborative learning environments. *Computers in Human Behavior, 21*, 623–643.

Beers, P. J., Boshuizen, H. P. A., Kirschner, P. A., & Gijselaers, W. H. (2007). The analysis of negotiation of common ground in CSCL. *Learning & Instruction, 17*, 427–435.

Beers, P. J., Boshuizen, H. P. A. E., & Kirschner, P. A. (2003). *Negotiating shared understanding in collaborative problem solving.* Paper presented at the 10th EARLI Conference, Padova, Italy.

Bekker, M. M., Olson, J. S., & Olson, G. M. (1995). *Analysis of gestures in face-to-face design teams provides guidance for how to use groupware in design.* Paper presented at the *conference on Designing Interactive Systems (DIS '95).* Proceedings of the Symposium on Designing interactive System design ACM. 157–166.

Blumer, H. (1969). *Symbolic interactionism: Perspective and method.* Berkeley, CA: University of California Press.

Boden, D. (1995). *The business of talk: Organizations in action.* London, UK: Blackwell.

Bourdieu, P. (1990). *The logic of practice* (R. Nice, Trans.). Stanford, CA: Stanford University Press.

Brett, C., Nason, R. A., & Woodruff, E. (2002). Communities of inquiry among preservice teachers investigating mathematics. *THEMES in Education, 3*(1), 39–62.

Brown, J. S., Collins, A., & Duguid, P. (1989). Situated cognition and the culture of learning. *Educational Researcher, 18*(1), 32–42.

Brown, S. I., & Walter, M. I. (1983). *The art of problem posing.* Philadelphia, PA: The Franklin Institute.

Bruner, J. (1990). *Acts of meaning.* Cambridge, MA: Harvard University Press.

Bruner, J. (1995). Meaning and self in cultural perspective. In D. Bakhurst & C. Sypnowich (Eds.), *The social self* (pp. 18–29). London: Sage.

Bunzl, M. (2002). Forward to Johannes Fabian's time and the other: Syntheses of a critical anthropology. In J. Fabian (Ed.), *Time and the other: How anthropology makes its object* (pp. ix–xxxvii). New York: Columbia University Press.

Bunzl, M. (2005). Anthropology beyond crisis: Toward an intellectual history of the extended present. *Anthropology & Humanism Quarterly, 30*(2), 187–195.

Button, G. Y. (Ed.). (1993). *Technology in working order: Studies of work, interaction, and technology*. London: Routledge.

Button, G. (2000). The ethnographic tradition and design. *Design Studies, 21*(4), 319–332.

Button, G. Y., & Dourish, P. (1996). *Technomethodology: Paradoxes and possibilities*. Paper presented at the ACM Conference on Human Factors in Computing Systems (CHI '96), Vancouver, Canada. Proceedings, pp. 19–26.

Cai, J., & Lester, F. K., Jr. (2005). Solution representations and pedagogical representations in Chinese and US classrooms. *Journal of Mathematical Behavior, 24*(3/4), 221–237.

Çakir, M. P. (2009). *How online small groups co-construct mathematical artifacts to do collaborative problem solving*. Unpublished Dissertation, Ph.D., College of Information Science and Technology, Drexel University, Philadelphia, PA, USA.

Çakir, M. P., Xhafa, F., Zhou, N., & Stahl, G. (2005). *Thread-based analysis of patterns of collaborative interaction in chat*. Paper presented at the international conference on AI in Education (AI-Ed 2005), Amsterdam, Netherlands. Retrieved from http://GerryStahl. net/pub/aied2005.pdf

Çakir, M. P., Zemel, A., & Stahl, G. (2009). The joint organization of interaction within a multimodal CSCL medium. *International Journal of Computer-Supported Collaborative Learning (ijCSCL), 4*(2), 115–149.

Campbell, C. (1998). *The myth of social action*. Cambridge, UK: Cambridge University Press.

Carmien, S., Kollar, I., Fischer, G., & Fischer, F. (2006). The interplay of internal and external scripts. In F. Fischer, H. Mandl, J. Haake, & I. Kollar (Eds.), *Scripting computer-supported collaborative learning: Cognitive, computational and educational perspectives* (pp. 303–325). Dodrecht, Netherlands: Kluwer-Springer Verlag.

Charles, E. S., & Kolodner, J. L. (in revision). *"In this classroom we are scientists!" Collective agency, its development, and its role in learning*. An extension of the paper presented at the annual meeting of the AERA, Montreal, 2005.

Chaudhuri, S., Kumar, R., Joshi, M., Terrell, E., Higgs, F., Aleven, V., et al. (2008). *It's not easy being green: Supporting collaborative "green design" learning*. Paper presented at the *Intelligent Tutoring Systems (ITS '08)*.

Chen, W., & Looi, C. K. (2007). Incorporating online discussion in face to face classroom learning: A new blended learning approach. *Australasian Journal of Educational Technology, 23*(3), 307–326.

Chi, M. T. H. (1997). Quantifying qualitative analysis of verbal data: A practical guide. *The Journal of the Learning Sciences, 6*, 271–315.

Chiu, M. M., & Khoo, L. (2003). Rudeness and status effects during group problem solving: Do they bias evaluations and reduce the likelihood of correct solutions? *Journal of Educational Psychology, 95*, 506–523.

Clark, H., & Brennan, S. (1991). Grounding in communication. In L. Resnick, J. Levine, & S. Teasley (Eds.), *Perspectives on socially-shared cognition* (pp. 127–149). Washington, DC: APA.

Clark, H. H., & Marshall, C. (1981). Definite reference and mutual knowledge. In A. K. Joshi, B. Weber, & I. A. Sag (Eds.), *Elements of discourse understanding* (pp. 10–63). New York: Cambridge University Press.

Clark, H. H., & Wilkes-Gibbs, D. (1986). Referring as a collaborative process. *Cognition & Instruction, 22*, 1–39.

Clifford, J., & Marcus, G. E. (Eds.). (1986). *Writing culture: The poetics and politics of ethnography*. Berkeley, CA: University of California Press.

Cobb, P. (1995). Mathematical learning and small-group interaction: Four case studies. In P. Cobb & H. Bauersfeld (Eds.), *The emergence of mathematical meaning* (pp. 25–130). Mahwah, NJ: Lawrence Erlbaum Associates.

Cobb, P. (2004). Mathematics, literacies, and identity. *Reading Research Quarterly, 39*(3), 333–337.

Cobb, P., Yackel, E., & McClain, K. (2000). *Symbolizing and communicating in mathematics classrooms: Perspectives on discourse, tools, and instructional design*. Mahwah, NJ: Lawrence Erlbaum Associates.

Cohen, E. G., Lotan, R. A., Abram, P. L., Scarloss, B. A., & Schultz, S. E. (2002). Can groups learn? *Teachers College Record, 104*(6), 1045–1068.

Condon, S. L. (2001). Discourse ok revisited: Default organization in verbal interaction. *Journal of Pragmatics, 33*(4), 491–513.

Cornelius, C., & Boos, M. (2003). Enhancing mutual understanding in synchronous computer-mediated communication by training: Trade-offs in judgmental tasks. *Communication Research, 30*, 147–177.

Coulon, A. (1995). *Ethnomethodology*. Thousand Oaks, CA: Sage.

Cress, U. (2008). The need for considering multilevel analysis in CSCL research: An appeal for more advanced statistical methods. *International Journal of Computer-Supported Collaborative Learning, 3*, 69–84.

Csikszentmihalyi, M. (1988). Society, culture, person: A systems view of creativity. In R. J. Sternberg (Ed.), *The nature of creativity* (pp. 325–339). Cambridge,UK: Cambridge University Press.

Csikszentmihalyi, M. (1990a). *Flow: The psychology of optimal experience*. Glasgow: Harper Collins.

Csikszentmihalyi, M. (1990b). The domain of creativity. In M. A. Runco & R. S. Albert (Eds.), *Theories of creativity* (pp. 190–212). Newbury Park, CA: Sage.

Daft, R. L., & Lengel, R. H. (1986). Organizational information requirements, media richness and structural design. *Management Science, 32*(5), 554–571.

D'Ambrosio, U. (2001). *Etnomatemática: Elo entre as tradições e a modernidade. [Ethnomathematics : Link between tradition and modernity]*. Belo Horizonte, Brazil: Autêntica.

Daradoumis, T., Martínez, A., & Xhafa, F. (2004). *An integrated approach for analysing and assessing the performance of virtual learning groups*. In Gert-Jan de Vreede, Luis A. Guerrero, Gabriela Marn Raventós (Eds.): Groupware: Design, Implementation and Use: 10th International Workshop, CRIWG 2004, San Carlos, Costa Rica, September 5–9, 2004. Proceedings. Lecture Notes in Computer Science 3198 Springer 2004, ISBN 3-540-23016-5 .

Davies, B., & Harré, R. (1990). Positioning: The discursive production of selves. *Journal for the Theory of Social Behaviour, 20*, 43–63.

Davis, B., Sumara, D., & Luce-Kapler, R. (2000). *Engaging minds: Learning and teaching in a complex world*. Mahwah, NJ: Lawrence Erlbaum.

de Saussure, F. (1959). *Course in general linguistics* (W. Baskin, Trans.). New York: Philosophical Library.

De Wever, B., Schellens, T., Valcke, M., & Van Keer, H. (2006). Content analysis schemes to analyze transcripts of online asynchronous discussion groups: A review. *Computers & Education, 46*, 6–28.

Dennis, A. R., & Valacich, J. S. (1999). *Rethinking media richness: Towards a theory of media synchronicity*. Paper presented at the Thirty-Second Annual Hawaii International Conference on System Sciences, Maui, Hawaii.

Descartes, R. (1633/1999). *Discourse on method and meditations on first philosophy*. New York: Hackett.

Design-Based Research Collective. (2003). Design-based research: An emerging paradigm for educational inquiry. *Educational Researcher, 32*(1), 5–8.

Dewey, J. (1938/1991). Logic: The theory of inquiry. In J. A. Boydston (Ed.), *John dewey: The later works, 1925–1953* (Vol. 12, pp. 1–5). Carbondale, IL: Southern Illinois University Press.

Dillenbourg, P. (1999). What do you mean by "Collaborative learning"? In P. Dillenbourg (Ed.), *Collaborative learning: Cognitive and computational approaches* (pp. 1–16). Amsterdam, NL: Pergamon, Elsevier Science.

Dillenbourg, P. (2005). Dual-interaction spaces. In T. Koschmann, D. D. Suthers, & T.-W. Chan (Eds.), *Computer-supported collaborative learning 2005: The next ten years! (Proceedings of CSCL 2005)*. Taipei, Taiwan: Mahwah, NJ: Lawrence Erlbaum Associates.

Dillenbourg, P., Baker, M., Blaye, A., & O'Malley, C. (1996). The evolution of research on collaborative learning. In P. Reimann & H. Spada (Eds.), *Learning in humans and machines: Towards an interdisciplinary learning science* (pp. 189–211). Oxford, UK: Elsevier.

Dillenbourg, P., & Jermann, P. (2006). Designing integrative scripts. In F. Fischer, H. Mandl, J. Haake, & I. Kollar (Eds.), *Scripting computer-supported collaborative learning: Cognitive, computational and educational perspectives* (pp. 275–301). Dodrecht, Netherlands: Kluwer-Springer Verlag.

Dillenbourg, P., & Traum, D. (2006). Sharing solutions: Persistence and grounding in multimodal collaborative problem solving. *Journal of the Learning Sciences, 15*(1), 121–151.

Dimitracopoulou, A. (2005). *Designing collaborative learning systems: Current trends & future research agenda.* Paper presented at the Computer Supported Collaborative Learning 2005. The Next 10 Years! (CSCL 2005). Mahwah, NJ: Lawrence Erlbaum Associates.

Dohn, N. B. (2009). Affordances revisited: Articulating a Merleau-Pontian view. *International Journal of Computer-Supported Collaborative Learning (ijCSCL), 4*(2), 151–170.

Donmez, P., Rose, C., Stegmann, K., Weinberger, A., & Fischer, F. (2005). *Supporting CSCL with automatic corpus analysis technology.* Paper presented at the International Conference of Computer Support for Collaborative Learning (CSCL 2005), Taipei, Taiwan.

Dörfler, W. (2000). Means for meaning. In E. Y. K. M. P. Cobb (Ed.), *Symbolizing and communicating in mathematics classrooms: Perspectives on discourse, tools and instructional design* (pp. 99–131). Mahwah, NJ: Lawrence Erlbaum.

Drew, P., & Heritage, J. (1993). *Talk at work: Interaction in institutional settings.* Cambridge, UK: Cambridge University Press.

Duranti, A. (1998). *Linguistic anthropology.* Cambridge, UK: Cambridge University Press.

Dwyer, N., & Suthers, D. (2006). Consistent practices in artifact-mediated collaboration. *International Journal of Computer-Supported Collaborative Learning (ijCSCL), 1*(4), 481–511.

Edwards, A. W. F. (1987). *Pascal's arithmetical triangle.* London: Griffin & Oxford.

EETI. (2007). *Effectiveness of reading and mathematics software products: Findings from the first student cohort.* US Congress.

Emirbayer, M., & Mische, A. (1998). What is agency? *American Journal of Sociology, 103*(4), 962–1023.

Engeström, Y. (1987). *Learning by expanding: An activity-theoretical approach to developmental research.* Helsinki, Finland: Orienta-Kosultit Oy.

Engeström, Y. (1999). Activity theory and individual and social transformation. In Y. Engeström, R. Miettinen, & R.-L. Punamäki (Eds.), *Perspectives on activity theory* (pp. 19–38). Cambridge, UK: Cambridge University Press.

Engeström, Y. (2008). *From teams to knots.* Cambridge, UK: Cambridge University Press.

Engeström, Y., & Toiviainen, H. (2009). Co-configurational design of learning instrumentalities: An activity-theoretical perspective. In S. Ludvigsen, A. Lund, & R. Säljö (Eds.), *Learning in social practices. ICT and new artifacts: Transformation of social and cultural practices.* New York, NY: Pergamon Press.

Engle, A. (1997). *Problem-solving strategies.* New York: Springer.

Engle, R. A. (2006). Framing interactions to foster generative learning: A situative explanation of transfer in a community of learners classroom. *Journal of the Learning Sciences, 15*(4), 451–498.

Engle, R. A., & Conant, F. R. (2002). Guiding principles for fostering productive disciplinary engagement: Explaining an emergent argument in a community of learners classroom. *Cognition & Instruction, 20*(4), 399–483.

Enyedy, N. (2005). Inventing mapping: Creating cultural forms to solve collective problems. *Cognition and Instruction, 23*(4), 427–466.

Erickson, T. (1999). Persistent conversation: An introduction. *Journal of Computer-Mediated Communication, 4*(4).

Erkens, G., & Janssen, J. (2008). Automatic coding of communication in collaboration protocols. *International Journal of Computer-Supported Collaborative Learning (ijCSCL), 3*(4), 447–470.

Evans, B. (2007). Introduction: Rethinking the disciplinary confluence of anthropology and literary studies. *Criticism, 49*(4), 429–445.

Fabian, J. (1971). History, language and anthropology. *Philosophy of the Social Sciences, 1*, 19–47.

Fabian, J. (1990a). *Power and performance: Ethnographic explorations through proverbial wisdom and theater in Shaba.* Madison, WI: University of Wisconsin Press.

Fabian, J. (1990b). Presence and representation: The other and anthropological writing. *Critical Inquiry, 16*(4), 753–772.

Fabian, J. (1991a). Dilemmas of critical anthropology. In L. Nencel & P. Pels (Eds.), *Constructing knowledge: Authority and critique in social science* (pp. 180–202). London: Sage.

Fabian, J. (1991b). *Time and the work of anthropology: Critical essays 1971–1991.* Chur, Switzerland: Harwood Academic Publishers.

Fabian, J. (2001). *Anthropology with an attitude: Critical essays.* Palo Alto, CA: Stanford University Press.

Fabian, J. (2002). *Time and the other: How anthropology makes its object* (2nd ed.). New York: Columbia University Press.

Fabian, J. (2007). *Memory against culture: Arguments and reminders.* Durham, NC: Duke University Press.

Firth, A. E. (1995). *The discourse of negotiation: Studies of language in the workplace.* Oxford, UK: Pergamon.

Fischer, F., Bruhn, J., Gräsel, C., & Mandl, H. (2002). Fostering collaborative knowledge construction with visualization tools. *Learning and Instruction. (Special issue on measurement challenges in collaborative learning research), 12*, 213–232.

Fischer, F., & Mandl, H. (2005). Knowledge convergence in computer-supported collaborative learning: The role of external representation tools. *The Journal of the Learning Sciences, 14*, 405–441.

Fischer, F., Mandl, H., Haake, J., & Kollar, I. (Eds.). (2006). *Scripting computer-supported collaborative learning: Cognitive, computational and educational perspectives* Computer-supported collaborative learning book series, Vol. 6. Dordrecht, Netherlands: Kluwer Academic Publishers.

Fischer, G., Nakakoji, K., Ostwald, J., Stahl, G., & Sumner, T. (1998). Embedding critics in design environments. In M. T. Maybury & W. Wahlster (Eds.), *Readings in intelligent user interfaces* (pp. 537–561). New York: Morgan Kaufman. Retrieved from http://GerryStahl.net/publications/journals/ker/index.html

Fischer, G., & Ostwald, J. (2005). Knowledge communication in design communities. In R. Bromme, F. Hesse, & H. Spada (Eds.), *Barriers and biases in computer-mediated knowledge communication–and how they may be overcome.* Dordrecht, Netherlands: Kluwer Academic Publisher.

Forsythe, D. E. (1999). "It's just a matter of common sense": Ethnography as invisible work. *Computer Supported Cooperative Work, 8*, 127–145.

Forsythe, D. E. (2001). *Studying those who study us: An anthropologist in the world of artificial intelligence.* Stanford, CA: Stanford University Press.

Fuks, H. (2000). Groupware technologies for education in AulaNet. *Computer Applications in Engineering Education, 8*(3 & 4), 170–177.

Fuks, H., & Assis, R. L. (2001). Facilitating perception on virtual learningware-based environments. *Journal of Systems and Information Technology, 5*(1), 93–113.

Fuks, H., Gerosa, M. A., & Lucena, C. J. P. (2002). The development and application of distance learning on the internet. *Open Learning – The Journal of Open and Distance Learning, 17*(1), 23–38.

Fuks, H., Pimentel, M., & Lucena, C. J. P. (2006). R-U-Typing-2-Me? Evolving a chat tool to increase understanding in learning activities. *International Journal of Computer-Supported Collaborative Learning (ijCSCL), 1*(1), 117–142. Retrieved from http://ijcscl.org/_preprints/volume1_issue1/fuks_pimentel_lucena.pdf

Gadamer, H.-G. (1960/1988). *Truth and method.* New York: Crossroads.

Garcia, A., & Jacobs, J. B. (1998). The interactional organization of computer mediated communication in the college classroom. *Qualitative Sociology, 21*(3), 299–317.

Garcia, A., & Jacobs, J. B. (1999). The eyes of the beholder: Understanding the turn-taking system in quasi-synchronous computer-mediated communication. *Research on Language and Social Interaction, 34*(4), 337–367.

Garfinkel, H. (1967). *Studies in ethnomethodology.* Englewood Cliffs, NJ: Prentice-Hall.

Garfinkel, H. (1972). Remarks on ethnomethodology. In J. J. Gumpertz & D. Hymes (Eds.), *Directions in socio-lingusitics* (pp. 301–324). New York: Rinehart & Winston.

Garfinkel, H. (2002). *Ethnomethodology's program: Working out Durkheim's aphorism.* Lanham, MD: Rowman & Littlefield.

Garfinkel, H., & Sacks, H. (1970). On formal structures of practical actions. In J. Mckinney & E. Tiryakian (Eds.), *Theoretical sociology: Perspectives and developments* (pp. 337–366). New York: Appleton-Century-Crofts.

Gattegno, C. (1988). *The science of education: Part 2b: The awareness of mathematization.* New York: Educational Solution.

Gee, J. P. (1992). *The social mind: Language, ideology, and social practice.* New York: Bergin & Garvey.

Geertz, C. (1973). *The interpretation of cultures.* New York: Basic Books.

Gerosa, M. A., Fuks, H., & Lucena, C. J. P. (2003). Analysis and design of awareness elements in collaborative digital environments: A case study in the AulaNet learning environment. *Journal of Interactive Learning Research, 14*(3), 315–332.

Getzels, J., & Csikszentmihalyi, M. (1976). *The creative vision: A longitudinal study of problem finding in art.* New York: Wiley & Sons.

Giddens, A. (1979). *Central problems in social theory: Action, structure and contradiction in social analysis.* London: Macmillan.

Giddens, A. (1984). *The constitution of society. Outline of the theory of structuration.* Berkeley, CA: University of California Press.

Glenn, P., Koschmann, T., & Conlee, M. (1999). Theory sequences in a problem-based learning group: A case study. *Discourse Processes, 27,* 119–133.

Goffman, E. (1963). *Behavior in public places.* New York: Free Press.

Goffman, E. (1981). *Forms of talk.* Philadelphia: University of Pennsylvania Press.

Goodwin, C. (1994). Professional vision. *American Anthropologist, 96*(3), 606–633.

Goodwin, C. (1995). Co-constructing meaning in conversations with an aphasic man. *Research on Language and Social Interaction, 28*(3), 233–260.

Goodwin, C. (2000a). Action and embodiment within situated human interaction. *Journal of Pragmatics, 32,* 1489–1522.

Goodwin, C. (2000b). Practices of color classification. *Mind, Culture, and Activity, 7*(1 & 2), 19–36.

Goodwin, C. (2004). A competent speaker who can't speak: The social life of aphasia. *Journal of Linguistic Anthropology, 14*(2), 151–170

Goodwin, C., & Heritage, J. (1990). Conversation analysis. *Annual Review of Anthropology, 19,* 283–307.

Greeno, J. G. (2006a). Authoritative, accountable positioning and connected, general knowing: Progressive themes in understanding transfer. *Journal of the Learning Sciences, 15*(4), 537–547.

Greeno, J. G. (2006b). Learning in activity. In R. K. Sawyer (Ed.), *The cambridge handbook of the learning sciences* (pp. 79–96). New York: Cambridge.

Gunawardena, C. N., Lowe, C. A., & Anderson, T. (1997). Analysis of a global online debate and the development of an interaction analysis model for examining social construction of knowledge in computer conferencing. *Journal of Educational Computing Research, 17,* 397–343.

Gutwin, C., & Greenberg, S. (2002). A descriptive framework of workspace awareness for real-time groupware. *Computer Supported Cooperative Work (CSCW), 11*(3–4), 411–446.

Gweon, G., Arguello, J., Pai, C., Carey, R., Zaiss, Z., & Rosé, C. P. (2005). *Towards a prototyping tool for behavior oriented authoring of conversational interfaces.* Paper presented at the ACL Workshop on Educational Applications of NLP.

Gweon, G., Rosé, C. P., Albright, E., & Cui, Y. (2007). *Evaluating the effect of feedback from a CSCL problem solving environment on learning, interaction, and perceived interdependence.* Paper presented at the CSCL 2007, Rutgers University.

Gweon, G., Rosé, C. P., Zaiss, Z., & Carey, R. (2006). *Providing support for adaptive scripting in an on-line collaborative learning environment.* Paper presented at the CHI 06: ACM conference on human factors in computer systems. New York: ACM Press.

Habermas, J. (1965/1971). *Knowledge and human interests.* Boston, MA: Beacon Press.

Habermas, J. (1967/1988). *On the logic of the social sciences.* Cambridge, UK: Polity Press.

Hacking, I. (1999). *The social construction of what?* Cambridge, MA: Harvard University Press.

Haine, S. (2008). Technology + information + collaboration = the virtual math teams project. *Bridge*, 2008(Fall), 2–3.

Hakken, D. (1999). *Cyborgs@cyberspace?: An ethnographer looks to the future.* New York: Routledge.

Hakken, D. (2003). *The knowledge landscapes of cyberspace.* New York: Routledge.

Halewood, C., Reeve, R., & Scardamalia, M. (2005). *Knowledge building in junior kindergarten: Gaining agency over ideas and process.* Paper presented at the American Educational Research Association (AERA), Montreal, CN.

Hall, R., & Stevens, R. (1995). Making space: A comparison of mathematical work in school and professional design practices. In S. L. Star (Ed.), *The cultures of computing.* Oxford, UK: Blackwell Publishers.

Halliday, M. A. K., & Hasan, R. (1976). *Cohesion in English.* London: Longman.

Hamann, E. T. (2003). Imagining the future of the anthropology of education if we take Laura Nader seriously. *Anthropology & Education Quarterly, 34*(4), 438–449.

Hammersley, M. (2003). Recent radical criticism of interview studies: Any implications for the sociology of education? *British Journal of Sociology of Education, 24*(1), 119–126.

Handelman, D. (1994). Critiques of anthropology: Literary turns, slippery bends. *Poetics Today, 15*(3), 341–381.

Hanks, W. (1992). The indexical ground of deictic reference. In C. Goodwin & A. Duranti (Eds.), *Rethinking context: Language as an interactive phenomenon.* Cambridge, UK: Cambridge University Press.

Hanks, W. (1996). *Language and communicative practices.* Boulder, CO: Westview.

Hanks, W. F. (2000). *Intertexts: Writings on language, utterance, and context.* Lanham: Rowman & Littlefield.

Haraway, D. J. (1991). *Simians, cyborgs, and women: The reinvention of nature.* New York: Routledge.

Harré, R., & Moghaddam, F. (2003). Introduction: The self and others in traditional psychology and in positioning theory. In R. Harré & F. Moghaddam (Eds.), *The self and others* (pp. 1–11). Westport, CT: Praeger.

Hausmann, R., Chi, M., & Roy, M. (2004). *Learning from collaborative problem solving: An analysis of three hypothesized mechanisms.* Paper presented at the 26nd annual conference of the Cognitive Science Society. Proceedings pp. 547–552.

Healy, L., & Hoyles, C. (1999). Visual and symbolic reasoning in mathematics: Making connections with computers. *Mathematical Thinking and Learning, 1*(1), 59–84.

Hegel, G. W. F. (1807/1967). *Phenomenology of spirit* (J. B. Baillie, Trans.). New York: Harper & Row.

Heidegger, M. (1927/1996). *Being and time: A translation of Sein und Zeit* (J. Stambaugh, Trans.). Albany, NY: SUNY Press.

Held, D. (1980). *Introduction to critical theory: Horkheimer to Habermas.* London: Hutchinson.

Henri, F. (1992). Computer conferencing and content analysis. In A. Kaye (Ed.), *Collaborative learning through computer conferencing: The Najaden papers* (pp. 117–136). London: Spinger Verlag.

Heritage, J. (1984). *Garfinkel and ethnomethodology.* Cambridge, UK: Polity Press.

Heritage, J. (1995). Conversation analysis: Methodological aspects. In U. Quasthoff (Ed.), *Aspects of oral communication* (pp. 391–418). Berlin: Walter de Gruyter.

Heritage, J., & Roth, A. (1995). Grammar and institution: Questions and questioning in the broadcast news interview. *Research on Language and Social Interaction, 28*(1), 1–60.

Herring, S. (1999). Interactional coherence in cmc. *Journal of Computer Mediated Communication, 4*(4) Retrieved from http://jcmc.indiana.edu/vol4/issue4/herring.html

Herring, S. C. (2001). Computer-mediated discourse. In D. Tannen, D. Schifrrin, & H. Hamilton (Eds.), *Handbook of discourse analysis*. Oxford, UK: Blackwell.

Hewett, T. (2005). Informing the design of computer-based environments to support creativity. *International Journal of Human-Computer Studies (IJHCS), 63*(4–5), 383–409.

Hicks, D. (1996). Contextual inquiries: A discourse-oriented study of classroom learning. In D. Hicks (Ed.), *Discourse, learning and schooling* (pp. 104–141). New York: Cambridge University Press.

Hmelo-Silver, C. (2003). Analyzing collaborative knowledge construction: Multiple methods for integrated understanding. *Computers & Education, 41*, 397–420.

Holland, D., Lachicotte, W., Jr., Skinner, D., & Cain, C. (1998). *Identity and agency in cultural worlds*. Cambridge, MA: Harvard University Press.

Holmer, T., Lukosch, S., & Kunz, V. (2008). *Addressing co-text loss with multiple visualizations for chat messages*. Paper presented at the 14th International Workshop, CRIWG 2008, Omaha, Nebraska. Proceedings, pp. 172–183.

Hurme, T. R., & Järvelä, S. (2005). Students' activity in computer-supported collaborative problem solving in mathematics. *International Journal of Computers for Mathematical Learning, 10*, 49–73.

Husserl, E. (1929/1960). *Cartesian meditations: An introduction to phenomenology* (D. Cairns, Trans.). The Hague, Netherlands: Martinus Nijhoff.

Husserl, E. (1936/1989). The origin of geometry (D. Carr, Trans.). In J. Derrida (Ed.), *Edmund Husserl's origin of geometry: An introduction* (pp. 157–180). Lincoln, NE: University of Nebraska Press.

Hutchins, E. (1996). *Cognition in the wild*. Cambridge, MA: MIT Press.

Hymes, D. H. (Ed.). (1972). *Reinventing anthropology* (1st ed.). New York: Pantheon Books.

Inokuchi, A., Washio, T., & Motodam, H. (2000). *An apriori-based algorithm for mining frequent substructures from graph data*. Paper presented at the PKDD 2000, Lyon, France. Proceedings, pp. 13–23.

Jameson, F. (1972). *The prison house of language*. Princeton, NJ: Princeton University Press.

Jeong, A. C. (2003). The sequential analysis of group interaction and critical thinking in online threaded discussion. *The American Journal of Distance Education, 17*(1), 25–43.

Jermann, P. (2002). *Task and interaction regulation in controlling a traffic simulation*. Paper presented at the Computer support for collaborative learning: Foundations for a CSCL community. Proceedings of CSCL 2002, Boulder, CO, pp. 601–602.

Jermann, P. (2004). *Computer support for interaction regulation in collaborative problem-solving*. Unpublished Dissertation, Ph.D., University of Geneva, Geneva, Switzerland.

Jermann, P., & Dillenbourg, P. (2005). Planning congruence in dual spaces. In T. Koschmann, D. D. Suthers, & T.-W. Chan (Eds.), *Computer-supported collaborative learning 2005: The next ten years! (Proceedings of CSCL 2005)*. Taipei, Taiwan; Mahwah, NJ: Lawrence Erlbaum Associates.

Johnson, D. W., & Johnson, R. T. (1989). *Cooperation and competition: Theory and research*. Edina, MN: Interaction Book Company.

Jonassen, D. H., & Kwon, H. I. (2001). Communication patterns in computer mediated and face-to-face group problem solving. *Educational Technology Research & Development, 49*, 35–51.

Jonassen, D. H., Peck, K. L., & Wilson, B. G. (1999). *Learning with technology: A constructivist perspective*. Upper Saddle River, NJ: Merrill/Prentice Hall.

Jones, C., Dirckinck-Holmfeld, L., & Lindström, B. (2006). A relational, indirect and meso level approach to design in CSCL in the next decade. *International Journal of Computer-Supported Collaborative Learning (ijCSCL), 1*(1), 35–56. Retrieved from http://ijcscl.org/_preprints/volume1_issue1/jones_holmfeld_lindstroem.pdf

Jordan, B., & Henderson, A. (1995). Interaction analysis: Foundations and practice. *Journal of the Learning Sciences, 4*(1), 39–103. Retrieved from http://lrs.ed.uiuc.edu/students/c-merkel/document4.HTM

Jordan, P., Hall, B., Ringenberg, M., Cui, Y., & Rosé, C. P. (2007). *Tools for authoring a dialogue agent that participates in learning studies.* Paper presented at the AIED 2007.

Joshi, M., & Rosé, C. P. (2007). *Using transactivity in conversation summarization of educational dialogue.* Paper presented at the SLaTE Workshp on Speech and Language Technology in Education.

Kang, M., Chaudhuri, S., Joshi, M., Rosé, C. P. (2008). *Side : The summarization integrated development environment.* Paper presented at the Association for Computational Linguistics.

Kanselaar, G., Erkens, G., Andriessen, J., Prangsma, M., Veerman, A., & Jaspers, J. (2003). Designing argumentation tools for collaborative learning. In P. A. Kirschner (Ed.), *Visualizing argumentation: Software tools for collaborative and educational sense-making* (pp. 51–73). New York, NY: Springer.

Kant, I. (1787/1999). *Critique of pure reason.* Cambridge, UK: Cambridge University Press.

Kaplan, A. (1964). *The conduct of inquiry: Methodology for behavioral science.* San Fransisco, CA: Chandler Publishing.

Kaptelinin, V., & Nardi, B. A. (2006). *Acting with technology: Activity theory and interaction design.* Cambridge, MA: MIT Press.

Kärkkäinen, E. (2003). *Epistemic stance in English conversation: A description of its interactional functions, with a focus on i think.* Amsterdam, NL: John Benjamins.

Kendon, A. (1985). Behavioral foundations for the process of frame attunement in face-to- interaction. In G. P. Ginsburg, M. Brenner, & M. V. Cranach (Eds.), *Discovery strategies in the psychology of action* (pp. 229–253). London: Academic Press.

Kilpatrick, J., Hoyles, C., Sokovsmose, O., & Valero, P. (Eds.). (2005). *Meaning in mathematics education.* New York: Springer.

King, F. B., & Mayall, H. J. (2001). *Asynchronous distributed problem-based learning.* Paper presented at the IEEE International Conference on Advanced Learning Technologies (ICALT '01). Proceedings, pp. *157–159.*

Kirsch, D. (2009). Problem solving and situated cognition. In P. Robbins & M. Aydede (Eds.), *Cambridge handbook of situated cognition.* Cambridge, UK: Cambridge University Press.

Kirschner, P. A., Buckingham Shum, S. J., & Carr, C. S. (Eds.). (2003). *Visualizing argumentation: Software tools for collaborative and educational sense-making.* London, UK: Springer Verlag.

Kobbe, L., Weinberger, A., Dillenbourg, P., Harrer, A., Hämäläinen, R., Häkkinen, P., et al. (2007). Specifying computer-supported collaboration scripts. *International Journal of Computer-Supported Collaborative Learning (ijCSCL), 2*(2–3), 211–224.

Kock, N. (2001). Compensatory adaptation to a lean medium: An action research investigation of electronic communication in process improvement groups. *IEEE Transactions on Professional Communication, 44*(4), 267–285.

Kock, N. (2004). The psychobiological model: Towards a new theory of computer-mediated communication based on darwinian evolution. *Organization Science, 15*(3), 327–348.

Kock, N. (2005). Media richness or media naturalness? The evolution of our biological communication apparatus and its influence on our behavior toward e-communication tools. *IEEE Transactions on Professional Communication, 48*(2), 117–130.

Komis, V., Avouris, N., & Fidas, C. (2002). Computer-supported collaborative concept mapping: Study of synchronous peer interaction. *Education and Information Technologies, 7*(2), 169–188.

Koschmann, T. (1996a). Paradigm shifts and instructional technology. In T. Koschmann (Ed.), *CSCL: Theory and practice of an emerging paradigm* (pp. 1–23). Mahwah, NJ: Lawrence Erlbaum.

Koschmann, T. (1999a). Meaning making: Special issue. *Discourse Processes, 27*(2).

Koschmann, T. (1999b). *Toward a dialogic theory of learning: Bakhtin's contribution to learning in settings of collaboration.* Paper presented at the Computer Supported Collaborative Learning

(CSCL '99), Palo Alto, CA: Lawrence Erlbaum. Proceedings, pp. 308–313. Retrieved from http://kn.cilt.org/cscl99/A38/A38.HTM

Koschmann, T. (2002). Dewey's contribution to the foundations of CSCL research. In G. Stahl (Ed.), *Computer support for collaborative learning: Foundations for a CSCL community: Proceedings of CSCL 2002* (pp. 17–22). Boulder, CO: Lawrence Erlbaum Associates.

Koschmann, T. (Ed.). (1996b). *CSCL: Theory and practice of an emerging paradigm.* Hillsdale, NJ: Lawrence Erlbaum Associates.

Koschmann, T., & LeBaron, C. (2003). *Reconsidering common ground: Examining clark's contribution theory in the operating room.* Paper presented at the European Computer-Supported Cooperative Work (ECSCW '03), Helsinki, Finland. Proceedings, pp. 81–98.

Koschmann, T., LeBaron, C., Goodwin, C., & Feltovich, P. J. (2001). Dissecting common ground: Examining an instance of reference repair. In J. D. Moore & K. Stenning (Eds.), *Proceedings of the twenty-third annual conference of the cognitive science society* (pp. 516–521). Mahwah, NJ: Lawrence Erlbaum Associates.

Koschmann, T., Stahl, G., & Zemel, A. (2007). The video analyst's manifesto (or the implications of Garfinkel's policies for the development of a program of video analytic research within the learning sciences). In R. Goldman, R. Pea, B. Barron, & S. Derry (Eds.), *Video research in the learning sciences* (pp. 133–144). Mahway, NJ: Lawrence Erlbaum Associates. Retrieved from http://GerryStahl.net/publications/journals/manifesto.pdf

Koschmann, T., & Zemel, A. (2006). *Optical pulsars and black arrows: Discovery's work in 'hot' and 'cold' science.* Paper presented at the International Conference of the Learning Sciences (ICLS 2006), Bloomington, IN. Proceedings, pp. 356–362.

Koschmann, T., Zemel, A., Conlee-Stevens, M., Young, N., Robbs, J., & Barnhart, A. (2005). How do people learn: Member's methods and communicative mediation. In R. Bromme, F. W. Hesse, & H. Spada (Eds.), *Barriers and biases in computer-mediated knowledge communication (and how they may be overcome)* (pp. 265–294). Amsterdam: Kluwer Academic Press.

Kotovsky, K., & Simon, H. A. (1990). Why are some problems really hard: Explorations in the problem space of difficulty. *Cognitive Psychology, 22,* 143–183.

Kozma, R. B., & Russell, J. (2005). Students becoming chemists: Developing representational competence. In J. Gilbert (Ed.), *Visualization in science education.* London: Kluwer.

Krange, I., & Ludvigsen, S. (2008). What does it mean? Students' procedural and conceptual problem solving in a CSCL environment designed within the field of science education. *International Journal of Computer-Supported Collaborative Learning (ijCSCL), 3*(1), 25–52.

Krause, E. (1986). *Taxicab geometry: An adventure in non-euclidean geometry.* New York: Dover.

Krippendorff, K. (2004). Reliability in content analysis: Some common misconceptions and recommendations. *Human Communication Research, 30,* 411–433.

Kumar, R., Gweon, G., Joshi, M., Cui, Y., & Rosé, C. P. (2007). *Supporting students working together on math with social dialogue.* Paper presented at the SLaTE Workshop on Speech and Language Technology in Education. Farmington, Pennsylvania, USA.

Kumar, R., Rosé, C. P., Aleven, V., Iglesias, A., & Robinson, A. (2006). *Evaluating the effectiveness of tutorial dialogue instruction in an exploratory learning context.* Paper presented at the Intelligent Tutoring Systems Conference. Taipei, Taiwan.

Kumar, R., Rosé, C. P., Wang, Y. C., Joshi, M., & Robinson, A. (2007). *Tutorial dialogue as adaptive collaborative learning support.* Paper presented at the AIED 2007. Marina del Rey, CA, USA.

Kuramochi, M., & Karypis, G. (2001). *Frequent subgraph discovery.* Paper presented at the 2001 IEEE International Conference on Data Mining, San Jose, CA. Proceedings, pp. 313–320.

Lakatos, I. (1976). *Proofs and refutations: The logic of mathematical discovery.* Cambridge, UK: Cambridge University Press.

Lakoff, G., & Núñez, R. (2000). *Where mathematics comes from: How the embodied mind brings mathematics into being.* New York City: Basic Books.

Landauer, T. K. (1996). *The trouble with computers: Usefulness, usability, and productivity.* Cambridge, MA: MIT Press.

Landis, J., & Koch, G. (1977). The measurement of observer agreement for categorical data. *Biometrics, 33*, 159–174.

Landsman, S., & Alterman, R. (2003). *Building groupware on thyme. Tech report cs-03-234.* Waltham, MA: Brandeis University.

Langenhove, L. v., & Harré, R. (Eds.). (1999). *Positioning theory.* Oxford, UK: Blackwell.

Latour, B. (1990). Drawing things together. In M. Lynch & S. Woolgar (Eds.), *Representation in scientific practice.* Cambridge, MA: MIT Press.

Latour, B. (2007). *Reassembling the social: An introduction to actor-network-theory.* Cambridge, UK: Cambridge University Press.

Lave, J. (1988). *Cognition in practice: Mind, mathematics and culture in everyday life.* Cambridge, UK: Cambridge University Press.

Lave, J. (1991). Situating learning in communities of practice. In L. Resnick, J. Levine, & S. Teasley (Eds.), *Perspectives on socially shared cognition* (pp. 63–83). Washington, DC: APA.

Lave, J., & Wenger, E. (1991). *Situated learning: Legitimate peripheral participation.* Cambridge, UK: Cambridge University Press.

LeBaron, C., & Streeck, J. (2000). Gesture, knowledge and the world. In D. McNeill (Ed.), *Language and gesture* (pp. 118–138). Cambridge, UK: Cambridge University Press.

Lee, Y.-J., & Roth, W.-M. (2003). Making a scientist: Discursive "doing" of identity and self-presentation during research interviews [37 paragraphs]. *Forum Qualitative Sozialforschung/ Forum: Qualitative Social Research [On-line Journal], 5*(1). Retrieved from http://www. qualitative-research.net/fqs-texte/1-04/1-04leeroth-e.htm

Lehrer, R., Schauble, L., Carpenter, S., & Penner, D. E. (2000). The inter-related development of inscriptions and conceptual understanding. In P. Cobb, E. Yackel, & K. McClain (Eds.), *Symbolizing and communicating in mathematics classrooms: Perspectives on discourse, tools, and instructional design* (pp. 325–360). Mahwah, NJ: Lawrence Erlbaum.

Lemke, J. L. (2001). The long and the short of it: Comments on multiple timescale studies of human activity. *Journal of The Learning Sciences, 10*(1–2), 17–26.

Lerner, G. (1993). Collectivities in action: Establishing the relevance of conjoined participation in conversation. *Text, 13*(2), 213–245.

Lesh, R., & Lehrer, R. (Eds.). (2000). *Handbook of research data design in mathematics and science education.* Mahwah, NJ: Lawrence Erlbaum.

Levin, J., Kim, H., & Riel, M. (1990). Analyzing instructional interactions on electronic message networks. In L. Harasim (Ed.), *Online education* (pp. 185–213). New York: Praeger.

Levinson, S. (1983). *Pragmatics.* Cambridge: Cambridge University Press.

Lim, L.-H., & Benbasat, I. (1993). A theoretical perspective on negotiation support systems. *Journal of Management Information Systems, 9*(3), 27–44.

Livingston, E. (1986). *The ethnomethodological foundations of mathematics.* London: Routledge & Kegan Paul.

Livingston, E. (1987). *Making sense of ethnomethodology.* London: Routledge & Kegan Paul.

Livingston, E. (1995). *An anthropology of reading.* Bloomington, IN: Indiana University Press.

Livingston, E. (2006). Ethnomethodological studies of mediated interaction and mundane expertise. *The Sociological Review, 54*(3), 405–425.

Lockhart, P. (2008). Lockhart's lament. *MAA Online, 2008*(March). Retrieved from http://www. maa.org/devlin/devlin_03_08.html

Lonchamp, J. (2006). Supporting synchronous collaborative learning: A generic, multi-dimensional model. *International Journal of Computer-Supported Collaborative Learning (ijCSCL), 1*(2). Retrieved from http://ijcscl.org/_preprints/volume1_issue2/lonchamp.pdf

Lucena, C. J. P., Fuks, H., Raposo, A., Gerosa, M. A., & Pimentel, M. (2007). Communication, coordination and cooperation in computer-supported learning: The AulaNet experience. In F. M. M. Neto & F. Brasileiro (Eds.), *Advances in computer-supported learning* (pp. 274–297). Idea Group Inc, Hershey, PA.

Lukacs, G. (1971). *History and class consciousness: Studies in Marxist dialectics.* Cambridge, MA: MIT Press.

Mahnkopf, C. S. (2002). Theory of polyphony. In C. S. Mahnkopf, F. Cox, & W. Schurig (Eds.), *Polyphony and complexity*. Hofheim, Germany: Wolke Verlag.

Manning, C., & Schutze, H. (1999). *Foundations of statistical natural language processing*. Cambridge, MA: MIT Press.

Marcus, G. E. (1995). Ethnography in/of the world system: The emergence of multi-sited ethnography. *Annual Review of Anthropology, 24*, 95–117.

Marcus, G. E. (1999a). Critical anthropology now: An introduction. In G. E. Marcus (Ed.), *Critical anthropology now: Unexpected contexts, shifting constituencies, changing agendas* (pp. 3–28). Santa Fe, NM: School of American Research Press.

Marcus, G. E. (Ed.). (1999b). *Critical anthropology now: Unexpected contexts, shifting constituencies, changing agendas*. Santa Fe, NM: School of American Research Press.

Marx, K. (1867/1976). *Capital* (B. Fowkes, Trans. Vol. I). New York: Vintage.

Mason, J., Burton, L., & Stacey, K. (1984). *Thinking mathematically*. London: Addison Wesley.

Mason, J. H. (1988). *Learning and doing mathematics*. London: Macmillan.

Mason, R. L., Gunst, R. F., & Hess, J. L. (2003). *Statistical design and analysis of experiments: With applications to engineering and science* (2nd ed.). Hoboken, NJ: Wiley.

Maxwell, J. (2004a). Causal explanation, qualitative research, and scientific inquiry in education. *Educational Researcher, 33*(2), 3–11. Retrieved from http://www.aera.net/pubs/er/pdf/vol33_02/2026-02_pp03-11.pdf

Maxwell, J. A. (2004b). Reemergent scientism, postmodernism, and dialogue across differences. *Qualitative Inquiry, 10*, 35–41.

Mayer, R. E. (1992). *Thinking, problem solving, cognition* (2nd ed.). New York: Freeman.

Mayer, R. E. (1999). Fifty years of creativity research. In R. J. Sternberg (Ed.), *Handbook of creativity* (pp. 449–460). Cambridge, UK: Cambridge University Press.

Mayer, R. E., & Wittrock, M. C. (1996). Problem-solving transfer. In D. C. Berlin & R. C. Calfee (Eds.), *Handbook of educational psychology* (pp. 47–62). New York: Macmillan.

Maynard, D. W. (1984). *Inside plea bargaining: The language of negotiation*. New York: Plenum Press.

Maynard, D. W. (2003). *Bad news, good news: Conversational order in everyday talk and clinical settings*. Chicago: University of Chicago Press.

McCarthy, J. C., & Monk, A. (1994). Channels, conversation, cooperation and relevance: All you wanted to know about communication but were afraid to ask. *Collaborative Computing, 1*, 35–60.

McGrath, J. E. (1990). Time matters in groups. In *Intellectual teamwork: Social and technical foundations of cooperative work*, (pp. 23–61). Hillsdale, NJ: Lawrence Erlbaum.

McGrath, J. E. (1991). Time, interaction, and performance (tip): A theory of groups. *Small Group Research, 22*(2), 147–174.

Medina, R., & Suthers, D. D. (2008). Bringing representational practice from log to light. *Proceedings of the International conference for the learning sciences*, Utrecht.

Mercer, N. (2000). *Words and minds. How we use language to think together*. London: Routledge.

Mercer, N., & Wegerif, R. (1999). Is "Exploratory talk" Productive talk? In K. Littleton & P. Light (Eds.), *Learning with computers: Analyzing productive interaction* (pp. 79–101). New York: Routledge.

Messick, S. (1989). Meaning and values in test validation: The science and ethics of assessment. *Educational Researcher, 18*(2), 5–11.

Messick, S. (1995). Validity of psychological assessment: Validation of inferences from persons' responses and performances as scientific inquiry into score meaning. *American Psychologist, 50*, 741–749.

Moss, J., & Beatty, R. A. (2006). Knowledge building in mathematics: Supporting collaborative learning in pattern problems. *International Journal of Computer-Supported Collaborative Learning (ijCSCL), 1*(4), 441–466.

Mühlpfordt, M. (2006). *The integration of synchronous communication across dual interaction spaces* (G. Stahl, Trans.). Paper presented at the German e-learning conference (DeLFI 2006).

Retrieved from http://GerryStahl.net/pub/delfi-german.pdf (in German) http://GerryStahl.net/pub/delfi-eng.pdf (in English).

Mühlpfordt, M., & Wessner, M. (2005). Explicit referencing in chat supports collaborative learning. In T. Koschmann, D. D. Suthers, & T.-W. Chan (Eds.), *Computer-supported collaborative learning 2005: The next ten years! (Proceedings of CSCL 2005)* (pp. 460–469). Taipei, Taiwan; Mahwah, NJ: Lawrence Erlbaum Associates.

Munn, N. D. (1992). The cultural anthropology of time: A critical essay. *Annual Review of Anthropology, 21,* 93–123

Murphy, K. L., & Collins, M. P. (1997). Development of communication conventions in electronic chats. *Journal of Distance Education, 12*(1–2), 177–200.

Murray, D. E. (2000). Protean communication: The language of computer mediated communication. *TESOL Quarterly, 34*(3), 397–421.

Nader, L. (1972). Up the anthropologist–perspectives gained from studying up. In D. Hymes (Ed.), *Reinventing anthropology* (pp. 284–311). New York: Pantheon Books.

Nader, L. (1996). Preface. In L. Nader (Ed.), *Naked science: Anthropological inquiry into boundaries, power, and knowledge* (pp. xi–xv). London: Routledge.

Nancy, J.-L. (2000). *Being singular plural* (R. Richardson, Trans.). Palo Alto, CA: Stanford University Press.

Nardi, B. (Ed.). (1996). *Context and consciousness: Activity theory and human-computer interaction.* Cambridge, MA: MIT Press.

Nash, C. M. (2005). *Cohesion and reference in English chatroom discourse.* Paper presented at the HICSS '05. Proceedings, pp. Track 4, (S. 108.103). IEEE Computer Society.

NCTM. (1989). *Curriculum and evaluation standards for school mathematics.* Alexandria, VA: National Council of Teachers of Mathematics.

Neuendorf, K. A. (2002). *The content analysis guidebook.* Thousand Oaks, CA: Sage.

Newell, A. (1980). Reasoning, problem solving and decision processes: The problem space as a fundamental category. In R. Nickerson (Ed.), *Attention and performance viii.* Hillsdale, NJ: Erlbaum.

Newell, A., & Simon, H. A. (1972). *Human problem solving.* Englewood Cliffs, NJ: Prentice-Hall.

Newmark, P. (1988). *A textbook of translation.* Hertfordshire, UK: Prentice Hall.

Nickerson, R. S. (1999). Enhancing creativity. In R. J. Sternberg (Ed.), *Handbook of creativity.* Cambridge, UK: Cambridge University Press.

Noam, E. (1995). Electronics and the dim future of the university. *Science, 270,* 247–249.

O'Neill, J., & Martin, D. (2003). *Text chat in action.* Paper presented at the ACM Conference on Groupware (GROUP 2003), Sanibel Island, FL.

Oikarinen, J., & Reed, D. (1993). *Internet relay chat protocol. Rfc 1459.* Network Working Group.

Oortwijn, M. B., Boekaerts, M., Vedder, P., & Strijbos, J. W. (2008). Helping behaviour during cooperative learning and learning gains: The role of the teacher and of pupils' prior knowledge and ethnic background. *Learning & Instruction, 18,* 146–159.

Outhwaite, W. (1994). *Habermas: A critical introduction.* Palo Alto, CA: Stanford University Press.

Pata, K., & Sarapuu, T. (2003). *Meta-communicative regulation patterns of expressive modeling on whiteboard tool.* Paper presented at the World Conference on E-Learning in Corporate, Government, Healthcare, and Higher Education 2003. Phoenix, AZ: AACE. Proceedings, pp. 1126–1129.

Patton, M. Q. (1990). *Qualitative evaluation and research methods.* (2nd ed.). Mewbury Park, CA: Sage.

Paulus, P. B. (Ed.). (2003). *Group creativity: Innovation through collaboration.* Oxford, UK: Oxford University Press.

Perret-Clermont, A.-N., & Schubauer-Leoni, M.-L. (1981). Conflict and cooperation as opportunities for learning. In W. P. Robinson (Ed.), *Communication in development* (pp. 203–234). New York: Academic Press.

Pfister, H.-R., & Mühlpfordt, M. (2002). *Supporting discourse in a synchronous learning environment: The learning protocol approach.* Paper presented at the CSCL 2002, Boulder, CO: Erlbaum. Proceedings, pp. 581–589.

Piaget, J. (1985). *The equilibrium of cognitive structures: The central problem of intellectual development.* Chicago: Chicago University Press.

Piaget, J. (1990). *The child's conception of the world.* New York: Littlefield Adams.

Pimentel, M. (2002). *Hiperdiálogo: Ferramenta de bate-papo para diminuir a perda de co-texto.* Unpublished Dissertation, MSc, Federal University of Rio de Janeiro.

Pimentel, M., Fuks, H., & Lucena, C. J. P. (2005). *Mediated chat development process: Avoiding chat confusion on educational debates.* Paper presented at the international conference of Computer Support for Collaborative Learning (CSCL 2005), Taipei, Taiwan. Proceedings, pp. 499–503.

Pimentel, M., & Sampaio, F. F. (2001). *Análise do bate-papo.* Paper presented at the XII Simpósio Brasileiro de Informática na Educação, Vitória, Brazil. Proceedings, pp. 545–549.

Pimentel, M. G., Fuks, H., & Lucena, C. J. P. (2003). *Co-text loss in textual chat tools.* Paper presented at the Fourth International and Interdisciplinary Conference on Modeling and Using Context (CONTEXT 2003), Stanford, CA. Proceedings, pp. 483–490.

Pirie, S., & Schwarzenberger, R. (1988). Mathematical discussion and mathematical understanding. *Educational Studies in Mathematics, 19*(4), 459–470.

Plato. (340 BC/1941). *The republic* (F. Cornford, Trans.). London: Oxford University Press.

Pollner, M. (1974). Mundane reasoning. *Philosophy of the Social Sciences, 4*(35), 35–54.

Polya, G. (1945/1973). *How to solve it: A new aspect of mathematical method.* Princeton, NJ: Princeton University Press.

Polyphony. (2005). *Polyphony.* Retrieved from http://cnx.rice.edu/content/m11634/latest

Pomerantz, A. (1986). Extreme case formulations: A way of legitimizing claims. *Human Studies, 9,* 219–229.

Pomerantz, A. (1988). Offering a candidate answer: An information seeking strategy. *Communication Monographs, 55,* 360–373.

Pomerantz, A., & Fehr, B. J. (1991). Conversation analysis: An approach to the study of social action as sense making practices. In T. A. van Dijk (Ed.), *Discourse as social interaction: Discourse studies, a multidisciplinary introduction* (Vol. 2, pp. 64–91). London: Sage.

Pomerantz, A. M. (1984). Giving a source or basis: The practice in conversation of telling 'how i know'. *Journal of Pragmatics, 8,* 607–625.

Poole, M. S., & van de Ven, A. H. (2004). Theories of organizational change and innovation processes. In M. S. Poole & A. H. v. d. Ven (Eds.), *Handbook of organizational change and innovation* (pp. 374–398). Oxford, UK: Oxford University Press.

Popolov, D., Callaghan, M., & Luker, P. (2000). *Conversation space: Visualising multi-threaded conversation.* Paper presented at the Working Conference on Advanced Visual Interfaces, Palermo, Italy. Proceedings, pp. 246–249.

Porpora, D. V. (1989). Four concepts of social strutcure. *Journal for the Theory of Social Behavior, 19*(2), 195–211.

Porpora, D. V. (1993). Cultural rules and material relations. *Sociological Theory, 11*(2), 212–229.

Powell, A. B. (2003). *"So let's prove it!": Emergent and elaborated mathematical ideas and reasoning in the discourse and inscriptions of learners engaged in a combinatorial task.* Unpublished Dissertation, Ph. D., Rutgers University, New Brunswick, NJ.

Powell, A. B., Francisco, J. M., & Maher, C. A. (2003). An analytical model for studying the development of mathematical ideas and reasoning using videotape data. *Journal of Mathematical Behavior, 22*(4), 405–435.

Powell, A. B., & Frankenstein, M. (Eds.). (1997). *Ethnomathematics: Challenging eurocentrism in mathematics education.* Albany, NY: SUNY.

Preece, J., Rogers, Y., & Sharp, H. (2007). *Interaction design: Beyond human-computer interaction* (2nd ed.). New York: John Wiley & Sons.

Pretz, J. E., Naples, A. J., & Sternberg, R. J. (2003). Recognizing, defining, and representing problems. In J. E. D. & R. J. Sternberg (Eds.), *The psychology of problem solving* (pp. 3–30). Cambridge, UK: Cambridge University Press.

Psathas, G. (1995). *Conversation analysis: The study of talk-in-interaction.* Thousand Oaks, CA: Sage.

Reimann, P. (2007). *Time is precious: Why process analysis is essential for CSCL.* Paper presented at the International Conference on Computer-supported Collaborative Learning (ICLS 2007), New Brunswick, NJ.

Reimann, P., & Zumbach, J. (2001). Design, diskurs und reflexion als zentrale elemente virtueller seminare. In F. Hesse & F. Friedrich (Eds.), *Partizipation und interaktion im virtuellen seminar* (pp. 135–163). München, Germany: Waxmann.

Renninger, K. A., & Farra, L. (2003). Mentor-participant exchange in the ask Dr. Math service: Design and implementation considerations. In M. Mardis (Ed.), *Digital libraries as complement to k-12 teaching and learning* (pp. 159–173). Syracuse, NY: ERIC Monograph Series.

Renninger, K. A., & Shumar, W. (1998). *Why and how students work with the math forum's problem(s) of the week: Implications for design.* Paper presented at the International Conference of the Learning Sciences (ICLS '98), Charlottesville, VA. Proceedings, pp. 348–350.

Rhee, H.-S., Pirkul, H., Varghese, J., & Barhki, R. (1995). *Effects of computer-mediated communication on group negotiation: An empirical study.* Paper presented at the 28th Annual Hawaii International Conference on System Sciences (HICSS '95), Hawaii.

Riffe, D., Lacy, S., & Fico, F. G. (1998). *Analyzing media messages: Using quantitative content analysis in research.* Mahwah, NJ: Lawrence Erlbaum Associates.

Rintel, E. S., Mulholland, J., & Pittam, J. (2001). First things first: Internet relay chat openings. *Journal Computer-Mediated Communication, 6*(3).

Robbins, P., & Aydede, M. (Eds.). (2009). *The Cambridge handbook of situated cognition.* Cambridge, UK: Cambridge University Press.

Rogoff, B. (1997). Evaluating development in the process of participation: Theory, methods, and practice building on each other. In E. Amsel & K. A. Renninger (Eds.), *Change and development: Issues of theory, method, and application.* Mahwah, NJ: Erlbaum.

Rosaldo, R. (1993). *Culture & truth: The remaking of social analysis.* Boston, MA: Beacon Press.

Roschelle, J. (1992). Learning by collaborating: Convergent conceptual change. *Journal of the Learning Sciences, 2*(3), 235–276.

Roschelle, J. (1996). Learning by collaborating: Convergent conceptual change. In T. Koschmann (Ed.), *CSCL: Theory and practice of an emerging paradigm* (pp. 209–248). Hillsdale, NJ: Lawrence Erlbaum Associates.

Roschelle, J., & Teasley, S. (1995). The construction of shared knowledge in collaborative problem solving. In C. O'Malley (Ed.), *Computer-supported collaborative learning* (pp. 69–197). Berlin, Germany: Springer Verlag.

Roscoe, P. B. (1995). The perils of 'positivism' in cultural anthropology. *American Anthropologist, 97*(3), 492–504.

Rosé, C., Wang, Y.-C., Cui, Y., Arguello, J., Stegmann, K., Weinberger, A., et al. (2008). Analyzing collaborative learning processes automatically: Exploiting the advances of computational linguistics in CSCL. *International Journal of Computer-Supported Collaborative Learning (ijCSCL), 3*(3), 237–272.

Rosé, C. P., Gweon, G., Arguello, J., Finger, S., Smailagic, A., & Siewiorek, D. (2007). *Towards an interactive assessment framework for engineering design learning.* Paper presented at the ASME 2007 International Design Engineering Technical Conferences & Computers and Information in Engineering Conference.

Rosé, C. P., Jordan, P., Ringenberg, M., Siler, S., VanLehn, K., & Weinstein, A. (2001). *Interactive conceptual tutoring in Atlas-Andes.* Paper presented at the AI in Education.

Rosé, C. P., & Torrey, C. (2005). *Interactivity versus expectation: Eliciting learning oriented behavior with tutorial dialogue systems.* Paper presented at the Interact '05.

Rosé, C. P., & VanLehn, K. (2005). An evaluation of a hybrid language understanding approach for robust selection of tutoring goals. *International Journal of AI in Education, 15*(4). 325–355.

Roth, W.-M. (2003). *Towards an anthropology of graphing: Semiotic and activity-theoretic perspectives.* The Netherlands: Kluwer Academic Publishers.

Rourke, L., & Anderson, T. (2004). Validity in quantitative content analysis. *Educational Technology Research & Development, 52*, 5–18.

Rourke, L., Anderson, T., Garrison, D. R., & Archer, W. (2001a). Assessing social presence in asynchronous text-based computer conferencing. *Journal of Distance Education, 14*(21), 50–71.

Rourke, L., Anderson, T., Garrison, D. R., & Archer, W. (2001b). Methodological issues in the content analysis of computer conference transcripts. *International Journal of Artificial Intelligence in Education, 12*, 8–22.

Ruby, J. (Ed.). (1982). *A crack in the mirror: Reflexive perspectives in anthropology.* Philadelphia: University of Pennsylvania Press.

Rummel, N., Spada, H., & Hauser, S. (2006). *Learning to collaborate in a computer-mediated setting: Observing a model beats learning from being scripted.* Paper presented at the Seventh International Conference of the Learning Sciences (ICLS 2006), Bloomsberg, IN: Lawrence Erlbaum Associates.

Ryle, G. (1949). *The concept of mind.* Chicago: University of Chicago Press.

Sacks, H. (1962/1995). *Lectures on conversation.* Oxford, UK: Blackwell.

Sacks, H., Schegloff, E. A., & Jefferson, G. (1974). A simplest systematics for the organization of turn-taking for conversation. *Language, 50*(4), 696–735. Retrieved from www.jstor.org

Salas, E., & Fiore, S. M. (Eds.). (2004). *Team cognition: Understanding the factors that drive process and performance.* Washington, DC: American Psychological Association.

Sandywell, B. (2008). Constructivism. In *International encyclopedia of the social sciences* (Vol. 2, pp. 96–99). Detroit, MI: Macmillan Reference USA.

Sarmiento, J., & Stahl, G. (2008a). *Extending the joint problem space: Time and sequence as essential features of knowledge building.* Paper presented at the International Conference of the Learning Sciences (ICLS 2008), Utrecht, Netherlands. Retrieved from http://GerryStahl.net/pub/icls2008johann.pdf

Sarmiento, J., & Stahl, G. (2008b). Group creativity in inter-action: Referencing, remembering and bridging. *International Journal of Human-Computer Interaction (IJHCI).* Retrieved from http://GerryStahl.net/pub/ijhci2007.pdf

Sarmiento-Klapper, J. W. (2009). *Bridging mechanisms in team-based online problem solving: Continuity in building collaborative knowledge.* Unpublished Dissertation, Ph.D., College of Information Science and Technology, Drexel University, Philadelphia, USA.

Sawyer, R. K. (2003). *Group creativity: Music, theater, collaboration.* Mahwah, NJ: Lawrence Erlbaum.

Sawyer, R. K. (Ed.). (2006). *Cambridge handbook of the learning sciences.* Cambridge, UK: Cambridge University Press.

Scardamalia, M. (2000). Can schools enter a knowledge society? In M. Selinger & J. Wynn (Eds.), *Educational technology and the impact on teaching and learning* (pp. 5–10). Abingdon, Oxfordshire: RM.

Scardamalia, M. (2002). Collective cognitive responsibility for the advancement of knowledge. In B. Smith (Ed.), *Liberal education in a knowledge society.* Chicago: Open Court.

Scardamalia, M., & Bereiter, C. (1991). Higher levels of agency in knowledge building: A challenge for the design of new knowledge media. *Journal of the Learning Sciences, 1*, 37–68.

Scardamalia, M., & Bereiter, C. (1996). Computer support for knowledge-building communities. In T. Koschmann (Ed.), *CSCL: Theory and practice of an emerging paradigm* (pp. 249–268). Hillsdale, NJ: Lawrence Erlbaum Associates.

Scardamalia, M., Bereiter, C., & Lamon, M. (1994). The CSILE project: Trying to bring the classroom into world 3. In K. McGilly (Ed.), *Classroom lessons: Integrating cognitive theory and educational practice.* Cambridge, MA: MIT Press.

Schank, R., & Abelson, R. P. (1977). *Scripts, plans, goals and understanding*. Hillsdale, NJ: Erlbaum.

Schank, R. C. (2002). *Designing world-class e-learning*. New York: McGraw-Hill Publishing.

Schegloff, E. (1991). Conversation analysis and socially shared cognition. In L. Resnick, J. Levine, & S. Teasley (Eds.), *Perspectives on socially shared cognition* (pp. 150–171). Washington, DC: APA.

Schegloff, E., & Sacks, H. (1973). Opening up closings. *Semiotica, 8*, 289–327.

Schegloff, E. A. (1968). Sequencing in conversational openings. *American Anthropologist, 70*, 1075–1095.

Schegloff, E. A. (1990). On the organization of sequences as a source of 'coherence' in talk-in-interaction. In B. Dorval (Ed.), *Conversational organization and its development* (pp. 51–77). Norwood, NJ: Ablex.

Schegloff, E. A. (2007). *Sequence organization in interaction: A primer in conversation analysis*. Cambridge, UK: Cambridge University Press.

Schellens, T., & Valcke, M. (2005). Collaborative learning in asynchronous discussion groups: What about the impact on cognitive processing? *Computers in Human Behavior, 21*, 957–975.

Schoenfeld, A. H. (1985). *Mathematical problem solving*. Orlando, FL: Academic Press.

Scholte, B. (1971). Discontents in anthropology. *Social Research, 38*, 777–807.

Scholte, B. (1972). Toward a reflexive and critical anthropology. In D. Hymes (Ed.), *Reinventing anthropology* (pp. 430–458). New York: Vintage Books.

Scholte, B. (1978a). Critical anthropology since it's reinvention: On the convergence between the concept of paradigm, the rationality of debate and critical anthropology. *Anthropology & Humanism Quarterly, 3*(1–2), 4–17.

Scholte, B. (1978b). On the ethnocentricity of scientistic logic. *Dialectical Anthropology, 3*(2), 177–189.

Schön, D. A. (1983). *The reflective practitioner: How professionals think in action*. New York: Basic Books.

Schönfeldt, J., & Golato, A. (2003). Repair in chats: A conversation analytic approach. *Research on Language and Social Interaction, 36*(3), 241–284.

Schutz, A. (1967). *Phenomenology of the social world* (F. Lehnert, Trans.). Evanston, IL: North-western University Press.

Schwartz, D. (1995). The emergence of abstract representations in dyad problem solving. *Journal of the Learning Sciences, 4*(3), 321–354.

Scott, J. (1991). *Social network analysis: A handbook*. Thousand Oaks, CA: Sage.

Sfard, A. (1998). On two metaphors for learning and the dangers of choosing just one. *Educational Researcher, 27*(2), 4–13.

Sfard, A. (2000a). On reform movement and the limits of mathematical discourse. *Mathematical Thinking and Learning, 2*(3), 157–189.

Sfard, A. (2000b). Symbolizing mathematical reality into being—Or how mathematical discourse and mathematical objects create each other. In P. Cobb, E. Yackel, & K. McClain (Eds.), *Symbolizing and communicating in mathematics classrooms: Perspectives on discourse, tools, and instructional design* (pp. 37–98). Mahwah, NJ: Lawrence Erlbaum Associates.

Sfard, A. (2002). There is more to discourse than meets the ears: Looking at thinking as communicating to learn more about mathematical learning. In C. Kieran, E. Forman, & A. Sfard (Eds.), *Learning discourse: Discursive approaches to research in mathematics education* (pp. 13–57). Dordrecht, Netherlands: Kluwer.

Sfard, A. (2005). Why cannot children see as the same what grown-ups cannot see as different?—early numerical thinking revisited. *Cognition and Instruction, 23*(2), 237–309.

Sfard, A. (2008). *Thinking as communicating: Human development, the growth of discourses and mathematizing*. Cambridge, UK: Cambridge University Press.

Sfard, A., & McClain, K. (2003). Analyzing tools: Perspectives on the role of designed artifacts in mathematics learning. *The Journal of the Learning Sciences, 11*(2 & 3), 153–161.

Shannon, C., & Weaver, W. (1949). *The mathematical theory of communication*. Chicago: University of Illinois Press.

Shirouzu, H., Miyake, N., & Masukawa, H. (2002). Cognitively active externalization for situated reflection. *Cognitive Science, 26*(4), 469–501.

Shneiderman, B., Fischer, G., Czerwinski, M., Resnick, M., Myers, B., & Candy, L. (2006). Creativity support tools: Report from a US NSF sponsored workshop. *International Journal of Human-Computer Interaction (IJHCI), 20*(2), 61–77.

Shumar, W., & Renninger, K. A. (2002). Introduction: On conceptualizing community. In K. A. Renninger & W. Shumar (Eds.), *Building virtual communities* (pp. 1–19). Cambridge, UK: Cambridge University Press.

Siemieniuch, C., & Sinclair, M. (1994). Concurrent engineering: People, organizations and technology or CSCW in manufacturing. In P. Lloyd (Ed.), *Groupware in the 21st century*. London: Adamantine Press.

Slavin, R. (1980). Cooperative learning. *Review of Educational Research, 50*(2), 315–342.

Smith, G. A. (1999). *Confronting the present: Towards a politically engaged anthropology*. Oxford, NY: Berg.

Smith, M., Cadiz, J., & Burkhalter, B. (2000). *Conversation trees and threaded chats*. Paper presented at the *ACM conference on Computer-Supported Cooperative Work (CSCW), Philadelphia, PA*. Proceedings, pp. 97–105.

Soller, A. (2004). Understanding knowledge sharing breakdowns: A meeting of quantitative and qualitative minds. *Journal of Computer Assisted Learning, 20*, 212–223.

Soller, A., & Lesgold, A. (2003). *A computational approach to analyzing online knowledge sharing interaction*. Paper presented at the 11th International Conference on Artificial Intelligence in Education, AI-ED 2003, Sydney, Australia. Amsterdam: IOS Press. Proceedings, pp. 253–260.

Speiser, B., Walter, C., & Maher, C. A. (2003). Representing motion: An experiment in learning. *The Journal of Mathematical Behavior, 22*(1), 1–35.

Speiser, B., Walter, C., & Shull, B. (2002). *Preservice teachers undertake division in base five: How inscriptions support thinking and communication*. Paper presented at the twenty-fourth annual meeting of the North American Chapter of the International Group for the Psychology of Mathematics Education. Athens, Georgia. Proceedings, pp. III, 1153–1162 ERIC.

Spencer, D. H., & Hiltz, S. R. (2003). *A field study of use of synchronous chat in online courses*. Paper presented at the 36th Annual Hawaii International Conference on System Sciences (HICSS'03), Hawaii.

Stahl, G. (1975a). *Marxian hermeneutics and Heideggerian social theory: Interpreting and transforming our world*. Unpublished Dissertation, Department of Philosophy, Northwestern University, Evanston, IL. Retrieved from http://GerryStahl.net/publications/dissertations/philosophy

Stahl, G. (1975b). The jargon of authenticity: An introduction to a Marxist critique of Heidegger. *Boundary 2, III*(2), 489–498. Retrieved from http://GerryStahl.net/publications/interpretations/jargon.htm

Stahl, G. (1976). Attuned to being: Heideggerian music in technological society. *Boundary 2, IV*(2), 637–664. Retrieved from http://GerryStahl.net/publications/interpretations/attuned.htm

Stahl, G. (1993a). *Interpretation in design: The problem of tacit and explicit understanding in computer support of cooperative design*. Unpublished Dissertation, Department of Computer Science, University of Colorado, Boulder, CO. Retrieved from http://GerryStahl.net/publications/dissertations/computer

Stahl, G. (1993b). *Supporting situated interpretation*. Paper presented at the Annual Meeting of the Cognitive Science Society (CogSci '93). Proceedings pp. 965–970 Boulder, CO: Lawrence Erlbaum. Retrieved from http://GerryStahl.net/cscl/papers/ch13.pdf

Stahl, G. (2002a). Groupware goes to school. In J. H. J. Pino (Ed.), *Groupware: Design, implementation and use: Proceedings of the 8th international workshop on groupware (CRIWG '02)* (Vol. LNCS 2440, pp. 7–24). La Serena, Chile: Springer. Retrieved from http://GerryStahl.net/cscl/papers/ch11.pdf

Stahl, G. (2002b). Rediscovering CSCL. In T. Koschmann, R. Hall, & N. Miyake (Eds.), *CSCL 2: Carrying forward the conversation* (pp. 169–181). Hillsdale, NJ: Lawrence Erlbaum Associates. Retrieved from http://GerryStahl.net/cscl/papers/ch01.pdf

Stahl, G. (2006a). Analyzing and designing the group cognitive experience. *International Journal of Cooperative Information Systems (IJCIS), 15,* 157–178. Retrieved from http://GerryStahl.net/pub/ijcis.pdf

Stahl, G. (2006b). *Group cognition: Computer support for building collaborative knowledge.* Cambridge, MA: MIT Press. Retrieved from http://GerryStahl.net/mit/

Stahl, G. (2006c). Scripting group cognition: The problem of guiding situated collaboration. In F. Fischer, H. Mandl, J. Haake, & I. Kollar (Eds.), *Scripting computer-supported collaborative learning: Cognitive, computational and educational perspectives* (pp. 327–335). Dodrecht, Netherlands: Kluwer-Springer Verlag. Retrieved from http://GerryStahl.net/pub/scripting.pdf

Stahl, G. (2006d). Supporting group cognition in an online math community: A cognitive tool for small-group referencing in text chat. *Journal of Educational Computing Research (JECR) special issue on cognitive tools for collaborative communities, 35*(2), 103–122. Retrieved from http://GerryStahl.net/pub/jecr.pdf

Stahl, G. (2006e). Sustaining group cognition in a math chat environment. *Research and Practice in Technology Enhanced Learning (RPTEL), 1*(2), 85–113. Retrieved from http://GerryStahl.net/pub/rptel.pdf

Stahl, G. (2007). *Meaning making in CSCL: Conditions and preconditions for cognitive processes by groups.* Paper presented at the international conference on Computer-Supported Collaborative Learning (CSCL '07), New Brunswick, NJ: ISLS. Retrieved from http://GerryStahl.net/pub/cscl07.pdf

Stahl, G. (2008a). Book review: Exploring thinking as communicating in CSCL. *International Journal of Computer-Supported Collaborative Learning (ijCSCL), 3*(3), 361-368. Retrieved from http://ijcscl.org/_preprints/volume3_issue3/stahl_3_3.pdf

Stahl, G. (2008b). Chat on collaborative knowledge building. *QWERTY, 3*(1), 67–78. Retrieved from http://GerryStahl.net/pub/qwerty08.pdf

Stahl, G. (2008c). *Human-human interaction and group learning.* Paper presented at the Human-Computer Interaction Consortium, Frasier, CO. Retrieved from http://GerryStahl.net/pub/hcic2008.pdf

Stahl, G. (2009a). *For a science of group interaction.* Paper presented at the Conference for Groupware (GROUP 2009), Sanibel Island, FL. Retrieved from http://GerryStahl.net/pub/group2009.pdf

Stahl, G. (2009b). Social practices of group cognition in virtual math teams. In S. Ludvigsen, A. Lund & R. Säljö (Eds.), *Learning in social practices. ICT and new artifacts: Transformation of social and cultural practices.* Pergamon. Retrieved from http://GerryStahl.net/pub/cmc.pdf

Stahl, G., & Herrmann, T. (1999). *Intertwining perspectives and negotiation.* Paper presented at the ACM SIGGROUP Conference on Supporting Group Work (Group '99), Phoenix, AZ. Proceedings pp. 316–324. Retrieved from http://GerryStahl.net/cscl/papers/ch07.pdf

Stahl, G., Koschmann, T., & Suthers, D. (2006). Computer-supported collaborative learning: An historical perspective. In R. K. Sawyer (Ed.), *Cambridge handbook of the learning sciences* (pp. 409–426). Cambridge, UK: Cambridge University Press. Retrieved from http://GerryStahl.net/cscl/CSCL_English.pdf in English, http://GerryStahl.net/cscl/CSCL_Chinese_simplified.pdf in simplified Chinese, http://GerryStahl.net/cscl/CSCL_Chinese_traditional.pdf in traditional Chinese, http://GerryStahl.net/cscl/CSCL_Spanish.pdf in Spanish, http://GerryStahl.net/cscl/CSCL_Portuguese.pdf in Portuguese, http://GerryStahl.net/cscl/CSCL_German.pdf in German, http://GerryStahl.net/cscl/CSCL_Romanian.pdf in Romanian

Stahl, G., Wee, J. D., & Looi, C.-K. (2007). *Using chat, whiteboard and wiki to support knowledge building.* Paper presented at the International Conference on Computers in Education (ICCE 07), Hiroshima, Japan. Retrieved from http://GerryStahl.net/pub/icce07.pdf

Stahl, G., & Zhou, N. (2006). *The virtual math teams project: A global math discourse community*. Paper presented at the International Conference on Computers and Education (ICCE '06), Beijing, China. Retrieved from http://GerryStahl.net/pub/icce2006.pdf

Star, S. L. (1989). The structure of ill-structured solutions: Boundary objects and heterogeneous distributed problem solving. In L. Gasser & M. N. Huhns (Eds.), *Distributed artificial intelligence* (pp. 37–54). San Mateo, CA: Morgan Kaufmann.

Stefik, M., Bobrow, D. G., Foster, G., Lanning, S., & Tatar, D. (1987). Wysiwis revised: Early experiences with multiuser interfaces. *ACM Transactions on Office Information Systems, 5*(2), 147–167.

Stigler, J. W., & Hiebert, J. (1999). *The teaching gap: Best ideas from the world's teachers for improving education in the classroom*. New York: Free Press.

Streeck, J., & Mehus, S. (2005). Microethnography: The study of practices. In K. L. Fitch & R. E. Sanders (Eds.), *Handbook of language and social interaction* (pp. 381–404). Mahwah, NJ: Lawrence Erlbaum Associates.

Strijbos, J. W. (2004). *The effect of roles on computer supported collaborative learning*. Unpublished Dissertation, Ph. D., Open Universiteit Nederland, Heerlen, the Netherlands.

Strijbos, J. W., & Fischer, F. (2007). Methodological challenges for collaborative learning research. *Learning & Instruction, 17*, 389–393.

Strijbos, J. W., Kirschner, P. A., & Martens, R. L. (Eds.). (2004). *What we know about CSCL: And implementing it in higher education*. Computer-supported collaborative learning book series, Vol. 3. Dordrecht, the Netherlands: Kluwer Academic Publishers.

Strijbos, J. W., Martens, R. L., Jochems, W. M. G., & Broers, N. J. (2004). The effect of functional roles on perceived group efficiency: Using multilevel modeling and content analysis to investigate computer-supported collaboration in small groups. *Small Group Research, 35*, 195–229.

Strijbos, J. W., Martens, R. L., Prins, F. J., & Jochems, W. M. G. (2006). Content analysis: What are they talking about? *Computers & Education, 46*, 29–48.

Strijbos, J. W., & Stahl, G. (2007). Methodological issues in developing a multi-dimensional coding procedure for small group chat communication. *Learning & Instruction. Special issue on measurement challenges in collaborative learning research, 17*(4), 394–404. Retrieved from http://GerryStahl.net/vmtwiki/jw.pdf

Struik, D. J. (1948/1967). *A concise history of mathematics* (3rd ed.). New York: Dover.

Suchman, L. (1987). *Plans and situated actions: The problem of human-machine communication*. Cambridge, UK: Cambridge University Press.

Suchman, L. A. (1990). Representing practice in cognitive science. In M. Lynch & S. Woolgar. (Ed.), *Representation in scientific practice*. Cambridge, MA: MIT Press.

Suchman, L. A. (2007). *Human-machine reconfigurations: Plans and situated actions* (2nd ed.). Cambridge, UK: Cambridge University Press.

Suchman, L. A., & Jordan, B. (1990). Interactional troubles in face-to-face survey interviews. *Journal of the American Statistical Association, 85*, 232–244.

Suthers, D. (2005a). Technology affordances for intersubjective learning, and how they may be exploited. In R. Bromme, F. W. Hesse, & H. Spada (Eds.), *Biases and barriers in computer-mediated knowledge communication: And how they may be overcome* (pp. 295–319). Boston: Kluwer Academic Publishers.

Suthers, D., Connelly, J., Lesgold, A., Paolucci, M., Toth, E., Toth, J., et al. (2001). Representational and advisory guidance for students learning scientific inquiry. In K. D. Forbus & P. J. Feltovich (Eds.), *Smart machines in education: The coming revolution in educational technology* (pp. 7–35). Menlo Park: AAAI Press.

Suthers, D., Girardeau, L., & Hundhausen, C. (2003). Deictic roles of external representations in face-to-face and online collaboration. In B. Wasson, S. Ludvigsen, & U. Hoppe (Eds.), *Designing for change in networked learning environments, Proceedings of the international conference on computer support for collaborative learning 2003* (pp. 173–182). Dordrecht: Kluwer Academic Publishers.

Suthers, D. D. (2001). *Collaborative representations: Supporting face to face and online knowledge-building discourse.* Paper presented at the 34th Hawai'i International Conference on the Systems Sciences (HICSS-34). Retrieved from http://lilt.ics.hawaii.edu/lilt/papers/2001/Suthers-HICSS-2001.pdf

Suthers, D. D. (2005b). *Collaborative knowledge construction through shared representations.* Paper presented at the 38th Hawai'i International Conference on the System Sciences (HICSS-38), Waikoloa, Hawai'i IEEE.

Suthers, D. D. (2006a). A qualitative analysis of collaborative knowledge construction through shared representations. *Research and practice in technology enhanced learning (RPTEL), 1*(2), 1–28. Retrieved from http://lilt.ics.hawaii.edu/lilt/2006/Suthers-2006-RPTEL.pdf

Suthers, D. D. (2006b). Technology affordances for intersubjective meaning making: A research agenda for CSCL. *International Journal of Computer-Supported Collaborative Learning (ijCSCL), 1*(3), 315–337.

Suthers, D. D., Dwyer, N., Medina, R., & Vatrapu, R. (2007). A framework for eclectic analysis of collaborative interaction. In C. Chinn, G. Erkens, & S. Puntambekar (Eds.), *The computer supported collaborative learning (CSCL) conference 2007* (pp. 694–703). New Brunswick: International Society of the Learning Sciences.

Suthers, D. D., & Hundhausen, C. (2003). An experimental study of the effects of representational guidance on collaborative learning. *Journal of the Learning Sciences, 12*(2), 183–219. Retrieved from http://lilt.ics.hawaii.edu/lilt/papers/2003/Suthers-Hundhausen-2003.pdf

Suthers, D. D., Vatrapu, R., Medina, R., Joseph, S., & Dwyer, N. (2008). Beyond threaded discussion: Representational guidance in asynchronous collaborative learning environments. *Computers & Education, 50*(4), 1103–1127. Retrieved from doi:10.1016/j.compedu.2006.10.007

Sweller, J., van Merrienboer, J., & Paas, F. (1998). Cognitive architecture and instructional design. *Educational Psychology Review, 10,* 251–296.

Tannen, D. (1989). *Talking voices: Repetition, dialogue, and imagery in conversational discourse.* Cambridge, UK: Cambridge University Press.

Tay, M. H., Hooi, C. M., & Chee, Y. S. (2002). *Discourse-based learning using a multimedia discussion forum.* Paper presented at the International Conference on Computers in Education (ICCE'02). Proceedings, pp. 293–299.

Teasley, S. D., & Roschelle, J. (1993). Constructing a joint problem space: The computer as a tool for sharing knowledge. In S. P. Lajoie & S. J. Derry (Eds.), *Computers as cognitive tools* (pp. 229–258). Mahwah, NJ: Lawrence Erlbaum Associates, Inc.

Tedlock, B. (1991). From participant observation to observation of participation: The emergence of narrative ethnography. *Journal of Anthropological Research, 47*(1), 69–94.

Tedlock, D. (1986). The analogical tradition and the emergence of a dialogical anthropology *Journal of Anthropological Research, 42*(3), 483–496.

Teli, M., Pisanu, F., & Hakken, D. (2007). The internet as a library-of-people: For a cyberethnography of online groups, *Forum Qualitative Sozialforschung/Forum: Qualitative Social Research* (Vol. 8). Retrieved from http://www.qualitative-research.net/fqs-texte/3-07/07-3-33-e.pdf

ten Have, P. (1999). *Doing conversation analysis: A practical guide.* Thousand Oaks, CA: Sage.

Thirunarayanan, M. O. (2000). Cutting down on chat confusion: A proposal for managing instructor-controlled chat systems. *Ubiquity, 1*(38) 2–es.

Thorndike, E. L. (1914). *Educational psychology* (Vol. I–III). New York: Teachers College.

Trausan-Matu, S., Rebedea, T., Dragan, A., & Alexandru, C. (2007). Visualisation of learners' contributions in chat conversations. In J. Fong. & P. Wang (Eds.), *Blended learning* (pp. 217–226): Pearson-Prentice Hal. Retrieved from http://www.cs.cityu.edu.hk/~wbl2007WBL2007_Proceedings_HTML/WBL2007_PP217-226_Trausan-Matu.pdf

Valsiner, J., & Veer, R. v. d. (2000). *The social mind: Development of the idea.* Cambridge, UK: Cambridge University Press.

van Bruggen, J. M. (2003). *Explorations in graphical argumentation. The use of external representations of argumentation in collaborative problem solving.* Unpublished Dissertation, Ph. D., Open Universiteit Nederland, Heerlen, NL.

van Bruggen, J. M., Kirschner, P. A., & Jochems, W. (2002). External representation of argumentation in CSCL and the management of cognitive load. *Learning & Instruction, 12*(1), 121–138.

VanLehn, K., Graesser, A., Jackson, G. T., Jordan, P., Olney, A., & Rosé, C. P. (2007). Natural language tutoring: A comparison of human tutors, computer tutors, and text. *Cognitive Science, 31*(1), 3–52.

Veerman, A., & Veldhuis-Diermanse, E. (2001). Collaborative learning through computer-mediated communication in academic education. In P. Dillenbourg, A. Eurelings, & K. Hakkarainen (Eds.), *European perspectives on computer-supported collaborative learning* (pp. 625–632). Maastricht, the Netherlands: University of Maastricht.

Venolia, G. D., & Neustaedter, C. (2003). *Understanding sequence and reply relationships within email conversations: A mixed-model visualization.* Paper presented at the SIGCHI'03, Ft. Lauderdale, FL. Proceedings, pp. 361–368.

Viegas, F. B., & Donath, J. S. (1999). *Chat circles.* Paper presented at the Conference on Human Factors in Computing Systems, Pittsburgh, PA.

Vogel, D., Nunamaker, J., Applegate, L., & Konsynski, B. (1987). *Group decision support systems: Determinants of success.* Paper presented at the Decision Support Systems (DSS '87). Proceedings, pp. 118–128.

Voloshinov, V. (1973). *Marxism and the philosophy of language.* New York: Seminar Press.

Vronay, D., Smith, M., & Drucker, S. (1999). *Alternative interfaces for chat.* Paper presented at the 12th Annual ACM Symposium on User Interface Software and Technology, Asheville, NC. Proceedings, pp. 19–26.

Vygotsky, L. (1930/1978). *Mind in society.* Cambridge, MA: Harvard University Press.

Vygotsky, L. (1934/1986). *Thought and language.* Cambridge, MA: MIT Press.

Wang, H. C., & Rosé, C. P. (2007). *Supporting collaborative idea generation: A closer look using statistical process analysis techniques.* Paper presented at the AIED 2007.

Wang, H. C., Rosé, C. P., Cui, Y., Chang, C. Y., Huang, C. C., & Li, T. Y. (2007). *Thinking hard together: The long and short of collaborative idea generation for scientific inquiry.* Paper presented at the CSCL 2007.

Wasserman, S., & Faust, K. (1992). *Social network analysis: Methods and applications.* Cambridge, UK: Cambridge University Press.

Watson, A., & Mason, J. (2005). *Mathematics as a constructive activity: Learners generating examples.* Mahwah, NJ: Lawrence Erlbaum Associates.

Webb, N., & Farivar, S. (1999). Developing productive group interaction. In O'Donnell & King (Eds.), *Cognitive perspectives on peer learning.* Mahwah, NJ: Lawrence Erlbaum Associates.

Webb, N., Nemer, K., & Zuniga, S. (2002). Short circuits or superconductors? Effects of group composition on high-achieving students' science assessment performance. *American Educational Research Journal, 39*(4), 943–989.

Webb, N. M., & Mastergeorge, A. M. (2003). The development of students' helping behaviour and learning in peer-directed small groups. *Cognition & Instruction, 21*, 361–428.

Wee, J. D. (2007a). *Construction of mathematical knowledge through the use of collaborative critiques in problem solving.* Paper presented at the Redesigning Pedagogy, Culture, Knowledge and Understanding Conference, Singapore.

Wee, J. D. (2007b). *Mathematical knowledge construction through the use of guided collaborative critique in a quasi-synchronous chat environment.* Paper presented at the Association for Active Educational Researchers Conference (AARE 2007), Perth, Australia.

Wegerif, R. (2006). A dialogical understanding of the relationship between CSCL and teaching thinking skills. *International Journal of Computer-Supported Collaborative Learning (ijCSCL), 1*(1), 143–157. Retrieved from http://ijcscl.org/_preprints/volume1_issue1/wegerif.pdf

Wegerif, R. (2007). *Dialogic, education and technology: Expanding the space of learning.* New York: Kluwer-Springer.

Wegner, D. (1986). Transactive memory: A contemporary analysis of the group mind. In B. Mullen & G. R. Goethals (Eds.), *Theories of group behavior* (pp. 185–208). New York: Springer Verlag.

Weinberger, A. (2003). *Scripts for computer-supported collaborative learning: Effects of social and epistemic cooperation scripts on collaborative knowledge construction.* Unpublished Dissertation, Ph. D., University of Munich.

Weinberger, A., & Fischer, F. (2006). A framework to analyze argumentative knowledge construction in computer-supported collaborative learning. *Computers & Education, 46,* 71–95.

Wessner, M., & Pfister, H.-R. (2001). *Group formation in computer-supported collaborative learning.* Paper presented at the ACM SIGGROUP Conference on Supporting Group Work (Group 2001). Proceedings, pp. 24–31 Boulder, CO: ACM Press.

Weusijana, B. K., Kumar, R., & Rosé, C. P. (2008). *Multitalker: Building conversational agents in second life using basilica.* Paper presented at the *SLcc08: The Second Life Community Convention,* Tampa, FL.

Whittaker, S. (2003). Things to talk about when talking about things. *Human-Computer Interaction, 18*(1–2), 149–170.

Winograd, T., & Flores, F. (1986). *Understanding computers and cognition: A new foundation of design.* Reading, MA: Addison-Wesley.

Wittgenstein, L. (1944/1956). *Remarks on the foundations of mathematics.* Cambridge, MA: MIT Press.

Wittgenstein, L. (1953). *Philosophical investigations.* New York: Macmillan.

Yukawa, J. (2006). Co-reflection in online learning: Collaborative critical thinking as narrative. *International Journal of Computer-Supported Collaborative Learning (ijCSCL), 1*(2), 203–228.

Zaki, M. J. (2002). *Efficiently mining frequent trees in a forest.* Paper presented at the ACM SIGKDD international conference on Knowledge Discovery and Data Mining, Edmonton, Canada. Proceedings, pp. 71–80.

Zemel, A., & Çakir, M. P. (2007). *Reading's work: The mechanisms of online chat as social interaction.* Paper presented at the National Communication Association Convention, Chicago. Retrieved from http://GerryStahl.net/vmtwiki/alan2.pdf

Zemel, A., Koschmann, T., LeBaron, C., & Feltovich, F. (2008). "What are we missing?" Usability's indexical ground. *Computer Supported Cooperative Work, 17,* 63–85.

Zemel, A., Shumar, W., & Çakir, M. P. (2007). *The disembodied act: Copresence and indexical symmetry in computer-mediated communication.* Paper presented at the The proceedings of CSCL 2007: Of mice, minds, and society, New Brunswick, NJ. Retrieved from http://GerryStahl.net/vmtwiki/alan.pdf

Zemel, A., Xhafa, F., & Çakir, M. P. (2007). What's in the mix? Combining coding and conversation analysis to investigate chat-based problem solving. *Learning & Instruction, 17*(4), 405–415. Retrieved from http://GerryStahl.net/vmtwiki/fatos.pdf

Zemel, A., Xhafa, F., & Stahl, G. (2005). *Analyzing the organization of collaborative math problem-solving in online chats using statistics and conversation analysis.* Paper presented at the CRIWG International Workshop on Groupware, Racife, Brazil. Retrieved from http://GerryStahl.net/pub/criwg2005zemel.pdf

Zhao, S. (2003). Toward a taxonomy of copresence. *Presence: Teleoperators and Virtual Environments, 12*(5), 445–455.

Zhou, N. (2009). *Investigating information practices of collaborative online small groups engaged in problem solving.* Unpublished Dissertation, Ph.D., College of Information Science and Technology, Drexel University, Philadelphia, USA.

Zhou, N., Zemel, A., & Stahl, G. (2008). *Questioning and responding in online small groups engaged in collaborative math problem solving.* Paper presented at the International Conference of the Learning Sciences (ICLS 2008), Utrecht, Netherlands. Retrieved from http://GerryStahl.net/pub/icls2008nan.pdf

Zitzen, M., & Stein, D. (2004). Chat and conversation: A case of transmedial stability? *Linguistics, 42*(5), 983–1021.

Zurn, C. F., (2008). Intersubjectivity. In W. A. Darity (Ed.), *International encyclopedia of the social sciences* (Vol. 4, pp. 116–117). Detroit, MI: Macmillan Reference USA.

Name Index

Subject Index

Note: Page numbers with 'f' and 't' in the index denote figures and tables in the text.

Lightning Source UK Ltd.
Milton Keynes UK
21 September 2009

144003UK00001BA/11/P